HANDBOOK OF PERCEPTION

Volume II

Psychophysical Judgment and Measurement

This is Volume II of

HANDBOOK OF PERCEPTION

EDITORS: *Edward C. Carterette and Morton P. Friedman*

A complete list of the books in this series appears at the end of this volume.

HANDBOOK
OF PERCEPTION

VOLUME II

PSYCHOPHYSICAL JUDGMENT
AND MEASUREMENT

EDITED BY

Edward C. Carterette and Morton P. Friedman

Department of Psychology
University of California
Los Angeles, California

ACADEMIC PRESS   New York   San Francisco   London   1974

A Subsidiary of Harcourt Brace Jovanovich, Publishers

ACADEMIC PRESS, INC.
111 Fifth Avenue, New York, New York 10003

United Kingdom Edition published by
ACADEMIC PRESS, INC. (LONDON) LTD.
24/28 Oval Road, London NW1

Library of Congress Cataloging in Publication Data

Carterette, Edward C
    Psychophysical judgement and measurement.

    (Their Handbook of perception, v. 2)
    Includes bibliographies.
    1.   Psychology, Physiological.   2.   Judgment.
3.   Psychometrics.   I.   Friedman, Morton P., joint
author.   II.   Title.   [DNLM: 1.   Perception.
2.   Sensation.   WL700 C325h]
QP360.C37   153.4′6   74-13803
ISBN 0−12−161902−8

CONTENTS

PART I. INTRODUCTION AND OVERVIEW

Chapter 1. History of Psychophysics and Judgment

F. Nowell Jones

PART II. PECEPTUAL CHOICE AND JUDGMENT

Chapter 2. Attention: The Processing of Multiple Sources of Information

W. R. Garner

Chapter 3.   Memory Processes and Judgment

Arthur Sandusky

Chapter 4.   Psychological Decision Mechanisms
             and Perception

Eugene Galanter

Chapter 5.   Contextual Effects: A Range–Frequency Analysis

Allen Parducci

Chapter 6.   Personality and Social Effects in Judgment

   Harry S. Upshaw

PART III.   MEASUREMENT MODELS AND APPLICATIONS

Chapter 7.   Stimulus and Response Measurement

   E. W. Holman and A. A. J. Marley

Chapter 8.   Algebraic Models in Perception

   Norman H. Anderson

Chapter 9.   Detection, Discrimination, and Recognition

   R. Duncan Luce and David M. Green

Chapter 13. Applications of Individual Differences Scaling to Studies of Human Perception and Judgment

Myron Wish and J. Douglas Carroll

Chapter 14. Applications of Multidimensional Scaling in Perception

Tarow Indow

LIST OF CONTRIBUTORS

Numbers in parentheses indicate the pages on which the authors' contributions begin.

NORMAN H. ANDERSON (215), Department of Psychology, University of California, San Diego, La Jolla, California

J. DOUGLAS CARROLL (391, 450), Bell Laboratories, Murray Hill, New Jersey

EUGENE GALANTER (85), Department of Psychology, Columbia University, New York, New York

W. R. GARNER (23), Department of Psychology, Yale University, New Haven, Connecticut

DAVID M. GREEN (299), Department of Psychology, University of California, San Diego, La Jolla, California

E. W. HOLMAN (173), Department of Psychology, University of California, Los Angeles, Los Angeles, California

TAROW INDOW (493), Department of Psychology, Keio University, Mita Minato-ku, Tokyo, Japan

F. NOWELL JONES (1, 343), Department of Psychology, University of California, Los Angeles, Los Angeles, California

R. DUNCAN LUCE (299), School of Social Science, University of California, Irvine, Irvine, California

A. A. J. MARLEY (173), Department of Psychology, McGill University, Montreal, Quebec, Canada

ALLEN PARDUCCI (127), Department of Psychology, University of California, Los Angeles, Los Angeles, California

ARTHUR SANDUSKY (61), Department of Psychology, University of California, Santa Barbara, Santa Barbara, California

S. S. STEVENS* (361), Laboratory of Psychophysics, Harvard University, Cambridge, Massachusetts

HARRY S. UPSHAW (143), Department of Psychology, University of Illinois at Chicago Circle, Chicago, Illinois

MYRON WISH (391, 450), Bell Laboratories, Murray Hill, New Jersey

* Deceased.

FOREWORD

The problem of perception is one of understanding the way in which the organism transforms, organizes, and structures information arising from the world in sense data or memory. With this definition of perception in mind, the aims of this treatise are to bring together essential aspects of the very large, diverse, and widely scattered literature on human perception and to give a précis of the state of knowledge in every area of perception. It is aimed at the psychologist in particular and at the natural scientist in general. A given topic is covered in a comprehensive survey in which fundamental facts and concepts are presented and important leads to journals and monographs of the specialized literature are provided. Perception is considered in its broadest sense. Therefore, the work will treat a wide range of experimental and theoretical work.

This ten-volume treatise is divided into two sections. Section One deals with the fundamentals of perceptual systems. It is comprised of six volumes covering (1) historical and philosophical roots of perception, (2) psychophysical judgment and measurement, (3) the biology of perceptual systems, (4) hearing, (5) seeing, and (6) feeling, tasting, smelling, and hurting.

Section Two, comprising four volumes, will cover the perceiving organism, which takes up the wider view and generally ignores specialty boundaries. The major areas will include speech and language, perception of space and objects, perception of form and pattern, cognitive performance, information processing, perceptual memory, perceptual aspects of thinking and problem solving, esthetics, and the ecology of the perceiver. Coverage will be given to theoretical issues and models of perceptual processes and also to central topics in perceptual judgment and decision.

The "Handbook of Perception" should serve as a basic source and reference work for all in the arts or sciences, indeed for all who are interested in human perception.

EDWARD C. CARTERETTE
MORTON P. FRIEDMAN

PREFACE

By *psychophysics* . . . I mean a theory which, although ancient as a problem, is new here insofar as its formulation and treatment are concerned; in short it is an exact theory of the relation of body and mind. Thus one finds its novel name neither unfitting nor unnecessary.

As an exact science psychophysics, like physics, must rest on experience and the mathematical connection of those empirical facts that demand a measure of what is experienced or, when such a measure is not available, a search for it. Since the measure of physical magnitudes is already known, the first and main task of this work will be to establish the as yet nonexistent measure of psychic magnitudes; the second will be to take up the applications and detailed arguments that develop from it.

It will be seen that the determination of a psychic measure is no mere matter of academic or philosophical abstraction but demands a broad empirical basis. This basis I believe I have been able to provide adequately from the results of my own and other investigations, so that the principle of this measure is now secure. In addition, I believe that I have shown its usefulness by many applications. The empirical basis, however, still needs considerable amplification; what has up to now been shown of the applications only serves to indicate that incomparably more can be provided.

G. T. FECHNER,
Preface, to his
"Elements of Psychophysics,"
Leipzig, 1860

Since Fechner wrote these words in 1859, the empirical basis of psychic measure has been extended enormously in every domain of sensation, perception, and cognition. The "incomparably more" applications have been provided. No one doubts now that properties of mind can be measured in the sense proposed by Fechner. What is in doubt is the theoretical basis of measurement.

In this volume we review the history of research on choice, judgment, and measurement in order to provide a background for contemporary work.

The basic psychological contexts in which choice and judgment occurs is considered in Section II. Fechner was, perhaps, very little concerned about such matters as attention, selection, memorial processes, the making of decisions under uncertainty, problems of perceptual context or the influence of the social milieu, and the way in which these matters influenced measurement.

The theoretical frame of measurement models has expanded greatly since Fechner, as may be seen by reading the chapters of Section III on measurement models and their applications.

Various psychophysical scaling methods, both those evolved from Fechner as well as his competitors, are reviewed in Section IV. In the same section, theories of scaling are treated.

Beyond Fechner there has developed a wide class of multidimensional models. Very recently their availability and use has expanded dramatically with the increased speed and cheapness of computing.

The present volume by no means exhausts the problems and theories or their applications to perceptual judgment and choice. In Section Two of the HANDBOOK OF PERCEPTION, the several volumes contained as *The Perceiving Organism* give further analyses of judgment and choice in such domains as decision making, problem solving and thinking, speech and language, information processing, and cognitive performance.

CONTENTS OF OTHER VOLUMES

Volume III: Biology of Perceptual Systems

Part I

Introduction and Overview

Chapter 1

HISTORY OF PSYCHOPHYSICS AND JUDGMENT

F. NOWELL JONES

It is ironic that the modern era of attention to the quantitative aspects of judgment should have been initiated by an attempt to prove, through rigorous analysis and measurement, a cosmology based on the German romantic philosophy of the nineteenth century. It was Fechner's publication of the *Elemente die Psychophysik* in 1860 that marked the beginning both of the modern interest in the quantification of judgment and probably even experimental psychology itself.

I. FECHNERIAN PSYCHOPHYSICS

A. The Origins

1. PHILOSOPHICAL BASE

What was Fechner about? He was very much concerned with the problems of German philosophy at the time, with its strong eastern influence. He had contributed to magnetism, had done some work on sensation, and had published some (not too well-received) philosophical work. He tells us that, lying in bed on October 22, 1850, he was suddenly struck with the idea that he could show the essential oneness of mind and body, of all existence, if he could demonstrate a mathematical relationship between bodily events and mind (inner psychophysics) and stimulus and mind (outer psychophysics). This idea was not without precedent. Pythagoras, perhaps influenced by the demonstration he had made between string length and pitch, had constructed a cosmology based on number. For him, numbers were the underlying reality both of man and cosmos. Following him, Plato was very much influenced by the same concept. The enormous difference between Plato and Fechner, however, was that Plato, the aristocrat, scorned the manipulation of material things, whereas Fechner set out at once to demonstrate his ideas empirically.

2. THE UNIT OF MEASUREMENT

Fechner had been impressed by some measurements of discrimination made by the physiologist, Weber (1834). It appeared that, for two stimuli of the same general kind to be discriminated, the difference between them had to be a constant proportion of the smaller. For Fechner, this generalization pointed to the solution of his most difficult problem—how does one measure sensations? Writing an equation between stimulus and sensation involves quantitative statements about both. Measuring the stimulus is relatively simple; one only need look to the standard methods of physics. Measuring sensation presented another problem. Fechner needed a unit, a zero point, and some way of applying the resulting scale to sensory magnitude. Fechner's approach was to appeal to the methods of physical measurement themselves. The reasoning goes as follows:

To measure, let us say, length, it is necessary to construct a yardstick, that is, the abstract property of length must be materialized, since it does not exist, at least in manipulable form, in and of itself. To measure a sensation we need to know the relationship between some actualizable scale and the property we wish to measure. The functional relationship is given by Weber's law, as generalized by Fechner. According to that law, the stimulus increment necessary for either a just noticeable difference between stimuli or for equal sensory differences between stimuli is a function of a proportional increase in the stimulus. This does not give us "the" unit of sensation, and Fechner proposed none, but it does tell us how such a unit is related to the stimulus units, hence we can use the stimulus to measure the sensation. Fechner thought of this, as just indicated, as analogous to the construction of a yardstick. The sensory unit thus conceived is not defined in and of itself, and is derived from sensitivity, that is, Weber's law, by integral calculus. Since measuring scales are arbitrary as to unit—our yardstick could just as well have been a meter stick—it makes no difference. Zero was given by the absolute or sensory threshold.

3. The Logarithmic Law: Bernoulli

Now since each successive unit on Fechner's sensory scale represents a constant fractional increase in the inducing stimulus, the relationship between stimuls and sensation—the "outer psychophysical law"—will be logarithmic and of the form $S = a \log(R/r)$, where R is the sensory threshold (cf. Fechner, 1964, Vol. II, pp. 33ff.). This "law" is also not without precedent, as acknowledged by Fechner. The topic of utility had been an important one and Bernoulli had introduced, in 1738, the idea that utility (a subjective concept, by the way) increased only logarithmically with return (Bernoulli, 1738) (see Fig. 1). So Fechner's law has much in common with the economist's law of diminishing returns.

4. Negative Sensations

Another aspect of Fechner's formulation requires comment. Because Fechner's sensory zero point corresponded not to zero physical energy but to some positive value of the stimulus (the threshold), his equation defines a class of negative sensations extending out to negative infinity. These are not really negative, of course, but may be interpreted more in line with Herbart's theoretical discussion of subliminal sensations (Herbart, 1824). At least, they were so interpreted some decades later by Freud, whose idea of an unconscious was inspired by Fechner's work.

5. Probabilistic Basis

Since repeated estimates of both the absolute and the differential thresholds show considerable variability, it was necessary for Fechner to define them statistically, and to devise methods for their measurement. Again, there were directions to which Fechner could turn for ideas. One consisted of a considerable literature in the area of probability and statistics, out of which Fechner gives primary credit to Euler (Fechner, 1860, Vol. II, pp. 548ff). Equally important was the body of work to which he could

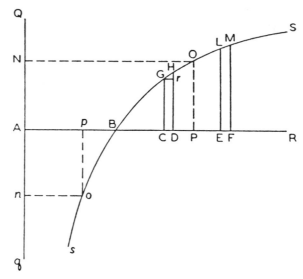

Fig. 1. From Bernoulli, p. 26 of the English translation. Possessions are plotted along the axis from *A* to *R*, utilities from *q* to *Q*. Note that equal increments along the possessions axis result in declining increments along the utilities axis.

turn for suggestions about experimental paradigms—thereafter to be known as psychophysical methods.

6. THE PSYCHOPHYSICAL METHODS

Fechner outlined three psychophysical methods. The first of these, usually known as the *method of limits,* Fechner ascribes to Delazenne, although Titchener (1905a, pp. 24–25), is inclined to give credit to Sauveur, whose work was published in 1700. What is relevant is that Fechner had a model on which to base his work. The *method of average error*—the "production" method—is, if we follow Titchener (1905a), ". . . a free gift to psychophysics from the exact sciences of physics and astronomy [p. 160]." Finally, the *method of right and wrong cases,* which we now call the *method of constant stimuli,* is probably best ascribed to Vierordt (cf. Hegelmaier, 1852). But here we must give the lion's share of credit to Fechner, who transformed a crude methodology into the most sophisticated of all his methods.

B. The Controversies

Fechner's work caught the immediate attention of the scientific community. The extensive controversies of the decades immediately following the publication of *Elemente die Psychophysik* has been exhaustively documented by Titchener (1905a). The controversies remain, their main features still much the same. At the risk of oversimplifying a rich literature we may consider two main foci of disputation, both with a familiar ring to the modern psychologist.

1. REALITY OF THE THRESHOLD.

The first question concerned the reality of the threshold. The issue was between those, on the one hand, who were inclined to consider the absolute threshold as basically a variety of difference threshold involving the discrimination of an external stimulus from the always-present internal sensations of the observer (we would probably say that we are dealing with a signal-in-noise discrimination, see the subsequent discussion of signal detection theory). Delboef (1883) attacked the concept of threshold on the ground that there is a continuum of sensory values associated with the continuum of stimuli. But at the same time, others were attempting to construct conceptual models of the threshold whose "reality" they accepted. One model was mechanical, and based on a concept expressed in modern engineering argot by the phrase "stiction is greater than friction." Suppose we have a galvanometer with a sticky pivot. For small imposed voltages there will be no observable response. At some point, however, the galvanometer will deflect a finite amount. As we increase the applied voltage, the instrument will tend to advance in small jerks. However, subsequent model building, as we shall observe, has been largely mathematical, not mechanical. Of course, Fechner, having postulated an inner as well as an outer psychophysics, gave some impetus to physiological speculation, a direction of interest that has resurged in the last few years.

2. SUBJECTIVE MEASUREMENT

a. PHILOSOPHICAL CONSIDERATION. The second broad area of concern was the question of subjective measurement. Fechner had attempted to construct a scale of equal units derived from the relationship between stimulus and sensory increments. This formulation has an unfortunate consequence. If Weber's law indeed holds, the unit is larger downward than upward. But this is a technical objection compared to the more fundamental issues raised during the decades before the turn of the century. The most basic question was, and is, whether one can "measure" a subjective event. To a large degree Wundt (1902), for example, contented himself with the measurement of sensitivity, not sensation. But few were content with this approach. The dominant thinking appears to have regarded subjective measurement as an example of indirect measurement, much like measuring an electric current by means of a galvanometer, in contrast to the direct measurement of, say, length by means of a meter stick. Even though considerable appeal was made to the uncontrolled observation of one's own subjective events, the direction has a modern, that is, positivistic aura. Specifically, the approach was to regard the differences between two sensations as subjective distances, and to deny the reality of difference thresholds (Delboef) or to regard them as facts of neural life, but not as defining units of measurement (Titchener). This position was bolstered by the development of the method of equal sense distances, or equal appearing intervals. We shall look briefly at the development of this method, since it represents the first of several quite divergent from the Fechnerian approach, and the theoretical positions of, among others, Delboef, require an understanding of it.

b. EQUAL SENSE DISTANCES. The first work is ascribable to Plateau who hit upon the idea, in the 1850s, of asking several artists to paint a gray subjectively midway between "white" and "black," examples of which were provided (Plateau, 1872). Unfortunately his work was not made public until 1872, and apparently had no chance to influence Fechner. In any event, when the resulting grays were measured photometrically he found that the reflectance of the middle gray was about $\frac{1}{8}$ of the lighter sample. Although he had plans to continue the bisection of the resulting new pairs, he never did. Since he determined that equal psychological ratios were apparently related to equal physical ratios, a little mathematical derivation showed that the two are related by a power function; that is, an equation of the $S = aI^b$, where S is sensation and I is intensity of the stimulus. This derivation is quite different from Fechner's, having a different theoretical base. At Plateau's suggestion Delbeof undertook to extend his work but had difficulties very likely ascribable to contrast effects that were improperly introduced. Others extended similar work to loudness and other senses. Inspection of some of the early data (Titchener, 1905b, p. 211) shows quite clearly that judgments fell much closer to the arithmetic mean of the bisected stimuli than to the geometric mean, a result that is particularly difficult to interpret for loudness. Subsequent work and argumentation helped matters very little. The experimental errors must have been enormous. At any rate, no one seems to have exploited Plateau's derivation. Except, perhaps, for William James! Although his contribution was not mathematical, he seems to have ascribed to the observer the ability to judge ratios among stimuli (James, 1890). It is unfortunate that he did not actually try it. Merkel (1888, etc.) and Fullerton and Cattell (1892) may be said to have gone part of the way when they asked observers to double the subjective magnitude resulting from a stimulus. Certainly the method implies that the subject is capable of a ratio judgment and thus it has a built-in zero point. Little was done with the method for several decades, although Wundt did dignify Merkel's results as providing a law of their own. (See the discussion in Wundt, 1902, beginning on p. 471, Vol. I. After all, Merkel's work had appeared in Wundt's journal.)

3. The Situation at Fechner's Death

As the brief description of issues given here shows, by the time of Fechner's death in 1887 there had accumulated a considerable—and sophisticated—literature in the field of psychophysics. Some of the discussion had a modern ring to it. Are there really thresholds? Can sensations be measured? Is there a reasonable neural model for the threshold? Can the concept of distance be applied to problems of measuring sensation? Can an observer follow an instruction to halve or double a sensation? These and other questions were considered. At the same time that these broad questions were demanding attention, methodological sophistication was increasing, partly by the consideration of experimental errors, including the question of observer attitude and his interpretation of instructions, and partly through mathematical refinement. Most of this latter effort was applied to the method of constant stimulus differences, and led to a line of development extending to the present.

Fechner had recommended his method of limits (minimal changes) for rough work only, and placed greater faith in the constant methods. His interpretation of the method of constant stimulus differences permitted three responses: greater, less, or equal—starting a tradition that was to generate debate for a hundred years. He did not, at least initially, calculate difference thresholds. Rather, he preferred to use a measure of precision derived from the Gaussian curve, calculated after apportioning the equal (or do not know) judgments equally between the other two categories. This term, h, is defined by the following equation for the normal ogive: $y = c \exp(-h^2 x^2)$.

II. OPPOSING DEVELOPMENT IN PSYCHOPHYSICAL MEASUREMENT

A. The Pragmatic View

1. The Conditions of Response

At the risk of oversimplification, we may regard the thrust of work following Fechner's death to have taken two general directions. One was pragmatic, and best represented by Cattell and by Urban. The aim was to specify the conditions under which a given probability of a certain response would be otained. Perhaps the most influential early paper in this vein was that by Fullerton and Cattell (1892). Here the central idea is accounting for "errors of observation," and the discussion utilizes underlying Gaussian distributions in accounting for response variability. It is very rewarding to examine their Figure 1 (Fig. 2 here) to see how near they came to what we now call the law of comparative judgment. But they were not thinking, as were Titchener and later Thurstone, of a sensory difference as analogous to a distance. In a similar vein, Urban's paper of 1933 is a sophisticated statement of this different point of view. Compatible with this approach was the attention paid to determining the proper form of the psychometric function—was it normal, log-normal, or perhaps some other function? (This topic, in modern form, is covered in considerable detail by Bock and Jones, 1968.) But, for the practical purpose of comparing subjects in sensitivity and the like, the exact function chosen makes little difference.

2. The "Stimulus Error"

Closely related to the debate between those who espoused the pragmatic view and those who felt that subjective distances could be measured was

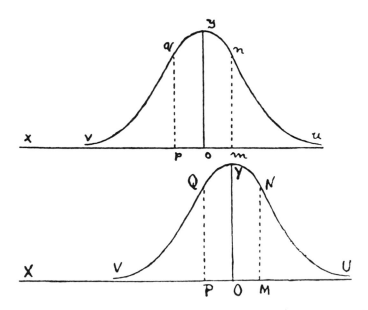

Fig. 2. From Fullerton and Cattell, 1892. The authors' discussions indicate that *X* and *x* may be considered to be "apparent" stimulus dimensions, that is, the actual stimulus strengths are at *o* and *O*, respectively, but errors of observation lead to their appearing at one or another point on the distribution according to a normal probability curve. When the perceived strength of *X* exceeds that of *x*, it will be judged greater. Although obviously much less frequently, the same holds for *x* versus *X*.

the Titchenerian concept of the "stimulus error." Although most properly applicable to genuine introspection, it also could affect subjective measurement, since perhaps all the subject was doing in some cases was making inferential judgments based on past experience with physical reality, rather than on the basis of "subjective" magnitude. In fact, Fullerton and Cattell so argued [this has again appeared in recent articles by Warren (cf. Warren & Warren, 1963)]. The stimulus error, according to Titchener, arises when one slips from the attitude of psychology—description of subjective events, "Beschreibung,"—to the attitude of physics—interpreted reports, or "Kundgabe." In the measurement of psychological magnitudes this issue tends to appear in the form of questions concerning the role of the subject. Is one really using the subject as a kind of physical instrument for the measurement of stimuli per se, or are his responses indicative in some systematic and discoverable way of an underlying subjective magnitude?

B. The Law of Comparative Judgment

1. DEVELOPMENT

Despite Woodworth's assertion in 1914 that the pragmatic approach had taken over research in psychophysics (Woodworth, 1914), another current was still flowing. Probably the clearest explanation of this other current is given by Dorothea Johannsen Crook (1941, pp. 13ff.) (whose monograph is also the best source for the literature to 1940). This current stemmed from the analogy to distance (cf. Titchener, 1905b, pp. xxiv ff. for a very clear statement), and has resulted in some of the most sophisticated work in the field of psychology.

The formulation of the law of comparative judgment by Thurstone (1927) marks the beginning of a line of scientific development which has had a profound influence on the general problem of psychological measurement. Thurstone himself indicated no specific antecedents—his *American Journal of Psychology* article introducing the theoretical derivations underlying the law has no references whatsoever. His argument now seems quite straightforward. Each stimulus to a subject gives rise to a hypothetical inner process, the "discriminal process." This is reminiscent of Fullerton and Cattell, of course, but where they stopped short, Thurstone made the leap forward. This inner process will vary from time to time and from subject to subject, and the result will be a "discriminal dispersion," either within the single subject or between subjects. Whether two stimuli with overlapping discriminal dispersions will be discriminated on a given presentation will depend upon the state of each discriminal dispersion, the distance separating the midpoints of the dispersions along some psychological continuum, and the distribution functions of the dispersions. By the consideration of assumptions concerning distribution functions and the like, Thurstone developed his famous five "cases" of comparative judgment (see Fig. 3). From the fundamental formula,

$$S_j - S_k = x_{jk}(G_j^2 + G_k^2 - 2r_{jk}G_jG_r^{1/2}),$$

where the Ss are scale values and x is the deviation from the mean of a normal distribution, it can be seen that simplifying assumptions about the correlations between the variances, and the form and homogeneity of the variances will lead to more immediately applicable formulas. The most simple case, Case V, assumes normal equal, noncorrelated variances, and leads to simple calculations. The further development of these concepts is summarized in Bock and Jones (1968).

2. IMPLICATIONS

It will be necessary to return to Thurstone again when we consider signal detection and choice, but some comments may be made here. First, the law of comparative judgment, although in the Fechnerian tradition (Thurstone mentions only Weber and Fechner) does not utilize the idea of a

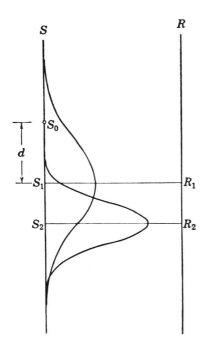

FIG. 3. From Thurstone. The R line refers to stimuli, the S line to apparent magnitudes. There will be a distribution of apparent magnitudes, the discriminal dispersion, corresponding to repeated presentations of R_1 and R_2. The distance between the average magnitudes is calculable by the application of the law of comparative judgment. In Case V, the two distributions are assumed to be identical in shape.

threshold. It is thus directly in the same category as signal detection and the work of Fullerton and Cattell. Second, the primary limitation of any confusion method of measuring psychological distance is that the distance between two perfectly (or nearly so) discriminated stimuli is in practice indeterminate. Third, and on the other hand, stimuli that have no simple physical referents may be scaled—for example, attitudes of various sorts, or objects of art. This has made the Thurstonian method very popular in such areas of research (cf. Guilford, 1954 for a summary to 1954).

III. THE THRESHOLD CONCEPT*

A. Signal Detection Theory

1. DEVELOPMENT

The old argument over the reality of the "threshold"—the "neural friction" of Titchener—was revived in modern form by a group at the University of Michigan (cf. Green & Swets, 1966). Much in the spirit of Fullerton and Cattell, but apparently quite independently, this group addressed its attention to the twin problems of separating observer attitude from sensitivity on the one hand, and the presumed "errors of observation" (to use Fullerton and Cattell's term, or "discriminal dispersions," to use Thurstone's) on the other. The power of their contribution arose from their choice of the electrical engineering analogy of signal detection. Briefly, the concept is this. All judgments—detections—must be made in the presence of noise. Making assumptions similar to those in Thurstone's Case V, this noise is considered to be Gaussian. A signal changes neither the shape nor variance of the distribution of hypothetical internal events, but rather simply shifts the mean along the continuum of interest. Whether the subject reports the signal will depend upon three things: first, the distance between the peaks of the noise and signal-plus-noise distributions; second, the particular point on the signal-plus-noise distribution at which the internal processes are to be found at the time of signal presentation; and third, the criterion adopted by the subject (see Fig. 4). It is not possible to discuss computational techniques in this chapter, so suffice it to say that the assumptions make it possible, as in the law of comparative judgment, to calculate a statistic d', which estimates the (psychological) distance between the mean of the noise and signal-plus-noise distributions. Altering the subject's criterion by manipulations such as changing the probability of the signal will not affect d' but will generate a curve, called the receiver operating characteristic (the ROC curve, see Fig. 5), which is the locus of points

* Corso (1963) has discussed the threshold concept in greater detail than is possible here, and the interested reader is referred to his article.

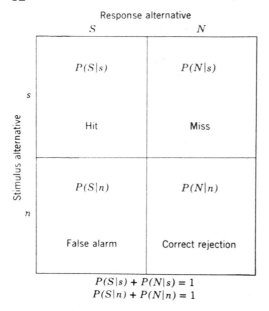

Response alternative

FIG. 4. From Green and Swets. In the two-choice situation where the subject is confronted with noise alone (*n*) or signal plus noise (*s*) he may respond correctly or incorrectly in each case. The terminology for the four possible combinations is shown. Note that as the subject increases or decreases his willingness to respond *S* (signal present), both hits and false alarms will increase.

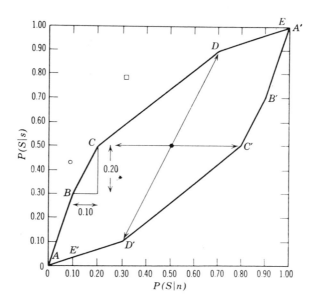

FIG. 5. A ROC graph (from Green and Swets). Ordinarily only the upper curve is plotted. Purely chance respones yield a line from 0 to *A*, whereas progressively easier discriminations yield ROC curves of increasing curvature.

for a given d' as the subject criterion changes. This has become a useful method of data analysis.

2. EVALUATION

Whether the signal detection model is completely adequate remains to be determined. Certainly some of the more recent model building has been assayed with the purpose of improving the fit. The general approach seems to have been absorbed into psychophysics for at least one important reason; it permits the separation of criterion from sensitivity variables to at least a first approximation, and therefore eliminates the worst feature of a psychophysics requiring errorless judgment; that is, based on the assumption that variability lies in the mechanisms presenting subjective events to the subject for judgment, not in the judgment process itself. This is similar to the difficulty that led to the unpopularity of genuine introspection—the experimenter had nothing unless he assumed perfect reporting by the "observer."

3. THE "FORCED-CHOICE" METHODS

Pari passu with the rise of signal detection theory was the development of the so-called "forced-choice" methods. Of course, the method of constant stimuli using only two categories of response, yes–no or greater–less, is a forced choice method of some seniority, but pair comparisons has considerable history also. The interesting extension of forced response has been to methods which require choice of place or interval rather than merely yes or no. Blackwell, for example, developed a method in which the subject was required to choose in which of four quadrants a visual signal had occurred (Blackwell, 1953). In auditory work a forced-choice method would require judgment about which of a series of n intervals, $n \geq 2$, contained the signal. Forced-choice methods have supplied the grist for the signal detector's mill, since they provide data in ideal form for analysis.

B. The Sensory Quantum

Not all have been willing to affirm the irreality or at least, uselessness, of the threshold. The idea of a sensory "quantum" may be regarded as an attempt to account for the process underlying the threshold, just as was Titchener's suggestion of neural friction. The original quantum concept is ascribable to von Békésy (1964a,b) although it was more fully developed by Stevens and others in his group (cf. Stevens, Morgan, & Volkmann, 1941). The basic concept is that as the stimulus increases in a continuous way, the neural response rises by discrete "jumps," the "quanta." Special methods are necessary to reveal these jumps, and needless to say, the issue has given rise to controversy. Much of this controversy is sum-marized by Corso (1967). Of course, should one be able to work at a level where one nerve impulse more or less (or even two) makes a differ-ence to judgment, the quantal argument must be correct. For some absolute thresholds this level may actually be approached (cf. Hensel & Boman, 1960, for example, for touch). In any event, the quantum idea indicates that the threshold concept has not been abandoned entirely.

IV. ORIGIN AND RISE OF THE "DIRECT METHODS" OF PSYCHOPHYSICS

A. Fractionation

Although some of the most recent developments in the general area of scaling, that is, psychological measurement, are generically related to the topics of the preceding sections, it is necessary for their understanding to consider other ideas that have profoundly influenced present thinking.

It has been mentioned previously that considerable work had been done using the technique of bisection or even of doubling of a given stimulus. Beginning in the early 1930s the method of fractionation, which the method of equal appearing intervals becomes when the interval is bounded by presumed zero on the lower end, was applied to a number of continua. Indeed it became popular to apply names to various presumed subjective dimensions scaled by the method—the *veg* for weight, the *mel* for pitch, and the *brill* for brightness are examples. This general methodology is dis-cussed more fully in another chapter. So far as history is concerned it is fair to say that this trend has not had a lasting effect. One does not rou-tinely use the named units and, what is more damaging, work by Garner (1954) leads to the conclusion that the results are so dependent upon the context within which the judgments are made as to render them suspect. Much the same conclusion was reached by Fullerton and Cattell in 1892! Perhaps the relative decline of the fractionation methods is also accounted for by the rise to prominence of a method, magnitude estimation, even more "direct" on the one hand, and by a shift in emphasis, which will be discussed later, on the other.

B. Magnitude Estimation

1. ORIGIN

In 1929 Richardson reported the results of his attempts to measure the intensity of images. This work grew out of his concern with the general issue of the measurability of subjective events. His method was indeed "direct." He simply estimated from time to time the strength of a fading image as a fraction of its original intensity. Encouraged by his results, and no doubt spurred by his critics, he and Ross next undertook to measure sensation in the same way (Richardson & Ross, 1930). Each of ten subjects was asked to judge, in numerical terms, a series of loudnesses against a standard designated "1.0." The results are reported for individuals and are described as power functions (loudness = constant $\times$ earphone current^n). Individual exponents varied considerably but averaged as .5.

This method lay fallow until the Steven's article of 1956. Perhaps the sheer volume of the American fractionation work tended to blanket it. In any event, having acquired a champion, what is now labeled the method of magnitude estimation has spawned an extensive literature, both substantive and theoretical. On the substantive side magnitude estimation shares with the Thurstone methods applicability to dimensions either with or without a measurable physical stimulus dimension (cf. Ekman & Sjöberg, 1965; Jones, Koor, & Humphrey, 1965; and Stevens, 1966). Perhaps an important appeal in this context is the relative ease of gathering and analyzing judgments. The theoretical side has not been such plane sailing, as might be expected from the long history of contention over the measurability of subjective events. Since the modern form of this controversy is central to much of the subsequent discussion, it is necessary to consider it, however briefly.

2. The Issue of Fundamental Measurement

In 1932 two sections of the British Association for the Advancement of Science appointed a joint committee to consider the measurability of subjective events. This Committee finally reported to the 1939 meeting (A. Ferguson et al., 1940). It was a "hung jury," unable, basically, to agree upon the meaning of "measurement." Specifically, the main split in opinion was between those who insisted on an additive operation for the subjective events allegedly being measured and those who wished to weaken the definition of measurement to include other procedures. The additive argument owes much of its development to Campbell (cf. Campbell, 1928). Following his lead, it has been widely held that true fundamental measurement obtains only where it can be shown that the actual physical juxtaposition of objects possessing the measured property results in the addition of the measured magnitudes of the properties in the objects separately. Length and mass are examples. In psychophysical measurement, one can add physical stimuli, but there is no way to add sensations directly. Hence one's conclusion concerning the measurability of subjective magnitudes is the direct outcome of one's adherence to the additive criterion. Those who argue that subjective magnitudes are measurable must find some other basis of validation. Since, as we have seen, basically the same problem had faced

Fechner and his critics, it must be said that the argument had not progressed far in almost a century.

3. THE POWER LAW

By far the most prolific and persuasive author in this context has been S. S. Stevens, whose espousal of magnitude estimation has been extremely influential. His thinking is summarized in several places although only one reference is given here (Stevens, 1957). Basically, the modern method of magnitude estimation uses the past learning of the subject to provide a scale of cardinal numbers which he is asked to assign to various stimuli. When the usual subject does this, the first-approximation relationship between physical stimulus and response is a power function (of the form $S = aI^b$). What validation is there for the assertion that this measures subjective magnitude? This question has been raised rather succinctly by Treisman (1964), and by Poulton (1968). Staying within the measurement system, for example, predicting cross-modality matches from the exponents for the continua judged separately, is not completely satisfying. Another line of evidence put forward involves scaling by strength of handgrip assigned by the subject to each magnitude. Unfortunately, this has two difficulties. First, this may be thought of as simply another case of cross-modality matching. Second, the correspondence between "grip measure" and "assigned number measure" is difficult to interpret since the number series is presumably infinite whereas there is a definite maximum to grip. Perhaps the numbers used by a subject are really a limited set (cf. Jones & Woskow, 1966), in which case they approach a set of categories.

Since contemporary problems of measurement are treated in considerable detail in another chapter, only a few highlights of more recent developments will be referred to here. The group surrounding Ekman has contributed a large literature that is closely related to the Stevens work. It was Ekman who first extended magnitude estimation to topics, such as occupational status, which have no underlying physical continuum. A good entry into the work of the Stockholm group is the bibliography in Ekman and Sjöberg (1965).

C. Constant Sum Method

Comrey (1950) is responsible for formalizing a ratio scaling technique, which is based on a suggestion by Metfessel (1947) (whose inspiration was betting behavior at horse racing tracks). Briefly, to scale a series of stimuli, the stimuli are given in all possible pairs and the subject is asked to divide 100 points among them according to their judged similarity. These judgments are transformed into proportions for further analysis. This method obviously requires more judgments than magnitude estimation, but, if it is assumed that the subject can make ratio judgments, a ratio scale results. The method has not had extensive application.

D. The Theory of Choice

During the past decade a new conceptual base for judgment has been emerging. Briefly, this new direction treats, not judgments, but choices. The initial contribution was by Luce (1959). The potential importance of this approach is that it encompasses any situation in which an organism makes one response rather than another, hence it includes both judgment and learning, in their traditional meanings. This way of looking at the problem is compatible with the mathematical learning theories developed over the past decade or so, and this circumstance, coupled with the mathematical sophistication of the workers in the field, has produced an interesting literature. This work has been reviewed by Zinnes (1969), and is very well treated in its application to psychophysical measurement by Luce and Galanter (1963). This latter reference, in conjunction with other essays in the same collection, shows how the development of choice models can be extended to cover a range of topics not directly related at first glance. It would appear that choice models may well lead away from the concept of sensory distances espoused by Titchener and underlying the essentially Euclidean assumptions of much scaling work.

E. Functional Measurement

Deserving of special comment is the recent work of Anderson on what he terms "functional measurement" (Anderson, 1971). Although he does not put it quite that way it appears that he regards the question of measurement to be bound up inseparably with empirical problems. An assertion concerning measurement is similar (identical?) to any other theoretical hypothesis concerning data of a certain sort. If, over a series of experiments or other kind of investigation, the hypotheses are empirically confirmed, the measure instrument is *pari passu* validated. Although Anderson puts this the most succinctly and directly it would appear that this way of going about things is what most psychologists do—witness the vast literature in mental testing, for example. This approach also removes much of the force from arguments concerning permissible arithmetic operations with various varieties of "scale" (cf. Stevens, 1951) since one does not prejudge the nature of the scale. In place of a simple additive criterion is put the impact of a convergent series of investigations, each presuming the existence of measurement and, if predictions are empirically verified, lending support to the presumption.

F. Cognitive Theory: Information Measures

Baird (1970a,b) has proposed a theoretical development based on the subject as a processor of information. Formally, this has its closest relationships with the work of Restle (1961) and Garner (1962). Interestingly enough, since the thrust of the argument is that the psychophysical results are determined by the particular coding system adopted by the subject and this is in turn influenced by the psychophysical method employed, we seem to have returned in spirit to the Fullerton and Cattell pragmatic approach. It would be unfair, however, to overlook the possible impact of work which self-confessedly aims at empirical verification of its features.

V. SPECIAL TOPICS

A. Multidimensional Psychophysics

1. THE EUCLIDIAN MODEL

So far the topics considered have been chosen to give a broad picture of the evolution of thinking about the central measurement problem in judgment. But there were developments not clearly in the mainstream of debate. One of the more important were the multidimensional methods. The scaling models of Fechner, Thurstone, Stevens, and others, are capable of assigning values to stimuli lying along a single dimension. Lack of transitivity is an embarrassment: How can one arrange three tennis players in order of skill when A beats B, B beats C, but C regularly beats A? And it does happen! Obviously no pair by pair comparison can generate more than one dimension. The first suggestion for extending judgmental methods to include the 2-, . . . , n-dimensional cases was made by Richardson (1938). His complete paper has not been published but has had private circulation. In it he introduced the method of triads. Here the subject is asked to choose the most similar pair from among three stimuli, and also the least similar. If one considers the stimuli to represent points in a (Euclidean) psychological space (distance again!), it is possible to apply essentially factor analytical techniques to determine the dimensionality of the judgments.

There are other ways of obtaining the original similarity judgments. Of course the hope underlying these techniques is that an unknown dimensionality will be revealed by analysis of the judgment data—a statistical application of Sir Francis Bacon's empiricism! An excellent explication of the general method is given by Torgerson (1958, Chap. 11).

2. NONPARAMETRIC ANALYSIS

Certain difficulties arise, largely surrounding the Euclidean assumption (cf. Attneave, 1950). There is no a priori reason why, even though we may accept a distance model, the law of cosines should hold in psychological space. Ordinarily it is necessary to seek the additive constant that will, on the one hand, give minimum dimensionality to the solution and, on the other, eliminate negative roots. An attempt to avoid these difficulties is due to Coombs (1950), whereas a more recent development is a method of analysis due to Shepard (1966). It is unfortunately the case, however, that application of multidimensional techniques to areas of unknown dimensionality have not been of outstanding usefulness, even though interesting! (A good entry into the literature to 1969 is Zinnes, 1969.)

B. Adaptation Level

Another concept that has been of considerable interest is "adaptation level." This has been extensively developed by Helson (cf. Helson, 1964). Now of course everyone has a vague awareness, at least, that judgments are relative. It would be unfair to suggest that adaptation level theory is so naive. Rather, it arose from some experimentation by Helson (1943) on induced color. If one observes a series of surfaces of different reflectance under (more or less) monochromatic light he will observe an interesting phenomenon—surfaces of greater than average reflectance appear to be the color of the illumination, the average surface appears gray, but the surfaces of less than average reflectance appear to be the complement of the illumination. In other words, judgment, so to speak, goes in opposite directions from some middle point. So far few would disagree with the idea of an adaptation level as a qualitatively reasonable suggestion. It is when quantificatification is attempted that difficulties arise. The most persistent testing of the precise predictions of adaptation level theory is due to Parducci. His substitution of a range-frequency model is based on extensive work with distorted distributions of stimuli which do not generate responses predictable by the Helson theory (Parducci & Perrett, 1971). It is possible that the further development of choice models will come to account for these results as most certainly they must if they are to be complete.

VI. FINAL COMMENTS

Little has been said in this chapter about the substantive contributions made in psychophysics and judgment over the last 100 years. All that has been discussed is basically methodological. Just as there is no inherent reason for measuring, say length, no matter how fundamentally, in the absence of some substantive context, so there is no reason for mathematical theorizing about psychological measurement unless it ultimately makes some difference outside its own context. As we have seen, the basic problems remain. So far, it would appear that no system of postulates and axioms has an adequate data base. Perhaps one will. Surely a general theory encompassing both judgment and learning would be of extreme importance. In the meantime, the psychologist interested in substantive problems may justifiably place his faith in pragmatism.

References

Anderson, N. H. Integration theory and attitude change. *Psychological Review,* 1971, 171–206.

Attneave, F. Dimensions of similarity. *American Journal of Psychology,* 1950, **63,** 516–556.

Baird, J. C. A cognitive theory of psychophysics. I. *Scandinavian Journal of Psychology,* 1970, **11,** 35–46. (a)

Baird, J. C. A cognitive theory of psychophysics. II. *Scandinavian Journal of Psychology,* 1970, **11,** 89–102. (b)

Békésy, G. von. Über die Herstellung und Messung langsamer sinusförmiger Luftdruckschwankungen. *Annelen der Physik,* 1936, **25,** 413–432. (a)

Békésy, G. von Über die Horschwelle und Fuhlgrenze langsamer sinusförmiger Luftruckschwankungen. *Annelen der Physik.,* 1936, **22,** 554–556. (b)

Bernoulli, Daniel. Specimen theoriae novae de mensura sortis. *Concentarii.* Academiae Scientiarum Imperiales Petopolotanae, 1738, **5,** 175–192. [This has been issued with German and English translations (by Fich and by Sommer) by the Gregg Press, 1967.]

Blackwell, H. R. Psychophysical thresholds: Experimental studies of methods of measurement. *Bulletin of the Engineering Research Institute of the University of Michigan,* No. 36, 1953.

Bock, R. D., & Jones, L. V. *The measurement and prediction of judgment and choice.* San Francisco: Holden-Day, 1968.

Campbell, N. R. *An account of the principles of measurement and calculation.* London: Longmans Green, 1928.

Comrey, A. L. A proposed method for absolute ratio scaling. *Psychometrika,* 1950, **15,** 317–325.

Coombs, C. H. Psychological scaling without a unit of measurement. *Psychological Review,* 1950, **56,** 145–158.

Corso, J. F. A theoretico-historical review of the threshold concept. *Psychological Bulletin,* 1963, **60,** 356–370.

Corso, J. F. *The Experimental Psychology of Sensory Behavior.* New York: Holt, 1967. Pp. 423ff.

Crook, Dorothea Johannsen. *The principles of psychophysics with laboratory Exercises.* Ann Arbor, Michigan: Edwards Brothers, 1941.

Delboef, J. R. L. *Examen critique de la loi psychophysique: Sa base et sa signification.* Paris: Bailliere, 1883.

Ekman, G., & Sjöberg, L. Scaling. *Annual Review of Psychology,* 1965, **16**, 451–474.

Fechner, Gustav T. *Elemente der Psychophysik.* Leipzig: Breitkopf and Hartel, 1860. [Reissued 1964 by Bonset, Amsterdam.]

Ferguson, A. (Chairman) *et al.* Final report. *Advances in Science,* 1940, No. 2, 331–349.

Fullerton, G. S., & Cattell, J. McK. On the perception of small differences, *Publications of the University of Pennsylvania,* **2**, Philadelphia: University of Pennsylvania Press, 1892.

Garner, W. R. Context effects and the validity of loudness scales. *Journal of Experimental Psychology,* 1954, **48**, 218–224.

Garner, W. R. *Uncertainty and structure as psychological concepts.* New York: Wiley, 1962.

Green, D. M., & Swets, J. A. *Signal detection theory and psychophysics.* New York: Wiley, 1966.

Guilford, J. P. *Psychometric methods* (2nd ed.). New York: McGraw-Hill, 1954.

Hegelmaier, F. Uber das Gedächtniss für Lineoranschauungen. *Archives of Physiolgie Heilk,* 1852, **11**, 844–853.

Helson, H. Some factors and implications of color constancy. *Journal of the Optical Society of America,* 1943, **33**, 555–567.

Helson, H. *Adaptation level theory.* New York: Harper & Row, 1964.

Hensel, H., & Bowman, K. K. A. Afferent impulses in cutaneous sensory nerves in human subjects. *Journal of Neurophysiology,* 1960, **23**, 564–578.

Herbert, J. F. *Psychologie als Wissenschaft.* Unzer, Königsberg, 1824.

James, William. *Principles of Psychology,* Vol. II. New York: Holt, 1890. Pp. 189ff.

Jones, F. N., Korr, A., & Humphrey, G. A direct scale of attitude toward the church. *Perceptual and Motor Skills,* 1965, **20**, 319–324.

Jones, F. N., & Woskow, M. J. Some effects of context on the slope in magnitude estimation. *Journal of Experimental Psychology,* 1966, **71**, 177–180.

Luce, R. D. *Individual choice behavior.* New York: Wiley, 1959.

Luce, R. D., & Galanter, E. Psychophysical scaling. In R. D. Luce, R. R. Bush, & E. Galanter (Eds.), *Handbook of Mathematical Psychology,* Chapter 5. New York: Wiley, 1963.

Merkel, J. Die Abhangigkeit zwischen Reiz und Empfindung. *Philosophical Studies,* 1888, **4**, 541–594; 1889, **5**, 245–291; and 499–557.

Metfessel, M. A proposal for quantitative reporting of comparative judgments. *Journal of Psychology,* 1947, **24**, 229–235.

Parducci, A., & Perrett, L. F. Category rating scales: Effects of relative spacing and frequency of stimulus values. *Journal of Experimental Psychological Monographs,* 1971.

Plateau, J. A. F. Sur la mesure des sensations physiques, et sur la loi qui lie l'intensité de ces sensations a l'intensité de l'intensité de la cause excitante. *Bulletin of the Academy of Royale, Belgique,* 1872, **33**, 376–385.

Poulton, E. C. The new psychophysics: Six models for magnitude estimation. *Psychological Bulletin,* 1968, **69**, 1–19.

Restle, F. *Psychology of judgment and choice.* New York: Wiley, 1961.

Richardson, L. F. Imagery, conation, and cerebral conductance. *Journal of General Psychology,* 1929, **2,** 324–352.

Richardson, L. F., & Ross, J. S. Loudness and telephone current. *Journal of General Psychology,* 1930, **3,** 288–306.

Richardson, M. W. Multidimensional psychophysics. *Psychological Bulletin,* 1938, **35,** 659–660.

Shepard, R. N. Metric structures in ordinal data. *Journal of Mathematical Psychology,* 1966, **3,** 287–316.

Stevens, S. S. Mathematics, measurement and psychophysics. In S. S. Stevens (Ed.), *Handbook of Experimental Psychology,* Chapter 1. New York: Wiley, 1951.

Stevens, S. S. On the psychophysical law. *Psychological Review,* 1957, **64,** 153–181.

Stevens, S. S. A metric for the social consensus. *Science,* 1966, **151,** 530–541.

Stevens, S. S., Morgan, C. T., & Volkmann, J. Theory of the neural quantum in the discrimination of loudness and pitch. *American Journal of Psychology,* 1941, **54,** 315–335.

Thurstone, L. L. Psychophysical analysis. *American Journal of Psychology,* 1927, **38,** 369–389.

Titchener, E. B. *Experimental psychology,* Vol. II. *Quantitative experiments. Part I. Student's manual* New York: Macmillan, 1905. [Reprinted 1927.] (a)

Titchener, E. B. *Experimental psychology,* Vol. II. *Quantitative experiments. Part II. Instructor's manual.* New York: Macmillan, 1905. [Reprinted 1927.] (b)

Torgerson, W. S. *Theory and methods of scaling.* New York: Wiley, 1958.

Treisman, M. Sensory scaling and the psychophysical laws. *Quarterly Journal of Experimental Psychology,* 1964, **16,** 11–22.

Urban, F. M. The Weber–Fechner law and mental measurement. *Journal of Experimental Psychology,* 1933, **16,** 221–238.

Warren, R. M., & Warren, R. P. A critique of S. S. Stevers New Psychophysics. *Percepual and Motor Skills,* 1963, **16,** 797–810.

Weber, E. H. *De pulsu, resorptione, auditu et tactu: Annotationes anatomical et physiologiae.* Leipzig, 1834.

Woodworth, R. S. Professor Cettell's psychophysical contributions. In Psychological researches of James McKeen Cattell. *Archives of Psychology,* 1914, **4** (No. 3), 60–74.

Wundt, W. *Grundzüge der Physiologischen Psychologie* (5th ed.). Leipzig: Engelmann, 1902. [Especially Vol. I.]

Zinnes, J. L. Scaling. *Annual Review of Psychology,* 1969, **20,** 447–478.

Part II

Perceptual Choice and Judgment

Chapter 2

ATTENTION: THE PROCESSING OF MULTIPLE SOURCES OF INFORMATION*

W. R. GARNER

I. INTRODUCTION

The human organism exists in an environment containing many different sources of information. It is patently impossible for the organism to process

* Preparation of this manuscript was supported by Grant MH 14229 from the National Institute of Mental Health to Yale University. The literature review for the chapter was completed in 1970.

all these sources, since it has a limited information capacity, and the amount of information available for processing is always much greater than the limited capacity. Therefore the organism must process information selectively. However, the fact that information must be processed selectively does not preclude the organism from processing more than a single source of information, and in fact it frequently does so. So nonselective as well as selective processing occurs with multiple sources of information, and both of these complementary areas are the subject of this chapter.

In line with most current ideas, the position taken here is that it is not stimulus energy that is processed, but the information contained in various stimuli. Information has various, but related, meanings to different authors writing in this field. Garner (1962) has used the term most nearly in its information–theoretic sense as having to do with the nature and number of the alternatives to a particular stimulus that could have occurred but did not. Although Neisser (1967) has not dealt with information in a quantitative sense, he has been concerned with the meaning, implication, or identifying referent of the stimulus rather than with its energic properties. Gibson (1966) has emphasized the meaning of information *about* the real world, rather than that carried in the specific stimulus itself. Broadbent (1958) used information both in its formal, quantifiable sense and also in its less formal sense as Neisser has done. These various authors, however, are simply emphasizing different aspects of the same fundamental concept, which is that what the organism processes is not stimulus energy, but information. What is important is not how much or what kind of energy exists, but rather what are the implications (e.g., what about the real world is represented) or the consequences (what must be done about it) of stimulation.

This introduction will consider several rational and logical aspects of the problem of information selection. In the past few years several excellent articles have been written on attention, and on the nature of the problem itself, and many of these have influenced the present analysis. Those most pertinent to the present discussion are Garner and Morton (1969), Garner (1970), Treisman (1969), Egeth (1967) and Egeth and Bevan (1973).

A. Some Definitions

1. SOURCE OF INFORMATION

The term *source* is a general term which refers to any stimulus property or characteristic that serves as the origin, outlet, or agent in providing information to the organism. It is an undifferentiated term, and may refer to channels, dimensions or attributes, distinctive features, levels of dimensions, etc.

2. DIMENSION OR VARIABLE

A dimension is any stimulus property which varies and thus serves as a source of information. The concept of a dimension includes that of variation, so there must either be more than one level of the dimension in existence or inferred by the organism in order for a dimension to serve as an information source. The different usages of the concept of information all emphasize different consequences of the variation: In the formal information–theoretic sense, the variation defines a set of alternative stimuli; it also defines relevant aspects of the real world that the stimulus represents; and it defines the behavioral or processing consequences of the stimulus.

Sometimes the term *attribute* is used instead of dimension, but this term has also been used to mean the level or single value on a dimension and it will not be used here. The general term *variable* is used here in the same sense as *dimension* and the two terms will be used interchangeably.

3. LEVEL OR VALUE

If there is a dimension or variable that defines a number of stimulus alternatives, then for any given stimulus event, the dimension exists with a given value or level. Thus if length is an informational dimension, the levels on this dimension will be specific lengths, such as 1 inch or 5 cm. Here level or value will be used interchangeably to mean the same thing.

4. TARGET

This is a term used by Treisman (1969), and she defines it as a level on a dimension. Such a definition is appropriate, since the specific level and the dimension must be distinguished. But target can also mean the conjunction of values on two or more different dimensions (e.g., a target is a red circle, where both hue and form are the dimensions). Here the term *target* will be used only when it is defined with respect to more than one dimension.

5. DISTINCTIVE FEATURE

A commonly used term in research on attention is distinctive feature, but it will not be used here because it has been used to mean either a level on a dimension, a target (as the conjunction of several levels), or as the dimension itself. For example, the term *distinctive feature* has been used to mean the property of curved lines in alphanumeric symbols, but it has also been used to mean the dimension of curved versus linear property.

6. CHANNEL

A frequently used term in information-processing work is channel. It is defined last here because its definition requires differentiation from other terms already defined. A channel is any property of a stimulus (or the organismic equivalent of the property) that makes information available but is not itself part of the information aspect of the stimulus. To illustrate, it may be considered that the visual modality is the information channel, but this modality does not produce information in the sense that it is one stimulus that is an alternative to another. It simply provides access to information that gets into the organism, but is not itself part of the information. Likewise, one ear may be a channel if all stimulus input is restricted to that channel, but the ear itself is not providing information. Still further, information may be provided by variations in the form of a visual stimulus presented 10° to the right of the fovea of a single eye. This lateral location defines a channel, but is itself not providing information. Variation in form provides the information, and retinal locus (or external locus) defines the information channel.

It should be clear that there is an intimate relation between levels on a dimension and the concept of a channel, and whether we consider a stimulus property to be a level on a dimension or a channel depends on its function for the organism in a particular setting. To illustrate, if two alternative stimuli are a 1000-Hz tone to the right ear or alternatively to the left ear, then the right ear is a level on an information-providing dimension, and not a channel. The auditory modality would be the channel in this case. Thus a particular property of a stimulus can in one situation be considered a channel, and in another a level on a dimension, the proper consideration depending on the information-providing role of the property.

To illustrate further, consider the preceding example in which the lateral location of a visual stimulus is considered a channel, because the information is provided by variations in form, not variations in retinal location. But clearly this channel can be a level on the dimension of lateral locus, and if variations in lateral locus are providing information, then laterality is a dimension, and particular location is a level on that dimension.

Thus channels do not enter into the definition of stimulus alternatives, but dimensions do.

B. Paradigmatic Experimental Tasks

Many experimental tasks have been used in the study of attention, but there is a particular set of experiments having logical relations that are critical to understanding the ability or inability of an organism to attend selectively to different sources of information. These experiments involve manipulations in the task requirements for the subject, but they also involve manipulations of the information relations in the two or more sources. If a subject succeeds in selectively attending, he has in some sense managed to treat two or more sources of information as independent. However, the sources themselves may or may not provide independent information, so the independence of information itself becomes a critical part of the experimental question.

1. SINGLE INFORMATION SOURCE: THE CONTROL EXPERIMENT

The control experiment is always one requiring the subject to perform some task with a single information source. How well he does in this case then provides the base measure to compare performance on other tasks. The performance measures are usually either time or accuracy.

2. ATTENTIVE SELECTION, INDEPENDENT INFORMATION

One comparison experiment provides more than one information source and by instruction requires the subject to respond only to one of the sources. To illustrate, continuous speech may be presented to the two ears and the subject required to "shadow" the speech in one ear by repeating it. Alternatively, a set of visual stimuli may be generated by varying size and color, and the subject required to sort the stimuli into two piles according to color only, ignoring size. If in these experiments the subject can shadow one ear as accurately when there is speech in the other ear as when there is not, or if he can sort the stimulus cards as fast when they vary in two dimensions as when they vary in color alone, it is concluded that the subject has managed to attend selectively to one ear as a channel, or to color as a single dimension.

Such experiments can be meaningfully interpreted only if it is known that the two sources of information (ears or dimensions) are providing independent information. If both ears receive the same speech, or if size and color are correlated, nothing can be learned about the ability of the organism to attend selectively, since it cannot be known to which source he was responding, or whether he was responding to a single source at all.

It should be noted that this task does not require an increased load for the subject if he is able to attend selectively. Only if there is a failure of selective attention (due to the inability of the subject to reject the undesired information channel), is there an increased task load. So interpretation of failure on the selective attention task is not complicated by an increased imposed task load.

3. ATTENTIVE COMBINATION, INDEPENDENT INFORMATION

An alternative task (which Treisman, 1969, called divided attention) is to provide two or more sources of independent information, but to require that the subject process both sources simultaneously. Thus he must shadow messages in both ears (or perhaps later be able to answer questions about them), or he must be able to sort the cards into piles based on both color and size. Performance is now considered satisfactory if he can do as well processing the multiple sources of information as he could with the control experiments for each source presented and processed alone. So successful attentive combination occurs if full information is obtained from both ears, or if there is no increase in sorting speed when the two dimensions must be processed simultaneously.

This task puts an increased information-processing load on the subject, and failure on this task (i.e., both sources cannot be processed as efficiently as one) implies an information-processing limitation somewhere. Such a limitation would produce either divided attention on the part of the subject (each source being processed less well than in its control experiment), or a resort to selective attention (only one source being processed, the other being ignored).

4. ATTENTIVE INTEGRATION, CORRELATED INFORMATION

A fourth experimental paradigm is one in which the multiple (usually two) sources of information provide correlated or redundant information rather than the independent information used with both the attentive selection and attentive combination tasks. For example, the same speech is presented to both ears, or the two dimensions of color and size are perfectly correlated. This type of experiment does not increase the information-processing load for the subject; thus there would be no expectation of any loss of performance due to an information-processing limitation. Rather, the normal expectation with this experiment would be an improvement in performance, either by a decrease in errors or by an increase in speed. This improvement is expected in the sense that the task requirements make it the ideal outcome, since redundant information is provided in this experimental paradigm. However, in order for the subject to make effective use of the redundant information, he must be able to integrate it. If the nature of the two sources of information is such that he cannot integrate information, then no improvement in performance will result.

Failure to obtain improvement with this experimental paradigm may also occur as an artifactual consequence of a performance limitation, and additional control experiments would be necessary to check for such a limitation. To illustrate, if errors in the control task are zero, there can be no improved performance, but such a result should not be interpreted as a failure of information integration. Likewise, there are minimum sorting times in card-sorting experiments, or minimum reaction times in discrete-reaction experiments, which cannot be lowered with any amount of redundant information. If an experiment fails to show improved speed of information processing with redundant information, control experiments are necessary to clarify the meaning of the result.

5. OTHER TASKS

a. LEARNING. Other experimental tasks that bear on problems of attention need brief mention. One is the learning task. An example is the Eckstrand and Wickens (1954) experiment in which 16 visual stimuli consisting of all combinations of four forms × four colors were used. Subjects were first trained to respond with key pressing to either color only or form only. Later they were trained with these two dimensions correlated, then were tested on just form or just color. Performance on the tests indicated that learning with correlated dimensions had occurred to that dimension first used in training—i.e., the initial training produced attention to the earlier relevant dimension in the training with correlated dimensions.

b. FREE CLASSIFICATION. Subjects may simply be asked to sort a set of stimuli into two or more groups in any manner they choose. As an example, Imai and Garner (1965) showed that there is dimensional salience (i.e., all stimulus dimensions are not used equally often as the basis of classification), although the relatively stronger attention value of some dimensions did not affect speed of sorting in a constrained classification task.

c. CONCEPT LEARNING. Attentional value (or salience) of particular dimensions in a set of stimuli will affect the rate at which concepts based on the different dimensions are learned. Furthermore, when concepts are based on two or more dimensions, the nature of the dimensions affects ease of learning. As an example, Shepard, Hovland, and Jenkins (1961) showed that stimulus dimensions such as color, size, and form of a single stimulus provide easier concept learning than stimulus dimensions of size of a triangle, circle, or square. Thus in the former case, attention is easily distributed, but not in the latter case.

C. Some Primary Attentive Concepts

These three paradigmatic experimental tasks, in conjunction with the necessary control experiments, provide a set of converging operations (Garner, Hake, & Eriksen, 1956) to delimit three major types of attentive processes or mechanisms. It is possible to dichotomize (for purposes of exposition) the outcomes of each of these three experiments with respect to the control experiments, and then to specify whether the task has been carried out successfully (indicated as "+" in Table I) or unsuccessfully (indicated as "−" in Table I). For the attentive selection task, successful

TABLE I

The Possible Outcomes of Three Paradigmatic Experiments Compared to a
Control Experiment and the Attentive Concepts They Imply[a]

	Task			
	Selection	Combination	Integration	Concept
a	+	−	−	Mandatory selection
b	+	+	+	Optional selection
c	+	−	+	Optional selection, process limit
d	+	+	−	Optional selection, performance limit
e	−	+	+	Mandatory distribution
f	−	−	+	Mandatory distribution, process limit
g	−	+	−	Mandatory distribution, performance limit
h	−	−	−	Mandatory distribution, process and performance limit

[a] A+ means that the task requirements have been satisfied compared to the control experiments. A− means that they have not.

performance is no loss of accuracy or speed when sources of independent information are added. For attentive combination, successful performance is no loss of accuracy or speed when sources of additional information are added and the subject actually processes the additional information. For the attentive integration task, a successful outcome is an improvement in either speed or accuracy when a source of redundant information is added.

With either successful or unsuccessful results for each of the three experiments, there are eight possible outcomes from all three experiments, and these are listed in Table I, along with the attentive concepts that each outcome implies. There are three ideal or prototypic outcomes, having to do with whether attention is selective or distributed, and whether the selectivity or distribution is mandatory or optional.

1. Mandatory Selection

Outcome *a* shows successful carrying out of the selection task, but failure on the other two tasks. Since selection does occur, selection is at least possible. But since information in the correlated task is not integrated, and since there is failure to process both sources of information on the combination task with independent information, it must be concluded that the subject in such a set of experiments had no choice but to attend selectively. Failure on both the combination and integration tasks could mean a combination of process limit and performance limit, and to be positive that mandatory selection is involved additional experiments would logically be required to establish that the subject can process more information, and that his performance is not limited.

2. OPTIONAL SELECTION

Outcome *b* shows successful carrying out of all three tasks, and this outcome indicates that the success with the selection task was due to an optional process, since each of the other two tasks requires distribution of attention, with information integration in one case and information combination in the other. Naturally, optional selection is the same as optional distribution.

3. MANDATORY DISTRIBUTION

Any outcome that shows a failure on the selection task implies that distributed attention is mandatory, since presumably the experimental subject is trying to carry out the task requirements. Such an outcome also implies that success should be obtained with both the combination and the integration tasks, since if attention must be distributed, it should be used. So Outcome *e* is the prototypical outcome for mandatory distributed attention.

The other five possible outcomes for the three experiments all require that some limiting factor be assumed, since the logic of the outcomes is contradictory. If there is a failure of integration when the other two experiments imply success, as in Outcome *d*, the most likely explanation is that there is a performance limitation. On the other hand, if there is a failure on the combination task when success is implied by the other two outcomes, as in Outcome *f*, then an information-processing limit (or channel capacity) is likely.

D. Some Related Concepts

1. INTEGRAL AND SEPARABLE DIMENSIONS

Garner (1970), following similar distinctions by Torgerson (1958), Shepard, Hovland, and Jenkins (1961), Shepard (1964), Hyman and Well (1968), Attneave (1962), and Lockhead (1966a), distinguished between integral and separable dimensions. The distinction was based on experimental data of Garner and Felfoldy (1970) involving use of both the attentive selection and integration tasks, but not the attentive combination task. The distinction was between dimensions that showed failure on the selection task and success on the integration task and dimensions that showed success on the selection task and failure on the integration task. This concept of integrality of dimensions satisfies the broader concept of mandatory distribution of attention; but the concept of separability does not fully satisfy the concept of mandatory selection. Failure on the integration task, combined with success on the selection task, implies mandatory selection, but failure on a combination task would argue for mandatory selection more strongly. Nevertheless, the stimulus concept of dimensional separability is nearly equivalent to the process concept of mandatory selection, whereas the stimulus concept of dimensional integrality is equivalent to the process concept of mandatory distributed attention.

The presently used process concepts are intended to be broader than the stimulus concepts in that they are not restricted to stimulus dimensions, and in that they allow the optional property as well.

2. SERIAL AND PARALLEL PROCESSING OF INFORMATION

A commonly made distinction about information processing (see Egeth, 1966) is whether two or more sources of information are processed in serial or in parallel mode (i.e., one at a time or both together). The distinction applies primarily to the attentive combination task, in which more than one source of information must be processed at the same time. If, in present terms, the combination task is carried out successfully, then no greater time is required to carry out two tasks than one, and processing is said to be in parallel. On the other hand, if attentive selection is mandatory, or alternatively if there is an information limit, then the tasks must be carried out one after the other, and processing is in the serial mode.

These concepts, as Garner (1970) has pointed out, are properly applicable only when it has been established that attentive selection exists, since only in that case can one be sure that there is more than a single information source for the subject. If attentive selection is mandatory, then clearly processing of multiple sources of information can only be accomplished with the serial mode. If attentive selection is optional, then either serial or parallel processing may occur, although a limit on information-processing capacity will force serial processing. On the other hand, if attention is mandatorily distributed, then all sources of information are attended to and processed simultaneously. In a naive sense, such a result implies parallel processing. And yet if attention is mandatorily distributed, there exists the very real question as to whether the information sources are indeed separate, since a parsimonious explanation of mandatory distribution is that the sources are not really separate at all. Thus the distinction between serial and parallel processing of information has some relevance to the problem of selective attention, but is clearly a secondary distinction.

3. SHORT-TERM MEMORY

A concept that deserves comment because of its implications for studies of attention is that of iconic memory, which can be defined as the very short-term persistence of visual or auditory input in basically its original form. Sperling (1960) and Averbach and Coriell (1961) have shown such persistence for vision; its existence in the auditory mode was a primary consideration in Broadbent's (1958) model of perceptual processing. More recently Crowder and Morton (1969) have demonstrated several effects of iconic auditory memory.

These concepts are not in themselves part of the attention problem, but they become important in that they mean that the stimulus is available for attentive processing for seconds or fractions of a second after the stimulus has been terminated. Furthermore, the short-term storage of stimulus information makes possible a serial processing of information which may at times seem like parallel processing, because that information that is not processed immediately is held for a short period for later processing.

II. INTERMODALITY ATTENTION

The rest of this chapter will be devoted to examining evidence for attentive factors. In particular, attempts will be made to determine the circumstances under which attentive selection and attentive distribution exist, and whether such processes are optional or mandatory. Since little research has been done on other modalities, only the visual and auditory modalities will be considered as primary information sources.

Of first concern is whether the two modalities themselves can be the basis of attentive selection or distribution. There is available the obvious fact that selection can occur in favor of audition, since the human organism can close its eyelids and thus exclude visual input, and this process is clearly optional. The ears cannot be closed so easily, since there is no mechanical device for shutting out sound. Nevertheless, there is ample evidence that auditory information can be excluded from attention.

A. Intermodality Attentive Combination

There has been little research showing the extent to which both visual and auditory information can be processed together, but the evidence nevertheless gives a quite clear picture of the extent to which combination tasks can be carried out.

1. ABSOLUTE JUDGMENTS

Tulving and Lindsay (1967) carried out an extensive experiment on absolute judgments of visual and auditory dimensions presented simultaneously. Their visual stimuli were circular patches of white light varying in intensity, and their auditory stimuli were pure tones, also varying in intensity. There were eight levels of each stimulus dimension. They used the single-dimension control tasks, the attentive-selection tasks for each dimension, and the attentive-combination task, although varying the order of report (as well as instructions about which dimension was to be considered primary).

Their results show that attentive selection occurs completely successfully, and that attentive combination is carried out with very little loss (the loss of accuracy occurring primarily for the dimension reported second). Thus this experiment has demonstrated optional selection with respect to the visual and auditory modalities: Intermodality selection can occur, but need not if the task demands require distributed attention. Furthermore, the ability to use distributed attention is not due to the use of short-term memory for the secondary dimension, since the effect is independent of stimulus duration up to 2 sec.

2. CONCEPT LEARNING

The fact that attention can be distributed among modalities is further demonstrated in two experiments requiring subjects to learn a conjunctive concept problem involving coincidence of levels on one auditory and one visual dimension presented simultaneously (Lordahl, 1961; Keele & Archer, 1967). In different ways, however, each of these experiments showed a tendency for greater attention to the visual modality than to the auditory modality. Lordahl showed that irrelevant auditory dimensions (such as pitch, intensity, steady or interrupted signal) interfered with concept learning less than irrelevant visual dimensions (such as size, shape, orientation, number of figures). Keele and Archer, on the other hand, showed that redundant relevant dimensions facilitated concept learning more if they were visual than if they were auditory. Such results concerning salience or dominance of modality must be interpreted with caution, however, since salience almost certainly depends both on modality and the particular dimensions used in each modality.

B. Information-Processing Limits

1. SIMPLE DISCRIMINATION TASKS

Lindsay (1970) has summarized several experiments carried out by himself and co-workers in which combined auditory and visual discrimination tasks were required for two levels on each stimulus dimension, with levels so close that errors occurred. In one of these experiments (Lindsay, Taylor, & Forbes, 1968), two auditory dimensions (pitch and intensity) and two visual dimensions (horizontal and vertical position of a dot) were used. The actual task required the subject to state which of two successively presented stimuli was, for example, higher in pitch, or to the right. Various conditions required discrimination of just one dimension, two dimensions within the same modality, two dimensions within different modalities, or all four dimensions. Those dimensions on which discrimination was not required in a particular series of trials were held constant between the two successive stimuli. Regardless of the number of dimensions the subject was required to attend and discriminate, he reported on only a single dimension specified to him after the presentation. Thus the problem of remembering several dimensions for reporting purposes was avoided.

The results of this experiment show a definite drop in discrimination accuracy as the number of dimensions to be discriminated increases. Arguing on the basis of a theoretical rationale involving the use of signal detection theory and the measure of d', the authors showed that *total* discrimination performance actually decreased with the attentive-combination task, and argued that this decrease was due to the necessity of channel sharing. Thus these results show an information-processing limit, with the consequent inability to carry out the attentive-combination task.

A secondary result, however, showed that performance was just as good whether discrimination was between two dimensions within different modalities or between two dimensions within the same modality. Thus intermodality distribution of attention does occur as an optional process, even though performance may be limited on a total information-processing basis.

Since the absolute-judgment experiment of Tulving and Lindsay (1967) showed little evidence of a processing limit, it must be concluded that the nature of the limiting factor in these two experiments is different. In the successive discrimination task this limit is almost certainly at or near the receptor periphery, while in the absolute-judgment task the limitation is at a judgmental or response level of processing, as Garner and Creelman (1964) have previously argued.

2. Prose Comprehension

An experiment by Mowbray (1953) further demonstrates that optional intermodality attentive selection exists, but that an information-processing limit may put a ceiling on actual performance. He had subjects both read and listen to ordinary prose passages (different for each), and tested comprehension for the material later. With easy prose passages, performance was well above chance for both modalities. With difficult passages, however, performance on the poorer modality was no better than chance, indicating that attention had been completely selective to a single modality. Thus attention *can* be shared or distributed, but there is an information limit. Broadbent (1958) discussed the consequences of this information limit more fully.

C. Modalities as Levels of a Dimension

So far, all the material discussed has been concerned with the use of the two modalities as information channels, in that they only provide access to information but do not in themselves provide the information. Handel and Buffardi (1968) have shown that the two modalities can be used as the levels of an information-providing dimension, however. They were investigating perception of temporal patterns formed from repeating sequences of two-element events. They found that one of the elements could be a light and the other a tone, and perception and learning of the patterns was essentially as good as when the two elements were two different tones or two different lights. Thus the two modalities can operate as levels on a dimension for some tasks.

D. Conclusions

The evidence is quite clear that intermodality selective attention is optional, since selective attention easily occurs, but considerable success is also found with the attentive-combination task. This conclusion would be stronger if there were any evidence on tasks where information is correlated in the two dimensions and the subject is expected to integrate it to improve performance. The fact that distributed attention is optional would suggest that improvement in performance should result if, for example, absolute judgments were required with correlated brightness and loudness, or if the same difficult prose material could be both read and heard.

Regardless of the fact that attention can be shared or distributed, there is clear evidence that total information-processing (or channel) limits exist that prevent perfect performance on attentive-combination tasks.

III. VISUAL ATTENTION

A. Interocular Attention

The two eyes could serve as separate information channels, or even possibly as the levels on an information-producing dimension. Usually when the two eyes are stimulated simultaneously with different inputs, binocular rivalry is experienced, in which the stimulus material from one eye or the other is perceived but not both simultaneously. This interocular attentive selection is mandatory. Ordinarily there is spontaneous alternation in attention, which is not subject to voluntary control to a great extent. This is an interesting aspect of vision, since by contrast, voluntary control of attention to information coming in one ear rather than the other appears to be rather easy.

When the two eyes are stimulated with identical input, a merged single percept occurs, although when there are slight differences in input of a special kind, depth perception occurs. It thus appears that the two eyes tend to operate as a single perceptual system, and therefore cannot easily be used as independent information channels.

B. Dimensional Attention

Research on attentive processes in vision has been centered on selective attention to different stimulus dimensions. Both some form of speed measurement and some form of accuracy measurement have been extensively used.

1. SPEEDED CLASSIFICATION

a. ATTENTIVE SELECTION. Many experiments have been carried out with this basic experimental paradigm: A set of stimuli is generated from orthogonal combinations of two or more stimulus dimensions, usually but not always dichotomous. The subject is required to respond differentially to just the levels on one dimension, either by sorting decks of cards or by a discrete reaction-time procedure. The dimension by which sorting or responding is to be done is the relevant dimension, and the other dimensions are irrelevant. The experimental question concerns whether the existence of irrelevant dimensions slows performance.

Gregg (1954) used a discrete reaction-time procedure, the response being movement of a lever to the right or left. Stimulus dimensions were all dichotomous: vertical position, horizontal position, brightness, and size. Various combinations of conditions were used in which reaction was to different dimensions, with different numbers of stimulus dimensions being irrelevant. The results of this experiment showed an average increase of about 4% in reaction time from the condition with no irrelevant dimensions to the condition with three irrelevant dimensions.

Archer (1954) carried out a similar experiment using six dichotomous dimensions (size, brightness, speed of movement, vertical position, horizontal position, and shape), and in some conditions subjects were required to identify as many as four relevant dimensions. A discrete, but self-paced, reaction-time procedure was used. He obtained no statistically significant effect of number of irrelevant dimensions, although there was actually an increase of about 7% in reaction time from the conditions with no irrelevant dimensions to those with two irrelevant dimensions.

Imai and Garner (1965) used a card-sorting task with stimuli generated from three dichotomous dimensions. The stimuli were two dots on a card; the dots varied in horizontal position, orientation, and distance separating them. These authors also used four different levels of discriminability of each dimension. They found no interference due to the addition of irrelevant dimensions, even when a highly discriminable dimension was irrelevant and a poorly discriminable one relevant. However, Morgan and Alluisi (1967) presented results showing that both accuracy of judgment of stimulus size and discrete reaction time are impaired if the size differences are small enough and if color is used as an irrelevant interfering dimension. Thus even though the Imai and Garner (1965) result showed no interference regardless of the relative discriminabilities of the relevant and irrelevant stimulus dimensions, the generality of the result for all kinds of tasks and all kinds of stimulus dimensions is limited.

The general result of these experiments and others summarized by Egeth (1967) is that there is little or no interfering effect from irrelevant dimensions.

b. ATTENTIVE INTEGRATION. Garner (1969) used the same stimuli (pairs of dots) previously used by Imai and Garner (1965) in a card-sorting experiment to determine whether the use of correlated dimensions in an integration task would increase the speed of card sorting. He found that the time (in seconds) to sort a deck of 32 cards decreased on the average (for three pairs of dimensions and four levels of discriminability) from 20.56 sec to 19.28 sec. However, in an experiment of this sort, it is common for a particular subject to be better on one dimension than on another, so that improvement would occur simply by his using a selective serial strategy, that is, sorting on the basis of the better dimension either first or only. Thus with correlated dimensions, the subject would always be able to use the better of two single dimensions, and a comparison of averages would show a decrease in sorting time. In order to correct for this effect, Garner compared the best of the three single-dimension cases with the best of the three correlated-dimension cases, and found a decrease from 17.84 sec to 17.04 sec. Thus the apparent improvement was somewhat less when correction for selective serial processing was made.

Biederman and Checkosky (1970) carried out a similar experiment with size and brightness of stimuli, using a discrete reaction-time procedure. They likewise found a slight improvement in reaction time, even when correcting for the selective serial effect by comparing each subject's best single dimension to the best of two runs on the correlated condition. The improvement was quite slight, however, mean reaction time being 378 msec for the fastest unidimensional condition and 364 msec for the fastest correlated condition, with highly discriminable dimensions.

c. INTEGRAL AND SEPARABLE DIMENSIONS. Taken together, these results on attentive selection and attentive integration lead to no clear conclusion concerning the nature of the attentive process. It appears that integration *may* be successful, or that selection *may* be successful. In order to clarify this problem, Garner and Felfoldy (1970) carried out a series of experiments which accomplished two primary goals: first, to have both the attentive selection and the attentive integration tasks carried out in the same experiment; and second, to provide systematic variation in the nature of the stimulus dimensions which were used.

They carried out several experiments whose logical form is that shown in Table II. Each experiment used two stimulus dimensions in a card-sorting task. The task always required sorting by a single dimension, but the three kinds of stimulus sets involved single dimensions (the control condition), correlated dimensions, and orthogonal dimensions. These last two stimulus sets provided attentive integration and attentive selection tasks. As already noted, the normal expectation with correlated dimensions is faster performance if attentive integration is successful, or performance equal to the control condition if it is not. The expectation with orthogonal (i.e., independent) dimensions is equal speed if attentive selection is successful, or slower speed if it is not and interference occurs.

The first experiment used value and chroma in a single color-chip as the two dimensions, and the results showed both facilitation with the correlated dimensions and interference with the orthogonal dimensions. This failure of attentive selection indicates mandatory distribution of attention, and this distributed attention also allows facilitation in the integration task. Unfortunately, an attentive combination task was not used in these experi-

TABLE II

THE EXPERIMENTAL DESIGN AND POSSIBLE EXPERIMENTAL OUTCOMES IN THE GARNER–FELFOLDY EXPERIMENTS[a]

	Stimulus set		
Dimension sorted	Single dimension	Correlated dimensions	Orthogonal dimensions
A or B	Base speed	Equal or faster	Equal or slower

[a] Sorting was always by a single dimension regardless of the nature of the stimulus set.

ments, so that a complete specification of the nature of attention as shown in Table I cannot be made.

A second experiment used the same two dimensions, but this time each was varied on a separate color chip. In this case there was no facilitation of performance with correlated dimensions nor interference with orthogonal dimensions. This result indicates mandatory attentive selection, although once again the conclusion would be clearer if the attentive combination task had been used.

A third experiment used the horizontal and vertical position of a dot as the two dimensions, and, as in the first experiment, facilitation occurred with correlated dimensions and interference with orthogonal dimensions. The interference effect was small, however. In fact, results with an absolute-judgment technique (Egeth & Pachella, 1969) showed no interference at all with these orthogonal dimensions, a result that would clearly imply optional attentive selection.

In a fourth experiment, the stimulus was a circle with a diameter drawn through it, and the two dimensions were the size of the circle and the angle of the diameter. The primary effect with these dimensions was no facilitation and no interference—again the result indicating mandatory distribution of attention.

Garner and Felfoldy (1970) and Garner (1970) have argued that these differences, generally being consistent between tasks, are clearly due to the nature of the stimulus dimensions themselves. They refer, as already mentioned, to integrality of stimulus dimensions when both facilitation and interference occur and to separability when neither occurs. Thus selective attention is not always possible with dimensions of visual stimuli. Rather, the nature of the relations between the stimulus dimensions is critical in determining whether selective attention is possible. This question is discussed further in Section III,C.

2. ABSOLUTE JUDGMENTS

a. ATTENTIVE INTEGRATION. One of the first experiments using multidimensional stimuli was carried out by Eriksen and Hake (1955). They used the absolute-judgment experimental paradigm, with 20 levels on each of three dimensions—hue, brightness, and size of color chips. They used each stimulus dimension alone, in all possible pairs, and all three dimensions together, always in correlated fashion. Their results showed an increase from 2.75 bits of information transmitted for single dimensions to 3.43 bits for two correlated dimensions, and 4.11 bits for three correlated dimensions. This result indicates either mandatory distributed attention or optional selective attention.

Lockhead (1966a) also showed an improvement in performance when the dimensions of length and vertical position of line were correlated. He used stimuli that were not highly discriminable, but obtained an improvement from 1.07 to 1.22 bits of information transmitted. When he further degraded the stimuli by decreasing the duration and contrast, he still obtained an increase from .47 to .58 of a bit of information transmitted. Thus the ability of correlated visual stimulus dimensions to improve accuracy is not limited to highly discriminable stimuli.

b. ATTENTIVE SELECTION AND COMBINATION. In this experiment, Lockhead also presented the stimuli with orthogonal dimensions and required responding to both stimulus dimensions—the attentive combination task. The result he obtained was that total information transmission with the combination task was slightly less than the sum of the information transmissions when each task was carried out separately with unidimensional stimuli. Many other similar experiments on the attentive combination task, summarized in Garner (1962), all lead to this same result. This result cannot be considered a complete success in the attentive combination task, but it more nearly constitutes evidence for distributed attention than for selective attention. Since most available evidence shows that the attentive integration task is carried out successfully, it must be tentatively concluded that most visual dimensions are processed with optional selection—i.e., any of the tasks of selection, integration, or combination can be carried out with reasonable success in the absolute-judgment task.

Nevertheless, it is very likely that the appropriate process concept for the absolute-judgment task depends on the particular stimulus dimensions involved, just as it does with speeded classification tasks. A strong suggestion of this effect is contained in an experiment by Egeth and Pachella (1969). They used the stimulus dimensions of color, size, and eccentricity of ellipses, and used as tasks the judgment of single dimensions varied alone, attentive selection with all three dimensions varied orthogonally, and attentive combination with the three orthogonal dimensions. They obtained the usual result with attentive combination of almost satisfactory performance. However, with attentive selection, there was no interference effect when color was being judged, but considerable interference when either size or eccentricity were being judged. This result suggests that size and eccentricity are integral dimensions, thus producing mutual interference, whereas color is separable from each. These authors did not carry out the attentive integration task to determine whether the selection was optional or mandatory. However, reference to the earlier result of Eriksen and Hake (1955), in which attentive integration was successfully carried out with color and size, suggests that color and size allow optional selective attention. Thus it is not unreasonable to assume that color is separable from other visual dimensions.

C. Spatial Factors

The visual system is ideally suited to the perception of spatial relations. While spatial location may be used as an information dimension, and that dimension can be attended selectively, it is also clear that the nature of the visual system makes it particularly easy to attend selectively to a single spatial location as a level on the dimension of spatial location. Such ease of attending selectively to a single spatial location suggests that location may provide specification of separate information channels, channels whose very separability makes distributed attention across them very difficult.

1. DIMENSIONAL SEPARABILITY

One question of considerable interest is what makes two or more stimulus dimensions integral or separable. Garner (1970) suggested that two dimensions are integral if in order for a level on one dimension to be realized, a dimensional level must be specified for the other. This requirement is certainly satisfied only if the dimensions are spatially in the same place. Thus brightness and color should be integral because both must coexist, and thus both must be represented in the same place. Lockhead (1966a) has argued that this spatial coincidence itself is the critical factor, suggesting that integral dimensions are those which can be presented simultaneously and in the same place. This definition would also include such dimensions as the superposed bar (varying in tilt, e.g.) on a colored circle.

We do not have a clear answer to what makes stimulus dimensions integral. The evidence is very strong, however, that stimulus information presented spatially separate does provide separability of dimensions with a process close to mandatory attentive selection. Lockhead (1966b), for example, used an absolute-judgment technique with hue and brightness of color chips, and found that the use of correlated dimensions gave a gain in information transmission only if the dimensions varied in the same chip rather than on two spatially separated chips. This result is the same as that found by Garner and Felfoldy (1970) with a speeded classification task. Garner and Lee (1962) had previously found no gain in accuracy when discrimination of X's or O's was required, and redundant stimulus elements (spatially separated) were added to the stimulus.

In a different type of experiment, Lappin (1967) required subjects to report the values of three stimulus dimensions (size, color, and angle of a diameter of a circle) with tachistoscopic exposure. In some conditions, subjects reported the values of the three dimensions in a single designated stimulus object, and in other cases they reported the value of a single dimension in three different objects. Accuracy was much poorer when attention had to be distributed spatially in the second case. An equivalent result was found by Neisser (1963), using an experimental task in which subjects searched for a single letter among different numbers of other letters in a single row. Speed of search was slower with more letters on a line, indicating an inability of subjects to distribute attention across several spatially separated items at once. In both this experiment and in Lappin's, the actual physical spacing was not a critical factor. Thus the critical factor is not a physical span, but rather the operation of different spatial locations as separate information channels.

The evidence certainly argues that spatial separation produces separable dimensions, and that these ordinarily lead to mandatory attentive selection—that is, neither the integration nor the combination tasks can be carried out successfully. It is not clear, however, that stimulus dimensions that are spatially coincident are integral. It is possible that some types of spatially coincident dimensions will lead to optional attentive selection, while others (those truly integral) will lead to mandatory distributed attention.

2. SPATIAL INTEGRATION

There are two types of situations in which complete separability of spatially separated stimulus dimensions is not the rule. One of these concerns the integration of spatially separate elements into a unified pattern, and the information processing is such that the stimulus can be redefined into an integrated pattern, such as reading a word, in which the letters are separate, and the word is an integrated pattern. Sekuler and Abrams (1968) used as stimuli up to four blackened cells of a 4×4 matrix. They presented pairs of these stimuli to subjects and measured the speed with which they stated that a pair was the same or different. In one condition, "same" meant that at least one blackened cell was in common between the two patterns, while in another condition "same" meant that all blackened cells were the same. Even when all blackened cells were in fact the same, this latter instruction produced faster responding. These authors argue that this instruction leads to a processing of the pattern as a gestalt whole, rather than as a series of stimulus elements.

Further evidence that stimuli consisting of several spatially separate items will be processed as whole patterns rather than as a series of elements comes from an experiment by Clement and Weiman (1970), using patterns of five dots in the imaginary cells of a 3×3 matrix. Previous research by Royer (1966) and Clement and Varnadoe (1967) had shown that speed of classification in a discrimination task was faster if two patterns to be discriminated had good gestalt (e.g., crosses, squares, T's) than if the patterns had poor gestalt. Clement and Weiman attempted to get rid of this advantage by instructing subjects that they could make the discrimination on the basis of the location of a single dot. Furthermore, prototype stimulus cards were used which showed only the two critical dots. In neither case was the advantage of the "good" patterns lost. Only when patterns were used in which it was impossible to carry out the task without using just a single dot location was the advantage of the figurally good patterns in discrimination lost.

Thus while spatial separation ordinarily leads to independent information channels, information is integrated across space if the information-processing task can be carried out on the basis of such redefined figures.

3. MULTIPLE PERCEPTUAL OPPORTUNITY

There is another information-processing task in which attention is distributed across two or more spatial locations, and that is the recognition task in which redundant stimulus information is presented, and each stimulus element is limited in visibility. For example, Eriksen and Lappin (1965) presented one, two, four, or six stimulus items tachistoscopically on the imaginary circumference of a circle, with visual fixation at the center of the circle. The stimuli were the capital letters A, T, or U, and were always the same on any single presentation. The results showed increased accuracy with increased number of items. In a similar experiment, Garner and Flowers (1969) presented either two or four X's or O's also on an imaginary circle and with fixation at the center of the circle. The increased number of elements improved accuracy of discrimination. Both of these experiments, however, involve what Garner (1970) has called state-limited processes, in that the failure of discrimination for the single stimulus item is not due to an inability to discriminate the letters, but rather is due to a failure to see the letters. If the letters in either of these experiments are seen, there is no question about what they are. Thus the redundant elements are providing additional perceptual opportunities, but a gain due to an increased number of opportunities does not imply any integration of information. Nevertheless, the fact that there is a gain does mean that attention has been distributed across spatial location.

If a gain in discrimination accuracy can be obtained with distributed attention in such experiments, why was it not obtained in the Garner and Lee (1962) experiment with patterns of X's and O's? In that experiment optional visual fixation had been allowed, and the subjects simply fixated an area where most accurate discrimination can be obtained. When some subjects were instructed to "distribute" their attention, their performance became poorer. Thus a gain with redundancy and distributed attention can be obtained with state-limited situations, but only at the expense of poorer performance caused by the failure to use foveal vision. In the free situation, foveal vision will be used; and in this situation there is no gain with re-dundant stimulus elements.

It is interesting to contrast this result with that found by Clement and Weiman (1970) concerning pattern discrimination. These authors found that subjects distributed their attention across space to form patterns, while Garner and Lee (1962) found that subjects focused in a single area. In both cases it was difficult to get subjects to change perceptual strategies. But in each case subjects were doing what produced optimum performance for the given stimulus and task conditions. This flexibility of performance is one of the most important properties of the human, even though this property makes it more difficult for psychological scientists to find answers to their questions. The answers, as Garner (1970) pointed out, are highly variable just because the organism adjusts to maximize performance for each separate situation.

D. Color Selection

It is clear that spatial location can be used to specify an information channel. The experiments on short-term memory by Sperling (1960) and Averbach and Coriell (1961) both used spatial location in specifying which items should be reported in partial-report conditions, and showed consider-ably more accurate reporting when only those items specified by a given row or column had to be reported. This technique of partial reporting was used more recently by von Wright (1968). His stimulus materials were either two rows of four letters or three rows of three letters, but these items differed (in addition to location) in chromatic color, brightness, size, and angular orientation. Thus for the partial-report conditions, any of these dimensions could be used to specify a "channel" for attentive selection (the letter being the information variable). This experimenter found that channel specification by chromatic color was nearly as effective in the par-tial-report condition as was channel specification by location. Brightness and size both provided some advantage in the partial-report condition, but orientation provided none at all.

It is clear, then, that the levels on a dimension may be used to specify an information channel, but that not all dimensions serve this purpose equally well. Certainly as a minimum it is necessary that subjects can attend to a level of a dimension, rather than to the dimension itself, in order for the channel function to be served. LaBerge, Tweedy, and Ricker (1967) have shown that subjects can attend to a particular one of three colors and thus have a faster reaction time when that color appears. It is interest-ing to note that their experimental design called for the attended color to have the same overt response as an unattended color, so that the differᴄ.ᴄe in reaction time was clearly established as a perceptual selective effect, not a response bias.

Color seems to be an especially important visual stimulus dimension, and it even seems to play this role in learning experiments. Weiss and Margolius (1954) and Underwood, Ham, and Ekstrand (1962) both showed that if nonsense syllables as stimulus items in paired-associate learning are framed in different colors, one color for each stimulus item, learning occurs more effectively to the color than it does to the nonsense syllable itself. Color seems, in other words, to be a very salient stimulus dimension.

E. Conclusions

Many different types of stimulus dimensions have been used in experiments involving speed and accuracy of information processing, with attentive selection, combination, and integration. There is no single conclusion that these experiments lead to concerning the appropriate attentive concept, and clearly whether attention must be or may be distributed or selective depends on the particular nature of the stimulus dimensions.

The evidence suggests that if two stimulus dimensions are spatially separate, mandatory attentive selection operates. In other words, different spatial locations operate as separate information channels, and it is difficult if not impossible to integrate information across them. Two special circumstances violate this principle, however. One circumstance is that in which redundant elements of a visual stimulus can be integrated into a spatial pattern. The other is that in which information processing is state-limited, in that simple ability to see the stimulus limits accuracy of perception. In this situation, redundancy provides multiple perceptual opportunities, which may improve performance.

If stimulus dimensions are effectively in the same spatial location, then attention is at least optionally distributed across dimensions. While some dimensions, such as hue and chroma of single color chips, operate as integral dimensions and produce mandatory distributed attention, other dimensions, such as vertical and horizontal location, tend to provide optional distributed attention in that information may be integrated when it is useful to do so, but may be selectively attended when it is useful to do that.

IV. AUDITORY ATTENTION

The visual modality may be used for language communication, but that is not its most natural function, and many adults never learn to use vision for that purpose. For humans language perception is probably the most important single function of the auditory modality. These natural differences in modality are, unfortunately, all too well reflected in the research that has been done. Whereas, as we have just seen, considerable research has been done with all of the paradigmatic attentive tasks on dimensional attention in vision, this has not been the case in auditory research. Rather, most of the auditory research has been done with speech perception. And contrariwise, much of the research done with speech perception has an analog in vision.

A. Dimensional Attention

1. ATTENTIVE COMBINATION

Pollack (1953) carried out an experiment in which absolute judgment of the pitch and loudness of tones was required. In the control condition, with just one dimension used, an average of about 1.8 bits of information transmitted was obtained for each dimension. When the combination task was used, with subjects making judgments of both the pitch and loudness of each stimulus (these dimensions being used orthogonally in generating the stimuli), total information transmitted increased to 3.1 bits—a result consistent with that found with visual dimensions in that information transmitted is considerably greater with two dimensions than with one, although the total is less than the sum from the two control conditions. Later Pollack and Ficks (1954) increased the stimulus dimensions to six by using an interrupted tone which varied in frequency, loudness, rate of interruption, percentage of time on, total duration, and direction of the sound source. With this number of dimensions, information transmitted increased to nearly 8 bits. Thus with these kinds of simple auditory dimensions, and with absolute-judgment tasks, the combination task is carried out quite effectively, although far from perfectly. Nevertheless, it must be concluded that either mandatory or optional distribution of attention operates.

2. ATTENTIVE SELECTION

Montague (1965) used as a stimulus a noise signal that varied in pitch, loudness, frequency of intensity modulation, and accenting of certain beats in the modulated signal. In addition, a tone that swept up or down, or warbled was added, the warbled tone being of high or low frequency. The task required was moderately complex, since the subject always had to identify the pitch and loudness of the basic signal, in addition to one other dimension. Thus this experiment required both attentive combination and attentive selection. The results showed that when irrelevant dimensions were added (the control condition always involved three dimensions), both accuracy and response latency became poorer. Thus there was interference. This result suggests mandatory distribution of attention.

And yet caution must be inserted, since these experiments do not differentiate the effects of particular pairs of dimensions in either the combination or selection task, and we have already seen how crucial that factor is for visual selective attention. In addition, there are no experiments in audition that use the attentive integration task, and results with this task would be useful in determining the extent to which the distributed attention is mandatory. Furthermore, Chapanis, Garner, and Morgan (1949), in reporting results of an experiment in which attempts were made to use auditory signals as information devices for pilots, point out that some signal systems were better than others because they prevented the pilot from attending to just one of the stimulus dimensions at a time. The kinds of stimulus dimensions used in that research were too complex, and the task itself (flying an airplane trainer) too complicated, for the specifics of that experiment to be of much help. But the possibility is strongly suggested that some stimulus dimensions will lead to mandatory distribution of attention, whereas others will lead to at least optional selective attention.

B. Speech

1. ATTENTIVE COMBINATION

It is common for humans to have difficulty listening to and comprehending two conversations at once; that is, they cannot successfully perform the attentive combination task. More scientific evidence for this fact can be found in an experiment by Webster and Thompson (1954). They carried out a fairly complicated experiment that more or less simulated the situation an airport control tower operator faces, in that planes radio in various messages to which the operator must respond. Sometimes two or more messages occur simultaneously, overlapping each other completely or partially. These authors determined the effects of such overlapping on accuracy of speech perception. The messages were of the form: "Lindbergh Tower, this is Navy 570," plus some standard test words. The subject (the operator) was required to repeat the identification message. This task could be carried out with nearly 100% accuracy when two messages did not overlap, but as low as 25% when messages were overlapping. If two messages were overlapping and of the same intensity, the leading message was responded to more accurately, unless it was less loud than the later message.

In another experiment, Mowbray (1964) had subjects listen to lists of 50 common English words presented at the rate of two words per second.

They were required to repeat these words as they came along—a technique frequently used in such research and called *shadowing*. These words were presented through an earphone to just one ear. During the list, one, two, or three ("target") words were also presented to the other ear, and the subject was supposed to remember these words and recall them at the end of the basic list. The results of this experiment were that fewer than half the target words were correctly recalled. Even more important, over 80% of the shadowed words that occurred simultaneously with the target words were missed. Thus the shadowing performance was almost completely disrupted, even though far less than perfect success was obtained with the disrupting target words.

So with speech, there is either a process limit (usually called a channel capacity limit with this research), or mandatory selective attention is the rule, as indicated in Table I.

2. ATTENTIVE SELECTION

If selective attention is necessary in speech perception, what are the stimulus properties that facilitate successful carrying out of an attentive selection task? In an experiment using only vowel sounds ("ah" or "ee"), Webster (1961) used stimuli that varied on four dichotomous dimensions—which sound, male or female, which ear, and rising or falling inflection. Pairs of stimuli were presented in succession, and the subject was required to describe one of the pair on the basis of an instruction concerning each of the possible dimensions. For example, he might be told to describe the stimulus in his left ear, or the one with the female voice. Thus one dimension was used to provide the basis of selection. Then the subject was required to describe the values of the other three dimensions. Results, in terms of accuracy, show that attentive selection and identification were most accurate with regard to the ear location. Voice quality and which particular sound also provided quite good accuracy, with poorest accuracy for inflection.

Spieth, Curtis, and Webster (1954), using the airport control tower situation, investigated variables that might improve the ability of operators to select a single message accurately. Two characteristics of the speech sources turned out to be particularly valuable in improving speech perception—the use of loudspeakers that were spatially separated, with best performance occurring when the speakers were 180° apart; and the use of a high-pass filter at 1600 Hz in one message with an equivalent low-pass filter in the other. This type of filtering still allows considerable intelligibility of most normal speech, so that its main effect is simply to make the two speech sources distinctively different qualitatively.

Further evidence for the importance of both spatial separation and qualitative differences in making attentive selection to speech possible comes from a series of experiments by Egan, Carterette, and Thwing (1954). With monaural listening, accuracy of sentence comprehension was greatly improved if either the desired speech signal or the interfering speech was put through a high-pass filter at about 500 Hz. Even stronger effects were obtained by putting the desired speech signal in one earphone and the interfering speech (or noise) signal in the other ear. The importance of ear separation of the signals can be understood clearly when the results are stated in terms of relative intensities. If average accuracy of perception was kept at 50%, the intensity of the message to be selected and understood could be decreased by 27 dB if the interfering signal is switched from the signal ear to the opposite ear.

Broadbent (1958) has far more completely summarized both his own and other research on the problem of selective listening to speech, and he arrives at the quite clear conclusion that selective listening is the rule. Furthermore, spatial separation is the most important stimulus characteristic making selective listening possible, although qualitative differences clearly are quite effective as well. This result gives an interesting parallel to the conclusion formed with visual attentive selection: Spatial separation is the most important stimulus property making attentive selection possible, but qualitative differences (in that case, color) provide an important additional means by which separate information channels may be established, thus making attentive selection possible.

3. How Suppressed Is the Unattended Material?

Broadbent (1958), in discussing this and related topics, devised his filter theory, which assumes an essentially complete exclusion mechanism for the unattended material. The bulk of the evidence now available, however, suggests that either the unattended material is attenuated rather than blocked, or that attention is at least partly distributed. Cherry (1953), in an experiment using dichotic speech, with shadowing of the speech in one ear required, showed that, after the test, listeners could identify whether the material in the unattended ear was speech or not, whether the voice used changed from male to female, or whether a 400-Hz tone was inserted. Moray (1959) showed that listeners frequently heard their own names when they occurred in the unattended message. Cherry (1953) and Treisman (1964) both found that identical speech in the unattended ear was noticed if it did not lag too far behind the same speech in the attended ear. And the experiment by Mowbray (1964), already described, is excellent evidence that speech in the unattended ear or channel is not completely blocked out.

Evidence from attentive combination tasks suggested that simultaneous listening to speech results in either mandatory attentive selection or to a process limit, i.e., a limited channel capacity. While the evidence from attentive selection tasks does not completely resolve the issue, there certainly is a strong suggestion that mandatory selection (at least in the sense of complete selection) is not the operative principle. Rather, attention is optionally distributed, but with such a severe limiting of total channel capacity that the attentive combination task cannot be carried out successfully.

V. ATTENTION AND MEANING

Attentive mechanisms discussed so far, whether selective or distributed, are related to identifiable stimulus properties or to clearly identifiable input channels such as modality, spatial location, or ear. It is worth noting that selective processes much like those that occur with respect to stimulus properties or input channel can operate with respect to the derived meaning of stimuli.

A series of related experiments on the use of classes of stimuli specified by meaning shows clearly that such selective attention does occur. Broadbent (1954) had shown that if two different lists of three digits are presented simultaneously to the two ears, recall of the six digits was better if done ear by ear rather than by successive pairs of items occurring at the same time. He concluded that this result demonstrated the importance of the ears as establishing separate information channels. Gray and Wedderburn (1960) challenged this conclusion with an experiment identical to Broadbent's, but in which, for example, words in one ear were: one, Aunt, three, while those in the other ear were: Dear, two, Jane. With such stimuli, recall was better by meaningful material, alternating between ears than by ear, and these authors concluded that the sequential meaning was critical.

Broadbent and Gregory (1964) then showed that the same result could be obtained if the successive items in the two ears were alternating digits and letters. They thus concluded that a sequential meaning was not necessarily critical, but rather that two classes of material form a basis for attentive selection, and that these classes need not have complicated interrelations at all.

This brief series of experiments is quite sufficient to demonstrate that the basis of effective attentive selection need not be simple physical or end-organ differences. Nevertheless, there is insufficient evidence to conclude whether such attentive mechanisms are optional or mandatory. Since such attention almost certainly occurs at higher neural centers than those

required for attention on the basis of stimulus or peripheral organ properties, however, it seems likely that such attentive processes would be
optional.

VI. OTHER INFORMATION COMBINATION

Ordinarily in speaking of attentive selection, combination, or integration
tasks the concern is with the processing of multiple sources of information
when they occur simultaneously. There are two types of perceptual tasks
involving the processing of multiple sources of information in which information is not presented simultaneously, and yet which are clearly related
to problems of attention. Both of these tasks involve one source of information that may have the effect of restricting the number of alternatives possible in a perceptual recognition task.

A. Perceptual Set and Restriction of Number of Alternatives

If the number of alternatives in a perceptual recognition task is limited,
then accuracy of recognition is greater with fewer alternatives. However,
the specification of number of alternatives may be viewed as one source
of information for the subject, whereas the visual or auditory presentation
of the stimulus is a second source of information (see Garner, 1962, pp.
85–87). If the problem is considered this way, and if recognition performance is measured in bits of information transmitted, then performance
does not necessarily improve with a restriction of number of alternatives,
because the greater the restriction, the more likely that the two sources
of information are not independent. Thus the restriction of number of alternatives will duplicate information which the subject could have obtained
anyway from the stimulus presentation.

It is not often easy to determine whether subjects can process two such
sources of information perfectly because of the difficulty of determining
exactly how much information is contained in the restriction of number
of alternatives and in the stimulus presentation. There is, however, a
secondary issue involving attentive selection rather than combination: If
the information contained in the restriction of number of alternatives allows
the subject to attend selectively so that he can get from the stimulus presentation information which is independent of that contained in the set restriction, then he can maximize his performance. Clearly, however, in order
to do this he must be able to attend selectively. Ordinarily this fact would
mean that restriction of alternatives prior to the stimulus presentation
would be much more effective than restriction after the presentation (al-

though short-term memory allows a brief period of potentially efficient attentive selection after the stimulus presentation).

A series of experiments has been done comparing the effect of restriction of number of alternatives before and after the stimulus presentation. Lawrence and Coles (1954) used pictures presented tachistoscopically, with alternatives specified as actual words describing the pictures. They found no advantage in telling the subject what the alternatives were before rather than after the stimulus presentation. In a similar experiment, Long, Reid, and Henneman (1960) presented distorted letters visually, and the number of alternatives specified to the subject ranged from 2 to 11. The number of alternatives had its expected effect on accuracy. In most cases there was no better effect when alternatives were presented both before and after rather than just after the stimulus presentation, although when the number of alternatives was only two, performance was better when the alternatives were known in advance. Thus under some circumstances it is possible to adjust what information is obtained in the stimulus presentation so that a greater gain is obtained by knowing the stimulus alternatives in advance of the presentation.

Egeth and Smith (1967) argued that such perceptual selectivity might have been possible in the Lawrence and Coles (1954) experiment if they had specified the alternatives with actual pictures rather than with words, since the actual pictures would make it more possible to attend selectively to differentiating distinguishing features. They used pictures as stimuli, with alternatives demonstrated as actual pictures, and did find that alternatives presented both before and after the stimulus presentation gave better performance than alternatives presented only after.

There is, of course, no reason whatsoever why the ability to attend selectively to certain aspects of a stimulus should be any different in this task than in tasks of absolute judgment and speeded classification discussed earlier. There is no single answer as to whether attentive selection will occur with alternatives specified in advance. Rather, it will depend on the particular stimulus dimensions used. The earlier evidence strongly suggests that selectivity by spatial location will be highly effective, as will selectivity by color. With stimulus dimensions for which mandatory distributed attention is the rule, however, selective attention cannot occur, and thus there should be little advantage to specification of alternatives before rather than after the stimulus presentation.

B. Effect of Context on Word Recognition

A closely related task requires the subject to recognize a tachistoscopically presented word after prior sentence context for the word has been provided. Tulving and Gold (1963), Tulving, Mandler, and Baumal (1964), Morton (1964), and Pollack (1964) all showed that visual recognition accuracy was improved with use of a sentence context presented before the word presentation. Stowe, Harris, and Hampton (1963) showed the same result when the sentence context was presented visually and the target word was heard in noise.

These results are all perfectly reasonable, and the effect of context can be understood as one way of restricting the number of alternatives. Furthermore, some context–word combinations should allow efficient selective attention, whereas others should not. If selective attention is possible, then context presented prior to stimulus presentation should be more effective than context presented after the stimulus presentation. There are no data directly bearing on this point, however.

VII. RESPONSE COMPETITION

Attention is a wide-ranging topic in psychology, and discussion of it here has been necessarily restricted. Even when topics such as activation, vigilance, and habituation are excluded, there is still a large body of problems. Because the primary purpose of this volume is to present material on perception, the research discussed has emphasized stimulus properties and early stages in information processing. But interaction in information processing exists even at the level of overt or implicit responding. Stroop (1935), in a now-classic experiment, showed that if printed words which are themselves the names of colors are printed in different colors than those named, reading time is substantially greater than when the same color names are printed in black. Morton (1969a) further demonstrated this same type of interference. He printed digits on cards, with the actual digit and the number of them (1 to 6) varying on the stimulus cards. When the digit disagreed with the number of them, classification by the number of them was slowed. And if the digit agreed with the number of them (Morton, 1969b), then facilitation occurred.

While such interference almost certainly occurs at the level of overt response competition, Hock and Egeth (1970) have shown that interference will occur even when it could only occur at a level of implicit response. These authors required the overt response of "yes" or "no" to stimulus cards with color names in contradictory colors, the positive response being required when the color was a member of a predefined set. Since the overt response required did not involve actual color names, and yet interference occurred, this experiment showed that there is a processing interaction at an earlier stage.

VIII. THEORIES IN CONCLUSION

The wide range of phenomena existing within the attentive problem area has inhibited any real attempt at a general theory. Different theories have emphasized different aspects of the problem, and even within the framework of the processing of multiple sources of information, various theories do not deal equally well with all types of process.

Broadbent's (1958) filter theory is certainly the most widely known, and it postulates a mechanism that can exclude input after a short-term storage in processing. This filter operates to prevent overload of a processing system with limited channel capacity. While he originally envisaged the filter as an all-or-none process, more recent evidence (see Treisman, 1969) strongly suggests that the filter simply attenuates, as noted in Section IV,B,3. Filter theory and its modifications are relatively input-oriented, and are properly classed as theories of perceptual attention. Other theories more strongly emphasize the response aspect of the problem.

Deutsch and Deutsch (1963) most strongly represent the response theorists, with a theory that combines the concept of a general level of arousal with a specific level of alertness for different possible input signals. Norman (1968) proposes a model of selective attention in which selection occurs after stimuli have had considerable processing, with additional pertinence added to possible items to be processed from other sources of information. In a similar model of attention, Morton (1969c) proposes a hypothetical *logogen* which accepts all kinds of information, whether directly stimulus, or contextual, or memorial information, and produces an available response when enough evidence for a particular word has occurred. None of these latter theories treats the overt response as the locus of information interaction, but all three assume considerably more information processing before the selective mechanisms can operate than do the theories of Broadbent and of Treisman.

Perhaps this problem area is not yet ready for an inclusive theory, since the evidence is so clear that informational interaction (whether attentive selection, combination, or integration) can occur at so many stages in processing. Certainly some form of selection can occur at the physical end-organs, such as the two eyes. And certainly some form of selection must take place if two overt responses are in direct competition. And selective processes can operate at almost any stage of meaning of stimulus information. It is probable that further clarification of the many ways in which the human organism can process multiple sources of information is required before reasonably broad and yet definitive theories of attention will be possible.

References

Archer, E. J. Identification of visual patterns as a function of information load. *Journal of Experimental Psychology,* 1954, **48,** 313–317.

Attneave, F. Perception and related areas. In S. Koch (Ed.), *Psychology: A study of a science,* Vol. 4. New York: McGraw-Hill, 1962. Pp. 619–659.

Averbach, E., & Coriell, A. S. Short term memory in vision. *Bell System Technical Journal,* 1961, **40,** 309–328.

Biederman, I., & Checkosky, S. F. Processing redundant information. *Journal of Experimental Psychology,* 1970, **83,** 486–490.

Broadbent, D. E. The role of auditory localization in attention and memory span. *Journal of Experimental Psychology,* 1954, **47,** 191–196.

Broadbent, D. E. *Perception and communication.* New York: Pergamon Press, 1958.

Broadbent, D. E., & Gregory, M. Stimulus set and response set: The alternation of attention. *Quarterly Journal of Experimental Psychology,* 1964, **16,** 309–317.

Chapanis, A., Garner, W. R., & Morgan, C. T. *Applied experimental psychology.* New York: Wiley, 1949.

Cherry, E. C. Some experiments on the recognition of speech with one and with two ears. *Journal of the Acoustical Society of America,* 1953, **25,** 975–979.

Clement, D. E., & Varnadoe, K. W. Pattern uncertainty and the discrimination of visual patterns. *Perception and Psychophysics,* 1967, **2,** 427–431.

Clement, D. E., & Weiman, C. F. R. Instructions, strategies, and pattern uncertainty in a visual discrimination task. *Perception and Psychophysics,* 1970, **7,** 333–336.

Crowder, R. G., & Morton, J. Precategorical acoustic storage (PAS). *Perception and Psychophysics,* 1969, **5,** 365–373.

Deutsch, J. A., and Deutsch, D. Attention: Some theoretical considerations. *Psychological Review,* 1963, **70,** 80–90.

Eckstrand, G. A., and Wickens, D. D. Transfer of perceptual set. *Journal of Experimental Psychology,* 1954, **47,** 274–278.

Egan, J. P., Carterette, E. C., & Thwing, E. J. Some factors affecting multi-channel listening. *Journal of the Acoustical Society of America,* 1954, **26,** 774–782.

Egeth, H. E. Parallel versus serial processes in multidimensional stimulus discrimination. *Perception and Psychophysics,* 1966, **1,** 245–252.

Egeth, H. Selective attention. *Psychological Bulletin,* 1967, **67,** 41–57.

Egeth, H., & Bevan, W. Attention. In B. Wolman (Ed.), *Handbook of general psychology.* Englewood Cliffs, New Jersey: Prentice-Hall, 1973.

Egeth, H., & Pachella, R. Multidimensional stimulus identification. *Perception and Psychophysics,* 1969, **5,** 341–346.

Egeth, H., & Smith, E. E. Perceptual selectivity in a visual recognition task. *Journal of Experimental Psychology,* 1967, **74,** 543–549.

Eriksen, C. W., & Hake, H. W. Multidimensional stimulus differences and accuracy of discrimination. *Journal of Experimental Psychology,* 1955, **50,** 153–160.

Eriksen, C. W., & Lappin, J. S. Internal perceptual system noise and redundancy in simultaneous inputs in form identification. *Psychonomic Science,* 1965, **2,** 351–352.

Garner, W. R. *Uncertainty and structure as psychological concepts.* New York: Wiley, 1962.

Garner, W. R. Speed of discrimination with redundant stimulus attributes. *Perception and Psychophysics*, 1969, **6**, 221–224.

Garner, W. R. The stimulus in information processing. *American Psychologist*, 1970. **25**, 350–358.

Garner, W. R., & Creelman, C. D. Effect of redundancy and duration on absolute judgments of visual stimuli. *Journal of Experimental Psychology*, 1964, **67**, 168–172.

Garner, W. R., & Felfoldy, G. L. Integrality of stimulus dimensions in various types of information processing. *Cognitive Psylmology*, 1970, **1**, 225–241.

Garner, W. R., & Flowers, J. H. The effect of redundant stimulus elements on visual discrimination as a function of element heterogeneity, equal discriminability, and position uncertainty. *Perception and Psychophysics*, 1969, **6**, 216–220.

Garner, W. R., Hake, H. W., & Eriksen, C. W. Operationism and the concept of perception. *Psychological Review*, 1956, **63**, 149–159.

Garner, W. R., & Lee, W. An analysis of redundancy in perceptual discrimination. *Perceptual and Motor Skills*, 1962, **15**, 367–388.

Garner, W. R., & Morton, J. Perceptual independence: Definitions, models, and experimental paradigms. *Psychological Bulletin*, 1969, **72**, 233–259.

Gibson, J. J. *The senses considered as perceptual systems*. Boston: Houghton Mifflin, 1966.

Gray, J. A., & Wedderburn, A. A. I. Grouping strategies with simultaneous stimuli. *Quarterly Journal of Experimental Psychology*, 1960, **12**, 180–184.

Gregg, L. W. The effect of stimulus complexity on discriminative responses. *Journal of Experimental Psychology*, 1954, **48**, 289–297.

Handel, S., & Buffardi, L. Pattern perception: Integrating information presented in two modalities. *Science*, 1968, **162**, 1026–1028.

Hock, H. S., & Egeth, H. Verbal interference with encoding in a perceptual classification task. *Journal of Experimental Psychology*. 1970, **83**, 299–303.

Hyman, R., & Well, A. Perceptual separability and spatial models. *Perception and Psychophysics*, 1968, **3**, 161–165.

Imai, S., & Garner, W. R. Discriminability and preference for attributes in free and constrained classification. *Journal of Experimental Psychology*, 1965, **69**, 596–608.

Keele, S. W., & Archer, E. J. A comparison of two types of information in concept identification. *Journal of Verbal Learning and Verbal Behavior*, 1967, **6**, 185–192.

LaBerge, D., Tweedy, J. R., & Ricker, J. Selective attention: Incentive variables and choice time. *Psychonomic Science*, 1967, **8**, 341–342.

Lappin, J. S. Attention in the identification of stimuli in complex visual displays. *Journal of Experimental Psychology*, 1967, **75**, 321–328.

Lawrence, D. H., & Coles, G. R. Accuracy of recognition with alternatives before and after the stimulus. *Journal of Experimental Psychology*, 1954, **47**, 208–214.

Lindsay, P. H. Multi-channel processing in perception. In D. E. Motofsky (Ed.), *Attention: A behavioral analysis*. New York: Appleton, 1970.

Lindsay, P. H., Taylor, M. M., & Forbes, S. M. Attention and multidimensional discrimination. *Perception and Psychophysics*, 1968, **4**, 113–117.

Lockhead, G. R. Effects of dimensional redundancy on visual discrimination. *Journal of Experimental Psychology*, 1966, **72**, 95–104. (a)

Lockhead, G. R. Visual discrimination and methods of presenting redundant stimuli. *Proceedings 74th Annual Convention of the American Psychological Association*, 1966, 67–68. (b)

Long, E. R., Reid, L. S., & Henneman, R. H. An experimental analysis of set: Variables influencing the identification of ambiguous, visual stimulus-objects. *American Journal of Psychology*, 1960, **73**, 553–562.

Lordahl, D. S. Concept identification using simultaneous auditory and visual signals. *Journal of Experimental Psychology*, 1961, **62**, 283–290.

Montague, W. E. Effect of irrelevant information on a complex auditory discrimination task. *Journal of Experimental Psychology*, 1965, **69**, 230–236.

Moray, N. Attention in dichotic listening: Affective cues and the influence of instructions. *Quarterly Journal of Experimental Psychology*, 1959, **11**, 56–60.

Morgan, B. B., Jr., & Alluisi, E. A. Effects of discriminability and irrelevant information on absolute judgments. *Perception and Psychophysics*, 1967, **2**, 54–58.

Morton, J. The effects of context on the visual duration threshold for words. *British Journal of Psychology*, 1964, **55**, 165–180.

Morton, J. Categories of interference: Verbal mediation and conflict in card sorting. *British Journal of Psychology*, 1969, **60**, 329–346. (a)

Morton, J. The use of correlated stimulus information in card sorting. *Perception and Psychophysics*, 1969, **5**, 374–376. (b)

Morton, J. Interaction of information in word recognition. *Psychological Review*, 1969, **76**, 165–178. (c)

Mowbray, G. H. Simultaneous vision and audition: The comprehension of prose passages with varying levels of difficulty. *Journal of Experimental Psychology*, 1953, **46**, 365–372.

Mowbray, G. H. Perception and retention of verbal information presented during auditory shadowing. *Journal of the Acoustical Society of America*, 1964, **36**, 1459–1464.

Neisser, U. Decision-time without reaction-time: Experiments in visual scanning. *American Journal of Psychology*, 1963, **76**, 376–385.

Neisser, U. *Cognitive psychology*. New York: Appleton, 1967.

Norman, D. A. Toward a theory of memory and attention. *Psychological Review*, 1968, **75**, 522–536.

Pollack, I. The information of elementary auditory displays. II. *Journal of the Acoustical Society of America*, 1953, **25**, 765–769.

Pollack, I. Interaction of two sources of verbal context in word identification. *Language and Speech*, 1964, **7**, 1–12.

Pollack, I., & Ficks, L. Information of elementary multidimensional auditory displays. *Journal of the Acoustical Society of America*, 1954, **26**, 155–158.

Royer, F. L. Figural goodness and internal structure in perceptual discrimination. *Perception and Psychophysics*, 1966, **1**, 311–314.

Sekuler, R. W., & Abrams, M. Visual sameness: A choice time analysis of pattern recognition processes. *Journal of Experimental Psychology*, 1968, **77**, 232–238.

Shepard, R. N. Attention and the metric structure of the stimulus space. *Journal of Mathematical Psychology*, 1964, **1**, 54–87.

Shepard, R. N., Hovland, C. I., & Jenkins, H. M. Learning and memorization of classifications. *Psychological Monographs*, 1961, **75**, 13 (Whole No. 517).

Sperling, G. The information available in brief visual presentations. *Psychological Monographs*, 1960, **74**, 11 (Whole No. 498).

Spieth, W., Curtis, J. F., & Webster, J. C. Responding to one of two simultaneous messages. *Journal of the Acoustical Society of America*, 1954, **26**, 391–396.

Stowe, A. N., Harris, W. P., & Hampton, D. B. Signal and context components of word-recognition behavior. *Journal of the Acoustical Society of America,* 1963, **35,** 639–644.

Stroop, J. R. Studies of interference in serial verbal reactions. *Journal of Experimental Psychology,* 1935, **18,** 643–661.

Torgerson, W. S. *Theory and methods of scaling.* New York: Wiley, 1958.

Treisman, A. M. Monitoring and storage of irrelevant messages in selective attention. *Journal of Verbal Learning and Verbal Behavior,* 1964, **3,** 449–459.

Treisman, A. M. Strategies and models of selective attention. *Psychological Review,* 1969, **76,** 282–299.

Tulving, E., & Gold, C. Stimulus information and contextual information as determinants of tachistoscopic recognition of words. *Journal of Experimental Psychology,* 1963, **66,** 319–327.

Tulving, E., & Lindsay, P. H. Identification of simultaneously presented simple visual and auditory stimuli. *Acta Psychologica,* 1967, **27,** 101–109.

Tulving, E., Mandler, G., & Baumal, R. Interaction of two sources of information in tachistoscopic word recognition. *Canadian Journal of Psychology,* 1964, **18,** 62–71.

Underwood, B. J., Ham, M., & Ekstrand, B. Cue selection in paired associate learning. *Journal of Experimental Psychology,* 1962, **64,** 405–409.

von Wright, J. M. Selection in visual immediate memory. *Quarterly Journal of Experimental Psychology,* 1968, **20,** 62–68.

Webster, J. C. Information in simple multidimensional speech messages. *Journal of the Acoustical Society of America,* 1961, **33,** 940–944.

Webster, J. C., & Thompson, P. O. Responding to both of two overlapping messages. *Journal of the Acoustical Society of America,* 1954, **26,** 396–402

Weiss, W., & Margolius, G. The effect of context stimuli on learning and retention. *Journal of Experimental Psychology,* 1954, **48,** 318–322.

Chapter 3

MEMORY PROCESSES AND JUDGMENT[*]

ARTHUR SANDUSKY

I. INTRODUCTION

With the application of the theory of signal detectability (Peterson, Birdsall, & Fox, 1954) to human detection performance, the separation of sensory processes from response–decision processes became explicit. Since then, the technique has been applied to a variety of judgmental tasks well beyond those included in the original scope of the theory (Banks, 1970). Basically, two statistical features of perceptual judgments are used to separate sensory effects from response effects. A systematic bias in judgment is identified with the response–decision process. The variability of responses is taken to reflect discriminability between stimuli.

However, in many tasks, the role of an additional judgmental process has been recognized, that of perceptual memory. When a stimulus is judged on an ordered perceptual dimension, it is compared to the perceptual memory of previously presented stimuli or to a remembered response

* This research was supported by NIMH Grant USPHS MH 21983.

criterion, either of which is subject to bias and variability effects. The introduction of a memory process into judgment makes the identification of bias with the response–decision process and of variability with sensitivity is less obvious. The goal of this chapter is to isolate the sources of bias and variability in judgmental processes in an effort to independently identify memory processes.

A. Bias

The problem of confounding sensory, memory and response–decision bias can be illustrated by a simple demonstration of a delayed comparison task for lifted weight. Lift a moderately heavy weight and set it down. Wait a few seconds and lift it again. Does the weight feel heavier or lighter on the second lifting? The emphasis must be on the word "feel," since obviously the object has not changed weight. Most persons judge the weight on second lifting as feeling slightly heavier. Why?

It can be argued that lifting the weight alters sensory processing characteristics temporarily. The first lifting "adapts" the receptor mechanism, and as a result the second lifting feels heavier. A perceptual memory explanation would suggest that the trace of the heaviness of the weight changes in memory from its original sensory value. The first lifting is remembered as light and by comparison, the same sensory experience at a later time is judged heavier. Finally, it can be asserted that no real difference between liftings is actually felt, but that "when in doubt," most people decide to respond "heavier" to the second lifting if pushed for a judgment.

These explanations of the judgmental bias in a delayed-comparison task identify three conceptual stages in perceptual processing, each of which can be a possible locus of bias effects in any judgmental task. They are: (1) sensory bias; the properties of the sensory or receptor mechanism alter, (2) memory bias; the memory trace or stored basis for comparison is displaced, and (3) response–decision bias; response preferences and tendencies operate to produce the observed judgmental effect. Currently, many judgmental bias phenomenon are attributed to sensory, memory, or response–decision stages as a matter of theoretical preference without a validating basis in the data.

B. Variability

Partitioning the sources of variability in judgment also presents a challenge. A second simple demonstration will illustrate this. Select 10 notes on a piano and assign a number or letter to each as an absolute (as opposed to relative) identification of the note. Practice associating the notes with their names. Then have someone play the notes a few times in a haphazard order, one at a time. Try to identify each note as it is played. When you have finished, compare your identifications with the actual order of presentation. Under these conditions, most listeners will make mistakes. The spacing between the notes and the amount of practice makes little difference. In fact, the limit of the ability to identify tones perfectly extends only to about seven or eight different values. This same limit holds for most other sensory dimensions (Miller, 1956), and does not depend on the mode of response.

Why should this be so? Most observers can easily discriminate two tones with as little as .3% difference in their frequencies. They ought to be able to identify hundreds of different tones. What processing feature limits the ability to make absolute identifications? To answer this, it is necessary to identify the sources of judgmental variance and their causes.

The variability of a remembered tone value may increase as a function of the time since its last presentation. In the language of memory studies, this is referred to as a trace decay theory of forgetting. The variability of the remembered tone value may also increase as a function of the tones intervening since its last presentation. This is called the interference theory of forgetting. Both of these memory factors would lead to an increasing number of errors as more and more tones were used, setting a limit on the number of absolute identifications possible.

Systematic changes in the judged value of each stimulus can occur as a function of a sensory or memory change that depends on the sequence of presentation. The judgment of tone may vary depending on whether a high or a low tone precedes it in the series. This would give rise to random variability in the responses and result in an apparent limit on identifications unless a sequential analysis were applied.

Finally, the naming of the tones itself is subject to variability. The response that was made to a particular tone on previous presentations may be forgotten. The criterion for naming a stimulus would then be the source of variability rather than the memory for the stimulus itself.

These accounts suggest some of the issues in partitioning the sources of variability in perceptual memory studies. Does variability increase only with time, or does it increase as a function of similar stimulation interfering with memory? To what extent do the observed confusions reflect random forgetting and to what extent a systematic change in memory dependent on the sequential nature of stimulus presentations? Is the source of variability in the stored value of a stimulus, or in the criterion used for identification?

Unfortunately these issues have not been clearly resolved. Each will be examined in the light of current research since they remain as obstacles to questions concerning the nature of perceptual memory, its extent and completeness, its form of coding, and its retrievability. Furthermore, these problems can obscure the contribution of perceptual memory to many features of sensory integration, including contrast and assimilation, the role of memory in illusions, and its function in psychophysical techniques in general.

II. DELAYED COMPARISONS

A. Data Representations

Much of the work is sensory memory uses a delayed-comparison method. A standard stimulus is presented, and following a time interval, a comparative stimulus is presented to be judged relative to the standard. The observer judges the comparative stimulus as "higher than" or "lower than" the standard.

1. PSYCHOMETRIC FUNCTIONS

Data from earlier psychophysical experiments using several comparative stimuli and a single standard, plotted the proportion of "higher" judgments against the physical value of the comparative stimuli (Guilford, 1954). This psychometric function plotted on log-normal coordinates is usually linear, indicating discriminability as a logarithmic-transformation of the physical scale with normally distributed sensory effects. The reciprocal of the slope in physical units reflects the variability of judgments and is called the difference limen (DL). The DL is a mixture of sensory, memory, and response variability. It is now seldom reported as a measure of discriminability.

The comparative stimulus value which would be called "higher" than the standard on just half of the trials is the point of subjective equality (PSE) and is still reported in many perceptual memory studies. The difference between the PSE and the standard in physical units is a bias measure called the constant error (CE).

2. RECEIVER OPERATING CHARACTERISTIC

More recently, two process theories like the theory of signal detection (TSD) (Green & Swets, 1966) have been applied to perceptual memory studies. These theories attempt to separate explicitly sensory processes from response processes. The form of data representation for this type of theory is the receiver operating characteristic (ROC). Generally, given two stimuli (S_1, S_2) and two identifing responses (R_1, R_2) the ROC is a plot of the probability of a correct identification, $\Pr(R_2|S_2)$, against the probability of a false identification $\Pr(R_2|S_1)$.

The measure of discriminability most commonly used is d', the normalized difference between the means of the two sensory distributions, and is derived from the two conditional probabilities.* This measure is inversely related to variability. The response criterion is a value on the sensory continuum or on some decisional transformation of it, such that values observed above the criterion are identified with response R_2. The sensory process and decision process are assumed to be independent and consequently, so are d' and the criterion measure.†

For a delayed-comparison task, this type of data representation can be applied when two values of the comparative stimuli are considered. The measure d' in this case confounds the sensory variability of the comparisons, the variability present in the memory for the standard, and criterion variability.

The response criterion for delayed comparisons has an unusual status. For TSD, the criterion value is usually assumed to represent response–decision bias only. If the comparison decision is based on a continuum of the comparative sensory value minus the trace of the standard, then the presentation of the standard is actually an instruction for criterion placement. The instructions for delayed comparisons essentially imply that if the observed value of the comparison is larger than the remembered value of the standard, judge it "higher"; if smaller, judge it "lower." The criterion is then the equivalent of the PSE and different values of the standard should produce shifts in the apparent criterion while leaving d' unchanged.‡

For example, five tone intensities were used in a delayed comparison with each intensity serving as standard and comparative stimuli (Needham, 1935a). Figure 1 shows the resultant ROC function for the 40- and 41-dB comparative stimuli for the five different standards of 38, 39, 40, 41, and 42 dB. The points fall approximately on a single isosensitivity curve with a d' of .80. It is important to note that, although the different points would

---

*A d' measure for two comparative stimuli, S_1 and S_2, can be derived from the DL (if they are close in value to the standard used to determine the DL) by the equation

$$d' = (S_2 - S_1)/\text{DL}.$$

Conversely for d' determined for S_1 and S_2,

$$\text{DL} = (S_2 - S_1)/d'.$$

† The PSE can be derived from the ROC point by the equation

$$\text{PSE} = S_1 - (S_2 - S_1)\Phi[\Pr(R_2|S_1)]/d',$$

where Φ is the normal transform.

‡ A less theoretically based measure is the area under the ROC (Green & Swets, 1966). An atheoretical bias measure for a fixed level of discriminability is the sum of the two conditional probabilities for one of the responses, $\Pr(R_2|S_2) + \Pr(R_2|S_1)$.

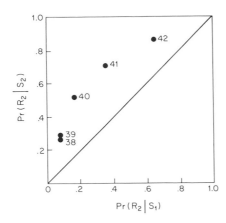

FIG. 1. The ROC plot for two comparative stimuli, $S_1 = 40$ and $S_2 = 41$ dB for the five different standards indicated by the adjacent numbers in decibels. (Data from Needham, 1935a.)

normally be considered as response-decision bias changes, in this case they actually represent the different values of the memory for the standards.

B. Bias

1. ADAPTATION-LEVEL

Systematic explanations of memory bias have been offered when the stimuli used in a delayed comparison are manipulated so as to displace the central tendency of the distribution of stimuli away from the perceptual value of the standard. Helson's (1964) adaptation-level theory proposes that the comparative basis for all category judgments is a weighted mean of the effective perceptual values relevant to the task. This average is the neutral point on the perceptual scale called the adaptation level (AL).

Translated into delayed comparisons, this implies that the trace of the standard, identified with the AL, is displaced toward the average of all stimuli presented in the judgment task. Formally, the adaptation level for delayed comparisons is given by:

$$AL = a(\overline{Co}) + (1 - a)(Std),$$

where a is an empirical weighting constant, $(\overline{Co})$ is the mean of the perceptual values of the comparative stimuli and (Std) is the perceptual value of the standard on presentation. For many physical dimensions, a logarithmic transformation of the physical values of the stimuli is a sufficient approximation to their perceptual values. In some cases, it is not (as, for example, line length on a card), and in other cases, a physical scale is not available (as for comparative pleasantness of odors). In those cases, functional scales should be derived (Anderson, 1970).

The memory for the standard can be manipulated according to this theory by changing the mean of the comparative stimuli. In general, it is a theory of contrast. Introducing larger stimuli raises AL and consequently lowers the judgmental categories applied to the stimuli.

Perhaps the cleanest delayed-comparison experiment, which shows the effect of manipulating the mean of the comparative stimuli relative to the standard, is the study of auditory intensity by Needham (1935a). Five intensities of pure tone were used in a delayed-comparison design, each intensity compared to every other intensity in a random series. Two delay intervals were used: 1 sec and 6 sec. Figure 2 plots the observed PSEs calculated from his data against the value of the standard.

The PSE shows a very slight CE at the 40-dB standard, which was reported to diminish with practice. As a consequence of the symmetric construction of the comparative stimuli, and the negligible CE at the central standard, we can rule out response bias as accounting for the other CEs. Each other PSE is drawn toward the mean of all the stimuli presented, 40 dB, with a greater effect for the 6-sec interval than for the 1-sec interval. Hollingsworth (1910) described this phenomenon as the "central tendency" effect, and Woodrow (1933) presented a verbal form of an averaging model for similar results.

The slopes of the lines indicate the weighting of the standard in the AL equation. The weighting for the standard is .7 for the 1-sec interval and .4 for the 6-sec interval. This recency effect for the weighting of the standard in determining the PSE is consistent with a perceptual memory interpretation of the CE.

2. RANGE-FREQUENCY THEORY

The method of delayed comparisons was developed assuming that judgments represented the results of sensory comparisons, uncontaminated by memory processes. Of course, in addition to systematic changes in the memory for the standard, response biases such as the observed tendency

FIG. 2. The observed delayed comparison PSEs for five different standards in decibels are shown for two delay periods. (Data from Needham, 1935a.)

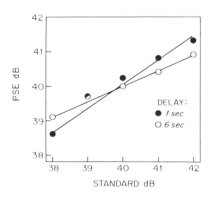

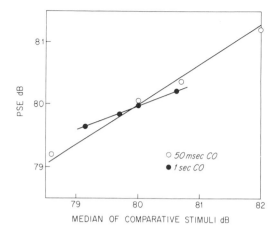

FIG. 3. The observed delayed comparisons PSEs are plotted against the median of the comparative stimuli in decibles for two comparative stimulus durations, 50 msec (○) and 1 sec (●). The standard was 80 dB. (Data are from Doughty, 1949.)

to use judgment categories with equal frequency affect the size of the CE (Parducci, 1965).

To separate response-decision bias from memory bias, the range-frequency model for comparative judgment (Parducci & Haugen, 1967) proposes that the PSE is a compromise between the true remembered value of the standard and the value that would give rise to an equal number of "higher" and "lower" judgments, namely, the median. Data from a comparative loudness experiment (Doughty, 1949), show the PSEs to be a linear function of the median of the comparative stimuli.* Figure 3 plots the observed PSE against the median of asymmetrical sets of comparative stimuli. The standard was 80 dB, and two durations of the comparative stimuli were used. The slopes ofthe lines, .65 and .35 for the 50-msec and the 1-sec comparative stimulus durations, respectively, indicate the relative contribution of the median comparative stimulus to the PSE. The greater response bias reflects the poorer perceptual performance for the shorter stimulus duration.

The theory proposes that the proportion of the CE attributable to the response equalization tendency can be factored out by use of the following equation:

$$PSE = bM + (1 - b)F,$$

where M is the true value of the memory for the standard, F is the median of the comparative stimuli and $(1 - b)$ is the proportionality constant of the contribution of the response frequency-equilization tendency (Parducci, Marshall, & Degner, 1966).

* The stimulus mean and median are confounded in this data, so, strictly speaking, the slopes may reflect some memory bias.

The AL as calculated by Helson's comparative judgment equation represents the memory for the standard and is equivalent to the M value in Parducci's equation. Substituting the AL equation for M we have

$$\text{PSE} = b[a(\overline{Co}) + (1 - a)(Std)] + (1 - b)F.$$

The observed PSE is then a weighted average of the standard (Std), the mean of the comparative stimuli ($\overline{Co}$), and the median of the comparative stimuli F.

3. TIME ERRORS

One of the first features of psychophysical data that was attributed to a perceptual memory process was the time error (TE), such as illustrated by the lifted weight illusion described earlier. This is a bias that varies solely as a function of the interval between the presentation of the standard and the comparative stimulus. The direction of the TE appears to vary in an idiosyncratic manner for different stimulus dimensions and for different time intervals (Postman, 1946). When the comparative stimuli are symmetric with respect to the standard on an equal-discriminability scale, the presence of TEs of varying direction has no unifying explanation. A sensory adaptation account is unlikely, because positive and negative TEs exist (Woodworth & Schlosberg, 1954). A simple response preference is rules out because presenting the comparative stimulus first, reverses the TE in sign, indicating a preponderance of responses opposite to the kind given when the standard is presented first (Woodrow, 1933). Furthermore, TEs appear to decrease with practice although this may be a result of the frequency-equilization response bias operating to reduce or eliminate them (Needham, 1934). These factors would argue for a memory trace explanation, although its idiosyncratic nature is unexplained. The TE must then be represented simply as an empirical constant in partitioning the overall bias.

4. RETROACTIVE INTERFERENCE

The mean of the stimulus distribution and consequently the AL can also be altered by introducing in the delay interval stimuli that are not judged. The terminology of verbal memory studies is often applied, referring to this type of design as a retroactive interference paradigm. Presentation of the standard is analogous to list acquisition, the interfering list, and the comparative stimulus equivalent to the test.

Guilford and Park (1931) presented a 100- or a 400-gm interfering weight in the delay interval with a 200-gm standard. The PSEs varied directly with the interfering weights. They interpreted this as a displacement in the memory for the standard toward the interfering value. Needham

(1935b) varied the delay interval between the standard and comparative stimulus from 1 to 6 sec with a .5-sec interfering tone in the middle of the interval. The interfering tone was either 20 dB greater or less than the 40-dB standard. The difference in the PSEs between the two interfering tone conditions was greatest for a 1-sec delay, and decreased to no difference for 6 sec.* The decrease could be attributed to decreasing recency of the interfering tone with respect to both the standard and comparative stimuli. In this case, there would have been a consequent increase in the effect of the entire distribution of stimuli on the memory for the standard. The mean of the entire distribution was 40 dB, the value of the standard. When the delay interval is completely filled by the interfering tone, an increase rather than a decrease in the displacement of the PSE toward the interfering tone is noted (Woodworth, 1938), consistent with a recency interpretation.

If only a single interfering stimulus value is used, the memory trace for the standard is very different from the median of the comparative stimuli, resulting in the preponderance in use of one of the categories. The CE would be reduced by the frequency-equalization response tendency. When one of two interfering values are used on different trials with one greater than the standard and one less than the standard, category usage is more readily equalized. The difference in PSEs following the two interfering values in a single experiment is actually greater than the difference when the interfering values are used singly in different experiments (Parducci et al., 1966). The range-frequency model for the retroactive design assumes that with a single interfering stimulus, the memory for the standard M_i, is a weighted average of the interfering weight and the trace of the standard with no interfering weight as follows:

$$M_i = cM + (1 - c)I$$

where the weighting factor c would depend on the delay between the interfering stimulus, I, and the comparison and possibly even the standard. It may also depend on the value of I, since very weak or very intense stimuli have been shown to have reduced effects on judgment (Sarris, 1967).

Combining this equation with the response frequency-equalization equation for the PSE, we have

$$PSE_i = bcM + b(1 - c)I + (1 - b)F$$

Varying the value of I and of F, holding the mean constant, for each standard in a factorial design will allow for solution of the weighting parameters from a simple regression equation. This experiment remains to be done.

---

* The actual PSEs were not reported, nor were data from which they could be tabulated. Needham (1935b) reported the proportion of "higher" judgments which would be highly correlated with the PSEs.

Consequently the quantitative effect of an interpolated weight on the memory for the standard is unknown.

5. PROACTIVE INTERFERENCE

Much less attention has been directed to the proactive interference design in delayed comparisons. For this design, the interfering stimulus precedes the standard. Although some studies have been concerned with carryover effects from previously judged comparative stimuli, the previous response is confounded with the stimulus, and the results are inconclusive (Fernberger, 1920; Turner, 1931).

An explicit proactive interference design for delayed comparisons was compared with a retroactive design by Glietman (1956). An interfering tone of 80 dB was presented either 2 sec before or after the 60-dB standard. Two delay intervals of 4 and 6 sec were used. The PSEs for both the proactive and the retroactive conditions were about 2 dB higher than the no-interference control. If the interfering effect were attributable to sensory contrast between the interfering stimulus and the following stimulus, then we should expect the PSE to be displaced away from the interfering stimulus in the proactive condition, and toward the interfering stimulus in the retroactive condition. Both effects must be attributable to a displacement of the memory trace for the standard toward the interfering stimulus.

Surprisingly, the time interval made little difference. This is probably because only one interfering stimulus and one standard were used. The subjects, who participated in all conditions, may have paid less attention to presentations of the standard and interfering stimuli than they might have if these stimuli had been varied. The frequency-equalization response bias would be expected to reduce the effect of a single interfering stimulus. What is needed for a firmer conclusion is a proactive experiment which varies the standard and the interfering stimulus.

C. Variability

The studies that have systematically explored variability in delayed comparisons have primarily used d' as an index of discriminability between two comparative stimuli. The use of this measure implies the assumption of a normal distribution of effects for each stimulus on some perceptual dimension with a fixed-criterion decision rule.* This measure actually combines variance from all sources, including the sensory variance of the com-

---

* A number of perceptual memory models are formulated in terms of the strength of the memory trace determined by the mean difference in the distributions of perceptual effects associated with the two comparative stimuli. However, changes in the difference between the means (decreases in strength) are perfectly indistinguishable from changes in the variance of the distributions (increases in variance).

parative-stimuli, the variance of the memory trace of the standard (Kinchla & Smyzer, 1967), and response criterion variance (Tanner, 1961).

1. Response Scales

Basically, two different types of response scales have been used, an ordered scale of "higher-lower" judgments and an unordered scale of "same-different" judgments. Wickelgren (1969) has argued that at least for the dimension of pitch, the ordered scale is inappropriate. He assumes that pitch is judged primarily on a familiarity dimension rather than on a pitch difference dimension. This suggests that pitch is, at least locally, a poorly ordered dimension. He shows that ROC functions for "higher–same–lower" judgments are nonlinear in normal–normal coordinates, contrary to expectations from TSD. However, nonlinearity has also been reported for "same-different" judgments (Moss, Myers, & Filmore, 1970; Bull & Cuddy, 1972).

Criterion variability for "same" judgments is very great, and their use on an ordered response scale has produced anomalous results for dimensions other than pitch (Turner, 1931; Needham, 1935a). Consequently, this category has been avoided in much research using ordered categories. However, recent studies of variability for delayed comparisons most often use the "same-different" scale.

2. Delay Time

The variance of judgment for delayed comparisons increases as a function of the delay interval (Harris, 1952). This increase is much less marked when one, rather than several standards, is used (Harris, 1952; Aiken & Lau, 1966). Repeated presentation of the same standard would act to reduce trace variance for the standard and also for criterion variability. Additionally, if the delay interval is filled with an interfering tone, then the variance is more strongly affected by the duration of the interval than if it is left blank (Bull & Cuddy, 1972). It has been argued that the presence of the interfering stimulus prevents rehearsal of the image of the standard (Wickelgren, 1969; Bull & Cuddy, 1972).

Two principle forms for the decay of d' (increase in variance) as a function of the delay interval have been postulated. Kinchla and Smyzer (1967) have developed a memory model for delayed comparisons that attempts to separate the sensory and memory components of variability. They assume that the comparative stimulus is judged relative to the memory trace of the standard. Using a random walk model of the memory trace over time, the variance of the trace increases linearly with time. Consequently, discrimination decreases as an inverse square root function of time according to the following equation:

$$d_t = a/(bt + c)^{1/2},$$

where d_t is the predicted sensitivity for delay time t, a is the absolute difference between the two comparative stimuli, and b is a diffusion rate parameter. The quantity bt represents the trace variance and c represents the input or sensory variance. The separation between sensory variance and memory variance is achieved for this model by plotting $1/d'^2$ against delay time. The plot should be linear with slope b and intercept c. For data on visual movement and auditory intensity, the sensory variance appeared to be negligible relative to the memory variance for delays from .5 to 2 sec.

Wicklegren has derived an alternative decay function from a memory strength theory. This theory postulates a decrease in the mean memory strength of a stimulus as a negative exponential decay function of time with the form:

$$d_t = ae^{-bt},$$

where d_t is as before, a is the sensory discriminability of the comparisons in the absence of a time difference (inversely proportional the sensory variability) and b is the decay rate (Wickelgren, 1969). A multipicative interaction between sensory and memory variance is implied. The plot of log d' against delay time would be linear with negative slope b and intercept a.

These two functions would not be readily distinguishable with available data. However, data for delayed comparisons for pitch show a less rapid decay for long time intervals than either function could handle (Wickelgren, 1969). A secondary trace with a slower decay rate relative to the primary trace was postulated and found to improve the fit to the data. The Kinchla and Smyzer model could similarly be elaborated to account for this data.

Massaro (1970a) has argued that the rate of forgetting is a decreasing function of the duration of the interfering stimulus as it would be for the item presentation rate in the verbal memory task. He links the sensory processing stage (acquisition) to forgetting by assuming that the processing time for a stimulus detracts from the memory strength for all other stimuli. Since processing is postulated to be a decreasing function of presentation time, memory strength for an item as measured by d', will decrease to an asymptote above zero. This interpretation requires only one memory trace rather than the two postulated for the other models. This, however, is an interpretation which rests on an interference model rather than a time-decay model of forgetting and will be taken up next.

3. INTERFERING STIMULI

The presence of an interfering stimulus in the delay interval may do more than simply prevent rehearsal. A number of authors have hypothesized that, in fact, the duration of the interval is irrelevant to the increase in memory variance and that the source of variance is the interfering stimulus itself. For example, one theory assumes that the perceptual processing of a stimulus (a negatively accelerating function of presentation time) detracts from the memory strength for stimuli that have been stored. This is equivalent to assuming that the variance of stored stimuli increases. Thus the predicted strength is a function of the memory strength after presentation multiplied by the memory strength remaining after processing of the interfering stimulus (Massaro, 1970a).

Massaro (1970b) has shown that for continuous interfering stimuli the addition of a blank delay interval before the interfering stimulus begins has no effect on d'. A decay theorist might point out that this is because of rehearsal of the image of the standard during the blank interval. However, the effectiveness of rehearsing a perceptual image has been asserted to be minimal (Wickelgren, 1966; Massaro, 1970c). In fact, it has been shown that instructions to rehearse the standard can actually degrade performance (Bull & Cuddy, 1972).

The effect of the similarity of the interfering tone to the standard and comparative stimuli shows mixed results. When the interfering stimulus is similar to the comparative stimuli, it has been reported to have a facilitating effect (Wickelgren, 1969; Massaro, 1970c) and a deteriorating effect (Deutsch, 1972) on performance. When the interfering stimulus fills the delay interval and is similar to the standard, the judgment may be made on the basis of successive difference judgments (Wickelgren, 1969) or the interfering stimulus may serve as the standard. In either case, this would increase d'. If the interfering stimulus is very different from the comparative stimuli, or is even on a different dimension (e.g., noise or digits interfering with pitch) the interfering stimuli produce little or no effect (Massaro, 1970c; Deutsch, 1970). It should be noted that this is not evidence for separate memory systems. Verbal memory studies have shown that highly dissimilar verbal material produces little interference without postulating a separate memory system for each type of verbal material.

In order to evaluate the contribution of time-decay and stimulus-interference to the increase in the variance for the trace of the standard, Massaro (1970b) covaried both the delay time and the number of interfering stimuli. Both of these variables had an independent effect on the variance.

If the effect of interfering stimuli is to displace the trace of the standard in their direction according to an AL averaging formulation, this would contribute to the variance of the trace by the simple additivity of variance rule. The more interfering stimuli that are included in the average, the more variance components there would be, with a consequent decrease in d'. This would explain the observed interference effects. A time controlled diffusion process such as that proposed by Kinchla and Smyzer (1967) would explain the independent delay-time effects. None of the memory strength theorists examining the effects of interfering stimuli seem to give any notice to the possibility of a memory bias and the consequent effects of the averaging process on the variance of the trace for the standard.

III. IDENTIFICATIONS

A. Data Representations

With identification methods, a set of stimuli are judged on an ordered scale without respect to an explicitly presented standard. These methods were developed to more efficiently accomplish the same ends as the comparison methods. Rather than present a physical standard on each trial, it was assumed that the subject could maintain internal criteria for the identification boundaries on the perceptual dimension. The observed stimulus values are assumed to be compared to internal criteria which serve as standards and result in classification.

For identifications, each stimulus is assigned a unique response. The memory for a stimulus is then identified with some measure of the accuracy of identification. Other judgment paradigms use relative categories which do not make a unique assignment of responses to stimuli. They will not be considered here because of the difficulty of isolating memory factors.

For the case of only two stimuli and two responses, the data are most conveniently represented by ROC functions using d' and bias measures. With multiple responses and stimuli, the mean and the variance of responses to a stimulus are calculated. Often, a psychological scaling procedure such as Thurstonian scaling is applied. This procedure results in a cumulative d' scale of the stimuli with arbitrary origin and unit (Torgerson, 1958).

B. Bias

1. TWO STIMULI

When stimulus presentation probabilities are varied in two-choice identification, probability contrast is observed (Parducci & Sandusky, 1965; Sandusky, 1971; Tanner, Haller, & Atkinson, 1967). Both conditional probabilities $\Pr(R_2|S_2)$ and $\Pr(R_2|S_1)$, decrease with an increase in the presentation probability of an S_2 stimulus. Figure 4 shows the effect of varying the presentation probability of the louder of the two tones on the bias. The direction of change, in the bias is opposite to that expected for a decision procedure that would optimize correct responses. However, contrast does tend to equalize the use of the response categories.

Response assimilation, not contrast, occurs in the signal detection task for which TSD was developed. It has been asserted that the difference in bias determination between identification and detection occurs because of the addition of memory requirements in the identification task. The detection task requires the subject to decide whether or not a faint tone has been added to the continuous noise background during brief observation intervals. The continuous background noise is presumed to function as a comparative basis for detecting the tone (Sandusky & Ahumada, 1971). With stimulus identifications, no background reference is presented. Recognizing a stimulus requires memory for the other stimuli or a remembered criterion which is displaced by the stimulus mean.

The sequential response dependencies are also quite marked for identifications and show strong sequential contrast. Both conditional probabilities are smaller following the presentation of S_2 on the preceding trial than following S_1. These dependencies are large enough that they alone account for the probability contrast.

Two alternative explanations have been offered for these sequential bias effects (Sandusky, 1971; Tanner et al., 1967). The memory trace regression model (MTR) is based on an adaptation-level displacement of the memory for the decision criterion. Each observation of a stimulus is compared to the current memory for the average of previous stimuli weighted for recency. This average serves as a momentary response criterion.

The memory state model (MS) is based on response contrast with respect to fixed memory-response states. Although the current observation

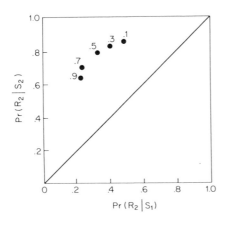

FIG. 4. The ROC plot for identifications of two loudness stimuli. The presentation probability of S_2 is shown in adjacent numbers. (Data from Tanner et al. 1967.)

of the stimulus may be on a continuous perceptual dimension, the memory states are assumed to be discrete. Each stimulus is recognized and correctly identified with fixed probability. When the stimulus is not recognized, the response depends on the memory state of the previous observation. If the previous stimulus was recognized, and the present one is not, the subject uses his response to discriminate the change of state and gives the response opposite to that given on the previous trial. If the previous stimulus was not recognized, and the present stimulus is also not recognized, the response is random with respect to the previous response.

Both of these models account for the probability contrast effect as resulting from the sequential response dependencies. The usual ROC plot is inappropriate in the presence of these dependencies because differential averaging may seriously distort the results. Instead, a sequential ROC is more representative of the data. The sequential ROC plots $Pr(R_2|S_2)$ against $Pr(R_2|S_1)$ as a function of the sequence of stimuli and responses on previous trials. For recognition data, the dependencies are confined largely to the stimulus and response on the single previous trial. Figure 5 shows a sequential ROC for four subjects in one condition of a two-choice visual position experiment. The four bias points for each subject represent the difference between S_2 and S_1 occurring on the preceding trial (squares versus circles) and the difference between R_1 and R_2 on the preceding trial (open versus closed symbols).

Both the memory state model (straight line–slashes) and the memory trace regression model (curved line–dots) predict the data quite well and there is little basis here for distinguishing between them.

This particular experiment used two types of Markov-chains with equiprobable stimuli for the presentation sequence, one chain with an 80% stim-

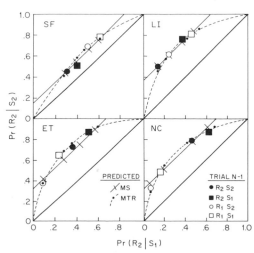

FIG. 5. The sequential ROC plots for identifications of two visual positions for four subjects. The four bias points are functions of the stimulus and response events on the preceding trial. The straight line–slashes are the memory state model predictions. The curve line–dots are the memory trace regression model predictions. (Data from Sandusky, 1971.)

ulus repetition rate, the other with an 80% stimulus alternation rate. The nonsequential ROC shows the surprising but predictable result that the alternation condition produces a higher apparent d' than the repetition condition for each of the four subjects. This is purely a result of differential averaging of the bias values and does not reflect a difference in discriminability between the two recognition stimuli. The sequential ROCs show no differences discriminability for the two conditions.

2. MULTIPLE STIMULI

When several stimuli are to be identified, varying the presentation probabilities and using differential spacing produce contrast effects on the mean judgments. These effects have been attributed variously to response bias (Parducci & Marshall, 1962; Ward & Lockhead, 1971) and memory bias (Holland & Lockhead, 1968; Malamed & Thurlow, 1971). Presumably, both the frequency-equalization response bias and an adaptation-level memory displacement process are occurring to produce the contrast.

However, the contrast is not as readily explained in terms of the sequential effects as in the two category case. The first order effects show that the judgment on the present trial is more like the judgment on the previous trial, i.e., assimilation (Garner, 1953). Dependencies on more remote trials show contrast. Initially, a memory hypothesis was offered for these effects, but they have since been demonstrated to be sequentially determined response bias effects (Ward & Lockhead, 1971). When feedback as to "correct" responses is given after each trial, the same response biases are present even when no stimuli are presented (i.e., when the subject only guesses which stimulus might have been presented).

The initial assimilation is accounted for by assuming that the subject tries to minimize the average error of his responses, and biases his response according to the probability distribution of successive stimulus differences. This distribution is very positively skewed, with a preponderence of small differences. The successive contrast for more remote trials represents any attempt at frequency-equalization over relatively short response sequences.

3. ANCHORS

For single-stimulus identifications, the introduction of unjudged anchors is comparable to the use of an interfering stimulus with delayed comparisons. An additional stimulus, usually one outside the range of the identified stimuli is presented before each judged stimulus. If the anchor stimulus is identified with a response, as is often done, then any effects it has can be attributed mainly to response bias (Parducci & Marshall, 1962). If the anchor is not judged, then other conditions being equal, the effects may be attributed to either sensory or memory bias. When the anchor is not judged, some contrast is still observed. It has been suggested that even when observers are instructed not to judge the anchor, they make an implicit response which may attribute the contrast to a response bias even in this case.

Anchors with extremely small or large values have a very reduced contrast effect. This presents difficulty for a sensory bias interpretation of the contrast, particularly at the lower end of the sensory continuum. Sarris (1967) has shown that very weak anchors have almost no effect on bias while moderate anchors produce contrast. In a case of true sensory bias such as brightness contrast, a disk would appear brightest with a completely dark background or anchor and decrease in brightness as the background increases in intensity. On the other hand, when no anchor produces less contrast then a moderate anchor, we may conclude that the effect of the anchor is to displace the memory for stimulus presentations in a manner described by adaptation level theory. When no anchor is presented, nothing is entered into the memory which will produce such a displacement.

C. Variability

It is a well-established fact that for stimulus identifications there is a limit on the number of different values on a single dimension that can be identified with any accuracy. This limit is well below that expected on the basis of discriminability. Only about seven or so different values on a single sensory dimension can be so identified (Miller, 1956). Manipulations of training and stimulus spacing help very little. This results from the fact that as the range of stimuli is increased, the variance of identifying responses also increases (Pollack, 1962).

If the range of stimuli is increased by presenting an unjudged anchor, the variance of identifying responses increases (Helson, 1964). Two confusable stimuli become even less well discriminated if a third stimulus outside their range is added (Lockhead, 1973). In general, the constant-ratio rule which implies constant discriminability for subsets of stimuli does not hold for single physical dimensions (Luce, 1959).

The source of this increased variability has been the subject of much theoretical research. Thurstone's model of judgment as applied to category identifications does not allow for a separate solution for the variance attributable to stimulus and response criterion effects (Torgerson, 1958). This model proposes that the responses are determined by comparison of the observed stimulus to each criterion. If we assume a perceptual scale value and a variance for each stimulus and a scale value and variance for each criterion, one of the sets of variances must be assumed to be a constant which affects only the value of the arbitrary scaling unit.

Gravetter and Lockhead (1970) suggest a way experimentally to separate stimulus and criterion variance. They calculated the average Thurstonian variance measure for the six central stimulus categories in an equally decibel-spaced array of ten loudness stimuli. The stimulus range was then symmetrically quadrupled by changing the intensities of the two highest and the two lowest tones. The variance was then recalculated for the six central stimulus categories. Since the physical spacing for these six stimuli remained the same in the two range conditions, the stimulus variance was assumed to be constant. The variance of the criterial boundaries has been shown to be a function for the stimulus range. Their equation for this relationship is:

$$\text{Var} = k^2 + (aR)^2,$$

where Var is the observed variance and k is the constant stimulus variance component. The criterion variance is $(aR)^2$, where R is the stimulus range and a is the constant of proportionality. Using an estimate of k from a previous experiment, the fit to the data proved to be quite good. However, more than two range conditions would be necessary to provide an adequate test for the goodness of fit.

A number of analogies have been proposed which describe this type of result. These suggest that a fixed response scale is adjusted to fit the entire range of stimulation as a voltmeter is adjusted to adapt the meter scale to the range of variation (Lockhead, 1973) or as a "rubber band" response measure is stretched to fit the stimulus range (Pollack, 1962). The results are described, but little insight is offered into the partitioning of variance into stimulus, memory and response components.

A more formal model has been proposed by Durlach and Braida (1969) which attempts to separate sensory variance from memory variance. Two modes of memory operation are assumed. The memory trace made is a memory of the image of the stimulus, subject to a diffusion process like the one proposed by Kinchla and Smyzer (1967), and is also subject to stimulus interference effects. The context-coding mode is a crude verbal representation of the stimulus relative to the stimulus context. The context coding depends principally on the range of stimuli.

Their model accounts for the difference between the fineness of discriminations and the crudeness of identifications by assuming that discrimination is based on the sensory trace whereas identifications are based on context coding. The variance effect of the stimulus range is also predicted. When the range is small, identifications are limited by sensory variance. When the range is large, identifications are limited by context coding.

Bower (1971) has similarly suggested that identifications are limited by the number of effective verbal memory codes. He posits that stimuli are first coded with respect to the context in a manner described by adaptation level theory. The result is then assigned to a member of a set of conceptual elements which are linearly ordered, transsituational and transdimensional. This implicit conceptual response set is either a verbal code such as "small–medium–large" or an order numerical series such as "first–middle–last." These models show much promise in accounting for a variety of variance effects in stimulus identifications including range and spacing effects.

IV. CONCLUSION

If memory processes are to be incorporated into the analysis of judgmental tasks, then bias and variance effects must be extended from their original interpretation as reflecting response and sensory effects respectively. Observed variance and bias must be partitioned into sensory, memory and response effects.

Sensory bias refers to a mean change in the level of sensory output such as occurs in brightness contrast. Sensory variability limits discriminability and in many judgmental tasks proves to be the smallest contributor to overall response variability. Memory bias can occur either as a systematic drift in the stored value of a stimulus as in the case of time errors, or as a distortion of the stored criterion for response choice as described by adaptation-level theory. Memory variability can occur as a random time process as suggested by decay theories or as a result of systematic distortions by randomly presented interfering stimuli. Finally, response bias can occur as the result of an effort to achieve some goal such as the response equalization specified by range–frequency theory of the optimization dictated by the theory of signal detectability. Response choice variability is then the result of random effects of response strategies.

The empirical partitioning of these effects can be accomplished through the use of a variety of experimental techniques and methods of data treatment. Sensory processes are affected by stimuli that are spatially or temporally contiguous with the judged simulus. Memory processes are studied by manipulating either the time of judgment or the sequence of stimulus events prior to presentation of the judged stimulus. Response choices depend on a variety of situational factors including instructions for judgment and stimulus probabilities, all of which determine the sequence of responses prior to the judged stimulus.

Research to date has not been completely successful in effecting a clear separation between these processes since they are so intertwined. For example, prior stimulus events affect not only the memory process but also establish a sequence of responses which can affect the response–decision process. It may in fact prove impossible to ever make a completely clear separation between the sensory, memory and response processes in judgment.

References

Anderson, N. H. Functional measurement and psychophysical judgment. *Psychological Review,* 1970, **77,** 153–170.

Aiken, E. G., & Lau, A. W. Memory for the pitch of a tone. *Perception and Psychophysics,* 1966, **1**, 231–233.

Banks, W. P. Signal detection theory and human memory. *Psychological Bulletin,* 1970, **74**, 81–99.

Bower, G. H. Adaption-level coding of stimuli and serial position effects. In M. H. Appley (Ed.) *Adaptation-level theory.* New York: Academic Press, 1971.

Bull, A. R., & Cuddy, L. L. Recognition memory for pitch of fixed and roving stimulus tones. *Perception and Psychophysics,* 1972, **11**, 105–109.

Deutsch, D. Effect of repetition of standard and comparison tones on recognition memory for pitch. *Journal of Experimental Psychology,* 1972, **93**, 156–162.

Deutsch, D. Tones and numbers: Specificity of interference in short term memory. *Science,* 1970, **168**, 1604–1605.

Doughty, J. The effect of psychophysical method and context on pitch and loudness functions. *Journal of Experimental Psychology,* 1949, **39**, 729–745.

Durlach, N. I., & Braida, J. F. Intensity perception. I. Preliminary theory of intensity resolution. *Journal of the Acoustical Society of America,* 1969, **46**, 372–383.

Fernberger, S. Interdependence of judgments within the series for the method of constant stimuli. *Journal of Experimental Psychology,* 1920, 126–150.

Garner, W. R. An informational analysis of absolute judgments of loudness. *Journal of Experimental Psychology,* 1953, **46**, 373–380.

Gleitman, H. Proactive and retroactive assimilation in the successive comparison of loudness. *American Journal of Psychology,* 1956, **67**, 117–119.

Gravetter, F. J., & Lockhead, G. R. Criterial dispersions and the stimulus range. *Proceedings of the 78th Annual Convention of the American Psychological Association,* 1970, **5**, 41–42.

Green, D., & Swets, J. A. *Signal detection theory and psychophysics.* New York: Wiley, 1966.

Guilford, J. P. *Psychometric methods.* Second edition. New York: McGraw-Hill, 1954.

Guilford, J. P., & Park, D. The effect of interpolated weights upon comparative judgments. *American Journal of Psychology,* 1931, **43**, 589–599.

Harris, J. D. The decline of pitch discrimination with time. *Journal of Experimental Psychology,* 1952, **43**, 96–99.

Helson, H. *Adaptation level theory.* New York: Harper & Row, 1964.

Holland, M. K., & Lockhead, G. R. Sequential effects in absolute judgments of loudness. *Perception and Psychophysics,* 1968, **3**, 409–414.

Hollingworth, H. The central tendency of judgment. *Journal of Philosophy, Psychology, and Scientific Method,* 1910, **7**, 461–468.

Kinchla, R., & Smyzer, F. A diffusion model of perceptual memory. *Perception and Psychophysics,* 1967, **2**, 219–229.

Lockhead, G. R. Choosing a response. In S. Kornblum (Ed.) *Attention and performance. IV.* New York: Academic Press, 1973.

Luce, R. D. *Individual choice behavior: A theoretical analysis.* New York: Wiley, 1959.

Malamed, L. E., & Thurlow, W. R. Analysis of contrast effects in loudness judgments. *Journal of Experimental Psychology,* 1971, **90**, 268–274.

Massaro, D. W. Perceptual processes and forgetting in memory tasks. *Psychological Review,* 1970a, **77**, 557–567.

Massaro, D. W. Forgetting: interference or decay? *Journal of Experimental Psychology,* 1970b, **83**, 238–243.

Massaro, D. W. Retroactive interference in short-term memory for pitch. *Journal of Experimental Psychology,* 1970c, **83**, 32–39.

Miller, G. A. The magical number seven, plus or minus two: Some limits on our capacity for processing information. *Psychological Review,* 1956, **63**, 81–97.

Moss, S. M., Myers, J. L., & Filmore, T. Short-term recognition memory of tones. *Perception and Psychophysics,* 1970, **7**, 369–373.

Needham, J. G. The time error as a function of continued experimentation. *American Journal of Psychology,* 1934, **46**, 558–567.

Needham, J. G. The effect of time interval upon the time-error at different intensive levels. *Journal of Experimental Psychology,* 1935a, **18**, 530–543.

Needham, J. G. Interpolation effects with different time intervals. *Journal of Experimental Psychology,* 1935b, **18**, 767–773.

Parducci, A. Category judgment: A range-frequency model. *Psychological Review,* 1965, **72**, 407–418.

Parducci, A., & Haugen, R. The frequency principle for comparative judgments. *Perception and Psychophysics,* 1967, **2**, 81–82.

Parducci, A., & Marshall, L. M. Assimilation vs. contrast in the anchoring of perceptual judgments of weight. *Journal of Experimental Psychology,* 1962, **63**, 426–437.

Parducci, A., Marshall, L., & Degner, M. Interference with memory for lifted weight. *Perception and Psychophysics,* 1966, **1**, 83–86.

Parducci, A., & Sandusky, A. Distribution and sequence effects in judgment. *Journal of Experimental Psychology,* 1965, **69**, 450–459.

Peterson, W. W., Birdsall, T. G., & Fox, W. C. The theory of signal detectability. *Transactions of the IRE Professional Group in Information Theory,* 1954, **PGIT 2–4,** 171–212.

Pollack, I. Selected developments in psychophysics, with implications for sensory organization. In W. A. Rosenblith (Ed.) *Sensory communication.* Massachusetts: M.I.T. Press, 1962.

Postman, L. The time-error in auditory perception. *American Journal of Psychology,* 1946, **59**, 193–219.

Sandusky, A. Signal recognition models compared for random and Markov presentation sequences. *Perception and Psychophysics,* 1971, **10**, 339–346.

Sandusky, A., & Ahumada, A. Contrast in detection with gated noise. *Journal of the Acoustical Society of America,* 1971, **49**, 1790–1794.

Sarris, V. Adaptation-level theory: Two critical experiments on Helson's weighted-average model. *American Journal of Psychology,* 1967, **80**, 331–344.

Tanner, T. A., Haller, R. W., & Atkinson, R. C. Signal recognition as influenced by presentation schedules. *Perception and Psychophysics,* 1967, **2**, 349–358.

Tanner, W. P., Jr. Physiological implications of psychophysical data. *Annals of the New York Academy of Sciences,* 1961, **89**, 752–765.

Torgerson, W. S. *Theory and methods of scaling.* New York: Wiley, 1958.

Turner, W. Intra-serial effects with lifted weights. *American Journal of Psychology,* 1931, **43**, 1–25.

Ward, L. M., & Lockhead, G. R. Response system processes in absolute judgment. *Perception and Psychophysics,* 1971, **9**, 73–78.

Woodworth, R. S. *Experimental psychology.* New York: Holt, 1938.

Woodworth, R. S., & Schlosberg, H. *Experimental psychology.* New York: Holt & Col., 1954.

Wickelgren, W. A. Associative strength theory of recognition memory for pitch. *Journal of Mathematical Psychology,* 1969, **6**, 13–61.

Wickelgren, W. Consolidation and retroactive interference in short-term recognition memory for pitch. *Journal of Experimental Psychology,* 1966, **72**, 250–259.

Woodrow, H. Weight discrimination with a varying standard. *American Journal of Psychology,* 1933, **45**, 391–416.

Chapter 4

PSYCHOLOGICAL DECISION MECHANISMS AND PERCEPTION*,†

EUGENE GALANTER

I. INTRODUCTION

The intention of this chapter is to show how psychologists have attempted to deal with the interconnections between motivation and perception. Motivation and perception, along with learning, have formed the central conceptual core of psychological science since its beginnings. But whereas the notion of perception and the idea of learning have fairly clear and simple intuitive interpretations (those external events that influence behavior are presumed to be mediated by perceptual processes, the effect of past experience on current behavior is the central notion of learning), the concept of motivation does not have such an ostensibly objectivistic intuitive basis. On the one hand, "motivation" may refer to purely psychological desires, aversions, feelings, attitudes, interests, and all of the other psychological quasi-synonyms that are inferred from behavior on the basis of very poorly defined primitive criteria. On the other hand, and most popu-

* Preparation of this chapter and some of the previously unpublished research herein described, was supported in part by the Office of Naval Research.

† I have had the immense advantage of extended discussions of the contents of this chapter with my colleague and friend, Julian Hochberg. Additionally, I am happy to acknowledge the technical assistance of Dr. Diana Jacobs, and the helpful comments of Prof. Donald Hood.

larly, the concept of specific motivations is objectified by construing them as the consequences of presumably objectively determinable changes in the physiological state of the organism. Classically these changes of physiological state were thought to generate physiological "needs" on whose consummation the survival of the organism rested. So, the argument goes, food deprivation gives rise to (ultimately objectively determinate) changes of internal physiological processes which in turn institute psychological presses that are consummated in food seeking behavior or in the ingestion of food if it is directly available. The psychological process that presumably mediates the behavior is termed "hunger" and, although some off-hand admission may be given that hunger may arise without food deprivation, the general consensus is that food deprivation produces the psychological event "hunger" and the existence of this event gives rise to food seeking and food ingesting behavior.

The proposal that motives, desires, and aversions are at bottom physiological events has in no way improved our understanding of the sources and consequences of an organism's desires and aversions. This is not to say that there are no physiological events that underlie such desires and aversions, but rather that the mere presence of a physiologically measurable antecedent will hardly enlighten us about the behavior of complicated organisms. Such enlightenment is probably too much to demand of a physiological psychologist at this point in history. The central source of the conceptual difficulty is that most people eat and drink when they are neither hungry nor thirsty in any physiologically describable way. Furthermore, even if they are hungry they have no difficulty in choosing from among a variety of possible foodstuffs those that are most preferred. Unless and until physiological information can provide us with evidence about differences in preferences that people exhibit, the study of people's preferences will have to be made without benefit of the recording electrode and scalpel. Once again the reader is cautioned not to believe that there are no unique and distinguishable physiological mechanisms that underlie differential preference, but only that such physiological mechanisms may not be invariant over people, nor may they be discoverable by any local investigation of the chemical and neurological machinery of the body.

The preceding remarks are all designed to warn the reader that for the remainder of this chapter, the concept of motivation will be dealt with in a physiologically neutral way. That is to say the motives we shall attempt to characterize, and the influence these motives may have on perceptual processes, will be examined without any detours through the physiological structure. The concept of motivation that we shall adhere to will have a strong cognitive component. Indeed, the preferences that a person exhibits in most of the experiments we discuss will be considered well understood when those preferences represent behavior to which the primitive term "rational," can be attached. The hallmark of an adequate theory of motivation will be to discover some appropriate transform of the exhibited preferences that provides a coherent rationality to a variety of behaviors modulated by these preferences. This criterion of rational behavior is quite close to the notion of derivability and predictability as it is used by theoreticians. The rationality guaranteed by some theory may, of course, not conform to any objective criterion of rationality based upon maximizing or optimizing some objective quantity. The very intrigue in the study of behavior is just to find those principles of coherence that explain why people do things that, in objective terms, could hardly be considered rational.

II. THE PSYCHOLOGICAL TRACE

One of the many arbitrary ways to divide psychological theories is by whether they construe man's actions as inner or outer directed. Roughly, the first position holds that people do what they do because of what they expect to happen to them after they do it. An auxiliary principle is that what does happen after they do it will be, relatively speaking, desirable. The outer-directed view of man's nature proposes that when certain external events occur certain behavioral reactions are their consequence. The auxiliary principle for this viewpoint takes one of several different forms. Usually the principle is a learning rule, and its form depends on how the connection between the environmental stimulus and different behavior becomes established.

The first, or inner-directed theory is a "motivational" view of human nature; the second, a "perceptual" one. Psychological scientists of either stripe would renounce as absurd the proposition that they did not take into account certain features of the alternative theory. Yet any reasonable reading of the experimental base of psychological science from 1860 to 1950 cannot fail to notice that both sides of the fence generally staked out work on the complementary side to be done at some future time. One purpose of this chapter is to show that motivational theories and the experiments that support them have, since 1950, attempted not to usurp but rather to reinforce the perceptual theories that have long been the mainstay of serious scientific work on psychological problems.* To forge a back-

* This sentence should not be understood to imply that the work of Sigmund Freud, that pioneer in the motivational treatment of human nature, was either unscientific or unconcerned with perceptual problems. But regardless of one's predilections, it should be acceptable to assert that Freud's influence in scientific psychology was less than it may now have become because of the renewed interest in the motivational features of behavior that are constrained by perceptual events.

ground for the introduction of motivational considerations into a psychology that has almost universally been viewed as a perceptual matter, we must review first (but briefly) the central conceptual and theoretical ideas of the major contributors to experimental and theoretical psychology during the quarter century from 1925 to 1950. There were three contributing theoreticians and one masterful critic.

Edwin R. Guthrie (1886–1959) was the man who hoped to preserve the classical view of the central role of the stimulus as the material and efficient cause of human behavior (Guthrie, 1935). He endeavored to make explicit the sufficiency of stimulus–response contiguity for the formation of novel S–R sequences. In several very important but often discounted experiments, he and his collaborator George P. Horton (Guthrie & Horton, 1937) showed that stimulus–response contiguity alone was sufficient on a single occasion to establish a strong likelihood that later, in the presence of that stimulus, the associated response would occur.

This attempt to sustain the immediate causal efficacy of the stimulus was Guthrie's answer to the challenges made to structural psychology by experiments on learning. If American psychology was to be viable, it had to cope with dynamic changes in behavior, and could not simply construe human reaction to perceptual configurations as some invariant aspect of the neurological structure of the sense organs and motor systems. Since the experiments of Thorndike and Pavlov psychologists had to account for alterations in the connections between sense organ activity and the responses they modulated. As Guthrie conceived the problem, the only way the classical causal view could be preserved was to replace the unacceptable, apparently teleological, conjectures that had been used by Thorndike (1903) as well as the theoretical musings of the Chicago school of functionalism with a form of associationism based on S_i–R contiguity, and to provide dynamism by letting i range fairly widely.

Unlike Guthrie, Clark Leonard Hull, Sterling Professor of Psychology in Yale University from 1929 until his death in 1952, directly and emphatically introduced motivational principles into the S–R paradigm. Hull (1943), fascinated by logic and mathematics and their application to scientific theory construction, introduced into psychology a theoretical solution to the teleological dilemma of behavioral consequences serving as part of the material cause of behavior. The salient structure of his argument was that although the stimulus configuration causes the behavior of the organism, both the stimulus configuration and the behavior leave small internal residues that are affected by the consequences of behavior: the "rewards" or "punishments." The effect that the consequences have is to strengthen or weaken postulated connection patterns between the postulated stimulus and response residues. Consequently, on subsequent presentations of the same (or similar?) stimulation, the particular response will occur with greater likelihood if reward had followed the response and with less likelihood if punishment had followed. Hull provided a more or less coherent explanation of the power of rewards and punishments. He accomplished this by transferring a theory of primary motivation based on primary biological need reduction, into an abstract motivational theory based in part on Pavlovian conditionability as a mediating mechanism for turning needs into drives and need reduction into rewards. By translating this theory through a series of subtle modifications into a set of working paradigms he constructed experiments in which the data represented confirmation or rejection of one or more of the components of the drive theory. By 1943 he had amassed enough data and so refined his theory that it still stands as the most complete (if currently least referred to) abstract conceptualization of, as he called it, "mammalian behavior." Hull's introduction of explicit motivational mechanisms to explain how different stimuli could lead to the same response, or how the same stimulus could lead to different responses on different occasions, became the first extensive incursion of motivational principles into academic psychology.

Hull's work with the white rat as the experimental subject par excellence challenged experimentalists and theoreticians to account for the occasionally unusual (but to Hull, explainable) forms of behavior that were observed in mazes, jumping stands, and other kinds of apparatus where the rat's locomotor behavior was the observable datum. The critical attack on Hull came from Edward Chace Tolman (1886–1959). The central critical judgment that Tolman made upon Hull's conceptualization was on the narrowness of Hull's specificity of stimulus and of reinforcement. Tolman was prepared to include relations among stimuli and other complex perceptual behavior as inferred "stimuli" (e.g., spatial learning), and argued that greater subtlety was needed to understand the role of motivational variables (e.g., latent learning). The result of these critiques was to introduce new experimental paradigms (latent learning, spatial learning, the existence of hypotheses, etc.) for Hull to explicate in his theoretical mill. Faced almost weekly with a new Tolmanian demonstration of the growing rationality of the white rat, Hull and his students and colleagues would pose a new formulation and many experiments to explain the anomaly within the month. As I picture the events described by some of my colleagues who were there, the charged atmosphere and general excitement in psychology must have been wonderful to see: notes and telephone calls at all hours of the day and night whipping back and forth to connect the three capitals, New Haven, Berkeley, and Iowa City, all working to illuminate the psychology of *Ratus norwegicus*. It has been said that the turnaround-time between conjecture and experiment in Hull's laboratory was often less than

3 days. The smell of success was in the air, and although there were mumbled arguments about what rats could ever tell us about people, it took World War II to slow down the action.

Meanwhile, the central role of reinforcement (and, therefore, motivation) in Hull's theory was becoming more and more widely recognized. Indeed, if a perceptual psychologist questioned these experimentalists about the nature of their stimuli or perceptual configurations, they were answered by a shrug, and the comment that any stimulus would serve if it was discriminable. A common answer was that albino rats could not see very well anyhow.

This clear lack of interest in the stimulus and consequent delegation of central importance to motivational processes as the cause of behavioral organization was recognized and capitalized upon by the third giant of animal psychology, B. F. Skinner 1904–   ). The enormous influence of Skinner's work was less recognized for its theoretical importance in the 1930s and early 1940s than for its contribution of a new experimental procedure. The lever-box apparatus made experiments with the white rat transparently clear in their structure, and animal data now became generally reproducible from laboratory to laboratory. There is no need here to review the well-documented invention of the lever-box, the food pellet, and the cumulative recorder. But each of these must be recognized not merely as an example of improvements in experimental apparatus and data reduction, but as the central tools of a revolutionary way of conceptualizing voluntary behavior.

Guthrie's attempt to preserve the power of the stimulus in the control of behavior, and Hull's acceptance of the S–R paradigm as the experimental and logical unit of analysis was simply overpowered by the invention of the lever box. The reproducible observation that the rate of response, made visible with a cumulative recorder, was only contingent upon the reinforcement schedule, dashed at one stroke the central role of the stimulus. After Skinner's publication of *The Behavior of Organisms* (1938) the function of the stimulus, at least in the study of learned behavior in animals, was abandoned. It did not reemerge until "Pigeons in a Pelican" (Skinner, 1960). But even in this context it was clear that the role of the stimulus S^D was merely technological, not scientific. After showing that one used discriminative stimuli simply to inform the organism about the reinforcement schedule, Skinner again withdrew from consideration of the stimulus as a fundamental variable, at least through the publication of *Schedules of Reinforcement* (Ferster & Skinner, 1957). It was not until a new generation of operant conditioners became interested in the role of stimulus control per se (Terrace, 1966), that the stimulus returned. Note, however, that the stimulus even in these new contexts serves only as a marker for the reinforcement contingencies. It is the informational properties of the stimuli that are relevant in the proper study of operant behavior.

Whereas these developments in theoretical psychology focused centrally on animal behavior as the paradigm for psychological research, World War II began with an immediate demand for some answers about the nature of human behavior. Generalizations from the existing theoretical framework based on animal behavior were not germane. Consequently many psychologists were innoculated with a Cartesian view about the importance of the distinction between animal nature and human nature. They abandoned the quest for theoretical models of human nature that rested upon the animal as a model of man. This abandonment of psychological Darwinism left psychologists with a model of human behavior and its organization no newer than Fechner on the one hand and Freud on the other. Let us turn now to a quick consideration of what had happened to Fechner and his ideas.*

Titchener's Americanization of Wundt's structural perceptualism depended on Fechner and his psychophysical methods only to provide the basic limenal information that was used to constrain the structural organization of the peripheral sense organs. After the stimulus was filtered by the receptor, the introspective method provided "context" variables and other larger components of perceptual organization that were not amenable to psychophysical measurement. When the vital Gestalt theory and the impatient functionalism dealt the death blow to perceptual structuralism (and incidentally, introspection as a "valid" method of psychological research) it accidently undercut psychophysics as a proper part of perceptual study. Psychophysics became and remained either a technical adjunct to other experimental methods or an honorable place for the outclassed structuralist who had nothing else to say, but who could still make behaviorally acceptable experiments. Within the coterie of psychophysicists, no one questioned the methods or the reliability and validity of the limens themselves. That is to say, no one raised any seriously embarassing questions until a particularly intractable methodological problem created consternation and confusion among the workers in the field.

This problem was the question of the "middle" category in constant stimulus experiments. In these experiments, two stimuli are presented either simultaneously or successively; one is the "standard," which does not vary from trial to trial, and the other is a "comparison" stimulus, which ranges over a set of values from trial to trial. The subject's task in these experiments is to say whether the comparison stimulus is "larger" or "smaller" than the standard (or to use some other, normally assymmetric, judgment). Some experimentalists found that observers could perform more accurately and reliably if they were given a middle category—"equality"—with which

---

* The Gestalt psychologists are overlooked because their program, as Lashley made so clear, failed to consider the American *sine qua non:* action, the name of the game.

to respond. The problem was that the use of the middle category did not seem to be under as much stimulus control as the inequality categories. Consequently, one would observe subjects making either extensive use of the center category or very little use of it, contingent upon features of the experiment that were not stimulus variables.

The upshot of the question about whether the center category should be used or not reached a climax with the publication of Fernberger's (1930) paper on the variables that control the use of the middle category. He observed that these factors were better construed as attitudinal or "subjective" (read here "motivational") than perceptual or sensory. Now this was some problem. If a perceptual psychophysicist like Samuel Fernberger could argue that attitudinal and motivational variables were controlling the responses that a subject made in a psychophysical experiment, the implicit assumption that the judgmental responses are a faithful translation of the stimulus effect could easily, instantly, and universally be called into question.

The implications of this notion were sufficiently harrowing to impede further exploration of these variables until the classical experiments in 1937 by Francis Irwin and Malcolm Preston, Fernberger's colleagues at the University of Pennsylvania. In a series of ingenious experiments, Irwin and Preston examined psychophysical judgments when the stimulus remained constant from trial to trial. In these experiments the subject was led to believe that he was listening to stimulus pairs that differed slightly, when in fact he was listening to stimulus pairs (or hefting weights) that were identical on every trial. Irwin and Preston analyzed each sequence of responses for trial independence, and demonstrated beyond question that the judgments made by the observers were strongly dependent on the responses that they had made on previous trials. The strength of the dependence related to the lag over which the statistic was measured. They went a step further by alternating acoustic stimuli and weight hefting from trial to trial. Still, the responses, even across perceptual modalities, continued to exhibit strong dependencies. This clear-cut demonstration of the effect of the preceding response on the subsequent judgment added just the necessary evidence of the decoupling between stimulus and response to cast doubt on the entire psychophysical enterprise.

So we arrive at the point where two major lines of scientific psychology lead to the uncomfortable position that stimulus variables have precious little to do with responses. At the infrahuman level Skinner displays a psychology without stimuli; in the psychophysical tradition, the stimulus again fails to cause the response. This vexing similarity was most clearly remarked in the important paper of Verplanck, Cotton, and Collier (1953), who refined the results of Irwin and Preston, and almost drew the conclusion we now recognize. Things that happen before a response are less important than things that happen after.

III. THE STATISTICAL TRACE

Meanwhile, among the statisticians, mathematicians, and philosophers, understanding human nature again became a fashionable enterprise as it had once been in the days of Daniel Bernoulli (1731). Bernoulli examined a popular puzzle about human nature. Since the formalization by Cardano in 1551, of the principles of probability that operate in games of chance, it was a known mathematical fact that if someone offered to let you play a game where you got $1 if she flipped a coin once and got a head, or $2 if she had to flip twice before she got a head, or $4 if she had to flip three times before she got a head, and generally 2^{n-1} if the first head appeared on the nth trial, then the expected value of the game is infinite. Bernoulli believed it was unlikely that one would ransom his life's savings to buy an opportunity to play this game. Consequently, he conjectured that people do not act on the basis of expected monetary return, but on the basis of the value of some numerical transform of money–utility. He proposed by the force of several arguments, that a logarithmic transformation on money would yield a utility scale for money that better represented how people appreciated it. So he "explained" the apparently irrational behavior of not buying into the St. Petersburg game by conjecturing a psychological transformation on the physical outcome of the experiment that preserved the notion that people did what led to something of value. It is what will happen that constrains what we do.

Bernoulli's utility theory represented an attempt to describe the consequences of action as a force to constrain the actor. We need not pause over the adequacy of Bernoulli's theory, we shall return to it and others prompted by it subsequently. Note only that an intelligent consideration of man's actions here, just as we have seen before, consistently includes some attempt to talk about the consequences of behavior as though they are an important cause of behavior. The problem with the problem is the inconvenient temporal sequence that Western science prohibits in any causal statements. As we all know now, having been brought up on feedback loops and servo-mechanisms, the problem is not serious. It simply requires that we make observations over an epoch, so that the consequences of behavior can have their effect on certain internal structures that guide new behavior in the new stimulus situation, just as Hull had suggested.

Hull's interest, of course, was in the dynamics of change in behavior.

He was a learning theorist. But we now note that using such time averaging does not require an analysis of learning, we may only be interested in the response values at an asymptote. Indeed, Skinner's concern, for example, is exactly with stationary response processes, even though he is categorized with theorists of learning. His own repudiation of such *theories,* might better have been directed toward illuminating his remarkable indifference to learning. But Bernoulli was not concerned with the nicities of a teleological analysis, he wanted to understand what appear to be irrational forms of behavior.

So, in addition to the notion of consequences of action as consequential for action, Daniel Bernoulli's "moral expectation" represents a further attempt to rationalize observable behavior. He proposed that people are guided by features of the environment whose quantitative characteristics are not directly represented by the accidents of our physical metrics. But there is even more to the idea. If a dog can catch a thrown stick, and if the description of a mechanism that would accomplish the same act requires the solution of several differential equations, then, whereas it is unreasonable to attribute to the dog the analytical power necessary to solve the equation, it may not be unreasonable to construe the dog's structure as the equivalent of a (analog) computer capable of solving the relevant equations. People make various decisions and engage in various actions that are generally on the positive side of the biological ledger, but we may never be sure how close they are to optimizing or maximizing some consequence without an analytical theory. The scientists who have attended to this problem have developed, since 1920, a body of knowledge that we shall call mathematical decision theory. It is not complete and coherent; there still are many arguments about fundamental philosophical issues within the theory itself and among its practitioners, but in general it purports to describe routine procedures for making decisions among alternative courses of action under conditions in which some uncertainty prevails about various aspects of the decision.

Because mathematical decision theory prescribes the procedures and action that *should* be taken, it represents what one may call a "normative" theory. That is, a theory that tells what one ought to do. On the other hand, many psychologists (and mathematical decision theorists, too, for that matter) have suggested that mathematical decision theory, like the differential equations that the dog must have known to catch the stick, are also descriptive of human nature and consequently, may be descriptive of human behavior. Which of these positions is valid, depends of course upon the value of the distinction between normative and descriptive theories. This distinction itself is very hard to formulate with real precision and involves philosophical issues that are not appropriately discussed here.

We shall concern ourselves with mathematical decision theory only because it may be suggestive of notions that may lead us to a deeper understanding of human nature. The central point is to recognize that if we abandon the stimulus as the nexus of behavior, we must find a characterization of its replacement—reinforcements, outcomes, payoffs—that can be as well described, repeated, and controlled as the experimentalists' stimuli had been. So now we abandon psychology for a time; turn our attention to the later-day descendants of Daniel Bernoulli and the subject of their discourse: mathematical decision theory, in the hope of finding the real cause of action.

People have been using mathematics to help them make decisions *not* involving uncertainty for a long time. Generally, the procedures have been informal, or they have been primarily concerned with estimating the values of physical measurement variables. Recently, however, an explicit formulation of the use of numbers in arriving at a basis for action in the face of uncertainty has resulted from the development of modern statistics. One of the two or three major problems of statistics is a search for the best method to evaluate incomplete or uncertain information in order to form an inference. If human action of some kind is based upon such an inference the problem of statistical inference leads to a decision-theoretic problem. The classical solution to the statistical problem did not, of course, concern itself with the nature and cost of the actions consequential to the inference. Rather, the question of the appropriate inference and its dependability was construed as the problem of statistics; the question of the action to be taken based upon the inferences that were made from statistical information were the problems of human prudence and judgment. Consequently, in the Neyman–Pearson formulation of the nature of statistical inference, statisticians were prepared to describe the limit of the relative frequencies of the error you would make by rejecting one hypothesis if it were true, or accepting another if it were false.

In attempting to avoid the philosophical consequences of incorporating the mysteries of man's judgmental mechanisms, classical statistical procedures developed without the excess baggage of deep philosophical worries. But Sir Ronald Fisher, the central spokesman for the developing statistical methods, attempted to educate the users of the new statistics. He would often point out, especially in his later writings, the relevant additional costs and benefits that collecting the data or using the statistical indexes would give rise to. Even though these comments were not central to the mathematical developments, the formulation by Fisher and others of the general structure of statistical inference created real excitement among intellectuals during the early part of this century. But the ramification of the ideas of statistical inference into the realm of judgment and choice did not grow from the statisticians themselves or from their considerations. In fact, it was the sophisticated understanding of statistical ideas by people in other fields, in particular economists and philosophers, that led to the examination of the use of inferential data in decisions, and the incorporation of theories of how data are used into the actual calculations on which inferences were based.

The beginning of the modern work that have led to the development of decision-theoretical statistical ideas seems to have been as a result of, and a reaction to, John Maynard Keynes's 1921 volume, *A Treatise on Probability*. Keynes offered an alternative to the classical empirical view of probability as a limit of a relative frequency by proposing that a probability is a logical relation between some statement and a collection of additional statements that constitute some set of evidence. The magnitude of the probability is represented as a "rational" degree of belief in the statement on the basis of the evidence. The difficulty of providing a practical measure of degrees of belief led Keynes to assume that not all degrees of belief are numerically measurable, and further that not all degrees of belief may be comparable.

In his review of Keynes's book, the French mathematician Emile Borel (1924, reprinted, 1964) urged that the measure of a person's degree of belief must depend upon observations of his behavior. Indeed he suggested the kinds of observations that should be made to circumvent Keynes's problems of incommensurability and lack of identifiability of degree of belief. Borel proposed to examine how people bet with respect to certain gambles. He then expected that a theory could be developed to determine with any desired precision the degree of belief the person exhibits from an analysis of his bets. He continued in this 1924 essay to make a prediction whose soundness today cannot be questioned.

> The deep study of certain games will perhaps lead to a new chapter of the theory of probabilities a theory whose origins go back to the study of games of chance of the simplest kind. It will be a new science where psychology will be no less useful than mathematics, but this new chapter will be added to previous areas without modifying them [1964, p. 58].

A first serious attempt to formulate exactly how behavioral experiments could be performed in order to obtain estimates of degree of belief appears explicitly in the 1926 article of Frank Plumpton Ramsey, "Truth and Probability" (reprinted, 1964). The central notion of this new subjectivist probability theory that Ramsey develops is the need for complementary estimates of the utility of the outcomes of gambles and the probabilities of outcomes. Ramsey solves this Bernoullian problem by postulating a particular event with probability .5 and then defining an interval scale of utility in terms of gambles made with this event. On the basis of this utility scale, he is then able to develop the notion of numerical degree of belief. The power of his ideas are revealed by the fact that Davidson, Suppes, and Siegal (1957) were able to exploit exactly these notions to develop a series of experiments from which they arrived at fairly reliable individual utility scales. Unhappily, the range of values over which these scales were constructed was not very large and consequently it is difficult to examine in empirical detail any psychophysical questions concerning the relation of utility and money. But these experimental questions aside, the fact is that Ramsey provided a basis for supporting subjectivist theories of probability through the development of utility measurement, and proposed that such probability structures were contingent on certain kinds of behavioral observations.

The question of whether these behavioral observations represented the existence of some psychological structure that corresponded to the theory being posed was not an issue for debate. For Ramsey, the theory was normative, and indeed behavior in conformity with the theory showed the existence of coherence among the various bets that a person would make. This notion of coherence represented the constraint that led to the identity between the degrees of belief that a person exhibited in a variety of situations, and the existing calculus of probabilities. Thus Borel's requirement was provided by Ramsey by simply denying rationality to anyone whose choice did not conform to the probability calculus.

The reformulation of the basis of probability theory and statistics remained fitful. Some marks along the path are the important paper by deFinnetti (1937, reprinted, 1964), and the very psychological *Foundations of Statistics* by L. J. Savage, (1956) whose first chapters read like an introduction to the psychology of choice. Readers interested in these developments are directed to the excellent textbook *Decision Theory and Human Behavior,* by Wayne Lee (1971), particularly Chapter 3, which traces these developments and makes sound judgments on their psychological import. What is now the classical source for these materials, and an interpretation from a modern philosophical point of view will be found in the introduction to the outstanding collection of papers, *Studies in Subjective Probability* by Kyburg and Smokler (1964), from which the preceding references were culled.

It remained, however, for Von Neuman and Morgenstern (1951), to develop the revised mathematics that Borel had anticipated, and to show how human nature might be modeled as a decision maker in the context of games with uncertain outcomes. A central contribution to this end is found in an appendix to the second edition on the measurement of utility. A coherent and useful explication of these materials is to be found in Luce and Raiffa (1963). As Von Neuman and Morgenstern conceptualized the problem, the root difficulty lay in finding a way to embed all the possible or conceivable outcomes of action into the real-number continuum. The search here is not simply for representation and uniqueness theorems that demonstrate the abstract existence of such a numbering scheme, but rather a characterization of outcomes, or a procedure of analysis that has intuitive appeal as, possibly, an empirically realizable operation. To form a continuum of what are intrinsically discrete outcomes, Von Neuman and Morgenstern hit upon the ingenious idea of converting these outcomes into gambles of the form: You receive outcome a if event e occurs and outcome b if event e does not occur. It seems intuitively reasonable that for these outcomes, the relative desirability of the gamble as a whole can be continuously varied by altering the probability of e. If all outcomes are construed as gambles of this kind then the problem is solved. For "pure," i.e., not uncertain, outcomes the gamble takes the form a with probability 1 and b with probability 0. Von Neuman and Morgenstern then show how to form an interval utility scale over gambles, and the problem is under control. When these utilities are inserted in the game matrices of the general theory, it is often presumed that the normative form of the game theory structure can be used as a descriptive theory contingent on the selection of an appropriate decision principle. Reviews of psychological research designed to evalute the theory of games as an appropriate description of psychological processes, both social and individual can be found in Edwards (1961), Becker and McClintock (1967), and Rappoport and Wallsten (1972).

At present, the power of game theory appears to reside in its psychologically appealing structure, rather than in either its analytical power for psychology in general or its predictive efficiency in experiments on decision making. Consequently, although widely quoted as the understructure of much research, the theory of games has not confirmed Borel's prediction vis-à-vis the role of psychology in revamping decision theory. It is also not clear that game theory has made a contribution to psychology over and above providing a paradigmatic design for experiments in social psychology or experiments on individual choices in the face of uncertain outcomes.

The decision theory ideas from Ramsey onward have concentrated on finding methods to measure abstract entities that are proposed as constraints on human behavior. The procedures aim for such measurement from two sides. First, the mathematical structure of a measurement model is explored. Then a set of empirical operations is devised that may lead to behavioral observations that are interpretable within the mathematical theory. Whereas game theory may not have lived up to its expectations as a mathematical structure into which behavior could be embedded, a part of a new look in measurement may, on the other hand, generate a quiet revolution in the analysis of experiments. This new measurement approach to some of the oldest problems in psychology currently takes two different forms. However, its emphasis is clear and its antecedents are overt. The emphasis of the new measurement is on the analysis of ordered data and their conversion to real-number scales. Its antecedents are the extended research efforts of Clyde Coombs and his collaborators and students. The background to Coombs's decades of work and his major results are available in his book, *A Theory of Data*, (1964). Here, the nature of the unfolding technique and its ramifications are discussed and developed. Coombs's work has an extremely persuasive quality. It seems obvious and reasonable that people can order their judgments, after all, this is the heart of most human and animal experiments. The question is whether there is any underlying structure to the orderings that suggests a psychological organization of one's mental processes. The variety of solutions Coombs suggested to this problem reveal its depth and nontrivial nature. But regardless of the importance of the problem, the solutions Coombs proposed never fired the imagination of the psychological community. The reason seems to be that the scale structures he was able to derive from experimental data were never compared extensively with the complimentary scales generated by techniques Coombs hoped to replace. It is always useful if you have a new method or technique, to show that it yields the old comfortable results before attacking the basis on which the old results were fashioned.

The newer analyses of ordinal data derive from the iterative data-processing schemes of Shepard (1962) and of Kruskul (1964a,b), and from the theory of conjoint measurement axiomatized by Luce and Tukey (1964). Roger Shepard's ingenuity made it possible to take a set of ordered judgments about pairs of sets of events, and to analyze them by an iterative computer processing scheme that extracts an embedding of the events that were ordered. The embedding will be represented by a real-number scale or scales on as many dimensions as are necessary to collapse the data and recover the orderings; and of course may say a great deal more. For example, in our laboratory Schneider and his student Carvellas (1972) had people order the dissimilarities of tones that varied in both frequency and amplitude. Using a modification of the Shepard–Kruskal procedure they found a representation for both loudness and pitch. The numerical values of these representations were themselves linearly related to the scales of loudness and pitch based on older magnitude estimation methods. Observe that if differential preference judgments about uncertain outcomes had been used, we would expect to find a representation of the preference orderings that might reveal a utility scale and a scale of subjective probability. What the combinatorial principle might be that welds these scales together to form the preference is not specified, just as the pitch and loudness that fuse to form a tone are simply described as "orthogonal," and consequently they may add in one or another way. Indeed Carvellas's thesis compared Euclidian and Minkowskian additivity, and unhappily reached no unimpeachable conclusion. The reason is, of course, that the data will never tell you. You must risk a theoretical conjecture, and then test its consequences. This is the line taken in the analysis of ordered data by the theory of conjoint measurement.

The main idea of conjoint measurement is this: The transparent decomposability of physical metrics and their independence is not immediately discernable when people act in response to variations of environmental events of one kind or another. Judging the relative weights of objects of varying sizes displays the problem. It may also help us see the conjoint measurement solution, i.e., to find the necessary and sufficient conditions under which we can assign numerical values to the effects of size and weight that preserves the rank order of the judgments, and to show how the two variables act when different values of each are concatenated. To illuminate the ideas of this new measurement method let us consider its application to the problem of utility and subjective probability as first formulated by Von Neuman and Morgenstern.

A gamble in the sense of Von Neuman and Morgenstern is defined objectively as a probability p of obtaining an outcome of objective (say, dollar) value v. A popular theory conjectures that people choose among gambles so as to maximize the subjective expected utility (SEU) of the gamble. The measurement problem is therefore to determine the dependence of SEU on p and v. The usual simplification of the problem hypothesizes that SEU is a simple function of the utility or subjective value of the outcome u and the subjective probability of its occurrence s. Furthermore, u is presumed to be a function only of v, and s a function of p. On these hypotheses there are consequently three subproblems to be solved: (*1*) Find the dependence of SEU on u and s. (2) Show how u depends on v. (3) Show how s depends on p. The experimental data are the rank order of a person's preferences for the various gambles. The gambles themselves can be construed to be (theoretically) all possible combinations of p and v. In practice, we would consider only m different p's and n different v's. The data are therefore the rank order of the $m \times n$ gambles (p_i, v_j).

An analysis of these data by the methods of conjoint measurement simultaneously determines whether the SEU hypothesis is tenable and if it is, the procedures also solve the three subproblems. The first part of the test of the SEU hypothesis examines whether p and v contribute independently to SEU. If the values of v show an invarient relation with the rank orders, regardless of which value of p is held constant and vice verse, then the data possess the montonicity property. Notice that the values of v and p are merely nominal, no relevance attaches to their numerical properties at this point. If the monotonicity property is observed then it is possible to examine other questions, for example whether SEU is a simple (additive) function of u and s. These numbers represent numerical values of v and p, that preserve the data ordering. The central condition for additivity of such component parts of confounded variables is the cancellation axiom of Luce and Tukey (1964). This axiom states that if gamble (p_i, v_l) is preferred to (p_j, v_m) and if (p_j, v_n) is preferred to (p_k, v_l), then (p_i, v_n) will be preferred to (p_k, v_m). Once it is shown that SEU is a simple additive* function of s and u it remains only to determine the empirical relations between utility and money or other value measure, and subjective and objective probability.

This elegant analysis of the SEU hypothesis was performed first in an experiment by Tversky (1967). We shall discuss his results later. Suffice it to say here that his experiment showed that subjective probability was approximately linear with objective probability or rather relative frequencies, thus closing Ramsey's circle and justifying Borel's belief that nothing about probability theory would have to be changed by examining the betting behavior of people.

IV. DESIRE AND PERCEPT

Suppose one believes that the consequences of action indeed altered one's judgment about future actions and consequently altered future action. How could this be accomplished: We have glossed over this problem twice before, and have offered nothing more profound than a thermostat and an averaging procedure. One is quite justified in finding these so-called explanations a bit lightweight. There are real possibilities for dealing with this issue which is, clearly, the problem of teleology. Some of them have even been subjected to experimental test. One conjecture to explain how outcomes affect future action that would please every stimulus–response psychologist would be to say that the effects of an outcome alter the perceptual properties of the stimulus. That is, on subsequent occasions when

---

* It should be noted that multiplication is a simple additive function for positive values of s and u in the sense used here because we can always convert multiplication to addition by defining new functions of s and u that are the logarithms of the old ones.

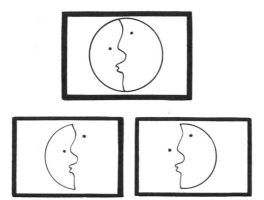

FIG. 1. Examples of the stimulus materials used by Shafer and Murphy. The two lower rectangles represent a pair of "training" stimuli. The upper rectangle shows the "test" stimulus made from these two figures. [From Shafer & Murphy, 1942.]

action is called for by a particular stimulus that has some consequential history, that consequential history may have resulted in a transformation of the perceptual effects of the stimulus, a change in perception if you like, that causes a response different from the response originally evoked by that external event. An early experiment to examine this question empirically was performed by Schafer and Murphy (1942). They showed subjects various drawings of semicircles bisected by a wavy line, with dots near the wavy line. An example is shown in Fig. 1. Each semicircle could be construed as a face. Various pairs of such faces interlock, and then display the "ambiguous figure" property of Rubin; a person will first see one then the other of the faces. By showing experimental subjects some faces that they rewarded and others they punished, Schafer and Murphy found that subjects who were subsequently shown ambiguous combinations tended to see the faces that were rewarded with high frequency and the faces that were punished with low. Because the faces were presented tachistoscopically, they interpreted these data as implying that the perceptual organization of the ambiguous figures was modulated by the rewards and punishments.

If rewards and punishments in an experimental context can alter what a person sees, then surely, one's lifetime acquaintanceship with rewards and punishments may alter the ways that symbols of reward are perceived by people with different experience. Taking this line, Jerome Bruner and his colleague, C. C. Goodman, conducted an experiment in which children adjusted the size of a variable diaphragm to set it equal to the perceived size of coins of different denominations (Bruner & Goodman, 1947). The results of their experiment took the psychological world by storm, and ushered in what came to be called the "new look" in perception. Their central finding, which was subsequently questioned by Carter and Schooler (1949), was that children of high socioeconomic levels (rich children) perceived the size of coins (as indicated by their adjustments of the diaphragm) as smaller than did children of low socioeconomic levels (poor children). Thus, Bruner and Goodman concluded, a personal history in which coins are objects of great value are perceived as larger than an unbiased observer would judge them, whereas among children for whom coins are of minor importance they are perceived as smaller.

This experiment suggested that motivational effects have direct consequences on perceptual events. In general the line taken was that our values, motives, and attitudes do not simply shape our responses, as a Skinnerian might assert, but alter in behaviorally diagnostic ways, our perceptions of the world. These changes in perception lead to changes in response by the same old classical stimulus–response mechanisms. Consequently the unique causal efficacy on behavior of the stimulus itself is unchanged by the introduction of motivational effects. At last the S–R paradigm can rest easily. After all if desires and aversions act simply to alter the proximal stimulus, then we can reinstate Titchner and give behavioral evidence for the existence of context variables.

Once this demonstration of the effect of desire on percept had been established, the experiments multiplied. Hungry people perceived ambiguous objects as food-related with greater frequency than nonhungry people. Sexually deprived people had lower tachistoscopic thresholds for certain kinds of scatological words. The tachistoscope and tachistoscopic thresholds became the primary tool and datum in the study of motivational influences on perceptual variables. It was not simply ambiguous perceptual judgments that were influenced, but the actual limens and other presumed capacity constants. This was a shocking idea, for it suggested that if, say, the acuity threshold could be reduced by appropriate motivational factors, we could eliminate the need for spectacles.

Such theoretically unpleasant ideas could not be allowed to go unchallenged. Perhaps the new look experimenters were only rediscovering Fernberger's original findings about the middle category in psychophysics, and consequently their results might represent only the response biasing effects of motivational variables. These decision theoretic attacks on the work of the "new look" psychologists took a variety of forms. Notice first that many of the "new look" experiments depended on the measurement of the flash threshold for the perception of words. A series of experiments by Solomon and Howes (1951) and subsequently additional work by Howes (1957), made clear that recognition thresholds for words depended almost exclusively upon the associative value of the words, i.e., upon their prior S–R history. Thus the only intrinsic changes that motivational variables appeared to make in these experiments was to increase the subjects' expectation of a particular word. His judgments might then be wrongly interpreted as a lowering of a perceptual threshold, whereas they were simply a change in his tendency to make certain responses.

Another line of attack on the new look was taken by Chapanis and Bricker (1953). Using the new tool of information theory for their analyses, they attacked the very notion of a tachistoscopic "threshold" by suggesting that there was information in the errors that subjects made in these experiments. In the usual interpretation of a "new look" tachistoscopic experiment, an error represented a value of the stimulus exposure time that was construed as below the subject's perceptual threshold. Chapanis showed, by allowing the subject to make several responses, that even though the subject had made an error, he had still extracted information from the stimulus display. Consequently, the notion of a "word threshold" in tachistoscopic presentations was probably as inappropriate in this context as it had been shown to be in classical psychophysical experiments where the phi-gamma hypothesis had been almost universally accepted. In general, then, the threshold idea itself was being attacked. The notion was being bruted about that a subject's responses could indeed be influenced by his motivation and the associated pay-offs but that one would be hard-pressed to justify the existence of alterations in the perceptual events themselves.

V. PSYCHOPHYSICS AND PAY-OFFS

The central experimental support for this point of view came from new studies on classical psychophysical problems. The nadir to which studies of the limen had fallen, as exemplified in the Verplanck *et al.* study mentioned earlier, represented a turning point. It was clear that the problems of classical psychophysics could not simply be brushed aside because response bias effects could conceal the psychophysical information. New methods were waiting just off-stage that promised to revitalize psychophysics, and to restore it to a central role in modern psychology. The need was for methods that would allow the separate contributions of stimulus and motivational variables to reveal themselves. Fitful attempts had been made, but the serious work began in earnest with the publication of a *Psychological Monograph* in 1953 by Moncrieff Smith and Edna Wilson. In a series of auditory experiments investigating whether more than one observer would significantly increase the accuracy of judgments about very weak signals; Smith and Wilson showed that the subject's attitudes strongly influenced the psychophysical data. In particular, if subjects were asked to change their criterion for reporting detectability and discriminability, they were able to do so. The psychometric functions showed a marked change

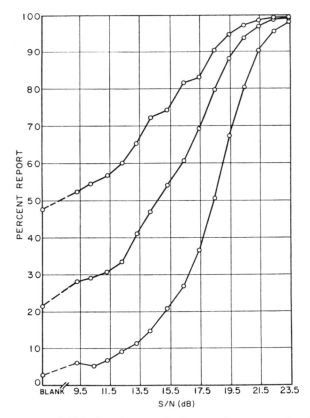

FIG. 2. Average poikilitic functions made by ten observers under three response biases. The lowest curve represents a "conservative" attitude toward reporting the signal, the middle curve a more "liberal" attitude toward reporting that the signal is present, and the top curve represents a "radical" response bias. [From Smith & Wilson, 1953.]

as a result of these criterion changes (Fig. 2). What Smith and Wilson did was to estimate a single parameter that represented these criterial values (they did it by using partial correlation techniques). Then after adjusting for the criterion, it could be shown that the threshold values, i.e., the stimulus effects themselves, had undergone no change at all.

Just before Smith and Wilson began their experiments at M.I.T., research there on the optimization of radar amplifiers had led to the formulation of engineering theories to provide figures of merit for electronic instrumentation that were more meaningful than the usual engineering specifications. This theory of signal detectability, and the accompanying theory of the ideal observer, were quickly translated into paradigms for psychological experiments at the University of Michigan by Wilson P. Tanner (1954). This new theory and the experiments that it generated, along with the ideas that were imminent in it, constituted no less than a revolution in the study of limenal psychophysics. This work led to a rapprochement among various generations of psychologists that cannot be overestimated.

We shall consider now only the central ideas that have emerged from the study of the theory of signal detectability, and the data on which it is based. An introductory review of these ideas and experiments can be found in Galanter (1962, 1966, Chap. 6). Details of the mathematical treatment of many variations on the signal detectability theme will be found in Chapter 3 of the *Handbook of Mathematical Psychology* (Luce, Bush, & Galanter, 1963). An excellent introduction to the notion of likelihood ratio and the decision statistics inherent in the theory of signal detectability are presented in a paper by David Green (1960), and a useful collection of experimental contributions to the theory will be found in Swets (1964). The main idea of the theory of signal detectability is that when a person tells you something about whether he perceives a stimulus or not, he is simultaneously telling you about his perception of the stimulus and about his tendency to make certain types of responses. The problem for the experimentalist is to separate the contribution made by the stimulus on the one hand, and by the variety of factors that could bias the response of the subject on the other. The situation is analogous to the teacher who gives a true–false examinaton and tries to find some computational formula that will take into account the fact that if some students guess part of the time they may get more questions correctly answered than their level of knowledge should permit. Consequently, the teacher believes that the test may not be a good estimator of what the student knows.

In principle this problem has been of concern to psychophysicists since Fechner's original work. Early in the experimental realization of psychophysical paradigms, the notion of the "catch" trial was introduced. The idea of the catch trial is to make occasional trials where the "correctness" of the response is determinable solely by the experimenter. For example, if the experimenter is measuring the absolute threshold for the loudness of an acoustic signal, a catch trial would be a trial on which no acoustic signal was presented. If a subject were to reply that he had heard the signal on such a trial, then in the classical experiment, our experimenter would have told the subject that he was not paying close enough attention to the task, and that he should improve his criterion for making judgments. This exhortation constituted a form of explicit payoff. The implicit pay-off throughout these experiments was, of course, that the subject should behave in such a way that he conformed to the experimenter's preconceptions. These preconceptions were normally quite reasonable; e.g., that the subject should respond "present" more frequently when an acoustic signal increases in intensity than when it does not. The problem with the catch-trials experiment was that the experimenter did not know how to use the information if subjects made errors on these catch trials. Of course he could always invalidate the entire experiment and throw away the data, but that was expensive. A better scheme was to invent some way of correcting the existing noncatch-trial information by using the information that had been secured on the catch trial. Various normalization procedures were proposed at various times. A good review and discussion of methods can be found in Blackwell's (1953) monograph.

Corrections for guessing might provide an improved estimate of the limenal value the experiment was designed to find. But still there was no underlying conceptualization that made one correction method better than another. Here is where the theory of signal detectability shone. The basic idea can best be understood as a variant on Thurstone's (1927) theory of category scaling. An experimental selection from two or more stimulus conditions confronts a subject on trial after trial. These stimuli may be thought of as generating distributions on some underlying perceptual continuum. The subject is presumed to establish one or more criterion points—category boundaries—on the perceptual continuum. He then uses a decision rule such as: say "yes" if the stimulus event on this trial is to the right of the cut point, and "no" if it is to the left. If the distributions on the perceptual continuum overlap at all, such a decision rule is bound to give rise to errors of one kind or another. An analysis of these errors makes it possible to assign a numerical index to the underlying psychological difference between the stimulus configuration distributions. This index will be independent of the location of the cut point on the perceptual continuum. Thus, the theory of signal detectability has the charming property that experimental variables that may move the cut point—the subject's expectations, his desires and aversions, his attitudes, and so on—cannot in principle influence the separate estimation of the stimulus effect upon his judgment.

The theory of signal detectability has given rise to a novel way to display the data from a variety of kinds of experiments that conform to the paradigm. Such graphs of data were originally called receiver operating characteristics (ROC) by the communications engineers. The initials ROC were preserved by the psychologists, the R now standing for "response." In preparing the *Handbook of Mathematical Psychology,* the editors considered a variety of alternative names for this graph. They proposed the name *isosensitivity function* to capture the psychological importance of this new form of data display. Figure 3 is an example of an isosensitivity function. Observe that the ordinate and abscissa run from 0 to 1, that is, the axes

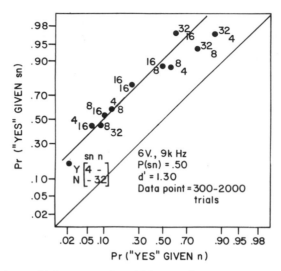

Fig. 3. An isosensitivity curve in which payoffs are varied. The probabilities on the axes are in normal coordinates. Beside each data point is a pair of numbers representing the payoff magnitudes for that datum for correct reports; false alarms and misses received constant negative outcome. [Huckle, 1972.]

represent probabilities. And in particular they conventionally represent conditional probabilities of reporting a signal when it is not present (a false alarm) on the abscissa, and reporting a signal when it is present (a hit) on the ordinate.

Let us consider this graphic representation more deeply, for it tells us a great deal about the kinds of problems that the theory of signal detectability endeavors to solve. First, note the following fact: If a data point represented an absolute failure of the subject to make any discrimination whatsoever, it could appear anywhere on the main diagonal. One might have thought that such an observation must appear at the 50% point on each axis, but a moment's consideration leads to the obvious truth that it hardly matters what the relative frequency of hits and false alarms are, provided they are exactly the same. After all, if a data point appears on the main diagonal, it represents only the relative frequency with which the subject enjoys using the word "yes," and tells nothing about his sensitivity to the differences in the stimulus configuration.

But notice further that even if the subject could discriminate between the (two) stimulus configurations, there is absolutely no reason that he would choose one response in the presence of one configuration and another response in the presence of another. That is, there is no reason to believe

that any data would be off the main diagnoal, even if the subject had ex-
quisite sensitivity. To appreciate this observation imagine for a moment
that the subject is a monkey or a rat. Thus Francis W. Irwin (1958) conjectured that, whereas it is clear that preference implies discrimination,
it may also be true that discrimination will not reveal itself without preference. Consequently, if one expects to obtain a data point off the main
diagonal, it will be necessary to arrange certain kinds of outcomes in a
way that is contingent upon using one response or the other in the presence
of one stimulus configuration or another. This is what made the actual
rat, whose data are shown in Fig. 3, behave as he did.

When this is arranged we establish a payoff function in the decision
theory sense, and we expect that if the subject is able to make the discrimination between the stimulus configurations, a data point will appear somewhere to the upper left of the main diagonal. Such a data point might
be expected to lie somewhere along the minor diagonal extending from
the midpoint in the square to the upper left-hand corner. That would be
true, if, as the subject detected the signal more and more easily, he increased
his hits and reduced his false alarms proportionately. This could be called
a form of "unbiased" judgment about the discriminability of the stimulus
configuration. Note, of course, that this is a very special use of the term
"unbiased." It simply means that a certain region of the unit square is
easy to find, and furthermore, that if discrimination is impossible with the
responses equally likely, or is perfect, the straight line connecting those
two points can be called the line of unbiased responses.

The heart of the theory of signal detectability is that for a fixed set of
stimulus configurations there is an infinite collection of data points, all of
which imply equal discriminability. Such an isosensitivity curve is shown
by the solid line in Fig. 3. It can be swept out by keeping the stimulus
configurations fixed and varying experimental variables that give rise to
the changes in the tendency of the subject to use the responses. Experiments have been performed that show that these functions can be swept
out by changing the stimulus presentation probabilities, the payoff matrices,
the instructions to subjects, and other attitude or motivation-inducing sets
communicated either by instruction or by the early experience of the subject in the experimental situation (see, for example, Galanter & Holman,
1967). Now in constructing this new kind of graph, and in sweeping out
this kind of function, we seem to have lost the classical psychometric or
poikilitic function of the dependence of response on stimulus magnitude.
Such a dependence could be graphed in this configuration by a set of data
points that might cleave to a line running from the main diagonal to the
upper-left corner. The solid line in Fig. 4 represents an example of such

an "isobias" function. These data were presumably collected by keeping all of the variables that could alter the response bias of the subject constant, and changing only the discriminability of the stimulus. They happen to be unpublished data from an experiment done by Herbert Huckle and the author (cf. Huckle, 1972). They were obtained from the same white rat shown in Fig. 3, but here making an auditory intensity discrimination at a frequency of 9 kHz. The payoff to the animal was a pellet of food if correct and a bright light in the face if incorrect. Animal experimentalists should take note that a decision-theoretic analysis of this animal's behavior implies nothing more about the decision-making power of this rat than catching a stick implies about the analytic power of the dog.

The performance that we have been referring to in the last few paragraphs represents stationary or asymptotic performance. The decision-theoretic concept of the perceptual processes inherent in these data presumes that in principle these data points could occur on a single trial. That is, if we had some neuromagical way to read the conditional probabilities directly, we would observe these values as inherent in the subject. One might be tempted to believe that such a stationary state of affairs may be true for a man or woman, but certainly it is not conceivable that an animal could so perform without training. Figure 5 shows how this rat looked making the auditory discrimination for the first 2500 trials. The early position biases are not unique to this animal. Five other subjects display similar effects.

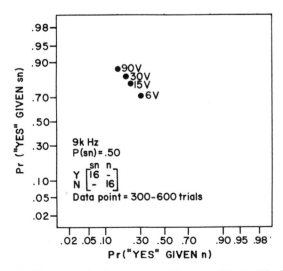

FIG. 4. An isobias curve in the same coordinates as Fig. 3. [Huckle, 1972.]

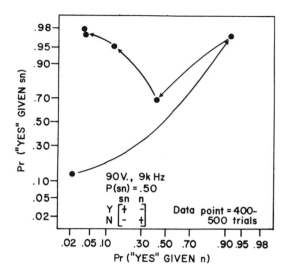

FIG. 5. The acquisition of a discrimination by a single animal. Positive reinforcement for correct responses was equal to circa "16" as represented in Figs. 3 and 4. [Huckle, 1972.]

VI. THE VALUE OF MONEY

Recall that the presence of discriminative behavior reveals itself only when the preferences of the observer lead him to respond in such a way that his discriminations become overt. The perceptual act is contingent upon the outcome structure of the experiment, in particular, the payoff matrices. In the original development of the theory of signal detectability it was believed that the subject maximized the expected monetary value that was available in the experiment. Empirical data to support that conjecture are shown in Fig. 6. Observe that the support is weak if present at all. But of course Bernoulli has explained why. We should search for a utility transform on the monetary rewards and losses of the payoff matrices. That is, we may find that the subject is maximizing a utility transform of the payoff matrix. The difficulty in finding such an incremental utility function of money is not a lack of possible conjectures; in addition to Bernoulli's there is also that of Cramer who, in 1728, proposed a power function with an exponent of .5. The difficulty is to collect a set of data that unequivocally supports one or another reasonable incremental utility function. To perform such an experiment we need to cast the problem into a form in which responses and relations among responses lead us to accept one or another utility function.

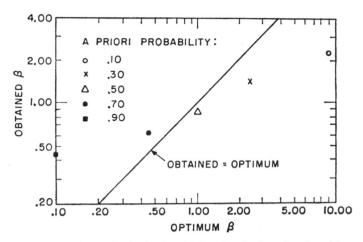

FIG. 6. A comparison of obtained criterion levels for signals with varying a priori probabilities and fixed payoffs plotted against the optimal criterion level calculated on the basis of "expected value" theory. [Green, 1960.]

Initially, the problem can be seen as theoretically equivalent to the scaling problem. Find some transformation of the physical metric that represents the psychological effect of the magnitude of the physical variable. But unlike signal intensity or other routinely scaled physical variables, the physical scale of wealth comes to us clearly marked with its numerical value. It is hard to get an observer to take seriously a request that he tell you whether $5 is worth more or less than $4, or whether $20 is worth twice as much as $10. The experimental tack originally taken to solve the problem is to direct the judgments of the subject not toward the money itself, but toward Ramsey-like or Von Neuman and Morgenstern-like, gambles. Leaving aside the classic study of Preston and Beratta (1948), who attempted to formulate the problem within the context of Helson's (1947) theory of adaptation level, and who therefore had other central concerns, an early experimental attempt to scale money was the work of Mosteller and Nogee (1951). They offered money gambles to various groups of subjects playing a game of poker-dice. The calculable probabilities of the various falls of the dice were sufficiently difficult to make that Mosteller and Nogee presumed the subjects were forming an estimate of the gamble itself. They then chose among the various gambles in their play of the game on the basis of some maximization principle involving the subjective probabilities of the various dice falls and the utilities in the Von Neuman and Morgenstern sense. The results show that for payoff functions over the small money-range used, one could not conclusively determine the form of the utility function.

As mentioned in passing before, by adopting Ramsey's conjecture to characterize the measurement of utility without assuming the linearity of objective and subjective probability, Davidson *et al.* (1957) engaged in an extensive series of experiments in which subjects chose among alternatives whose occurrence depended on the outcome of the roll of a die that had independently been shown to have the desired Ramsey property of equal degree of belief for each of its two outcomes. A reasonable conclusion that can be drawn from the many experiments described in their monograph is that one may expect to observe over a limited monetary range utility functions that are roughly linear, concave downward, or concave upward.

Galanter (1962) reported an experiment in which he attempted to assess incremental utilities for money by asking subjects to assign numbers not to the amounts of money being scaled but rather to the relative happiness that additional monetary increments would provide. The question in its starkest form is, "If $10 will make you happy to a certain degree, how much would you have to receive to be twice as happy?" Subjects consistently report that more than $20 is required to make them twice as happy as $10. Indeed, if you strike an average over what multitudes of people

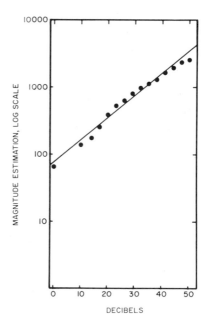

FIG. 7. Magnitude estimations of loudness of a 400-Hz tone varying amplitude. The slope is .33.

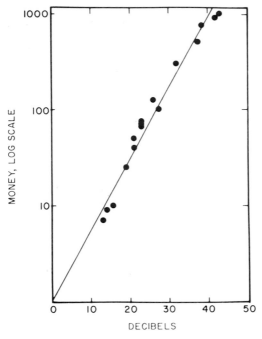

Fig. 8. A cross-modality matching function in which subjects adjusted a Sone potentiometer to match the value of hypothetical monetary increments. The exponent is .74.

say, it turns out that about $50 is required to make a person twice as happy as $10. Because this ratio reappears almost independent of the modulus, the experiment supports the hypothesis that the utility function of money is a power function, just as many other subjective scales are (cf. Stevens & Galanter, 1957). The exponent for this utility function, .43, is quite close to Cramer's conjectured square root. In attempts to confirm both the form and the exponent of this utility function, the author and his students have conducted several additional experiments. In one of them, subjects first scale (by the method of magnitude estimation) the loudness of a 400-Hz tone. The results are shown in Fig. 7. The subjects are then given control over the amplitude of the tone and asked to adjust it so that the loudness of the tone corresponds to the value of different monetary increments. Using a sone potentiometer to make the auditory stimulus match the hypothetical monetary increments, the subjects generate the cross-modality matching function shown in Fig. 8. The exponent of the observed loudness function is .33, and the exponent of the cross-modality matching function is .74. A little algebra shows that if, given an appropriate choice of units, two continua are governed by the equations

$$\Psi_1 = \Phi_1{}^m,$$

$$\Psi_2 = \Phi_2{}^n,$$

and if the values of Ψ_1 and Ψ_2 are equated at various levels, then Φ_1 and Φ_2 are related by

$$\log \Phi_1 = (n/m)\log \Phi_2.$$

Consequently, if the utility function for money is a power function, then the cross-modality match estimates its exponent, n/m, as .45. This is quite close to the directly estimated exponent for positive monetary increments.

Because attempts by us to obtain direct estimates of negative increments of money had consistently produced extremely variable data, this method of cross-modality matching was attempted (Galanter & Pliner, 1974) with the instructions that subjects adjust the loudness of a tone to equal how unhappy they would be with losses of different amounts of money. Figure 9 shows the cross-modality match, which has an exponent of .64. The loudness function for this group of subjects had an exponent of .38; the ratio of the two exponents gives a negative utility function of .59. Because this number departs significantly from the value of the positive exponent, we believed it was reasonable to examine further the negative branch of the utility function. With the help of Professor Carl Pfaffman who supplied the chemicals and the experimental lore to conduct the experiment, we scaled the bitterness of the exceedingly bitter substance, sodium octa-ace-

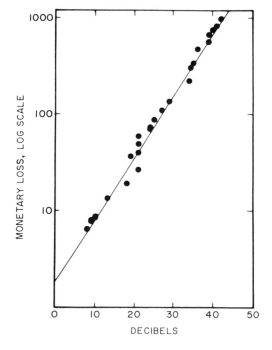

FIG. 9. A cross-modality matching function in which the loudness of a 400-Hz tone was adjusted to match the "unhappiness" associated with various monetary decrements. The exponent is .64.

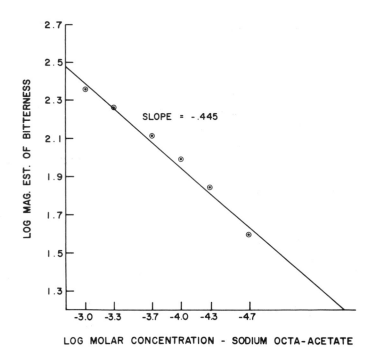

Fɪɢ. 10. Magnitude estimates of varying concentrations of the bitter substance sodium octa-acetate.

tate. Figure 10 is the magnitude estimation scale representing the subjective bitterness of this substance. The experimental observers were then told that these liquids would be used in another experiment in which other people would be asked to drink 8 oz of it. They were then asked for estimates of how much should be paid to subjects to drink liquids at these various concentrations. Once again they tasted the substances and made cross-modality matches to provide monetary values that represented the noisomeness of the substance to the observer. These data are shown in Fig. 11, and reveal a cross-modality exponent of .705. Taking the appropriate ratio of exponents we calculated that the disutility function for monetary decrements was .63, confirming quite strongly the results of the cross-modality loudness judgment experiments.

On a visit to her home in England just before the decimalization of British currency, Diana Jacobs asked English men and women to answer the question about the relation between monetary increments and happiness described by Galanter (1962). The results confirm that the utility function was again a concave downward function, the exponent being .44 when averages were struck in reasonable ways. This result compromises the criticism that the earlier findings may be an accidental consequence of the decimal character of the United States currency. Galanter and Holman (1967) have also confirmed the power function form of the utility function in a signal detection experiment by multiplying the payoff matrix by a positive constant and recovering the original data points under this new payoff. Jacobs and Galanter (1974) also showed that if in classical signal detection experiments the subjects were attempting to maximize the (power function) utility of the payoff, and were limited only by their capacity to detect the signals, then, if the payoff matrices were all of one sign rather than the usual loss for error, gain for correct types, it would be possible to estimate the exponent of their utility transform. The experiment gave estimates of the slope of the conjectured power function for utility which, for positive increments of utility and for reasonably discriminable stimuli, confirmed our earlier observation. The estimate of the exponent of the negative utility function gave a function of the right shape, but was not numerically consonant with our previous observations.

We must recognize that the differential increments in the payoff matrices

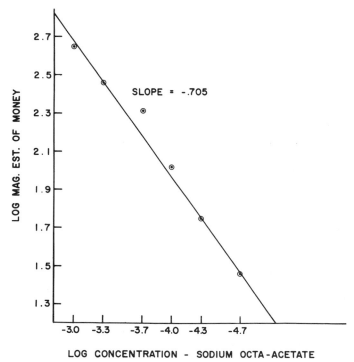

FIG. 11. A cross-modality matching function of monetary decrements presumably equivalent to the drinking of a fixed quantity of these bitter solutions.

in these experiments are, on each trial, extremely small. Insofar as we have no knowledge of the unit of the scale that we are using, we may be observing behavior constrained to the region of fractional utility increments, a region in which the rate of growth of utility is greater than the rate of growth of the monetary increments.

Returning at this point to Tversky's (1967) scaling experiment we may reasonably inquire into the form of the utility function he observed. Does it confirm the power law, and if so, is the exponent of the same magnitude as we have observed in the preceding experiments? Unfortunately the results of the conjoint measurement inquiry yield a utility function that is linear with money. A power function to be sure, but not one of great interest. The only possibility of reconciling these data is to examine further an aspect of Tversky's study that shows a component of the judgments contingent upon a presumed utility for gambling. This phenomenon may have interacted with the competing desire for money to generate the observed utility function.

VII. CONCLUDING EXPECTORATIONS

At this point, a tentative summary of the role of decision mechanisms in the study of perception seems appropriate. As the last few paragraphs have demonstrated, there is no question that the perceptual tasks and the techniques developed in perceptual studies may serve to augment our understanding of motivational variables and decision-making mechanisms. That is, we may learn something about motivational variables from the response biases observed in various perceptual tasks. In addition, insights from decision theory lead to increased sophistication in the design of perceptual experiments. We avoid the confusion of interpreting as "perceptual," behavior that is a consequence of motivational processes. In all fairness, however, we must point out that these more sophisticated perceptual experiments have not altered the general form nor the approximate magnitude of the perceptual functions that were first observed late in the nineteenth century. We may no longer construe the absolute threshold as we once did, but our newer experiments have not forced us to revise completely the tabled values of the various psychological limens and threshold functions. These numerical tables form a central part of the data base for the analytical study of the mechanisms of vision and audition. These considerations suggest that an understanding of decision mechanisms may improve the precision with which we characterize perceptual processes, but at this moment they add nothing to our understanding of the perceptual processes, themselves. We must repeat, however, that techniques used in the study of perception may indeed contribute importantly to a further elucidation of the psychological processes implicated in decision making.

Whereas the previous summary might sound disheartening in its rather off-hand treatment of the importance of decision mechanisms in perception, because the processes reveal themselves only as modulators of responses, it suggests that the place one might search for the power of decision-making principles on perceptual processes may be where perception is central in the actual guidance of behavior. Even though the determination of a limen may be minimally influenced or influenced not at all by attitudinal or motivational factors, the fact is that behavioral judgments about the stimulus take certain decision making principles into account. This means that if one were responding in a continuous way, but were modulated by certain perceptual inputs, then the decision making mechanisms might have a greater role to play in the perceptual process *in extenso*.

If you accept, in a general way, the conceptual ideas expounded in Miller, Galanter, and Pribram's, *Plans and the Structure of Behavior* (1960) the great majority of representable human action will be under conceptual, and not perceptual, control. The trip I plan to California involves sequences of acts where perceptual events are remarkably interchangeable. The central guidance is provided by tests against conceptualizations, and so I check to see if I have my airline ticket, go out into the street to hail a taxi cab, get aboard the airliner, and finally arrive at my destination all without being aware of any perceptual regulation of my behavior. The fact is of course, that it was there, but it was hard to observe (unless the taxi turned out not to be painted yellow!) and in general, perceptual guidance is hard to observe in the majority of human contexts. Normally, our actions have a ballistic quality. We go from here to there with hardly a glance on the way. We are creatures guided by images only poorly represented by punctiform transforms of a retinal mosaic, or pulse modulation patterns of the hair cell discharges of the cochlea bending under the swish of their fluid humours.

The few places where perceptual control over ongoing behavior *can* be construed as paramount are, unexpectedly, of recent origin in man's history. The first, and unquestionably most prominent demonstration of the preceptual control of behavior, is in the act of reading. The second locus of clear-cut perceptual control of ongoing behavior is in the perceptual–motor acts involved in the guidance of (relatively speaking) high-speed vehicles. I shall conclude this discussion of psychological decision mechanisms and their connection to perceptual processing by a brief sketch of certain possible avenues of research that may bring together the motivational features of human nature with perceptual factors in ways that our simple psychophysical tasks have not been able to do.

There is very little question that the ballistic saccades of the eye are the consequences of some strong interaction between the printed page and intrinsic decisional structures (Hochberg, 1970a). We might mimic the atomic unit of the reading task by the tachistoscopic recognition threshold of the Solomon and Howes experiment described earlier. What was observed there is that the values of the word recognition threshold interacted with the response biases of the past experience of the subject. By an appropriate analysis (informational, signal detection, etc.) one can show that the sensory thresholds themselves remain unaltered, and only the response habits of the subject induced variations in the correctness of the response. Let us now consider the limiting case of this experiment first performed by Goldiamond and Hawkins (1958), in which no stimulus at all is presented. The subjects are asked to report the words that are flashed. The relative frequency of word reports corresponds again to the Thorndike–Lorge word count. The experiment is an exact analog of the Irwin and Preston constant stimulus experiment. Response bias alone controls the response frequencies. Consider now the act of reading as a perceptual–motor task. The relevant responses in the act are the saccadic movements of the eye. These saccades (Hochberg & Brooks, 1970) depend not only on the textual material being read, but also on the intentions of the reader. Saccades during proofreading are small; saccades in reading for pleasure are large. The movements themselves, being ballistic (Saslow 1967), must be determined by sensory information in the peripheral retina that represents the target toward which the saccade is directed. But insofar as the intentions of the reader have been shown to determine saccade excursion, the retinal information must be processed in such a way that the intentional information can bias the responses. These response biases are exactly analogous to the response biases in a simple psychophysical yes–no experiment, where the subject is expected to report seeing a signal or not, contingent upon certain pay-offs. However, because the response is so intimately stimulus-connected in the sense of "plans," the bias is really a perceptual bias.

A similar analysis can be found in Hochberg's (1970b) explication of the span of tachistoscopic recognition and the conflicting evidence of iconic storage. It is known that the number of discrete letters that can be reported after tachistoscopic presentations is of the order of four or five. This also corresponds roughly to the number of discrete and unconnected letters that can be remembered. On the other hand Sperling (1960) has shown that the presentation of a matrix of nine disconnected letters yields positive identification for any single letter subsequently cued. Apparently nine letters are represented in the sensory system immediately following their exposure as demonstrated by the fact that subjects can recover any of them: Consequently, the postexposure bias induced by the cueing stimulus represents the intrusion of a decision-making process into the actual transformation and transmission of the perceptual information itself. This kind of extremely tight coupling between the decision process and the perceptual event must be preserved in reading. The latency of a saccade being of the order of 250 msec, and its ballistic nature make it unreasonable to conjecture that saccadic movements converge on an appropriate "next" point by some stepwise corrective process that could be captured in stimulus–response terms. One may anticipate that such molecular analyses of behavior as here suggested, and not the usual molar arguments will serve as the coup-de-grace that will lead us finally to abandon the stimulus–response paradigm.

As a last example of this sort of analysis, consider the task of vehicular guidance. The field of motor skills, tracking, or sensory–motor performance, has routinely been viewed as a form of response-shadowing of a variable stimulus. The quasi-linear analysis of Licklider (1960), as well as reviews of the tracking literature (Bilodeau & Bilodeau, 1969), all support the notion that stimulus information is used to guide responses that occur slightly behind the stimulus but with more or less linear fidelity. Descriptions of the motor tasks in this context may leave out, of course, all forms of increments and decrements that can be attributed to concentration, attention, motivation, attitude, and so on. Experience alone is presumed to reduce the error term in the tracking equation, and a few free parameters are construed as absorbing the remainder of the nonperceptual variance. Treated as we parody it above, the vehicle guidance task can be conceived in quite a different fashion. Rather than formalize the subject as making certain corrections to reduce perceptual error, we can construe his role as one of extracting perceptual information from some environmental display, and then by imposing a bias determined by some decision process, acting to induce the appropriate motion to the vehicle. At some future point the perceptual system is presumed to provide information to formulate a new target region, and decisional procedures then constrain further responses in the new direction.

A potential criticism of this formulation for vehicle guidance rests on an important distinction between this task and reading. After all, guidance of a vehicle is not accomplished by necessarily ballistic responses. Consequently, as long as information is available on a continuing real-time basis, why not correct the motor system to conform to the visual information? In reality, the only answer to a criticism of this kind is some experimental demonstration to show that the conjectured conception is more faithful to the observed data than is a continuous tracking model. Experimental evidence to support this "plan-and-execute" conceptualization is now being collected and analyzed. The early data suggest that vehicle operators who are given only "saccadic" glimpses of the environment can make psychophysical judgments about the future state of the vehicle, and consequently they have information necessary to make corrective movements of the vehicle itself. Their judgments are indistinguishable from the performance of vehicle operators who have the visual scene constantly available. The task we are using is the approach and landing of an aircraft, an intrinsically difficult and artful maneuver. It turns out, however, that the artistry is contained in the formulation of three fairly bulky but essentially unitary actions: approach path control, flare, and touchdown and roll-out. There are indeed minor corrections made during the execution of each of these major acts, but the minor corrections are intrinsically distinguishable from the central task itself, landing the airplane. These control acts take the form of maintaining the wings level and maintaining latitudinal parallelism with the runway and its center line, i.e., they provide a stable platform. I make here no serious suggestion that three quick glimpses would enable a pilot to land an airplane, at least I would not suggest it if I were a passenger. On the other hand, I would be no less nervous if the guidance of an aircraft to the ground were accomplished by continuous corrections based on maintaining particular x–y–z-coordinate values (even with some time smoothing) at each point in the approach. It seems quite reasonable to feel uncomfortable in the hands of a machine that guides your physical destiny when that machine has no information about the final state of affairs you desire. Eventually, we may all be in the hands of such Cyclopean devices, but nobody says we have to like it.

References

Becker, G. N., & McClintock, C. G. Behavioral decision theory. *Annual Review of Psychology,* 1967, **18,** 239–286.

Bernoulli, D. Specimen theoriae novae de mensura sortis. *Commentarii academiae scientiarum imperiales petropolitanae.* 1738. **5,** 175–192. [Trans. by L. Sommer in *Econometrica,* 1954, **22,** 23–36.]

Bilodeau, E. A., & Bilodeau, I. M. (Eds.), *Principles of skill acquisition.* New York: Academic Press, 1969.

Blackwell, H. R. *Psychophysical threshold: Experimental studies of methods of measurement.* Ann Arbor Engineering Research Institute, University of Michigan, 1953.

Borel, E. Apropos of a treatise of probability. 1924. [Trans. by Smokler.] In H. E. Kyburg, Jr., & H. E. Smokler (Eds.), *Studies in subjective probability.* New York: Wiley, 1964.

Bricker, P. D., & Chapanis, A. Do incorrectly perceived tachistoscopic stimuli convey some information? *Psychological Review*, 1953, **40**, 181–188.

Bruner, J. S., & Goodman, C. C. Value and need as organizing factors in perception. *Journal of Abnormal and Social Psychology*, 1947, **42**, 33–44.

Carter, L. F., & Schooler, K. Value, need and other factors in perception. *Psychological Review*, 1949, **59**, 200–207.

Carvellas, T., & Schneider, B. Direct estimation of multidimensional tonal dissimilarity. *Journal of the Acoustical Society of America*, 1972, **51**, 1839–1848.

Coombs, C. *A theory of data.* New York: Wiley, 1964.

Davidson, D., Suppes, P., & Siegel, S. *Decision making: An experimental approach.* Stanford, California: Stanford Univ. Press, 1957.

deFinetti, B. La prevision: se lois logiques ses sources subjectives. 1937. Trans. and reprinted in H. E. Kyburg, Jr., & H. E. Smokler (Eds.), *Studies in Subjective Probability*. New York: Wiley, 1964.

Edwards, W. Behavioral decision theory. *Annual Review of Psychology*, 1961, **12**, 473–498.

Fernberger, S. W. The use of equality judgments in psychophysical procedures. *Psychological Review*, 1930, **37**, 107–112.

Ferster, C. B., & Skinner, B. F. *Schedules of reinforcement.* New York: Appleton, 1957.

Galanter, E. Contemporary psychophysics. In R. Brown, E. Galanter, E. H. Hess, & G. Mandler (Eds.), *New directions in psychology*. New York: Holt, 1962. (a)

Galanter, E. The direct measurement of utility and subjective probability. *American Journal of Psychology*, 1962, **75**, 208–220.(b)

Galanter, E. *Textbook of elementary psychology.* San Francisco: Holden-Day, 1966. (c)

Galanter, E., & Holman, G. L. Some invariances of the isosensitivity function and their implications for the utility function of money. *Journal of Experimental Psychology*, 1967, **73**, 333–339.

Galanter, E., & Pliner, P. Cross-modality matching of money against other continua. In H. Moskowitz, B. Sharf, & J. C. Stevens (Eds.), *Sensation and measurement: Papers in honor of S. S. Stevens*. Dordrecht, Netherlands: Reidel, 1974.

Glanville, A. D., & Dallenbach, K. M. The range of attention. *American Journal of Psychology*, 1929, **41**, 207–236.

Goldiamond, I., & Hawkins, W. F. Vexierversuch: The log relationship between word frequency and recognition obtained in the absence of stimulus words. *Journal of Experimental Psychology*, 1958, **56**, 457–456.

Green, D. M. Psychoacoustics and detection theory. *Journal of the Acoustical Society of America*, 1960, **32**, 1189–1203.

Guthrie, E. R. *The psychology of learning.* New York: Harper, 1935.

Guthrie, E. R., & Horton, G. P. A study of the cat in the puzzle box. *Psychological Bulletin*, 1937, **34**, 774.

Helson, H. Adaptation level as a frame of reference for prediction of psychophysical data. *American Journal of Psychology*, 1947, **60**, 1–29.

Hochberg, J. Components of literacy: Speculations and exploratory research. In H. Levin & J. Williams (Eds.), *Basic studies on reading*. New York, Basic Books, 1970. (a)

Hochberg, J. Attention, organization and consciousness. In D. I. Mostofsky (Ed.) *Attention: Contemporary theory and analysis*. New York Appleton, 1970. (b)

Hochberg, J., & Brooks, V. Reading as an intentional behavior. In H. Singe, & R. Ruddekk (Eds.), *Theoretical models and processes of reading*. Newark, Delaware. International Reading Assoc., 1970.

Howes, D. H., & Solomon, R. L. Visual duration thresholds as a function of word-probability. *Journal of Experimental Psychology,* 1951, **41,** 401–410.

Howes, D. H. On the relation between intelligibility and frequency of occurrence of English words. *Journal of the Acoustical Society of America,* 1957, **29,** 296–305.

Huckle, H. Signal detection in the albino rat. Unpublished Doctoral Dissertation, University of Washington, 1972.

Hull, C. L. *Principles of behavior.* New York: Appleton, 1943.

Irwin, F. W. An analysis of the concepts of discrimination and preference. *American Journal of Psychology,* 1958, **71,** 152–165.

Irwin, F. W., & Preston, M. G. Avoidance of repetition of judgments across sense modalities. *Journal of Experimental Psychology,* 1937, **21,** 511–520.

Jacobs, D. E., & Galanter, E. Estimates of utility function parameters from signal detection experiments. Tech. Rept. 32, Psychophysics Laboratory Columbia University, 1974.

Keynes, J. M. *A treatise on probability.* London: Macmillan, 1921.

Kruskal, J. B. Multidimensional scaling by optimizing goodness of fit to a nonmetric hypothesis. *Psychometrika,* 1964, **29,** 1–27. (a)

Kruskal, J. B. Nonmetric multidimensional scaling: A numerical method. *Psychometrika.* 1964. **29,** 115–129. (b)

Kyburg, H. E., & Smokler, H. E. *Studies in subjective probability.* New York: Wiley, 1971.

Lee, W. *Decision theory and human behavior.* New York: Wiley, 1971.

Licklider, J. C. R. Quasi-linear operator models in the study of manual tracking. In R. D. Luce (Ed.), *Developments in mathematical psychology.* Glencoe, Illinois: Free Press, 1960. Pp. 166–279.

Luce, R. D. Detection and recognition. In R. D. Luce, R. R. Bush, & E. Galanter (Eds.), *Handbook of mathematical psychology,* Vol. I. New York: Wiley, 1963.

Luce, R. D., Bush, R. R., & Galanter, E. *Handbook of mathematical psychology,* Vol. I. New York: Wiley, 1963.

Luce, R. D., & Raiffa, H. *Games and decisions.* New York: Wiley, 1963.

Luce, R. D., & Tukey, J. W. Simultaneous conjoint measurement: A new type of fundamental measurement. *Journal of Mathematical Psychology,* 1964, **1,** 1–27.

Miller, G. A., Galanter, E., & Pribram, K. *Plans and the Structure of behavior.* New York: Holt, 1960.

Mosteller, R., & Nogee, P. An experimental measurement of utility. *Journal of Political Economy,* 1951, **59,** 371–404.

Preston, M. G., & Beratta, P. An experimental study of the auction-value of an uncertain outcome. *American Journal of Psychology,* 1948, **61,** 183–193.

Ramsey, F. P. Truth and probability. (1926). Reprinted in H. E. Kyburg Jr., & H. E. Smokler (Eds.), *Studies in subjective probability.* New York: Wiley, 1964.

Rappoport, A., & Wallsten, T. S. Individual decision behavior. *Annual Review of Psychology* 1972, **23,** 131–176.

Saslow, M. G. Effects of components of displacement-step stimuli upon latency for saccadic eye movement. *Journal of the Optical Society of America,* 1967, **57,** 1024–1029.

Savage, L. J. *Foundations of statistics.* New York: Wiley, 1956.

Schafer, R., & Murphy, G. The role of autism in a visual figure ground relationship. *Journal of Experimental Psychology,* 1942, **32,** 335–343.

Skinner, B. F. Are theories of learning necessary? *Psychological Review,* 1950, **57,** 193–216.

Skinner, B. F. *The behavior of organisms: An experimental analysis.* New York: Appleton, 1938.

Skinner, B. F. Pigeons in a pelican. *American Psychologist,* 1960, **15,** 28–37.

Shepard, R. N. Analysis of proximities: multidimensional scaling with an unknown distance function I & II. *Psychometrika,* 1962, **27,** 125–140.

Smith, M., & Wilson, E. A. A model of the auditory threshold and its application to the problem of the multiple observer. *Psychological Monographs: General and Applied,* 1953, **67** (9, Whole No. 359).

Solomon, R. L., & Howes, D. H. Word probability, personal values, and visual duration thresholds. *Psychological Review,* 1951, **58,** 256–270.

Sperling, G. The information available in brief visual presentations. *Psychological Monographs,* 1960, **74** (Whole No. 11).

Stevens, S. S., & Galanter, E. Ratio scales and category scales for a dozen perceptual continua. *Journal of Experimental Psychology,* 1957, **54,** 377–411.

Swets, J. A. (Ed.). *Signal detection and recognition by human observers.* New York: Wiley, 1964.

Tanner, W. P., & Swets, J. A. The human use of information. I. Signal detection for the case of signal known exactly. *IRE Transactions of Professional Group in Information Theory,* 1954, **4,** 213–221.

Terrace, H. S. Stimulus control. In W. K. Honig (Ed.), *Operant behavior.* New York: Appleton, 1966.

Thorndike, E. L. *Educational psychology.* New York: Lemike and Buechner. 1903.

Thurstone, L. L. A law of comparative judgment. *Psychological Review,* 1927, **34,** 273–286.

Tolman, E. C. Purposive Behavior in Animals and Men. New York: Appleton, 1932.

Tversky, A. Additivity, utility and subjective probability. *Journal of Mathematical Psychology,* 1967, **4,** 31–48.

Verplanck, W. S., Cotton, J. W., & Collier, G. H. Previous training as a determinant of response dependency at the threshold. *Journal of Experimental Psychology,* 1953, **45,** 10–14.

Von Neuman, J., & Morgenstern. O. *Theory of games and economic behavior* (3rd ed.), Princeton, New Jersey : Princeton Univ. Press, 1951.

Chapter 5

CONTEXTUAL EFFECTS: A RANGE–FREQUENCY ANALYSIS*

ALLEN PARDUCCI

I. INTRODUCTION

This chapter is concerned with how the judgment of a psychophysical stimulus depends upon the other stimuli with which it is presented. Attention is restricted to research using successive presentations of single stimuli that differ on a univariate dimension.† In contrast to traditional scaling, where the interest is in assigning each stimulus a psychological value that is independent of context, the present review is directed to those experiments in which judgments are most clearly dependent upon context. This

* This work was supported in part by United States Public Health Service Grant HD-00923. Special thanks to Michael H. Birnbaum for helpful suggestions.
† The effects of context upon social judgment, multidimensional scaling, and perceptual illusions are not included in the present review.

focus reflects the assumption that relativism is a basic characteristic of judgment. It is the special susceptibility of psychophysical judgments to the immediate stimulus context that recommends this type of research as a source of general principles.

In the tradition of adaptation-level theory (Helson, 1964), the present discussion treats the context or frame of reference as a frequency distribution of stimulus values. Consider a typical experiment on "absolute" judgment. The task might be to rate each of a succession of lifted weights, using naturalistic verbal categories varying from *very light* to *very heavy*. In the absence of explicit standards, the instructions imply that each weight is to be compared with the others in the series. Indeed, the experimental subject tends to match the range of permissible categories to the range of weights presented, judging the lightest *very light* and the heaviest *very heavy*. The judgment of any particular weight thus depends upon the other weights: The same 100-gm weight is *very heavy* relative to a series varying from 50 to 100 gm but *very light* in a series from 100 to 200 gm. The judgment also depends upon the relative frequencies with which the different weights are presented, tending to be "lighter" when the heavier weights are presented more frequently.

Despite considerable adjustment to the series he is judging, the subject could of course discriminate it from a prior series of much heavier or lighter weights. One can picture Stevens's (1958) example of "a large mouse that ran up the trunk of the small elephant" without confusing the relative sizes of the two beasts. There are greater contexts which include the different experimental series or the different species of animal. Whatever the difficulties of determining the relevant context, it is clear that judgments are made with respect to some stimulus context.

The appeal of simple psychophysical research is that the relevant context is under almost complete experimental control. By judicious selection of the series of stimuli, the experimenter can elicit any rating he wishes for a particular physical stimulus. Although there seems little practical reason for controlling ratings of lifted weight, the study of such contextual effects is presumed to reveal basic processes also operating in situations in which it would be difficult to identify the stimulus context.

This type of study suggests the practical importance of contextual considerations with important value dimensions (Brickman & Campbell, 1971; Parducci, 1968). For example, when choosing a career, a man anticipates how pleased he will be with his future income. However, his actual satisfaction will depend upon where this income falls in a context of other incomes, such as those of associates and competitors. This future context will differ from the one determining his ratings of satisfaction at the time of choice. The large expected income of a banker may seem meager in a later context that includes the astronomical possibilities of the world of high finance;

a much smaller but regularly increasing salary in civil service may actually yield a greater sense of affluence. Progress toward understanding the relativism of judgment should make it easier to take the future context into account when anticipating the psychological consequences of a decision.

II. RANGE EFFECTS

The most obviously effective feature of the stimulus context is its *range,* the difference between the two extreme stimuli. The primary effect of range can be summarized as a matching of successive categories to successive subranges of the stimuli (Volkmann, 1951).

In psychophysical research, the stimuli are presented repeatedly, usually in random order, and the mean rating of each stimulus is taken across its different presentations and also across the different subjects rating a particular set of stimuli. When judgments are made using verbal categories, it is customary to assign successive integers to the categories (e.g., 1–6 for a six-category scale) and then to average these to obtain a mean rating for each stimulus. When mean ratings are plotted against stimulus values, the slope of the plot varies inversely with the range of values in the set presented for judgment, as illustrated in Fig. 1.

The function relating these mean ratings to the log-physical values of the stimuli approaches linearity (Stevens & Galanter, 1957), particularly

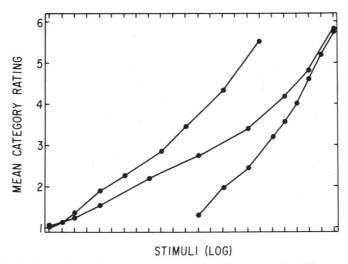

FIG. 1. Ratings of the sizes of squares presented in sets with different endpoints. Slope varies inversely with log–range of stimulus widths. [Data from Parducci & Perrett, 1971.]

when the stimuli have been selected to form a geometric or logarithmic series whose different members are presented with equal frequency. Thus, equal differences in mean rating tend to correspond to equal ratios of stimulus magnitudes. Once the extreme ratings are matched to the stimulus endpoints, the rest of the judgment function is at least partially determined. However, as will be described in the section on frequency effects, the specific form of the scale also depends on the relative spacing and frequency of the stimuli.

A. Psychological Endpoints and Magnitude Estimations

Subjects sometimes avoid the use of one of the end categories, as though comparison were being made with a stimulus value more extreme than any in the set presented for judgment. This psychological endpoint may represent some expected value or even a background feature of the stimulus situation. For example, the subject's rating of the size of the largest square in a series varies inversely with the size of the immediate background against which it is projected, and the upper psychological endpoint can be described as an average of the largest square and the size of the background (Parducci & Perrett, 1971).

Extension of the scale to cover a broader psychological range seems particularly important when subjects are instructed to estimate the ratios of stimulus magnitudes (cf. Chapter 1 by Jones). Teghtsoonian (1971) uses this distinction between psychological and physical ranges to explain the differences between the slopes for different dimensions when these are obtained from log–log plots of magnitude estimations against physical magnitudes. He assumes that the psychological range is determined by the ratio of the greatest and smallest of the *likely* stimulus magnitudes. Teghtsoonian also assumes that the subject matches this range with a constant log-range of numerical estimations in which the greatest value is about 100 times the smallest. Consequently, the log–log slope for each dimension is inversely proportional to its characteristic psychological log-range. Although scaling experiments often employ as great a range of physical values as possible, the slope does vary inversely with the log-range of stimuli actually presented for magnitude estimations (Di Lollo & Kirkham, 1969; Poulton, 1968). It thus seems that magnitude estimations are governed by a range effect analogous to the one so prominent with category ratings.

B. Regression, Central Tendency, and Adaptation Level

This summary of range effects as a matching of end categories to end stimuli is presented as a general rule, but it is rare that actual experimental

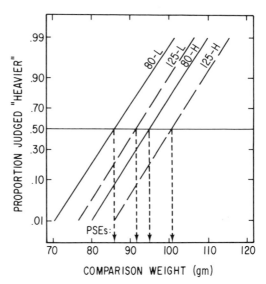

FIG. 2. Psychometric functions and points of subjective equality (PSE) for 100-gm standard when followed by unjudged interpolated weight of either 80 or 125 gm and by comparison weight sampled from one of two sets. Median weight was 90 gm for light set (L), 110 gm for heavy set (H). Mean was 100 gm for both comparison sets. [Generalized from Parducci & Haugen, 1967.]

data can be described so simply. For example, Johnson (1972) has called attention to a regression effect in which the slope of the plot of category ratings against log-stimulus values reflects the less than perfect correlation between stimuli and responses. The magnitude of this correlation varies directly with the duration of the stimulus exposures (Johnson & Mullally, 1969).

In the classic research by Hollingworth (1909), subjects' reproductions of each standard length regressed toward some central value of the different standards presented for reproduction. This central tendency effect is qualitatively consistent with the theory of adaptation level (Helson, 1964) which asserts that the point of subjective equality (PSE) for the standard is a weighted mean of the different stimulus values. Figure 2 illustrates the central tendency effect for an experiment in which each of a set of comparison weights is rated either *heavier* or *lighter* than a constant standard. In this example, an irrelevant weight of either 80 or 125 gm is interpolated between the standard and comparison weights. As shown in Fig. 2, the inferred PSE (in this case, the value of the comparison weight rated *heavier* on half its presentations) varies directly with the value of the irrelevant, interpolated weight.

C. Anchoring

As pointed out by Guilford (1954; cf. Bieri, Atkins, Briar, Leaman, Miller, & Tripodi, 1966; Johnson, 1972, for more recent reviews), "anchoring" is a theoretical concept which seems itself in need of anchoring. The term has most often been applied to shifts in scale that depend upon extension of the range, i.e., upon introduction of a stimulus (the anchor) whose value is either higher or lower than any in the set originally presented for judgment. The instructions sometimes assign a specific category to the new stimulus, but anchoring effects are also obtained when the new stimulus is unlabeled by the experimenter and even when the subject is instructed not to judge it. Unless the subject can be persuaded to employ a new, more extreme rating, he must stretch his old scale to include the new stimulus. This shifts the rating of the old endpoint to a less extreme value. More generally, the ratings of the original set of stimuli shift toward the values that the subject would have assigned to them in the extended set—had the latter been presented from the beginning (as in Fig. 1). Although the degree of shift increases with distance of the new stimulus, Sarris (1967) demonstrated that there is a critical distance beyond which the effect of unlabeled and unjudged anchors decreases, as though these more extreme values were considered too remote to be included in the context for judgment.

Attempts to anchor the endpoints of psychophysical scales by special verbal instructions (e.g., "always call this stimulus 6") are surprisingly ineffective. It is much easier to recall the requested label than to recognize the particular stimulus to which it is supposed to be applied. Consequently, the anchor stimulus becomes a standard whose PSE shifts toward other stimulus values. When the shift is toward less extreme stimuli (as in Parducci and Marshall, 1962), category ratings exhibit the central tendency effect described for comparative judgments. In such cases, the anchor is said to produce "assimilation" rather than the usual "contrast" (Sherif, Taub, & Hovland, 1958).

D. Discriminability

In agreement with the psychological importance attributed to the range, the consistency or precision of judgment is greatest for the two values defining the range, i.e., the stimulus endpoints. There is abundant evidence that the variance in ratings is lower for a particular physical stimulus when it is one of the endpoints (Eriksen & Hake, 1957). More recent research demonstrates that the discriminability of particular physical values is also greater when they are closer to an endpoint (Braida & Durlach, 1972; Parducci & Perrett, 1971; Tabachnick, 1971). The measure of discriminability in this research is the difference between the normal deviates corresponding to the proportion of times each is judged above a particular limen (see the sections on successive-interval scaling in Bock and Jones, 1968, and the chapter by Torgerson in the present volume). This measure of discriminability varies as a linear function of the stimulus range: The same pair of stimuli are harder to discriminate when presented with a broader range of contextual stimuli, even when one of them is an endpoint in both sets. This type of range effect is another aspect of the well-known finding that increases in range have surprisingly little effect on the amount of information transmitted (Pollack, 1953).

III. FREQUENCY EFFECTS

A. Absolute Judgment

Although it seems useful to describe category ratings as a matching of the range of available ratings to the psychological range of stimulation, the particular form of the scale depends upon the relative spacing and frequency of the stimuli. The empirical data points in Fig. 3 illustrate the typical finding that the form of the judgment function is steeper for those portions of the range where the stimuli are more closely spaced or presented with greater relative frequency. Such functions can cross and recross (Parducci, 1963) so that no rescaling of the stimulus or response values could produce the linear functions implied by either a strict range analysis or by the assumption, basic to adaptation-level theory (Helson, 1964), that

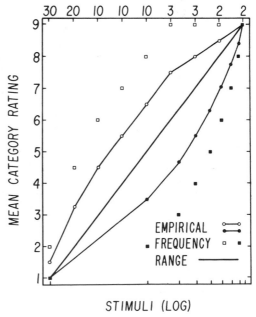

Fig. 3. Category ratings of stimuli presented with unequal frequencies (upper abscissa and open points) or unequal spacing (lower abscissa and solid points). For each condition, "empirical" ratings are halfway between range and frequency values. [Generalized from Parducci & Perrett, 1971.]

ratings are linearly related to differences from the stimulus mean. Instead, the effects of variation in stimulus frequency reflect a general tendency to place the same number of stimuli in each of the available categories.

B. Comparative Judgment

The most striking demonstration of an equal-frequency tendency comes from an experiment on comparative judgment (Garner, 1954) in which the task was to judge whether the second tone in each pair was more or less than half as loud as the first (a constant standard). Although the comparison sets for the different conditions consisted of nonoverlapping ranges of tones, the proportion of "louder" judgments was the same for each comparison set. In this case, variation in the relationship between the standard tone and the general level of the comparison series was completely without effect.

In a more conventional comparative task requiring subjects simply to judge whether each of two comparison tones was *louder* or *softer* than the standard (Parducci & Sandusky, 1970), the total proportion of "louder" judgments remained at .5 despite large variation in the proportion of comparison presentations actually of greater amplitude than the standard (.2 versus .8). Although there was considerable discrimination, PSE shifted toward whichever comparison value was presented more frequently. This equal-frequency tendency is illustrated by Fig. 2: PSE shifts directly with the value of an interpolated stimulus, but it also shifts toward the median or equal-frequency value of the comparison series.

Even when judgments are made in terms of a familiar metric, such as inches or ounces, the scale adapts to the immediate context (Krantz & Campbell, 1961). Similarly, practice with an arbitrary scale established by the experimenter does not prevent a subsequent shift toward equalization of response frequencies (Parducci, Perrett, & Marsh, 1969). This equalization, along with the central tendency effect described earlier, suggests why it is so difficult to anchor unidimensional scales.

C. Discriminability Scaling

The conventional measure of discriminability seems largely impervious to these frequency effects. Although PSEs shift with the value of the interpolated stimulus, slopes of the psychometric functions remain relatively constant—as idealized in Fig. 2. Shifts in discriminability would be indicated by nonparallelism in these curves. Parallelism is also the rule with the psychometric functions for "absolute" judgments (Braida & Durlach, 1972; Parducci & Perrett, 1971; Tabachnick, 1971). Typical findings are shown

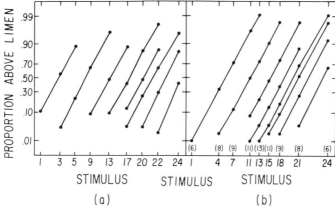

FIG. 4. Proportion of presentations of each stimulus rated above each category limen for Set a scaled by Thurstone model and Set b whose Thurstone values were obtained by interpolation from A. Stimuli were squares of varying size, presented with equal frequency for a but with frequencies shown in parentheses for b. Goodness of fit of Thurstone model indicated by parallelism in a; independence of context by parallelism in b. [Data from Parducci & Perrett, 1971.]

in Fig. 4. Different sizes of squares were presented with equal frequency and plotted on the abscissa of Fig. 4a so as to make the psychometric functions as parallel as possible. Figure 4b shows the psychometric functions for a second set of squares, consisting of the same two endpoints but with intermediate sizes that are more closely spaced and presented with greater relative frequency near the midrange. Since the abscissa for Fig. 4b was scaled from the data of Fig. 4a, the parallelism of the empirical plot in Fig. 4b is a testimonial to the independence of discriminability scaling from frequency effects.

Although the slope of the psychometric function (i.e., the conventional measure of discriminability) is independent of the relative spacing and frequency of the stimuli, the intercept shifts systematically: Differences between successive limens tend to be smaller in those portions of the scale where stimuli are packed more closely. Discriminability scaling does not account for these shifts in the locations of the limens, nor is that approach concerned with contextual shifts in the mean ratings of particular stimuli. However, these effects of context can be explained using the simple algebraic model to be described next.

IV. A RANGE–FREQUENCY MODEL

Range and frequency effects have been incorporated into contextual models that predict the category ratings of each of the stimuli presented for judgment (Parducci, 1965; Parducci & Perrett, 1971). In the simplest range–frequency model, R_i, the *range value* of the ith stimulus, is the hypothetical rating that stimulus would have elicited if there were no frequency effects. The range value is assumed to depend solely upon the physical relationship between stimulus i and the two end stimuli. The range value can be inferred from empirical data obtained from a condition in which the ith stimulus has been presented with another set of stimuli having the same endpoints. The inference is based upon the model so that scaling of the stimuli is a by-product of the model's description of contextual effects.

The *frequency value* F_i is what the mean rating of the ith stimulus would have been if each category had been assigned to some fixed proportion of the stimulus presentations. In the simplest model, frequency values are calculated under the assumption that different categories are used with equal frequency, maintaining a perfectly ordinal scale. For example, the lower abscissa of Fig. 3 shows the log–physical values for nine stimuli presented with equal frequency and judged with category ratings from 1 to 9. The solid squares show the corresponding frequency values which, in this case, are simply the stimulus ranks.

The set whose log–physical values are marked off along the upper abscissa is composed of stimuli presented with the varying frequencies shown at the top of Fig. 3, i.e., with the lower stimulus values presented more frequently. Dividing the total number of presentations, 90, by the number of categories, 9, yields 10 presentations per category. The frequency values can be calculated a priori by counting off presentations into successive categories of 10 and averaging the category ratings for each stimulus. For example, since the lowest value is presented 30 times, it must be divided equally between the three lowest ratings, 1, 2, and 3, yielding a mean frequency value of 2.0 (the leftmost of the open squares). Since the frequencies for the four highest values total to 10, all four are assigned the highest possible frequency value, 9.0. Although the two sets have the same endpoints, the frequency values for the stimulus at the log-midrange differ by three-fourths the possible range of ratings.

The combined effect of range and frequency upon the judgment of the ith stimulus, J_i, is described by the model as the mean of the associated range and frequency values:

$$J_i = (R_i + F_i)/2. \tag{1}$$

This is illustrated in Fig. 3, where each of the "empirical" ratings is located halfway between its associated range and frequency values. Since frequency values are calculated without reference to data, ratings from one set can be used to infer the range function common to both sets. Alternatively, a best-fitting range function can be calculated for values inferred from ratings of a number of different sets with the same endpoints. For simplicity of illustration, the range values in Fig. 3 fall on the solid line that describes a linear relationship to the log–physical values, matching the end categories to the end stimuli. Of course, this would not be the typical case, since the psychological range may either be narrower or broader than the actual range of physical values presented for judgment. However, the model assumes that all sets of stimuli sharing common endpoints and procedures for presentation have the same range function.

A. Tests of the Model

In the most extensive of the experimental tests of contextual models (Parducci & Perrett, 1971), different groups of subjects rated 34 different sets of squares whose frequency distributions of sizes represented different ranges, different degrees of either negative or positive skewing, and also U-shaped, normal, and other, more irregular frequency distributions of size. The sets were formed by varying the spacing, the relative frequency of presentation, or both spacing and frequency. Some subjects were instructed to establish a six-category scale, others to use nine categories. As implied by the model, the form of the mean judgment function is independent of the number of categories. The general differences in form between judgment functions for the different sets are successfully predicted by the model. These differences are qualitatively inconsistent with both the strict-range and the adaptation-level approaches. In statistical analyses of the ratings of test stimuli common to different sets with the same endpoints, the simple range–frequency model of Eq. (1) accounts for some 80% of the variance associated with contextual differences in spacing and frequency. This simple model, which assumes perfect discriminability for the computation of frequency values and also equal weighting of range and frequency values, describes the data nearly as well as more general range–frequency models that leave these parameters free to vary.

To the degree that the model fits the data, the inferred range values represent a context-free scaling of the stimuli. A stimulus has the same range value in different contextual sets with the same endpoints, regardless of variations in the spacing or frequencies of the other stimuli. However, it is not yet clear whether the range values have any psychological significance beyond their role in testing the model; insofar as the scale values inferred from this model of judgment correspond to those obtained when applying models of other psychological processes to other tasks with the same stimuli, these common values might acquire a more general status as a psychological scale (cf. Chapter 8 by Anderson).

B. Further Implications

The range–frequency model entails a trading relationship between the effects of differences in the spacing or frequencies of the stimuli. Using the model as a basis for selecting stimulus values, sets have been constructed whose positively skewed spacing (i.e., lower values more closely spaced) are balanced by negatively skewed frequencies (upper values presented more frequently) so that the empirical category-rating function is almost identical to that of a rectangular set with equal spacing and frequencies (Parducci & Perrett, 1971). As predicted by the model, contextual effects are greater when both spacing and frequency vary in the same direction than when either is varied separately.

Although the judgment function is lower for negatively skewed sets, the grand mean of all the ratings is higher. This is illustrated in Fig. 3. The majority of the ratings of the negatively skewed set are from the upper half of the scale, and the mean of all the ratings is almost 6.0. This is a quarter of the range higher than the overall mean rating (4.0) for the positively skewed set. The overall mean rarely corresponds to the center of the scale, particularly when the distributions are skewed; nor are the categories actually used with equal frequency. As entailed by the model, the relative frequency of higher categories (and hence the grand mean of all the ratings) is increased by negative skewing of the frequency distribution of the stimuli presented for judgment.

C. Sequential Effects

In tests of the range–frequency model, stimuli are presented for repeated judgments in long, random sequences. Other research demonstrates that the rating of particular presentations varies *directly* with the values of the two immediately preceding stimuli and *inversely* with the values of stimuli further back in the sequence (Ward & Lockhead, 1971); however, these trial-by-trial effects are small in comparison with the overall range and frequency effects. As suggested by the range–frequency approach, big trial-to-trial shifts in scale occur only for the initial presentations or when the range is suddenly extended. Although extension of the range, as by adding higher values of the stimuli at later points in the sequence, produces an immediate readjustment of the scale, restriction of the range does not have the complementary effect (Parducci, 1956). The missing values continue to define the effective endpoints of the stimulus context. This seems consistent with the independence of range and frequency effects postulated by the range–frequency model.

D. Information Integration

Unlike the experiments in which a separate rating is obtained for each successive stimulus in the sequence, everyday judgments often represent an integrated impression of a sequence or set of events (cf. Chapter 8 by Anderson). Once the impression of a set is formed, its overt rating appears to depend upon its place in a distribution of similar sets. The effect of this between-set context appears consistent with the range frequency model described here for single stimuli (Parducci, Thaler, & Anderson, 1968). To the degree that changes in context produce nonlinear shifts in judgment, as in Fig. 3, the distribution constituting the context between sets will affect the outcome of the usual tests of integration models (see Birnbaum, Parducci, & Gifford, 1971, Expt. V).

V. COMMENTS

Controversy about the psychological significance of the kinds of contextual effects described by the range–frequency model raises the question of whether they are "truly perceptual" or "merely semantic." Such terms usually carry vague, introspective meanings that are not defined with respect to particular models of judgment. There has been a general disposition to label range–frequency effects "semantic" insofar as they can be overcome by changing the judgment task. For example, although a particular stimulus in the upper set of Fig. 3 receives the same rating as a much greater stimulus in the lower set, subjects exposed to both sets might be able to report at least the direction of this difference. The sets then assume the character of large mice and small elephants. However, the point of using psychophysical stimuli to study contextual effects is to establish a world inhabited *only* by mice—or only by elephants—where there is no opportunity for comparison. Indeed, the attraction of psychophysical stimuli is that the presented values represent the entire context for judgment. Application to a practical situation must consequently be concerned with the entire context relevant to that situation.

Category ratings, analogous to the type of psychophysical judgment emphasized in this review, provide the dependent variable for a great portion of psychological research, with different verbal categories representative of everyday evaluative judgments of degree of satisfaction, favorableness, approval, etc. Such ratings are presumably less dependent upon the immediate context and more dependent upon the grander contexts of past experience. For example, it is usually assumed that the psychotherapist's scale for assessing a patient's adjustment is stabilized by clinical experience with many patients. However, the evaluation would also depend upon the special context established by his experience with the particular patient. Just as the experimental subject rates the comparison weight *heavier* following a lighter interpolated weight, the therapist may mistakenly rate the patient *much improved* when the latter has simply returned to his initial level of maladjustment following a period of even poorer adjustment.

It would be difficult to identify the range and frequency values of the events with which everyday ratings are concerned. However, psychophysical research alerts us to the likelihood of contextual effects wherever ratings are made. The pervasiveness of range and frequency effects in those situations in which the effective context is under experimental control suggests that these effects are characteristic of the basic relativism of judgment and thus fundamental to the study of psychology.

References

Bieri, J., Atkins, A. L., Briar, S., Leaman, R. L., Miller, H., & Tripodi, T. *Clinical and social judgment.* New York: Wiley, 1966.

Birnbaum, M. H., Parducci, A., & Gifford, R. K. Contextual effects in information integration. *Journal of Experimental Psychology,* 1971, **88**, 158–170.

Brickman, P., & Campbell, D. T. Hedonic relativism and planning the good society. In M. H. Appley (Ed.), *Adaptation-level theory: A symposium.* New York: Academic Press, 1971.

Bock, R. D., & Jones, L. V. *The measurement and prediction of judgment and choice.* San Francisco: Holden-Day, 1968.

Braida, L. D., & Durlach, N. I. Intensity perception. II. Resolution in one interval paradigms. *Journal of the Acoustical Society of America,* 1972, **51**, 483–495.

Di Lollo, V., & Kirkham, R. Judgmental contrast effects in relation to range of stimulus values. *Journal of Experimental Psychology,* 1969, **81**, 421–427.

Eriksen, C. W., & Hake, H. W. Anchor effects in absolute judgments. *Journal of Experimental Psychology,* 1957, **53**, 132–138.

Garner, W. R. Context effects and the validity of loudness scales. *Journal of Experimental Psychology,* 1954, **48**, 218–224.

Guilford, J. P. *Psychometric methods.* New York: McGraw-Hill, 1954.

Helson, H. *Adaptation-level theory: An experimental and systematic approach to behavior.* New York: Harper & Row, 1964.

Hollingworth, H. L. The inaccuracy of movement. *Archives of Psychology,* 1909, No. 13.

Johnson, D. M. *A systematic introduction to the psychology of thinking.* New York: Harper & Row, 1972.

Johnson, D. M., & Mullally, C. R. Correlation-and-regression model for category judgments. *Psychological Review,* 1969, **76**, 205–215.

Krantz, D. L., & Campbell, D. T. Separating perceptual and linguistic effects of context shifts upon absolute judgments. *Journal of Experimental Psychology,* 1961, **62**, 35–42.

Parducci, A. Direction of shift in the judgment of single stimuli. *Journal of Experimental Psychology*, 1956, **51**, 169–178.

Parducci, A. Range-frequency compromise in judgment. *Psychological Monographs*, 1963, **77**(2, Whole No. 565).

Parducci, A. Category judgment: A range-frequency model. *Psychological Review*, 1965, **72**, 407–418.

Parducci, A. The relativism of absolute judgments. *Scientific American*, 1968, **219**, 84–90.

Parducci, A., & Haugen, R. The frequency principle for comparative judgments. *Perception and Psychophysics*, 1967, **2**, 81–82.

Parducci, A., & Marshall, L. M. Assimilation vs. contrast in the anchoring of perceptual judgments of weight. *Journal of Experimental Psychology*, 1962, **63**, 426–437.

Parducci, A., Perrett, D. S., & Marsh, H. W. Assimilation and contrast as range-frequency effects of anchors. *Journal of Experimental Psychology*, 1969, **81**, 281–288.

Parducci, A., & Perrett, L. F. Category rating scales: Effects of relative spacing and frequency of stimulus values. *Journal of Experimental Psychology Monograph*, 1971, **89**, 427–452.

Parducci, A., & Sandusky, A. J. Limits on the applicability of signal detection theories. *Perception and Psychophysics*, 1970, **7**, 63–64.

Parducci, A., Thaler, H., & Anderson, N. H. Stimulus averaging and the context for judgment. *Perception and Psychophysics*, 1968, **3**, 145–150.

Pollack, I. The information in elementary auditory displays. II. *Journal of the Acoustical Society of America*, 1953, **25**, 765–769.

Poulton, E. C. The new psychophysics: Six models for magnitude estimation. *Psychological Bulletin*, 1968, **69**, 1–19.

Sarris, V. Adaptation-level theory: Two critical experiments on Helson's weighted average model. *American Journal of Psychology*, 1967, **80**, 331–355.

Sherif, M., Taub, D., & Hovland, C. I. Assimilation and contrast effects of anchoring stimuli on judgments. *Journal of Experimental Psychology*, 1958, **55**, 150–155.

Stevens, S. S. Adaptation-level vs. the relativity of judgment. *American Journal of Psychology*, 1958, **71**, 633–646.

Stevens, S. S., & Galanter, E. H. Ratio scales and category scales for a dozen perceptual continua. *Journal of Experimental Psychology*, 1957, **54**, 377–411.

Tabachnick, B. J. *Contextual effects in discriminability scaling*. Ph.D. Dissertation, University of California, Los Angeles, 1971.

Teghtsoonian, R. On the exponents in Stevens' law and the constant in Ekman's law. *Psychological Review*, 1971, **78**, 71–80.

Volkmann, J. Scales of judgment and their implications for social psychology. In J. H. Rohrer & M. Sherif (Eds.), *Social psychology at the crossroads*. New York: Harper, 1951.

Ward, L. M., & Lockhead, G. R. Response system processes in absolute judgment. *Perception and Psychophysics*, 1971, **9**, 73–78.

Chapter 6

PERSONALITY AND SOCIAL EFFECTS IN JUDGMENT*

HARRY S. UPSHAW

I. INTRODUCTION

According to Stevens (1966), the essence of judgment is the establishment of a correspondence between a stimulus domain and a response domain. This view of judgment implies an interest in variables representing stimulus properties, response properties, and the processes whereby the judge conjoins stimulus and response. Most psychophysical research deals explicitly with these variables. Most of the work on personality and social effects in judgment could be analyzed in terms of these variables, but the distinguishing characteristic of that subarea of the judgmental literature to which the present chapter is devoted is a concern for the social context of judgment. A judgment is a communication, and as such, it is relevant to consider the message it conveys, the stimulus to which it refers, characteristics of the source (the judge), and characteristics of the recipient. The concept of judgment as communication invites a functional approach that

* The preparation of this chapter was supported by Grant No. 2303 from the National Science Foundation. Helpful comments by Thomas Ostrom on an earlier draft are gratefully acknowledged.

is more traditional in research on personality and social effects in judgment than in psychophysical research.

There is a specialty within personality and social psychology that has come to be known as *social judgment*. As presently constituted, this specialty concentrates on the application of psychophysical principles as explanations of social phenomena. The potential scope of social judgment, however, is considerably broader. There are many variables in the literature of personality and social psychology with obvious judgmental relevance, but which are not commonly analyzed in judgmental terms. This chapter describes several problem areas relating to social functions of judgment. In some cases the terms of the present discussion are not conventional, whereas in others, especially those encompassed by the social judgment specialty, the discussions here and in the original literature are more obviously compatible. The primary aims of the chapter are to suggest areas of contact between the psychology of judgment and social psychology, to define the judgmental issues in these areas and to convey in general terms the current state of fact and thought about those issues. By this approach it is hoped that new research leads may be formulated to the benefit of both of the intersecting fields of psychology.

II. SOCIAL FUNCTIONS OF JUDGMENT

Recognition that judgment normally occurs within the context of social interaction suggests that the interactional goals of the judge serve as a determinant of his behavoir. That is, the relationship between the judge and his audience is likely to affect the nature of the judgment that he makes. Three possible relationships come immediately to mind. First, the recipient may be nothing more than the witness to the judge's self-expression. Second, he may acquire information from the judge about an object of common concern. Third, he may be the target of the judge's attempt to persuade him to adopt a point of view about the referent stimulus. The fact that self-expression, stimulus description, and persuasion can be distinguished as three social functions of judgment does not imply that each act of judgment fulfills one, and only one, function. It is probably true that the typical act of social judgment fulfills all these functions to some degree, for the reason that most social encounters are likely to engage all three interactional goals to some degree.

Although social functions are plausible determinants of judgment, they have not apparently been studied as such. For that reason, this review does not describe a systematic literature on the effect of social purpose on judgment. Instead, what must be described is a set of three more-or-less separate traditions that have yet to be integrated effectively.

A. Self-Expression

The notion of judgment as the matching of a stimulus domain to a response domain imposes virtually no limit upon the types of stimuli that may be judged nor upon the kinds of behavior that may be employed as responses. The literature in cross-modal psychophysics documents the principle that there are two basic ingredients of judgment: a stimulus quantity that is presented for judgment, and any other quantity over which the subject has control to serve as a response language. Judgmental responses may be made with the aid of mechanical devices, but they may also be unaided behaviors, such as verbal utterances and facial or other bodily movements. Any behavioral dimension that becomes correlated with a stimulus dimension might profitably be analyzed in terms of judgmental principles. Thus, the gestures, postural changes, verbalizations, and other activities associated with emotional states are, by this concept, interpretable as judgments provided only that they correspond systematically to referent stimuli.

Under the hypothesis that nonverbal behaviors are more valid indices of referent private states than are deliberately better-controlled verbal behaviors, investigators who are particularly interested in psychotherapeutic processes are building an impressive literature on self-expressive behaviors in the clinical context (see Ekman & Friesen, 1968, for a recent survey). Many of these behaviors qualify under the terms of the present discussion as judgments. At issue in much of this type of research are the determinants of a subject's accuracy in estimating on the basis of behavioral cues the feelings or traits of a target person. Thus, in many studies the self-expressive judgments of one group of persons serve as stimuli to be described in the judgments of another group. To date relatively greater attention has been devoted to understanding the judgmental activities of the second group than the first. However, increasing attention has been paid in recent years to the psychological processes underlying nonverbal communication and self-expression (Duncan, 1969; Exline & Winters, 1965; Meltzer, Morris, & Hayes, 1971).

An approach to communication that promises to yield insight and data to the area of self-expressive judgment is that represented by social psychologists who, with roots both in psychology and sociology, study the encounters among people in terms of more-or-less skilled performances by the various participants. See Argyle and Kendon (1967) for a review of the literature in this area. The social psychologist views people as attempting to control their social encounters (see Goffman, 1955, 1959). The type of behavior that is designated here as self-expressive judgment is thought to intrude involuntarily upon the person's otherwise managed social performance, arising when there is a disruption in the social interaction.

The literature dealing with self-expressive judgments contains evidence that certain presumed expressive behaviors provide reliable interpretive cues for others to use, and it suggests some antecedents of self-expressive behavior. A judgmental approach to the area would hopefully add to existing knowledge something about the process of encoding feelings into expressive behaviors. It might illuminate questions such as how a judge selects and controls a particular behavioral dimension, and whether value associated with a particular behavioral dimension affects its use as a judgmental language.

B. Stimulus Descriptions: The Detection and Identification of Social Stimuli

It is probable that most communication among people concerns attributes of their environment. The stimulus-descriptive judgments that comprise so much of normal communication are highly similar to the judgments that psychophysicists study. In a very readable essay Galanter (1962) distinguished four experimental tasks in contemporary psychophysics: stimulus detection, recognition (or identification), discrimination, and scaling. Galanter's distinctions are drawn in terms of problems that the judge attempts to solve: The detection problem is that of determining whether a signal exists within the noisy background; the recognition or identification problem is that of determining which of a set of alternative signals is present, assuming it is known that some signal exists; the discrimination problem is that of determining whether one stimulus magnitude is subjectively different from another; and the scaling problem is that of determining the subjective magnitude of particular stimuli.

Psychophysicists usually study detection and identification by presenting relatively simple stimuli to subjects who are instructed to decide on each trial whether a particular stimulus was displayed or which of several alternative stimuli was displayed. In a major type of social psychological study involving detection and identification the subject is asked to decide on the basis of photographs which of a set of persons belongs to a particular ethnic group. In another line of social psychological research subjects are asked to detect or identify emotional or motivational states in themselves or in others following manipulations of social context.

1. ETHNIC GROUP IDENTIFICATION

A principal concern in the literature on ethnic identification has been the relationship between the accuracy of a judge and his attitudes or personality traits. The two primary issues in this line of research have been: (1) whether a reliable relationship exists between a judge's attitude and his judgments of ethnic membership, and (2) if there is such a relationship, whether it is due to a perceptual or a response process. There is strong evidence that attitude is related to the frequency of labeling stimulus persons as members of the particular ethnic group. Prejudiced judges tend to identify group members correctly (G. W. Allport & Kramer, 1946; Lindzey & Rogolsky, 1950), but they also tend more often than "nonprejudiced" judges to ascribe membership to nonmembers (Elliott & Wittenberg, 1955; Scodel & Austrin, 1957). Research in which response biases have been controlled seems to indicate that prejudiced subjects are, in fact, more sensitive judges (Dorfman, Keeve, & Saslow, 1971; Pulos & Spilka, 1961; Scodel & Austrin, 1957). Although the differences in judgmental performances between prejudiced and non prejudiced subjects in these studies have been small, they suggest that prejudice is related both to accuracy of identification and to a tendency to identify falsely people as members of the rejected "out-group." This conclusion has obvious relevance to social issues, but its implication for the psychology of judgment is not clear. It is difficult to establish a basis for generalizing the results of these studies because the subjects are specially selected.

2. LABELING EMOTIONS AND DRIVES IN SELF AND OTHERS

An important current area of study relates the social context in which an emotion or drive state is experienced to the judge's identification of the emotion or drive. In most of this research, the dependent variables have been behavioral, with implicit judgments mediating the relationship between independent and dependent variables. The two guiding principles in the area have been the following: (1) The behavioral manifestations of an emotional or motivational state depend in part upon judgments by the subject concerning the cause and nature (identification) of the state. (2) The subject's judgments concerning such states depend jointly upon cues associated with internal physiological processes and external cues deriving from the environment (see, Schachter, 1964, 1971). Several generalizations relative to the issues of this chapter seem to be supported by the accumulated research in the area.

(1) Social cues may be critical in determining the nature of the subject's ultimate identification of an otherwise ambiguous state of arousal (Schachter & Singer, 1962).

(2) Environmental cues are most effective in determining the subject's identification of an arousal state if they are consistent with internal cues (Schachter & Wheeler, 1962), and to the extent that they provide a plausible explanation of the internal state.

(3) There are individual differences in sensitivity to internal and ex-

ternal determinants of at least one motivational state—hunger (Nisbett, 1968; Schachter, Goldman, & Gordon, 1968; Goldman, Jaffa, & Schachter 1968; Stunkard & Koch, 1964)—and these differences appear to refer to general environmental sensitivity, not just to hunger cues (Schachter, 1971).

C. Stimulus Descriptions: The Discrimination and Scaling of Social Stimuli

In the typical psychophysical study involving discrimination and scaling the judge is asked to assess the comparative or absolute sensory impact of a set of stimuli that differ according to a single physical dimension. The equivalent study in social psychology is likely to require that the judge evaluate stimuli according to a subjective attribute. Sometimes the focal attribute is, in principle, idiosyncratic, such as the case when the subject reports his preferences among stimuli. At other times the attribute is defined consensually, as in studies in which subjects are asked to determine how favorable or unfavorable toward some object a stated opinion is. In almost all cases, however, the attribute in terms of which social stimuli are judged is less objectively defined than in psychophysical research. There have been discussions of the implications of this difference in the nature of the judgmental continuum in sensory and social studies involving discrimination and scaling (e.g., M. Sherif & Hovland, 1961; Stevens, 1958). However, there appear to be no experimental data bearing on the question of whether the variable of objectivity–subjectivity with respect to the judgmental continuum has consequences for any measurable judgmental behavior. In part, this deficiency in the literature may be due to the fact that the traditional dependent variables that are examined in judgmental research are not equally appropriate for studying sensory and social processes. The issues of original concern in the two areas are different: Psychophysics began as the study of the sensitivity of the human organism, and social judgment was originally concerned with the distortions of judgments that are traceable to social factors. Understandably the dependent variables that developed in psychophysics referred to comparisons of a physical with a judgmental continuum (e.g., category limens and a mathematically stated psychophysical function), whereas those that developed in social psychology referred to comparisons among individuals or groups of people.

Working independently Upshaw (1969) and Johnson and Mullally (1969) described similar approaches to judgment, which imply a distinctive set of dependent variables that appear to be equally appropriate for psychophysics and social judgment. Theirs is a response system involving the comparison of two distributions in terms of statistics appropriate to distributional comparisons. In some cases a distribution of stimuli may be compared to a distribution of judgments, and in others the distribution of judgments of two subjects or groups of subjects may be compared. The information to be obtained from such an analysis refers to differential level and spread of the distributions, the degree of correlation within the two distributions, and information about the stability of these measures over judgmental trials (where appropriate). Although they have apparently not been used for that purpose, these variables appear to be appropriate for the study of the influence on judgments of the relative subjectivity–objectivity of the stimulus dimension.

1. ATTRIBUTION OF TRAITS AND DISPOSITIONAL STATES TO PERSONS

In attributing a more-or-less permanent trait or temporary dispositional state to someone, a person attains at least the illusion of understanding a part of the other person's specific behaviors. With this understanding, even if it is illusory, comes an assumption that future behavior is predictable. Presumably it is the failure of predictions that leads the subject to revise his attributional judgments if, in fact, he does revise them. It is usual in discussions of person perception to assume that the judge seeks only a plausible explanation of the target's behavior, and that he revises his attributional judgments until he finds a sufficient set (cf., Heider, 1958; Jones & Davis, 1965; Kelley, 1967).

a. STEREOTYPES. A short-cut in the cognitive labors of judging the causes of the behavior of others is the use of stereotypes. Walter Lippmann (1922) introduced the concept of stereotype, defining it as a culturally determined, simplified perception of a complex stimulus. The most frequently studied class of stereotypes has been that by which the subject attributes a single set of traits to all members of an ethnic group. Much of the research effort dealing with ethnic stereotypes has been devoted to determining the content of particular stereotypes and assessing the extent of agreement with given stereotypes by members of specific populations. Some attention has been given to the age at which particular stereotypes are first noticed, to the stability of stereotypes over time, and to the effects of familiarity with the target group on the endorsement of a stereotype. Brigham (1971) has reviewed the literature on these and other aspects of ethnic stereotypes.

The ethnic stereotype is a special form of judgment. However, principles of judgment formulated in the psychophysics laboratory do not appear to facilitate understanding of the stereotyping process, nor do concepts derived from research on stereotypes appear to hold great promise for psychophysics. This seeming irrelevance suggests a gap in the general psychology of judgment. Traditionally, judgment studies involve an experimental task of evaluating specific stimuli in terms of attributes specified by the investigator. That paradigm offers no insight into the selection of the object of judgment or into the selection of those attributes in terms of which judgments are made. There is no obvious reason why these facets of human judgment cannot be brought into the laboratory. In view of the fact that a defining characteristic of an ethnic stereotype is the selection of a group rather than an individual as the object of judgment, and that stereotypes involve selection among alternative traits as judgmental dimensions, perhaps the area of ethnic stereotyping can be profitably integrated with an expanded psychology of judgment. No signs of activity in this direction are visible, however, in the current literature.

b. IMPRESSION FORMATION. A major research problem concerning stereotypes has been that of determining the causal relationship between a judge's attitude toward a group and the content of the stereotypes he endorses about that group. It has often been assumed that a hostile attitude toward a group leads to the stereotyped ascription of socially undesirable traits to members of the group. Another problem area in social psychology proceeds from the inverse of the same relationship; that is, that the relative desirability of the traits attributed to a person determines how favorably another person evaluates him initially.

The basic paradigm for research on impression formation is due to Asch (1946). It entails the presentation of a set of trait adjectives that are attributed to a person with the requirement that the subject respond by indicating his impression of the person. The results of studies based upon this paradigm clearly support the notion that the attitude of a judge toward a target person is predictable from the social desirability of the traits attributed to him. The major issues in this line of research concern the process by which the prediction is made possible.

Subjects in one of Asch's original experiments were asked to describe in their own words and by choosing between paired adjectives a person with the following attributes: intelligent, skillful, industrious, determined, practical, cautious. In one experimental group the attribute *warm* was included, whereas in the countercondition the attribute list included *cold*. The substitution of cold for warm in the list of traits greatly influenced the impressions reported by subjects. The associated traits that comprised the impressions were generally much more favorable in the *warm* than in the *cold* condition. Asch concluded from these and similar data that impression formation follows a Gestalt principle whereby the target person's traits are integrated to form a unitary concept. He claimed indirect support for the hypothesis that the individual traits change their meanings when placed in combinations, assuming meanings that correspond to the emerging unitary impression.

More recent studies of impression formation have typically involved variations in properties of the list of traits ascribed to the focal person, with the experimental task of describing the impression by means of rating scales. From the accumulated research, three kinds of evidence support the meaning-change hypothesis: (*1*) introspection by subjects, (*2*) the primacy effect, and (*3*) a positive context effect. Introspecting about the experimental task subjects have reported greater ease when it is known at the outset that a set of traits all describe a single individual, as opposed to learning this fact after the presentation of all traits (Asch, 1946). A primacy effect has been demonstrated when the trait adjectives are presented serially (Asch, 1946; Anderson, 1965; Anderson & Barrios, 1961). The primacy effect is represented in results that show a more favorable impression when traits are in the desirable–undesirable order than when they are presented in the reverse order. The meaning-change hypothesis assumes a process underlying the primacy effect whereby the emerging unitary impression causes the subject to select special meanings of the later traits that would possibly not have been selected if they had been presented first. The third kind of evidence supporting the meaning-change hypothesis, a positive context effect, has been observed when the subject was instructed to rate the desirability of a component trait from the set on the basis of which the impression was made. Anderson (1966, 1971), Anderson and Lampel (1965), Kaplan (1971), Wyer and Dermer (1968), and Wyer and Watson (1969) have all reported a displacement of the desirability rating of a component trait *toward* the average value of the set, suggesting some kind of assimilation to the composite. The displacement was not observed, however, when the traits were rated singly and without any emphasis by the investigators upon the set of which they were part (Anderson, 1971; Anderson & Lampel, 1965; Wyer & Dermer, 1968).

A major alternative to the meaning-change hypothesis in impression formation is derivable from Anderson's (1968) information integration theory. According to that theory the judgment of how likable one expects a person to be is a weighted average of the impression that was held prior to receipt of the information (measured on a scale of likableness) and the likableness values of the traits attributed to him. Support for the information integration explanation has generally been claimed on the basis of confirmation of precise experimental predictions regarding primacy and context effects. The meaning-change interpretation of the primacy effect assumes that traits presented later in a list acquire special meanings that facilitate the development of a single, unitary impression. The information integration interpretation, on the other hand, assumes that the later traits are given smaller weights. According to the latter formulation any experimental device for increasing the weights assigned to traits that appear late in the list would be expected to diminish the primacy effect. Thus, the information integration theory is supported by Anderson and Hubert (1963) who eliminated primacy by having subjects recall all traits in the set prior to rating their impressions, and by Stewart (1965) who eliminated primacy by having subjects report their developing impressions after each trait adjective was presented. Further support for the theory comes from a detailed analysis of context effects in terms of a model suggested by Anderson (1966). This model specifies that the effective value of a trait on the likeability scale is a weighted average of its context-free value and the value of the composite of which it is part. From this formulation Anderson (1971) and Kaplan (1971) predicted that the magnitude of context effects depends upon the number of traits in the set. The prediction was confirmed in both studies. The meaning-change hypothesis apparently cannot account for these results.

Anderson's approach to context effects in impression formation is clearly applicable to the judgment of a component in any stimulus set, provided that the set has a single value on the same scale as the component. It is interesting to note that the predicted effect is a displacement toward rather than away from the context stimuli, in apparent contradiction to most theories of context effects, which predict contrast effects. The fact that positive context effects (assimilation) have been reliably reported in the impression-formation literature but not in many other judgmental situations provides a challenge to judgment theory.

A very large literature on impression formation has accumulated, most of which has been shaped by Asch's experimental paradigm and directed to the dependent variable of rated likableness based upon a set of trait adjectives. Jones and Goethals (1972) have pointed out that this paradigm does not encompass many features of social situations in which impression formation is a meaningful topic of study. Specifically, they noted that some situations imply that successive items of information are all simultaneously valid, as, for example, when the person who forms an impression witnesses some unfolding behavioral episode involving the target person. Other situations, however, imply that later information effectively supplants what was received earlier, as, for example, when the subject is led to believe that he has witnessed a change in the characteristics of the target person. In addition to situational factors there are variables relating to the past history and present state of the person who forms an impression that Jones and Goethals believe to have been left out of research on impression formation.

Examples are variables such as the amount of prior experience with processing information about the target person and the subject's commitment to a preliminary impression.

The critique by Jones and Goethals may be viewed as a plea to expand the scope of inquiry in the area of impression formation to examine additional independent variables. An equivalent plea could be made for the examination of additional dependent variables and for consideration of the way in which people organize fairly complex impressions based upon beliefs concerning component traits. Anderson (1974) has presented impressive evidence that his information integration theory can account for the attribution of virtually any type of trait to a target person, and that it is in no sense limited to the study of simple impressions of varying favorability. The organization of a set of traits into a coherent impression of the target person is beginning to receive rigorous attention (see, for example, Rosenberg & Sedlak, 1972; Wyer, 1973).

c. CAUSAL ATTRIBUTIONS. The special topic of impression formation illustrates a currently popular personality and social psychology conception of man as a seeker and integrator of information. The notion that receipt of information is a recurring need in life has inspired a literature on observational learning and imitation (Bandura & Walters, 1963; Miller & Dollard, 1941), on the consequences of being dependent upon another for needed information (Jones & Gerard, 1967; Kelley & Thibaut, 1969), and on the instigation to compare oneself with others (Festinger, 1954; Latane, 1966). Concern with information processes has also been manifested by interest in the phenomenology of the human experimental subject, and in the more general questions regarding judged causes of observed behavior.

In the personality area, interest has focused on a trait referring to the perceived locus of control over reinforcement. At one extreme the subject may perceive that he himself has primary responsibility for the rewards and punishments that he receives (internal control), and at the other extreme he may perceive that others have that responsibility (external control). The trait, which derives from Rotter's (1954) learning theory, is conceived as a recurring assessment of the extent of one's own power over his outcomes in relation to the power of others. That assessment is assumed to result from a learned, generalized expectancy (Rotter, 1966), and it is assumed to mediate various types of behaviors. The general picture of the "internal-control" person is that of a confident, task-oriented, active individual who credits himself for his successes and blames himself for his failures. By contrast the "external-control" person is pictured as less confident, more hedonistically oriented, and passive, with a tendency to hold external agents responsible for both good and bad outcomes (Davis

& Phares, 1967; Lefcourt, 1966, 1972; Phares, Ritchie, & Davis, 1968; Phares, Wilson, & Klyver, 1971; Rotter, 1966; Rotter, Seeman, & Liverant, 1962).

There are at least two points of contact between the psychology of judgment and work on the locus of perceived control, neither of which has been explored. One is at the theoretical underpinnings of the area, in the conception of the trait as a learned, generalized expectancy, and the other is higher in the structure at the point of attributing responsibility for particular outcomes. It is a common notion in judgment theories that standards of judgment are expectancies. Thus, Parducci (1968), Upshaw (1965, 1969b,c, 1970), and Volkmann (1951), all of whom invoke a stimulus-range principle as central to their systems, more-or-less explicitly relate the effective range to the judge's expectations concerning the stimuli he will experience. Thibaut and Kelley (1959), who invoke a concept of comparison level to define affective neutrality, conceive of that level as an expectancy concerning the quality of outcomes. Helson (1964) conceives of the adaptation level as determined by the integration of immediate experience with remembered (learned, expected?) experience. The expectancy that defines the locus-of-control trait refers to the subject's estimation of how much influence his own activities are likely to have in the determination of his rewards and costs, whereas the expectancies that define judgmental standards refer to more general dimensions. It seems a reasonable hypothesis that the judgmental standards of at least some socially relevant dimensions are affected by expectancies concerning personal power. The identification of those dimensions and the processes by which the hypothesized influence occurs are research questions to be dealt with in the integration of the two theoretical areas.

In recent years, social psychologists have become increasingly interested in the situational determinants of causal judgments, particularly those which attribute causality to persons. The pioneer in this field was Heider (1944, 1958), who formulated basic issues and suggested many insights bearing on those issues. More recently Jones and Davis (1965) and Kelley (1967, 1972) have suggested approaches to the field that lead more directly than Heider's work to testable propositions. The various approaches all seek to account for judgments of the following sort:

> To what extent was a particular action intended by the actor?
> What outcomes were expected by the actor?
> What motives or personality traits led to the actor's intentions?
> How free was the actor to choose his actions?

Heider's approach to the area draws heavily from Gestalt principles as applied to perception. The approaches of Jones and Davis and Kelley may be described as problem-solving approaches. To date, judgmental principles have not been incorporated into any of the systems in a manner that leads to explicit hypotheses. Because the major issues in the area appear to be judgmental in at least some facets, it seems reasonable to anticipate future efforts toward a judgmental analysis of some of the characteristic phenomena.

2. ESTIMATION OF THE ATTITUDES OF OTHERS

For methodological as well as substantive reasons, judgment of the attitudes of others is an area that has received considerable attention by psychologists. The methodological spur was Thurstone's (1928) approach to measurement of attitudes. That approach assigns a scale value to each of a set of opinion statements on the basis of the consensual judgment of a group of subjects concerning the sentiment implied by the statement. Subsequently, other subjects are asked to endorse or reject the scaled items, and they are assigned attitude scores according to the mean scale value of the statements they endorse. As Thurstone noted, the utility of his approach would be impaired if the scale values proved to be critically dependent upon the attitude of the judge who supplies the data for scaling. Many experiments have been conducted to determine how seriously the Thurstone model may be threatened by this source of invalidity (see Upshaw, 1968a). Research on the issue indicates no apparent effect of attitude upon comparative judgments of attitude statements (Kelley, Hovland, Schwartz, & Abelson, 1955), and with absolute judgments, an effect of attitude only upon the central tendency and dispersion of the distribution of judgments (Upshaw 1965). It should be noted that the validity of Thurstone's attitude-measurement procedures requires nothing more stringent than a linear relationship among values assigned by groups of judges. By that criterion the accumulated research on this topic does not seriously threaten the Thurstone model.

The judgment of others' attitudes is a critical dependent variable for several theoretical questions in social psychology. With some risk of superficiality two major theoretical contexts can be distinguished in terms of which the variable has been studied. One is focused on the interaction of the judge with someone else, such as a partner or a propagandist. The other is focused on the judge as an individual. For no apparent reason with the more complex setting the explanatory approaches have tended to assume that observed effects on the dependent variables are perceptual phenomena, whereas with the simpler setting the effects are assumed to be response phenomena.

Two examples of theories that view the judge in an interaction setting are Newcomb's (1956, 1961, 1968) theory of social attraction and

Feather's (1964, 1967) theory of persuasive communication. Both of these approaches are based upon Heider's (1946, 1958) formulation of the "balance principle" which provides that a person (p) is motivated to achieve and retain harmony among three elements: his sentiments regarding the other person (o) with whom he interacts, the relationship of p to a particular object, (X), and the relationship of o to X. According to these theories the attitude attributed to o is determined in part by p's striving for balance.

M. Sherif and his co-workers (Hovland, Harvey, Sherif, 1958; Sherif & Hovland, 1961; C. Sherif, M. Sherif, & Nebergall 1965) have developed an approach to the judgment of the attitudinal position advocated by a propagandist. According to their theory, the person who is the target of persuasion evaluates the position advocated in terms both of its acceptability to him as an expression of his own attitude and its implied affect toward the attitude object. The theory holds that his judgment of implied affect is dependent upon his judgment of personal acceptability. A second phase of the theory relates attitude change (presumably personal acceptability at a later time) to the degree of implied affect that the target person perceived in the advocated position. As with the Newcomb and Feather theories, the Sherif theory apparently assumes perceptual rather than linguistic effects.

Focusing on the judge as an individual, Upshaw (1962, 1964a, 1965, 1969b,c 1970) and Ostrom (Ostrom, 1966; Ostrom & Upshaw, 1970) have developed an approach that concentrates upon the linguistic aspects of judgment. This approach views the basic judgmental process as fitting a response scale, with its origin and unit parameters, to a perceptual continuum. Much of the data that have been collected in this line of research have referred to the estimation of the attitudes of others, although the theory is not restricted to that dependent variable. The judgment of others' attitudes has also been studied from the perspective of other general judgmental theories, such as adaptation-level (e.g., Fehrer, 1952; Segall, 1959; Ward, 1965, 1966) enhancement of contrast (Eiser, 1971) and various personality approaches (e.g., Bieri, Atkins, Briar, Leaman, Miller, & Tripodi, 1966; Larsen, 1971; White, Alter, & Rardin, 1965; White & Harvey, 1965).

From the viewpoint of the general psychology of judgment, research in the area of estimating attitudes appears to offer several potential benefits. The dependent variable is defined with enough precision to provide an opportunity for testing the generality of psychophysical principles. Furthermore, because the variable is easily linked to personality and social psychological theory, it provides an opportunity to broaden the prevailing scope of judgmental approaches to take into account new types of problems.

3. EVALUATION OF INTERACTION OUTCOMES

Central to the Thibaut and Kelley (1959; Kelley & Thibaut, 1969) theory of social groups is the notion that group members individually seek to maximize their outcomes. The theory accounts for social behavior by what is essentially an economic analysis of interaction based upon each individual's judgment of his own utility and his estimate, assuming various contingencies, of the utilities of his partners. The authors have specified certain determinants of utility judgments in addition to the objective values of the outcomes that are judged. These include a personality variable referring to the subject's tendency to weight more heavily either the reward or cost aspects of complex outcomes, the person's estimate of his power to achieve high outcome states and avoid low ones, and the relative salience of good and bad outcomes. Thibaut and Kelley assume that these various determinants of utility judgments operate directly upon the point of affective neutrality, the *comparison level* (CL), and through the CL upon the judgments.

The Thibaut and Kelley theory is rich in leads for understanding several facets of social interaction, and many of these leads have been followed in the literature. Although CL is a central concept in many applications of the theory, it has not, itself, been the target of much research. Unfortunately, what was said of the concept in an earlier, more detailed review still holds:

> As a theory of judgment, comparison level has received very little attention. This is regrettable for it appears to be distinctly different in some of its implications from its acknowledged conceptual parent, adaptation level. These unique features derive from special considerations regarding utility judgments which are of less importance in judgments of stimulus attributes. Because the concept of CL was developed as an adjunct to the theory of social interaction, it offers a valuable potential link between the psychology of judgment, on the one hand, and the traditional social psychological domain, on the other [Upshaw, 1969a, p. 350].

Utility is the dimension in terms of which people evaluate outcomes; and comparison level was formulated to account for utility judgments. Another dimension of judgment in outcome evaluation is equity. Homans (1974) contends that the governing principle in many interactions is the social norm of "distributive justice," which specifies that rewards and costs should be equitably distributed among the participants in the interaction. As each participant applies the norm of distributive justice it is assumed that he makes several judgments, which combine to determine his ultimate judgments of equity.

(1) He estimates, for every participant, including himself, the net balance of rewards and costs that have accrued in the group.

(2) He estimates the investments of each participant.

(3) He forms a subjective ratio of each participant's reward–cost balance to his investments.

(4) He judges the variability of these ratios over participants. The greater the variance of the ratios, the greater the individual's sense of inequity.

More of the research related to questions of judged equity has dealt with the consequences of the judgment than with its antecedents and the process by which it is made. The most general prediction based upon considerations of equity is that dissatisfaction follows in proportion to the judged degree of inequity. In turn, this dissatisfaction is said to provide the motive for many alternative behaviors, the goal of which is the establishment of equity in the group (see, Adams, 1963, 1965; Homans, 1974; Patchen, 1961; Walster Berscheid, & Walster 1973). Among alternative equity-producing behaviors are reevaluations of the rewards, costs, and investments of participants. Because the equity area deeply involves judgmental considerations both at the conceptual and data levels, it appears to be an area in which the collaboration of social and judgmental psychologists would be particularly rewarding. From the exchange the social psychologist could hope to attain greater theoretical precision, and the judgment psychologist could hope to attain knowledge concerning topics such as the motivational determinants of judgment as a behavior (in contrast to alternative behaviors), the combination of elemental judgments to form more complex judgments, and the function of judgment as a determinant of other behaviors.

Festinger's (1957) theory of cognitive dissonance, which applies to many subareas of personality and social psychology, has received a great deal of attention as an approach to the evaluation of outcomes. The theory is a special case of the "cognitive consistency theories" (Abelson, Aronson, McGuire, Newcomb, Rosenberg, & Tannenbaum, 1968). The relationship between the class of theories and the psychology of judgment was discussed in a paper by Upshaw (1968b). The present discussion is limited to the orientation of Festinger's particular formulation to outcome evaluation.

According to dissonance theory an unpleasant state of tension is produced by a person simultaneously holding cognitions (i.e., items of knowledge or belief) that have psychologically opposite implications. Given any particular cognition, all other cognitions are either irrelevant to it, consonant with it, or dissonant. In principle, the amount of dissonance is measurable by the ratio of the number of dissonant cognitions, weighted by their importance, to the number of consonant cognitions, weighted by their importance. The magnitude of the unpleasant tension that provides the motive force in this theory is assumed to be a monotonic function of the amount of cognitive dissonance. It is hypothesized that to reduce the discomfort of the tension, the subject seeks, with minimal effort, a better balance between consonant and dissonant elements. The reduction of dissonance can be achieved by discovering new information that is consonant with the basic cognition, by discrediting dissonant information, or by reevaluating the relative importance of cognitions in the set.

Dissonance theory is particularly relevant to the cognitive functioning of an individual before and after making a choice among alternatives. A comprehensive review of the literature organized by phases of the choice situation has been made by Jones and Gerard (1967). For present purposes it should be noted that, in general, any information suggesting undesirable aspects of the chosen alternative is dissonant with knowledge of the choice that was made. The ensuing process of dissonance reduction presumably produces effects on a number of dependent variables, including outcome evaluation. Thus, Aronson and Mills (1959) reported an overvaluation of group membership by subjects in the high-dissonance condition; Weick (1964) reported differences in effort, accuracy, and ratings of interest-value of the task as a function of dissonance; Brehm (1956) reported a postdecisional change in the difference in judged attractiveness of chosen and rejected alternatives, etc.

As an approach to outcome evaluation dissonance theory seems to offer the same opportunity and challenge to the judgment specialist that is offered by comparison-level theory and the prevailing approaches to equity phenomena. Perhaps more than the other theories, this one focuses upon the important issue of the motivation of judgment.

It has been shown that stimulus context influences judgments of desirability in the same way that it influences judgments of the extent to which stimuli possess particular attributes (e.g., Messick, 1964; Parducci, 1968; Thibaut & Ross, 1969). It is not known, however, whether the influence on judged desirability is mediated by a judgment of stimulus characteristics or whether it is direct. The theoretical positions described in this section seem to imply a direct effect, whereas theories such as adaptation-level theory, which emerged from the psychophysical tradition, seem to imply an indirect effect. This question appears to be an important one, both for personality and social psychology and for the psychology of judgment. It is therefore surprising that it does not appear to have been dealt with explicitly.

4. Interpersonal Attraction and Dependence

A significant variable in personality and social psychology is the degree to which one person likes another. The determinants of attraction are the subject of several theories. Newcomb's theory based upon the balance principle was described in the earlier section on the estimation of the attitudes of others. It holds that people like others who share their attitudes. The same hypothesis has been derived from reinforcement principles by Byrne (1961, 1969). Both theories relate a judgment of attraction to a prior judgment of attitudinal similarity. The possibility of purely judgmental influences on either of the components has apparently not been explored.

Thibaut and Kelley (1959) relate attraction to the evaluation of those outcomes of the person for which he believes the other to be responsible. The evaluation of outcomes, it was noted earlier, is subject to influence by means of context manipulations and from factors other than the objective value of the outcomes. It may be inferred from the position of Thibaut and Kelley that any change in outcome evaluation influences the associated attraction jugments, but there are apparently no data bearing on the question. A related question is whether partner attractiveness can be influenced by manipulating the context of available partners (without varying the associated outcome context), and whether any effects of context upon partner evaluation produce corresponding effects upon the evaluation of outcomes.

Thibaut and Kelley made an important distinction between *attraction* and *dependence*. The former represents the absolute judgment of degree of liking for a partner, whereas the latter represents the comparative judgment between the partner and the best alternative to him. The degree of attraction is assumed to be a function of the distance on the outcome utility scale between the comparison level (CL) and the typical outcome associated with the partner. The degree of dependence, on the other hand, is assumed to be a function of the scale separation between the typical outcome associated with the partner and that which is estimated for the best alternative. The latter comparison point is called the *comparison level for alternatives* (CL alt). It is on the basis of comparison with CL alt that people are predicted to disrupt old relationships and enter into new ones.

Representing dependency judgments as pair comparisons suggests the possibility of "time-order errors" and related phenomena (Guilford, 1954, pp. 305ff.) in decisions to enter or leave groups. Time-order errors are systematic biases in pair comparisons which are related to the order in which members of each pair are presented for judgment. It is known that stimuli interpolated between pair members are strong determinants of the direction and magnitude of the time-order errors. In the present application, it would be interesting to know if judged dependency is related to how the judge orders the pair of partners for judgment; that is whether he compares the present partner to the CL alt or the CL alt to the present partner. Furthermore, the psychophysical analogue suggests that information about other conceivable partners presented to the subject while he is deciding whether to go or stay might function as interpolated stimuli, thereby biasing the final judgment. It is possible that none of these expectations based upon consideration of the time-order error would be observed for dependency judgments. Beebe-Center (1932) observed the phenomenon with affective judgments, but most instances of time-order errors have been with sensory judgments. Because dependency is so clearly nonsensory, its formulation in terms of comparative judgment may provide a critical test of major theories of time-order errors that are based upon sensory considerations (e.g., Helson, 1964; Koehler, 1923; Lauenstein, 1932).

D. Persuasion

Sometimes people render judgments with a persuasive intent as, for example, in flattery or other forms of ingratiation. Persuasive judgments present special methodological problems in that they differ from other types only in intent. A person may thus cloak his real feelings by feigned self-expressive judgments, and he may deliberately convey false information in a setting that is appropriate to stimulus-descriptive judgments. Because persuasive judgments cannot easily be distinguised from other forms of judgment, their analysis requires special experimental and statistical approaches.

The persuasive bias of judgments is likely to vary in degree according to the social demands that are made upon the judge. Under some conditions he may be encouraged to engage in obvious dissimulation, whereas in others he may be required to do nothing more than accommodate himself to an interaction situation by tempering some of his responses. Persuasive judgment has not been studied as a separate topic. However, several subareas within social psychology may be identified according to the degree to which the phenomena under study are assumed to reflect interpersonal pressures upon the subject to misrepresent his beliefs or his sensory data. At the one extreme is research on impression management, including ingratiation (Jones, 1964) and "faking" on personality inventories (e.g., Edwards, 1957). At the other extreme are studies of so-called social facilitation, which are oriented to assessing the effects of performing various behaviors in a group setting as opposed to an individual setting (F. Allport, 1924; Dashiell 1935; Zajonc, 1965). Somewhere between these extremes is research dealing with the social psychology of experiments, in which results of psychological experiments are analyzed as possible artifacts produced by demands upon the subject which are imposed by virtue of his interaction with the experimenter (e.g., McDavid, 1965; Orne, 1962; Riecken, 1962; Rosenberg, 1965).

1. CONFORMITY

Research on conformity represents many of the problems and the promises of research on persuasive judgments. The experimental paradigm for much of the work on this topic was introduced by Asch (1951, 1956). It consists of an apparent psychophysical task to be conducted in a group setting in which all or most of the judgments of other group members are falsified. The subject is, therefore, placed in a conflict situation whereby he must either give stimulus-descriptive judgments at the cost of appearing deviant in the group, or he must conform to the group at the cost of misrepresenting his sensory impressions on a task that has been described to him as requiring valid sensory information. In the original studies based upon this paradigm many subjects chose to conform, most of whom freely confessed during debriefing that they had knowingly falsified their judgments in order to "go along" with the group (Asch, 1956).

There are several good reviews of the voluminous literature on conformity (e.g., Allen, 1965; Jones & Gerard, 1967; Kiesler, 1969). Much of the research deals with the manner in which subjects resolve the conflict created as part of the experimental paradigm. Among the independent variables in these studies are the subject's task competence and his confidence, his personality, the conditions under which the response is made (public versus private, and degree of commitment to the response), the group's size, attractiveness, and unanimity, the discrepancy between the group's response and that which the subject would be expected to make in private, and the ambiguity of the stimuli that are judged.

A recurring question in conformity studies is whether a subject's adoption of the group's judgment represents private acceptance of the judgment or merely public compliance. Protocols of individual subjects indicate that typically they are aware of the conflicting demands made upon them (Asch, 1956; Tuddenham & McBride, 1959). Furthermore, the pattern of results of experimental studies indicates that conformity increases when group pressures are made more salient by requiring public responses, by increasing dependence on or attraction to the group, etc. It seems, therefore, that there is much evidence for interpreting conformity responses as judgments intended to persuade an audience (most often, the experimenter) that the judge privately accepts the norms of the group, while, in fact, his behavior represents only public compliance with those norms.

Based upon principles of dissonance theory (Festinger, 1957), a mechanism by which public compliance in the conformity study situation might lead to private acceptance has been suggested by Kiesler (1969). It assumes that increasing group pressure leads to an increasing willingness to comply and to increasing justification for the act of compliance. Cognitive dissonance is expected following compliance in an amount inversely proportional to its justification. Hence, subjects who are targets of just enough pressure to produce compliance are expected to experience greater dissonance than those who receive more pressure, and who can easily justify their behavior by reference to that pressure. One avenue for the reduction of dissonance is the internalization of the group norm, that is, the private acceptance of the judgment that was originally rendered as an act of conformity.

It should be noted that the dissonance model, of which Kiesler's application to conformity experiments is a special case, is the subject of some controversy. A leading alternative formulation assumes a change toward the position advocated in a forced compliance response in proportion to the rewards one obtains in exchange for the compliant act (Janis & Gilmore, 1965; Rosenberg, 1965; Scott, 1957, 1959). Aronson (1966) noted that both theories can be correct in a single instance. Linder, Cooper, and Jones (1967) have presented data showing the dissonance effect when subjects have at least the illusion of having been free to perform the dissonant act, and the incentive effect when the subject felt himself to have been coerced. Both formulations of the forced-compliance–private-acceptance phenomenon seem worth pursuing in the general context of persuasive judgments.

2. REFERENCE SCALE ACCOMMODATION

Volkmann (1951) discussed the need for common frames of reference if communication is to be effective, and he stressed the function of education in providing these common perspectives. Only when everyone agrees about the scale can there be clear communication about positions along the scale. As a judgmental theorist Volkmann emphasized the stimulus range as the principal determinant of the judgmental scale. Thus, in his analysis of communication he stressed the need to establish at an early stage in the interaction a set of end-anchors for judging the topic at issue.

Following Volkmann's analysis, it appears likely that much persuasive communication has two distinct targets: the parameters of the reference scale in terms of which alternative positions are to be judged, and a particular position which the communication source wishes the recipient to adopt. Ostrom and Upshaw (1968), Upshaw (1964b, 1969a), and Upshaw, Ostrom, and Ward (1970) have reported research that indicates that the two targets are separately subject to influence, and that suggests some of the determinants of change on each.

In the previous section on conformity, it was suggested that one might comply with the normative demands of a group by means of a persuasive judgment designed to create the impression of private acceptance. The present discussion of the reference scale as a target of influence suggests that it, too, may be adopted as an act of compliance, possibly with little reluctance since the essential arbitrariness of reference scales must be generally recognized. Having adopted a scale, however, the person's judgment of his own position, as well as those of others, is determined. If he does not like the judgment which he must now make of himself, he may either change his position to which the judgment refers, or reject the reference scale and its supporting perspective (see, Upshaw, 1964b, 1968b). Ostrom (1970) has reported some conditions under which one or the other mechanism is invoked. Thus, the person who perhaps innocently complies with normative pressure to adopt a reference scale may find himself caught in a web that requires considerable cognitive labor for extrication.

III. THE RELATIONSHIP OF PERSONALITY AND SOCIAL PSYCHOLOGY TO THE PSYCHOLOGY OF JUDGMENT

Personality and social psychology, on the one hand, and the psychology of judgment, on the other, have developed as more-or-less independent branches of psychology. The influence across their boundaries, when it has occurred, has tended to be asymmetric, with principles of judgment invoked as explanatory concepts in personality and social psychology. The review in this chapter of research at the intersection of the two branches has disclosed a number of problem areas for which established judgmental principles provide inadequate explanations. Furthermore, some of these areas suggest conceptual and research issues of direct relevance to the psychology of judgment. There appears to be a need to broaden the scope of both of the intersecting branches of psychology and to forge a more rigorous link between them.

It was noted earlier that judgmental behavior is often an alternative to other behavior that may be produced in response to the independent variables in a personality or social psychological experiment. In such cases it is not sufficient to understand properties of the resulting judgment. It is also important to understand why a judgment occurred rather than some other form of behavior. The social psychologist needs to know the conditions under which self-expressive, stimulus descriptive, and persuasive judgments are made. The determinants of the particular type of judgment may not hold great interest for the student of the general psychology of judgment. However, the determinants of whether any judgment at all is made would appear to be highly relevant to his concerns.

Another issue bearing upon the relationship of the two branches of psychology refers to the status of judgmental processes as mediators of other behaviors. The social psychologist is likely to be interested in the consequences of particular judgments, as well as in their determinants and content. A broadly defined psychology of judgment would surely be concerned with this topic, particularly as it is represented in certain sequential judgments in which one is consequent upon the other.

It seems a reasonable gamble that attention given to the borders of personality and social psychology and judgment will be beneficial to both branches. In any event incorporating such issues into the literature would make future reviews of the domain covered by this chapter easier to write and more rewarding to read.

References

Abelson, R. P., Aronson, E., McGuire, W. J., Newcomb, T. M., Rosenberg, M. S., & Tannenbaum, P. H. (Eds), *Theories of cognitive consistency: A sourcebook.* Chicago: Rand McNally, 1968.

Adams, J. S. Toward an understanding of inequity. *Journal of Abnormal and Social Psychology,* 1963, **67,** 422–436.

Adams, J. S. Inequity in social exchange. In L. Berkowitz (Ed.), *Advances in experimental social psychology,* Vol. 2. New York: Academic Press, 1965. Pp. 267–299.

Allen, V. L. Situational factors in conformity. In L. Berkowitz (Ed.), *Advances in experimental social psychology,* Vol. 2. New York: Academic Press, 1965. Pp. 133–175.

Allport, F. *Social psychology.* Cambridge, Massachusetts: Riverside, 1924.

Allport, G. W., & Kramer, B. M. Some roots of prejudice. *Journal of Psychology,* 1946, **22,** 9–39.

Anderson, N. H. Primacy effects in personality impression formation using a generalized order effect paradigm. *Journal of Personality and Social Psychology,* 1965, **2,** 1–9.

Anderson, N. H. Component ratings in impression formation. *Psychonomic Science,* 1966, **6,** 279–280.

Anderson, N. H. A simple model for information integration. In R. P. Abelson, E. Aronson, W. J. McGuire, T. M. Newcomb, M. J. Rosenberg, & P. H. Tannenbaum (Eds.), *Theories of cognitive consistency: A sourcebook.* Chicago: Rand McNally, 1968.

Anderson, N. H. Two more tests against change of meaning in adjective combinations. *Journal of Verbal Learning and Verbal Behavior,* 1971, **10,** 73–85.

Anderson, N. H. Cognitive algebra: Integration theory applied to social attribution.

In L. Berkowitz (Ed.), *Advances in experimental social psychology,* Vol. 7. New York: Academic Press, 1974. Pp. 1–101.

Anderson, N. H., & Barrios, A. A. Primacy effects in personality impression formation. *Journal of Abnormal and Social Psychology,* 1961, **63,** 346–350.

Anderson, N. H., & Hubert, S. Effects of concomitant verbal recall on order effects in personality impression formation. *Journal of Verbal Learning and Verbal Behavior,* 1963, **2,** 379–391.

Anderson, N. H., & Lampel, A. K. Effect of context on ratings of personality traits. *Psychonomic Science,* 1965, **3,** 433–434.

Argyle, M., & Kendon, A. The experimental analysis of social performance. In L. Berkowitz (Ed.), *Advances in experimental social psychology,* Vol. 3. New York: Academic Press, 1967. Pp. 55–98.

Aronson, E. The psychology of insufficient justification: an analysis of some conflicting data. In S. Feldman (Ed.), *Cognitive consistency.* New York: Academic Press, 1966. Pp. 115–133.

Aronson, E., & Mills, J. The effect of severity of initiation on liking for a group. *Journal of Abnormal and Social Psychology,* 1959, **59,** 177–181.

Asch, S. E. Forming impressions of personality. *Journal of Abnormal and Social Phychology,* 1946, **41,** 258–290.

Asch, S. E. Effects of group pressure upon the modification and distortion of judgment. In H. Guetzkow (Ed.), *Groups, leadership and men.* Pittsburgh: Carnegie Univ. Press, 1951. Pp. 177–190.

Asch, S. E. Studies of independence and submission to group pressure: *I.* A minority of one against a unanimous majority. *Psychological Monographs,* 1956, **70,** No. 9 (Whole No. 417).

Bandura, A., & Walters, R. H. *Social learning and personality development.* New York: Holt, 1963.

Beebe-Center, J. G. *The psychology of pleasantness and unpleasantness.* New York: Van Nostrand, 1932.

Bieri, J., Atkins, A. L., Briar, S., Leaman, R. L., Miller, H., & Tripodi, T. *Clinical and social judgment.* New York: Wiley, 1966.

Brehm, J. W. Postdecision changes in the desirability of alternatives. *Journal of Abnormal and Social Psychology,* 1956, **52,** 384–389.

Brigham, J. C. Ethnic stereotypes. *Psychological Bulletin,* 1971, **76,** 15–38.

Byrne, D. Interpersonal attraction and attitude similarity. *Journal of Abnormal and Social Psychology,* 1961, **62,** 713–715.

Byrne, D. Attitudes and attraction. In L. Berkowitz (Ed.), *Advances in experimental social psychology,* Vol. 4. New York: Academic Press, 1969. Pp. 35–89.

Dashiell, J. F. Experimental studies of the influence of social situations on the behavior of individual human adults. In C. Murchison (Ed.), *Handbook of social psychology.* Worcester, Massachusetts: Clark Univ. Press, 1935. Pp. 1097–1158.

Davis, W. L., & Phares, E. J. Internal–external control as a determinant of information-seeking in a social influence situation. *Journal of Personality,* 1967, **35,** 547–561.

Dorfman, D. D., Keeve, S., & Saslow, C. Ethnic identification: A signal detection analysis. *Journal of Personality and Social Psychology,* 1971, **18,** 373–379.

Duncan, S. Nonverbal Communication. *Psychological Bulletin,* 1969, **72,** 118–137.

Eiser, J. R. Enhancement of contrast in the absolute judgment of attitude statements. *Journal of Personality and Social Psychology,* 1971, **17,** 1–10.

Edwards, A. L. *The social desirability variable in personality assessment and research.* New York: Dryden, 1957.

Ekman, P., & Friesen, W. V. Nonverbal behavior in psychotherapy research. In J. M. Shlien (Ed.), *Research in Psychotherapy,* Vol. 3. Washington: American Psychological Association, 1968. Pp. 179–216.

Elliott, D. H., & Wittenberg, B. H. Accuracy of identification of Jewish and non-Jewish photographs. *Journal of Abnormal and Social Psychology,* 1955, **51,** 339–341.

Exline, R. V., & Winters, L. C. Affective relations and mutual glances in dyads. In S. Tomkins & C. Izard (Eds.), *Affect, cognition and personality.* New York: Springer, 1965. Pp. 319–351.

Feather, N. T. A structural balance model of communication effects. *Psychological Review,* 1964, **71,** 291–313.

Feather, N. T. A structural balance approach to the analysis of communication effects. In L. Berkowitz (Ed.), *Advances in experimental social psychology,* Vol. 3. New York: Academic Press, 1967. Pp. 99–165.

Fehrer, E. Shifts in scale values of attitude statements as a function of the composition of the scale. *Journal of Experimental Psychology,* 1952, **44,** 179–188.

Festinger, L. A theory of social comparison processes. *Human Relations,* 1954, **7,** 117–140.

Festinger, L. *A theory of cognitive dissonance.* Evanston, Illinois: Row, Peterson, 1957.

Galanter, E. Contemporary psychophysics. In R. W. Brown, E. Galanter, E. H. Hess, & G. Mandler (Eds.), *New directions in psychology.* New York: Holt, 1962. Pp. 87–156.

Goffman, E. On face-work: an analysis of ritual elements in social interaction. *Psychiatry,* 1955, **18,** 213–231.

Goffman, E. *Presentation of self in everyday life.* New York: Doubleday, 1959.

Goldman, R., Jaffa, M., & Schachter, S. Yom Kippur, Air France, dormitory food and the eating behavior of obese and normal persons. *Journal of Personality and Social Psychology,* 1968, **10,** 117–123.

Guilford, J. P. *Psychometric methods,* 2nd. ed. New York: McGraw-Hill, 1954.

Heider, F. Social perception and phenomenal causality. *Psychological Review,* 1944, **51,** 358–374.

Heider, F. Attitudes and cognitive organization. *Journal of Psychology,* 1946, **21,** 107–112.

Heider, F. *The psychology of interpersonal relations.* New York: Wiley, 1958.

Helson, H. *Adaptation-level theory.* New York: Harper, 1964.

Homans, G. C. *Social behavior: Its elementary forms,* Rev. Ed. New York: Harcourt, 1974.

Hovland, C. I., Harvey, O. J., & Sherif, M. Assimilation and contrast effects in reactions to communication and attitude change. *Journal of Abnormal and Social Psychology,* 1957, **55,** 244–252.

Janis, I. L., & Gilmore, J. B. The influence of incentive conditions on the success of role playing in modifying attitudes. *Journal of Personality and Social Psychology,* 1965, **1,** 17–27.

Johnson, D. M., & Mullally, C. R. Correlation-and-regression model for category judgments. *Psychological Review,* 1969, **76,** 205–215.

Jones, E. E. *Ingratiation: A social psychological analysis.* New York: Appleton, 1964.

Jones, E. E., & Davis, K. E. From acts to dispositions. In L. Berkowitz (Ed.), *Advances in experimental social psychology,* Vol. 2. New York: Academic Press, 1965, Pp. 219–266.

Jones, E. E., & Gerard, H. B. *Foundations of social psychology.* New York: Wiley, 1967.

Jones, E. E., & Goethals, G. R. Order effects in impression formation: Attribution context and the nature of the entity. In E. E. Jones, D. E. Kanouse, H. H. Kelley, R. E. Nisbett, S. Valins, & B. Weiner (Eds.), *Attribution: Perceiving the causes of behavior.* Morristown, N.J.: General Learning Press, 1972. Pp. 27–46.

Kaplan, M. Context effects in impression formation: The weighted average versus the meaning-change formulation. *Journal of Personality and Social Psychology,* 1971, **19,** 92–99.

Kelley, H. H. Attribution theory in social psychology. *Nebraska Symposium on Motivation,* 1967, **15,** 192–238.

Kelley, H. H. Attribution in social interaction. In E. E. Jones, D. E. Kanouse, H. H. Kelley, R. E. Nisbett, S. Valins, & B. Weiner (Eds.), *Attribution: Perceiving the causes of behavior.* Morristown, N.J.: General Learning Press, 1972. Pp. 1–26.

Kelley, H. H., Hovland, C. I., Schwartz, M., & Abelson, R. P. The influence of judges' attitudes in three methods of attitude scaling. *Journal of Social Psychology,* 1955, **42,** 147–158.

Kelley, H. H., & Thibaut, J. W. Group problem solving. In G. Lindzey & H. E. Aronson (Eds.), *The handbook of social psychology,* Vol. 4. Reading, Massachusetts: Addison-Wesley, 1969. Pp. 1–101.

Kiesler, C. A. Group pressure and conformity. In J. Mills (Ed.), *Experimental social psychology.* New York: Macmillan, 1969. Pp. 233–306.

Koehler, W. Zur Theories des Suksessiv-vergleichs und der Zeitfehler. *Psychologische Forschung,* 1923, **4,** 115–175. Cited in J. P. Guilford, *Psychometric methods,* 2nd ed. New York: McGraw-Hill, 1954. P. 305.

Larsen, K. S. Affectivity, cognitive style, and social judgment. *Journal of Personality and Social Psychology,* 1971, **12,** 119–127.

Latane, B. (Ed.) Studies in social comparison. *Journal of Experimental Social Psychology, Suppl.* **1,** 1966.

Laurenstein, O. Ansatz zu einer physiologischen Theorie des Vergleichs und der Zeitfehler. *Psychologische Forschung,* 1932, **17,** 130–177. Cited in J. P. Guilford, *Psychometric methods,* 2nd ed. New York: McGraw-Hill, 1954. P. 305.

Lefcourt, H. M. Internal versus external control of reinforcement: A review. *Psychological Bulletin,* 1966, **65,** 206–220.

Lefcourt, H. M. Recent developments in the study of locus of control. In B. A. Maher (Ed.), *Progress in Experimental Personality Research, V. 6.* New York: Academic Press, 1972. Pp. 1–38.

Linder, D. E., Cooper, J., & Jones, E. E. Decision freedom as a determinant of the role of incentive magnitude in attitude change. *Journal of Personality and Social Psychology,* 1967, **6,** 245–254.

Lindzey, G., & Rogolsky, S. Prejudice and identification of minority group membership. *Journal of Abnormal and Social Psychology,* 1950, **45,** 37–53.

Lippmann, W. *Public opinion.* New York: Harcourt, 1922.

McDavid, J. W. Approval-seeking motivation and the volunteer subject. *Journal of Personality and Social Psychology,* 1965, **2,** 115–117.

Meltzer, L., Morris, W. N., & Hayes, D. P. Interruption outcomes and vocal amplitude: Explorations in social psychophysics. *Journal of Personality and Social Psychology,* 1971, **18**, 392–402.

Messick, D. M. Some effects of the temporal distribution of outcomes on the evaluation of social stimuli. Unpublished Masters Thesis. Chapel Hill: University of North Carolina, 1964.

Miller, N. E., & Dollard, J. *Social learning and imitation.* New Haven: Yale Univ. Press, 1941.

Newcomb, T. M. The prediction of interpersonal attraction. *American Psychologist,* 1956, **11**, 575–586.

Newcomb, T. M. *The acquaintance process.* New York: Holt, 1961.

Newcomb, T. M. Interpersonal balance. In R. B. Abelson, E. Aronson, W. J. McGuire, T. M. Newcomb, M. J. Rosenberg, & P. H. Tannenbaum (Eds.), *Theories of Cognitive Consistency: A sourcebook.* Chicago: Rand McNally, 1968. Pp. 28–51.

Nisbett, R. E. Taste, deprivation, and weight determinants of eating behavior. *Journal of Personality and Social Psychology,* 1968, **10**, 107–116.

Orne, M. On the social psychology of the psychological experiment. *American Psychologist,* 1962, **17**, 776–783.

Ostrom, T. M. Perspective as an intervening construct in the judgment of attitude statements. *Journal of Personality and Social Psychology,* 1966, **3**, 135–144.

Ostrom, T. M. Perspective as a determinant of attitude change. *Journal of Experimental Social Psychology,* 1970, **6**, 280–292.

Ostrom, T. M., & Upshaw, H. S. Psychological perspective and attitude change. In A. G. Greenwald, T. M. Brock, & T. M. Ostrom (Eds.), *Psychological foundations of attitudes.* New York: Academic Press, 1968. Pp. 217–242.

Ostrom, T. M., & Upshaw, H. S. Race differences in the judgment of attitude statements over a thirty-five year period. *Journal of Personality,* 1970, **38**, 235–248.

Parducci, A. The relativism of absolute judgments. *Scientific American,* 1968, **219**, No. 6, 84–90.

Patchen, M. *The choice of wage comparisons.* Englewood Cliffs, New Jersey: Prentice-Hall, 1961.

Phares, E. J., Ritchie, D. E., & Davis, W. L. Internal–external control and reaction to threat. *Journal of Personality and Social Psychology,* 1968, **10**, 402–405.

Phares, E. J., Wilson, K. G., & Klyver, N. W. Internal–external control and the attribution of blame under neutral and distractive conditions. *Journal of Personality and Social Psychology,* 1971, **18**, 285–288.

Pulos, L., & Spilka, B. Perceptual selectivity, memory, and anti-semitism. *Journal of Abnormal and Social Psychology,* 1961, **62**, 690–692.

Riecken, H. W. A program for research on experiments in social psychology. In F. F. Washburne (Ed.), *Decision, values and groups,* Vol. 2. New York: Pergamon, 1962. Pp. 25–41.

Rosenberg, M. J. When dissonance fails: On eliminating evaluation apprehension from attitude measurement. *Journal of Personality and Social Psychology,* 1965, **1**, 28–42.

Rosenberg, S. & Sedlak, A. Structural representations of implicit personality theory. In L. Berkowitz (Ed.), *Advances in Experimental Social Psychology, V. 6.* New York: Academic Press, 1972. Pp. 235–297.

Rotter, J. B. *Social learning and clinical psychology.* Englewood Cliffs, New Jersey: Prentice-Hall, 1954.

Rotter, J. B. Generalized expectancies for internal versus external control of reinforcement. *Psychological Monographs,* 1966, **80,** No. 1 (Whole No. 609).

Rotter, J. B., Seeman, M. R., & Liverant, S. Internal versus external control of reinforcements: A major variable in behavior theory. In N. F. Washburn (Ed.), *Decisions, values, and groups,* Vol. 2. New York: Pergamon, 1962. Pp. 473–516.

Schachter, S. The interaction of cognitive and physiological determinants of emotional state. In L. Berkowitz (Ed.), *Advances in experimental social psychology,* Vol. 1. New York: Academic Press, 1964. Pp. 49–80.

Schachter, S. Some extraordinary facts about obese humans and rats. *American Psychologist,* 1971, **26,** 129–144.

Schachter, S., Goldman, R., & Gordon, A. Effects of food deprivation and fear on eating behavior. *Journal of Personality and Social Psychology,* 1968, **10,** 91–97.

Schachter, S., & Singer, J. E. Cognitive, social, and physiological determinants of emotional state. *Psychological Review,* 1962, **69,** 379–399.

Schachter, S., & Wheeler, L. Epinephrine, chlorpromazine, and amusement. *Journal of Abnormal and Social Psychology,* 1962, **65,** 121–128.

Scodel, A., & Austrin, H. The perception of Jewish photographs by non-Jews and Jews. *Journal of Abnormal and Social Psychology,* 1957, **54,** 278–280.

Scott, W. A. Attitude change through reward of verbal behavior. *Journal of Abnormal and Social Psychology,* 1957, **55,** 72–75.

Scott, W. A. Cognitive consistency, response reinforcement, and attitude change. *Sociometry,* 1959, **22,** 219–229.

Segall, M. H. The effect of attitude and experience on judgments of controversial statements. *Journal of Abnormal and Social Psychology,* 1959, **58,** 61–68.

Sherif, C. W., Sherif, M., & Nebergall, R. E. *Attitude and attitude change.* Philadelphia: Saunders, 1965.

Sherif, M., & Hovland, C. I. *Social judgment.* New Haven: Yale Univ. Press, 1961.

Stevens, S. S. Adaptation-level vs. the relativity of judgment. *American Journal of Psychology,* 1958, **71,** 633–646.

Stevens, S. S. On the operation known as judgment. *American Scientist,* 1966, **54,** 385–401.

Stewart, R. H. Effect of continuous responding on the order effect in personality impression formation. *Journal of Personality and Social Psychology,* 1965, **1,** 161–165.

Stunkard, A. J., & Koch, C. The interpretation of gastric motility. I. Apparent bias in the reports of hunger by obese persons. *Archives of General Psychiatry,* 1964, **11,** 74–82.

Thibaut, J. W., & Kelley, H. H. *The social psychology of groups.* New York: Wiley, 1959.

Thibaut, J. W., & Ross, M. Commitment and experience as determinants of assimilation and contrast. *Journal of Personality and Social Psychology,* 1969, **13,** 322–329.

Thurstone, L. L. Attitudes can be measured. *American Journal of Sociology,* 1928, **33,** 529–554.

Tuddenham, R. D., & McBride, P. D. The yielding experiment from the subject's point of view. *Journal of Personality,* 1959, **27,** 259–271.

Upshaw, H. S. Own attitude as an anchor in equal-appearing intervals. *Journal of Abnormal and Social Psychology,* 1962, **64,** 85–96.

Upshaw, H. S. A linear alternative to assimilation and contrast: A reply to Manis. *Journal of Abnormal and Social Psychology,* 1964, **68,** 691–693. (a)

Upshaw, H. S. Opinion Change vs. Reference Scale Change in the Study of Attitudes. Paper delivered at the 72nd Annual Convention of the American Psychological Association, Los Angeles, 1964. (b)

Upshaw, H. S. The effects of variable perspectives on judgments of opinion statements for Thurstone scales. *Journal of Personality and Social Psychology,* 1965, **2,** 60–69.

Upshaw, H. S. Attitude measurement. In H. M. Blalock, Jr. & A. B. Blalock (Eds.), *Methodology in social research.* New York: McGraw-Hill, 1968. Pp. 60–111. (a)

Upshaw, H. S. Cognitive consistency and the psychology of judgment. In R. P. Abelson, E. Aronson, W. J. McGuire, T. M. Newcomb, M. J. Rosenberg, & P. H. Tannenbaum (Eds.), *Theories of cognitive consistency: A sourcebook.* Chicago: Rand McNally, 1968. Pp. 210–217. (b)

Upshaw, H. S. Judgmental Language in Attitude Research. Paper presented at the Annual Convention of the Western Psychological Association, Vancouver, B.C., 1969. (a)

Upshaw, H. S. The personal reference scale: An approach to social judgment. In L. Berkowitz (Ed.), *Advances in experimental social psychology,* Vol. 4. New York: Academic Press, 1969. Pp. 315–371. (b)

Upshaw, H. S. Stimulus range and the judgmental unit. *Journal of Experimental Social Psychology,* 1969, **5,** 1–11. (c)

Upshaw, H. S. The effect of unit size on the range of the reference scale. *Journal of Experimental Social Psychology,* 1970, **6,** 129–139.

Upshaw, H. S., Ostrom, T. M., & Ward, C. D. Content versus self-rating in attitude research. *Journal of Experimental Social Psychology,* 1970, **6,** 272–279.

Volkmann, J. Scales of judgment and their implications for social psychology. In J. H. Rohrer & M. Sherif (Eds.), *Social psychology at the crossroads.* New York: Harper, 1951. Pp. 273–294.

Walster, E., Berscheid, E., & Walster, G. W. New directions in equity research. *Journal of Personality and Social Psychology,* 1973, **25,** 151–176.

Ward, C. D. Ego involvement and the absolute judgment of attitude statements. *Journal of Personality and Social Psychology,* 1965, **2,** 202–208.

Ward, C. D. Attitude and involvement in the absolute judgment of attitude statements, *Journal of Personality and Social Psychology,* 1966, **4,** 465–476.

Weick, K. E. Reduction of cognitive dissonance through task enhancement and effort expenditure. *Journal of Abnormal and Social Psychology,* 1964, **68,** 533–539.

White, B. J., Alter, R. D., & Rardin, M. Authoritarianism, dogmatism, and usage of conceptual categories. *Journal of Personality and Social Psychology,* 1965, **2,** 293–295.

White, B. J., & Harvey, O. J. Effects of personality and own stand on judgment and production of statements about a central issue. *Journal of Experimental Social Psychology,* 1965, **1,** 334–347.

Wyer, R. S., Jr. Category ratings as "subjective expected values": Implications for attitude formation and change. *Psychological Review,* 1973, **80,** 446–467.

Wyer, R. S., Jr., & Dermer, M. Effect of context and instructional set upon evaluations of personality trait adjectives. *Journal of Personality and Social Psychology,* 1968, **9,** 7–14.

Wyer, R. S., Jr., & Watson, S. F. Context effects in impression formation. *Journal of Personality and Social Psychology,* 1969, **12,** 22–33.

Zajonc, R. B. Social facilitation, *Science,* 1965, **149,** 269–274.

Part III

Measurement Models and Applications

Chapter 7

STIMULUS AND RESPONSE MEASUREMENT[*]

E. W. HOLMAN and A. A. J. MARLEY

I. INTRODUCTION

Stevens (1951) has defined measurement as "the assignment of numerals to objects or events according to rules." Most applications of measurement have emphasized the numerals themselves, either as convenient summaries of observable properties or as variables appearing in scientific laws. This approach, however, has been notoriously less successful in psychology than in the physical sciences. Indeed, there is still some controversy about whether the numerical results of formal psychological measurements are any more useful practically or lawful scientifically than the original observations from which they are derived. These difficulties suggest that particularly in psychology, the numerals generated in measurement may be of

[*] This work was supported by National Science Foundation Grant GB-13588X and by National Research Council of Canada Grant A-8124.

We thank Edward C. Carterette, David H. Krantz, R. Duncan Luce, Donald G. MacKay, J. O. Ramsay, and Amos Tversky for their helpful comments and suggestions.

less importance than the rule by which they are assigned. This rule embodies a mathematical model for the objects being measured; the numerals assigned to the objects are the parameters of the model. In physical measurement, to be sure, the testable consequences of most models are rather obvious empirically; for instance, few would deny that under most conditions, the total length of two rigid objects placed end to end is equal to the sum of the lengths of the individual objects. A corresponding statement for psychological entities, however, would be much more controversial; and unless the measurement model is correct, the numerals produced will be of little value. Therefore, this chapter will emphasize tests of models rather than techniques for assigning numerals. More extensive general treatments of measurement are given by Bock and Jones (1968), Krantz, Luce, Suppes, and Tversky (1971), Pfanzagl (1968), and Suppes and Zinnes (1963).

Measurement models differ from most other mathematical models in having many more free parameters. Psychophysical measurement, for instance, typically assigns at least one numerical scale value to each stimulus in an experiment. Neverthless, despite the famous theorem that with five free parameters one can fit an elephant, measurement models are eminently testable, and not always confirmed. One common method for testing such a model is to estimate the scale values that best describe a given set of data, and then evaluate how well the model fits the data with these parameter values. In many cases, computer programs have been developed for parameter estimation; but evaluation procedures remain largely informal. An alternative approach is to test parameter-free axioms that are necessary or sufficient for the model. A theorem that derives a model from a set of sufficient conditions is usually called a *representation* theorem. Since the several axioms can be tested independently, such tests can give information about exactly which aspects of the model are correct and which should be modified.

Because measurement models have so many parameters, the values of these parameters are usually not uniquely determined by data. Nevertheless, the alternative sets of scale values assigned by a given model to a given set of objects are usually related to each other in a well-defined way. For instance, the model for measuring length does not specify whether lengths are to be expressed in miles, meters, or some other unit; but obviously any lengths can be transformed to different units by just multiplying by a positive constant. A theorem that states the transformation relating alternative numerical assignments for a given model is usually called a *uniqueness* theorem. Since scale values are not absolutely unique, certain statements about them may be ambiguous and therefore empirically meaningless. An example would be, "The distance (along the surface of the earth) from Los Angeles to New York is about 2500." As Suppes and Zinnes (1963) demonstrate, one way to avoid such ambiguity is to show that a statement applies equally well to any numerical assignment permitted by the measurement model. Such a statement would be, "The distance from Los Angeles to New York is about twice the distance from Los Angeles to Dallas." Fortunately, it is a straightforward mathematical exercise to determine whether any particular statement or class of statements is invariant over the transformations permitted by the uniqueness theorem for any given model. Such determinations have been made for many important cases by Adams, Fagot, and Robinson (1965), Luce (1959, 1962, 1967), Rozeboom (1962), Stevens (1951), and Suppes and Zinnes (1963). Another more direct way to eliminate ambiguity is just to specify the numerical assignment or class of assignments to which the statement applies. For instance, "The distance from Los Angeles to New York is about 2500 miles." Other more complex examples are discussed by Anderson (1961, 1974) and Lord (1953). Statements that hold for a specified set of numerical assignments may be less general than statements that are completely invariant, but they are no less testable.

Measurement models can be classified according to the sorts of data they describe. *Algebraic* models deal with events that occur, at least in principle, with probabilities of 0, $\frac{1}{2}$, or 1 only; whereas *probabilistic* models attempt to describe other probabilities as well. Algebraic models can be further divided into two subclasses. Models for *fundamental* measurement, also called *nonmetric* models, refer only to qualitative or nonnumerical data. Such models may also be applied to numerical observations, but they describe only qualitative properties such as the rank-order of the observations. On the other hand, models for *derived* measurement, also called *metric* models, are based on numerical information from previous fundamental or derived measurement, and perhaps upon qualitative data in addition. Probabilistic models inevitably involve derived measurement, because they require previously measured probabilities. In this chapter, examples of algebraic fundamental measurement are discussed in Sections II,A–C, algebraic derived measurement in Section II,D, and probabilistic derived measurement in Section III.

II. ALGEBRAIC MODELS

A. Equivalence and Order Relations

The class of data described by algebraic measurement models is relatively limited. Such models always refer to relations among objects, and in particular usually include either *equivalence relations* or *weak orders*.

To define these types of relations, let X be a set of objects such as stimuli, with individual objects in X denoted x, y, z, etc. A relation $\approx$ is an equivalence relation if and only if the following three conditions hold for all x, y, and z in X.

E1. $x \approx x$.

E2. $x \approx y$ implies $y \approx x$.

E3. $x \approx y$ and $y \approx z$ implies $x \approx z$.

Examples might be $x \approx y$ whenever subjects are indifferent between x and y, or whenever they cannot distinguish between x and y. A relation $\gtrsim$ is a weak order relation if and only if the following two conditions hold for all x, y, and z in X.

W1. $x \gtrsim y$ or $y \gtrsim x$ or both.

W2. $x \gtrsim y$ and $y \gtrsim z$ implies $x \gtrsim z$.

Examples might be $x \gtrsim y$ whenever subjects do not prefer y over x, or whenever they say that x has at least as much of a given attribute as y has. If $\gtrsim$ is a weak order, and if $\approx$ is defined so that $x \approx y$ whenever $x \gtrsim y$ and $y \gtrsim x$, then $\approx$ is an equivalence relation. On the other hand, given only an equivalence relation, it is not necessarily possible to define a weak order. Consequently, weak orders are stronger than equivalence relations.

Empirically, the conditions for equivalence relations and weak orders generally hold only to a first approximation, and are frequently wrong in detail. For instance, the symmetry requirement of Condition E2 and the connectedness requirement of Condition W1 are inconsistent with time–order errors and response biases in psychophysical data. These effects have been extensively studied in their own right, and are generally included in probabilistic models if not in algebraic models.

Also, the transitivity requirement of Conditions E3 and W2 is frequently invalidated by limitations on the sensitivity of subjects to very small differences. Thus, it is often possible to find three stimuli of which the two most extreme are easily discriminable from each other, whereas the middle stimulus is not reliably discriminable from the other two. Again, this problem has been thoroughly investigated, and in fact it constitutes a central issue for probabilistic models in psychophysics. Algebraic models have dealt with the problem in two ways. One approach is to replace equivalence relations and weak orders by other relations in which the transitivity requirement is eliminated or weakened. Theoretical work on such alternatives has been done by Fishburn (1970), Luce (1956), Krantz (1967a), Roberts (1970), and Scott and Suppes (1958); but few experimental tests of these models have been performed. Another possibility is to define relations in terms of probabilities, so that random fluctuations in behavior will not destroy transitivity. For instance, if $\gtrsim$ is defined such that $x \gtrsim y$ whenever subjects choose x over y with probability at least $\frac{1}{2}$, then Condition W2 is equivalent to *weak stochastic transitivity:* if x is chosen over y with probability at least $\frac{1}{2}$, and y is chosen over z with probability at least $\frac{1}{2}$, then x is chosen over z with probability at least $\frac{1}{2}$. Although this condition seems to be consistent with most of the relevant experimental data, two important counterexamples have been found. Shepard (1964) has constructed a series of complex tones, which continuously increases in pitch, yet after ascending an octave has returned to its starting point. Also, Tversky (1969) has demonstrated stochastic intransitivities in preferences among alternatives that vary on several dimensions of differing importance.

Given that an empirical relation does satisfy the conditions for an equivalence relation or a weak order, the following simple representation and uniqueness statements hold when the set X, on which the relation is defined, is finite or countably infinite. First, if and only if $\approx$ is an equivalence relation, then there is a function ϕ on X such that for all x, y in X,

$$\phi(x) = \phi(y) \quad \text{if and only if} \quad x \approx y. \tag{1}$$

Moreover, another function ϕ' will also satisfy (1) if and only if ϕ and ϕ' are related by a one-to-one transformation; in the terminology of Stevens (1951), this model defines a nominal scale. Second, if and only if $\approx$ is a weak order, then there is a function ϕ on X such that for all x, y in X,

$$\phi(x) \geq \phi(y) \quad \text{if and only if} \quad x \gtrsim y. \tag{2}$$

Moreover, another function ϕ' will satisfy (2) if and only if ϕ and ϕ' are related by a strictly increasing transformation; in Stevens's (1951) terms, this model defines an ordinal scale.

The representations in (1) and (2) state correspondences between the empirical relations $\approx$ or $\gtrsim$, and the mathematical relations $=$ or $\geq$, respectively. These mathematical models are relatively simple, however, and the resulting scale values are only loosely constrained by the uniqueness statements. Other algebraic models state further correspondence between empirical and mathematical structures, and impose more uniqueness on their scale values. Each of the more complicated models nevertheless still includes a correspondence between relations similar to either (1) or (2). Consequently, each model will require either an equivalence relation or a weak order, whose experimental verification will be subject to the problems already mentioned.

B. Additive Structures

As well as describing relations that compare one object with another, some models attempt also to describe relations among groups or combinations of objects, or better yet, to predict relations among combinations from properties of individual objects. One obvious way to study combinations of objects is simply to add objects together and then order the results. The two most important types of additive structures occur in *extensive* measurement and *conjoint* measurement.

In extensive measurement, the objects combined and the results of the combination are qualitatively similar, in the sense that they can all be included in the same ordering. Most physical quantities are extensive; in measuring length, for instance, objects are combined by placing them end to end, and the lengths of such combinations are easily compared to the lengths of single objects. A less directly physical example of an extensive structure is probability, in which unions of disjoint events can be compared to individual events. Krantz *et al.* (1971) review work on extensive measurement.

In psychology, however, extensive structures are much less frequent than conjoint structures. In conjoint measurement, the objects to be combined are qualitatively different from the combinations, and are not ordered along with them. Factorial experiments provide the most common examples: Experimental treatments are combinations of several factors, which are not observed in isolation. To simplify notation, two-factor experiments will be discussed here; the generalization to more factors is straightforward.

Let the sets X_1 and X_2 be the two factors; and let the elements x_1, y_1, etc. in X_1 and x_2, y_2, etc. in X_2 be the levels of these factors. Each pair such as x_1x_2, composed of one level from each factor, determines an experimental group; the set of all such pairs is denoted $X_1 \times X_2$. If the experiment yields numerical data, then the group means define a function f on $X_1 \times X_2$. The simplest additive model for such an experiment expresses the data as the sum of a row effect and a column effect. According to such a model, there are functions ϕ_1 on X_1 and ϕ_2 on X_2 such that for any x_1 in X_1 and x_2 in X_2,

$$\phi_1(x_1) + \phi_2(x_2) = f(x_1 x_2). \tag{3}$$

The model is usually tested by means of the analysis of variance; (3) holds if and only if no interaction is present in the analysis.

This model has perhaps its longest history in reaction-time experiments, where the factors are various information-processing tasks that subjects must perform before completing their response. Donders (1868) first used an additive model for reaction time; Sternberg (1969) gives a definitive modern treatment. Confirmation of (3) for a given pair of tasks would suggest that subjects must perform the tasks in successive stages rather than simultaneously.

Although sequential processing stages are directly reflected in additive mean reaction times, other types of additive underlying structures may be only monotonically related to the observable data. In other words, if the data define a weak order $\gtrsim$ on the experimental groups, then there may be functions ϕ_1 on X_1 and ϕ_2 on X_2 such that for any x_1, y_1 in X_1 and x_2, y_2 in X_2,

$$\phi_1(x_1) + \phi_2(x_2) \geq \phi_1(y_1) + \phi_2(y_2) \quad \text{if and only if} \quad x_1x_2 \gtrsim y_1y_2. \quad (4)$$

Statment (4) is the representation for conjoint measurement; in a conjoint structure, therefore, the order of the data is determined additively even though the data themselves may not be. Debreu (1960) and Luce and Tukey (1964) stated the first sets of axioms sufficient for (4); Krantz et al. (1971) review later work. These axioms imply not only the conjoint representation but also the following uniqueness statement. Other functions ϕ_1' and ϕ_2' will also satisfy (4) if and only if $\phi_1' = \alpha\phi_1 + \beta_1$ and $\phi_2' = \alpha\phi_2 + \beta_2$ for some constants $\alpha > 0$, β_1, and β_2; in Stevens's (1951) terms, conjoint measurement defines interval scales with a common unit.

Anderson (1970, 1974) has used additive models to describe the numerical ratings subjects gave to stimulus displays, where the factors were different aspects of the displays. In many of his experiments, (3) holds directly; and in others, additivity holds for a relatively simple transformation of the ratings, such as the logarithm or a power function. For cases where the appropriate transformation is not obvious, Kruskal (1965), Kruskal and Carmona (1969), and Lingoes (1967) have provided computer programs for iterative algorithms that converge to a best-fitting conjoint representation. The analysis of variance can then be applied to the output of the program; if an interaction still exists, then conjoint measurement is not possible.

Even when additivity in the sense of (4) does not hold, a more general representation may still be possible. There may be functions ϕ_1 on X_1, ϕ_2 on X_2, and F on pairs of real numbers, such that F is strictly increasing on both its arguments, and also for all x_1, y_1 in X_1 and x_2, y_2 in X_2,

$$F[\phi_1(x_1), \phi_2(x_2)] \geq F[\phi_1(y_1), \phi_2(y_2)] \quad \text{if and only if} \quad x_1x_2 \gtrsim y_1y_2. \quad (5)$$

This representation replaces addition in (4) with the general monotonic function F, but it still allows the separate scales ϕ_1 and ϕ_2 to be constructed on the two factors. The following two axioms are necessary for (5), and also sufficient if the sets X_1 and X_2 are finite.

C1. $\gtrsim$ is a weak order on $X_1 \times X_2$.

C2.   For any x_1, y_1, in X_1 and x_2, y_2 in X_2, $x_1x_2 \gtrsim y_1x_2$ implies $x_1y_2 \gtrsim y_1y_2$, and $x_1x_2 \gtrsim x_1y_2$ implies $y_1x_2 \gtrsim y_1y_2$.

These axioms are of course necessary conditions for (4) as well; they are, in fact, the only conjoint measurement axioms that have been tested at all frequently. Axiom C1 was discussed in the previous section. In the analysis of variance, interactions that contradict Axiom C2 are called crossover interactions, and cannot be removed by any monotonic transformation of the data.

Two special cases of (5) are of particular importance in psychophysical measurement. First, suppose that X_1 and X_2 are the same set of stimuli, and let the order $\gtrsim$ be determined by the probability that subjects choose the first stimulus over the second when presented with a pair of stimuli. In this case, (5) is equivalent to the condition of *simple scalability* introduced by Krantz (1967b) and discussed in Section III,B.

For another example of the model expressed in (5), suppose that X_1 is a set of discriminative stimuli, X_2 is a set of responses or reinforcing stimuli, and the order $\gtrsim$ reflects the speed or accuracy of discriminative responding. In this case, Axiom C2 expresses the common belief that the relative discriminability of stimuli does not depend upon the responses required of the subject or the stimuli used to reinforce these responses. Several counterexamples to this axiom have recently been discovered, however. According to the experiments of Lawicka (1964), dogs can learn to turn left or right depending upon whether a tone is presented above or below them, and they can learn to perform or withhold a response depending upon the pitch of a tone, but they are practically incapable of learning the directional response to the pitch cue or the yes–no response to the directional cue. Similarly, in studies of stimulus–response compatibility in human choice-reaction time, reviewed by Welford (1963, pp. 82–87, 180–189), subjects make faster reaction times and fewer errors when the stimuli and responses are similar in modality or in spatial configuration than when they are different. These results suggest an interaction between discriminative stimuli and responses. Also, Garcia, McGowan, Ervin, and Koelling (1968) found that rats can learn to avoid a distinctively flavored food if they are punished after eating it by an overdose of X rays that makes them sick, and they can learn to avoid a food of distinctive visual appearance if they are punished by painful electric shock, but they do not avoid the flavor after shock punishment, or the visual cue after X rays. These findings indicate an interaction between stimuli and reinforcers.

C. Metric Spaces

Another simple property of objects taken in combination is the difference between two objects. Since Carroll and Wish (1974), Indow (1974), and Wish and Carroll (1974) review work on the measurement of differences and similarities, this chapter will give only a general introduction to the topic.

Examples of psychological data that reflect differences between stimuli are subjects' direct ratings of differences, the frequency with which subjects place two stimuli in different classes when asked to sort a large set, and the numbers of errors or lengths of reaction times made by subjects instructed or trained to perform different responses to two stimuli. Mathematical models for such data attempt to represent the stimuli as points in a psychological space, so that the distances between the points are at least monotonically related to the data. Unfortunately, most experiments have studied only one empirical measure of difference at a time; thus, little is known about the conditions under which the measures are monotonically related to each other and thus consistent with the same model. Falmagne (1971) describes some cases where monotonicity does hold, and the examples at the end of Section II,B indicated nonmonotonic relationships in other instances.

To describe possible models, let X, with elements x, y, etc., be a set of objects such as stimuli; let $X \times X$ be the set of all pairs of objects in X; and let $\gtrsim$ be a relation that orders these pairs according to difference. The usual mathematical model for this situation is a metric space, which requires a function δ on $X \times X$, with the following properties for all w, x, y, z in X:

$$\delta(w, x) \geq \delta(y, z) \quad \text{if and only if} \quad wx \gtrsim yz. \tag{6}$$

$$\delta(x, x) = 0, \quad \text{and} \quad \delta(x, y) > 0 \quad \text{if} \quad x \neq y. \tag{7}$$

$$\delta(x, y) = \delta(y, x). \tag{8}$$

$$\delta(x, z) \leq \delta(x, y) + \delta(y, z). \tag{9}$$

The following three axioms are necessary for this representation, and also sufficient if the set X is finite. The axioms apply to all x, y in X.

M1. $\gtrsim$ is a weak order on $X \times X$.

M2. $xx \approx yy$, and $xy > xx$ if $x \neq y$.

M3. $xy \approx yx$.

The ordering axiom is standard, and the next axiom seems at least a reasonable approximation. The symmetry assumption of Axiom M3, however, does not always hold in real data. In many applications, for instance, the distance from stimulus x to stimulus y is supposed to be inversely related to the probability with which subjects make the response appropriate to y when x is actually presented; but subjects sometimes say "y" when *x* is presented more often than they say "*x*" when *y* is presented. Usually such asymmetries are attributed to extrinsic factors, such as response biases, context effects, or sampling errors, superimposed upon a basically symmetric structure; experimenters therefore tend to reanalyze their data to make them symmetric, and then apply a metric-space model. Alternatively, however, the asymmetries could be regarded as intrinsic; this approach would require a different model. There does not yet seem to be any convincing way to choose between these possibilities.

Even when the axioms are satisfied, the general metric-space model is rather weak in two respects. First, it defines only a function on pairs of objects, rather than specifying an underlying structure on individual objects. Second, the function δ is scarcely more unique than an ordinal scale. Most research has therefore been devoted to various special cases of metric spaces, which remedy these two deficiencies at the price of making more assumptions about the data. The two most commonly used of these special metric spaces are the *hierarchical clustering model* and the *multidimensional Euclidean model*.

The hierarchical clustering model assumes that people classify objects such as stimuli by dividing them into nonoverlapping clusters, then subdividing the clusters into smaller clusters, and so on. Such classification schemes are sometimes used in linguistics. For instance, nouns can be divided into names of animate and inanimate objects, names of animate objects can then be divided into names of human beings and nonhuman beings, etc. Similarly, phonemes can be divided into consonants and vowels, consonants can be divided into voiced and unvoiced, etc. The psychological question is whether subjects actually follow such classifications in responding to differences between stimuli.

A hierarchical clustering model for a given set of objects can be represented by a tree diagram like Fig. 1. Individual objects are at the bottom of the tree, and clusters are nodes in the tree. The distance δ(*x*, *y*) between the objects *x* and *y* is determined by how far the tree must be climbed

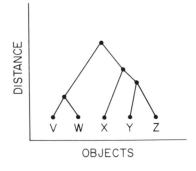

Fig. 1. Example of a tree diagram for a hierarchy of clusters.

before x and y are in the same cluster. This distance thus appears on the ordinate in Fig. 1, and would predict for instance that $vw \lesssim yz \lesssim xy \approx xz \lesssim vx$. Although the distance function in the hierarchical model is still only unique up to strictly increasing transformations, the tree structure of clusers is absolutely unique.

In addition to the usual properties of a metric space, the hierarchical model has the property that any two objects in the same cluster are equidistant from any object outside the cluster. It follows that for any three objects in a hierarchy, the two that are least different from each other must be equally different from the third. This condition is equivalent to the *ultrametric inequality:*

M4.   For all x, y, z in X, $xz \lesssim xy$ or $xz \lesssim yz$ or both.

Johnson (1967) has shown that Axioms M1–M4 are not only necessary for the hierarchical clustering model, but also sufficient if the set X is finite.

Axiom M4 does not allow any object to be strictly between two other objects in the sense of being less different from each of the other objects than they are from each other. Thus, a hierarchical model cannot describe stimuli that are continuously variable, such as colors or tones, but the model may be appropriate for stimuli that are, in a sense, discrete, such as phonemes or words. More specific tests of the axiom with discrete stimuli would be difficult, because the axiom requires strict equalities that would be contradicted even by unsystematic errors in the data. Instead, several computer algorithms have been developed to find hierarchical representations that maximize various measures of goodness of fit to data. These methods are described by Jardine and Sibson (1971), Johnson (1967), and Sokal and Sneath (1963), among others. The most extensive and successful psychological applications have been to judgments of the similarity in meaning of words; examples are Fillenbaum and Rapoport (1971) and Miller (1969).

The multidimensional Euclidean model assumes that people place objects such as stimuli in a psychological space that is similar to physical space except perhaps for its dimensionality. Thus, if a set of stimuli vary on only one psychological dimension, then they would be represented as points on a straight line; if the stimuli vary on two dimensions, they would be represented in a plane; and so on. In general, for k dimensions, the model defines k real-valued functions $\phi_1, \phi_2, \ldots, \phi_k$ on the set X of objects, which give the coordinates of each object in the space. For any two objects x and y, the distance $\delta(x, y)$ is equal to the Euclidean distance

$$\left\{ \sum_{i=1}^{k} [\phi_i(x) - \phi_i(y)]^2 \right\}^{1/2}.$$

As Shepard (1962a) remarks, any set of n objects that satisfy Axioms M1–M3 can be trivially represented in a Euclidean space of $n - 1$ dimensions. Thus, the interesting problem is to specify the conditions under which the representation is possible in fewer dimensions. Holman (1972) and Lingoes (1971) show that $n - 2$ or fewer dimensions will suffice if and only if the objects do not all satisfy the ultrametric inequality of Axiom M4, which characterizes the hierarchical clustering model. At the opposite extreme from the hierarchical model, Suppes and Winet (1955) and Krantz et al. (1971) have stated axioms for the one-dimensional (linear) case. Also, Beals and Krantz (1967), Beals, Krantz, and Tversky (1968), and Tversky and Krantz (1970) give axioms for various generalizations of Euclidean spaces. For all practical purposes, however, these axioms have not been tested.

Rather than studying axioms, most research on the Euclidean model has attempted to find best-fitting representations directly by means of iterative computer algorithms. This technique is frequently called *nonmetric multidimensional scaling*. Shepard (1962a,b) described the first program for this purpose. Kruskal (1964a,b) and Torgerson (1965), among others, give alternative versions, which determine the dimensionality differently, maximize different measures of goodness of fit, and allow certain non-Euclidean representations. Needless to say, for any given set of data, the fit of the model increases with the number of dimensions, until a trivially perfect fit is reached with one fewer dimensions than objects represented. Unfortunately, no rigorous methods seem to be available for deciding the point at which deviations from the model are attributable to random errors in the data rather than to insufficient dimensions in the model.

Benzécri (1964) and Shepard (1966) give some theoretical results on the uniqueness of the Euclidean representation. Uniqueness has also been investigated empirically by comparing the representations produced for a given set of data when different algorithms are used, various monotonic transformations are applied to the data, and random or even systematic errors are added to the data. The results of all these studies indicate that as the number of objects in the set becomes appreciably larger than the number of dimensions, the uniqueness of the presentation rapidly approaches the uniqueness of a geometric figure in Euclidean space: The configuration is essentially unique up to translations, rotations, and uniform dilations and contractions.

Indow (1974) reviews the extensive literature on empirical applications of the multidimensional Euclidean model. Suffice it to say here that in virtually all cases, the model seems to have fit the data adequately using at most three or four dimensions. Possibly subjects cannot usually respond to more than three or four dimensions at once; on the other hand, perhaps the fit of the model is not very sensitive to higher dimensionality in the data, or else maybe experimenters do not report higher-dimensional solutions because they are harder to interpret.

D. Vector Spaces

Many stimuli can be characterized physically in terms of intensity distributions. To describe such situations, let X be a set of stimuli, with elements x, y, etc.; let P be another set with elements p, q, etc.; and let f be a function on the set of pairs $P \times X$, which can be written $f(p, x)$. For instance, if X is a set of homogeneous colors, then P is the set of visible wavelengths, and f gives the distribution of energy over wavelengths for each color. If X is a set of continuous sounds, then P is the set of audible frequencies, and f gives the energy distribution over frequencies for each sound. If X is a set of monochromatic visual patterns, then P is a plane, and f gives the energy distribution over positions for each pattern. If X is a set of solutions to be tasted or smelled, then P is the set of chemical substances with detectable taste or odor, and f gives the amount of each of these substances in each solution. In these examples, the function f completely specifies the stimuli, in the sense that for any x, y in X:

$$x = y \quad \text{if and only if} \quad f(p, x) = f(p, y) \quad \text{for all } p \text{ in } P. \qquad (10)$$

Moreover, for any two stimuli x and y in X, it is possible to define a combined stimulus $x + y$ in X, such that:

$$f(p, x + y) = f(p, x) + f(p, y) \quad \text{for all } p \text{ in } P. \qquad (11)$$

Also, for any stimulus x in X, and any positive constant λ, it is possible to define a multiplied stimulus λx in X, such that:

$$f(p, \lambda x) = \lambda f(p, x) \quad \text{for all } p \text{ in } P. \qquad (12)$$

Since the function f is previously defined by physical measurement, models for this situation will be examples of derived measurement. Given stimuli with so much physical structure, subjects do not have to provide an ordering, but only an equivalence relation $\approx$, interpreted as matching or indistinguishability. Obviously, subjects will not be able to distinguish many stimuli that are different physically. The task of a model is therefore to describe stimuli by functions that do not differentiate between indistinguishable stimuli yet can be added and multiplied as in (11) and (12). In other words, the model should define functions ϕ_1, ϕ_2, . . . , ϕ_k on

X, with the following properties for all x, y in X, $i = 1, \ldots, k$, and $\lambda > 0$:

$$x \approx y \quad \text{if and only if} \quad \phi_i(x) = \phi_i(y) \quad \text{for all} \quad i = 1, \ldots, k. \quad (13)$$

$$\phi_i(x + y) = \phi_i(x) + \phi_i(y). \quad (14)$$

$$\phi_i(\lambda x) = \lambda \phi_i(x). \quad (15)$$

Consequently, the model represents the objects in X as points in a k-dimensional vector space, with coordinates given by the ϕ_i.

Krantz (1971a,b) shows that given a physical characterization satisfying (10)–(12), the representation in k dimensions is possible if the following axioms hold for all x, y, z in X, and all $\lambda > 0$.

V1. $\approx$ is an equivalence relation.

V2. $x \approx y$ if and only if $x + z \approx y + z$.

V3. $x \approx y$ implies $\lambda x \approx \lambda y$.

V4.   For any $x_0, x_1, \ldots, x_k$ in X, there are nonnegative real numbers $\lambda_0, \lambda_1, \ldots, \lambda_k$, and $\mu_0, \mu_1, \ldots, \mu_k$, such that $\lambda_i \neq \mu_i$ for at least one i, and

$$\sum_{i=0}^{k} \lambda_i x_i \approx \sum_{i=0}^{k} \mu_i x_i.$$

Given these axioms, the representation is also unique up to rotations of the coordinate axes and changes of unit on any axis.

Possible empirical objections to Axiom V1 were discussed in Section II,A. One clear exception to Axiom V2 is the phenomenon of masking: If the same masking stimulus is added to each of two distinguishable stimuli, the resulting stimuli may be indistinguishable from each other. Although masking has received much empirical study, it does not seem to have been incorporated into measurement models. On the face of it, Axiom V3 appears inconsistent with the observation that for many stimuli, changes in intensity produce changes in perceived quality, such as hue, pitch, taste, or odor. Actually, however, these data are not directly comparable to the axiom, because the matching relation in the axiom holds only when the stimuli match in all respects, whereas the experiments asked whether the stimuli matched in quality while clearly differing in intensity. In fact, qualitative changes contradict the axiom if and only if the stimuli change in different directions, so that two stimuli appear different from each other at one intensity but not at another. Since this distinction has not been emphasized in the experimental literature, it is difficult to state the conditions under which the axiom becomes invalid.

Axioms V1–V3 establish the vector space; Axiom V4 implies that k dimensions are enough to represent the stimuli. In most psychophysical applications, Axiom V4 can be satisfied rather trivially if k is set equal to the number of stimuli in X that are just noticeably different when intensity is matched. Although k defined in this way will probably be considerably less than the number of elements in P, it will still be much too large for the representation to be of any practical use. In order for k to be reduced further, there must exist pairs of stimuli that are indistinguishable for subjects even though they are less similar physically than other stimuli that can be distinguished. Using the terminology of color theory, stimuli that match in this way can be called metameric. The existence of metameric stimuli means that the perceptual system is reducing information without reducing the discriminability of physically adjacent stimuli.

This kind of information reduction is particularly important in color vision. As is well known, so many colors are metameric that any color can be matched by a suitably defined mixture of three primary colors. This finding is equivalent (given the other axioms) to Axiom V4 with k equal to three. Thus, each color corresponds to a point in a three-dimensional vector space, and two colors will match if and only if they correspond to the same point. Moreover, the configuration of colors in this space is very similar to the configuration that results when the multidimensional scaling methods of Section II,C are applied to rankings of the similarity of colors that do not match. Consequently, the different responses of matching mixtures and judging similarities seem to be derived, according to their respective response rules, from the same underlying three-dimensional representation for color stimuli.

Other stimulus modalities differ greatly in the prevalence of metameric stimuli. Tastes are frequently described by a vector space with four primary tastes, although the experimental evidence for this model is much less extensive for taste than for color. The data for odors are even less conclusive. Some metameric pairs have apparently been demonstrated, but estimates of the number of primary odors range from about five to about twenty or even higher. Finally, in audition and pattern vision, metameric stimuli are rare or absent, the dimensionality of the space would have to be comparable to the number of just noticeable differences in pitch or position, and consequently vector space models are not used. In general, it seems that metameric stimuli tend to occur, and low-dimensional vector representations are thus possible, in modalities that Erickson (1968) has classified on physiological grounds as nontopographic, but not in modalities classified as topographic.

III. PROBABILISTIC MODELS

Luce (1964) suggested that the available psychophysical models fell into two quite distinct classes, which he called the *internal state* models, and the *choice* models. Much of the empirical and theoretical literature relevant to these models is summarized in Krantz (1972a), Luce (1963), Luce and Galanter (1963a,b), Luce and Green (1974), and Zinnes (1969). The internal state models suppose that each possible stimulus presentation activates, in a probabilistic fashion, an internal state, which in turn leads, via some decision mechanism, to a response. The choice models suppose that there is a measure of similarity over the possible stimulus presentations, and a measure of response tendency, that are combined in some suitable fashion to give a measure of response tendency for a given response in the presence of a given stimulus. Although special cases of these models are equivalent (Marley, 1971), it does not appear that this is generally true. Nonetheless, several internal state and choice models have been applied to psychophysical data, without any single model consistently appearing superior to the others (Luce, 1963; Luce & Green, 1974). For this reason, it appears worthwhile to explore how much content these models have; in other words, to what extent is it possible on the basis of a relatively small amount of data to discriminate among the various realizations of models within these two classes. To allow our discussion to be quite detailed, we focus our attention on internal state models for certain two-alternative absolute judgment experiments, discrimination experiments, and direct estimation experiments. We demonstrate that many such models for absolute judgment have little empirical content, and that a quite general class of internal state models for magnitude estimation predicts many of the results that are usually quoted as valid in such experiments. (It would be interesting to have a similar body of results for other classes of models.) Having illustrated the preceding points, in the discussion we consider their implications for future research in psychophysics: Our main conclusion is that it is now reasonable to explore models that, by appropriate specialization, can be applied to many different psychophysical designs.

A. Two-Alternative Absolute Judgment

The typical two-alternative absolute judgment experiment has the following form: We have available some stimulus set X, from which we select two distinct stimuli x, y. At the beginning of the experiment, the subject is informed that response 1 is correct when x is presented, and response 2 is correct when y is presented. During the body of the experiment, he may or may not be correctly informed of which stimulus occurred on a particular trial and he may or may not be rewarded with a sum of money depending on his response on that trial. In different experiments using the same stimuli, the experimenter may use different presentation probabilities for the stimuli, and different monetary rewards. Data and theory relevant to such experiments are summarized in Luce (1963), Green and Swets (1966), and Luce and Green (1974). We confine our discussion to the simplest and most commonly studied models and experiments.

So assume that response 1 is correct for x, response 2 is correct for y, and that during the body of the experiment the subject receives monetary payoffs consistent with this identification of correct responses. Important data in such experiments are the probabilities $p(1|z)$, $z = x, y$, which denote the probability of response 1 when stimulus z is presented; since we suppress reference to trial numbers, p may be thought of as an estimate of asymptotic response probabilities. For notational convenience we write $(a, b) \in [x, y]$ if we have data with $a = p(1|x)$, $b = p(1|y)$. The *absolute judgment isosensitivity curve* $[x, y]$ consists of the pairs $(0, 0)$, $(1, 1)$, and the data pairs (a, b) obtained as we vary such things as presentation probabilities and payoffs; an example is given in Fig. 2.

Turning to theory, the *univariate internal state model under a simple cutpoint criterion* (Luce, 1964; Wickelgren, 1968) requires that there exists a family of distribution functions $\{F_x, x \in X\}$ such that for each $x, y \in X$, if $(a, b) \in [x, y]$, then there exists a (real number or $\pm \infty$) t with $a = F_x(t)$, $b = F_y(t)$. The intended interpretation is that for each $x \in X$, F_x is the cumulative distribution associated with some "sensation" random variable, and the subject responds 1 on a particular trial if and only if the value of the sensation random variable is less than the value of the cutpoint t; as we change payoffs, presentation probabilities, etc., but keep the same stimuli x, y, only the value of t is assumed to change. Marley (1971) investigated necessary and sufficient conditions for a set of absolute judgment data to be so representable. For simplicity, he assumed that the set X is ordered by a relation $\lesssim$, and that the subject is instructed and rewarded to respond consistently with this order in the sense that of $x, y \in X$ with $x < y$ are the stimulus presentations, then response 1 is correct for x, response 2 is correct for y. Under quite weak regularity conditions, any *pair* of isosensitivity curves are representable by the preceding model; the major additional constraint required for three or more curves is a generalization of the following condition:

If $(a, b) \in [x, y]$, and $(b, c) \in [y, z]$ with $b \in (0, 1)$, then $(a, c) \in [x, z]$. Figure 3 illustrates its interpretation. [The condition has to be generalized because, as it stands, it requires that the pair (a, c) be obtained as a *data point* on the isosensitivity curve $[x, y]$, whereas the model does not imply

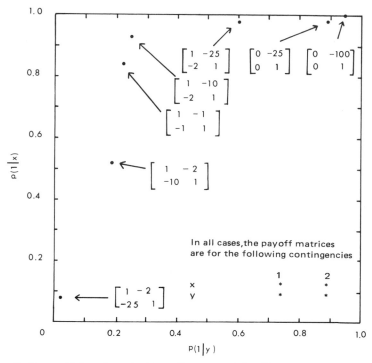

FIG. 2. Isosensitivity data (subject 6) reported by Norman (1962). x denotes a fixed energy, 1000–Hz pure tone, y denotes this tone incremented 2.2% in energy; the presentation probability of x was .5; and the payoff matrices (in cents) are shown. Each point is estimated from 200–300 observations.

that we must have collected such data.] Marley (1971) also demonstrated that the absolute judgment curves specify the representing family fairly weakly to the extent that if $\{F_x, x \in X\}$ is a representing family, then (essentially so is $\{F_x g, x \in X\}$ for any real-valued, strictly monotonic increasing, 1–1 function g.

Once we are convinced that the curves are representable by a family of distribution functions, we can start exploring the question of more specific representations. For instance, we can ask under what conditions the curves are representable by a *scale family* of distribution functions: A family of distributions $\{F_x, x \in X\}$ is a scale family if there exists a cumulative distribution function G that is strictly monotonic increasing whenever it is different from 0 and 1, and a positive function η on X such that for each $x \in X$, and each real t such that $F_x(t) \neq 0, 1$,

$$F_x(t) = G\left(\frac{t}{\eta(x)}\right)$$

Marley (1971) has explored necessary conditions for such representations; related questions are considered by Aczel (1965), Falmagne (1971), and Levine (1970).

In most applications, the obverse of the above axiomatic approach has been taken. Specific assumptions are made regarding the form of the underlying (univariate) distributions, and the available data are analyzed using the usual methods of parameter estimation, etc. A very common assumption is that the representing family $\{F_x, x \in X\}$ is a particular scale family. Such an assumption is usually motivated on the basis of mathematical simplicity, or on the basis of an explicit model of the sensory system being studied.

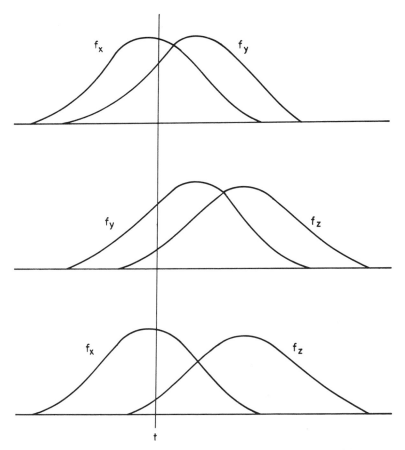

FIG. 3. A diagram illustrating a necessary condition for representability. $a = F_x(t)$, $b = F_y(t)$, $c = F_z(t)$, where t is the fixed cutpoint that is associated with the pairs of points $(a, b) \in [x, y]$, $(b,c) \in [y, z]$, $(a, c) \in [x, z]$.

In the former category are most of the cases in which it is assumed that for $s \geq 0$,

$$G(s) = \Phi(\log s),$$

where Φ is the cumulative normal distribution; Swets (1964) and Green and Swets (1966) present detailed theoretical and empirical support for this particular assumption. A second common scale-family assumption is that for $s \geq 0$,

$$G(s) = s/(1 + s).$$

This distribution represents Luce's *choice model* (Luce, 1959a, 1963; Marley, 1971). The motivations behind the normal model and the choice model are quite distinct, yet their predictions are frequently extremely similar (Burke & Zinnes, 1965; Chambers & Cox, 1967; Dawkins, 1969; Yellott, 1970).

Examples of the second motivation, i.e., an explicit model of the sensory system, abound in psychoacoustics where various models of the auditory system specify the form of G. For instance, Green and McGill (1970) present a model for discrimination of bursts of noise which is such that if each waveform is of bandwidth W and duration T, and if $\eta(x)$ denotes the average noise power per unit bandwidth for the burst x, then G is χ^2 with $2WT$ degrees of freedom. Various other detailed suggestions are explored in the Green and McGill paper, and also in Swets (1964), Green and Swets (1966), McGill (1967, 1968), Jeffress (1968), and Siebert (1968).

One means of obtaining additional support for a particular theory is to use information from one set of experiments to predict performance in one or more other experiments using a subset of the same stimuli. For instance, suppose that the theory asserts that the distribution of internal states are n-dimensional normal, these distributions having different means but equal covariance matrices, and that the subject uses a likelihood-ratio decision mechanism (Luce, 1963, p. 109) in deciding his response. Anderson (1958, pp. 133–135 and p. 13) shows that each isosensitivity curve $[x, y]$ is characterized by a distance $\delta(x, y)$ in n-dimensional Euclidean space, this distance being a function of the relevant means and covariance matrix. If the univariate version of the model is correct, then for stimuli x, y, z, we can estimate $\delta(x, z)$ from estimates of $\delta(x, y)$ and $\delta(y, z)$. If the multivariate model is correct, no such estimate of $\delta(x, z)$ is available, and in order to discriminate between the univariate and multivariate model, we need to obtain at least three, suitably related, isosensitivity curves. This is the kind of result we might expect on the basis of Marley's (1971) condition introduced earlier. Other cross-validation studies are summarized by

Green and Swets (1966), Luce (1963), Luce and Green (1974), and Swets (1964).

So far, we have ignored the possibility of explaining the dependence of the cutpoint t of the univariate models on such variables as the payoffs and the stimulus presentation probabilities. In this case, the theory will not only predict the shape of the isosensitivity curve, but also the relative location of points corresponding to different payoffs, etc.; Green and Swets (1966), Luce (1964), and Luce and Green (1974) summarize the relevant models and data. Nonetheless, two-alternative absolute judgment data only allows us to specify the scale t up to a monotone transformation (Marley, 1971), which complicates the interpretation of the fit of the predictions.

The foregoing applications concern the detailed form of the sensory distributions, and all assume a simple cutpoint decision rule. Clearly, much more complex decision rules can be formulated, which might, in fact, be more appropriate. Henning (1967) presents an interesting rule for pure-tone discrimination based on the assumption that the internal state u is filtered in a suitable manner, and that the decision is based on the output of one or more such filters. Wickelgren (1968) presents the following model based on a distribution of cutpoints. Let A denote the class of absolute judgment experiments that we can generate by altering payoffs, presentation probabilities, etc. Wickelgren's model requires that there exist families of distribution functions $\{H_x, x \in X\}$, $\{K_{\alpha(a)}, a \in A\}$, α a real-valued function, such that for any data point $(p_a(1|x), p_a(1|y))$ obtained from a particular absolute judgment experiment $a \in A$,

$$p_a(1|x) = \int_{-\infty}^{\infty} H_x(c) \, dK_{\alpha(a)}(c) \stackrel{\text{def}}{=} F_x(\alpha(a)),$$

$$p_a(1|y) = \int_{-\infty}^{\infty} H_y(c) \, dK_{\alpha(a)}(c) \stackrel{\text{def}}{=} F_y(\alpha(a)),$$

i.e., H_x, H_y represent distributions of "sensation" values, $K_{\alpha(a)}$ represents the criterion distribution, and the subject responds 1 on a particular trial if and only if the value of the sensation random variable is less than the value of the criterion random variable. Changing the experiment $a \in A$ now changes the cutpoint $\alpha(a)$, and without the preceding analysis we might interpret the family $\{F_x, x \in X\}$ as a family of "sensation" distributions (as we have done in our discussion to this point). Such an interpretation might lead to error in analyzing data obtained in other experiments using stimuli from the set X: For example, assume that when discriminating between $x, y \in X$, the subject says that element that has the larger sensation value on a particular trial is "greater." The discriminability of x from y predicted using $\{F_x, x \in X\}$ as the family of "sensation" distributions is poorer than that predicted using the (true) "sensation" distributions $\{H_x, x \in X\}$. Although the particular model might not be appropriate (since we might also expect criterion variance to play a part in discrimination tasks), it does indicate that careful consideration should be given to criterion variances. Wickelgren (1968) gives detailed examples, confining his discussion to the case where both the sensation and the criterion random variables are normally distributed. The assumption of normality for the sensation distribution can be defended for the reasons given earlier, and also on the basis of appropriate central limit theorems (Thompson & Singh, 1967). Norman (1972, Sect. 17.4) shows that a large class of learning models for criterion change leads to normal distributions for the asymptotic values of the criterion, provided that learning is "slow."

Owing partly to the complexities that arise as a result of various possible combinations of distributional assumptions and decision rules, several authors have seriously investigated internal state models that assume a small, finite number of internal states, plus a quite general decision mechanism. Krantz (1969) has explored several such models, and concluded that a particular three-state model provides good fits to various threshold data. However, he notes that the isosensitivity curves that he has studied appear to be fit equally well by assuming that the underlying distributions of sensory states are normal with different means and variances; he concludes that it will be difficult to make a final decision between finite state (or threshold) models and continuous models on the basis of isosensitivity curves. His conclusions are based to a considerable extent on the comparative fit of these models to isosensitivity curves of the form $[n, s + n]$, where n is a noise stimulus, and $s + n$ is some signal embedded in that noise. Again, a stronger test of the model necessitates studying three interrelated curves $[n, s_1 + n]$, $[n, s_2 + n]$, $[s_1 + n, s_2 + n]$. To give the model an even break (as is necessary for any "univariate" model), we should confine our attention to "unidimensional" stimuli: say, n, s_1, and s_2 bursts of acoustic white noise, as opposed to n acoustic white noise, and s_1, s_2 pure tones of equal amplitude but different frequencies.

B. Discrimination

Considerable theory and data related to discrimination can be encompassed by the assumption that for various pairs of stimuli x, y, there is a measure $r(x, y)$ of the discriminability of x from y (Krantz, 1972a; Falmagne, 1971). For instance, if x, y are patches of light, $r(x, y)$ might be the probability that a subject judges x to be "redder" than y in a two-alternative forced-choice experiment, or it might be the reaction time of the subject in deciding that x is "redder" than y when x, y are presented simultaneously. Falmagne (1971), Krantz (1972a), Levine (1970), Luce and Galanter (1963a), Luce and Suppes (1965), Morrison (1963), and Zinnes (1969) give detailed summaries of data and theory related to such discriminability measures, so in this section we highlight certain results that appear in those summaries, and discuss several other results that are not included there.

As in the previous section, suppose that we have some set X, weakly ordered by a relation $\precsim$ that has a "natural" psychological counterpart. For elements $x, y \in X$, let $p(x, y)$ denote the (binary choice) probability of a subject deciding that x is "greater" than y in some suitably designed experiment. As in our discussion of absolute judgment, two distinct approaches can be taken to models for such data. We can either search for necessary and/or sufficient conditions for a set of data to satisfy a particular class of models, or we can suggest specific forms for the functions defining the model, and investigate the appropriateness of such assumptions. We apply each approach in turn to two broad classes of models.

The first class assumes that the binary choice probabilities satisfy *simple scalability* (Krantz, 1967b), which requires that there are real valued functions F and u, with F strictly increasing in its first argument and strictly decreasing in the second, such that for all, $x, y \in X$,

$$p(x,y) = F[u(x), u(y)].$$

Independence is both necessary and sufficient for the probabilities to satisfy simple scalability (Tversky & Russo, 1969): For $a, b, c, d \in X$,

$$p(a, c) \geq p(b, c) \quad \text{if and only if} \quad p(a, d) \geq p(b, d).$$

(The authors also introduce other equivalent conditions.) Krantz (1967b) and Tversky and Russo (1969) found relatively serious violations of independence, Krantz studying similarity judgments between pairs of monochromatic colors, and Tversky and Russo studying judgments of area with stimuli that differed in size and shape. The authors do not provide an alternative model that fits their data, but discuss the fact that judgments are affected by overall "similarity" of stimuli as well as by the relevant scale values: Thus in Tversky and Russo's case, the irrelevant dimension of shape, and the similarity of objects on this dimension, affects the difficulty of deciding which of two objects has the larger area. Tversky (1972) presents a model that potentially contributes to our understanding of these phenomena.

The second class of models assumes that the binary-choice probabilities satisfy a (*binary*) *random utility model* (Luce & Suppes, 1965), which is a set of (binary) choice probabilities defined on a set X for which there is a random vector **u** on X such that for $x, y \in X$,

$$p(x, y) = \mathrm{Pr}[\mathbf{u}(x) \geq \mathbf{u}(y)].$$

If the random vector **u** consists of components that are independent random variables, then the model is an *independent* random utility model. When X contains at most three elements, the *triangle condition* (Marschak, 1960) is both necessary and sufficient for the probabilities to satisfy a random utility model: For $a, b, c \in X$,

$$1 \leq p(a, b) + p(b, c) + p(c, a) \leq 2.$$

When X has more than three elements, no necessary and sufficient set of conditions is known; Marschak (1960) discusses various necessary conditions. If we require that the probabilities satisfy an independent random utility model, then, when X contains at most three elements, the following condition is necessary and sufficient (Trybula, 1961): For $a, b, c \in X$,

if $p(a, b) + p(b, c) > 1$, then either $p(a, b)p(b, c) \leq p(a, c)$,
$$\text{or } p(b, c)p(c, a) \leq p(b, a),$$
$$\text{or } p(c, a)p(a, b) \leq p(c, b).$$

Again, when X has more than three elements, no necessary and sufficient set of conditions is known. Further discussion of the independent model, with no restriction on the set size, can be found in Chang (1961), Steinhaus and Trybula (1959), Trybula (1965), and Usiskin (1964).

For all set sizes, there are (binary) independent random utility models that do not satisfy simple scalability. On the other hand, if X contains at most three elements, then any set of (binary) choice probabilities that satisfies simple scalability also satisfies an independent random utility model; it is unknown whether this statement is true for larger set sizes.* To our knowledge, no experiments have been carried out with the specific aim of testing Marschak's or Trybula's conditions. However, by noting their relation to other conditions (see footnote), and referring to the data in Krantz (1967b), Luce and Suppes (1965), Tversky (1969), and Tversky and Russo (1969), we conclude that if the stimulus domain X is suit-

---

* These conclusions follow by combining various results in the papers referenced above with those of Luce and Suppes (1965). An independent random utility model may not satisfy strong stochastic transitivity, which is equivalent to simple scalability (Trybula, 1965; Tversky & Russo, 1969). Strong stochastic transitivity implies the triangle condition (Fig. 5 of Luce & Suppes, 1965) and also implies Trybula's (1961) condition (use the method of proof in Theorem 38 of Luce & Suppes, 1965).

ably "unidimensional," then the conditions are valid; the trick, of course, is to give an independent definition of what we mean by "unidimensional."

Turning to more specific models that satisfy simple scalability, a *strong* (or *Fechnerian*) *binary utility model* (Luce & Suppes, 1965) is a set of binary choice probabilities for which there exist a real-valued function w on X, and a cumulative distribution ϕ such that

(i) $\phi(0) = \frac{1}{2}$ and
(ii) for all $x, y \in X$ for which $p(x, y) \neq 0, 1$,
$\qquad p(x, y) = \phi[w(x) - w(y)]$.

Strong utility models are appealing because of their connection with the *Weber-Fechner* problem (Luce & Galanter, 1963a). For each $\pi \in (0, 1)$ and (real-valued) $x \in X$, we define the *Weber function* $\Delta_\pi(x)$ by

$$p(x + \Delta_\pi(x), x) = \pi.$$

The following set of relations is compatible with a strong utility model: There exist $x_0 \in X$, constants $A > 0$ and B, and a strictly monotonic function k such that

$$\Delta_\pi(x) = k(\pi)(x + x_0),$$
$$w(x) = A \log(x + x_0) + B,$$

and

$$\phi(a) = k^{-1}[\exp(a/A) - 1].$$

The first relation is *Weber's law,* the second *Fechner's law;* the idea of Fechner's law is that w gives *the* relation between *the* physical measure x and *the* "sensation" $w(x)$. However, when the probabilities satisfy a strong utility model, we may equally write

$$p(x, y) = \phi'\left(\frac{w'(x)}{w'(y)}\right)$$

for appropriately constructed functions ϕ', w', and call w' *the* "sensation" measure. Thus, as pointed out by Luce and Galanter (1963a), it is not appropriate to call the relation specified by w (or w'), a "law" until w (or w') has been independently defined: In Section III,C we discuss how we might approach such definition.

Table I describes three commonly studied random utility models that are also strong utility models; Luce and Suppes (1965) discuss the general relation between these two classes of models. Burke and Zinnes (1965), Chambers and Cox (1967), Dawkins (1969), and Yellott (1970) discuss the fact that it is difficult to obtain data that discriminate between the mod-

TABLE I

Three Commonly Studied Random Utility Models[a]

Name of model	$\Pr[\varepsilon(x) \leq t]$	$\phi(a)$	References
1. Thurstone's Case V	$(2\pi)^{-1/2} \int_{-\infty}^{t} \exp(-u^2/2)\,du, \quad -\infty < t < \infty$	$(2\pi)^{-1/2} \int_{-\infty}^{a} \exp-(u^2/4)\,du, \quad -\infty < a < \infty$	Luce and Galanter, 1963a; Bock and Jones, 1968
2. Strict utility	$1 - \exp(-e^t), \quad t \geq 0$	$\dfrac{1}{1 + e^{-a}}, \quad -\infty < a < \infty$	Luce and Suppes, 1965
3. Dawkins	$1 - e^{-t}, \quad t \geq 0$	$\left. \begin{cases} \frac{1}{2}e^{-\lvert a \rvert} \\ 1 - \frac{1}{2}e^{-\lvert a \rvert} \end{cases} \right\}$ if $\begin{cases} a \leq 0 \\ a \geq 0 \end{cases}$	Dawkins, 1969; Yellott, 1970

[a] In each case, there is a real-valued function u on X such that for x, $y \in X$, $\mathbf{u}(x) = u(x) + \varepsilon(x)$, and $p(x, y) = \Pr[\mathbf{u}(x) \geq \mathbf{u}(y)]$ $= \phi[u(x) - u(y)]$, where ϕ is the distribution of the difference $\varepsilon(x) - \varepsilon(y)$.

els of Table I, particularly between Thurstone's Case V and the strict utility model.

C. Direct Estimation

Direct estimation refers to situations such as magnitude estimation, category scaling, and rating of similarity, where the subject's response is a number that represents some property of the stimulus presentation under observation. As Zinnes (1969) emphasizes, there is no sense in which a numerical response is more direct than any other response, and our use of the term here is a matter of terminological convenience. Ekman and Sjöberg (1965), Krantz (1972b), Luce and Galanter (1963b), Poulton (1968), and Zinnes (1969) give summaries of theory and data in such direct estimation experiments. Most of this research has focused attention on the average response to various stimuli, and the relation of the average response to some physical measure of these stimuli. Krantz (1972b) develops the most complete models in this genre: He presents axioms that capture the content of various empirical generalizations concerning average responses in magnitude estimation, pair estimation, and cross-modality matching, and shows that a particular representation theorem follows from these axioms. A major exception to the concern with average responses is a magnitude estimation model due to Luce and Galanter (1963b) that was tested by Luce and Mo (1965).

We begin this section with a class of models motivated by Luce and Galanter's work, and then discuss how these models can be generated by internal state models. The models are compatible with the five generalizations that Krantz (1972b) requires any satisfactory model to handle. We conclude the section with a discussion of how to extend the models to category experiments, and how to explore subjects' ability to evaluate sensation "ratios" as opposed to sensation "differences."

Consider a *magnitude estimation experiment,* in which a series of stimuli from some set X is presented one at a time, and the subject has to report a (nonnegative) real number that represents the magnitude of the presented stimulus, relative to the magnitude of a standard stimulus x_0 that is assigned the finite (response) value $r_0 > 0$ by the experimenter. Let $P(r|x)$ indicate the probability that the subject responds with a number less than or equal to r when x is presented. We initially suppose that there exists a cumulative distribution function Φ with $\Phi(0) = 0$, and a positive-valued function ψ on X such that

$$P(r|x) = \Phi\left(\frac{r/r_0}{\psi(x)/\psi(x_0)}\right).$$

If we let $\mathbf{r}(x)$ denote the (response) random variable associated with r in the quantity $P(r|x)$, and if M is a real-valued function such that for each $x \in X$, and real constant c,

$$M(c\mathbf{r}(x)) = cM(\mathbf{r}(x)),$$

then it follows (Marley, 1972) that for each $x \in X$,

$$M(\mathbf{r}(x)) = [M(\mathbf{r}(x_0))/\psi(x_0)] \cdot \psi(x).$$

Calling ψ the *psychophysical function*, $M(\mathbf{r}(x))$ is proportional to the psychophysical function. Examples of suitable M are the nth root of the nth raw or central moment (including the arithmetic mean and the standard deviation), the geometric mean, and the percentiles (including the median). In the remainder of this section, we loosely refer to such functions M as measures of the *average* response.

In particular, when ψ is a power function, the average response is also a power function; this result is approximately true in magnitude estimation (Krantz, 1971b; Stevens, Mack, & Stevens, 1960). Second, the average response to a particular stimulus x must be proportional to the standard deviation of the responses to that stimulus, since both are proportional to $\psi(x)$; Luce and Mo (1965) give evidence, both favorable and unfavorable, on this point. Also, for a pair of magnitude estimation experiments that differ only in the value of the standard stimulus and/or the value of the standard response, the average response to a stimulus x in the one experiment is proportional to the average response to x in the second experiment, the constant of proportionality depending only on the form of M, and the values of the standard stimuli and responses; Krantz (1972b) calls this *magnitude consistency*. Finally,

$$\Pr\left[\frac{\mathbf{r}(x)}{M(\mathbf{r}(x))} \le t\right] = \Phi\left(\frac{M(\mathbf{r}(x_0))}{r_0} \cdot t\right),$$

i.e., for each stimulus x, the distribution of the response, $\mathbf{r}(x)$, normalized by the average response, $M(\mathbf{r}(x))$, is independent of the stimulus. This property is not commonly tested on magnitude estimation data, although Luce and Mo (1965) give some evidence in its favor, using a particular function Φ that is motivated by Luce and Galanter's (1963b) choice model of magnitude estimation.

Attneave (1962) suggests that magnitude estimation entails two stages: in the first (input) stage, the subject evaluates the relationship between stimuli, and in the second (output) stage, he maps this relationship onto the number system. Rule, Curtis, and Markley (1970) tested a version of these ideas in magnitude estimation, and in difference estimation (defined later). Both papers are restricted to mean responses, and both fit each stage with power functions. Marley (1972) discusses a class of internal state models, based on similar intuitions, that in certain special cases predicts choice probabilities compatible with the form suggested above for $P(r|x)$. He supposes that associated with each stimulus $x \in X$ is a nonnegative random variable $\mathbf{u}(x)$, which represents the effect of a presentation of x, and a nonnegative random variable $\mathbf{v}(x_0)$, which represents the memory for the standard x_0. When x is presented, the subject evaluates the ratio $\mathbf{u}(x)/\mathbf{v}(x_0)$, and emits a response based on this ratio; in particular there exists a probability $P(r|u)$ that the subject responds with a number less than or equal to r when the ratio equals u. If it is now assumed that there exist functions η, G, H, K, and a constant $\gamma > 0$ such that

$$\mathrm{Pr}(\mathbf{u}(x) \leq t) = G\left(\frac{t}{\eta(x)}\right),$$

$$\mathrm{Pr}(\mathbf{v}(x_0) \leq t) = H\left(\frac{t}{\eta(x_0)}\right),$$

and

$$P(r|u) = K\left(\frac{r/r_0}{u^{\gamma}}\right),$$

then a routine demonstration (Marley, 1972) shows that

$$P(r|x) = \Phi\left(\frac{r/r_0}{[\eta(x)/\eta(x_0)]^{\gamma}}\right),$$

where Φ is an integral defined in terms of G, H, and K. Provided that the integral exists, this is clearly of the form considered earlier. Marley (1972) also discusses specific forms for G, H, and K that either directly match the model tested by Luce and Mo (1965), or that approximate this model in certain limiting cases.

Appropriate extensions of the preceding internal state model generate predictions for related experiments (Marley, 1972). The extended model possesses various of the properties regarding average responses that Krantz (1972b) feels must be handled by any satisfactory model.

We now briefly describe a category experiment, and mention relations that are sometimes found between data obtained in such experiments and in magnitude estimation experiments. We discuss how to extend the internal state models to category situations, and inquire whether we obtain the expected relations between category and magnitude data.

The experimenter selects a set of stimuli, numbering from about 20 to 100, which he presents to the subject one at a time. If there is a "natural" physical dimension, then the experimenter might also present the smallest stimulus x_1, and say that it belongs to category 1, and the largest stimulus x_m and say that it belongs to category k. The subject is instructed to use the remaining categories as if they were "equally spaced" along the sensation continuum between these two stimuli. The simplest response measure studied is the mean category assigned to each stimulus. If we plot the mean category scale against the mean magnitude scale for a set of stimuli, various relations are found including logarithmic and power functions (Ekman & Sjöberg, 1965; Engen & McBurney, 1964).

What is the form of the appropriate internal state model? If the subject interprets the instructions to mean that he should pay attention to sensation "differences" as opposed to sensation "ratios," then we might assume that for each stimulus x, he "evaluates" the quantity

$$c = \frac{\mathbf{u}(x) - \mathbf{u}(x_1)}{\mathbf{u}(x_m) - \mathbf{u}(x_1)},$$

and emits a response based on c. However, the properties of the model then depend crucially on the relation of the response to values of c—by using suitable mappings, essentially any relation can be obtained between the category and magnitude scales. And we are without a satisfactory response theory to limit our assumptions. These points have been made by various authors, whose views are summarized by Ekman and Sjöberg (1965), Krantz (1972a), and Zinnes (1969).

We can ask, however, whether it makes sense to talk of a subject using sensation "ratios" in magnitude estimation, and sensation "differences" in category scaling; or, more generally, does it make sense to talk of sensation "differences" as opposed to "ratios," or vice versa. To explore this question, we introduce two further classes of experiments. Krantz (1972b) calls the first *pair estimation,* but to distinguish between the two experiments we call it *ratio estimation:* A pair of stimuli (x, y) is presented, and the subject is instructed to respond with a number that corresponds to the "sensation ratio" of x to y. The second experiment is *difference estimation:* A pair (x, y) is presented, and the subject responds with a number corresponding to the "sensation difference" of x and y. Pursuing our earlier class of models, we assume that the subject's "sensation" values are generated by a scale family: There exist functions η, G, and random variables $\mathbf{u}(x)$, $x \in X$, such that for $t > 0$,

$$\Pr(\mathbf{u}(x) \leq t) = G\left(\frac{t}{\eta(x)}\right).$$

If we are to apply this distribution in explaining data obtained in ratio and difference estimation experiments, and yet avoid the debate regarding mappings between sensory quantities and responses, then we seem forced to study only the most obvious assumptions: In ratio estimation, the subject evaluates the ratio $\mathbf{u}(x)/\mathbf{u}(y)$, and emits this value as his response; in difference estimation, the subject evaluates the difference $\mathbf{u}(x) - \mathbf{u}(y)$, and emits this value as his response. Under these conditions, the mean ratio-estimation response to a pair (x, y) is proportional to $\eta(x)/\eta(y)$, and the mean difference-estimation response is proportional to $\eta(x) - \eta(y)$. There are three related ways to check the appropriateness of these (and other) representations.

First, we can test whether certain quantitative relations hold between the mean responses to various pairs. In the present case, we have, for $x, y, z \in X$:

(a) for ratio estimation, the mean response to (x, y) multiplied by the mean response to (y, z) equals the mean response to (x, z) [Krantz (1972b) calls a similar condition *pair consistency*];

(b) for difference estimation, the mean response to (x, y) plus the mean response to (y, z) equals the mean response to (x, z).

Fagot and Stewart (1969) failed to find support for either condition using brightness judgments.

Second, we can construct certain functions and see if they are related in the way specified by the model being considered. In the present case, we construct a function f that represents the mean ratio responses as accurately as possible as a ratio of f values, construct a function f' that represents the mean difference responses as accurately as possible as a difference of f' values, and check whether f' is linearly related to some suitable power transformation of f.

Essentially this approach was taken by Rule, Curtis, and Markley (1970). Their data suggest generalizing the conclusions regarding mean responses by assuming that there is a constant $\gamma > 0$ such that the mean ratio-estimation response is linearly related to $[\eta(x)/\eta(y)]^\gamma$, and that the mean difference-estimation response is linearly related to $[\eta(x) - \eta(y)]^\gamma$. They were satisfied with the fit of such a model to mean magnitude and difference estimation data with η a power function, and with circles and weights as stimuli. If we generalize the internal state model to include the assumption that there is a power function with exponent γ mapping the appropriate sensory quantity onto a response, then the representations for mean responses can approximate those suggested by Rule *et al.* (1970). Any data that satisfies this more general model will satisfy Condition (a), but need not satisfy Condition (b). Since Fagot and Stewart's (1969) data failed on both (a), (b), the present model does not explain their ratio estimation data, although it might fit their difference estimation data.

Finally, we can test whether certain qualitative relations hold between the mean responses to various pairs of stimuli in the two classes of experiments (Krantz, 1972b; Krantz *et al.,* 1971); because these conditions are complex, and so far untested, we do not include specific examples—they are similar in nature to the conditions considered in Section II.

The specific representation for mean responses considered above followed from a complex internal state model. Changing certain of the assumptions leads to rather different theoretical positions, and changed form for the relation between mean-ratio responses and mean-difference responses. By using both "ratio" and "difference" instructions, and (presumably) obtaining different results in the two cases, we should be able to pin down the appropriate internal state model, and avoid some of the arbitrariness of representations that was discussed in the discrimination section. For instance, if the above basic model is supported by data, then it seems appropriate to call η *the* sensation measure—partly because it is the measure that gives the simplest description of the data. Nonetheless, we still must discover whether the appropriate model for biased discrimination (Luce & Galanter, 1963a, p. 224) is based on sensation ratios or sensation differences (or neither or both depending on the circumstances?) of these *same* random variables $\mathbf{u}(x)$.

Although in the preceding example, the scale-family representation seems to be the most parsimonious description of the data, it is also possible for a set of data to be equally well described by two alternative representations; such a case is illustrated in Table II. If we take the scale family representation, then the underlying assumption is that the subject is able

TABLE II

A Pair of Equivalent Models for Ratio and Difference Judgment

Representation[a]	Task	Basis for response	Mean response[b]
Scale family	Ratio judgment	$\mathbf{u}(x)/\mathbf{u}(y)$	$\eta(x)/\eta(y)$
	Difference judgment	$\log \dfrac{\mathbf{u}(x)}{\mathbf{u}(y)}$	$\log \dfrac{\eta(x)}{\eta(y)}$
Shift family	Ratio judgment	$\exp[\mathbf{v}(x) - \mathbf{v}(y)]$	$\exp[v(x) - v(y)]$
	Difference judgment	$\mathbf{v}(x) - \mathbf{v}(y)$	$v(x) - v(y)$

[a] The scale family representation requires that there exist functions η, G, and random variables $\mathbf{u}(x)$, $x \in X$, such that for $t \geq 0$, $\Pr(\mathbf{u}(x) \leq t) = G(t/\eta(x))$, whereas the shift family representation requires that there exist functions v, H, and random variables $\mathbf{v}(x)$, $x \in X$, such that for real t, $\Pr(\mathbf{v}(x) \leq t) = H(t - v(x))$.

[b] Only that part of the mean response that depends on the stimuli x, y is listed.

to evaluate sensation ratios, but only makes sense of difference instructions by applying a logarithmic transform to sensation ratios. The appropriate reversal of the roles of ratios and differences gives the model as represented by a shift family of distributions. And, clearly, with $v(x) = \log \eta(x)$ the two models are equivalent. If we choose the scale-family representation, then we expect biased discrimination to be based on sensation ratios, whereas if we choose the shift-family representation, such judgments will be based on sensation differences. But we have no means of saying one is the correct representation, which is exactly the problem we originally faced in discussing discrimination models. In summary, if the data have certain configurations (for example, compatible with the first set of assumptions that we considered) then the most parsimonious model may be essentially unique; but other data configurations (for example, those just considered) do not yield a unique representation.

D. Summary

With the appropriate interpretation, many of the models discussed in previous sections can be simultaneously applied to absolute judgment, discrimination, and direct estimation. For example, suppose that there are random variables $\mathbf{u}(x)$, $x \in X$, of the form: for $t \geq 0$,

$$\Pr(\mathbf{u}(x) \leq t) = 1 - \exp(-t/x^\alpha),$$

where $\alpha > 0$, constant. This family gives a plausible internal state model for absolute judgment; similar models have been proposed by Egan, Schulman, and Greenberg (1961) (discussed by Green & Swets, 1966, p. 81), and by Luce and Green (1972). The parallel (binary) independent random utility model gives

$$p(x, y) = x^\alpha/(x^\alpha + y^\alpha);$$

this is of the form suggested by the choice model (Luce, 1959a), and in particular Weber's law holds (Section III,B). Finally, we can approximate Luce and Mo's (1965) magnitude estimation model by an internal state model that uses the random variables $\mathbf{u}(x)$, $x \in X$, for the distributions of internal states (Marley, 1972); for this model, the mean magnitude-estimation response will be a power function of the stimulus measure.

The thrust of this example, and of our presentation regarding probabilistic models to this point, is that the present framework includes many of the models presently available in the psychophysical literature, and that it is all too easy to suggest variants that can be experimentally tested. In the discussion to follow, we propose that we now need a slightly different strategy than we have used in the past; it no longer seems appropriate to suggest special models for individual experiments, but we should try to cover various data within the same framework. The first major empirical attack on this problem occurs in Farrell, Pynn and Braida (1968), and Durlach and Braida (1969), both of which fit data from various psychophysical experiments using a univariate normal model, with the estimated parameters suitably invariant across experiments. Luce and Mo (1965) and Shipley and Luce (1964) are more limited studies of parameter invariance in the choice model. Finally, Luce and Green (1972) present a quite general theory that is applicable to many psychophysical experiments, and they are carrying out extensive empirical studies related to this theory (Green & Luce, 1967, 1971; Luce & Green, 1970).

E. Discussion

If we wish to pursue, say, internal state models as descriptors of classical psychophysical data, and if we are either unwilling or unable to consider explicit peripheral sensory and central decision mechanisms, then the approach taken by Durlach and his co-workers, and by Luce and Green, is valuable. For, as we hope we have illustrated in the previous sections, it is very difficult to test a given internal state model satisfactorily in a particular experimental situation; perhaps by obtaining a model, and a particular set of parameters, that simultaneously describes the data of several experiments, we can feel reasonably confident of the model's validity, even though its fit in any one of the experiments is not impressive.

This argument is rather negative. We are essentially admitting that either our data base is not strong enough to test our theory critically, or that our theory is not of sufficient depth to be rejectable. We therefore have two, possibly related, alternative avenues of attack. One, to obtain more data, or two, to study more explicit theories. We discuss each in turn.

One way to obtain more data is to look at aspects of the responses other than their occurrence or nonoccurrence. One such aspect that has frequently fascinated psychologists is reaction time. Thus we include reaction time from stimulus onset to response onset, etc., in our data. There is already a large literature in psychophysics on this topic, but in this case the lack of acceptable theories is quite apparent, and so we are lead to our second alternative, more explicit theories.

Perhaps our criterion for a reasonable model is faulty. In recent years, many modelers interested in psychophysics, and other areas, have tended to be satisfied with models that seem to be reasonable descriptors of the data. Few such models have been concerned with possible brain mechanisms that would be compatible with the given formulation. This is partly because of our vast ignorance of such mechanisms; however, if we already knew the mechanisms, the task of model building would be (relatively) simple. Therefore, perhaps we should start being rather more explicit in stating where, say, our various distributions and criteria are generated, and what are the properties of the system generating them. We have available various rather sophisticated ideas regarding peripheral processing by the eye and ear, but there is a shortage of equally sophisticated ideas for more central processes. This is not to imply that there are presently no models that lie between the "simple-minded" approach, and the preceding requirement of "explicit mechanisms." Many of the models in psychoacoustics mentioned in earlier sections belong in this middle ground, although their emphasis tends to be on the sensory, rather than the decision, component of the problem. Luce and Green's (1972) pulse modulation model provides a single sensory mechanism with alternative decision rules applied to the sensory information in different experiments; Baron (1970) has an interesting, fairly explicit mechanism for recognition and recall; the models of Siebert (1968), Sperling (1970), and van de Grind, Koenderick, and Bouman (1970a,b) are strong on the sensory end. However, overall one is impressed by how much detail these models accord the sensory transforms, and with how superficial is their treatment of any later (say, decision) processes. This may be because the kinds of experiments carried out in psychophysics are really mainly studying sensory processes. If we see psychophysics as limited to the study of such processes, all is well. However, in this case psychophysics will always be dealing with "sensation" rather than "perception," or with the mechanisms of sensory information transmission, rather than with the content of such transmission. This would be unfortunate, for it seems more appropriate to think of our understanding of sensory processes as a foundation on which to build an understanding of more complex phenomena. Finally, however, we should keep in mind Cornsweet's (1970, p. 370) statement to the effect that "perception" is a description of those phenomena that we do not yet understand.

References

Aczél, J. Ouasigroups, nets, and nomograms. In *Advances in Mathematics,* Vol. I. New York: Academic Press, 1965. Pp. 383–450.

Adams, E. W., Fagot, R. F., & Robinson, R. E. A theory of appropriate statistics. *Psychometrika,* 1965, **30,** 99–127.

Anderson, N. H. Scales and statistics: parametric and non-parametric. *Psychological Bulletin,* 1961, **58**, 305–316.

Anderson, N. H. Functional measurement and psychophysical judgment. *Psychological Review,* 1970, **77**, 153–170.

Anderson, N. H. Integration of information. In E. C. Carterette & M. P. Friedman (Eds.) *Handbook of Perception,* Vol. II. New York: Academic Press, 1974.

Anderson, T. W. *An introduction to multivariate statistical analysis.* New York: Wiley, 1958.

Attneave, F. Perception and related areas. In S. Koch (Ed.) *Psychology: A study of a science.* Vol. IV. New York: McGraw-Hill, 1962.

Baron, R. J. A model for cortical memory. *Journal of Mathematical Psychology,* 1970, **7**, 37–59.

Beals, R., & Krantz, D. H. Metrics and geodesics induced by order relations. *Mathematische Zeitschrift,* 1967, **101**, 285–298.

Beals, R., Krantz, D. H., & Tversky, A. Foundations of multidimensional scaling. *Psychological Review,* 1968, **75**, 127–142.

Benzécri, J. P. Analyse factorielle des proximités. *Publications de l'Institut de Statistique de l'Université de Paris,* I. 1964, **13**, II. 1965, **14**.

Bock, R. D., & Jones, L. V. *The measurement and prediction of judgment and choice.* San Francisco: Holden-Day, 1968.

Burke, C. J., & Zinnes, J. L. A paired comparison of pair comparisons. *Journal of Mathematical Psychology,* 1965, **2**, 53–76.

Carroll, J. D., & Wish, M. Multidimensional scaling models for measurement of human perception. In E. C. Carterette & M. P. Friedman (Eds.), *Handbook of Perception,* Vol. II. New York: Academic Press, 1974.

Chambers, E. A., & Cox, D. E. Discrimination between alternative binary response models. *Biometrika,* 1967, **54**, 573–578.

Chang, Li-Chien. On the maximum probability of cyclic random inequalities. *Scientia Sinica,* 1961, **10**, 499–504.

Cornsweet, T. N. *Visual Perception.* New York: Academic Press, 1970.

Dawkins, R. A threshold model of choice behavior. *Animal Behavior,* 1969, **17**, 120–133.

Debreu, G. Topological methods in cardinal utility theory. In K. J. Arrow, S. Karlin, & P. Suppes (Eds.) *Mathematical methods in the social sciences, 1959.* Stanford, California: Stanford University Press, 1960. Pp. 16–26.

Donders, F. C. Over de snelheid van psychische processen. Ouderzoekingen gedaan in het Physiologisch Laboratorium der Utrechtsche Hoogeschool, 1868–1869, *Tweede veeks,* **II** 92–120. [Transl. by W. C. Koster, *Acta Psychologica,* 1969, **30**, 412–431.]

Durlach, N. I., & Braida, L. D. Intensity perception. I. Preliminary theory of intensity resolution. *Journal of the Acoustical Society of America,* 1969, **46**, 372–383.

Egan, J. P., Schulman, A. I., & Greenberg, G. Z. Operating characteristics, signal detectability, and the method of free response. *Journal of the Acoustical Society of America,* 1961, **33**, 993–1007.

Eisler, H. The connection between magnitude and discrimination scales and direct and indirect scaling methods. *Psychometrika,* 1965, **30**, 271–289.

Ekman, G., & Sjöberg, L. Scaling. *Annual Review of Psychology,* 1965, **16**, 451–474.

Egan, T., & McBurney, D. H. Magnitude and category scales of the pleasantness of odors. *Journal of Experimental Psychology,* 1964, **68**, 435–440.

Erickson, R. P. Stimulus coding in topographic and nontopographic afferent modalities: on the significance of the activity of individual sensory neurons. *Psychological Review,* 1968, **75,** 447–465.

Fagot, R. F., & Stewart, M. Tests of product and additive scaling axioms. *Perception and Psychophysics,* 1969, **5,** 117–123.

Falmagne, J. C. The generalized Fechner problem and discrimination. *Journal of Mathematical Psychology,* 1971, **8,** 22–43.

Farrell, R. M., Pynn, C. T., & Braida, L. D. Determination of intensity discrimination and detection capabilities by absolute identification procedure. *Journal of the Acoustical Society of America,* 1968, **44,** 389.

Fillenbaum, S., & Rapoport, A. *Structures in the subjective lexicon.* New York: Academic Press, 1971.

Fishburn, T. C. Intransitive indifference with unequal indifference intervals. *Journal of Mathematical Psychology,* 1970, **7,** 144–149.

Garcia, J., McGowan, B. K., Ervin, R. F., & Koelling, R. A. Cues: their relative effectiveness as a function of the reinforcer. *Science,* 1968, **160,** 794–795.

Green, D. M., & Luce, R. D. Detection of auditory signals presented at random times. *Perception and Psychophysics,* 1967, **2,** 441–450.

Green, D. M., & Luce, R. D. Detection of auditory signals presented at random times, III. *Perception and Psychophysics,* 1971, **9,** 257–268.

Green, D. M., & McGill, W. J. On the equivalence of detection probabilities and well-known statistical quantities. *Psychological Review,* 1970, **77,** 294–301.

Green, D. M., & Swets, J. A. *Signal detection theory and psychophysics.* New York: Wiley, 1966.

Henning, G. B. A model for auditory discrimination and detection. *Journal of the Acoustical Society of America,* 1967, **42,** 1325–1334.

Holman, E. W. The relation between hierarchical and Euclidean models for psychological distances. *Psychometrika,* 1972, **37,** 417–423.

Indow, T. Applications of multidimensional scaling in perception. In E. C. Carterette & M. P. Friedman (Eds.) *Handbook of Perception,* Vol. II. New York: Academic Press, 1974.

Jardine, N., & Sibson, R. *Mathematical taxonomy.* New York: Wiley, 1971.

Jeffress, L. A. Mathematical and electrical models of auditory detection. *Journal of the Acoustical Society of America,* 1968, **44,** 187–203.

Johnson, S. C. Hierarchical clustering schemes. *Psychometrika,* 1967, **32,** 241–254.

Krantz, D. H. Extensive measurement in semiorders. *Philosophy of Science,* 1967, **34,** 348–362. (a)

Krantz, D. H. Rational distance functions for multidimensional scaling. *Journal of Mathematical Psychology,* 1967, **4,** 226–245. (b)

Krantz, D. H. Threshold theories of signal detection. *Psychological Review,* 1969, **76,** 308–324.

Krantz, D. H. Color measurement and color theory—I. Representation theorem for Grassman structures. Michigan Mathematical Psychology Program, MMPP 71-3. Department of Psychology, University of Michigan, 1971. (a)

Krantz, D. H. Color measurement and color theory—II. Opponent-colors theory. Michigan Mathematical Psychology Program, MMPP 71-4. Department of Psychology, University of Michigan, 1971. (b)

Krantz, D. H. Visual scaling. In D. Jameson & L. M. Hurvich (Eds.), *Visual psychophysics.* Berlin: Springer-Verlag, 1972. (a)

Krantz, D. H. A theory of magnitude estimation and cross-modality matching. *Journal of Mathematical Psychology.* 1972, **9,** 168–199. (b)

Krantz, D. H., Luce, R. D., Suppes, P., & Tversky, A. *Foundations of measurement.* Vol. I. New York: Academic Press, 1971.

Kruskal, J. B. Multidimensional scaling by optimizing goodness of fit to a nonmetric hypothesis. *Psychometrika,* 1964, **29,** 1–28. (a)

Kruskal, J. B. Nonmetric multidimensional scaling: A numerical method. *Psychometrika,* 1964, **29,** 115–130. (b)

Kruskal, J. B. Analysis of factorial experiments by estimating monotone transformations of the data. *Journal of the Royal Statistical Society. Series B,* 1965, **27,** 251–263.

Kruskal, J. B., & Carmona, F. J., Jr. MONANOVA: A FORTRAN IV program for monotone analysis of variance (non-metric analysis of factorial experiments). *Behavioral Science,* 1969, **14,** 165–166.

Lawicka, W. The role of stimuli modality in successive discrimination and differentiation learning. *Bulletin de l'Académie Polonaise des Sciences, Classe II,* 1964, **12,** 35–38.

Levine, M. Transformations which render curves parallel. *Journal of Mathematical Psychology,* 1970, **7,** 410–443.

Lingoes, J. C. An IBM-7090 program for Guttman–Lingoes conjoint measurement, I. *Behavioral Science,* 1967, **12,** 501–502.

Lingoes, J. C. Some boundary conditions for a monotone analysis of symmetric matrices. *Psychometrika,* 1971, **36,** 195–203.

Lord, F. M. On the statistical treatment of football numbers. *American Psychologist,* 1953, **8,** 750–751.

Luce, R. D. Semiorders and a theory of utility discrimination. *Econometrica,* 1956, **24,** 178–191.

Luce, R. D. *Individual choice behavior.* New York: Wiley, 1959. (a)

Luce, R. D. On the possible psychophysical laws. *Psychological Review,* 1959, **66,** 81–95. (b)

Luce, R. D. Comments on Rozeboom's criticisms of "On the possible psychophysical laws." *Psychological Review,* 1962, **69,** 542–551.

Luce, R. D. Detection and recognition. In R. D. Luce, R. R. Bush, & E. Galanter (Eds.) *Handbook of Mathematical Psychology,* Vol. I., New York: Wiley, 1963, 103–189.

Luce, R. D., Asymptotic learning in psychophysical theories. *British Journal of Statistical Psychology,* 1964, **17,** 1–14.

Luce, R. D. Remarks on the theory of measurement and its relation to psychology. In *Les modèles et la formalisation du comportement.* Paris: Editions du Centre National de la Récherche Scientifique, 1967.

Luce, R. D., & Galanter, E. Discrimination. In R. D. Luce, R. R. Bush, & E. Galanter (Eds.) *Handbook of Mathematical Psychology,* Vol. I. New York: Wiley, 1963, Pp. 191–243. (a)

Luce, R. D., & Galanter, E. Pychophysical scaling. In R. D. Luce, R. R. Bush, & E. Galanter (Eds.) *Handbook of Mathematical Psychology,* Vol. I. New York: Wiley, 1963, Pp. 245–307. (b)

Luce, R. D., & Green, D. M. Detection of auditory signals presented at random times, II. *Perception and Psychophysics,* 1970, **7,** 1–14.

Luce, R. D., & Green, D. M. A neural timing theory for response times and the psychophysics of intensity on inter-arrival times of "neural" pulses. *Psychological Review,* 1972, **79,** 14–57.

Luce, R. D., & Green, D. M. Detection, discrimination, and recognition. In E. C. Carterette & M. P. Friedman (Eds.), *Handbook of perception,* Vol. II. New York: Academic Press, 1974.

Luce, R. D., & Mo, S. S. Magnitude estimation of heaviness and loudness by Individual subjects: A test of a probabilistic response theory. *British Journal of Mathematical and Statistical Psychology,* 1965, **18,** 159–174.

Luce, R. D., & Suppes, P. Preference, utility, and subjective probability. In R. D. Luce, R. R. Bush, & E. Galanter (Eds.) *Hankbook of Mathematical Psychology,* Vol. III. New York: Wiley, 1965, Pp. 249–410.

Luce, R. D., & Tukey, J. W. Simultaneous conjoint measurement: a new type of fundamental measurement. *Journal of Mathematical Psychology,* 1964, **1,** 1–27.

Marley, A. A. J. Conditions for the representation of absolute judgment and pair comparison isosensitivity curves by cumulative distributions. *Journal of Mathematical Psychology,* 1971, **8,** 554–590.

Marley, A. A. J. Internal state models for magnitude estimation and related expediments. *Journal of Mathematical Psychology,* 1972, **9,** 306–319.

Marschak, J. Binary choice constraints and random utility indicators. In K. J. Arrow, S. Karlin, & P. Suppes (Eds.) *Mathematical methods in the social sciences,* 1959. Stanford: Stanford University Press, 1960. Pp. 312–329.

McGill, W. J. Neural counting mechanisms and energy detection in audition. *Journal of Mathematical Psychology,* 1967, **4,** 351–376.

McGill, W. J. Polynomial psychometric functions in audition. *Journal of Mathematical Psychology,* 1968, **5,** 369–376.

Miller, G. A. A psychological method to investigate verbal concepts. *Journal of Mathematical Psychology,* 1969, **6,** 169–191.

Morrison, H. W. Testable conditions for triads of paired comparison choices. *Psychometrika,* 1963, **28,** 369–390.

Norman, D. A. *Sensory thresholds and response biases in detection experiments: A theoretical and experimental analysis.* Ph.D. Thesis, Department of Psychology, University of Pennsylvania, 1962.

Norman, M. F. *Markov processes and learning models.* New York: Academic Press, 1972.

Pfanzagl, J. *Theory of measurement.* New York: Wiley, 1968.

Poulton, E. C. The new psychophysics: six models for magnitude estimation. *Psychological Bulletin,* 1968, 1–19.

Roberts, F. S. On nontransitive indifference. *Journal of Mathematical Psychology,* 1970, **7,** 243–258.

Rozeboom, W. W. The untenability of Luce's principle. *Psychological Review,* 1962, **69,** 542–547.

Rule, S. J., Curtis, D. W., & Markley, R. P. Input and output transformations from magnitude estimation. *Journal of Experimental Psychology,* 1970, **86,** 343–349.

Scott, D., & Suppes, P. Foundational aspects of theories of measurement. *Journal of Symbolic Logic,* 1958, **23,** 113–128.

Shepard, R. N. The analysis of proximities: multidimensional scaling with an unknown distance function. I. *Psychometrika,* 1962, **27,** 125–140. (a)

Shepard, R. N. The analysis of proximities: multidimensional scaling with an unknown distance function. II. *Psychometrika,* 1962, **27,** 219–246. (b)

Shepard, R. N. Circularity in judgments of relative pitch. *Journal of the Acoustical Society of America,* 1964, **36,** 2346–2353.

Shepard, R. N. Metric structures in ordinal data. *Journal of Mathematical Psychology,* 1966, **3,** 287–315.

Shipley, Elizabeth F., & Luce, R. D. Discrimination among two- and three-element sets of weights. In R. C. Atkinson (Ed.) *Studies in Mathematical Psychology.* Stanford: Stanford University Press, 1964, Pp. 218–232.

Siebert, W. M. Stimulus transformations in the peripheral auditory system. In P. A. Kolers & M. Eden (Eds.) *Recognizing Patterns.* Boston: M.I.T. Press, 1968, Pp. 104–133.

Sokal, R. R., & Sneath, P. H. A. *Principles of numerical taxonomy.* San Francisco: W. H. Freeman, 1963.

Sperling, G. Model of visual adaptation and contrast detection. *Perception and Psychophysics,* 1970, **8,** 143–157.

Steinhaus, H., & Trybula, S. On a paradox in applied probabilities. *Bulletin de l'Académie Polonaise des Sciences,* 1959, **7,** 67–69.

Sternberg, S. The discovery of processing stages: extensions of Donders' method. *Acta Psychologica,* 1969, **30,** 276–315.

Stevens, J. C., Mack, J. D., & Stevens, S. S. Growth of sensation on seven continua as measured by force of handgrip. *Journal of Experimental Psychology,* 1960, **59,** 60–67.

Stevens, S. S. Mathematics, measurement, and psychophysics. In S. S. Stevens (Ed.) *Handbook of experimental psychology.* New York: Wiley, 1951, Pp. 1–41.

Suppes, P., & Winet, M. An axiomatization of utility based on the notion of utility differences. *Management Science,* 1955, **1,** 259–270.

Suppes, P., & Zinnes, J. L. Basic measurement theory. In R. D. Luce, R. R. Bush, & E. Galanter (Eds.) *Handbook of Mathematical Psychology,* Vol. I. New York: Wiley, 1963, Pp. 1–76.

Swets, J. A. (Ed.) *Signal detection and recognition by human observers: Contemporary readings.* New York: Wiley, 1964.

Thompson, W. A., & Singh, J. The use of limit theorems in paired comparison model building. *Psychometrika,* 1967, **32,** 255–264.

Torgerson, W. S. Multidimensional scaling of similarity. *Psychometrika,* 1965, **30,** 293–310.

Trybula, S. On the paradox of three random variables. *Zastosowania Matematyki,* 1961, **5,** 321–332.

Trybula, S. On the paradox of n random variables. *Zastosowania Matematyki Applicationes Mathematicae,* 1965, **8,** 143–156.

Tversky, A. The intransitivity of preferences. *Psychological Review,* 1969, **76,** 31–48.

Tversky, A., & Russo, J. E. Substitutability and similarity in binary choices. *Journal of Mathematical Psychology,* 1969, **6,** 1–12.

Tversky, A. Elimination by aspects: A probabilistic theory of choice. *Journal of Mathematical Psychology,* 1972, **9,** 341–367.

Tversky, A., & Krantz, D. H. The dimensional representation and the metric structure of similarity data. *Journal of Mathematical Psychology,* 1970, **7,** 572–596.

Usiskin, Z. Max-min probabilities in the voting paradox. *Annals of Mathematical Statistics,* 1964, **35,** 857–862.

van de Grind, W. A., Koenderink, J. J., & Bouman, M. A. Models of the processing of quantum signals by the human peripheral retina. *Kybernetik,* 1970, **6,** 213–227. (a)

van de Grind, W. A., Koenderink, J. J., & Bouman, M. A. Models of retinal processing at high luminances. *Kybernetik,* 1970, **6,** 227–237. (b)

Welford, A. T. *Fundamentals of skill.* London: Methuen, 1963.

Wickelgren, W. A. Unidimensional strength theory and component analysis of noise in absolute and comparative judgments. *Journal of Mathematical Psychology,* 1968, **5,** 102–122.

Wish, M., & Carroll, J. D. Applications of INDSCAL to studies of human perception and judgment. In E. C. Carterette & M. P. Friedman (Eds.), *Handbook of Perception,* Vol. II. New York: Academic Press, 1974.

Yellott, J. The relationship between Thurstone's, Luce's, and Dawkin's models for pair comparison. Paper presented at Mathematical Psychology Meetings, Miami, 1970.

Zinnes, J. L. Scaling. *Annual Review of Psychology,* 1969, **20,** 447–478.

Chapter 8

ALGEBRAIC MODELS IN PERCEPTION*

NORMAN H. ANDERSON

I. INTRODUCTION

A. Information Integration

There is a long tradition of viewing perception as integration of stimulus information. The organism resides in a multitudinous stimulus field, and the job of the perceptual apparatus is to combine or integrate the varied stimulus cues into some more-or-less unitary percept. Depth perception, involving the combined action of interposition, stereopsis, texture, and other cues is one classic example; the dependence of size constancy on the coacting depth cues is a well-known result. The same principle is found

* This work has been supported by grants from the Psychobiology Program of the National Science Foundation, and facilitated by grants from the National Institute of Mental Health to the Center for Human Information Processing, University of California, San Diego. I wish to express my appreciation to M. H. Birnbaum, E. C. Carterette, L. E. Marks, A. Parducci, G. S. Reynolds, G. Stanley, and D. J. Weiss for various helpful comments on various sections of this paper. I also wish to express my deep indebtedness to J. C. Shanteau and D. J. Weiss who have been my co-workers in developing functional measurement methodology.

in the classroom example of the "taste" of soda pop, conditioned by smell, pain, and cold senses, as well as the various taste receptors.

To say, then, that perception depends on information integration is to stress the obvious. To translate this view to an experimental counterpart leads to a synthetic approach—studying how the several separate cues are combined or integrated into the overall percept. Synthesis is inverse to analysis. Where analysis aims to isolate and define specific sensory mechanisms and stimulus cues, synthesis studies the response to a complex stimulus field. Where analysis seeks to simplify the stimulus field, synthesis seeks to complicate it, in specific experimental ways.

Examples of synthetic studies abound: Contrast, assimilation, illusions and ambiguous figures, bisection, temporal and spatial summation, size constancy, and depth perception all involve an integrative response to a field of many stimuli. However, these problems have been studied largely because of their individual interest. Little has emerged in the form of general principles of synthesis.

This chapter gives a unified approach to stimulus integration. Its scope is limited in certain respects, but it does combine precision with breadth. Furthermore, it rests on a substantial empirical base. Much of this supportive experimentation has been done in various areas of judgment, especially person perception. However, the same processes and principles appear in numerous problems of traditional perception.

This theoretical approach has a dual basis—in substantive theory and in measurement theory. The substantive base rests on problems of information integration. Extensive use is made of algebraic models to represent the integration processes. The measurement base is a theory of functional measurement. It provides the scales required for the algebraic models. The substantive aspects and the measurement aspects are woven together; the measurement theory is organically related to the substantive theory.

The beginnings of this development appeared in two articles—one theoretical and one experimental (Anderson, 1962a,b)—which gave the essential ideas of the functional measurement approach, and an empirical test of a very simple averaging model. Since then, primary concern has been with the experimental development of this approach, especially to more complex models and to a wider variety of judgment tasks. Summary articles have discussed applications in psychophysics (Anderson, 1970a, 1972c), person perception (Anderson, 1968a), social judgment (Anderson, 1971a, 1974c) and general judgment theory (Anderson, 1972b, 1974b).

B. Algebraic Models

Many investigations in perception and judgment have used some form of simple algebraic model. Adding models can be used for spatial and temporal summation, subtracting models for preference and difference judgments, averaging models for bisection and for contrast effects, multiplying models for size constancy, and dividing models for ratio settings and for comparative judgment. These models have arisen naturally in a variety of experimental situations, and they are alike in specifying the response to be some simple algebraic function of the subjective values of the physical stimuli.

To illustrate, consider the response to a combination of two stimuli, S_1 and S_2. In a simple but still fairly general form, the algebraic judgment model may be written,

$$R = w_1 s_1 + w_2 s_2. \tag{0}$$

Here s_1 and w_1 represent the subjective-scale value and subjective weight of the physical stimulus S_1, and, similarly, s_2 and w_2 represent the value and weight of the physical stimulus S_2. These value and weight parameters are the ones that are effective in the overall judgment.

As it stands, Eq. (0) is an adding model. If the weights sum to unity, then it becomes an averaging model, which has some different properties that become extremely important in the general theory. Preference or difference judgments can be represented by setting $w_1 = 1$, $w_2 = -1$. With a single stimulus, Eq. (0) reduces formally to a multiplying model, $w \times s$. Other cases, as well as some direct generalizations, are considered in what follows.

The algebraic model involves two basic psychological operations. One of these is the integration process itself, and this is the focus of much of this chapter. The other is the valuation process, by which the overt physical stimuli receive their subjective values, both scale value and weight. The scale value s will depend primarily on the focal stimulus in perceptual tasks and secondarily on other factors such as contrast and adaptation. In more judgmental tasks, the instructions will often define the dimension of judgment on which the scale value lies. The scale value of a given stimulus might be quite different for different judgment dimensions.

The weight parameter w reflects the importance of the given stimulus in the judgment. It can depend on temporal or spatial properties of the stimulus field, as in the serial position curve for serial integration (Section II,B,10). In more judgmental tasks, weight will reflect the felt relevance of the stimulus to the judgment. Conceptually, weight is more important than scale value because of its dependence on numerous stimulus factors.

The response R is assumed to be numerical, although choice data can be handled by pooling trials to get a proportion. For present convenience, the response, and the stimulus values as well, are treated as point concepts. Introspectively, of course, sensations such as loudness or heaviness do not seem to have a precise value, but rather a certain degree of indefiniteness.

A more realistic representation would treat the terms of Eq. (0) as distributions, either as random variables (Anderson, 1961, 1964a), or as confidence distributions. The point concepts may be considered as the means of such distributions. The distributional aspects are then lumped into an additive "error" term, as in Eq. (2) in Section II. This treatment is adequate for present purposes, but the problem of structure in the stimulus and the response needs to be kept in mind.

As will be seen later, most of the algebraic models have a simple mathematical structure. Their analysis is equally simple. Except for the response-scaling problem, which can get technically complex, little more than elementary algebra is required. Even tests of goodness of fit can be made graphically.

C. Functional Measurement

Functional measurement has a triple goal:

1. to measure the subjective values of the stimuli on interval scales,
2. to measure the subjective value of the response on an interval scale, and
3. to determine the psychological law relating stimuli and response.

These three goals are to be accomplished together. That this is feasible, indeed rather simple, is demonstrated in the experiments discussed in Section II,B.

The guiding idea of functional measurement is that substantive theory is the foundation of measurement. This view leads to an orientation and approach that are in many ways exactly opposite to the customary approach. Too often, measurement is viewed as a methodological preliminary to substantive inquiry; only after the stimuli have been scaled does the study of the psychological law begin. In contrast, the functional view is that measurement is woven into the fabric and structure of the substantive laws. Measurement theory and substantive theory are organically related. They are cofunctional in development.

No measurement theory is worth much unless it works. That functional measurement does work has been shown in repeated experiments. This is a piece of good luck. It reflects the fact that stimulus information is integrated according to simple algebraic models in a considerable range of tasks. This fact, which has been slowly emerging from the experimental work, allows simple solutions to the problems of measuring the stimulus and, more valuably, the response.

One caution should be added. Functional measurement is well established for tasks that require integration of verbal or symbolic stimuli. In perception, however, the multiplying model (Section III) has an uncertain status, and the linear models (Section II) have exceptions whose interpretation is not yet definite.

D. Comment

Three basic concepts underlie the discussion of this chapter. They are stimulus integration, algebraic models, and functional measurement. The pervasiveness of stimulus integration in perception has already been noted. Special cases of the general algebraic model have been considered by numerous investigators in many areas. When they begin to be collected together, it is surprising how many such applications have been made. It is also striking how investigators in unrelated areas have tended to adopt similar models. This formal similarity apparently represents common integration processes operative in diverse substantive tasks.

It is not possible in this chapter to refer to more than a small part of the relevant work on algebraic models of stimulus integration. A few references will be cited here to indicate the extent of previous work.

Among the earliest attempts to use algebraic models in psychophysical measurement are those of Fletcher and Munson (1933) on loudness summation, and of Geiger and Firestone (1933) on loudness fractionation. Stevens (1955) discusses loudness fractionation, among other methods, and summarizes other previous work on loudness. Garner (1954a,b) and McGill (1960) have also made important contributions to the study of loudness. This work exemplifies an approach in which the primary goal has been scaling, and the algebraic models are employed as tools for that purpose.

Extensive and concerted study of algebraic models in perception has been made by the Scandinavians (e.g., Ekman, 1958; Goude, 1962; Mashhour, 1964; Öttander, 1967; Sjöberg, 1966; Svenson, 1970), and by the Oregonians (e.g., Beck & Shaw, 1968; Curtis, Attneave, & Harrington, 1968; Curtis & Fox, 1969; Fagot & Stewart, 1969a,b). This work is considered later, but it deserves more attention than can be given here.

Other investigators have been more concerned with judgmental factors in perception. This includes the work of Guilford (1954), Poulton (1968), and Parducci (1965). Treisman (e.g., 1964) has taken a similar conceptual view, but with an emphasis on more articulated stage models. Carterette's (1967) paper on vowel perception represents an interesting attempt to delineate the perceptual structure of complex stimuli using a linear model combined with experimental manipulation. Baird (1970) has reviewed the factors that affect judgments of distance and size, and Gogel's (1970) numerous papers in this area should be noted.

More general theoretical formulations have been given by several writers. Helson's (1964) theory of adaptation-level is the best known and takes a very broad approach. Attneave (1959), Garner (1962), and Garner and Morton (1969) have explored the implications of mathematical information theory. Brunswik (1956) has been especially concerned with the combining of stimulus cues, and has attempted to apply multiple regression analysis to the study of this problem.

A number of the preceding developments have simultaneously adopted some of the basic concepts of the functional measurement approach. However, many of them have suffered, often severely, from the lack of an adequate theory of measurement. Measurement problems are often central to the use of an algebraic model. This chapter presents a unified approach based on functional measurement theory.

II. LINEAR MODELS AND AVERAGING MODELS

A. Assumptions and Analyses

1. EXPERIMENTAL ILLUSTRATION

Functional measurement with linear models can be extremely simple. Before taking up the general method, therefore, one empirical application will be used to illustrate the main ideas.

Figure 1 is a plot of data from an experiment on weight-averaging. Subjects lifted two unseen weights, one after the other, and judged their "average heaviness" on a 1–20 rating scale. The 25 combinations of two weights formed a two-way factorial design with first and second weight as the two factors. Each factor had 5 levels, from 200 gm, to 600 gm, as listed in Figure 1.

The theoretical question is how the subject integrates the sensory inputs from the two lifts into a single judgment. An obvious hypothesis is that the integration rule is an arithmetic mean. The lifting of each weight produces a heaviness sensation, and the response is the average of the two sensations. Under the assumptions to be discussed, this averaging model has a linear or additive form.

The data of Figure 1 exhibit a pattern of parallelism. The linear model predicts parallelism, so the observed parallelism supports the model.

Furthermore, the vertical spacing of the five curves constitutes an interval scale of the heaviness sensation. The subjective distance between 500 and 600 gm is visibly a little less than the subjective distance between 200 and 300 gm.

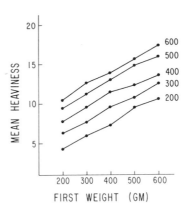

FIG. 1. Subjects rate the average heaviness of two unseen weights. The first weight is listed on horizontal axis, with one curve for each value of the second weight. The data obey the parallelism prediction of the averaging model for stimulus integration. [From Anderson, 1972c.]

This experiment, therefore, has accomplished three goals simultaneously:

1. It validates the integration model, or psychological law.
2. It validates the response scale.
3. It yields an interval scale of sensation.

These three points will be developed in more detail later, but the point about the response scale deserves a brief remark.

A priori, there is no great reason to think that ordinary ratings constitute an interval scale of the response. However, if the overt response were a nonlinear function of the underlying response, then the data would not plot as parallel lines even if the model were true. Parallelism thus provides a joint validation of the psychological law, and of the response scale.

The simplicity and directness of the functional measurement approach are noteworthy. All that is necessary is to plot the raw data. No parameters need to be estimated, and even the test of goodness of fit can be made by visual inspection.

This analysis has far-reaching consequences. It solves the measurement problem in psychology in a way that is both simple and useful. The success of the model establishes interval scales on both the stimulus side and on the response side. This is done in the context of establishing a substantive psychological law. Substantive theory and measurement theory are thus cofunctional in development. This experiment is discussed later in Section II,B,1. At this point, it is necessary to take up the model analysis in more detail.

2. MODEL AND ASSUMPTIONS

For simplicity, only the case in which the subject receives combinations of two stimuli will be considered. The physical stimuli will be denoted by

$S_{\mathrm{R}i}$ and $S_{\mathrm{C}j}$, where R and C stand for rows and columns of a two-way matrix or factorial design, and i and j index the levels of the row and column factors.

The simple linear model can then be written as

$$R_{ij} = C_0 + w_{\mathrm{R}}s_{\mathrm{R}i} + w_{\mathrm{C}}s_{\mathrm{C}j} + \epsilon_{ij}. \tag{1}$$

Here R_{ij} is the response to the stimulus combination $(S_{\mathrm{R}i}, S_{\mathrm{C}j})$; $s_{\mathrm{R}i}$ and $s_{\mathrm{C}j}$ are the (subjective) scale values of the stimuli $S_{\mathrm{R}i}$ and $S_{\mathrm{C}j}$; w_{R} and w_{C} are constant mathematical weighting parameters; and C_0 is a constant that allows for an arbitrary zero in the measured response. The additive error terms ϵ_{ij} represent response variability. For simplicity, they will usually be ignored hereafter because the difference between the "true" and "observed" values of R_{ij} will be clear from context. The C_0 term will also be ignored.

Implicit in Eq. (1) are two independence assumptions. First, the scale value of each stimulus is assumed to be constant, regardless of what other stimulus it may be combined with. Contrast, assimilation, and other stimulus interactions are not allowed (but see Sections II,B,2 and III,B,5). Second, equal weighting is assumed within each design factor; w_{R} is constant for all rows, and w_{C} is constant for all columns.

a. INTERVAL RESPONSE SCALES. For simplicity, it will be assumed in most of this chapter that the overt response is numerical, measured on an interval scale. This is only a provisional, working assumption, since it is tested in the analysis. A successful test implies an interval response as already noted. Strictly speaking, a successful test implies that the response measure is "theoretically adequate" (Anderson, 1962b). For a linear model, that corresponds to the so-called interval scale: Any linear transformation of the response would also satisfy the model, and nonlinear transformations would, in general, not satisfy the model.

b. ORDINAL RESPONSE SCALES. In some situations, the observed response will not be on an interval scale. Brightness bisection is an example. Bisection can be represented as a linear averaging model, since the bisector is just the mean of the two given stimuli. But the subject bisects on the subjective continuum, whereas the measured response is on the physical continuum. These two dimensions, the psychological and the physical, are nonlinearly related. The parallelism test would fail, therefore, even though the model was correct.

Functional measurement handles this problem in a straightforward way with monotone transformations (Anderson, 1962b; Bogartz & Wackwitz, 1970, 1971; Weiss, 1973a,b). In the brightness example, it can be assumed that the overt response measure and the underlying psychological response are related by a monotone transformation. The leverage for finding that transformation is given by the algebraic model and the factorial stimulus design. For the bisection model the data would be transformed to eliminate the nonparallelism. In this example, incidentally, the monotone transformation would be the psychophysical law relating sensation to physical intensity.

In principle, ordinal scales present no problem in functional measurement. Actually, monotone transformations have not been used much in practice because the rating scales have worked so well. Monotone analysis does introduce statistical complications. However, routine methods are available, and these are discussed further in Section II,A,6.

3. TEST OF FIT

a. PARALLELISM TEST. Linear models are easily tested, both graphically and statistically. Because of its additive form, Eq. (1) leads directly to a prediction of parallelism. To illustrate, consider the differences between the entries in Rows 1 and 2 (with response variability neglected):

$$R_{1j} - R_{2j} = C_0 + w_R s_{R1} + w_C s_{Cj}$$
$$- C_0 - w_R s_{R2} - w_C s_{Cj}.$$

Cancellation yields

$$R_{1j} - R_{2j} = w_R(s_{R1} - s_{R2}). \tag{2}$$

Since the right side of Eq. (2) is independent of the column index j, it follows that the difference between Rows 1 and 2 is the same constant in every column. That is equivalent to parallelism in the graphical form.

b. ANALYSIS OF VARIANCE TEST. Ordinary analysis of variance can supplement the graphical test of parallelism with a rigorous statistical test. Equation (1) can readily be rewritten in the form of an additive model used in analysis of variance (e.g., Mandel, 1961, 1964; Scheffé, 1959; Winer, 1971). In that form, the statistical interaction terms are absent from the model. They should, therefore, be nonsignificant in the data analysis. The graphical test of parallelism is equivalent to the statistical test of the Row × Column interaction.

The analysis of variance generalizes directly to any number of stimulus variables, a useful feature for preliminary screening of data from larger experiments. Experimental applications that illustrate various pertinent features of analysis of variance are given in Anderson (1962a, 1964b, 1972a), Anderson and Jacobson (1968), Anderson and Shanteau (1970), Birnbaum and Veit (1973), Shanteau (1972), Shanteau and Anderson (1969, 1972), Weiss (1972, 1973b), and Weiss and Anderson (1969, 1972). The ability to analyze data for single subjects is especially important.

4. FUNCTIONAL SCALES OF THE STIMULUS

If the model passes the test of fit, estimates of the subjective stimulus values are immediately available. These are simply the marginal means of the factorial design; see Section II,B,1 for an experimental illustration. The row means, for instance, estimate the scale values of the row stimuli on an interval scale. To see this, the marginal mean for Row i can be obtained by averaging Eq. (1) over the other stimulus factors to yield

$$\bar{R}_{i\cdot} = C_0 + w_R s_{Ri} + w_C \bar{s}_C,$$

or   (3)

$$\bar{R}_{i\cdot} = w_R s_{Ri} + \text{const.}$$

Equation (3) states that the row mean is a linear function of the scale values of the row stimulus, and conversely. Within the model, therefore, the row means constitute an interval scale of the s_{Ri}.

In the data, therefore, the observed marginal means constitute estimates of the subjective values of the row stimuli on an interval scale. Given statistical independence and homogeneous variance (Scheffé, 1959), these are unbiased least squares estimates with minimum variance.

The interval character of the stimulus values derives from the interval character of the response. For a fixed response scale, the row means estimate the total effect $w_R s_{Ri}$ of the row stimuli. Comparisons between rows and columns are not appropriate in general, a reflection of the ability to use qualitatively different stimuli in the row and column factors.

To estimate the weights requires some additional constraint. One important case is that in which the same scale values are used in each factor of the design (e.g.. Weiss & Anderson, 1969). In that case, the several sets of marginal means may be averaged to obtain an overall set of marginal means. Each separate set is plotted as a function of the overall set. Each such plot should be linear, and its slope is an estimate of the corresponding weight parameter on a ratio scale. The weight scale has a natural zero corresponding to a line of zero slope.

To ensure that the scale values are equal, up to an additive constant, in each factor of the design, it would usually be necessary to use the same stimuli in each factor (for an exception, see Anderson, 1964b). That is not sufficient, however, since order of presentation or spatial position might affect the scale values as well as the weights. Nonlinear changes in scale values can be guarded against since the several sets of marginal means would then violate the bilinear form (Section III,A). However, it is not possible to distinguish between linear changes in the scale values and changes in the associated weight without additional information.

5. AVERAGING MODEL

Averaging processes appear to be pervasive in stimulus integration. Under special circumstances, the averaging model has a linear form and can be analyzed by the methods already given. Indeed, the weight-averaging task of Figure 1 is one such example. This equal-weight averaging model is discussed later.

a. GENERAL AVERAGING MODEL. The averaging model for two stimulus factors can be written in somewhat simplified form as

$$R_{ij} = C_0 + \frac{w_{Ri}s_{Ri} + w_{Cj}s_{Cj}}{w_{Ri} + w_{Cj}}. \tag{4}$$

This form is analogous to the linear model of Eq. (1), but each stimulus is allowed a separate weight. The sum of weights in the denominator normalizes the sum of the *relative* weights of the two stimuli to add to unity. Since this normalization applies to every stimulus combination separately, Eq. (4) is nonlinear, in general.

The nonlinear case is considerably harder to handle than the linear case. Preliminary information on the rank order of the weight parameters can allow prediction of direction of nonparallelism (Anderson, 1971a, pp. 183–185; 1974b, Section 5.1). Numerical techniques can also be used to estimate all the parameters (Anderson, 1972a; Leon, Oden, & Anderson, 1973). The next section discusses a special case of differential weighting that has a straightforward analysis.

b. SEMILINEAR AVERAGING MODEL. A special case of Eq. (4) results if all the row stimuli have the same weight w_R. Then the row means of Eq. (4) can be written,

$$\bar{R}_{i\cdot} = c_1 s_{Ri} + c_2, \tag{5}$$

where c_1 and c_2 are complicated constants of no present interest. The row means thus constitute an interval scale of the row stimuli. More important, the data of each column should plot as a straight-line function of the row means. That provides a test of goodness of fit. An interval scale of column weight can also be obtained (Anderson, 1971a, Eq. 12), though that estimation procedure seems to be susceptible to serious bias or unreliability.

c. EQUAL-WEIGHT AVERAGING MODEL. When all row weights equal w_R, and all column weights equal w_C, Eq. (4) becomes

$$R_{ij} = \frac{w_R s_{Ri} + w_C s_{Cj}}{w_R + w_C}. \tag{6}$$

This model is linear because the denominator is constant. For any fixed number of stimulus dimensions, the equal-weight averaging model has the same mathematical properties as the linear model. The parallelism property and the analysis of variance test both apply as before. Similarly, the marginal means provide interval scales of the stimulus values.

d. COMMENTS ON THE AVERAGING HYPOTHESIS. The averaging hypothesis has assumed considerable importance in the general theory of stimulus integration. It has had extensive development, both qualitative and quantitative, for integration tasks with verbal stimuli (Anderson, 1974b). For psychophysical integration, however, its status is less clear. Quite a number of successful applications have been made (see Section II,B), but there are a few reports (e.g., Birnbaum, Parducci, & Gifford, 1971; Parducci Thaler, & Anderson, 1968) whose interpretation is uncertain.

Much of the interest has centered on the question of averaging versus adding. Adding models of stimulus integration have seemed reasonable in many tasks on a priori grounds. However, critical qualitative tests have almost always shown that an averaging process is actually involved (see Anderson, 1973, 1974b). In fact, there is virtually no evidence that any integration task follows an adding model in an exact quantitative sense (but see Anderson 1974a). Even simple commodity bundles, the most likely candidate, appear to exhibit diminishing returns (Shanteau, 1970).

Averaging theory allows for an internal state variable S_0 that is averaged in with the overt stimuli. This aspect of the theory has been omitted here because such an internal stimulus is not necessary for most perceptual integration tasks. However, it becomes quite important theoretically in many tasks with verbal stimuli. In person perception, for example, it represents an "initial impression," or generalized expectation about the person in the absence of specific information. It is thus possible to account for the increase in response produced by adding isovalent information, a fact that cannot be handled by the simple averaging model (Anderson, 1967b, 1974b). Illustrations of some aspects of estimating w_0 and s_0 are in Anderson (1967b), Leon, Oden, and Anderson (1973), and Shanteau (1972).

It is interesting that the averaging model has a gestalt character. Although the absolute weight of each stimulus is assumed to be constant, its relative or effective weight will depend on the other stimuli with which it is combined. The role of each part thus depends upon the whole. Nevertheless, the response to the whole is completely predictable from knowledge of the parts.

The averaging hypothesis has three important implications for measurement theory. The first is that two parameters, weight and scale value, are both necessary to characterize a stimulus. Traditionally, measurement has been viewed in terms of scale values only. That was adequate when only adding or linear models were considered. In such models, the weight parameter can typically be treated as a scale unit without independent existence. In averaging theory, however, weight and value are distinct, conceptually and mathematically. Moreover, the weight parameter seems to be theoretically more interesting because of the variety of factors that affect it.

The second implication of the averaging hypothesis is that deviations from parallelism must be expected in many situations. With differential weighting, adding and linear models still predict parallelism. But that is not true of the averaging model; differential weighting will produce systematic nonparallelism. Such nonadditivities, being real, clearly should not be eliminated by response transformation. With a metric response, it becomes feasible to work with such situations. Nonmetric methods that use only order properties of the data have great difficulty with averaging models.

The third implication of the averaging hypothesis is that it can provide scales of weight and value that are comparable across stimulus factors. This property can be extremely important. In certain situations, it is desirable to compare the importance of two qualitatively different stimulus variables. Such comparisons are not allowed by the simple linear models, because they do not separate weight and scale value. Consequently, there is no way to distinguish between a stimulus variable that is effective by virtue of a large range in scale value, and a stimulus variable that is effective by virtue of a high weight-parameter.

The nonlinearity of the general averaging model thus becomes a virtue. Equation (4) allows weight estimates on a common ratio scale, comparable across diverse stimuli. However, scale value estimates lose all uniqueness in the usual factorial design, though they can be evaluated on a common interval scale in a triangular design (Anderson, 1972a) or by varying set size.

6. Monotone Response Transformation

a. The monotone rescaling principle. Numerical response scales will, in practice, be at some uncertain position between mere rank-order scales and interval scales. An adequate theory of measurement cannot rest on the assumption of an interval scale, yet ought to be able to utilize whatever metric information the observed response may contain. Functional measurement meets this criterion. In principle, it assumes no more than an ordinal scale, yet it includes systematic methods for extracting the metric information in the data.

The essential idea is quite simple (Anderson, 1962b). An ordinal response can be transformed into an interval response by a monotone transformation. The algebraic model provides the scaling frame. In a simple linear model, the monotone transformation would be chosen to eliminate nonparallelism. For example, the magnitude estimation data in the right panel of Fig. 5 (page 237) can be transformed to parallelism. A correct model, therefore, need not be infirmed by an invalid response scale, but instead can serve as a frame to transform that response to a valid scale. On the other hand, if no monotone transformation can be found, then the model would need to be rejected.

b. FUNPOT. Bogartz and Wackwitz (1971) have developed a general method for response scaling within the analysis of variance framework. Their procedure has been expanded and computerized by Weiss (1973a) in his FUNPOT program, which he has used in a successful analysis of psychophysical bisection (Weiss, 1973b). The FUNPOT method is quite powerful. It applies a stepwise power-series expansion to the observed response, with coefficients chosen to minimize statistical interaction terms in the analysis of variance. In multifactor designs, selected interactions can be chosen for elimination. Thus, the method is especially useful for the compound adding–multiplying models of Section III,A,5. Elimination of the interaction between two variables that add should also transform into bilinear form the interaction between two variables that multiply.

FUNPOT is not constrained to yield a monotone transformation. A crossover interaction in a 2×2 design, for example, can always be eliminated with a nonmonotone quadratic expansion (E. F. Alf, personal communication). Nonmonotone transformations would usually be unacceptable and cause rejection of the model. Mild nonmonotonicity may be difficult to interpret, of course, since there are no simple, routine methods for testing whether observed deviations from monotonicity are statistically significant.

c. OTHER TRANSFORMATIONS. Prior knowledge sometimes provides a basis for choosing a monotone transformation of a specific form. The "stretching transformation,"

$$R' = R + a \operatorname{sign}(R - b)|R - b|^c, \tag{7}$$

can be useful in eliminating floor and ceiling effects (Anderson & Jacobson, 1968). The value of b would be set at the center of the response scale for symmetrical stretching, off-center for asymmetrical stretching. The parameter c could be chosen at some convenient value greater than zero. Positive and negative values of a would then produce stretching or compression, respectively. The amount of stretching or compression would increase with distance from b. The stretching function is appropriate for removing response nonlinearity that has a general U-shape.

Power-function transformations may be applicable in certain situations. This approach has been applied in a number of experiments by Curtis, Fagot, and their associates (e.g., Curtis, 1970; Curtis, Attneave, & Harrington, 1968; Fagot & Stewart, 1969b; Rule, Curtis, & Markley, 1970).

These experiments, however, have also used a power function on the physical stimulus measure (Section II,B,6).

Ogive-type transformations can be expected in certain cases. One example is the normal deviate transformation used in Thurstonian scaling and signal detection theory (Section II,B,9). Other transformations with the same general effect may also be useful (Mosteller, 1958). Choice proportions can be handled in this way, and direct percentage ratings might show similar nonlinearity.

Use of a specific function has certain advantages. It can be required to be monotone, as in the stretching function, and an appropriate choice would require estimation of only a few parameters. Chandler's (1969) general purpose STEPIT program could be quite useful in that respect.

It should be emphasized that there have been relatively few applications of the monotone rescaling procedures. This mirrors the pleasant fact that rating methods, with suitable precautions, seem to be able to provide interval scales without the need for transformation. As a consequence, unfortunately, knowledge of the various practical aspects of the transformation problem is as yet rudimentary. For example, it seems likely that FUNPOT will work better if a preliminary transformation of a suitable specific form is applied to handle the major component of the nonlinearity. Possible preliminary transformations would include the stretching transformation of Eq. (7), and power functions, both of which are flexible and useful in curve fitting. FUNPOT would then be used to remove residual nonlinearity. On this and similar questions, however, little is known.

Analyses of mathematical functions that do and do not allow monotone transformation to parallelism have been given by Scheffé (1959, Sect. 4.1) and by Levine (1970, 1972). Their results seem most useful when theoretically given functions are studied. For example, it is easy to show from Scheffé's theorem that the averaging model (Section II,A,5) cannot, in general, be transformed to parallelism. For actual data analysis, however, these theorems may not be too useful, either in determining whether it is appropriate to transform, or in finding a suitable transformation.

d. RANK-ORDER DATA. Functional measurement can also be used with data only in rank-order form. Weiss and Anderson (1972) illustrate the use of Kruskal's (1965) MONANOVA procedure with some angle-averaging data. The original data were numerical and satisfied the parallelism property. They were then reduced to ranks, and MONANOVA was applied to recover the original metric information. The functional scale from the original data was equivalent to that reconstituted from the ranks.

In general, however, nonmetric, rank-order analyses do not seem very promising. The statistical theory is almost nonexistent and there seems little prospect for developing it. Moreover, nonmetric methods tend to hang up on small crossovers that represent nothing but error variability. To work at all, they would seem to require widely spaced stimulus values. Unfortunately, the wider the stimulus spacing, the weaker the constraints imposed by the model on the data.

e. WHEN NOT TO TRANSFORM. Although there are various practical problems in finding a suitable monotone transformation, the really troublesome problem is in knowing when not to transform. It will often be too easy to transform given data to fit a model even though that model is wrong (Anderson, 1962b, Birnbaum & Veit, 1974).

One part of this problem is that the data may not impose very much constraint on the transformation. This depends in part on the design, in part on the nature of the data. A 2 × 2 design, for example, will disallow monotone transformation in the special case of a crossover interaction, as in certain tests of the averaging model. Except in that case, it imposes very little constraint. Shepard's work on multidimensional scaling (e.g., Shepard, 1966) suggests that the constraints build up very rapidly as the size of the design increases. The results of Weiss and Anderson (1972) indicate that a 5 × 5 design can be adequate in certain circumstances. However, the problem depends also on the spacing of the stimuli, and requires systematic study.

Another part of this problem is that the justification for transformation depends on accumulated knowledge. For example, rating methods have been shown to be capable of giving interval scales in a variety of tasks. This accumulated knowledge produces confidence in the rating procedure, one of the benefits of working with metric response measures. But deviations from a model cannot then be lightly attributed to nonlinearities in the rating scale. Such deviations need serious consideration even when they can be eliminated by transformation.

In a similar way, the justification for transformation rests on the correctness of the model that is used as the scaling frame. This aspect of the problem has already been noted in the discussion of the averaging model (Section II,A,5). The averaging model is known to hold over a considerable range of tasks, but it predicts parallelism only under the special condition of equal weighting. In such tasks, it would clearly be wrong to transform the data to parallelism unless there was good reason to expect equal weighting.

Some writers have argued that if it is possible to eliminate an interaction by monotone rescaling, then the interaction has no real meaning and is attributable to the rating scale. That position is clearly incorrect. It fails to recognize that the formal, mathematical aspects of the transformation problem are subsidiary to substantive, empirical consideration.

f. FORMALLY EQUIVALENT SYSTEMS. One final aspect of the transformation problem needs a brief discussion. This is the trade-off relation between scale and model, a relation that can be illustrated by reference to the weight-averaging data of Section II,B,1, page 233. As is pointed out there, the parallelism of the curves in Fig. 1 gives joint validation to the response scale and the integration rule based on the arithmetic mean. Nevertheless, it would still be possible to argue a different interpretation based on an exponential transformation of the data. That would transform the parallel lines to a diverging fan of lines; at the same time, it would transform the arithmetic mean to a geometric mean. Since the exponential transformation is an allowable monotone transformation in functional measurement, it is evident that the arithmetic and the geometric averaging models are formally equivalent interpretations of these data. From a mathematical viewpoint, one model cannot be said to be better than the other.

Three aspects of this problem require comment. First, the integration models as a group appear to work well in terms of the rating scales that have been used. Thus, the arithmetic mean forms the basis of a consistent system. Even if there is an ultimate element of convention in the model, working within a consistent system will be adequate for many purposes.

Second, arithmetic means make sense in almost all situations, whereas geometric means do not. In intuitive averaging of number or position (Anderson, 1964b, 1968c), or of angle (Weiss & Anderson, 1972), it is hard to see any reasonable basis for the hypothesis that the underlying mechanism is a geometric average. This point illustrates how much the interpretation of any single experiment depends on the entire network of empirical knowledge (Anderson, 1972c).

Third, the given indeterminacy is not peculiar to the present approach, but applies equally well to physics. In general, if M is any arbitrary, strictly monotone transformation, then $y = f(x)$ is formally equivalent to $y = fM^{-1}(M(x))$. To say that f is the functional law and x the independent variable is formally equivalent to saying that fM^{-1} is the functional law, and $M(x)$ is the independent variable. In the same way, to say that f is the functional law and y is the dependent variable is formally equivalent to saying that Mf is the functional law and My is the dependent variable. A sensible discussion of these questions from a philosopher's standpoint is given by Ellis (1966), but no ultimate solution is visible. In practice, the well-known criteria of simplicity and unity seem to operate almost silently so that only certain kinds of simple algebraic models are used in most of physics. The data now to be considered give a reasonable basis for expecting the same in a substantial part of psychology.

7. NOTE ON USING RATING SCALES

Several precautions have been standard with rating scales in functional measurement. First is the use of preliminary practice, which has several functions. The general range of stimuli is not known to the subject initially, and the rating scale itself is arbitrary. Accordingly, the subject needs to develop a frame of reference for the stimuli and correlate it with the given response scale. The practice stimuli should be chosen to facilitate the subject's adjustment to the simulus–response framework. In addition, practice can decrease variability by giving the subject an opportunity to stabilize his valuation and integration operations. With a difficult task, a complete practice session may be desirable (Anderson & Shanteau, 1970). In many tasks, however, a few minutes practice seems to be adequate.

Stimulus end-anchors are extremely important. These are additional stimuli that are more extreme than the experimental stimuli to be studied. One function of the end-anchors is to help define the frame of reference. Indeed, they can often be included in the practice with explicit instructions like, "This is the smallest stimulus you will see—call it 1."

The main function of the end-anchor stimuli is to tie down the ends of the rating scale so that the data come from the interior of the scale. Various evidence suggests that judgmental processes are different near the ends of the scale (e.g., Anderson, 1967b; Eriksen & Hake, 1955, 1957; Garner, 1953; Jones, 1960, Fig. 2.6; Parducci & Perrett, 1971). The first-cited report gives a striking demonstration of one such end-effect. The end-anchors help eliminate end-biases such as floor and ceiling effects, end-response preferences, etc.

Much of the work has used a 20-step scale which seems to leave ample room interior to the end-anchors. A 10-step scale is probably minimal. Some subjects complain initially about using 20 steps and going beyond that may cause lumping.

Graphic ratings offer several advantages over numerical ratings, as they are less susceptible to number preferences, and to possible memory effects when stimuli are repeated. Residual number preferences can remain even under the best of conditions (Shanteau & Anderson, 1969). Memory effects, however, do not seem to be much trouble except perhaps with continuous responding in serial integration (e.g., Anderson, 1968b). Graphic ratings are more tedious, and are probably only necessary in the most careful work.

Not much systematic work has been done on the experimental procedures needed to get interval data out of rating scales. The preceding precautions have been adopted on grounds of common sense and have appeared to work reasonably well. The question deserves further methodological work, though that might best be conducted as part of substantive experiments (e.g., Anderson, 1967b). All response measures will have some bias, and their development must be considered a continuing task.

Residual bias in a rating scale can be removed with a monotone transformation (Section II,A,6). It should be recognized, however, that the overall experimental situation itself defines a response transformation, from the internal to the overt response. The effect of the response scale itself can be seen in the comparison between category ratings and magnitude estimation in Fig. 5 of Section II,B,5. Functional measurement can sometimes rectify a biased scale, of course, but generally it is preferable to do that by experimental rather than statistical means.

B. Applications

1. WEIGHT-AVERAGING

This section resumes the analysis of the weight-averaging data of Section II,A,1. The data of Figure 1 are reproduced in Table I. Goodness of fit of the equal-weight averaging model was tested by analysis of variance. The interaction between the first and second weights was $F(16, 304) = 1.04$, which is far from significant. The statistical test thus agrees with the graphical test of parallelism.

These data, therefore, support the averaging model for this weight-averaging task. At the same time, they also imply that the rating response is an interval scale since a nonlinear scale would of itself tend to invalidate the model. The test of goodness of fit has thus provided a joint validation of the model and of the response scale. These results are in line with previous work on weight-averaging (Anderson, 1967a; Anderson & Jacobson, 1968).

TABLE I

MEAN RATED "AVERAGE HEAVINESS" OF TWO WEIGHTS LIFTED IN SUCCESSION[a]

First weight	Second weight					Mean
	200	300	400	500	600	
600	10.45	12.38	13.57	15.85	17.27	13.90
500	9.43	10.70	12.25	14.77	15.43	12.52
400	7.30	9.55	11.42	12.97	13.77	11.00
300	5.93	7.65	9.53	11.12	12.60	9.37
200	4.35	6.30	7.77	9.53	10.50	7.69
Mean	7.49	9.32	10.91	12.85	13.91	10.90

[a] Each data point is based on three judgments by each of 20 subjects on a 1–20, light–heavy, rating scale. End-anchors were a pair of 100-gm and a pair of 700-gm weights that were specified as 1 and 20, respectively. Data after Anderson (1972c).

Table I shows a very slight recency effect. The range of the marginal means is 6.21 and 6.42 for first and second weights, respectively. Thus, the weight lifted second has slightly more effect than the weight lifted first. This recency effect is insignificant, of course, but longer sequences have yielded reliable recency. Indeed, recency seems to be the rule for psychophysical averaging (see Section II,B,10).

2. SIZE–WEIGHT ILLUSION

When the lifted weight is visible, its size affects its judged heaviness. There are thus two cues to be integrated, and the linear integration model can be written,

$$R_{ij} = w_R s_{Ri} - w_C s_{C_j}^*, \tag{8}$$

where w_R and s_{Ri} are the (mathematical) weight and scale value of the weight cue, and w_C and $s_{C_j}^*$ are the weight and scale value of the size cue. The negative sign on w_C reflects the contrast effect; the same physical weight feels heavier when it is smaller.

This linear model can be tested directly in a two-way, Weight × Size factorial design. Figure 2 summarizes one such experiment. Subjects rated apparent heaviness of cylinders varying in weight and height as listed in the graph. The parallelism of the curves supports the linear integration model, in agreement with previous work on the size–weight illusion (Anderson, 1970b). Parallelism also implies that the rating scale is an interval response measure, by the logic already noted.

An incidental but notable feature of Figure 2 is the functional scale of the size cue, s^*. The trend of the curves reflects the inverse effect of size on heaviness. The effect is not linear, however, but shows diminishing effects with taller cylinders. That seems consistent with the previous experiment in which s^* was a linear function of the cube root of the volume

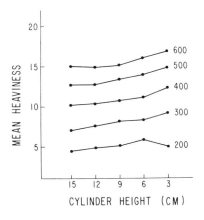

FIG. 2. Subjects rate the heaviness of visible cylinders in a 5 × 5 design. Cylinder height is listed on the horizontal axis, with one curve for each value of cylinder weight in grams. The data obey the parallelism prediction of the integration model. [From Anderson, 1972c.]

of cubes. The value of s^* presumably derives from the operation of a learned expectancy and would be difficult to measure in any other way. The present method would apply to objects of any size, shape, and appearance.

3. Cross-Task Validation and the Psychophysical Law

Both the weight-averaging task, and the size–weight data yield functional scales of subjective heaviness. If functional measurement procedure is valid, these two scales should be equivalent. This test has particular interest since the two tasks involve rather different integration processes.

The heaviness scale from the weight-averaging data is given by the marginal means of Table I. For simplicity, these two sets of marginal means were averaged to yield a single scale. The heaviness scale from the size–weight data can be obtained similarly by taking the mean elevation of the curves in Figure 2.

If both scales are interval scales, then one should plot as a linear function of the other. Figure 3 verifies this, thus providing cross-task validation of the stimulus scales. Of course, this also constitutes a cross-task validation of the rating response scale, and the linear integration model from which the stimulus values derive (see also Section II,B,10).

The psychophysical law for lifted weight is plotted in Figure 4. This is just the plot of subjective heaviness s against objective gram weight S. Both curves are nearly linear, but slightly convex downward.

4. Comment on Magnitude Estimation

The results of the three previous subsections conflict with those obtained when magnitude estimation is used as a response measure. Stevens and

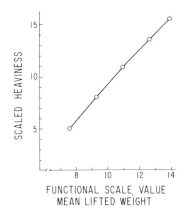

Fig. 3. Cross-task validation of integration models for lifted weight. Functional scale of heaviness from a size–weight task is plotted on the vertical axis with the functional scale of heaviness from a weight-averaging task on the horizontal axis. The data should fall on a straight line if both scales are interval scales. [From Anderson, 1972c.]

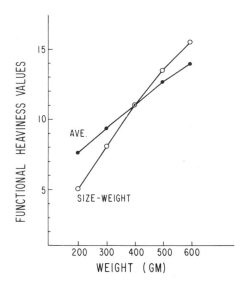

FIG. 4. Psychophysical law for lifted weight. Subjective heaviness is plotted against physical weight on the horizontal axis. Data from Table I and Fig. 2. Both curves are slightly convex downward. [From Anderson, 1972c.]

Galanter (1957) report an exponent of 1.45 for the power function for lifted weight. The data of Figure 4 would require an exponent less than unity. More generally, Stevens (1957, 1971) has repeatedly asserted that rating scales are biased for "prothetic" dimensions such as heaviness. Certainly, it is true that ratings and magnitude estimations are nonlinearly related. Both cannot be correct.

There is a fundamental difference between functional measurement procedure and Stevens's method of magnitude estimation. Functional measurement includes a validational base, whereas Stevens does not (Section IV,B,4; Anderson, 1972c, 1974a). In the previous subsections, the validational base is represented by the parallelism prediction, and by the cross-task agreement. Since the rating response has been validated, it follows that magnitude estimation yields a biased, nonlinear response scale.

5. GRAYNESS AVERAGING

A direct comparison between ratings and magnitude estimates was made by Weiss (1972). Subjects judged the average grayness of two Munsell chips using both response modes. Stimulus combinations were constructed using a 5 × 5 factorial design.

The rating data are given in the left panel of Figure 5. The five curves from the 5 × 5 design are essentially parallel, in agreement with the averaging model. This test is made directly on the raw data. Thus, the observed parallelism jointly validates the model and the rating response.

The magnitude estimation data, in the right panel of Figure 5, are markedly nonparallel. Presumably the stimulus-integration process is independent of the response requirements. It follows, therefore, that magnitude estimation suffers from a severe nonlinear bias, in agreement with the discussion of the previous section. As Weiss comments, "The response techniques are not merely discrepant; one is valid and the other is not."

6. SUM AND DIFFERENCE JUDGMENTS

Numerous investigators have tried to solve the measurement problem in psychophysics by using some kind of integration task, bisection, or loudness summation, for example (see Anderson, 1970a, 1972c). These attempts have not been generally successful, although recent studies by Curtis, Fagot, and their associates (e.g., Curtis, 1970; Fagot & Stewart, 1969a; Rule, Curtis, & Markley, 1970) have shown greater promise; see also Birnbaum and Veit (1974) and Weiss (1973b). The difficulties may reflect a basically incorrect integration model, but in most cases the issue

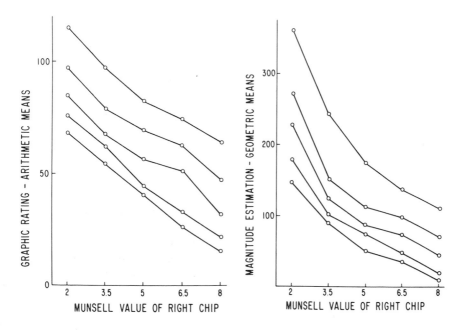

FIG. 5. Subjects judged the average grayness of two Munsell chips presented together. Value of the right-hand chip is shown on the horizontal axis, with one curve for each value of the left-hand chip. Graphic rating response in the left panel obeys the parallelism prediction of the integration model. Magnitude estimations in the right panel are nonparallel, which reflects the nonlinear bias of this response procedure. [Data after Weiss, 1972.]

remains unclear because previous analytical techniques have not been optimal. The algebraic integration model has been assumed to be true, but it has seldom been tested adequately. Fagot and Stewart (1969a), who have been attentive to this problem, found substantial deviations from the model. If the model is not correct, then the scale values derived from it may not be very meaningful.

A report by Feldman and Baird (1971) has double interest in this regard. On the positive side, it illustrates an integration task that has considerable potential importance. On the negative side, it illustrates the weaknesses of traditional methods of analyzing integration models.

Feldman and Baird obtained judgments of "total intensity" of a sound–light pair. Their second experiment employed a 5×5, Sound $\times$ Light design with 25 stimulus pairs. One hypothesis they wished to test was that the "total intensity" was an additive or linear function of the components. They actually tested the more restrictive model,

$$R = a(S_1^{n_1} + S_2^{n_2}) + b, \qquad (9)$$

where R is the predicted response, S_1 and S_2 are the measured intensities of the physical stimuli, n_1 and n_2 are power law exponents, and a and b are constants.

Feldman and Baird followed the traditional approach in testing their model. They carefully measured the values of S_1, and of S_2, on the physical scales; a power law was assumed so that $s_1 = S_1^{n_1}$, $s_2 = S_2^{n_2}$, where s and S denote subjective and objective values; n_1 and n_2 were estimated from judgments of the stimuli presented singly in the first experiment; and a and b were estimated by least squares to maximize the fit between the predicted values of R and the actual judgments. This model gave a better graphical fit than an alternative model, but no test of goodness of fit was possible.

It is striking how much simpler the analysis is with functional measurement. Every step in Feldman and Baird's test can be bypassed, and the resultant test is more general and much more powerful.

All that is needed is to plot the raw responses as a two-way data table, in the manner of Fig. 5, for example. The linear model predicts parallelism; it is as simple as that. No parameters need estimation, and the power law assumption is unnecessary. Furthermore, functional measurement procedure is superior on technical statistical grounds.

The cited studies by Curtis, Fagot, and their associates have used models similar to Eq. (9) to study sum and difference judgments for stimulus pairs from the same dimension. However, they also allow for one form of nonlinearity in the overt response. Their model can be written in one form as

$$(R_{ij})^{1/m} = a(S_i^k \pm S_j^k), \qquad (10)$$

where k and $1/m$ are exponent parameters. This is essentially the same as Eq. (9), except that a power transformation is allowed for the response. If the model is basically correct, then m should be near 1 if the overt response is on an interval scale. Values of m different from 1 would suggest a nonlinear response measure.

The overall result of these studies has been that m is near 1 when category ratings are used. However, magnitude estimation typically yields exponents quite different from 1. These results are consistent with the preceding studies, since they suggest that ratings are an interval response, and that magnitude estimation is severely biased. However, these conclusions are provisional since they rest on specialized assumptions, and since only one or two of the studies have adequately tested the model itself; see also Anderson (1974a).

7. Binaural Loudness Summation

Fletcher and Munson (1933) assumed that a tone presented binaurally should be twice as loud as when presented monaurally. With that assumption, they could obtain a loudness function from binaural–monaural loudness matches. As a strictly empirical result, they found that the binaural–monaural intensity difference for matching was not constant, but increased from about 5 to about 10 dB over the base range of 20 to 100 dB. Their result was replicated by Reynolds and Stevens (1960) with noise.

Reynolds and Stevens had initially questioned the Fletcher–Munson results on the stated ground that if loudness is a power function of intensity, then the binaural–monaural intensity difference should be constant. To allow for the nonconstant difference, they assumed that both binaural and monaural loudness are power functions, but that the binaural loudness function has a larger exponent. This interpretation was shown to be consistent with independent estimates of binaural and monaural loudness of noise, using three different techniques, magnitude estimation, magnitude production, and cross-modality matching. Work by Scharf and Fishken (1970) has verified their results for noise, though tones apparently give different results.

All this work suffers from a well-known theoretical difficulty. It is concerned with the subjective attribute of loudness, and the conclusions that are drawn depend on the assumption that the loudness scale is known. Yet none of this work has provided a criterion for validating the obtained loudness scale. Reynolds and Stevens's assumption of a power function is just as arbitrary as Fletcher and Munson's assumption of perfect summation. Resolution of the difficulty requires methodology that can validate the subjective scale.

Functional measurement may help elucidate this problem. A two-ear design would be used, the same sound being presented to both ears but with independently varied intensities, in a factorial design. If row and column represent the right and left ears, the summation hypothesis can be written

$$r_{ij} = w_R s_{Ri} + w_L s_{Lj}, \tag{11}$$

where s_{Ri} and s_{Lj} are the monaural loudnesses, w_R and w_L are the weights of the right and left ears, and r_{ij} is the binaural loudness. The subject is assumed to give a numerical estimate of loudness.

This functional-measurement design may be compared to the traditional monaural–binaural design, which is an odd fraction of a complete design. In the traditional design, either one ear is stimulated alone, or both ears receive the same stimulation. Thus the monaural data represent one row, and the binaural data represent the diagonal of a complete factorial design.

To use the traditional design, it is almost necessary to assume that the two ears have the same loudness functions, at least up to a linear transformation. If also the observed response is an interval scale of loudness, then the summation hypothesis [Eq. (11)] implies that the binaural data will be a linear function of the monaural data. Equivalently, the two sets of data should follow the bilinear form of Section III,A.

It is interesting to speculate on the interpretation of existing data in the light of the preceding analysis. The noise data of Reynolds and Stevens follow the bilinear form as plotted. The noise data of Scharf and Fishken also appear to follow the bilinear form, though not as a power function of decibel level. Both reports are thus consistent with the joint hypothesis that the summation model is correct, and that the response measure actually plotted is an interval scale of loudness. But, the response measure actually plotted is not the magnitude estimation but its logarithm. Thus, these data suggest that magnitude estimation is severely biased, a conclusion that has more direct support (Section II,B,5; Anderson, 1972c, 1974a; Weiss, 1972, 1973b).

This interpretation of the cited data is speculative. The tone data of Scharf and Fishken show apparent parallelism, rather than bilinear divergence, and the needed statistical analyses have not been performed for any of these data. More importantly, the traditional monaural–binaural design is inherently too weak to test the summation model adequately. If the monaural–binaural relation is linear with zero intercept, then it will remain linear under a power transformation of the response. Since two response measures could satisfy the bilinearity condition even though they were nonlinearly related, the traditional design is not adequate to validate the response scale. Furthermore, the obvious monotone relationships among the monaural response, binaural response, and stimulus intensity imply that it will always be possible to find some monotone transformation that will produce parallelism (Levine, 1970), and hence also bilinearity by an exponential transformation. In short, it is always formally possible to transform monaural–binaural data from the traditional design to satisfy the summation hypothesis.

An alternative is to use a monaural matching response instead of a numerical estimate. This is attractive because it rests on direct sensory comparison instead of an extraneous response language. But since the matching response is on the physical intensity scale, it requires transformation to a subjective metric. This procedure was used by Fletcher and Munson (1933) and studied more extensively by Treisman and Irwin (1967). Both reports assume perfect summation, and that assumption allows a solution to the transformation problem. Treisman and Irwin also assume a power function for the loudness–intensity relation but allow a variable exponent to handle the nonconstant binaural–monaural intensity difference already discussed. But neither of these reports tests the summation assumption per se, nor does it seem possible to do so with the traditional design. Since the monaural response must be a strictly monotone function of the binaural intensity, it can always be monotonically transformed to a linear function thereof, or indeed to have any other prescribed monotone relation (see also Section III,B,2). However, it should be noted that Treisman and Irwin did attempt to check their loudness function by also obtaining monaural matches to unequal binaural stimulation of the two ears.

Functional measurement procedure provides for a more powerful attack on binaural summation. Intensity at each ear would be varied independently in a factorial design. Imperfect summation is allowed, and no assumption about the psychophysical function is needed. Indeed, the two ears could even differ radically in sensitivity. A monaural matching response could be used if the binaural stimulation was varied independently in the two ears in a factorial design as already noted. Monotone transformation (Section II,A,6) would then be required, so that more than two rows of data would be needed. It might be preferable, of course, to seek a response measure that is an interval scale in its raw form (Section II,A,7). The parallelism prediction would then apply directly to the raw data, just as in Section II,B,1.

An experiment of this general type (Levelt, Riemersma, & Bunt, 1972) was overlooked in the draft of this chapter, but a brief note may be added here. This experiment has special interest as one of the few applications of a nonmetric approach. The two subjects chose the louder of two binaural stimuli in which the intensities to the two ears were varied independently in a modified factorial design. These choice data were converted to rank orders and analyzed by nonmetric methods to yield power functions with exponents modally around .45. One reservation about these results is the extremely low stress values of the additive solutions, which seem almost too good. Very low stress values suggest that the stimulus spacing was very coarse. With a coarse spacing, however, the analysis lacks power to detect discrepancies from the summation hypothesis. Unfortunately, satisfactory tests of goodness of fit are not available for nonmetric analysis.

8. RANGE–FREQUENCY THEORY OF CATEGORY JUDGMENTS

This section discusses Parducci's theory of how people use category rating scales to portray their judgments. Although not well-known, his theory has had reasonably good quantitative success, and is markedly superior to its closest competitor, Helson's (1964) theory of adaptation-level.

a. RANGE PRINCIPLE AND FREQUENCY PRINCIPLE. Parducci's (1965) theory of category judgments assumes that two principles govern judgments made on an ordinal category scale. The *frequency principle* postulates that each category has a characteristic frequency of usage. Equal frequency of usage would be the simplest case, as might be expected on an ordinary numerical rating scale. The *range principle* postulates a division of the total (subjective) stimulus range into subranges, one for each category. The characteristic frequency of each category, and the relative size of its subrange, are assumed to depend on the verbal definition of that category. However, both are assumed to be independent of the set or distribution of stimuli that is presented for judgment.

These two principles will often conflict. With a U-shaped distribution and an equal-frequency category scale, the range principle implies a U-shaped distribution of responses, whereas the frequency principle implies a uniform distribution of response.

In Parducci's theory, the overt judgments are a compromise between these two principles. In Parducci's earlier papers, this compromise was assumed to apply to the category boundaries, and the stimuli were judged relative to them, as in Thurstone's theory of successive categories. More recently, Parducci and Perrett (1971) have assumed that the range–frequency compromise applies to each individual stimulus. The percentile range–frequency model presented here is essentially the same as that used by Parducci and Perrett.

b. PERCENTILE RANGE–FREQUENCY MODEL. This section shows how to apply the functional-measurement approach to range–frequency theory. The basic assumptions are those used by Parducci, but the functional-measurement procedure allows a simpler and more powerful analysis. It is assumed that the rank order of the stimuli is known, and that both the stimulus distributions and the response measure are effectively continuous.

Each stimulus is assumed to have two percentile values: f is the ordinary frequency percentile, calculable directly from the stimulus distribution; s

is the range percentile, that is, 100 times the subjective distance between the stimulus and the lower end of the range, divided by the subjective distance between the upper and lower ends of the range. The model assumes that the judgment value is a weighted average:

$$R = a[ws + (1 - w)f], \tag{12}$$

where a is a scale factor that adjusts the percentile scale to the overt response scale. For simplicity, a will be taken equal to one.

To illustrate the method of analysis, consider two stimulus distributions that have the same range. Because the ranges are equal, any stimulus common to both distributions has the same range percentile s in both distributions. Let f_1 and f_2 be the frequency percentile functions for the two distributions, and let R_1 and R_2 be the overt response to a given common stimulus. From Eq. (12)

$$R_1 = ws + (1 - w)f_1,$$
$$R_2 = ws + (1 - w)f_2, \tag{13}$$

so that

$$R_1 - R_2 = (1 - w)(f_1 - f_2). \tag{14}$$

Equation (14) provides a solution for w, since $R_1 - R_2$ is observable, and $(f_1 - f_2)$ is calculable directly from the stimulus distributions. The model implies that w is the same for all common stimuli, and a test of goodness of fit is straightforward on that basis. Once w has been obtained, Eqs. (13) may be used for estimating the subjective stimulus values s.

This functional-measurement approach has the great advantage that it does not require prior estimates of the scale values of the stimuli. In his earlier work, Parducci typically started with Thurstonian scaling methods and used these values in his further analyses. Even if the Thurstone values are valid, they have an uncertain variability that complicates testing the basic model.

Besides the basic model of Eq. (12), the present approach retains two of Parducci's assumptions that need explicit comment. The first is that the overt response is a theoretically adequate scale. The second is that all categories tend to be used equally often. This latter assumption is implicit in the use of the frequency percentile function. Thus the test of fit is a joint test of all three assumptions.

Some direct leverage is available even on these last two assumptions. For example, if the range is held constant and the stimulus distribution is varied, then R is a linear function of f for a fixed stimulus. This property could be used to linearize the f-scale or the R-scale. In the latter case, a test of fit could be obtained by extending the stimulus range. A somewhat different application of functional measurement methodology to this problem has been given by Birnbaum (1974), who also provides an impressive experimental comparison of several theories of category judgment.

One strong implication of the range–frequency model is worth noting. Consider two stimulus distributions with the same range, and identical except for an interior "hole" at different locations toward the upper end of each distribution. Both distributions are thus identical up to the lower edge of the lower hole, so that each stimulus below that edge has the same range percentile and the same frequency percentile in both distributions. Each such stimulus should, therefore, receive the same judgment in both distributions. This prediction has apparently not been tested, and it may be worth pursuing, since it provides a strong, parameter-free test of the basic range-frequency assumption.

c. CONTRAST EFFECTS. It has long been recognized that "contrast" may be an artifact, reflecting merely linguistic habits, not true change in stimulus value (see Anderson, 1971a, pp. 189–190, 200). The artifact interpretation of contrast becomes especially clear in range–frequency theory. The frequency principle acts directly to produce apparent contrast; if the frequency of some stimulus is increased, its neighbors will shift away in order to reequalize the category frequencies. But the shift is in the category judgments; the stimulus value, s in Eq. (12) remains constant.

The matter is complicated because true changes in perceptual value certainly do occur in certain cases. Temperature adaptation is one; lukewarm water will feel warm or cold to fingers preadapted in cold or warm water, respectively. The size–weight illusion (Section II,B,2) and the Ebbinghaus illusion (Section III,B,5) are others. However, even simple psychophysical stimuli sometimes show small assimilation effects where contrast effects would be expected on adaptation or range–frequency grounds (Garner 1953; Anderson, 1791b). And it seems safe to say that satisfactory evidence for true contrast with verbal or symbolic stimuli has yet to be obtained.

Range–frequency theory itself does not disallow true contrast. Such effects, if they exist, could appear as a shift in the affective zero of the scale. Shifts in scale zero are outside the scope of the theory, since the range values, being percentiles, are unaffected by such shifts.

d. STIMULUS SCALING. The present analysis suggests that range–frequency theory may be especially useful for stimulus scaling, since it can factor out the category frequency habits. Indeed, the frequency habits provide the leverage, so that response bias is put to good use. An especially interesting application is given by Parducci, Marshall, and Degner (1966). A very similar theoretical analysis has been given by Erlebacher and Sekuler (1971). This kind of application could perhaps be extended to analyze the influence of anchors on the scale value. Such influences might be expected if anchors affect discriminability and thereby also scale value.

Scaling the effective stimulus could also be useful in stimulus integration tasks. Most of Parducci's work has been with judgments of single stimuli, but Birnbaum, Parducci, and Gifford (1971) had subjects rate average length of pairs of lines. They found nonlinear changes in the ratings of given pairs of lines between two different distributions of lines. Range–frequency theory would apply to the judgments of average length, considered as the effective distribution of stimuli to be rated. Here again, an appropriate design would factor out the biasing effects of the verbal frequency habits. In general, of course, it is preferable to avoid such biases with experimental procedure, by using stimulus end-anchors and graphic ratings, for example (Section II,A,7).

e. RANGE–FREQUENCY VERSUS ADAPTATION-LEVEL. Parducci's range–frequency theory may be compared most directly with Helson's theory of adaptation-level. Both deal with category judgment, and both have been developed mainly with reference to magnitude judgments of single psychophysical stimuli. Range–frequency theory has been shown to be overwhelmingly superior to adaptation-level theory in predicting category judgments (e.g., Parducci & Perrett, 1971).

An illustrative comparison between range–frequency theory and adaptation-level theory is shown in Fig. 6. Subjects rated apparent size of squares on a nine-category scale. Mean category judgments are plotted as a function of the Thurstone scale values of square size. Two different distributions

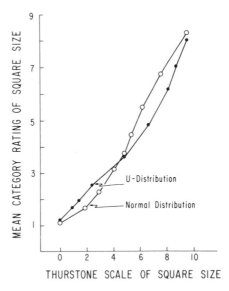

FIG. 6. Mean rating of squares on a 9-step scale. Two different distributions of square sizes produce crossover in the category scales. This crossover is predicted by Parducci's range-frequency theory, but cannot be accounted for by Helson's adaptation-level theory. [After Parducci & Perrett, 1971.]

of square sizes were used. One distribution was normal, with mostly middle-sized squares, and relatively few large or small squares. The other distribution was U-shaped, with mostly large and small squares, and very few middle-sized squares. The crossover of the judgment curves for the two conditions was predicted by range–frequency theory, with reasonable quantitative accuracy. Adaptation-level theory assumes that the judgments are a linear function of distance from adaptation-level. If these two distributions have a different adaptation-level, then one curve must always lie above the other. Thus, adaptation-level theory cannot account for the crossover.

However, adaptation-level theory does deal with one phenomenon not considered in range–frequency theory, namely, perceptual adaptation. In Helson's approach, the adaptation-level is the stimulus at the affective zero. In range–frequency theory, the stimulus scale has an arbitrary zero and unit. Thus it is silent on a question that is central for adaptation-level theory (see also Section III,B,4).

9. SIGNAL DETECTION

Most of the methods discussed in this chapter assume a numerical response measure. It is a major problem how they may be applied in the analysis of choice data. One standard approach is to assume that the integration model applies to an underlying response variable, and that the overt choice is made by referring the covert numerical response to some criterion. For analysis, it is then desired to reconstruct the underlying response measure from the observed discrete choices. Such an approach is used in this section to study a linear integration model. This model was developed using the decision apparatus of signal-detection theory. In some respects, however, it is more similar to Thurstonian scaling methods. Particular mention should be made of Bock and Jones (1968; Sects. 7.3.3, 8.5), who consider a linear integration model within the framework of the Thurstonian methods.

a. INTEGRATION DECISION MODEL. Consider a stimulus field of N sources, each of which can be in various states. Each source–state combination is assumed to correspond to an independent normal distribution of information values x_{ij} for Source i in State j. On any trial, the total accumulated information is taken to be a weighted sum

$$y(A) = \sum_A w_i x_{ij}, \tag{15}$$

where w_i is the relative importance of Source i, x_{ij} is the random value of Source i in State j, and the sum is over all sources in some given array A of states.

Since the x_{ij} are independent normal, $y(A)$ is also normal, with mean and variance:

$$s_y(A) = \Sigma w_i s_{ij}, \tag{16}$$

$$\sigma_y{}^2 = \Sigma w_i{}^2 \sigma_i{}^2, \tag{17}$$

where s_{ij} and $\sigma_i{}^2$ are the mean and variance of x_{ij}. As the notation indicates, the variance is assumed constant over states within a source, so that the variance of $y(A)$ is independent of the particular array A on any trial. For simplicity, $\sigma_y{}^2$ is set equal to unity which may be done without loss of generality for fixed N.

In line with current decision theory, the subject is assumed to make categorical responses using some criterion. For a yes–no task, the response would be "yes" or "no" depending on whether the value of y is above or below the criterion k. The observed proportion of "yes" responses, conditional on a given array of source states, corresponds to the unit normal deviate

$$z_{\mathrm{Yes}}(A) = s_y(A) - k = -k + \sum_A w_i s_{ij}. \tag{18}$$

Thus, $s_y(A)$ is a linear function of the observable $z_{\mathrm{Yes}}(A)$, which is itself a linear function of the source values, and the criterion.

b. APPLICATIONS. Equation (18) is the basic result, and several applications are possible. Suppose that the stimulus arrays are constructed from factorial designs in which the sources are the factors, each with several states or levels of equal weight and variance. If z_{Yes} is used as the dependent variable, Eq. (18) implies that all interactions are zero. If the model passes this test of fit, it may be used for scaling. Indeed, the marginal means estimate the values of the information states s_{ij} on interval scales. In practice, this simple scheme might need modification to allow for missing cells that would result from choice proportions near 0 or 1.

Criterion scaling represents an important application that could be accomplished by manipulating the criterion as a factor in the design. Standard methods for controlling the criterion are by instruction, or by varying stimulus probabilities. Or several criteria could be maintained simultaneously by requiring a rating response. Since Eq. (18) is linear in k, the marginal means of the criterion factor would give interval scale estimates of the criterion values.

Two other experimental applications may be noted. First, serial presentation of the simulus sources would be expected to introduce memory effects. The present approach allows weight to depend on serial position, and a complete serial curve can be obtained (Section II,B,10). Such curves could be useful in studying memory factors. Previous models for serial integration in signal detection (Green & Swets, 1966, Chap. 9) have disallowed imperfect memory.

Second, the case of unordered homogeneous sources can rise in recognition memory. For example, subjects might be required to categorize as "old" or "new" items in sets with both old and new items in varied proportion. All items in the set then represent sources having, in the simplest case, equal weight and the same two states. For fixed set size, z_{Yes} would be a linear function of the number of old items.

Finally, the case of one source with two states has special interest. It is the case usually considered in signal-detection theory. The two states are called *signal* and *noise,* with scale values s_S and s_N. These may be considered as the rows in a two-way factorial design in which the column stimuli represent the criterion value, k_j. Equation (18) then becomes

$$z_{Yes,j}(S) = -k_j + ws_S, \qquad z_{Yes,j}(N) = -k_j + ws_N. \tag{19}$$

The difference between these two expressions is the well-known symbol, d':

$$d' = z_{Yes}(S) - z_{Yes}(N) = w(s_S - s_N), \tag{20}$$

which is seen to be theoretically independent of the criterion k_j.

The constancy of d' is equivalent to the parallelism property of functional measurement. In signal-detection theory, the standard test of the model is in terms of the ROC curve; varying the criterion should leave d' unchanged. This ROC test is equivalent to the test of interaction in a two-way design: One factor is the criterion, the other factor is the two-state source. The data should plot as two parallel curves. There is no necessary restriction to two-state sources, of course. Multistate sources, corresponding to several signal intensities, for example, would imply several parallel curves.

In signal-detection theory, response bias, payoff, and other "motivational" factors are considered to affect k only, so that d' is a true measure of sensory discriminability. That this view may be limited in its generality has been suggested by R. Kinchla (personal communication), who has independently arrived at much of the analysis presented here. In Kinchla's view, the criterion variable is no less a stimulus than the ostensible signal and both enter linearly in the model equation. Thus, to interpret d' as a true sensory measure must rest on external considerations in each experimental application.

c. TECHNICAL COMMENTS. The formal similarity between Eqs. (15) and (18) deserves emphasis in two respects. In Eq. (15), the informational state of the subject is a numerical variable, but this is mapped into a discrete yes–no response by the decision output system. The z-transformation of the observed proportions allows a reconstruction of the structure of the original informational state as it depends on the stimulus design. One main effect of the z-transformation is to invert the choice dichotomization, allowing a recovery of the basic numerical information. In addition, the criterion value gets worked into Eq. (18) and may be estimated with suitable design.

From the present view, the preoccupation with choice data in signal-detection theory and Thurstonian scaling is surprising and perhaps unfortunate. Even when ratings are obtained, they are treated as choices. Yet it is clear that if there were any way to observe the $y(A)$ in Eq. (15) directly, that would be much more efficient than having to accumulate enough trials to estimate a choice proportion.

As an alternative to choice data, therefore, ratings, latencies, or other numerical response measures might provide a more efficient analysis in many situations. A possible application to reaction time is given in Section III,B,3. Ratings themselves will ordinarily contain more information than choices; they are obtainable from suprathreshold stimuli; and they could eliminate the problem of empty data cells that result from extreme choice proportions. A linearizing transformation would probably still be needed, but existing data suggest that getting such a transformation would not be difficult (Section II,A,6). Such a monotone transformation would serve the same function as the z-transformation, though at the cost of one or two degrees of freedom. Such an approach may seem overly empirical, but it would avoid the traditional reliance on untestable assumptions about underlying response distributions, and address itself directly to the integration process.

10. SERIAL INTEGRATION

When the stimuli are presented serially in time, primacy and recency effects are often obtained. The averaging model can be extended to handle serial integration by allowing the weight parameter to depend on serial position. The essential idea is to make the serial positions correspond to the factors in the design, as in the weight-averaging experiment of Section II,B,1.

Only one special case will be considered here. Suppose that the same two stimuli S_1 and S_2 are used at each serial position. Assume that their scale values s_1 and s_2 are constant across serial position, and that their weights are equal except as weight depends on serial position. Then the difference between the two marginal means at the kth serial position D_k has the theoretical expression,

$$D_k = w_k(s_1 - s_2), \tag{21}$$

where w_k is the weight parameter associated with the kth serial position.

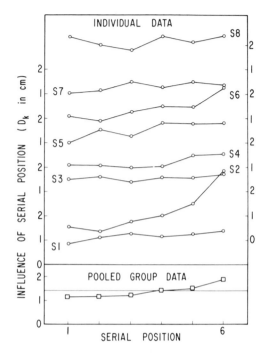

FIG. 7. Serial position curves for length-averaging. Six lines were presented in sequence, and the subject gave a graphic judgment of their average length. The plotted data are proportional to the weight parameter at each serial position. Curves for individual subjects are displaced vertically. [From Weiss & Anderson, 1969.]

Since $(s_1 - s_2)$ is constant, Eq. (21) implies that the observed value of D_k is proportional to w_k. These observable differences thus provide direct estimates of the complete serial position curve. This methodology is developed in more detail in Anderson (1974b), Shanteau (1972), and Weiss and Anderson (1969).

Figure 7 shows such curves from a length averaging task. Subjects saw six lines in succession for several seconds each. When the last line had vanished, the subject estimated the average length of the lines by adjusting a marker on a rod. The two possible lengths at each position were 16 and 24 cm. With six serial positions, there were then 64 possible sequences to be judged.

The D_k values of Eq. (21) are plotted in Fig. 7. Recency is reflected in the upward trend in the group curve at the bottom. The curves for the individual subjects (staggered vertically) show relatively small individual differences.

The recency in Fig. 7 is typical of psychophysical averaging tasks (Anderson, 1967a; Anderson & Jacobson, 1968; Levin, Craft, & Norman, 1971; Parducci, Thaler, & Anderson, 1968; Weiss & Anderson, 1969). Little is known about its cause. Requiring a response at each serial position can produce a considerably different curve (Weiss & Anderson, 1969).

Two memory-type hypotheses were tested by Weiss and Anderson (1969) with minimal success. The recency does not appear to be an adaptation-level effect (Anderson, 1971b). Also it is interesting that primacy is typically obtained in analogous experiments with verbal stimuli (e.g., Anderson, 1974c).

Serial integration has numerous possible applications besides estimating serial position curves. It might be used to scale subjective velocity or time, for example, which could be difficult to pin down in other ways. Or it could serve a cross-task validation, as illustrated in the linear models for weight-averaging and the size–weight illusion (Sections II,B,1–3). An arithmetic averaging model might seem almost trivial for the weight-averaging task. However, it provided useful support for the treatment of the size–weight illusion for which the linear model is by no means so obvious.

11. TWO-STAGE INTEGRATION MODEL

Two-stage models have special potential in integration theory. They can be used to study valuation processes, especially in stimulus interaction. The essential idea is to study a complex integration process by adding a second stage based on a simple integration process. For example, judgments might be asked of the difference in area of two complex figures, or of their total area. The first stage involves the perception of the area of the individual figures. The second stage, in contrast, requires only a simple algebraic operation. Success of the second-stage model would yield functional scales for the complex figures, and so provide a basis for the further analysis of the first stage integration.

a. GENERAL TWO-STAGE INTEGRATION MODEL. An explicit statement of the general two-stage integration model is complicated to no good purpose. Since the essential ideas are simple, they will be developed by illustration in a simple case.

Two integration stages are assumed. The output of the first, A-stage, is considered as input to the second, B-stage. For simplicity, the B-stage is assumed to follow a binary operation, although any of the algebraic models discussed here would do. The model can then be written,

$$R_{ij} = H_{\mathrm{R}}(S_{\mathrm{R}i}) \circ H_{\mathrm{C}}(S_{\mathrm{C}j}). \tag{22}$$

In this equation, R_{ij} is the overt response to the pair of stimuli, $S_{\mathrm{R}i}$ and $S_{\mathrm{C}j}$; H_{R} and H_{C} are the A-stage integration functions, and $\circ$ denotes the B-stage integration rule.

In the example of area judgments, H_{R} and H_{C} would represent the initial integration that yielded the subjective area of each complex figure. The B-stage integration rule would be subtracting or adding in the two respective judgment tasks. The main result would be the construction of functional scales of subjective area of the figures. These could then be further related to the physical characteristics of the stimulus.

The two-stage approach is important for its potential in studying integration processes that do not follow a simple model. Judged area of rectangles, for example, exhibits certain discrepancies from a simple base-times-height model (Anderson & Weiss, 1971). More generally, contrast, assimilation, and other kinds of stimulus interaction can involve complicated integration rules. Interpretation of such results is often uncertain because the response may not be on an interval scale. When such stimulus complexes can be embedded in a second integration task, it will often be possible to use the second stage to validate the stimulus and response scales.

Much of the work of Section II,B can be considered as a limiting case of the two-stage approach, in which H_R and H_C are the ordinary psychophysical functions. In the size–weight illusion (Section II,B,2), for instance, H_R would be the psychophysical function for subjective heaviness, and H_C would be the psychophysical function for the size cue s^*. The s^*-scale is of special interest, since it will depend strongly on several aspects of the visual field, and since it would be hard to obtain by any kind of direct estimation.

As yet, however, not a great deal has been done with the two-stage approach in perception. Applications in decision making may have some analogical interest. For example, Shanteau (1970) used a two-stage model to verify a subadditivity effect in utility theory. In this case, a multiplying model was used in the A-stage to validate a deviation from additivity in the B-stage.

b. TWO-STAGE DIMENSIONAL INTEGRATION MODEL. An important special case of the general two-stage integration model arises when the stimuli have a common dimensional construction. The integration in the A-stage may then proceed on a dimension-by-dimension basis, with these partial integrations being combined in the B-stage.

For illustration, suppose that a subject makes successive paired observations on two sources of variable loudness and judges the difference in average loudness of the two sources. The successive observations correspond to the dimensions; each observation yields one loudness difference, and the response is taken to be the average of these differences, much as in the serial integration models of Section II,B,10. Certain models for similarity judgment, in the next subsection, are also of this type. Other dimensional integration models, based on preference and averaging judgments, are noted in the last subsection.

For simplicity, only an adding operation in the B-stage will be considered here. Consider combinations of two stimuli, each defined along several dimensions so that stimulus i can be represented as $(S_i, T_i, U_i, \ldots)$, where S_i is its physical value on dimension S, etc. No metric is assumed for these physical stimulus values which may be discrete and nominal.

In the two-stage model, the response to the combination of stimuli i and j is

$$R_{ij} = w_S H_S(S_i, S_j) + w_T H_T(T_i, T_j) + w_U H_U(U_i, U_j) + \cdots, \quad (23)$$

where the w's are weighting coefficients. The arbitrary functions, H_S, H_T, etc, represent the A-stage integration, and need not be the same for different dimensions.

In the illustrative loudness task, $H_S(S_i, S_j)$ would be just the loudness difference between the first observation from source i, and the first observation from source j. The successive terms in Eq. (23) would represent successive paired observations, and the w's would be the serial position weights. In the simplest case, $H_S(S_i, S_j)$ would be just the difference, $(s_i - s_j)$, between the loudnesses. However, Eq. (23) could still hold even if S_i and S_j interacted in some way to yield a nonlinear H_S.

The key to the analysis of the two-stage dimensional model is in factorial design. Each dimension corresponds to a factor in the design. The levels of each factor are *pairs* of stimulus values from that dimension. The standard analysis for strict adding models may then be applied: The model predicts parallelism and the marginal means are the scale values of the partial integrations of the A-stage.

Table II gives a 2×3 illustration. The upper half shows the six stimulus combinations; the lower half shows the theoretical response values for the

TABLE II

Illustrative 2×3 Design for Two-Stage Dimensional Model, with Adding Process in B-Stage, Showing Stimulus Design and Zero Interaction Prediction

Dimension S	Dimension T		
	(T_1, T_2)	$(T_3 T_4)$	(T_5, T_6)
a. Stimulus combinations			
(S_1, S_2)	(S_1, T_1) & (S_2, T_2)	(S_1, T_3) & (S_2, T_4)	(S_1, T_5) & (S_2, T_6)
(S_3, S_4)	(S_3, T_1) & (S_4, T_2)	(S_3, T_3) & (S_4, T_4)	(S_3, T_5) & (S_4, T_6)
b. Response values			
	$H_S(S_1, S_2) + H_T(T_1, T_2)$	$H_S(S_1, S_2) + H_T(T_3, T_4)$	$H_S(S_1, S_2) + H_T(T_5, T_6)$
	$H_S(S_3, S_4) + H_T(T_1, T_2)$	$H_S(S_3, S_4) + H_T(T_3, T_4)$	$H_S(S_3, S_4) + H_T(T_5, T_6)$
	$c + H_T(T_1, T_2)$	$c + H_T(T_3, T_4)$	$c + H_T(T_5, T_6)$

case of unit weighting. The difference between the two rows is constant across columns. With this design, therefore, the two-stage model makes the parallelism prediction.

Functional scale values are obtainable as marginal means, illustrated here for the column stimuli. The column means in the last row of Table II are the values of $H_T(T_i, T_j)$ on an interval scale. Estimation of these values would help define the nature of the integration in the A-stage. For example, the values of all six pairs of T_1, T_2, T_3, T_4 could be measured in a 2×6 design even though each pair combined in an arbitrary way. Such information could be especially useful in the study of nonlinear or configural integration.

Both stages might be additive in certain tasks. That can be tested simply by extending the procedure just mentioned so that the column pairs, say, form a factorial design. For example, the four columns, (T_1, T_2), (T_3, T_4), (T_1, T_3) and (T_2, T_4), would form a 2×2 design. If H_T is a linear rule, then this design should show no interaction. That would be the case in the illustrative loudness experiment if indeed $H_S(S_i, S_j) = s_i - s_j$ etc. One statistical analysis suffices to handle the tests of both stages, as exemplified in analogous work in utility theory (Anderson & Shanteau, 1970; Shanteau, 1970).

The two-stage dimensional model can be extended directly to combinations of more than two stimuli. For three stimuli, Eq. (23) would become

$$R_{ijk} = w_S H_S(S_i, S_j, S_k) + w_T H_T(T_i, T_j, T_k) + \cdots . \qquad (24)$$

The levels of each factor would be the stimulus triples, (S_i, S_j, S_k), etc. The marginal means of the design would be the effective values output from the A-stage and input to the B-stage.

c. SIMILARITY MODELS. Similarity judgments will be treated very briefly here, mainly to illustrate some potential applications of functional-measurement procedure. Most work on similarity has been done in the context of multidimensional scaling, in which the aim has been to delineate the effective stimulus dimensions and to obtain a spatial representation of the stimulus. In contrast, integration theory emphasizes the study of judgmental processes and a spatial representation becomes secondary. This approach agrees with Hyman and Well (1967, p. 248), who question the need for spatial models, and who note also that mathematical elaboration of similarity models has far outrun the data.

1. ADDING DISSIMILARITY. Much of the work on similarity judgments has employed some form of an additive-difference model first investigated by Attneave (1950) and studied with increasing sophistication in numerous papers of which those by Shepard (1964), Torgerson (1965), Hake

(1966, p. 520), Hyman and Well (1967, 1968) Gregson (1970), Beals, Krantz and Tversky (1968), and Tversky and Krantz (1969) are most immediately relevant. The last two papers are notable in two respects, for relaxing the assumption that the dissimilarity within any dimension is a difference, and for concern with testing goodness of fit. They rely on non-metric rank-order tests, whereas the metric approach is emphasized here, as in the original experiment by Attneave (1950).

The basic idea of the additive dissimilarities model is simple. It assumes that a dissimilarity value is obtained for each separate stimulus dimension, and that these dissimilarity values are added across dimensions to yield the total dissimilarity. It is thus a two-stage integration model of the type studied in the two previous subsections, and can be analyzed in the same way.

Let stimuli i and j be defined on dimensions $S, T, \ldots$, and let d_S be the dissimilarity function on dimension S, etc. Following Eq. (23), the overall dissimilarity between stimuli i and j is

$$R_{ij} = w_S d_S(S_i, S_j) + w_T d_T(T_i, T_j) + \cdots . \tag{25}$$

Factorial stimulus design allows a test of this model in the manner already illustrated in Table II. If the model passes the test, then the marginal means of the data table are interval-scale estimates of the within-dimensional dissimilarities, $d_S(S_i, S_j)$, etc.

It is frequently assumed that within-dimensional dissimilarity follows an absolute difference model,

$$d_S(S_i, S_j) = |s_i - s_j|, \tag{26}$$

where s_i and s_j are the scale values of S_i and S_j. The present formulation, like that of Beals, Krantz, and Tversky (1968), does not require the restrictive assumption of Eq. (26). But it has the added advantage of providing a relatively straightforward test of Eq. (26), since it yields direct interval scales of the $d_S(S_i, S_j)$, etc.

Two problems about the response scale should be specifically noted here. First, only an interval scale is required for the overall test of the two-stage model. The additive constant problem, raised by Hake (1966) in connection with Attneave's treatment, concerns only the absolute difference assumption of Eq. (26).

Second, the observed response may be ordinal rather than interval, so that a monotone transformation would be required. Such an assumption has been embodied in the multidimensional scaling approach stemming from the work of Shepard (1962) as well as in the nonmetric tests of fit used by Tversky and Krantz (1969). The functional measurement approach also allows for possible monotone transformation (Anderson, 1962b; see also Section II,A,6).

2. AVERAGING SIMILARITY. Almost without exception, similarity models have been formulated in terms of addition of dissimilarities. This approach seems questionable in two respects, and it will be suggested that the judgments are based on integration of similarities, probably by an averaging rule.

The difficulty with the dissimilarity approach may be seen in the following two pairs:

$$
\begin{aligned}
S_1 &= C, & S_3 &= A\ B\ C\ E\ F, \\
S_2 &= D, & S_4 &= A\ B\ D\ E\ F.
\end{aligned} \tag{27}
$$

The addition of common letters seems to increase the similarity so that S_3 and S_4 are more similar than S_1 and S_2. This suggests that the hypothesis of additive dissimilarities is not tenable. Addition of common elements cannot decrease dissimilarity, or increase similarity, unless negative dissimilarities are allowed, and that is difficultly compatible with the representation of dissimilarity as distance.

On this basis, similarity analysis should be in terms of similarities, not dissimilarities. The next question is whether similarities are added or averaged. Presumably the addition of noncommon letters to S_3 and S_4 in (27) would decrease the similarity. To handle this, an adding model would need to allow for positive and negative similarity values. A critical test between averaging and adding is then possible on the same basis as in previous work on the averaging hypothesis (Section II,A,5). Addition of a near-neutral element should decrease either similarity or dissimilarity if it is averaged in. Some evidence that supports the averaging hypothesis for similarity judgments is given by Simmonds (1971).

The standard approach based on adding of dissimilarities seems to stem from the attempts to obtain a spatial representation. This approach has the mathematical convenience of providing a rational zero, namely, the dissimilarity of two identical stimuli. And it is directly associated with the treatment of dissimilarity as a distance measure in spatial models. This approach is not theoretically neutral, however, and may be misleading if the averaging hypothesis is correct.

The averaging hypothesis for similarity judgments has some important implications. Since the weights appear in the denominator, the averaging model will be linear only with certain constraints on the weight parameter (Section II,A,5). Recent evidence suggests that the weight parameter is not always independent of the stimulus value, but can vary directly with stimulus intensity. In that case, the averaging model will not generally be linear. Attempts to handle such data with an inappropriate integration model would presumably produce distorted spatial representations.

3. NONLINEAR SIMILARITY FUNCTIONS. Similarity of unitary stimuli is probably a nonlinear function of stimulus magnitude in many situations. Loudness or brightness, for example, might follow a rule such as $|s_1 - s_2|/(s_1 + s_2)$. An approach of this general type, often formulated in set theoretic terms, has been employed by numerous investigators (see Gregson, 1970, p. 54). The given algebraic model is quite similar to the Eisler-Ekman (1959) similarity equation $s_1/(s_1 + s_2)$. Despite its nonlinearity, it could be tested fairly readily using computerized numerical estimation routines.

An alternative is to attempt a two-stage approach as discussed in the two previous subsections. If nonunitary stimuli can be constructed to combine on a simple between-dimensional integration rule, that can be used to evaluate the within-dimensional similarity function. Between-dimensional averaging is plausible on a priori grounds, and would be qualitatively similar to the usual set theoretical formulation.

d. POTENTIAL APPLICATIONS. To illustrate the potential power of the two-stage approach, some possible applications will be noted briefly.

In the first example, already mentioned, two shapes are presented in a factorial design. The subject judges their average or total area, say, or perhaps the difference in area. Each of these three judgments suggests a simple linear model and that can be tested simply and directly by the parallelism prediction, exactly as illustrated in Section II,A,1. If the linear model succeeds, then the marginal data means of the factorial design constitute interval scales of subjective area. Since an absolute zero is evidently available in this particular case, these interval scales could readily be made into ratio scales.

In this task, the first integration stage yields the subjective area of each single shape. For complex shapes, this first integration might not follow any simple rule. The second integration stage is the assigned task of averaging, adding, or subtracting. This stage has the important role of validating the stimulus scales. Such scales could be useful in studying illusions and contextual effects in judgments of area (Anderson & Weiss, 1971) and in studying subjective area of complex shapes.

For certain shapes, the first integration stage might also follow a simple rule. Perceived area of rectangles, for instance, might be expected to follow a multiplying model, base times height (Section III,A,1). The complete model could then be written as $B_1H_1 + B_2H_2$, a multilinear model that has a simple analysis (Section III,A,5).

The second example deals with spatial summation of warmth which appears to extend over wide areas of the skin (see Stevens & Marks, 1971). Two separate regions would be stimulated with independently varied intensity to form a two-way factorial design. The subject's task would be to judge apparent warmth. The summation hypothesis implies that the data should obey the parallelism prediction. If successful, the model would yield functional scales of subjective warmth as a function of intensity. Functional scaling of the stimuli, and a validated response measure could be quite useful for quantitative study of summation.

As an extension of the above design, both area and intensity could be varied independently in each region. If summation occurs within each region, then intensity and area would combine by multiplying. The complete model could then be written as $I_1A_1 + I_2A_2$, which is a multilinear model with a simple analysis (Section III,A,5).

The third, and last, example is concerned with evaluating the joint dependence of pitch on frequency and intensity. This dependence would be treated as the first integration stage, one that would not be expected to follow a simple algebraic model. The second stage could consist of judging the average pitch of two such tones. A successful averaging model would yield functional scales of pitch as a joint function of the two physical parameters.

Many other problems in perception seem amenable to similar analysis. Each experimental task has its own complexities that would need to be considered in applying the algebraic model approach. To the extent that this approach does apply, however, it provides results that might not be available from other methods.

The function of the simple adding, averaging, and subtracting tasks deserves notice. These tasks may seem somewhat artificial, but they play an important theoretical role because they provide a validational base for scaling response and stimuli. That allows closer study of the valuation process in the first integration stage. It also provides a base for examining other response measures, such as reaction time, that may not follow any simple integration rule. Because of this potential importance, the simple adding, averaging, and subtracting tasks deserve more extensive study.

12. INTERACTION IN JUDGMENTS OF TIME AND DISTANCE

If two lamps are flashed to mark the beginning and end of a time interval, the judged duration depends on the distance between the lamps. The time interval seems longer when the lamps are farther apart (e.g., Price-Williams, 1954). This so-called kappa effect has sometimes been considered to result from "imputed movement," but how that might work has never been made clear.

One possible interpretation follows a previous suggestion that the effect is an illusion of positive context (Anderson, 1970b). One cue for the judgment is the actual time interval. The other cue is an expectancy, based on the time that would be required to traverse the distance at a fixed velocity. The actual judgment is assumed to be a weighted average of these two cues.

An important property of this model is that it implies parallelism in a two-way, Time × Distance design. This agrees with the results of Price-Williams (1954, Expt. 2). Evidence for the expectancy assumption comes from work utilizing the Müller–Lyer illusion (e.g., Lebensfeld & Wapner, 1968), which indicates that the expected time is based on phenomenal rather than physical distance, and by the data, somewhat uncertain, of Newman and Lee (1972), who claim no effect when expectancy is prevented by making the distance zero on an unpredictable portion of the trials.

An inverse effect also exists for two points farther apart in time also seem farther apart in space. An exactly analogous formulation should apply to this case. Further tests of both models might be obtainable by experimental manipulation of the velocity of the imputed movement, or of the relative weights of the two cues, or by using various probabilistic spatial arrangements beyond that of Newman and Lee.

III. MULTIPLYING MODELS

This section discusses models in which two stimulus factors multiply rather than add. Multiplying models, like adding models, are characterized by a certain pattern that appears in the data from a factorial design. This pattern is one of bilinearity instead of parallelism. After the bilinearity analysis has been developed, some composite adding–multiplying models will be considered in Section III,A,5.

A. Assumptions and Analyses

1. EXPERIMENTAL ILLUSTRATION

A very simple illustration of the nature of multiplying models is given in Fig. 8. Subjects judged the area of rectangles varied in base and height. Both base and height varied from 3 to 18 cm in equal steps in a 6 × 6 design. The data are plotted as a function of height with one curve for each value of the base. The subjects were instructed to judge intuitively, on the basis of appearance, and the responses were on a linear graphic rating scale.

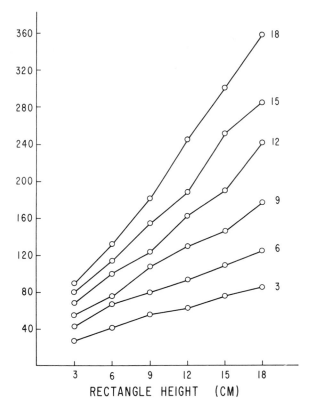

FIG. 8. Mean graphic rating of area of rectangles in a 6 × 6 design. Rectangle height is shown on the horizontal axis, with one curve for each value of the base. The data show mild deviations from the bilinear form of a diverging fan of straight lines; long, slim rectangles were overestimated. [After Anderson & Weiss, 1971.]

A multiplying model is an obvious candidate for this task, of course. In physical measures,

$$\text{Area} = \text{Base} \times \text{Height}. \tag{28}$$

Equation (28) has a bilinear form. With height on the horizontal axis, each value of the base yields a straight line whose slope is proportional to the value of the base.

The data of Fig. 8 follow this bilinear form approximately. The curves are roughly linear, and their slopes increase directly with the value of the base. There is, however, some curvilinearity apparent, especially in the upper curves.

It is important to recognize that Fig. 8, as it is plotted, is not critical for the multiplying model. The horizontal axis uses the physical measure of length. But the multiplying model, if it is psychologically valid, must be tested in terms of subjective length. If subjective and objective length are not linearly related, then the points on the horizontal axis would need to be moved about. That would change the shapes of the curves. It is possible, therefore, that the observed curvilinearity would disappear if the heights were plotted in terms of subjective length rather than objective length.

The key idea in the analysis of the multiplying model is therefore quite simple. In Fig. 8, the points on the horizontal would be moved about until the set of curves come into maximum congruence with the bilinear form. If curvilinearity is still found, then the model is infirmed. There is a routine procedure for doing this as is shown later.

Two further comments should be added with regard to this particular set of data. First, the bilinearity analysis does not completely eliminate the discrepancies. Bilinearity analysis is not a general curve-fitting procedure, but is strictly limited in what it can do. This outcome can be foreseen in Fig. 8. To make the top curve linear would require an increasing rightward displacement of the points on the horizontal. However, that would produce a greater downward curvature in the bottom curve.

The second point relates to a general problem in the interpretation of algebraic models. In the report (Anderson & Weiss, 1971), it was argued that the integration process is really one of adding. For rectangles, that would mimic a multiplying model, which would then have only an "as if" status. This possibility, incidentally, could be tested by getting judgments of total area of two separate figures using a factorial design as in Section II. That procedure could also yield the subjective areas of complex shapes (see Section II,B,11,d).

2. MODEL AND ASSUMPTIONS

If two stimulus variables combine by multiplying, the response to the combination (S_{Ri}, S_{Cj}) can be written as

$$R_{ij} = C_0 + s_{Ri}s_{Cj} + \epsilon_{ij}, \qquad (29)$$

where s_{Ri} and s_{Cj} are the subjective values of the physical stimuli, C_0 is a constant, and ϵ_{ij} is an additive random term with zero mean that represents response variability.

The main assumption is one of independence. The subjective value of any stimulus is assumed to be independent of what other stimulus it may be combined with. The C_0 term allows for an arbitrary zero in the response scale. Treating response variability as additive is reasonable in some situations (Anderson & Shanteau, 1970), though a multiplicative error may be necessary in others. As in the discussion of linear models, C_0 and ϵ_{ij} will be ignored unless explicitly mentioned.

Only the two-factor multiplying model will be discussed explicitly. However, the same analysis generalizes simply and directly to higher-order models discussed in Section III,A,5.

3. FUNCTIONAL SCALES OF THE STIMULUS

These are obtained in the same way as for linear models (Section II,A,4). If the multiplying model is correct, then the marginal means of the stimulus design are interval-scale estimates of the subjective values. If Eq. (29) is averaged over rows, it yields the column means,

$$\bar{R}_{\cdot j} = C_0 + \bar{s}_R s_{Cj} + \bar{\epsilon}_{\cdot j}, \qquad (30)$$

where $\bar{s}_R$ is the mean value of the s_{Ri}. The column means are thus a linear function of the column scale values, and conversely. The observed column means thus provide estimates of the column scale-values on an interval scale.

Estimates obtained from Eq. (30) are unbiased if s_{Ri} and s_{Cj} are statistically independent. However, they may not have minimum variance. In a two-row design with $s_{R_1} = -s_{R_2}$, $\bar{s}_R = 0$ so that the observed column means would be pure error. This problem can be handled by reversing the sign of the data for each row or column for which the scale values are negative. In addition, both variables should cover a reasonably wide range.

4. TEST OF FIT

a. GRAPHICAL TEST. An easy graphical test of fit can be obtained by using the observed column means as provisional scale values. These means are spaced on the horizontal axis according to their value. Equations (29) and (30) then imply that each row of data should plot as a straight line, with slope $\bar{s}_{Ri}/\bar{s}_R$, except for sampling error. The complete set of curves should thus form a diverging fan of straight lines. Deviations from this bilinear form would infirm the model and also, of course, the provisional estimates of the stimulus values. A quick version of the graphical test can be obtained by plotting one row as a function of another. Each such plot should be a straight line.

b. ANALYSIS OF VARIANCE TEST. Ordinary analysis of variance can be applied to test the multiplying model. The row–column interaction is non-zero, of course, since the curves are theoretically nonparallel. If the model is correct, however, this interaction should be concentrated in the bilinear component of the interaction. The residual interaction should then be nonsignificant.

To calculate the sums of squares for the bilinear and residual components of the interaction, assume that there are n independent observations in each cell of the design with T_{ij} the total of the n scores in cell ij. The bilinear sum of squares (see also Section III,A,5) can then be expressed as

$$\text{SS}_{\text{bilinear}} = \frac{[\Sigma(\bar{R}_{i\cdot} - \bar{R}_{\cdot\cdot})(\bar{R}_{\cdot j} - \bar{R}_{\cdot\cdot})T_{ij}]^2}{n\Sigma[(\bar{R}_{i\cdot} - \bar{R}_{\cdot\cdot})(\bar{R}_{\cdot j} - \bar{R}_{\cdot\cdot})]^2} \tag{31}$$

Here $\bar{R}_{i\cdot}$, $\bar{R}_{\cdot j}$, and $\bar{R}_{\cdot\cdot}$ are the row, column, and overall means, and the sum is over all cells of the design. $\text{SS}_{\text{interaction}}$ is calculated in the usual way and $\text{SS}_{\text{bilinear}}$ subtracted from it to leave $\text{SS}_{\text{residual}}$ on one less degree of freedom. This residual is tested in the usual way. If the model is correct, the residual is zero in principle, and should be nonsignificant in practice.

The statistical basis of the preceding test was developed by Tukey (1949) and Scheffé (1959, Sect. 4.8). Both writers were concerned with developing a more sensitive test of interaction, not with the multiplying model. Indeed, Tukey advocated the use of transformations to remove the nonadditive component. That would ordinarily be inappropriate in the analysis of multiplying models, although it has some purely statistical advantages for testing main effects. Mandel's (1961, 1964, Chaps. 11, 13) work is more directly relevant, since he was concerned with the study of functional relations.

The preceding test is limited by the assumption of statistical independence among the observations. Although this independence assumption can be satisfied by using independent groups of subjects in each cell of the design, the resulting test would be much less powerful than if each subject served in all cells of the design.

Fortunately, this independence assumption seems reasonable in many experimental tasks when applied to the data of a single subject. More than one replication is required, of course, but the resulting within-cells variability is used as the error term for all the tests. Most of the published applications have been made in this way at the single-subject level.

Two limitations on such single-subject analysis should be noted. First, the independence assumption will be violated to the extent that there are order or carryover effects from one condition to the next. That would not seem to be a serious problem in most perceptual experiments, at least with reasonable procedural precautions. Second, there could be a correlation across replications if they were run at different times, say, that allowed potential changes in the stimulus parameters. In that case, it might become necessary to treat replications within an individual subject in the same way as subjects are treated in the repeated-measurements designs that are discussed next.

The term repeated-measurements design ordinarily refers to designs in which each subject serves in a complete design, but with the analysis done for the group of subjects as a whole. The observations are not then independent, being correlated across subjects. It is still possible to apply the analysis of variance, but in general each systematic source must be tested against its own interaction with subjects (Winer, 1971). As a consequence, the above analysis requires certain modifications.

In the two-way repeated-measurements design, the error term for the Row $\times$ Column interaction is the Row $\times$ Column $\times$ Subjects interaction. The Row $\times$ Column interaction needs to be broken down into its bilinear and residual components as already indicated. Its error term must be broken down in a parallel way. Details on computing procedure are given in Graesser and Anderson (1974).

5. Multilinear Models

The multilinear models form a general class based on the simple adding and multiplying models as building blocks. Multilinear models arise fairly frequently in the general study of judgment. Examples from perception are discussed in later sections on adaptation-level theory and comparative judgment. Experimental applications in utility theory are given by Shanteau and Anderson (1972) and Anderson and Shanteau (1970).

A few examples will be considered here to illustrate how functional measurement can be applied directly to the analysis of these extended models. Three stimulus variables will be considered, the third "Layer" variable being denoted as S_{Lk}, with values s_{Lk}. The weight parameter will be ignored for simplicity. The three variables will be considered to form a three-way factorial design. As usual, it is assumed that the stimulus values are constant over the various combinations. Finally, an interval response scale is assumed.

Some examples of multilinear models are:

$$R_{ijk} = s_{Ri}s_{Cj}s_{Lk}; \tag{32}$$

$$R_{ijk} = s_{Ri}s_{Cj} + s_{Lk}; \tag{33}$$

$$R_{ijk} = s_{Ri}(1 + s_{Cj} + s_{Lk}). \tag{34}$$

In general, the multilinear models may be defined as a sum of products of the stimulus factors, such that each factor occurs in each product in all-or-none fashion.

Stimulus scaling for multilinear models is essentially the same as for the simple adding and multiplying models. The marginal means of the data tables estimate the subjective stimulus values on interval scales. Of course, the validity of these stimulus values depends on the correctness of the model which needs a test of goodness of fit. These tests can be obtained by applying analysis of variance.

Model (32) is a three-factor multiplying model of the kind used in adaptation-level theory (Section III,B,4). For each value of k, it is a two-factor model that should follow the bilinearity analysis already outlined. The same holds, therefore, for the averages taken over k. Analogous statements hold for each other pair of stimulus variables. In the complete analysis of variance, therefore, each of the three two-way interactions should be concentrated in its bilinear component, and each two-way residual should be nonsignificant. The three-way interaction should similarly be concentrated in the trilinear component, and its residual should also be nonsignificant.

Model (33) is a compound adding–multiplying model of the type that arises in utility theory and decision making. All interactions are theoretically zero except the Row $\times$ Column interaction; it should be concentrated in its bilinear component with a zero residual. The Row $\times$ Layer and Column $\times$ Layer data should obey the parallelism prediction. If the response scale were thought to be nonlinear, Weiss' (1973a) FUNPOT program could be applied to eliminate any interaction between layer and row or column. This transformation to additivity should simultaneously transform the Row $\times$ Column interaction to bilinearity.

Model (34) is also a compound model, one that arises in comparative judgment (Section III,B,5). Its characterizing properties are that the Row $\times$ Column and the Row $\times$ Layer interactions should each be concentrated in its bilinear component, with nonsignificant residual. The Column $\times$ Layer interaction should be nonsignificant and so also the three-way interaction.

The model,

$$s_{Ri}s_{Cj} + s_{Lk}(s_{Ri} + s_{Cj}),$$

has a similar analysis. Each two-way interaction is all in its bilinear component, as with Model (32), and the three-way interaction is zero.

In general, each multilinear model implies a particular pattern of interaction, and that provides a basis for testing goodness of fit. Even more important, the observed pattern of interactions can diagnose which, if any, model is applicable. An experimental illustration of this diagnostic capacity of the data is given by Shanteau and Anderson (1972). This paper is also of interest because it illustrates the methodological importance of including a third variable in the experimental design.

One precaution should be kept in mind when using the multilinear tests. As already noted in Section II,A,3, stimulus estimates may be unreliable when the data curves have both positive and negative slopes. When the slope signs are known a priori, as would often be the case, reliability can be increased by a simple procedure. The curves of negative slope can be complemented to produce curves of equal positive slope. The marginal means from these data would be used as the various R-values in Eqs. (30) and (31). The T_{ij} in Eq. (31), however, would still be obtained from the original data.

B. Applications of Multiplying Models

The bulk of the applications of multiplying models in psychophysics have been to some form of ratio judgments. Ratio judgments fall in two main classes. In *ratio ratings,* two stimuli are presented, and the subject is instructed to judge the ratio of their magnitudes. In *ratio adjustment,* one standard stimulus is presented, and the subject is instructed to adjust a variable stimulus so that it stands in a prescribed ratio to the standard. When the prescribed ratio is less than one, ratio adjustment is called fractionation. In both methods, the term "ratio" refers only to the instructions given to the subjects. That the responses really do represent ratios is a presumption that needs to be validated.

Neither of these two methods is in a satisfactory state. Ratio adjustment appears to have an inherent indeterminacy that makes it insufficient for scaling. Ratio rating avoids this indeterminacy, but has had limited success in experimental applications. Both ratio methods are discussed next. Applications of multiplying models to reaction time, adaptation-level theory, and to comparative judgment are also considered.

1. RATIO RATING

a. MODEL ANALYSIS. In a typical experiment with the method of ratio rating, subjects are shown pairs of stimuli and instructed to judge the ratio of their magnitudes on a numerical scale. Suppose that the stimulus pairs are constructed from a factorial design, with the row stimuli S_{Ri} to be judged relative to various standards represented by the column stimuli S_{Cj}.

The model for this task may be written:

$$R_{ij} = C_0 + s_{Ri}/s_{Cj}, \tag{35}$$

where C_0 is a constant, and s_{Ri} and s_{Cj} are the subjective values of S_{Ri} and S_{Cj}.

This model has a dividing form, but it can be analyzed by a fairly direct application of the methods just given. The theoretical expression for the row means is obtained by averaging over the column index j:

$$\bar{R}_{i.} = C_0 + cs_{Ri}, \tag{36}$$

where c is a constant that equals the harmonic mean of the s_{Cj}. This equation implies that the row means constitute an interval scale of the subjective values of the row stimuli, if the model is correct. If $C_0 = 0$, then these estimates are on a ratio scale.

The column means are slightly different. The average over the row index i, is:

$$\bar{R}_{.j} = C_0 + c'/s_{Cj}, \tag{37}$$

where c' is a constant that equals the mean of the s_{Ri}. This equation implies that the marginal column means constitute an interval scale of the *reciprocals* of the subjective values of the column stimuli. If $C_0 = 0$, then these estimates can be directly inverted to yield an interval scale of the column stimuli.

Nothing in the present analysis requires a given stimulus to have the same scale value if it appears both in a row and in a column. That is necessary for a general method, of course, since the row and column stimuli need not be psychologically equivalent. Attentional factors, for example, can affect stimulus salience.

To use the model for scaling requires a test of goodness of fit. The graphical and bilinear analyses already discussed may be applied directly for this purpose.

b. EXPERIMENTAL TESTS. The complete analysis of the method of ratio rating has emerged very slowly, with contributions by a number of different workers. One of the earliest formal treatments of ratio rating is Comrey's (1950) consant-sum method in which the subject apportions 100 points between the two stimuli to represent the ratio of their magnitudes. The statistical analysis (Torgerson, 1958) is somewhat complicated.

If the model underlying the constant-sum method is written out explicitly, it is seen to be somewhat different from the basic ratio rating model. Since the points within each pair must sum to 100, the points for S_{Ri} paired with S_{Cj} are

$$R_{ij} = 100s_{Ri}/(s_{Ri} + s_{Cj}). \tag{38}$$

The constant-sum method is interesting because, in contrast to the basic ratio-rating model, it can be generalized directly to sets of three or more stimuli. For three stimuli, for example,

$$R_{ijk} = 100s_{Ri}/(s_{Ri} + s_{Cj} + s_{Lk}).$$

Equation (38) is formally similar to a ratio rule that has been studied by Bradley and Terry (1952) and by Luce (1959). Both those models, however, require that R_{ij} be a choice probability, not a numerical response. Luce's choice axiom, in particular, applies only to imperfectly discriminable objects, not the suprathreshold differences studied in ratio judgments.

Ekman (1958) made an important simplification of the constant-sum method by using instructions to rate all ratios directly in comparable terms. That leads to a model fairly similar to Eq. (35). Ekman assumed that C_0 was zero and that a given stimulus had the same value in a row as in a column. He noted that the row and column means would then provide estimates of the stimulus values. He also noted the advantages of factorial design, although his illustrative data were apparently obtained from a tri-angular, paired comparisons design. Ekman did not provide a test of fit, but he did attempt a cross-task comparison between ratio rating and ratio adjustment.

Since magnitude estimation employs an instruction to judge ratios, the above analyses should be directly applicable if at least two standards are employed. This follows Stevens's (1956) precept to "use various standards, for it is risky to decide the form of a magnitude function on the basis of data obtained with only one standard [p. 6]." Unfortunately, different standards tend to yield different exponents in a power function as Poulton (1968) has pointed out in his review (see also Anderson, 1970a, p. 166; Baird, 1970, p. 45; Stevens, 1956, Figs. 2 and 4). Changing the exponent is not a "permissible transformation" on a true ratio scale, or even on an interval scale. Stevens (1971) has since adopted a position that no assigned standard should be used which would eliminate a test of fit.

Fagot and Stewart (1969a) tested a product axiom that is derivative from the basic model under two further assumptions. If $C_0 = 0$, and if a stimulus has the same value in a row as in a column, then it follows directly from the basic model that

$$R_{ij} = R_{ia}R_{aj},$$

where a indexes any stimulus common to both row and column. Their paper applied analysis of variance tests to conclude that "The product axiom was rejected for all six Ss." The deviations from prediction in their Fig. 1 are quite substantial. The possibility still remains, however, that the basic model is correct, and that the deviations reflect a failure of their two further assumptions.

Extensive work by the Swedish investigators, especially Goude (1962), Mashhour (1964), Öttander (1967), and Sjöberg (1971), has been gener-ally negative on the simple ratio-rating model. Attempts to extend the model to allow for asymmetry between the variable (row) and standard (column) stimuli have not yielded a completely clear picture. Sjöberg's (1971) later experiments fit his generalized ratio model rather well, but yielded unusually large exponents of 1.7 and up for lifted weight (see Sec-tion II,B,3–4).

Present methods may be useful in obtaining a definitive assessment of the method of ratio rating. As already noted, it allows for different subjective scales on the row and column stimuli. That this is necessary is suggested by the cited work of the Swedish investigators. No assumption about a power function is required.

2. Ratio Adjustment

Ratio adjustment requests the subject to set a variable stimulus so that it stands in some fixed ratio to a given standard stimulus. For ratios less than one, this is the traditional fractionation task. Ratio adjustment seems psychologically simpler than ratio rating because it depends less on the subject's use of numbers. As it turns out, however, ratio adjustment is at best not very satisfactory.

The natural model for ratio adjustment is a simple multiplying model:

$$r = ws, \qquad (39)$$

where w is the effective ratio. The response is written in lowercase to emphasize that it is the subjective values that enter into the model. The measured response R is on the physical scale, and would ordinarily require monotone transformation to the psychological scale.

Traditionally, the interest in the method of ratio adjustment has been to measure sensation. If the model is correct, and if the subject uses that ratio, typically $\frac{1}{2}$, that is prescribed by the experimenter, then a ratio scale of s can be obtained in a straightforward way. But both assumptions are uncertain, and some means for testing the underlying model is needed.

a. Reciprocal ratio test. Three main procedures can be used in the analysis of ratio adjustment. The traditional procedure has been with reciprocal ratios. The responses based on ratios of $\frac{1}{2}$ and 2, for example, should be consistent with each other if the subject does use the prescribed ratios. This procedure has seen considerable use, especially in work on loudness measurement summarized by Stevens (1955, Tables I–IV). These data indicate moderate, systematic discrepancies between halving and doubling which naturally puts the results under suspicion. Stevens suggested that halving and doubling might be biased in opposite directions and took an average of the two to get a loudness scale. Such averaging is questionable in view of the extreme context effects in loudness fractionation noted by Geiger and Firestone (1933), and more dramatically by Garner (1954b).

b. Constant fractionation ratio. The second procedure, stemming from an analysis by Ekman (1958), is interesting because it applies directly to the physical stimulus scale. It assumes that the psychophysical function is a power function, that is, that

$$s = (S - S_0)^a, \qquad (40)$$

where S_0 is a threshold constant, and a is the power function exponent. Equations (39) and (40) together imply that the observed response is a weighted average of the standard and threshold stimuli on the physical scale. Straightforward arithmetic yields:

$$R = w^{1/a}S + (1 - w^{1/a})S_0. \qquad (41)$$

Since R is thus a linear function of S, the model can be tested directly in terms of the observables.

In most applications, S_0 would be negligible. In that case, Eq. (41) implies that the physical fractionation ratio is constant:

$$R/S = w^{1/a}. \qquad (42)$$

This constancy prediction has received some support for lifted weights (Guilford & Dingman, 1954; Warren & Warren, 1956; see Anderson, 1972c). It does not hold for loudness since Stevens's (1955) compilations show that the decibel difference between R and S is a function of S. In Pollack's data, the decibel reduction required for half-loudness for tones increases steadily from 3.2 to 8.9 dB over the base range from 10–20 to 100–110 dB. Garner's data over this same range increase from 6.3 to 18.0 dB, and then decline to 14.6 dB.

The most extensive treatment of fractionation data has been given by Fagot and Stewart (1969b) who fit Eq. (35) to single-subject data on brightness fractionation using both experimental and statistical methods of estimating S_0. The model fit poorly, though it should be noted that it was based on the assumption that $w = \frac{1}{2}$, as well as the assumption of a power function.

Some improvement was obtained if an additive constant was allowed in Eq. (39) analogous to an additive constant used in ratio ratings by McGill (1960). This analogy seems inappropriate because of the difference in the response scales in the rating and adjustment tasks. In any case, this model also fit poorly.

There is an indeterminacy in the analysis based on the physical fractionation ratio. The right side of Eq. (42) contains two unknown parameters, w and a. A scale of sensation can be obtained only if one parameter can be determined from other information. This procedure, therefore, is not useful for actual scaling.

c. BILINEARITY ANALYSIS. The third procedure is to scale the data in an attempt to produce the bilinear form implied by the basic model of

Eq. (39). If a power function applies, then the physical response measure will satisfy the bilinear form. Otherwise the response may need monotone transformation, either to bilinearity or to additivity.

In all three procedures, the stimulus scale is unique only up to a power transformation unless auxiliary information on w is available. Some additional comments can be found elsewhere (Anderson, 1970a, 1972c).

d. THE ACHILLES HEEL OF RATIO ADJUSTMENT. There is a reasonable alternative for ratio adjustment that will fit the data equally well. This alternative model allows the adjustment ratio to depend on stimulus intensity. Specifically, each prescribed adjustment ratio w would be represented as the product of a constant and some function $f(S)$. In all the analyses based on the assumption that w is constant $f(S)$ would be automatically absorbed into the stimulus scale. The two models would be indistinguishable, therefore, but would correspond to quite different psychophysical functions.

That the subject's criterion may change with intensity is a very real possibility in view of the dramatic effects of context on half-loudness judgments demonstrated by Garner (1954b). It is doubtful, therefore, that the method of ratio adjustment has much value for scaling purposes. Ratio adjustment may be an interesting task from a judgmental standpoint, but it might be better approached with a psychophysical function known from some other integration task.

3. REACTION TIME

Models for reaction time (RT) have followed two main approaches. One approach makes detailed assumptions about the stochastic character of the stages in the neural transmission process (e.g., Green & Luce, 1971; Luce, 1966; McGill, 1963, 1967; Restle & Davis, 1962). Detailed predictions about the complete latency distribution and the number of stages are then obtained. The other approach makes minimal assumptions and restricts itself largely to predictions about mean RT. The latter approach has been advocated by Sternberg (1969a), Grice (1968), and Anderson (1969) on two grounds: First, that the detailed stochastic assumptions are unrealistic; second, that cogent tests can be obtained with minimal assumptions as illustrated here and in the cited articles.

Many approaches to reaction time assume a succession of distinct processing stages that are additive. In a fundamental paper, Sternberg (1969a) has developed a powerful additive-factor method to determine the number and interrelation of the various stages. The basic idea is simple. If two stimulus factors influence different stages, then their interactions would be expected to be zero; if they influence the same stage, then their interaction would in general be nonzero.

To illustrate this, it is useful to represent the stages as additive terms in a multilinear model (Section III,A,5). Just as the model defines the interaction pattern, so conversely the interaction pattern defines the additivity structure of the model. With judicious choice of stimulus factors, the observed pattern of interaction can provide valuable though not definitive clues to the number and nature of the stages.

Sternberg's method is not actually a multilinear model, because it makes no claim that the interactions are concentrated in their linear components. Nonlinear interactions that would invalidate an algebraic model could be quite useful in delineating the stage structure of the reaction. However, certain simple scanning models (Sternberg, 1969b) can be represented as algebraic models (see also Briggs & Swanson, 1970).

A somewhat different approach to reaction time has been employed by Grice and his associates (e.g., Grice, 1968; Kohfeld, 1968, 1969, 1971; Murray 1970). Their approach emphasizes the importance of the response criterion, in the manner of current decision theory. For simple reaction time, it leads to a multiplying model.

Grice assumes that the signal produces impulses or counts at a constant rate that accumulate at a decision center. When the cumulative count reaches some criterion, the response is initiated. Impulse rate is assumed to depend on signal intensity but to be otherwise constant. The criterion is assumed to depend on instructions, payoffs, adaptation, etc., and to vary randomly from trial to trial.

Grice's formulation is similar to that of Stone (1960) and McGill (1963, 1967) in its use of an impulse counter, as well as in its emphasis on variability in the criterion instead of in the sequence of impulses. This ignores the sequential stochastic structure of the reaction. However, it does provide a method of analysis based on joint variation of impulse rate and criterion in a factorial design. Indeed, Grice's graphic presentations of the predictions of his model are equivalent to the bilinearity analysis discussed above. A somewhat more general treatment will be given here.

The total reaction time can be considered as the sum of input and output times, plus an internal reaction or decision time (Anderson, 1959, 1969; McGill, 1963; Stone, 1960). Since the decision time is of primary concern, the input and output times will be represented as a random variable, C_0, assumed independent of the manipulated stimulus variables. On any trial, the internal reaction time itself is considered as the sum of N impulse times, where N is a random variable that represents the criterion. Thus, the total reaction time can be written,

$$R = C_0 + \sum_{j=1}^{N} at_j, \tag{43}$$

where a is a constant and at_j is the time for the jth impulse. The t_j are assumed only to have the same distribution, independent of N, and may be correlated among themselves. In terms of mean values, Eq. (43) reads

$$\bar{R} = \bar{C}_0 + \bar{N}(a\bar{t}). \tag{44}$$

Equation (44) forms the basis of the analysis. The experimental requirement is to vary $\bar{N}$ and $\bar{t}$ jointly in a factorial design. In Grice's work, for example, the mean criterion $\bar{N}$ is manipulated by instructions, preadaptation, etc., and the mean impulse time $\bar{t}$ is manipulated by signal intensity. Equation (44) must then follow the bilinearity analysis, since it is formally a simple multiplying model.

The generality of Grice's formulation is unclear. The same analysis should apply to choice reaction-times no less than simple reaction-times. Such applications do not seem to have been made, although they would be most interesting. On the other hand, the attempts to apply the model to conditioning experiments seem inappropriate. Such experiments typically show substantial numbers of no-response trials, but they are disallowed by the assumption of a constant impulse rate. Grice (1971) has more recently considered a somewhat different model for conditioning experiments that incorporates additional decision-theoretical notions.

Figure 9 shows an experimental test of Grice's model for a simple reaction time experiment by Kohfeld (1969). Subjects pressed a key to an auditory response signal of 30, 60, or 90 dB, under one of five ready-signal conditions. The data are plotted as in the graphical test for bilinearity (Section III,A,4,a), but in a manner designed to mirror the model. Each upward-sloping curve represents one response-signal intensity; the slope of the curve is taken to be the rate at which "impulses" accumulate as a function of time on the horizontal axis. Each horizontal line of three data points corresponds to one ready-signal condition which was assumed to set the criterion. As the cumulated number of impulses passed this criterion, the response was made. Thus, the reaction occurs earlier for stronger response-signals because the impulse rate is higher. Similarly, the reaction occurs later for louder ready-signals because they raise the criterion. The bilinear form agrees with the formal description as a multiplying model.

Despite the impressive nature of Fig. 9 and similar graphs in the cited reports, some doubt may be expressed about the model. Grice (1968, Figs. 12 and 13) shows comparable graphs, but the data on which they are based (Kohfeld, 1968, Fig. 1) do not show the bilinear form; instead, they show parallelism that infirms Grice's model instead of supporting it. Several other sets of data in the cited reports also show nonsignificant interaction, contrary to Grice's interpretation. Evidently it can be misleading

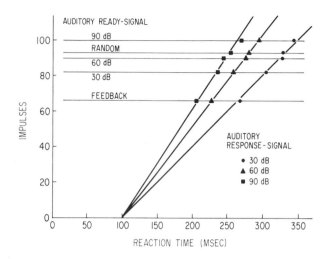

Fig. 9. Reaction time (on the horizontal axis) for each of three intensities of a response-signal (upward sloping lines) under each of five ready-signal conditions (horizontal lines). Vertical placement of data points is arbitrary, chosen to maximize fit to bilinear form; see text. [From Kohfeld, 1969.]

to depend on visual curve fitting without also using a proper statistical test. Kohfeld's data in the present Figure 9 did show a significant interaction term, but on the whole the bilinear component does not seem to be very large in these studies.

4. Adaptation-Level Theory

The theory of adaptation level propounded by Helson (1964) represents one of the broadest attempts at a general theory of perception and judgment. It attempts, moreover, to be quantitative though in this regard it is weak. In the theory, the perceptual value of any stimulus is determined by its relation to the prevailing level of adaptation. "Adaptation level represents the zero of function" and is considered as an average or pooling of all relevant stimuli, focal and contextual. Two basic postulates of the theory will be considered here, for rating responses to a set S_i of stimuli measured on some physical scale, such as weight or length. Functional measurement procedure will be shown to give a simple and rigorous test of the basic postulates of adaptation-level theory.

a. Power product model for AL. The basic equation of the theory expresses the adaptation-level (AL) as a power product:

$$AL = \bar{S}^w B^b R^r. \tag{45}$$

Here $\bar{S}$ is the geometric mean of the focal stimuli S_i that are to be rated;

B represents background or context stimuli; R represents stimulus residuals from past experience; and the exponents w, b, and r are weighting constants whose sum is one.

It is important to note that Eq. (45) defines AL in the physical metric. There is no problem of response transformation, since the theory postulates the validity of the physical metric.

Equation (45) is formally the same as (32) of Section III,A,5, and may be tested as outlined there. In many applications, the residual stimulus will be constant, and Eq. (45) then becomes a two-factor multiplying model. The present methods of analysis avoid difficulties produced by the additive correction term that Helson uses in his applications of this model. Moreover, the present analysis requires explicit measurement only for the AL itself; this has marked advantages, since R will generally be unknown, and B will often be difficult to determine. Indeed, if the model passes the test of fit, it may then be used to obtain functional scales of B.

b. Logarithmic difference model for ratings. Although Eq. (45) is basic in adaptation-level theory, it extracts only part of the information in the rating response. Helson also gives a model for the ratings themselves in terms of the "reformulated Fechner law" (Helson, 1964, Eq. 49):

$$
\begin{aligned}
J_i &= C_0 + K \log (S_i/AL) \\
&= C_0 + K[\log S_i - \log AL],
\end{aligned} \tag{46}
$$

where J_i is the rating of stimulus S_i, AL is the adaptation level, C_0 and K are constants (Helson, 1964; pp 197ff).

Equation (46) is additive in the two terms, $\log S_i$, and $\log AL$. To apply the test of parallelism, therefore, it is only necessary to vary S_i and AL in factorial design, following Section II,A. The AL can be varied by manipulating value or frequency of anchor stimuli, for example. The anchor effect should be additive in terms of the raw rating response, and the curves for different anchor conditions should be parallel when plotted against S_i on the horizontal. No stimulus metric is required since parallelism is invariant under all transformations.

This parallelism prediction has apparently not been noticed, possibly because Helson uses two different equations for ratings (Helson, 1964, Eqs. 41 and 49). Helson's Eq. 41 is apparently used for fitting actual data. Helson's Eq. 49 [Eq. (46) here], is introduced with the statement, "For theoretical purposes, however, a much more powerful tool will be found in the reformulated Fechner law (Michels & Helson, 1949) to which we now turn [Helson, 1964, p. 196]." Helson's Eq. 49 makes the parallelism prediction, as already noted, but his Eq. 41 does not. No attempt seems to have been made to resolve this theoretical inconsistency.

There are a number of such sets of curves in the literature (see Helson, 1964), some showing apparent parallelism, others not. Extreme nonparallelism was obtained by Helson and Kozaki (1968) for numerosity judgments of plates of dots for different anchor stimuli (see Fig. 10). It does not seem that either of Helson's equations could account for these data and the discrepancy is the more important because the work was considered to be an *"experimentum crucis."* The bilinear form that was actually obtained agrees with the model for comparative judgment of the next section.

5. COMPARATIVE JUDGMENT

The judged magnitude of a stimulus will, in certain tasks, depend on both "absolute" and "relative" factors. Contextual stimuli in the neighborhood of the focal stimulus may have a yardstick function, serving as referents to calibrate the magnitude of the focal stimulus.

Let S denote the focal stimulus, and let T_1 and T_2 denote two yardstick stimuli. The "absolute" value of S may be represented by $V(S)$ where V is an arbitrary psychophysical function. The value of S relative to the first yardstick may be represented by $V(S)/Y_1(T_1)$, where Y_1 is an arbitrary yardstick function. A similar relation is assumed for the second yardstick. The judged magnitude of S is assumed to be a composite of absolute and relative factors. Specifically, the model assumes this composite to be a linear combination (Anderson, 1970b) which, in the present case, would be

$$R = V(S) + V(S)/Y_1(T_1) + V(S)/Y_2(T_2). \tag{47}$$

Equation (47) is a multilinear model and can be tested by the techniques already discussed. Suppose that S, T_1, and T_2 can be independently varied in a factorial design. Since T_1 and T_2 have additive effects, they should follow the parallelism prediction. However, S and T_1 combine by a dividing rule. Hence they should follow the bilinear form, and the same holds for S and T_2. Plotted as a function of S, following the bilinear analysis, the curves for T_1 should form a diverging fan of straight lines, and similarly for T_2. This analysis can be made directly on the raw response; nothing need be known about the functions V, Y_1, and Y_2.

The comparative judgment model relates most closely to Helson's adaptation-level theory in its emphasis on the influence of context on judgment. However, the theoretical predictions are different. Helson predicts that anchor yardsticks should produce parallelism or near-parallelism (Section III,B,4), whereas the comparative judgment model predicts a bilinear form. The data of Helson and Kozaki, reproduced in Fig. 10, provide a comparative test.

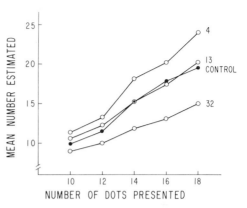

FIG. 10. Numerosity judgments of plates of 10 to 18 dots under each of three anchor conditions and no-anchor control. Comparative judgment theory predicts a fan of diverging lines; adaptation-level theory predicts parallelism or near-parallelism. [After Helson & Kozaki, 1968.]

In the experiment of Fig. 10, subjects judged numerosity of plates that contained from 10 to 18 dots presented tachistoscopically for .3 sec. Each such presentation was preceded by a .3-sec presentation of an unjudged anchor plate containing 4, 13, or 32 dots, or by a no-anchor control. Subjects were instructed to judge the actual number of dots.

This design is a two-way, $S \times T_1$, design. If the anchor does serve as a comparative yardstick, then the data should obey the bilinear form, a diverging fan of lines. That is almost exactly true of Fig. 10. Adaptation-level theory cannot account for these data (Section III,B,4). Very similar results have been reported by Steger, Wilkinson, and Carter (1973).

An interesting feature of Fig. 10 is that the actual number of dots is plotted on the horizontal axis. That the data are nearly bilinear in this plot implies that subjective and objective numerosity are near-linearly related in this experiment. That is not necessary for the use of the method, however. Indeed, the subjective scale for numerosity is a byproduct of the method.

A somewhat different application of the comparative judgment model to the Ebbinghaus illusion was made by Massaro and Anderson (1971). This illusion is shown in the left panel of Fig. 11; the center circle has equal size in both cases, but appears different because it is being judged relative to the surrounding yardstick circles. The right panel of Fig. 11 shows the magnitude of the illusion as a function of two variables: the number of surrounding circles, and their size relative to the focal center circle. The curves are theoretical and fit the data points quite well.

The idea that perception depends on both absolute and relative factors is long-standing, but relatively little quantitative work has been done. The broadest approach has been taken by Helson (1964), whose adaptation-

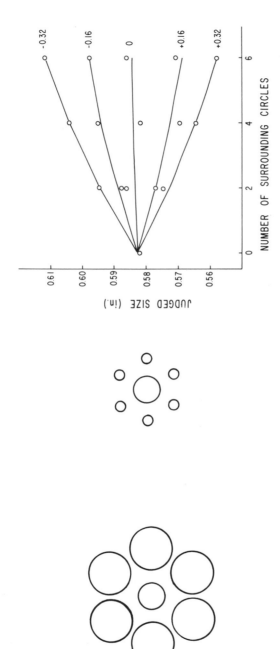

FIG. 11. The Ebbinghaus illusion is shown on the left; the center circle is the same size in both figures. Magnitude of the illusion is shown on the right as a function of the number of surrounding circles (on the horizontal axis), and the size of the surrounding circles relative to the center circle (curve parameter). [From Massaro & Anderson, 1971.]

level theory was discussed in the previous section. Restle's work on illusions (e.g., Restle & Greeno, 1970; Restle & Merryman, 1969) is based on Helson's theory, and employs a more adequate mathematical analysis. Hake and his associates (e.g., Hake, Faust, McIntyre, & Murray, 1967) have made an interesting attack on this problem using discriminant function methodology. Unfortunately the discriminant function itself is not fully adequate because it disallows differential weighting within a stimulus dimension (Massaro & Anderson, 1971). Kinchla's (1971) analysis of threshold discriminability using signal-detection theory also deserves notice. Kinchla used a very interesting task of movement perception that might readily be adapted to suprathreshold effects to which the present formulation would apply directly.

6. SIZE–NUMBER JUDGMENTS

An interesting application of a multilinear model to size–number judgments has been made by Birnbaum and Veit (1973). Subjects judged numerosity of dots distributed randomly on cards of varied size in a 5×4, Size $\times$ Number design. The judgment was assumed to follow an additive contrast model as in the size–weight illusion of Section II,B,2. If the weight parameters and subscripts are omitted for simplicity, then the model can be written,

$$R = s_N - s_S^*, \qquad (48)$$

where s_N is the subjective value corresponding to the actual number of dots, and s_S^* is an expectancy based on card size. In effect, s_S^* corresponds to the expected number of dots for a card of given size S.

Equation (48) states that size and number combine additively. Hence the data for the Size $\times$ Number design should obey the parallelism prediction. The alternative hypothesis, that the judgment depends on the density of the dots on the card, would imply systematic deviations from parallelism. In fact, the data were parallel, in agreement with the additive contrast model.

Birnbaum and Veit were also concerned with the experiential basis of the expectancy. Indeed, the size–number task was chosen on the ground that the expectancy based on prior experience should not be strong, and hence could readily be manipulated by learning experiences within the experimental situation.

Accordingly, three different expectancy conditions were run, in which contextual stimuli were added in such a way that the actual, physical correlation between size and number was .57, .00, and —.57, respectively. In the —.57 condition, for example, the contextual stimuli included large cards with few dots, and small cards with many dots. In this condition, subjects presumably develop an expectancy for an inverse relation between size and number. The expectancy was hypothesized to follow a multiplying model,

$$s_\mathrm{S}{}^* = s_\rho s_\mathrm{S} , \tag{49}$$

where s_ρ is the subjective size–number correlation, and s_S is the subjective size. Equation (49) implies that the interaction between expectancy and size should be significant, and concentrated in the bilinear component. This prediction was verified.

An interesting aspect of the data was that the subjective correlation, measured by the slopes of the curves in the Size $\times$ Number graph, was positive in the condition in which the physical correlation was zero. This reflects preexperimental experience. However, the subjective correlation did become negative in the condition in which the physical correlation was negative, demonstrating that the effect of size could be reversed by the learned correlation.

If Eq. (49) is substituted into Eq. (48), then the complete model for this experiment is obtained:

$$R = s_\mathrm{N} - s_\rho s_\mathrm{S} . \tag{50}$$

This is a multilinear model of the form of Eq. (33) of Section III,A,5, and has the same analysis. An experimental test is given by Birnbaum, Kobernick, and Veit (1974).

IV. PSYCHOLOGICAL MEASUREMENT

A. Functional Measurement

1. FUNCTIONAL MEASUREMENT DIAGRAMS

Figure 12 shows a useful expositional diagram that brings out the general nature of functional measurement. Physical stimuli, S_1, S_2, . . . , impinge on the organism to produce an overt response, R. Two different conceptions of the organism are shown.

The organism of strict behaviorism is in the upper part of the diagram. Unobservables within the organism are conceptually illegitimate. The focus of investigation is on the physical law relating the observable response to the observable stimuli. This behavioristic conception is discussed further in Section IV,A,5.

A more cognitive conception is given in the lower part of the diagram. The physical stimuli S produce subjective representations within the orga-

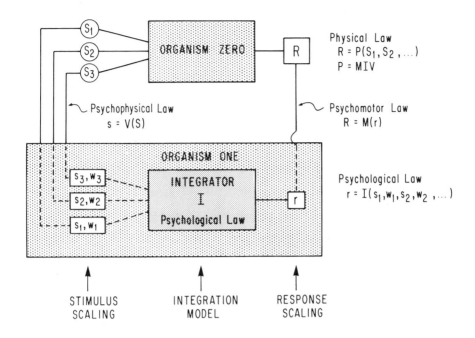

FIG. 12. Functional measurement diagram.

nism. These subjective values are combined by an integrating mechanism I to produce an implicit response r. This implicit response leads to the overt response R. Variations of this conception are widely used, Hull (1952), Guilford (1954), and Garner, Hake, and Eriksen (1956) being representative cases.

Integration theory and functional measurement focus primarily on the integration process. In molar form, this is the psychological law I that relates r to s. The three vertical arrows point to three problems that need solution:

1. scaling the subjective stimulus values,
2. scaling the subjective response value, and
3. determining the form of the psychological law.

Functional measurement solves these three problems simultaneously. This is an interesting property that deserves two or three comments. The most important comment is practical: Although the simultaneous attack may seem unnecessarily complex, it can be quite simple. This has been illustrated in the discussion of lifted weights in Section II,B.

Conceptually, measurement thus becomes an integral part of establishing the psychological law. The measurement scales obtain their existence by virtue of the laws that they enter into, so that scaling is derivative from substantive theory. This differs from the usual emphasis in psychological measurement in which scaling is viewed as a methodological preliminary to the study of psychological laws.

2. THE PSYCHOLOGICAL LAW, I

The psychological law is the function that relates the implicit response r to the subjective stimulus values s_i and weights w_i. This chapter has been concerned with one special class of psychological laws, those that can be represented as algebraic models. It is a fortunate chance that these simple models have a reasonable breadth of validity, both in perception and in general judgment theory.

Extension of these algebraic models to handle more complex integration tasks may be feasible. The independence assumption, for example, might seem to rule out the possibility of handling stimulus interactions such as contrast. Yet contrast effects have been handled in a straightforward manner in three different applications (Sections II,B,2, II,B,8, and III,B,5). This illustrates the flexibility of the general approach.

How far this will extend is uncertain. It is easy to feel that only very simple processes can be handled using simple quantitative models, and that quantification is premature for more complex processes. But the converse argument has no less logical force, that complex process interaction can be disentangled only with a quantitative approach.

One technical feature of the functional measurement approach has particular interest in this respect. That is the use of two or more stimulus variables in factorial designs. Postman and Tolman (1959, p. 531) contrast the technique of "successive accumulation of cues" used in classical psychophysics with Brunswik's reverse procedure of "successive omission of cues." Functional measurement uses simultaneous variation of cues, in accord with its aim of studying synthesis. Simultaneous cue variation in factorial design is more effective than Brunswik's representative design at discovering how the organism utilizes stimulus information, even within the organism's normal operating range. Moreover, it contributes simultaneously to analysis by uncovering the weighting of the cues.

3. THE PSYCHOPHYSICAL LAW, V

In the diagram, the psychophysical law is the function V that relates the subjective and objective scale values of the stimuli, s and S, respectively. Since measuring S presents no conceptual problem, the difficulty lies in measuring s. Once s is known, the plot of s against S is the psychophysical law, at least in a numerical form. Section II,B,3 illustrates this.

In the functional measurement approach, therefore, the psychophysical law assumes secondary importance. It is derivative from the more basic psychological law. This orientation is exactly opposite to that of traditional psychophysics.

The original purpose of the psychophysical law was as a means to measure the unobservable sensation value. This is mirrored in the controversies over the "true" measure of sensation. The implicit hope was that V would assume some simple, rational form. However, without a validity criterion, it became necessary to rely on untestable arguments about equality of just noticeable differences (jnd's), or about the meaning of verbal number habits.

Whereas traditional psychophysics attempted to work from the outside in, functional measurement works from the inside out. This is illustrated in the diagram. Primary focus is on the integration function I. The s-scale is derivative from I, and the V-function is derivative from s. From this standpoint, the psychophysical law does not have fundamental interest.

4. THE PSYCHOMOTOR LAW, M

The M-function relates the implicit response r to the overt response R. To round out the nomenclature, it may, with some apology, be called the psychomotor law. This term may be more appropriate for reaction time than for ratings, but it does emphasize the constraints that the organism's response apparatus can place on the overt behavior.

The psychomotor law has minimal scientific standing. In part, this reflects the peripheral place that psychology has generally accorded motor behavior. In most psychophysical views, the M-function is inessential if linear, and an obstructive bias if nonlinear.

The M-function has a special role in functional measurement. If M is nonlinear, then the inverse transformation M^{-1} is needed to assess the psychological law and to scale the stimuli. In that sense, a nonlinear M complicates the analysis. However, to dismiss M as a bias is hardly appropriate. There is no more reason to expect M than V to be linear, and the nature of response evocation is at least as important as the sensory transducer. From that standpoint, the M-function is a worthy object of study.

5. THE PHYSICAL LAW, P

The physical law relates the overt response R to the physical values of the stimulus. Quite properly, much psychological research is concerned only with the physical law. Parametric studies in perception are often of this type. However, some schools of thought, such as strict behaviorism, go one step further. They take as their credo that the only proper province of psychology is the physical law.

The attractions of strict behaviorism are plain to see. By considering only observables, it avoids the uncertainty and confusion that can result from the introduction of subjective quantities. Strict behaviorism would have avoided the long muddle over the psychophysical law. A power function, $R = S^\alpha$, obtained from magnitude estimation would be treated as a strictly observable physical relation. Only trouble results from unvalidatable assertions that the observable R is a veridical measure of the unobservable "sensation," s.

All science seeks to base itself on observables, and no one quarrels with an objectivist emphasis. The issue is whether the physical law is a sufficient base for a science of psychology, or whether the inferred psychological law is necessary.

Strict behaviorism often works very well in restricted domains. But it does not form an adequate basis for physics, and there is no reason to suppose it can do so in psychology. This can be seen quite clearly in the concepts of "hue" or of "loudness." Graham and Ratoosh (1962, p. 499), who adopt a behavioristic stand, speak of the "difficulty posed by this fact" that "hue varies with other factors than wavelength." It is to their great credit that they recognize the problem and face it squarely.

That they speak of this "fact" shows that they recognize hue as a psychological entity. The "difficulty" is that banishing the term *hue* leads at best to very awkward phraseology. It is a reasonable working hypothesis that such subjective terms mirror processes by which the organism perceives. If that is correct, then banishing the subjective terms will hobble and distort the investigation.

In terms of the diagram, P is the composition of the three psychological functions: $P = MIV$. To understand the organism, which is the goal of the science, cannot be done with P alone. Understanding requires a decomposition of P into its three psychological components.

B. Comparative Comments on Psychological Measurement

1. FIVE PRACTICAL CRITERIA FOR MEASUREMENT THEORIES

The final measure of any measurement theory is its empirical value. That is sometimes lost to sight amid elaborate mathematical development. It is appropriate, therefore, to emphasize five practical criteria that any general theory of measurement must satisfy.

1. It should be testable.
2. It should have been tested with some measure of success.
3. It should apply to psychophysical stimuli with a physical metric.

4. It should apply to verbal and symbolic stimuli without a physical metric.

5. It should apply to the single subject.

These criteria need little discussion. The first duty of a proper theory is to provide for its testability; that is the first criterion. And until it has shown some empirical success, as required by the second criterion, it is a theory only by courtesy or promise.

The next two criteria are both necessary for a general theory. Special theories have been developed for psychophysical stimuli that lean on the physical metric. However, a general theory clearly must be able to handle verbal stimuli, whose value is strictly internal or subjective.

Finally, the fifth criterion recognizes that individuals differ, and that any psychological theory of measurement must be able to operate at the level of the individual. It might seem unnecessary to state this criterion explicitly, but it often is not met.

One further criterion might be needed: the ability to scale weight as well as value. According to averaging theory, both parameters are necessary to represent a stimulus. Measurement has traditionally been concerned only with scale value, but that is not adequate (Section II,A,5,d).

2. FUNCTIONAL MEASUREMENT

This formulation satisfies all five criteria. The first three have been considered in detail in Sections II and III. The last two criteria were satisfied in an early application of functional measurement procedure (Anderson, 1962a) to person perception. That experiment used personality-trait stimuli and found good support for a simple averaging model with single-subject design and analysis. Later work (see Anderson, 1974b) has found extensive empirical support over a broad range of applications.

The present emphasis on adding and averaging tasks of stimulus integration calls to mind Campbell's (1957) attempts to place measurement on a foundation of additive physical operations. However, many of the integration models do not require any kind of physical addition.

Moreover, simple algebraic models are not a necessary basis for a theory of measurement. It is a great convenience that simple algebraic models have had some degree of success, because that markedly simplifies the work. The necessary requirement, however, would seem to be no more than a psychological law in two independent variables, together with an ordinal response measure. Monotone rescaling can then be applied, with degrees of freedom left over to test goodness of fit. With only one independent variable, the data could always be transformed to fit the law.

The essential requirement, therefore, would seem to be a functional relation in two independent variables. Measurement is implicit in the functional relation, and it provides the basis and frame for explicit scaling. This approach should hold equally well in all sciences; there is no reason to restrict it to psychology. On this view, Campbell's partial success with physical addition is an interesting but misleading coincidence.

The monotone rescaling principle is, of course, conceptually vital to functional measurement theory. This point (Section II,A,6) may need reemphasis in view of the extensive reliance on direct ratings in the preceding applications. Success of a model will simultaneously validate the rating scale, as already noted, and it is fortunate that ratings have worked so well. In general, however, the raw response will not be on an interval scale, so that monotone transformation will be necessary. Without allowing for monotone response transformation, functional measurement could not claim to be a general theory of measurement.

It is interesting that two theoretical developments based on monotone transformation were given independently at about the same time (Anderson, 1962b; Shepard, 1962). These two developments have had considerably different emphasis. Shepard's work on multidimensional scaling has been largely concerned with determining the dimensional structure of various kinds of nonsimple stimuli. The work on functional measurement, in contrast, has been largely concerned with the stimulus integration rule. Multidimensional stimuli are used, but their components are manipulated experimentally in order to ascertain what integration rule the subject is using. Because of their different emphases, there has been little interaction between these two approaches. Some unifying trends seem to appear in work by Wish and Carroll (Chapter 13 in this volume), which allows for weight parameters and individual differences in multidimensional scaling.

3. CONJOINT MEASUREMENT

Subsequent to the introduction of functional measurement procedure, Luce and Tukey (1964) introduced conjoint measurement, which has certain similarities to functional measurement. The term conjoint itself refers to simultaneous scaling of two or more stimulus variables, analogous to the functional scales for the factors of a factorial design. Because of such surface similarities, conjoint measurement and functional measurement are frequently confused, even though they have fundamentally different orientations. Conjoint measurement has been primarily concerned with abstract mathematical analysis of certain axiom systems; functional measurement is primarily concerned with substantive, empirical theory.

This difference is reflected in the experimental applications of the two approaches. Functional measurement has provided a wealth of applications in several areas (see references in Section I,1). In contrast, applications of conjoint measurement are rare as has been observed by Tukey (1969), Zinnes (1969), and Rapoport and Wallsten (1972). One main cause of this difference is the treatment of numerical response measures.

In conjoint measurement, order relations are taken as basic, and the axioms allow only for rank-order properties of the data. This restriction has severely limited attempts to apply conjoint measurement because it does not provide a satisfactory error theory for handling the response variability in real data. This problem is generally recognized, and the few attempts that have been made to analyze real data illustrate the difficulties of even an approximate analysis.

Functional measurement, in contrast, places first emphasis on numerical response measures. Even when these are not interval scales, they will ordinarily contain a good deal of metric information. Functional measurement uses that metric information. As a consequence, it is possible to employ standard statistical tests based on analysis of variance. The usefulness of the functional measurement approach is a direct consequence of its use of numerical response measures.

It may not be appropriate to compare functional measurement and conjoint measurement on empirical grounds. Krantz, Luce, Suppes, and Tversky (1971) claim to be concerned with "fundamentals" of measurement theory. In their development, that becomes essentially a search for sets of abstract axioms that will imply an additive model, for example, based only on order relations among error-free data. Such implications are called existence theorems. But such abstract existence theorems do not imply that anything actually exists in the empirical world. This point should be self-evident. Indeed, the additive model of conjoint measurement is known to be false in many situations (Section II,A,5). Moreover, neither the abstract axioms, nor the proof of the existence theorem specifies the empirical situations in which the additive model holds.

The abstract existence theorems could, of course, serve as a basis for a test of goodness of fit. In that respect, they would be nonparametric tests, parallel to the parametric tests of functional measurement. Such tests could be extremely valuable. But very few applications have been made; almost all the evidence on algebraic models has been obtained outside the axiomatic approach.

Existence theorems are also obtained in functional measurement, but these are empirical rather than abstract. Establishing the empirical validity of the model also establishes the existence of the associated measurement scales. Thus, each successful application of functional measurement can be considered as an empirical existence theorem (Anderson, 1973).

In general, abstract measurement theory seeks to reduce the concept of measurement to a certain type of formal, axiomatic structure. The axiomatic approach is attractive because it reaches conclusions that are mathematically rigorous and certain, regardless of any empirical relevance they may have. This approach seems to reflect a preference for a certain intellectual view, one that stems from mathematics and formal logic where, necessarily, formal interrelations are the sole object of study. This view deserves a serious hearing, but it is doubtful that it is epistemologically adequate.

A comparison with physics may illuminate the issue. Functional measurement is similar in spirit to the approach used in physics. Measurement is vital in physics, yet the laws of classical physics antedate abstract measurement theory and contemporary physics virtually ignores it. This fact, which Krantz et al. (1971, pp. 31ff) acknowledge, demonstrates that abstract measurement theory is not necessary to science.

The functional view is that measurement is woven into the fabric of empirical knowledge. The foundations of measurement are not theory-free, but the theoretical component is substantive, not abstract, axiomatic assumptions. Measurement exists only within the framework of substantive empirical laws. The measurement of any quantity is organically related to the empirical-theoretical network into which that quantity enters; that is the true foundation of measurement theory.

4. THURSTONIAN SCALING

The Thurstonian system is the first proper theory of measurement in psychology. Because it provided a validating criterion, it promised a way out of the Fechnerian controversy.

But though it has enjoyed continued popularity, the success of the Thurstonian system is open to question. It does not seem to have had a great deal of use in sensory scaling in psychophysics. The reasons for this are not entirely clear, though the Case V–Case VI indeterminacy may be involved (Bock & Jones, 1968, Section 6.4.1; Eisler, 1965).

More seriously, the Thurstonian system does not seem to be generally applicable for single subjects with most classes of verbal stimuli. The reason, in brief, is that the methods require imperfect discrimination or choice confusions. Choice proportions of 0 or 1 are not usable. Repeated presentations of identifiable stimuli to a single subject would not, therefore, yield usable data except in special cases (Bock & Jones, 1968, pp. 1–4; Torgerson, 1958, p. 167).

In practice, paired-comparison scales of verbal or symbolic stimuli are obtained by pooling data from many subjects. Such group scales can be useful in many ways, but real individual differences are lost in the process. That can be a serious limitation when scaling attitudes, personality-traits, foods, or similar stimuli.

Instead of paired comparisons, Thurstone's method of categorical judgment might be adapted to get individual scales in certain cases, though such attempts do not seem to have been made (Bock & Jones, 1968, p. 2). However, this method would require a close stimulus spacing that would not be feasible with certain stimulus classes. It is uncertain, therefore, whether the Thurstonian system can be considered as a general theory of measurement.

5. MAGNITUDE ESTIMATION

Magnitude estimation is a particular method of obtaining numerical responses. As such, it is not a theory of measurement. However, Stevens (1957, 1971) has claimed that such responses give a direct veridical measure of sensation on a ratio scale. A great deal of work and controversy has developed around this claim.

The central issue is simple and well-known. Such a claim requires a validity criterion, together with empirical evidence that the criterion is satisfied. Such criteria have been proposed, and magnitude estimation has repeatedly failed to satisfy them.

One of the earliest criteria was Stevens's (1960) claim that the exponent of a power function fit to the data should be a characteristic of the sensory transducer. The exponent should be constant, therefore, independent of stimulus range. That is far from true (Poulton, 1968).

Other criteria have also been proposed, several of which have already been discussed (Sections II,B and III,B). Numerous investigators have considered these problems (see references in Anderson, 1970a, p. 166, 1972c, 1974a; Garner & Creelman, 1967; Poulton, 1968; Weiss, 1972; Zinnes, 1969). On the whole, it seems fair to say the results uniformly infirm the magnitude estimation procedure. Two other criteria deserve a brief remark.

A common empirical finding is that a power function gives a fairly good fit to the data. It is sometimes thought, apparently, that this validates magnitude estimation. That this is not correct can be seen, for instance, in the recent finding that category rating data can be fit equally well by power functions (Marks, 1968; Stevens, 1971). Since category responses and magnitude estimations are nonlinearly related, not both power functions can be the true measure of sensation. Stevens claims that it is magnitude estimation that gives the true exponent, but that reverts to the original question of the validity criterion for his claim.

As an incidental comment, it would be advisable to divorce the power function from the magnitude estimation problem. Power functions are simple and convenient, and statisticians have long advocated them for curve fitting (Mandel, 1964). Their usefulness reflects their ability to fit a class of simple monotone functions. It is doubtful that that reflects any deeper psychophysical truth as Guilford (1932, 1954) and Stevens (1957, 1971) have argued. Magnitude estimation itself is a response procedure that is subject to the validity tests that have been discussed.

One final validity criterion remains to be considered. That is cross-modality matching. In addition to obtaining magnitude estimates for two sensory continua, one may be judged in terms of the other. Three power functions are then possible, and the ratio of two of the exponents should equal the third. Stevens has taken this prediction as a validity criterion.

Empirically, it is uncertain whether the cross-modal exponent prediction is true. If the data are taken at face value, it is false. Different exponents are obtained depending on which of the two sensory continua is adjusted to match the other (Stevens & Greenbaum, 1966). At least one exponent must be biased and invalid. Stevens has handled these data by averaging the two exponents, but averaging biases is an uncertain path to truth.

No less seriously, Attneave (1962) has pointed out that the cross-modal exponent prediction can be satisfied even with a severely biased response (see also Anderson, 1972c). If the bias is approximately a power function of number, it cancels out, so that the same result is predicted. Therefore, cross-modality matching does not validate magnitude estimation. Nor does it validate the power law since Treisman (1964) showed that a log law would predict the same relation among the exponents.

It should be made clear that Stevens has disavowed most of the validity criteria that have been proposed for magnitude estimation. Sum and difference judgments, for example, are claimed to suffer from invalidating response bias. The same holds for bisection and even for fractionation (Stevens, 1971). This stand leaves magnitude estimation without a validational base.

Without a validational base, however, the controversy over magnitude estimation becomes meaningless. From that standpoint, the claims that have been made for magnitude estimation are not so much invalid, as devoid of meaning or content. Stevens (1971) appears to recognize this problem in his discussion of validity since he concludes that "the answer becomes a matter of opinion [Stevens, 1971, p. 448]."

To the many workers who have employed one or another of the algebraic models, response validity is not " a matter of opinion." The model provides a criterion against which to validate the response measure. Magnitude estimation and rating scales have equal opportunity to meet this criterion. Judged on this ground, magnitude estimation fails.

6. STIMULUS INTEGRATION

The fundamental concern of this chapter has been with stimulus integration. This point merits a final emphasis to balance an undue prominence that has been given to measurement theory. The starting point of the present approach and its continuing concern is with questions of how stimulus information is integrated to form perceptions or judgments.

The unifying theme across a wide range of experimental situations has been the idea of a perceptual algebra. The analysis of each situation rested on the assumption that the stimulus information was integrated according to a simple algebraic rule. The study of these algebraic integration rules becomes a focal point of theory and experiment.

Within this framework, problems of measurement arise in a natural way. The very statement of an algebraic model involves the concept of scales of the dependent and independent variables. The integration model is primary because the scales obtain their existence by virtue of the model, at least in the functional measurement approach. Measurement is thus an organic part of experimental analysis. Measurement theory is not a separate discipline but rather a working part of substantive inquiry. Measurement and substantive theory are cofunctional in their development.

This approach is well illustrated by the shift in concern away from the psychophysical law to the psychological law. It is the psychological law that governs stimulus integration. The psychophysical law, which is more a problem of measurement, emerges as a by-product of the larger theoretical development.

The idea of a perceptual algebra is quite natural. Numerous investigators, especially over the last four decades, have studied algebraic models in many experimental situations. The present approach is in the spirit of much previous work. The special value of functional measurement is that it provides a unified approach to the study of algebraic models in perception.

References

Anderson, N. H. Temporal properties of response evocation. In R. R. Bush and W. K. Estes (Eds), *Studies in mathematical learning theory.* Stanford: Stanford University Press, 1959.

Anderson, N. H. Two learning models for responses measured on a continuous scale. *Psychometrika,* 1961, **26,** 391–403.

Anderson, N. H. Application of an additive model to impression formation. *Science,* 1962, **138,** 817–818. (a)

Anderson, N. H. On the quantification of Miller's conflict theory. *Psychological Review,* 1962, **69,** 400–414. (b)

Anderson, N. H. Linear models for responses measured on a continuous scale. *Journal of Mathematical Psychology,* 1964, **1,** 121–142. (a)

Anderson, N. H. Test of a model for number-averaging behavior. *Psychonomic Science,* 1964, **1,** 191–192. (b)

Anderson, N. H. Application of a weighted average model to a psychophysical averaging task. *Psychonomic Science,* 1967, **8,** 227–228. (a)

Anderson, N. H. Averaging model analysis of set size effect in impression formation. *Journal of Experimental Psychology,* 1967, **75,** 158–165. (b)

Anderson, N. H. A Simple model for information integration. In R. P. Abelson, E. Aronson, W. J. McGuire, T. M. Newcomb, M. J. Rosenberg, & P. H. Tannenbaum (Eds.), *Theories of cognitive consistency: A sourcebook.* Chicago: Rand McNally, 1968. (a)

Anderson, N. H. Application of a linear-serial model to a personality-impression task using serial presentation. *Journal of Personality and Social Psychology,* 1968, **10,** 354–362. (b)

Anderson, N. H. Averaging of space and number stimuli with simultaneous presentation. *Journal of Experimental Psychology,* 1968, **77,** 383–392. (c)

Anderson, N. H. A search task. In J. F. Voss (Ed.), *Approaches to thought.* Columbus: Charles E. Merrill, 1969.

Anderson, N. H. Functional measurement and psychophysical judgment. *Psychological Review,* 1970, **77,** 153–170. (a)

Anderson, N. H. Averaging model applied to the size-weight illusion. *Perception & Psychophysics,* 1970, **8,** 1–4. (b)

Anderson, N. H. Integration theory and attitude change. *Psychological Review,* 1971, **78,** 171–206. (a)

Anderson, N. H. Test of adaptation-level theory as an explanation of a recency effect in psychophysical integration. *Journal of Experimental Psychology,* 1971, **87,** 57–63. (b)

Anderson, N. H. Looking for configurality in clinical judgment. *Psychological Bulletin.* 1972, **78,** 93–102. (a)

Anderson, N. H. Information integration theory: A brief survey. Technical Report No. 24, Center for Human Information Processing, University of California, San Diego, April 1972. (b)

Anderson, N. H. Cross-task validation of functional measurement. *Perception & Psychophysics,* 1972, **12,** 389–395. (c)

Anderson, N. H. Comments on the papers of Hodges, and of Schonemann, Cafferty, and Rotton. *Psychological Review,* 1973, **80,** 88–92.

Anderson, N. H. Cross-task validation of functional measurement using judgments of total magnitude. *Journal of Experimental Psychology,* 1974, **102,** 226–233. (a)

Anderson, N. H. Information integration theory: A brief survey. In D. H. Krantz, R. C. Atkinson, R. D. Luce, & P. Suppes (Eds.), *Contemporary developments in mathematical psychology,* Volume 2. San Francisco: Freeman, 1974. (b)

Anderson, N. H. Cognitive algebra. In L. Berkowitz (Ed.), *Advances in experimental social psychology,* Vol. 7. New York: Academic Press, 1974. (c)

Anderson, N. H., & Jacobson, A. Further data on a weighted average model for judgment in a lifted weight task. *Perception & Psychophysics,* 1968, **4,** 81–84.

Anderson, N. H., & Shanteau, J. C. Information integration in risky decision making. *Journal of Experimental Psychology,* 1970, **84,** 441–451.

Anderson, N. H., & Weiss, D. J. Test of a multiplying model for estimated area of rectangles. *American Journal of Psychology,* 1971, **84,** 543–548.

Attneave, F. Dimensions of similarity. *American Journal of Psychology,* 1950, **63,** 516–556.

Attneave, F. *Applications of information theory to psychology.* New York: Holt, 1959.

Attneave, F. Perception and related areas. In S. Koch (Ed.), *Psychology: A study of a science*. Volume 4. New York: McGraw-Hill, 1962.

Baird, J. *Psychophysical analysis of visual space*. New York: Pergamon, 1970.

Beals, R., Krantz, D. H., & Tversky, A. Foundations of multidimensional scaling. *Psychological Review*, 1968, **75**, 127–142.

Beck, J., & Shaw, W. A. Discrimination of loudness similarity. *Perception & Psychophysics*, 1968, **3**, 105–108.

Birnbaum, M. H. Using contextual effects to derive psychophysical scales. *Perception & Psychophysics*, 1974, **15**, 89–96.

Birnbaum, M. H., Kobernick, M., & Veit, C. T. Subjective correlation and the size-numerosity illusion. *Journal of Experimental Psychology*, 1974, **102**, 537–539.

Birnbaum, M. H., Parducci, A., & Gifford, R. K. Contextual effects in information integration. *Journal of Experimental Psychology*, 1971, **88**, 158–170.

Birnbaum, M. H., & Veit, C. T. Judgmental illusion produced by contrast with expectancy. *Perception & Psychophysics*, 1973, **13**, 149–152.

Birnbaum, M. H., & Veit, C. T. Psychophysical measurement: Information integration with difference, ratio, and averaging tasks. *Perception & Psychophysics*, 1974, **15**, 7–15.

Bock, R. D., & Jones, L. V. *The measurement and prediction of judgment and choice*. San Francisco: Holden-Day, 1968.

Bogartz, R. S., & Wackwitz, J. H. Transforming response measures to remove interactions or other sources of variance. *Psychonomic Science*, 1970, **19**, 87–89.

Bogartz, R. S., & Wackwitz, J. H. Polynomial response scaling and functional measurement. *Journal of Mathematical Psychology*, 1971, **8**, 418–443.

Bradley, R. A., & Terry, M. E. Rank analysis of incomplete block designs. I. The method of paired comparisons. *Biometrika*, 1952, **39**, 324–345.

Briggs, G. E., & Swanson, J. M. Encoding, decoding, and central functions in human information processing. *Journal of Experimental Psychology*, 1970, **86**, 296–308.

Brunswik, E. *Perception and the representative design of psychological experiments*. Berkeley, California: University of California Press, 1956.

Campbell, N. R. *Foundations of science: the philosophy of theory and experiment*. New York: Dover, 1957.

Carterette, E. C. A simple linear model for vowel perception. In W. Wathen-Dunn (Ed.), *Models for the perception of speech and visual form*. Cambridge, Massachusetts: M. I. T. Press, 1967.

Chandler, J. P. Subroutine STEPIT—Finds local minima of a smooth function of several parameters. *Behavioral Science*, 1969, **14**, 81–82.

Comrey, A. L. A proposed method for absolute ratio scaling. *Psychometrika*, 1950 **15**, 317–325.

Curtis, D. W. Magnitude estimations and category judgments of brightness and brightness intervals: A two-stage interpretation. *Journal of Experimental Psychology*, 1970, **83**, 201–208.

Curtis, D. W., Attneave, F., & Harrington, T. L. A test of a two-stage model of magnitude estimation. *Perception & Psychophysics*, 1968, **3**, 25–31.

Curtis, D. W., & Fox, B. E. Direct quantitative judgments of sums and a two-stage model for psychophysical judgments. *Perception & Psychophysics*, 1969, **5**, 89–93.

Eisler, H. The connection between magnitude and discrimination scales and direct and indirect scaling methods. *Psychometrika,* 1965, **30,** 271–289.

Eisler, H., & Ekman, G. A mechanism of subjective similarity. *Acta Psychologica,* 1959, **16,** 1–10.

Ekman, G. Two generalized ratio scaling methods. *Journal of General Psychology,* 1958, **45,** 287–295.

Ellis, B. *Basic concepts of measurement.* Cambridge University Press, 1966.

Eriksen, C. W., & Hake, H. W. Absolute judgments as a function of stimulus range and number of stimulus and response categories. *Journal of Experimental Psychology,* 1955, **49,** 323–332.

Eriksen, C. W., & Hake, H. W. Anchor effects in absolute judgments. *Journal of Experimental Psychology,* 1957, **53,** 132–138.

Erlebacher, A., & Sekuler, R. Response frequency equalization: A bias model for psychophysics. *Perception & Psychophysics,* 1971, **9,** 315–320.

Fagot, R. F., & Stewart, M. Tests of product and additive scaling axioms. *Perception & Psychophysics,* 1969, **5,** 117–123. (a)

Fagot, R. F., & Stewart, M. R. Individual half-judgment brightness functions. *Perception & Psychophysics,* 1969, **5,** 165–170. (b)

Feldman, J., & Baird, J. C. Magnitude estimation of multidimensional stimuli. *Perception & Psychophysics,* 1971, **10,** 418–422.

Fletcher, H., & Munson, W. A. Loudness, its definition, measurement and calculation. *Journal of the Acoustical Society of America,* 1933, **5,** 82–108.

Garner, W. R. An informational analysis of absolute judgments of loudness. *Journal of Experimental Psychology,* 1953, **46,** 373–380.

Garner, W. R. A technique and a scale for loudness measurement. *Journal of the Acoustical Society of America,* 1954, **26,** 73–88. (a)

Garner, W. R. Context effects and the validity of loudness scales. *Journal of Experimental Psychology,* 1954, **48,** 218–224. (b)

Garner, W. R. *Uncertainty and structure as psychological concepts.* New York: Wiley, 1962.

Garner, W. R., & Creelman, C. D. Problems and methods of psychological scaling. In H. Helson & W. Bevan (Eds.), *Contemporary approaches to psychology.* Princeton, New Jersey.: van Nostrand Reinhold, 1967.

Garner, W. R., Hake, H. W., & Eriksen, C. W. Operationism and the concept of perception. *Psychological Review,* 1956, **63,** 149–159.

Garner, W. R., & Morton, J. Perceptual independence: Definitions, models, and experimental paradigms. *Psychological Bulletin,* 1969, **72,** 233–259.

Geiger, P. H., & Firestone, F. A. The estimation of fractional loudness. *Journal of the Acoustical Society of America,* 1933, **5,** 25–30.

Gogel, W. C. The adjacency principle and three-dimensional visual illusions. *Psychonomic Science, Monograph Supplement,* 1970, **3,** Whole No. 45, 153–219.

Goude, G. *On fundamental measurement in psychology.* Stockholm: Almquist & Wiksell, 1962.

Graesser, C. A., & Anderson, N. H. Cognitive algebra of the equation: Gift size = generosity $\times$ income. *Journal of Experimental Psychology,* 1974, in press.

Graham, C. H., & Ratoosh, P. Notes on some interrelations of sensory psychology, perception, and behavior. In S. Koch (Ed.), *Psychology: A study of a science,* Vol. 4. New York: McGraw-Hill, 1962.

Green, D. M., & Luce, R. D. Detection of auditory signals presented at random times: III. *Perception & Psychophysics,* 1971, **9,** 257–268.

Green, D. M., & Swets, J. A. *Signal detection theory and psychophysics.* New York: Wiley, 1966.

Gregson, R. A. M. Quadratic similarities. *British Journal of Mathematical and Statistical Psychology,* 1970, **23,** 53–68.

Grice, G. R. Stimulus intensity and response evocation. *Psychological Review,* 1968, **75,** 359–373.

Grice, G. R. A threshold model for drive. In H. H. Kendler & J. T. Spence (Eds.), *Essays in neobehaviorism.* New York: Appleton, 1971.

Guilford, J. P. A generalized psychophysical law. *Psychological Review,* 1932, **39,** 73–85.

Guilford, J. P. *Psychometric methods.* Second edition. New York: McGraw-Hill, 1954.

Guilford, J. P., & Dingman, H. F. A validation study of ratio-judgment methods. *American Journal of Psychology,* 1954, **67,** 395–410.

Hake, H. W. The study of perception in the light of multivariate methods. In R. B. Cattell (Ed.), *Handbook of multivariate experimental psychology.* Chicago: Rand McNally, 1966.

Hake, H. W., Faust, G. W., McIntyre, J. S., & Murray, H. G. Relational perception and modes of perceiver operation. *Perception & Psychophysics,* 1967, **2,** 469–478.

Helson, H. *Adaptation-level theory.* New York: Harper & Row, 1964.

Helson, H., & Kozaki, A. Anchor effects using numerical estimates of simple dot patterns. *Perception & Psychophysics,* 1968, **4,** 163–164.

Hull, C. L. *A behavior system.* New Haven: Yale University Press, 1952.

Hyman, R., & Well, A. Judgment of similarity and spatial models. *Perception & Psychophysics,* 1967, **2,** 233–248.

Hyman, R., & Well, A. Perceptual separability and spatial models. *Perception & Psychophysics,* 1968, **3,** 161–165.

Jones, L. V. Some invariant findings under the method of successive intervals. In H. Gulliksen & S. Messick (Eds.), *Psychological scaling.* New York: Wiley, 1960.

Kinchla, R. A. Visual movement perception: A comparison of absolute and relative movement discrimination. *Perception & Psychophysics,* 1971, **9,** 165–171.

Kohfeld, D. L. Stimulus intensity and adaptation level as determinants of simple reaction time. *Journal of Experimental Psychology,* 1968, **76,** 468–473.

Kohfeld, D. L. Effects of the intensity of auditory and visual ready signals on simple reaction time. *Journal of Experimental Psychology,* 1969, **82,** 88–95.

Kohfeld, D. L. Simple reaction time as a function of stimulus intensity in decibels of light and sound. *Journal of Experimental Psychology,* 1971, **88,** 251–257.

Krantz, D. H., Luce, R. D., Suppes, P., & Tversky, A. *Foundations of measurement,* Vol. 1. New York: Academic Press, 1971.

Kruskal, J. B. Analysis of factorial experiments by estimating monotone transformations of the data. *Journal of the Royal Statistical Society (B),* 1965, **27,** 251–263.

Lebensfeld, P., & Wapner, S. Configuration and space-time interdependence. *American Journal of Psychology,* 1968, **81,** 106–110.

Leon, M., Oden, G. C., & Anderson, N. H. Functional measurement of social values. *Journal of Personality and Social Psychology,* 1973, **27,** 301–310.

Levelt, W. J. M., Riemersma, J. B., & Bunt, A. A. Binaural additivity of loudness. *British Journal of Mathematical and Statistical Psychology,* 1972, **25,** 51–68.

Levin, I. P., Craft, J. L., & Norman, K. L. Averaging of motor movements: Tests of an additive model. *Journal of Experimental Psychology*, 1971, **91**, 287–294.

Levine, M. V. Transformations that render curves parallel. *Journal of Mathematical Psychology*, 1970, **7**, 410–443.

Levine, M. V. Transforming curves into curves with the same shape. *Journal of Mathematical Psychology*, 1972, **9**, 1–16.

Luce, R. D. *Individual choice behavior*. New York: Wiley, 1959.

Luce, R. D. A model for detection in temporally unstructured experiments with a Poisson distribution of signal presentations. *Journal of Mathematical Psychology*, 1966, **3**, 48–64.

Luce, R. D., & Tukey, J. W. Simultaneous conjoint measurement: A new type of fundamental measurement. *Journal of Mathematical Psychology*, 1964, **1**, 1–27.

Mandel, J. Non-additivity in two-way analysis of variance. *Journal of the American Statistical Association*, 1961, **56**, 878–888.

Mandel, J. *The statistical analysis of experimental data*. New York: Wiley, 1964.

Marks, L. E. Stimulus-range, number of categories, and form of category scale. *American Journal of Psychology*, 1968, **81**, 467–479.

Mashhour, M. *Psychophysical relations in the perception of velocity*. Stockholm: Almquist & Wiksell, 1964.

Massaro, D. W., & Anderson, N. H. Judgmental model of the Ebbinghaus illusion. *Journal of Experimental Psychology*, 1971, **89**, 147–151.

McGill, W. J. The slope of the loudness function: A puzzle. In H. Gulliksen & S. Messick (Eds.), *Psychological scaling*. New York: Wiley, 1960.

McGill, W. J. Stochastic latency mechanisms. In R. D. Luce, R. R. Bush, & E. Galanter (Eds.), *Handbook of mathematical psychology*, Vol. 1. New York: Wiley, 1963.

McGill, W. J. Neural counting mechanisms and energy detection in audition. *Journal of Mathematical Psychology*, 1967, **4**, 351–376.

Michels, W. C., & Helson, H. A reformulation of the Fechner law in terms of adaptation-level applied to rating-scale data. *American Journal of Psychology*, 1949, **62**, 355–368.

Mosteller, F. The mystery of the missing corpus. *Psychometrika*, 1958, **23**, 279–289.

Murray, H. G. Stimulus intensity and reaction time: Evaluation of a decision-theory model. *Journal of Experimental Psychology*, 1970, **84**, 383–391.

Newman, C. V., & Lee, S. G. The effect of real and imputed distance on judgments of time. *Psychonomic Science*, 1972, **29**, 207–211.

Öttander, C. *On sensory interaction in judgment of velocity and its measurement by psychophysical scaling methods*. Stockholm: Ivar Haeggström, 1967.

Parducci, A. Category judgment: A range-frequency model. *Psychological Review*, 1965, **72**, 407–418.

Parducci, A., Marshall, L. M., & Degner, M. Interference with memory for lifted weight. *Perception & Psychophysics*, 1966, **1**, 83–86.

Parducci, A., & Perrett, L. F. Category rating scales. *Journal of Experimental Psychology*, 1971, **89**, 427–452.

Parducci, A., Thaler, L., & Anderson, N. H. Stimulus averaging and the context for judgment. *Perception & Psychophysics*, 1968, **3**, 145–150.

Postman, L., & Tolman, E. C. Brunswik's probabilistic functionalism. In S. Koch (Ed.), *Psychology: A study of a science*, Vol. 1. New York: McGraw-Hill, 1959.

Poulton, E. C. The new psychophysics: Six models for magnitude estimation. *Psychological Bulletin*, 1968, **69**, 1–19.

Price-Williams, D. R. The kappa effect. *Nature*, 1954, **173**, 363–364.

Rapoport, A., & Wallsten, T. S. Individual decision behavior. *Annual Review of Psychology*, 1972, **23**, 131–176.

Restle, F., & Davis, J. H. Success and speed of problem solving by individuals and groups. *Psychological Review*, 1962, **69**, 520–536.

Restle, F., & Greeno, J. G. *Introduction to mathematical psychology*. Reading, Massachusetts: Addison-Wesley, 1970.

Restle, F., & Merryman, C. Distance and an illusion of length of line. *Journal of Experimental Psychology*, 1969, **81**, 297–302.

Reynolds, G. S., & Stevens, S. S. Binaural summation of loudness. *Journal of the Acoustical Society of America*, 1960, **32**, 1337–1344.

Rule, S. J., Curtis, D. W., & Markley, R. P. Input and output transformations from magnitude estimation. *Journal of Experimental Psychology*, 1970, **86**, 343–349.

Scharf, B., & Fishken, D. Binaural summation of loudness reconsidered. *Journal of Experimental Psychology*, 1970, **86**, 374–379.

Scheffé, H. *The analysis of variance*. New York: Wiley, 1959.

Shanteau, J. C. Component processes in risky decision judgments. Unpublished doctoral dissertation, University of California, San Diego, 1970.

Shanteau, J. C. Descriptive versus normative models of sequential inference judgment. *Journal of Experimental Psychology*, 1972, **93**, 63–68.

Shanteau, J. C., & Anderson, N. H. Test of a conflict model for preference judgment. *Journal of Mathematical Psychology*, 1969, **6**, 312–325.

Shanteau, J. C., & Anderson, N. H. Integration theory applied to judgments of the value of information. *Journal of Experimental Psychology*, 1972, **92**, 266–275.

Shepard, R. N. The analysis of proximities. Multidimensional scaling with an unknown distance function. II. *Psychometrika*, 1962, **27**, 219–246.

Shepard, R. N. Attention and the metric structure of the stimulus space. *Journal of Mathematical Psychology*, 1964, **1**, 54–87.

Shepard, R. N. Metric structures in ordinal data. *Journal of Mathematical Psychology*, 1966, **3**, 287–315.

Simmonds, M. B. Verbal factors modifying similarity judgments. Unpublished Ph.D. dissertation. Christchurch, New Zealand: University of Canterbury, 1971.

Sjöberg, L. A method for sensation scaling based on an analogy between perception and judgment. *Perception & Psychophysics*, 1966, **1**, 131–136.

Sjöberg, L. Three models for the analysis of subjective ratio. *Scandinavian Journal of Psychology*, 1971, **12**, 217–240.

Steger, J. A., Wilkinson, J., & Carter, R. Test of integration theory and adaptation level theory in anchored judgments. *Perceptual and Motor Skills*, 1973, **36**, 271–274.

Sternberg, S. The discovery of processing stages: Extensions of Donders' method. *Acta Psychologica*, 1969, **30**, 276–315. (a)

Sternberg, S. Memory-scanning: Mental processes revealed by reaction-time experiments. *American Scientist*, 1969, **57**, 421–457. (b)

Stevens, J. C., & Marks, L. E. Spatial summation and the dynamics of warmth sensation. *Perception & Psychophysics*, 1971, **9**, 391–398.

Stevens, S. S. The measurement of loudness. *Journal of the Acoustical Society of America*, 1955, **27**, 815–829.

Stevens, S. S. The direct estimation of sensory magnitudes—loudness. *American Journal of Psychology*, 1956, **69**, 1–25.

Stevens, S. S. On the psychophysical law. *The Psychological Review*, 1957, **64**, 153–181.

Stevens, S. S. The psychophysics of sensory function. *American Scientist*, 1960, **48**, 226–253.

Stevens, S. S. Issues in psychophysical measurement. *Psychological Review*, 1971, **78**, 426–450.

Stevens, S. S., & Galanter, E. H. Ratio scales and category scales for a dozen perceptual continua. *Journal of Experimental Psychology*, 1957, **54**, 377–411.

Stevens, S. S., & Greenbaum, H. B. Regression effect in psychophysical judgment. *Perception & Psychophysics*, 1966, **1**, 439–446.

Stone, M. Models for choice-reaction time. *Psychometrika*, 1960, **25**, 251–260.

Svenson, O. A functional measurement approach to intuitive estimation as exemplified by estimated time savings. *Journal of Experimental Psychology*, 1970, **86**, 204–210.

Torgerson, W. S. *Theory and methods of scaling*. New York: Wiley, 1958.

Torgerson, W. S. Multidimensional scaling of similarity. *Psychometrika*, 1965, **30**, 379–393.

Treisman, M. Sensory scaling and the psychophysical law. *Quarterly Journal of Experimental Psychology*, 1964, **16**, 11–22.

Treisman, M., & Irwin, R. J. Auditory intensity discriminal scale. I. Evidence derived from binaural intensity summation. *Journal of the Acoustical Society of America*, 1967, **42**, 586–592.

Tukey, J. W. One degree of freedom for nonadditivity. *Biometrics*, 1949, **5**, 232–242.

Tukey, J. W. Analyzing data: Sanctification or detective work? *American Psychologist*, 1969, **24**, 83–91.

Tversky, A., & Krantz, D. H. Similarity of schematic faces: A test of interdimensional additivity. *Perception & Psychophysics*, 1969, **5**, 124–128.

Warren, R. M., & Warren, R. P. Effect of the relative volume of standard and comparison-object on half-heaviness judgments. *American Journal of Psychology*, 1956, **69**, 640–643.

Weiss, D. J. Averaging: An empirical validity criterion for magnitude estimation. *Perception & Psychophysics*, 1972, **12**, 385–388.

Weiss, D. J. FUNPOT, a FORTRAN program for finding a polynomial transformation to reduce any source of variance in a factorial design. *Behavioral Science*, 1973, **18**, 150. (a)

Weiss, D. J. A functional measurement analysis of equisection. Unpublished doctoral dissertation. University of California, San Diego, 1973. (b)

Weiss, D. J., & Anderson, N. H. Subjective averaging of length with serial presentation. *Journal of Experimental Psychology*, 1969, **82**, 52–63.

Weiss, D. J., & Anderson, N. H. Use of rank order data in functional measurement. *Psychological Bulletin*, 1972, **78**, 64–69.

Winer, B. J. *Statistical principles in experimental design*. Second edition. New York: McGraw-Hill, 1971.

Zinnes, J. L. Scaling. *Annual Review of Psychology*, 1969, **20**, 447–478.

Chapter 9

DETECTION, DISCRIMINATION, AND RECOGNITION*

R. DUNCAN LUCE and DAVID M. GREEN

* This work was supported in part by a grant from the Alfred P. Sloan Foundation to The Institute for Advanced Study and in part by grants from the National Institutes of Health, Public Health Service, U.S. Department of Health, Education, and Welfare, and from the National Science Foundation to the University of California, San Diego. Manuscript was completed January, 1971.

1. INTRODUCTION

During the period 1955–1970 many attempts were made to formulate precisely the basic mechanisms thought to underlie the processing of simple physical signals and to isolate some of the factors that affect subjects' responses to such signals. The main impetus for this work was the application of the theory of signal detectability to psychophysics by Tanner and Swets (1954). This work is well known and is adequately summarized elsewhere (Green & Swets, 1966; Luce, 1963a; Swets, 1964), and we will not review the basic ideas again. Rather, we will report some of the later developments sparked by these early studies.

Despite the diversity of extant models, all are able to predict certain basic features of the relevant data, and competing pairs of models tend to be about equally parsimonious as measured by the number of free parameters that one must estimate from data. Moreover, the predictions are often so similar that rather elaborate statistical tests are needed to ascertain which theory best accounts for a particular experiment. For those hoping to find a single, clearly superior theory, this chapter will prove disappointing. Our tentative conclusion is that among existing theories, different ones are appropriate to different situations. Or put another way, no current theory is really correct and which one better approximates the data varies with the experiment being analyzed. That state of affairs, though not ideal, would be acceptable if we were able to state clearly which experimental features serve to bound the region of reasonable application of a given theory. For example, we would like a rule such as: Threshold theories best handle discrimination of small changes in intensity when there is no noise background, whereas continuous theories are best when the signal is in noise. The sad fact is that no such rules have yet been formulated.

Another criterion for the worth of a theory, in addition to its accuracy, is the class of experimental designs for which it makes significant predictions. A minimum requirement of any theory is that it unify data from most of the simple (one and two stimulus) psychophysical tasks. Practically all current theories make predictions that can be cross validated in the simple yes–no (YN) and forced-choice (FC) experiments and in the single stimulus design with a rating response.* By "cross validate" we mean that certain parameters which, on theoretical grounds, should be the same in different experimental designs, appear to be so. It is our particular bias

---

* We abbreviate certain recurrent terms. At the first use of the term, we place the abbreviation in parentheses after it; thereafter we use the abbreviation.

that an adequate theory should apply to experimental situations in which the stimulus interval is not precisely marked as well as those in which it is. Experiments in which the signal can occur at any time mimic many practical detection and discrimination situations better than do the usual fixed interval (FI) designs. To generate models that account for behavior in these so-called free-response designs and to relate their parameters to those from the discrete FI tasks is a challenging and largely unsolved problem.

Applying the criterion of generality usually involves an element of individual taste, because one theory generalizes easily in one direction, another theory in a different direction. For example, choice theory is readily stated for any finite number of stimuli and responses, but the connection between its parameters and physical properties of the stimuli is exceedingly vague. The theory of signal detectability (TSD) is easily couched in very stimulus-oriented terms, but its extension to more than two responses produces so many free parameters that prediction becomes virtually impossible.

Let us consider further some of the problems that arise when we generalize designs and theories from $n = 2$ to $n > 2$ stimuli. Recall that the standard $n = 2$, YN design involves a noise background or null signal, $\emptyset$, a signal in noise, s, and a single observation interval in which one of these alternatives is presented. If we retain the single observation interval, then the natural way to generalize the YN design is to increase the number of signals that can be presented. We might do this by using several different frequencies or hues or by presenting several different levels of intensity. In contrast, we can keep only two signals, but increase the number of possible stimuli. If we allow all possible combinations of two signals in k observation intervals, there are 2^k possible stimuli. Thus, in the most general two-alternative forced-choice (2AFC) task there are four possible ordered pairs—stimuli—$\langle s, \emptyset \rangle$, $\langle \emptyset, s \rangle$, $\langle \emptyset, \emptyset \rangle$, and $\langle s, s \rangle$. Usually, the signal s is permitted to appear only once, which restricts the number of stimuli to the number of intervals. Under that restriction, a 3AFC design has the stimuli $\langle s, \emptyset, \emptyset \rangle$, $\langle \emptyset, s, \emptyset \rangle$, and $\langle \emptyset, \emptyset, s \rangle$. Most empirical studies have imposed this restriction; however, Markowitz (1966) explored the most general case of 2AFC.

The compass of such terms as detection, discrimination, and recognition for $n > 2$ is still confused. When there is one interval and n different non-null signals in one-to-one relation with n responses, we speak of the design as a recognition task except when $n = 2$ and the stimuli differ only in intensity, in which case it is called an *intensity discrimination* task. However, if one of the n signals is replaced by the null signal $\emptyset$, we call it *simultaneous recognition and detection* except when $n = 2$ (one nonnull signal), in which case it is called a *yes–no detection* task. Any FC design having a signal in one interval and the null signal in the other $n - 1$ intervals is also called a detection design. For more details, see Luce (1963a) and Green and Swets (1966). There is, of course, an obvious sense in which all of these designs are asking the subject to recognize which of n possible stimulus presentations has been presented. Were the terminology not so deeply ingrained in the psychophysical literature, we might be tempted to reserve the use of "detection" for FR designs concerned with the detection of a signal whose time of onset is uncertain, and refer to all of the FI designs as recognition experiments.

As the numbers n of stimuli and m of responses increase, programming problems and costs rise rapidly. Specifically, we must increase the number of trials by the factor $n(m - 1)/2$ in order to have, on the average, a constant number of observations per independent estimated probability. Thus, considerable experimental selectiveness is required. Most of the studies that have been performed have been motivated by specific considerations. In addition, there are theoretical difficulties of two types. First, several viable two-stimuli theories exist and each of them can be generalized in a variety of ways (many of the logical possibilities have not yet been worked out). Moreover, all of these generalizations proliferate free parameters at a spectacular rate. Often postulates not needed in the two-stimulus case must be added in order to test the general model. Even so, a great number of parameters must be estimated. This leads to the second difficulty: how to estimate optimally the many parameters from data and how to compare the adequacy of theories with different numbers of parameters? We have barely begun to face these problems.

Our review begins with a general classification scheme. It is first used to organize various general theories for situations with n signals and m responses. Following this, we turn to the special cases of $n = 2$ stimuli which have received the most careful attention in the literature. We first deal with operating characteristics and psychometric functions on the assumption of stationary mechanisms. We next turn to the limited literature dealing with sequential effects in the data. And, finally, we turn to the relatively few attempts to deal with FR data in which responses may occur at any time.

II. CLASSIFICATION SCHEME

Our classification of theories is based on guiding principles clearly evident in all of the theories so far proposed. First, they all postulate a sensory or perceptual stage followed by a memory process that stores a hypothetical representation of the stimulus. Second, following the sensory–memory process is a decision stage, which operates on the representation of the stimulus. This two-stage structure is characteristic of the successful two-stimulus theories, and it has been uniformly maintained in generalizing them. So we will class theories according to the two types of stages assumed.

A. Sensory–Memory Processes

The sensory–memory processes are of three general types, which provides the first dimension of our classification system:

1. FINITE STATE

There are assumed to be k internal states of which one is activated with some probability when a stimulus is presented. These states may or may not be ordered. Two special cases are of importance.

(a) $k = n$, in which case the states are identified with the stimuli; these are *stimulus generalization* models.

(b) $k = m$, in which case the states are identified with the possible responses (*implicit responses*).

Note that, without further assumptions, the conditional probabilities relating states to stimuli constitute $n(k - 1)$ free parameters.

2. CONTINUOUS STATE

The internal states are assumed to form a continuum, usually in Euclidean space. In the one-dimensional case, the continuum is naturally ordered. Usually, each signal is represented by some distribution over the continuum. Such assumed distributions constitute, in a sense, a continuum of free parameters unless there are strong a priori arguments for restricting them to a particular family. Frequently, though not always, the family is assumed to be normal, in which case the parameters are reduced to two, namely the mean and variance of each normal distribution.

3. STOCHASTIC PROCESS

A signal is assumed to generate in time a train of pulses (neural, perhaps), which is described by some stochastic process. Most often, the process is assumed to be Poisson—in which case the interarrival times are independent and exponentially distributed, and so it can be viewed as a special type of continuous state process; however, the decision processes associated with continuous state and stochastic sensory models usually differ somewhat.

B. Response Processes

The response or decision processes are of three types; they provide the second dimension of our classification system.

1. RESPONSE GENERALIZATION

This is only compatible with the finite state representation in which $k = m$; it assumes that when the sensory process indicates one response, there is some tendency (possibly, probability) of another response occurring.

2. RESPONSE BIAS

Response bias models postulate that among the possible responses or implicit responses, there are differential tendencies to employ one rather than another. The most widely used variant, called a choice model, assigns a weight $b(r) > 0$ to each response r and calculates the probability of choosing r out of a set R of possible responses as $b(r)/\sum b(x)$.

3. RESPONSE CRITERION

Such models are compatible only with an ordered set of states; they are a natural generalization of TSD. Most often, the criteria are assumed to be fixed, but in some models they are assumed to be distributed in some manner and in others to be adjusted systematically, according to a fixed learning model.

III. THEORIES FOR FIXED-INTERVAL DESIGNS

In talking about the various theories that have actually been developed in any detail, we will identify them by the names used by their authors followed by a symbol i–j, where i identifies the sensory and j the decision process in the preceding classification. No model is described fully, and little more than mention is made of experiments that seem especially relevant to it. When a model has been tested for $n > 2$, we discuss the test in this section. All of the experimental work for $n = 2$ is dealt with in the following sections. Little by way of systematic confrontation of alternative models has yet taken place for $n > 2$.

A. Constant-Ratio Rule (CRR) (1a–)

Let $p(r|s)$ denote the typical entry of a confusion matrix when s is in the stimulus set S and r is in the response set R. The CRR asserts that if S' is a subset of S and R' is the response set corresponding to S', then the recognition experiment based on S' and R' has the confusion matrix

$$p(r'|s') \Big/ \sum_{x \text{ in } R'} p(x|s'),$$

where s' is in S and r' is in R' (Clarke, 1957). Supporting experimental evidence can be found in Anderson (1959), Clarke (1957, 1960), Clarke and Anderson (1957), Conrad (1964), Egan (1957a,b), Hodge (1962, 1967), Hodge, Crawford, and Piercy (1961); Hodge, Piercy, and Crawford (1961); Hodge and Pollack (1962), and Pollack and Decker (1960). Hodge and Pollack (1962) and Lee (1968) have suggested that the CRR may be a good empirical generalization when the stimuli are multidimensional but is less accurate when they are unidimensional. Clearly, this rule is of limited generality, since by varying the presentation probabilities, payoffs, or instructions, $p(r|s)$ can be affected [Nakatani (1968) and Shipley and Luce (1964) report such data]. Nonetheless, it suggests that the special case of a theory without response bias should predict the CRR or something close to it.

B. Stimulus and Response Generalization (1a–1)

Shepard (1957) proposed a recognition model ($m = n$) which has the matrix form $P_{SS}JP_{RR}$ where P_{SS} is a stochastic matrix representing stimulus generalization, J is an experimenter assigned permutation matrix mapping stimuli into responses, and P_{RR} is a response generalization matrix. He suggested how to estimate P_{SS} by running several experiments with different J's. In addition, he postulated that these probabilities of the stimulus matrix are exponentially related to an Euclidean distance, and he provided supporting experimental evidence (Shepard, 1958a,b). Applications are given in Shepard (1961a,b). These ideas grew ultimately into Shepard's very fruitful nonmetric scaling procedure (Kruskal, 1964a,b; Shepard, 1962a,b, 1963, 1966; see Carroll and Wish (Chapter 12) and Wish and Carroll (Chapter 13) of this volume), but they do not seem to have been pursued as a theory of recognition.

C. Choice Theory (1a–2)

Shipley (1960) generalized to various experimental designs some of the psychophysical models in Luce (1959); a general statement of these models was given in Luce (1963a); and they were modified to account for experimental data by Shipley (1965). Consider an $n = m$ experiment where response r_i corresponds to stimulus s_i. Assume there is a stimulus generalization function η_{ij} (not necessarily a probability measure) and a response bias function b_j such that

$$p(r_j|s_i) = \frac{\eta_{ij}b_j}{\sum_{k=1}^{n}\eta_{ik}b_k}.$$

The scale values, though not the probabilities, can be written in matrix form as

$$
\begin{bmatrix} & & \cdot & & \\ & & \cdot & & \\ & & \cdot & & \\ \cdots & \eta_{ij}b_j & \cdots & \\ & & \cdot & & \\ & & \cdot & & \\ & & \cdot & & \end{bmatrix} = \begin{bmatrix} & & \cdot & & \\ & & \cdot & & \\ & & \cdot & & \\ \cdots & \eta_{ij} & \cdots & \\ & & \cdot & & \\ & & \cdot & & \\ & & \cdot & & \end{bmatrix} \begin{bmatrix} b_1 & 0 & \cdots & 0 \\ 0 & b_2 & \cdots & 0 \\ & \cdot & & \\ & \cdot & & \\ & \cdot & & \\ 0 & 0 & \cdots & b_n \end{bmatrix}.
$$

Note that in the unbiased case, i.e., b_j is independent of j, this model predicts the CRR. To reduce the number of free parameters, it is assumed, as in Shepard's work, that $-\log \eta_{ij}$ acts like a distance (in particular, it is symmetric, i.e., $\eta_{ij} = \eta_{ji}$); if the stimuli have components (as when there are several listening intervals), the squared distances add like orthogonal components of an Euclidean space; and if the stimuli vary in only one dimension, distances are assumed to be additive. For complex stimuli, such as words, which account for much of the recognition data, none of these assumptions has much bite. Only by holding the stimuli fixed and manipulating the response bias by, say, varying the presentation probabilities, do the number of free parameters increase more slowly than the number of independent data. However Broadbent (1967) has shown that the word frequency effect can be predicted simply by assuming η_{ij} is related to the frequency of the word in the language, and that theories based on pure response bias, $b_i \neq b_j(\eta_{ij} = 1)$ are inadequate. This paper is criticized by Catlin (1969) and Nakatani (1970), but defended by Treisman (1971).

An experiment on lifted weights was reported by Shipley and Luce (1964). Both $n = 2$ and $n = 3$ data were collected and fit reasonably well by the choice models using the same stimulus parameters where appropriate.

Using two tones and noise, Shipley (1965) investigated 12 different YN and FC detection, recognition, and simultaneous detection-and-recognition experiments. She was led to postulate that in the mixed case, a two-stage process is involved in which recognition of the stimulus precedes a detection decision; and when only detection is required in the uncertain frequency experiment the subject behaves as if he made covert recognition responses and simply ignored them later. These ideas given an adequate account of her data which, so far, have not been analyzed in detail in terms of any other theory. However, these choice models are surely wrong because they predict symmetric ROC curves for both YN and 2AFC experiments, whereas empirically the former is usually asymmetric and the latter appears to be linear (Atkinson & Kinchla, 1965; E. F. Shipley's data in Norman 1964a).

See also the discussion of the uncertain frequency experiments in Section III,F on discriminal dispersion theory.

D. Confusion-Choice Recognition Theory (1b–2)

Nakatani (1968, 1972) proposed a theory in which the internal states are implicit responses that correspond to the possible responses. When stimulus s_i is presented, implicit response j occurs with probability a_{ij}. Thus, any subset T of the set $M = (1, 2, \ldots, m)$ of implicit responses can occur. The probability that T occurs, called an equivocation probability, is

$$\prod_{k \text{ in } T} a_{ik} \prod_{k \text{ in } M-T} (1 - a_{ik}).$$

Given that a nonempty set T occurs, the decision process is assumed to select one response from T; If $T = \varnothing$, then the process treats it as if $T = M$. It is postulated that there is a response bias vector $(b_1, b_2, \ldots, b_m)$ such that j in T is selected with probability $b_j / \sum_{k \text{ in } T} b_k$. Thus, summing over all possible sets T such that T is a subset of M and j is in T yields

$$p(r_j | s_i) = \sum_{T} \prod_{k \text{ in } T} a_{ik} \prod_{k \text{ in } M-T} (1 - a_{ik}) \left(b_j / \sum_{k \text{ in } T} b_k \right).$$

When $m = n$, the data suggest making the auxiliary assumption that the matrix A is symmetric, $a_{ij} = a_{ji}$. With this, there are $\frac{1}{2}n(n+1) + n - 1 = \frac{1}{2}n(n+3) - 1$ parameters, and so only for $n \geq 5$ do the number of independent probabilities exceed the number of parameters.

In his model, Nakatani views the probabilities a_{ij} as areas under the tails of normal distributions. By itself, this does not affect the fit to the data. However, in his 1971 paper, he used this as a way to estimate the similarity between the stimuli and responses and then used Kruskal's (1964a,b) nonmetric multidimensional scaling technique to locate stimuli and responses as points in a Euclidean space. If that space has k dimensions, this reduces the number of parameters to $(n - 2)k + 1$ stimulus ones (the arbitrariness of the origin and rotations of the space drops $2k - 1$) and $n - 1$ bias ones.

Considering word-confusion data, Nakatani (1968) had considerable success with his model. Using the special case where the matrix A has identical main diagonal entries and identical off-diagonal ones and no response bias, he accounted nicely for plots of the probability of a correct response versus the number n of words, with S/N ratio as a parameter, from data of Miller, Heise and Lichten (1951), Pollack (1959) and Rubenstein and Pollack (1963). Again, assuming no response bias, he gave as good an account as the CRR of the data in Clarke (1957) and Egan (1957a). Dorfman (1967) reported a series of 2×2 recognition experiments using four presentation probabilities and three tachistoscopic times. The key prediction of Nakatani's theory in this case is that, for each time, the data points should lie on a linear ROC curve. The data do not reject this, although a symmetric curve (as in the choice theory) appears equally adequate. In a study of his own, Nakatani used six nonsense syllables at two S/N levels and three presentation distributions. One A matrix and three b vectors were estimated and they gave a satisfactory account of the data. In a second experiment, he chose three pairs of words with little confusion between pairs and a great deal within. Presentation distributions were chosen so that, in one case, the absolute probability of a word remained about constant whereas its relative probability to its mate varied, and in the other the relative probability remained constant whereas the absolute one varied. The model predicts that articulation scores should change in the former case and not in the latter, and this was confirmed.

Using Kruskal's nonmetric multidimensional scaling technique, Nakatani (1971) analyzed confusion data for Munsell color chips (Shepard, 1958b) and for pure tones (Hodge & Pollack, 1962). The fits are impressive: The model accounts for 99.8% of the variance with 49 df and 99.2% with 30 df, respectively.

A direct confrontation of these models with the choice model, which with analogous assumptions has about the same number of parameters, has not been carried out.

E. Threshold Theory (1–2, 3)

Basically, all threshold models involve a discrete set of states, some probabilistic rule for their activation, and a response bias or a criterion response rule, or both. Many can be viewed as a discrete version of Thurstone's (1959) discriminal dispersion model (see Section III,F).

One body of literature, called neural quantum theory, is concerned with the shape of the distribution over states induced by the signal (Békésy, 1930; Stevens, Morgan, & Volkman, 1941; Corso, 1956); relevant data are discussed in Section IV,F. The other body of literature, much influenced by TSD, concerns the nature of the response criterion and the resulting ROC curve in the two-stimulus case (for a summary, see Luce, 1963a, Krantz, 1969, and Sections IV,A,D, and F).

The only attempt to use the theory for $n > 2$ was in connection with

Shipley's (1965) simultaneous detection-and-recognition data. Luce (1963a) pointed out that when one of two signals of different frequency was presented in a YN design and the subject was required to state which signal it was (independent of his detection response), there was no evidence of any residual recognition when he responded "no." Lindner (1968) carried out a systematic study in which the response bias was varied; his data suggested the opposite conclusion and rejected, at least, a two-state threshold model.

F. Discriminal Dispersion Theory (2–3)

The natural generalization of TSD to $n > 2$ was presented by Tanner (1956). Each signal relative to noise defines a likelihood ratio axis. These axes are thought of as directions in some multidimensional Euclidean space. Each signal is represented as a multinormal density in such a way that the likelihood ratio of one signal to another can be mapped to the straight line connecting the two signal points. Not only do the means and covariance matrices required to define the normal distributions introduce many parameters, but the response criteria of the $n = 2$ case generalize, even in the simplest generalization, to $\frac{1}{2}n(n - 1)$ likelihood ratio criteria. As a result of this multiplicity of free parameters, this model has not been seriously pursued, and no useful generalization of TSD has been proposed. This remains the gravest weakness of TSD.

Much earlier, the successive interval or categorical judgment generalization of Thurstone's (1959) discriminal dispersion model was proposed (see Torgerson, 1958). One continued to assume an abstract one-dimensional representation (definitely not likelihood ratio) of the stimuli in which each signal is described by a normal distribution, and the m responses are represented as a partition of the continuum into m intervals. This model may be suitable for acoustic signals that vary only in intensity, but it is doubtful for word-recognition studies. If the normal distributions are correlated, the model has $\frac{1}{2}n(n - 1) + n - 1 + n - 1 + m - 1 = \frac{1}{2}(n - 1)(n + 4) + m - 1$ free parameters. For references to the relevant literature see Torgerson (1958, p. 208) and Bock and Jones (1968, p. 213).

A careful, very general study of the discriminal dispersion model for both comparative and categorical judgments—called unidimensional strength theory—is given by Wicklegren (1968a).

A special dispersion model was used by Green and Birdsall (1964) to reanalyze the data of Miller *et al.* (1951). Essentially they assumed that the representation of a stimulus (word) is cross correlated with templates corresponding to the possible responses, that each correlation is a normally distributed random variable with unit variance and mean 0 except for the correct one, which has mean d. It is assumed that the response is determined by the largest of the correlations. It appeared that a single function related signal-to-noise ratio to d independent of the number of words on the list, except for the 1000 word list. The distinctive feature of this theory is that each stimulus is represented as a random point in an n-dimensional space, and the decision rule does not involve any free parameters.

A key model-free phenomenon of the YN design when either of two signals ($n = 3$, $m = 2$) may be presented is that an appreciable decrement in detectability results as compared with the single signal case (Gundy, 1961; Shipley, 1965; Swets, Shipley, McKey, & Green, 1959; Tanner & Norman, 1954; Tanner, Swets, & Green, 1956; Veniar, 1958). Tanner *et al.* (1956) suggested that the hearing mechanism acts like a single filter that has to be shifted from one frequency to another. Later Green (1958) proposed a multiple filter model. Some subjects seem in accord with the one model, others with the other model. Shipley (1960) pointed out that a single stage, covert, choice model admits two solutions, which correspond closely to the two filter models. Swets and Sewall (1961) argued that a decision between the perceptual and response explanations can be made by comparing performance with a presignal presentation cue identifying the signal (if any) to that with a postsignal presentation cue. If the phenomenon is perceptual, the precue should result in the same performance as for a single signal, whereas the postcue should leave the decrement unaffected; if it is a response matter, both cues should return the performance to the level of a single signal. Swets and Sewall interpreted their data as supporting the perceptual hypothesis; actually neither cue was very effective and the support to either theory is most marginal. Their conclusion is at variance with Pollack (1959) in another context. Shipley's (1965) later two-stage, recognition-then-detection model does not allow for this differential prediction.

Greenberg and Larkin (1968) and Greenberg (1969a,b) have explored a design in which the detectabilities of various probe signals are measured when they are introduced without prior warning to the subject who is expecting only a single signal frequency. Detection is best at the expected signal frequency and decreases systematically at frequencies different from it. They failed to observe any decrement in detection when either of two signals might be used on a YN trial, despite a highly asymmetric payoff matrix favoring one of the two signals (Larkin & Greenberg, 1970). Thus, they found no evidence for a "listening strategy." However, Penner (1970), using a 2AFC design with asymmetric reward over the various signal frequencies, found detection best at the most highly rewarded frequency. If all frequencies were equally rewarded, then detection was the same at all frequencies.

G. Counter Theory (3–3)

McGill (1967) and Siebert (1965) have proposed that the sensory system converts signal energy into a "neural" pulse train with a rate that increases with intensity. Moreover, as an idealization they assume that the process is Poisson, i.e., the times between successive pulses are independent and exponentially distributed. Kiang's (1965) data on periphal auditory fibers supports the independence assumption; however, refractoriness and equilibration make the full Poisson assumption a considerable idealization. Ultimately, the exponential assumption will probably have to be replaced by a more descriptive one, but the mathematical complications will be considerable and, in all likelihood, more precise assumptions will have to be simulated on a computer.

The basic decision process assumed in the FI design is that the pulses occurring during the observation interval are counted and this number is compared with a criterion (in YN design) or with another count (in 2AFC designs). Under the Poisson assumption, explicit expressions can be calculated for all the relevant probabilities and, in general, it provides a good account of the data (McGill, 1967; McGill & Goldberg, 1968). Because the sum of a number of identically distributed random variables is approximately normally distributed, the predictions of the counter models tend to be similar to those of TSD, but without requiring the likelihood interpretation.

A modification of this theory to FR designs is outlined in Section VI,D.

IV. OPERATING CHARACTERISTICS AND PSYCHOMETRIC FUNCTIONS FOR FIXED-INTERVAL DESIGNS WITH TWO STIMULI

As we have already noted, little has been done to compare one model against another for $n > 2$. For $n = 2$, the main comparison has been between discrete and continuous sensory–memory states—this distinction served as the first component of our classificatory scheme. The issue is, basically, whether a sensory threshold exists in any measurable form. Some investigators have attempted to assess this question by examining the shape of the ROC curve.

A. The Shape of the ROC Curve

Given the same decision process—usually, a response criterion one—different theories about the sensory process predict qualitative differences in the ROC curve [$p(Y|s)$ versus $P(Y|\varnothing)$ as the response criterion is varied]. Thus, one is led to collect such data. More often than not, the shape exhibited by the data is found largely in the eye of the beholder. Any data point estimates a point on the ROC curve with variability appearing in both dimensions, and even binomial variability, which is at best a lower bound on experimental variability, is sufficient to obscure somewhat the shape of any empirically determined curve (see Green & Swets, 1966, pp. 402–403). The only sure generalization from these earlier studies is that the high threshold model is definitely wrong (Swets, 1961; Tanner & Swets, 1954). A large amount of data appear to be fit adequately by the two straight-line segments of low threshold theory, and there are also considerable data that appear to be better fit by continuous curves. Krantz (1969) has provided a careful critique of the attempts to discriminate these hypotheses.

For data consistent with the Gaussian assumptions of TSD, the slope of the ROC curve on double probability paper is often interpreted as the ratio of the noise to the signal-plus-noise standard deviations. Wickelgren (1968b) and Nachmias (1968) have emphasized that this slope is also affected by criterion variability. Shipley (1970) found an apparent increase in criterion variance when the subject was asked to increase the number of response criteria. Markowitz and Swets (1967), who found systematic differences in the shape of binary and rating ROC curves (see Section IV,D) although the detection indices ($d's$) were nearly the same, suggested that the slope is related to the a priori probability of the signal's occurrence. Schulman and Greenberg (1970) found similar effects.

One safe generalization is that one seldom obtains data with a slope less than one (an exception being Shipley, 1970).* Thus, either the signal distribution is seldom less variable than the noise distribution or the criterion variability is so large compared with the variance of the sensory distributions that such changes cannot be observed.

B. Fitting a Theoretical ROC Curve to Data Points

A persistent problem in evaluating the shape of the ROC curve is the estimation of parameters. Recent work has improved this somewhat.

---

* Dr. Angus Craig (personal communication, 1974) has reanalyzed vigilance data reported by Colquhoun and Baddeley (1967) and by Colquhoun, Blake, and Edwards (1968) and has found that somewhat more than half of the individual ROC curves have slopes greater than one. Of course, the procedure for these experiments is somewhat different from the usual YN one, from which we made our "safe" generalization; in particular, the probability of a signal recurring is low and the subject does not make a response of no signal.

When we have only two data points, we can reformulate the question as a test of the following null hypothesis: Given a particular theory, the two points lie on the same theoretical curve. Gourevitch and Galanter (1967) gave a parametric analysis for large samples from normal distributions with equal variances. They presented an approximate estimate for the asymptotic variance of d'. Smith (1969) provided an approximate estimate for the variance of the criterion β associated with a single data point.

With three or more data points, the null hypothesis approach is awkward and is replaced by attempts to estimate the best fitting member of some family of ROC curves and to provide a measure of goodness of fit. The most general case so far studied (Abrahamson & Levitt, 1969) is the location-scale family where, for some probability density g, the noise and signal densities are given by

$$g_\varnothing(x) = \frac{1}{\sigma^g}g\left(\frac{x}{\sigma}\right) \quad \text{and} \quad g_s(x) = \frac{1}{\sigma_s}g\left(\frac{x-d}{\sigma_s}\right).$$

The hit and false alarm probabilities are given by

$$p_H(\beta) = p(Y|s) = \int_\beta^\infty g_s(x)\,dx \quad \text{and} \quad p_F(\beta) = P(Y/\varnothing) = \int_\beta^\infty g_\varnothing(x)\,dx.$$

If G is the distribution function of g and if we define

$$\xi = G^{-1}(1 - p_F) \quad \text{and} \quad \eta = G^{-1}(1 - p_H),$$

then the (G-transformed) ROC curve is given by the linear relation

$$\xi = (\sigma_s/\sigma)\eta + d.$$

The problem is to estimate σ_s/σ and d. This is not a conventional linear regression because both ξ and η are estimated, and the joint distribution varies with (ξ, η). Madansky (1959) has given one general approximate treatment of such problems. Within the context of YN and rating-scale designs, Abrahamson and Levitt (1969) used numerical iteration to solve the resulting maximum likelihood (ML) equations. By Monte Carlo methods, they showed that Madansky's approximation is virtually identical to the ML method. They defined a goodness-of-fit statistic which is, asymptotically, related to a χ^2 variable. These results generalize earlier ones for the logistic and normal distributions applied to YN and rating methods (Ogilvie & Creelman, 1968; Dorfman & Alf, 1968, 1969; the latter is a specialization of Schonemann & Tucker's 1967 analysis of the Thurstonian model for successive intervals with unequal variances).

Various threshold models (Luce, 1963b; Norman, 1963, 1964a; Krantz, 1969) suggest that the ROC curve may be composed of several linear pieces. No statistical treatment has been given for these cases. The heart of the difficulty is in deciding which data points belong with each linear piece.

C. Sampling Variability of the Area under the ROC Curve

Green (1964; Green & Swets, 1966, p. 47) showed that the area under the YN ROC curve (as a proportion A of the unit square) equals the percentage of correct responses in the unbiased 2AFC model, and that this result is independent of the form of the assumed distributions. Pollack and Norman (1964) have provided a reasonable scheme for estimating A given only a single point on the ROC curve; see also Norman (1964b). Pollack, Norman, and Galanter (1964) have illustrated its use in a recognition memory experiment. Because of the nonparametric (although not model-free) character of Green's result, much interest is shown in A as a general unidimensional measure of sensitivity. Therefore, it is important to know something about its sampling variability. Green and Moses (1966) assumed a binomial sampling distribution, in which case the variance is $A(1 - A)/N$. This is not obviously true, and no one has yet worked out the actual sampling distribution for, say, the ML member of a location-scale family or even of a logistic or normal family. The only detailed study (Pollack & Hsieh, 1969) is a Monte Carlo exploration of A under step functions fitted to "data" points generated from normal, uniform, and exponential families. The relation between A and its standard deviation is roughly independent of the family and is slightly less than the binomial standard deviation. Among other things, they showed that correlations in the samples had little effect on this relationship.

D. Rating Operating Characteristics

Egan, Schulman, and Greenberg (1959) were the first to compare the operating characteristics determined from binary (YN) responses and ratings responses in which the subject indicated his confidence about the presence of the signal by choosing among a limited ($\sim$6) number of categories. They found good agreement between the two methods, and their results were replicated by Emmerich (1968). Markowitz and Swets (1967), however, found systematic differences between the methods as the a priori probability of the signals was varied.

Impatient with the slow accumulation of information in both of these methods, Watson, Rilling, and Bourbon (1964) pioneered the use of the rating method with a very large number of response categories. Using an auditory single-interval detection design in which the signal was a pure tone partially masked by noise, they asked subjects to position a movable rod to indicate their degree of confidence about the signal's presence. The possible positions of the rod were categorized into 31 distinct "ratings," and the operating characteristics produced by the procedure have been widely cited. The curves are remarkably smooth (as they must be, since they are cumulative in character) and the slope appears to change continuously.

Unfortunately, these plots have tended to be somewhat overinterpreted in attempts to decide whether the internal sensory states are continuous or discrete. The crux of the problem is that specific assumptions about the response process must be made in order to draw unambiguous inferences about the sensory mechanism from the data. The central issue is the assumption one makes about the decision or response process, in particular about the mapping relating responses to the internal sensory states.

It is generally admitted that the same internal state may lead to different responses—in effect, this is an assumption that some generalization takes place. There is considerable disagreement about the extent of this generalization. Clearly, the more responses that a single sensory state elicits, the less certain are the inferences made from responses to internal states. Sensory psychologists have tended to assume that extreme rating responses indicate, unambiguously, extreme detection states, whereas only the medium rating responses may be caused by either sensory state.

If such a view is adopted, a two-state threshold model predicts a rating operating characteristic that begins and ends with straight-line segments and is curved only in the middle portion, where medium ratings are encountered. This mapping between detection states and responses is clearly what Watson et al. (1964) had in mind in their original paper, and Nachmias and Steinman (1963) and Green and Moses (1966) assumed it explicitly. Broadbent (1966) and Larkin (1965) challenged this assumption, and the alternative hypothesis was defended by Wickelgren (1968b). Krantz (1969) has presented the most complete statement of the alternative view.

The key assumption of that alternative view is, of course, that any sensory state can lead to any response. The rationale for this position is simple and compelling. Suppose an observer has, in fact, only two sensory states, but that other, nonsensory, internal states affect his disposition toward a certain response. Then these other internal states can bias the rating responses and produce high confidence responses, even when the signal is undetected, or low ones when it is detected. So long as these other variables are partially independent of the sensory states, any sensory state may, with some probability, elicit one of the possible responses. We might think of these nonsensory variables as attentional factors.

If R_i, $i = 1, \ldots, r$, denote the possible ratings and D and $\bar{D}$ the two states, we let $\sigma_D(i) = p(R_i|D)$ and $\sigma_{\bar{D}}(i) = p(R_i|\bar{D})$. Let us make the following two assumptions about these parameters. First, they are sto-chastic, i.e., $\sigma_D(i)$, $\sigma_{\bar{D}}(i) \geq 0$ and $\sum_i \sigma_D(i) = \sum \sigma_{\bar{D}}(i) = 1$. Second, $\sigma_D(i)/$ $\sigma_D(i)$ is nonincreasing as i moves from 1 to r, i.e., there is more likelihood that a high rating response is chosen in the presence of a detect state than a nondetect state. Thus the effect of these nonsensory states coupled with only two sensory states determines the relation between the ratio $\sigma_D(i)/$ $\sigma_{\bar{D}}(i)$ and the response emitted.

From these assumptions and letting $q(s) = p(D|s)$ and $q(\varnothing) = p(D|\varnothing)$, the kth point on the ROC has coordinates

$$P(R \leq k|s) = q(s) \sum_i \sigma_D(i) + [1 - q(s)] \sum_i \sigma_{\bar{D}}(i)$$

$$= \sum_i \sigma_{\bar{D}}(i) + q(s) \sum_i [\sigma_D(i) - \sigma_{\bar{D}}(i)];$$

$$P(R \leq k|\varnothing) = q(\varnothing) \sum_i \sigma_D(i) + [1 - q(\varnothing)] \sum_i \sigma_{\bar{D}}(i)$$

$$= \sum_i \sigma_{\bar{D}}(i) + q(\varnothing) \sum_i [\sigma_D(i) - \sigma_{\bar{D}}(i)].$$

Thus the kth point can be considered as the sum of two vectors, lying along the major diagonal one with coordinates $(\sum_i \sigma_{\bar{D}}(i), \sum_i \sigma_{\bar{D}}(i))$ and the other with coordinates $[q(s) \sum_i [\sigma_D(i) - \sigma_{\bar{D}}(i)], q(\varnothing) \sum_i [\sigma_D(i) - \sigma_{\bar{D}}(i)]]$. The term $\sum_i [\sigma_D(i) - \sigma_{\bar{D}}(i)]$ is a scaler which ranges between 0 and 1 (because of the stochastic assumptions).

Observe that the slope between successive points is simply

$$\frac{1 + q(s)\{[\sigma_D(i)/\sigma_{\bar{D}}(i)] - 1\}}{1 + q(\varnothing)\{[\sigma_D(i)/\sigma_{\bar{D}}(i)] - 1\}},$$

and so it is monotonic decreasing because $\sigma_D(i)/\sigma_{\bar{D}}(i)$ never increases. The limiting slope is $[1 - q(s)]/[1 - q(\varnothing)]$.

There is no intention of fitting data using all of these parameters, but it does suggest a plausible account of how a two-state theory can predict the smooth, apparently continuous, data of rating experiments. Krantz's assumptions (especially as expressed here) are, in effect, a multistate theory if one considers the two sensory states and the several nonsensory states needed to provide the different values for the ratio $\sigma_D(i)/\sigma_{\bar{D}}(i)$.

There is, in fact, little difference between the way continuous theory and multistate theory handle the comparison between YN and rating data. Note that if one starts by assuming two equal variance Gaussian distribu-tions and a number of fixed response criteria, then replacing D by s and $\bar{D}$ by $\varnothing$ means that $\sigma_D(i) = p(R_i|s)$ and $\sigma_{\bar{D}}(i) = p(R_i|\varnothing)$. The parame-ters are clearly stochastic and the assumption that $\sigma_D(i)/\sigma_{\bar{D}}(i) =$

$p(R_i|s)/p(R_i|\varnothing)$ is nonincreasing follows simply from the likelihood ratio being monotonic in the equal variance Gaussian case. About the only observation damaging to either theory would be rating operating characteristics that lie above (i.e., include more area) than the YN ROC curves.

E. Latency Operating Characteristics

Another recent development has been the attempt to use latency measures as a means of determining the observer's confidence in his response, and from these data to construct curves claimed to be analogous to the rating operating characteristics. In this method, the subject is seldom informed that his response time is being measured, and no emphasis on speed is ever given—latencies greater than 1 sec are common. Moreover, the results of these experiments are not used, as are the reaction-time data discussed in Section VI,E, to make inferences concerning stochastic delays within the sensory processing. Rather, the idea is that latency of a response is an index of the confidence of the subject concerning his response. The basic argument, as expressed by Norman and Wickelgren (1969), is that if the response is quick, then the subject is probably sure; if it is slow, he is probably uncertain.

Consider a simple YN task of the type described earlier. Associated with each cell of the response matrix is a corresponding latency distribution. For example, let l_{sY} be the latency associated with a "yes" response given that the signal was present on that trial. Similarly, $l_{\varnothing Y}$ is the latency associated with a false alarm, $l_{\varnothing N}$ the latency of a correct rejection, and l_{sN} the latency of a false "no." Note that there is no obvious dependency among the latencies as there was among the probabilities in the stimulus–response matrix. Over many trials, the four different latency distributions can be estimated. Two treatments of these data have been suggested, one by Carterette, Friedman, and Cosmides (1965) (CFC) and the other by Norman and Wickelgren (1969) (NW). A more recent example of such curves is in Katz (1970). Because they are different, yet related, and because the techniques are new, we explain both in some detail.

The CFC method constructs two curves from the data. One is constructed from the latencies of the "yes" responses by passing a temporal criterion through the two Y distributions:

$$y_1(k) = P(l_{sY} \geq k) \cong N(l_{sY} \geq k)/N_{sY}, \qquad 0 \leq k < \infty;$$
$$x_1(k) = P(l_{\varnothing Y} \geq k) \cong N(l_{\varnothing Y} \geq k)/N_{\varnothing Y}, \qquad 0 \leq k < \infty;$$

where $N(l_{sY} \geq k)$ is the number of latencies equal to or exceeding k and N_{sY} is the total number of such latencies. Thus, both y and x range from

0 to 1 and the curve is monotonic increasing. There is no mathematical necessity that $y > x$ and, in fact, some empirical data have shown the reverse order over the entire range of k.

Another curve is constructed in an analogous fashion from the negative responses, namely,

$$y_2(k) = P(l_{\varnothing N} > k) \cong N(l_{\varnothing N} \geq k)/N_{\varnothing N}, \qquad 0 \leq k < \infty;$$
$$x_2(k) = P(l_{sN} > k) \cong N(l_{sN} \geq k)/N_{sN}, \qquad 0 \leq k < \infty.$$

In the NW scheme, these two curves are composed into a single graph by rescaling the two CFC curves as follows:

$$\beta_1(k) = P(l_{sY} \geq k)p(Y|s) = y_1(k)p(Y|s)$$

versus

$$\alpha_1(k) = P(l_{\varnothing Y} \geq k)p(Y|n) = x_1(k)p(Y|s)$$

and

$$\beta_2(c) = p(Y|s) + [1 - p(Y|s)]P(l_{nY} \geq c)$$
$$= p(Y|s) + [1 - p(Y|s)]y_2(c)$$

versus

$$\alpha_2(c) = p(Y|n) + [1 - p(Y|n)]P(l_{nN} \geq c)$$
$$= p(Y|n) + [1 - p(Y|n)]x_2(c).$$

Although the two curves are related and are designed to analyze similar kinds of data, neither has any great theoretical rationale. They are both simply ways of presenting data and it is as pointless to argue whether one treatment is superior to the other as it is to argue that the median is a better measure of central tendency than the mean. Either curve may be useful in certain circumstances. It is clear that theoretical work is needed to reveal their exact relation to other, more traditional ROC curves. On the face of it, there is no apparent relation.

F. Psychometric Functions

By a "psychometric function" we mean a plot of some measure of detectability against physical signal intensity, $I(s)$. The examination of such functions, as a source of information about the nature of the sensory system, has a long and venerable history (Boring, 1942). A popular approach is to deduce the shape of the function from a consideration of physical fluctuations of the stimulus. In these theories the observer is treated as having either no threshold or one that is small compared with the fluctuations in the stimulus. The physical quantum theory in vision (Hecht, Schlaer, & Pirenne, 1942; Cornsweet, 1970) or the "ideal" detector theories in audition (Green & McGill, 1970; Green & Swets, 1966; Jeffress, 1964; Pfafflin & Mathews, 1962) are examples of this approach.

We will not consider this approach further at this time, but rather we will emphasize that potentially the psychometric function can be used to try to determine whether or not the observer possesses a threshold and to estimate its size. The problem is what dependent variable one should use in determining the detectability of the signal. The classic one is $p(Y|s)$. Since TSD and our awareness of ROC curves, there has been a temptation to plot d' versus signal-to-noise ratio, especially since a special case of TSD predicts that d' is proportional to $(E/N_0)^{1/2}$. The objection to the first measure is that it is highly affected by the subject's location on the ROC curve and that location may very well not be independent of $I(s)$. The objection to the latter measure is that it is special to a particular theory.

An alternative proposal is to use A, the area under the YN ROC curve, which obviously is independent of response criterion and which, as was already noted, is equal in a broad class of models to the percentage correct $p(C)$ in the (symmetric) 2AFC design. Closely related is the proposal to use

$$\Delta = p(1|\langle s, \varnothing \rangle) - p(1|\langle \varnothing, s \rangle),$$

which has the following advantage. If the presentation probabilities are equal in the 2AFC design, $\Delta = 2p(C) - 1 = 2A - 1$, and if they are not equal, all of the threshold theories predict that Δ should be independent of the response bias or criterion (which is equivalent to saying that the 2AFC ROC curve is a straight line with slope 1). The surprising fact is that even though the advantages of using $p(C) = A$ have been known since at least 1964 and of Δ since 1963, we do not know of any plots of these functions against signal intensity.

It was early recognized that some appropriate psychometric function should be able to decide between a threshold and a continuous theory. In particular, as Krantz (1969) later emphasized, such a test is best made at low signal levels, where threshold theories imply that there is no detection whatsoever. In practice, the attempts to see this (as well as other features expected in the psychometric function) have been based upon plots of $p(Y|s)$ versus $I(s)$ for pure tones, with no artificial noise in the background, and for light flashes. Békésy (1930) and later Stevens, Morgan, and Volkmann (1941) reported such functions as favoring a particular threshold theory known as neural quantum theory. Blackwell (1963) drew the opposite conclusion for light. A survey article by Corso (1956), summarizing many studies, was inconclusive. Luce (1963b) pointed out that the ROC literature suggests that there can be serious and complex biasing of such functions; Larkin and Norman (1964) and Norman (1963) demonstrated this empirically. These studies made clear that threshold theories could account for a wide range of shapes of psychometric functions arising from YN designs, and so these functions could not possibly decide between the two classes of theories. The conclusion does not, however, apply to Δ, and so there is much to recommend a careful 2AFC study in which Δ is determined as a function of $I(s)$.

G. Efficient Estimates of Single Psychometric Points

With the advent of sequential analyses in statistics (Wald, 1947; Wetherill, 1966), the early introduction of sequential or tracking methods into psychophysics (Békésy, 1947) and the widespread availability of digital computers for on-line control of psychophysical experiments, adaptive control of stimulus presentation schedules has become increasingly common. The goal is a procedure to estimate the physical stimulus required to achieve a preassigned response probability. The procedure is to be efficient (not necessarily optimal), not too complex, not too biased, and robust (insensitive to the exact underlying model). The initially widely used method of limits has come under severe theoretical criticism (Brown & Cane, 1959; Herrick, 1967, 1969, 1970; Pollack, 1968), and it has been largely replaced by one or another variant of the up-and-down (or staircase) method. The original method, apparently due to Békésy (1947) and Dixon and Mood (1948), was designed to use fixed step size to ascertain the 50% point on a distribution function (Brownlee, Hodges, & Rosenblatt, 1953; Cornsweet, 1962; Wetherill, 1963; Wetherill & Levitt, 1965; Wetherill, Chen, & Vasudeva, 1966). Variable step size was early proposed and studied (Chung, 1954; Robbins & Munro, 1951) and is now commonly used. Cornsweet (1962) and Smith (1961) suggested that by randomly interleaving two up-and-down procedures the subject will not detect the strategy of presentation, and Levitt (1968) suggested a nonrandom interleaving to test for the existence of sequential dependencies. To estimate points other than 50% on a distribution function, transformed up-and-down methods have been proposed (Campbell, 1963; Cardozo, 1966; Heinemann, 1961; Levitt & Bock, 1967; Levitt & Treisman, 1969; Wetherill & Levitt, 1965; Zwislocki, Maire, Feldman, & Rubin, 1958).

Applications of these methods include, among other studies, Adler and Dalland (1959); Békésy (1947); Blough (1955, 1958); Blough and Schrier (1963); Elliott, Frazier, and Riach (1962); Gourevitch, Hack, and Hawkins (1960); Levitt (1968); Levitt and Rabiner (1967); Symmes (1962); and Zwislocki et al. (1958).

When on-line computer control is available, much more complicated adaptive procedures can be entertained: Hall (1968) suggested placing the next signal at the current ML estimate, and Smith (1966) proposed a strategy that maximizes the information gained on each trial. A somewhat different adaptive procedure, based on the concepts of sequential testing, is Taylor and Creelman's (1967) PEST procedure, for which a computer program is available.

For an excellent general survey of these methods see Levitt (undated, but not earlier than 1969), and for a complementary survey of their use in animal psychophysics see Blough (1966).

V. NONSTATIONARY RESPONSE PROCESSES

Differences in assumptions about the nature of the sensory–memory process and the resulting internal representation of the stimulus has been a major focus of the previous section and will be taken up again in Section VI. Whereas the impact of the response process on the observed behavior is generally acknowledged, it is often treated as a necessary evil—something that merely clouds our view of the sensory systems. Others find the decision processes inherently interesting. Over the past 15 years a number of studies have attempted to clarify their nature and to develop an organized theory for them comparable in scope to those of the sensory processes.

The corresponding empirical investigations have centered around sequential dependencies and the effect of stimulus presentation probability on the hit and false-alarm rate. The latter is closely related to questions about ROC curves. The emphasis on sequential effects is easily understood. With only one exception (Atkinson, 1963), all theories assume that the sensory processes are statistically stationary; thus, any evidence of nonstationary behavior is interpreted as trial-by-trial changes in the decision–response process. The emphasis on how the response criterion is affected by a priori probability was stimulated in part by the glaring failure in both TSD and threshold models of the postulate that the criterion is set so as to maximize the expected payoff.

Despite the rapid development of response theories, a number of empirical factors are still not completely understood. We attempt to summarize the better-established empirical generalizations. Often, some of the earlier studies used conditions that, in retrospect, were far from optimum and hence the effects demonstrated in these studies are not impressive. It is to be hoped that the bootstrap phase is nearly over and that future work, utilizing more judicious experimental conditions, will obtain more sizable effects.

A. Studies of Sequential Effects

Although judgments in psychophysical tasks are often treated as if they arise from a Bernoulli process, it has long been known that this is, at best, an idealization. Preston (1936a,b) clearly established response dependencies in psychophysical data, and a number of later papers have repeated his basic finding. Senders and Soward (1952) present a good history of these studies as well as some data of their own. In the early 1950s, a number of papers on this topic were published, reporting studies that used mainly visual detection tasks. Verplanck, Collier, and Cotton (1952) reported a tendency to repeat the last response. Correlations among the responses extended over a period of about 1 min in their study. Similar effects were also reported by Verplanck, Cotton, and Collier (1953) and Howarth and Bulmer (1956). Sequential dependencies using auditory detection were also demonstrated by Day (1956), Shipley (1961) and Speeth and Mathews (1961). Day also showed that the size of the sequential effect diminishes as a function of the length of the interstimulus interval. Since about 1960, a number of studies have investigated various determinants of sequential effects and have contrasted experimental results with theoretical models of the response process.

Sequential dependencies arise naturally in models that postulate a decision criterion that is updated from trial to trial. Among the models of this type are those of Atkinson (1963), Atkinson, Carterette, and Kinchla (1962), Dorfman and Biderman (1971), Kac (1962), Luce (1963b, 1964), Bush, Luce, and Rose (1964), Norman (1962, 1964a), and Schoeffler (1965). The advantage of these models over purely empirical estimates of the sequential probability is that they require much less data in order to estimate the magnitude of the effect.

B. Size of the Sequential Effects

Stating the size of a sequential effect is still largely a subjective matter. There simply is no standard way to record the results or for assessing the magnitude of the effects. The null hypothesis is that the occurrence of some response is a Bernoulli process with an unknown probability p. By computing various conditional probabilities, one may show that the occurrence of some response deviates significantly from the value p. A subjective element arises both in determining how large a deviation one believes is really important and in evaluating how much of the past history is needed in order to achieve the given deviation. For example, if the overall probability of a "yes" response is .5, and the conditional probability of a "yes" response given a previous "yes" response is .6, then clearly a fairly interesting sequential dependency has been uncovered. On the other hand, if one needs a sequence of five or six previous responses in order to achieve deviations of 10% from the overall mean, then because such sequences occur so infrequently, the deviation is less important. No one has yet suggested a method for combining the size of the deviation and the length of the conditioning sequence into a single measure. Thus, it is frequently impossible to compare the magnitudes of the sequential effects in two different experiments, despite the fact that the authors used the same number of responses and conditionalized on very similar events.

C. Generalizations about Sequential Dependencies

Although the preceding remarks make clear why it is difficult to compare different studies, we nonetheless offer the following generalizations concerning response dependencies. Each conclusion is stated in terms of a single variable because there have been very few studies that provide information about potential interactions among variables. Sequential effects are as follows:

1. small in simple auditory detection situations (Atkinson, 1963; Atkinson & Kinchla, 1965; Carterette, Friedman, & Wyman, 1966; Friedman, Carterette, Nakatani, & Ahumada, 1968a,b);

2. possibly large in simple visual detection situations (Kinchla, 1964); however, the design of this study may mean it was really a probability prediction rather than a detection design, and it is well known that sequential effects are large in probability prediction designs;

3. relatively large in recognition situations (at least of intensity) (Kinchla, 1966; Tanner, Haller, & Atkinson, 1967; Tanner, Rauk, & Atkinson,1970);

4. smaller when feedback is given then when it is not (Atkinson & Kinchla, 1965; Kinchla, 1966; Tanner, Haller, & Atkinson, 1967; Tanner, Rauk, & Atkinson, 1970).

Based in part on these generalizations, Tanner, Rauk, and Atkinson (1970) have attempted to state a fairly complete model dealing with these various factors. The following summary illustrates the general nature of models in this area. Given a stimulus presentation, the observer is assumed to compare it with whatever standard is available to him. For a sine wave in noise, the noise itself plays the role of the standard. In this case, very little memory is involved in the decision making, and, hence, the sequential effects are small. In experiments in which the task is to recognize the more intense of two 1000-Hz tones, the basic decision process is treated as a comparison of the stimulus presentation with a memory trace, which is influenced by the past presentations and so changes from trial to trial. The observer's response is assumed to result from a weighted combination of two tendencies: One is to repeat the response he made on the previous trial and the other is to report the signal labeled correct by the feedback that occurred on the preceding trial. These tendencies are combined according to a linear weight. If there is no feedback, the tendency to repeat the previous response is given all of the weight. Thus the model can account for the smaller sequential effects observed with feedback.

This model exhibits several interesting effects. One is sequential dependencies (because the pattern of previous stimuli and responses influence the present decision). A second is a very interesting prediction about the effect of presentation probabilities on the response probabilities, a topic we take up in the next section. A third implication of this general view concerns the role played by a standard in a psychophysical judgment task. Although relatively large sequential effects have been found in the intensive discrimination task, Parducci and Sandusky (1970) report relatively small ones in an experiment having, as an explicit standard, a constant intensity signal preceding each trial. The view of memory introduced by Tanner *et al.* is reminiscent of adaptation level theory, Helson (1964), a similarity which has been pursued in papers by Parducci and Marshall (1962) and Parducci and Sandusky (1965).

D. The Effect of a Priori Probability on Response Bias

As we noted previously, the original impetus for many of the adaptive models of response criteria was the attempt to specify how the subject's response changes as a function of values and costs and the a priori probability of the stimulus alternatives. One of the early dramatic findings was that the change in the criterion as a function of a priori probability could be opposite to that predicted by the expected-value model. Kinchla (1966) and Tanner *et al.* (1967) reported data in which the observer decreased his false-alarm rate when the a priori probability of the signal was increased. This finding is at odds with considerable previous data obtained in simple detection experiments. The crucial difference appears to be whether or not the subject is given feedback and his degree of experience in these experiments. Naive subjects with no feedback invariably reduce their false-alarm rates as the signal probability is increased. With feedback, the opposite tendency is observed (Tanner *et al.*, 1967).

Although this finding is accounted for by the general model proposed by Tanner *et al.*, another quite simple explanation of it can be given. Suppose that the observer is trying to maintain an equal number of yes and no responses in the experimental situation. A tendency to equalize the frequency of all the available responses is a well-known property of many judgment tasks, as was first demonstrated by Arons and Irwin (1932). If one attempts to achieve this goal by dividing a sensory scale in such a way that half the responses will be yes and the other half no, then the criterion must be increased when the signal is presented more frequently (since more drawings are presented from the signal distribution) and so the false-alarm rate will decrease. Note that this view is consistent with a stationary observer, one whose response dependencies do not change from trial to trial. For more complete discussions of the matching hypothesis to account for the change in the hit and false-alarm rate caused by altering the a priori probabilities, see Creelman and Donaldson (1968), Dorfman (1969), Parks (1966), and Thomas and Legge (1970).

Tanner *et al.* argued that both the change in false-alarm rate with a priori probability and the large sequential effects support their view that a memory process is heavily involved in these kinds of tasks. Parducci and Sandusky (1970), however, exhibit this change in false-alarm rate with a priori probability without finding any sequential effects. Thus, presumably, the presence of the standard in the Parducci and Sandusky experiment minimizes the changes in criterion on a trial by trial basis, but nonetheless the criterion did change systematically in response to changes in a priori probability. Further work is needed to clarify this general area. Unfortunately, the next series of studies must concentrate on various interactions among the major variables.

VI. THEORIES FOR FREE RESPONSE DATA

Although we do not wish to contend that the setting for all laboratory measurements must simulate natural ones, one should realize that the study of detection and discrimination by means of fixed interval (FI) designs is highly artificial. Most signals in nature occur at unpredictable times, and one is seldom quizzed in an interval just following a potential signal about whether or not one seemed to be present. The reason for using a FI procedure is that it allows one to avoid several thorny questions concerning the temporal properties of the detection process. It is exactly these questions that one must face in trying to extend the analysis of a detection or discrimination mechanism to more practical and realistic situations.

A. A Methodological Note

In all free response (FR) experiments, an attempt is made to schedule signal presentations so that the subject is unable to predict their arrival.

The complete achievement of this goal is, perhaps, more subtle than is often realized. In any event, the schedules employed in some of the studies do not achieve the desired ends and, in fact, should strongly reinforce behavior that is highly nonuniform over time. Because this problem has not been discussed explicitly in many of the papers and because it is important, the following remarks seem in order.

Probably because of ease of programming, the most common presentation schedule is the discrete approximation to the rectangular (uniform) distribution over a fixed interval. For example, with an interval of 100 sec, signals might be presented with equal probability at each of the second marks of the 100 sec after the preceding signal. The mean time to the next signal is approximately 50 sec, and there is considerable randomness in the time of presentation. The difficulty with this schedule is that the conditional density of the signal is not uniform throughout the interval: Given that it has failed to occur up to some point in time, the probability that it will occur in the next second is a monotonic increasing function of the duration of the wait. In particular, the probability that it will occur in the first interval is $1/100$, whereas the probability that it will occur in the last interval, given that it has not occurred in any of the previous ones, is 100 times as great. The potential bias that can result from this depends upon the degree to which the subject can estimate when the last signal occurred, and so it will interact with signal level. Even if no bias is evident at low intensities, this may not be true for higher intensities. It is clear that, in some circumstances, subjects make use of this information and, in fact, in a reaction time experiment by Nickerson (1967), the number of false anticipations increased monotonically with the wait from the warning light.

To avoid this problem and so the possibility of encouraging subjects to adopt nonhomogeneous response strategies, one should use the correct temporal analogue to uniform uncertainty, namely the Poisson process in which the times between successive events are independent and have a common exponential distribution. A crucial property of this distribution is the fact that the probability of an event occurring in the next instant in time is independent of how long it has been since the last event. Put another way, the conditional density of a signal occurring is constant. Experimentally, the major difficulty in using this distribution is that successive events are often quite close together in time, and so it becomes difficult to distinguish which event caused a later response (see Luce & Green, 1970). With a low signal rate, this is rarely a problem, and so it is unfortunate that the exponential schedule (or its discrete analogue, the geometric distribution) is seldom used in vigilance tasks, for the bias introduced by the uniform distribution may be considerable.

B. Temporal Partitioning

Although FI designs are special cases of FR ones, most analyses have attempted to reduce FR data to FI models. In practice, the motivation has been largely expediency, not a belief that the organism actually quantizes time and so is a kind of sample data system. If the latter were actually true and if we could divide time so as to agree with the natural quanta, then it would be perfectly reasonable to treat the FR situation as a sequence of yes–no experiments. Although the hypothesis that organisms quantize time has existed for some time (e.g., Stroud, 1955; and White, 1963), Kristofferson (1965, 1966, 1967a,b, 1969) is the only contemporary psychophysicist who argues seriously for it. His evidence consists of the numerical agreement of three parameters estimated from successive discrimination and two reaction experiments. From these data, he estimates the time quantum to be about 50 msec, which it should be noted is about half the alpha rhythm period. Although both of the present authors are skeptical, as are others (for example, Carterette, 1969), it is important to realize how crucial this unresolved point is for finding the appropriate generalization of present detection models.

The simplest practical procedure for partitioning time, one often followed in the analysis of vigilance data and first adopted by Broadbent and Gregory (1963) and Mackworth and Taylor (1963), divides time into nonoverlapping intervals of equal duration, usually about 1 sec, although other durations have been used both by the original authors and by subsequent investigators. They estimate the hit probability as the relative frequency of positive responses in the interval following the signal and estimate the false-alarm probability as the relative frequency of positive responses in all other intervals. The interval is chosen to be sufficiently large so that even the slowest responses are not misclassified as false alarms. Because the density of false alarms is usually quite low, there is little chance of making the opposite misclassification. These probabilities are then used in a TSD yes–no analysis to estimate d' and β.

Egan, Greenberg, and Shulman (1961) and Watson and Nichols (1966) carried out a somewhat more subtle analysis. In their experiments the number of false positive responses was at least an order of magnitude higher than usually is encountered in vigilance experiments; hence, the problem of misclassifying false alarms as hits becomes much more serious, and so requires more care. They constructed empirical histograms showing the frequency of response following the onset of a signal. Naturally, there is a high response rate immediately following signal onset; this is especially so with loud signals. By 1 or 2 sec after the signal interval, this rate returns to a fairly stable value, which they treated as a quantity similar to the false-alarm probability in the FI design. Their analogue of the hit probability in the FI design is the proportion of responses occurring between the signal onset and the return to the base rate. They then proceeded as follows: Suppose the observer "divides time into a succession of subjective intervals, each of duration T_σ. It will be considered that each of these subjective intervals implicitly defines a trial for the listener, and that he makes a decision after each interval." Obviously the observed rate is then proportional to the probability of each response, the constant of proportionality being T_σ. The ROC data generalized by varying the subject's criterion yields an estimate of d' which is close to the FI one, e.g., 1.29 and 1.55. Egan *et al.* pointed out two major defects with this procedure. As the subject relaxes his criterion, the data suggest an apparent increase in the detection index, and the method does not lead to an independent estimate of the subject's criterion.

Another important approach involving temporal partitioning is based on sequential decision making. One class of empirical studies allows the observer to determine how many intervals he observes before making a response (Swets & Green, 1961; Swets & Birdsall, 1967). And one class of theoretical studies of reaction time assumes that the subject partitions time, observes a random variable in each interval, and arrives at a response decision by means of a sequential decision procedure (Carterette, 1966; Edwards, 1965; La Berge, 1962; Laming, 1968; Stone, 1960).

C. Vigilance

A vigilance task is, by definition, a free response one in which the signal rate is low (perhaps one per minute) and the total observation period is long (an hour or two); a general reference is Buckner and McGrath (1963). A major empirical generalization from a long history of research in this area is that there is a very marked decrement in performance as the period of the watch increases (a good summary of these data is Jerison and Pickett, 1963).

Broadbent and Gregory (1963) applied TSD to the data simply by dividing the FR situation into 1-sec intervals, as already explained. Assuming the signal and noise distributions are both Gaussian, with equal variance, they estimated both d' and β. The surprising finding was that although β changed during the course of the watch, d' appeared to remain constant. They argued that the decline in performance was, in fact, simply a shift on the part of the observer to a more conservative response criterion. They argued from the apparent constancy of d' that sensitivity is independent of the period on the watch. At about the same time, however, Mackworth and Taylor (1963) applied TSD to a continuous visual display and found a systematic decline in d' as a function of watch time. It appears that the modality of the display plays an important role in whether or not a decline in sensitivity is observed. Apparently the decline is related to some sort of attentional variable and may be related to observing responses, as argued by Loeb and Binford (1964), Jerison, Pickett, and Stenson (1965), and Jerison (1967). In auditory experiments, where no orienting or observing responses are required, the data show little change in sensitivity but large changes in criterion as a function of the time in the watch (Broadbent & Gregory, 1965; Davenport, 1968; Levine, 1966; Loeb & Binford, 1964; Mackworth, 1968; Hatfield & Soderquist, 1970).

Mackworth (1965) tried a variety of different temporal intervals to estimate the hit and false alarm rate. She concluded that a 30-fold change in the size of the interval has little effect upon the conclusion one draws. Although such stability is impressive, it must be remembered that in vigilance situations the false-alarm rate is extremely low. Indeed, in many of the experiments, when something like 10^4 responses are counted as hits, the number of false alarms is of the order of 10. With such tiny probabilities, it is hardly surprising that the size of the interval used to estimate them has little effect on the estimate. A more serious problem, one recognized by practically all investigators, is the stability of the estimates. Given the paucity of false alarms, the confidence intervals on both d' and β are enormous. Also, as Mackworth and Taylor (1963) pointed out, the estimates depend heavily on the assumed form of the distribution. This is not too serious as long as we only wish to compare parameter estimates within similar conditions of an experiment, but the extrapolation of these parameter estimates to other situations, especially to FI ones, is indeed hazardous. This point, along with some other cautions about the overacceptance of TSD, is well expressed in Jerison's paper (1967).

D. A Continuous Free-Response Model

Luce (1966) proposed an approach to the analysis of free response data which does not involve any arbitrary division of time into decision intervals. The most striking feature of this approach is that it redefines the basic data of a free response experiment as a family of temporal distributions: the distribution of times from a signal to the next response, the distribution of times between successive responses given that no signal has intervened, and so forth. What a theory of free-response behavior must account for are these temporal distributions, rather than some artificially constructed quantities analogous to the hit and false-alarm rate of an FI experiment.

Such notions as the hit and false-alarm probabilities are, at best, uncertain concepts because, when false alarms can occur and when the time between a stimulus initiating a response and its response is not constant, it is impossible to be sure what preceding event caused a given response.

The original model has undergone considerable experimental testing and modification in Green and Luce (1967, 1971) and Luce and Green (1970, 1971). The present version can be formulated in terms of three main ideas. First, as in the counter models (Section III,G), the intensity of a signal is assumed to be transduced and ultimately represented at the observer's decision center as a temporal pulse train of (perhaps, neural) events whose average rate is assumed to increase with signal intensity. A more specific assumption, which ultimately may have to be abandoned, is that the transduction of a signal of constant intensity is a Poisson process. In this case, the pulse rate, which is the reciprocal of the expected interpulse time, completely characterizes the process. The pulse rate due to noise v and that due to signal-plus-noise μ play roles somewhat similar to β and d' in TSD.

The second assumption is that this pulse train is subjected to a decision process which determines when and which response is to be activated. The time taken to reach such a decision, which depends upon the pulse rate, is called the *sensory-decision latency*. A variety of decision rules in addition to counter models are possible. Initially, Green and Luce investigated the simplest possible rule, namely that the arrival of each pulse activates a response. (If so, these theoretical pulses are surely not the same as the peripheral ones which, even in the absence of an auditory signal, often have rates of about 10 per second.) Ultimately, they showed that this rule is untenable (see the next subsection). The next simplest model, still not involving a time partition, assumes that the momentary pulse rate (and hence, by the first assumption, the intensity of the signal) is estimated from the reciprocal of the interarrival times (IAT) of the pulses and that certain sums of IATs are compared with a criterion or with another sum of IATs, much as likelihood ratios are compared with a criterion or with each other in TSD. Such rules can be applied to a variety of psychophysical designs, including all the usual FI ones as well as free response types (Luce & Green, 1972).

The third and last feature of the theory concerns delays introduced by the afferent and motor systems. The sum of all these is called the *residual latency*. This latency is assumed to convolve independently with the decision latency to produce the observed response time. The only assumption made about the residual latency is that it is a bounded random variable. According to the theory, reaction times to intense signals are approximately the residual latencies, so the bound is probably about 200–300 msec. Aside from being bounded, the distribution of residual times is not otherwise constrained in the theory; undoubtedly, it depends on the input channel and on the exact response required.

The key role of the boundedness assumption is this: any observable density that is a convolution of a decision latency whose tail is exponential with a residual latency has a tail (beyond the bound) that is entirely dictated by the tail of the decision density. This is of great interest because the tail of the decision latency reflects something of the decision rule and the interpulse density. With weak signals, these tails represent an appreciable fraction of all the data, and so they can be used to test hypotheses about the nature of the decision process and to estimate mean pulse rates. For example, in Green and Luce (1967) and Luce and Green (1970) certain signal–response and response–response densities were shown to have approximately exponential tails; from these the pulse rates v and μ were estimated, μ/v was shown to increase smoothly with S/N in decibels, and criterion changes altered both in a way such that $\mu-v$ is approximately constant.

A basic difficulty in applying this type of analysis to FR data arises when two signals occur close together, in which case the response to the second may be initiated before the response to the first is completed. This is especially an issue when the signal presentation schedule of the signals is Poisson, since short intersignal times are common. Using schedules other than the Poisson for the signal presentation greatly complicates the mathematical analysis and is bound to invite nonhomogeneous strategies on the part of the observer, as we already discussed.) Some simple assumptions were explored and rejected, and more complex ones have so far proved mathematically intractable. This led to consideration of experiments in which freedom not to respond was retained, but in which multiple responses were avoided; we turn to these next.

E. Related Reaction Time Experiments

For the stochastic models of the detection process just outlined, a natural source of information about them is a reaction-time (RT) experiment with exponentially distributed foreperiods and weak signals. Although the literature on simple RT is enormous, that having to do with very weak signals is quite small. Yet such signals are admirably suited to study the decision process since they generate processing delays that are appreciable with respect to other lags in the system. In a sense, weak signals serve as a microscope to provide a more detailed view of the sensory part of the perceptual system. The nature of these delays is predicted in detail by the stochastic model. Green and Luce (1971) and Luce and Green (1970, 1972) have pursued this approach. They show an increase in RT of over an order of magnitude as signal-to-noise ratio is decreased. In addition, sizable effects were observed when the criterion of the subject was altered and some dependence on mean signal wait was also noted.

Using the assumptions stated in the preceding section and assuming that each pulse initiates a response, they employed Fourier transforms of the observed RT distribution to try to deconvolve the sensory decision process from the remaining residual distribution. They found that the calculated residual distribution was bounded, as predicted by the theory, but was negative for a short period after the bound (which, of course, is impossible). Moreover, the mean of this inferred residual distribution was about 100 msec longer than the response times observed in simple RT to very strong signals. This is inconsistent with their model since if a bounded number of IATs enter into any response decision, as would be the case with a finite buffer store, the time for processing the pulse train vanishes as $\mu \to \infty$; hence the RT to a very strong signal should be identical to the residual distribution. Although some aspect of that model, most likely the assumption that single pulses activate responses, is surely incorrect, the authors believe that the approach has considerable promise.

Since the observed RT distribution for strong signals approximates the residual latency distribution, and the RT distribution for weak and moderate signals is the convolution of the corresponding decision latency with this RT distribution for strong ones, there is no reason to expect this convolution to have any simple mathematical form. The extraction of information from RT distributions is therefore a matter of considerable delicacy and probably requires more complicated techniques of analysis than has been traditionally assumed.

References

Abrahamson, I. G., & Levitt, H. Statistical analysis of data from experiments in human signal detection. *Journal of Mathematical Psychology,* 1969, **6,** 391–417.

Adler, H. E., & Dalland, J. I. Spectral thresholds in the starling. *Journal of Comparative and Physiological Psychology,* 1959, **52,** 438–445.

Anderson, C. D. The constant-ratio rule as a predictor of confusions among visual stimuli of brief exposure duration. Indiana University, Hearing and Communication Lab., TN-58–60, 1959.

Arons, L., & Irwin, F. W. Equal weights and psychophysical judgments. *Journal of Experimental Psychology,* 1932, **15,** 733–751.

Atkinson, R. C. A variable sensitivity theory of signal detection. *Psychological Review,* 1963, **70,** 91–106.

Atkinson, R. C., Carterette, E. C., & Kinchla, R. A. Sequential phenomena in psychophysical judgments: a theoretical analysis. *I.R.E. Transactions of Information Theory,* 1962, **8,** 155–162.

Atkinson, R. C., & Kinchla, R. A. A learning model for forced-choice detection experiments. *British Journal of Mathematical and Statistical Psychology,* 1965, **18,** 183–206.

Békésy, G. von. Über das Fechneresche Gesetz und seine Bedeutung für die Theorie der akustishe Beobachtungsfehler und die Theorie des Hörens. *Annalen der Physik,* 1930, **7,** 329–359.

Békésy, G. von. A new audiometer. *Acta Oto-laryn,* 1947, **35,** 411–422.

Blackwell, H. R. Neural theories of simple visual detection. *Journal of the Optical Society of America,* 1963, **53,** 129–160.

Blough, D. S. A method for tracing dark adaptation in the pigeon. *Science,* 1955, **121,** 703–704.

Blough, D. S. A method for obtaining psychophysical thresholds from the pigeon. *Journal of the Experimental Analysis of Behavior,* 1958, **1,** 31–43.

Blough, D. S. The study of animal sensory processes by operant methods. In W. K. Honig (Ed.), *Operant behavior.* New York: Appleton 1966. Pp. 345–379.

Blough, D. S., & Schrier, A. M. Scotopic spectral sensitivity in the rhesus monkey. *Science,* 1963, **139,** 493–494.

Bock, R. D., & Jones, L. V. *The measurement and prediction of judgment and choice.* San Francisco: Holden-Day, 1968.

Boring, E. *Sensation and perception in the history of experimental psychology.* New York-London: D. Appleton-Century, 1942.

Broadbent, D. E. Two-state threshold model and rating scale experiments. *Journal of the Acoustical Society of America,* 1966, **40,** 244–245.

Broadbent, D. E. Word-frequency effect and response bias. *Psychology Review,* 1967, **74,** 1–15.

Broadbent, D. E., & Gregory, Margaret. Vigilance considered as a statistical decision. *British Journal of Psychology,* 1963, **54,** 309–323.

Broadbent, D. E., & Gregory, M. Effects of noise and of signal rate upon vigilance analyzed by means of decision theory. *Human Factors* 1965, **7,** 155–162.

Brown, J., & Cane, Violet An analysis of the limiting method. *British Journal of Statistical Psychology,* 1959, **12,** 119–126.

Brownlee, K. A., Hodges, J. L., & Rosenblatt, M. The up-and-down method with small samples. *Journal of the American Statistical Association,* 1953, **48,** 262–277.

Buckner, D. N., & McGrath, J. J. (Eds.), *Vigilance: A symposium.* New York: McGraw-Hill, 1963.

Bush, R. R., Luce, R. D., & Rose, R. M. Learning models for psychophysics. In R. C. Atkinson (Ed.), *Studies in mathematical psychology.* Stanford: Stanford University Press, 1964. Pp. 201–217.

Campbell, R. A. Detection of a noise signal if varying duration. *Journal of the Acoustical Society of America,* 1963, **35,** 1732–1737.

Cardozo, B. L. A sequential up-and-down method. *Institut voor Perceptie Onderzock, Annual Progress Report,* 1966, **1,** 110–114.

Carterette, E. C. Random walk models for reaction times in signal detection and recognition. *Proceedings of the XVIII International Congress on Psychology,* 1966, **16,** 84–95.

Carterette, E. C. Symposium on attention. *Proceedings of the XIX International Congress on Psychology,* 1969, London: British Psychological Society, 1971. Pp. 226–227.

Carterette, E. C., Friedman, M. P., & Cosmides, R. Reaction-time distributions in the detection of weak signals in noise. *Journal of the Acoustical Society of America,* 1965, **38,** 531–542.

Carterette, E. C., Friedman, M. P., & Wyman, M. J. Feedback and psychophysical variables in signal detection. *Journal of the Acoustical Society of America,* 1966, **39,** 1051–1055.

Catlin, J. On the word-frequency effect. *Psychology Review,* 1969, **76,** 504–506.

Chung, K. L. On a stochastic approximation method. *Annals of Mathematical Statistics,* 1954, **25,** 463–483.

Clarke, F. R. Constant-ratio rule for confusion matrices in speech communication. *Journal of the Acoustical Society of America,* 1957, **29,** 715–720.

Clarke, F. R. Confidence ratings, second-choice responses, and confusion matrices in intelligibility tests. *Journal of the Acoustical Society of America,* 1960, **32,** 35–46. Reprinted in J. A. Swets (Ed.), *Signal detection and recognition by human observers.* New York: Wiley, 1964. Pp. 620–648.

Clarke, F. R., & Anderson, C. D. Further test of the constant-ratio rule in speech communication. *Journal of the Acoustical Society of America,* 1957, **29,** 1318–1320.

Colquhoun, W. P. & Baddeley, A. D. Influence of signal probability during pre-training on vigilance decrement. *Journal of Experimental Psychology,* 1967, **73,** 153–155.

Colquhoun, W. P., Blake, M. J., & Edwards, R. S. Experimental studies of shift-work I: a comparison of "rotating" and "stabilized" 4-hour shift systems. *Ergonomics,* 1968, **11,** 437–453.

Conrad, R. Acoustic confusions in immediate memory. *British Journal of Psychology,* 1964, **55,** 75–84.

Cornsweet, T. N. The staircase-method in psychophysics. *American Journal of Psychology,* 1962, **75,** 485–491.

Cornsweet, T. N. *Visual perception.* New York: Academic Press, 1970.

Corso, J. F. The neural quantum theory of sensory discrimination. *Psychology Bulletin,* 1956, **53,** 371–393.

Creelman, C. D., & Donaldson, W. ROC curves for discrimination of linear extent. *Journal of Experimental Psychology,* 1968, **77,** 514–516.

Davenport, W. G. Auditory vigilance: the effects of costs and values on signals. *Australian Journal of Psychology,* 1968, **20,** 213–218.

Day, W. F. Serial non-randomness in auditory differential thresholds as a function of interstimulus interval. *American Journal of Psychology,* 1956, **69,** 387–394.

Dixon, W. J., & Mood, A. M. A method for obtaining and analyzing sensitivity data. *Journal of the American Statistical Association,* 1948, **43,** 109–126.

Dorfman, D. D. Recognition of taboo words as a function of a priori probability. *Journal of Personality and Social Psychology,* 1967, **7,** 1–10.

Dorfman, D. D. Probability matching in signal detection. *Psychonomic Science,* 1969, **17,** 103.

Dorfman, D. D., & Alf, E., Jr., Maximum likelihood estimation of parameters of signal detection theory—a direct solution. *Psychometrika,* 1968, **33,** 117–124.

Dorfman, D. D., & Alf, E. Jr. Maximum-likelihood estimation of parameters of signal-detection theory and determination of confidence intervals—rating-method data. *Journal of Mathematical Psychology,* 1969, **6,** 487–496.

Dorfman, D. D., & Biderman, M. A learning model for a continuum of sensory states. *Journal of Mathematical Psychology,* 1971, **8,** 264–284.

Edwards, W. Optimal strategies for seeking information: models for statistics, choice reaction times and human information processing. *Journal of Mathematical Psychology,* 1965, **2,** 312–329.

Egan, J. P. Message repetition, operating characteristics, and confusion matrices in speech communication. Indiana Univ., Hearing and Communication Lab., Tech. Rep. 57-50, 1957. (a)

Egan, J. P. Monitoring task in speech communication. *Journal of the Acoustical Society of America,* 1957, **29,** 482–489. (b)

Egan, J. P., Greenberg, G. Z., & Schulman, A. I. Operating characteristics, signal detectability, and the method of free response. *Journal of the Acoustical Society of America,* 1961, **33,** 993–1007. [Reprinted in J. A. Swets (Ed.), *Signal detection and recognition by human observers.* New York: Wiley, 1964. Pp. 316–348.]

Egan, J. P., Schulman, A. I., & Greenberg, G. Z. Operating characteristics determined by binary decisions and by ratings. *Journal of the Acoustical Society of America,* 1959, **31,** 768–773. [Reprinted in J. A. Swets (Ed.), *Signal detection and recognition by human observers.* New York: Wiley, 1964. Pp. 172–186.]

Emmerich, D. S. ROCs obtained with two signal intensities presented in random order, and a comparison between yes–no and rating ROCs. *Perception & Psychophysics,* 1968, **3,** 35–40.

Elliott, D. N., Frazier, L., & Riach, W. A tracking procedure for determining cat's frequency discrimination. *Journal of the Experimental Analysis of Behavior,* 1962, **5,** 323–328.

Friedman, M. P., Carterette, E. C., Nakatani, L. H., & Ahumada, A. Comparison of some learning models for response bias in signal detection. *Perception & Psychophysics,* 1968, **3,** 5–11. (a)

Friedman, M. P., Carterette, E. C., Nakatani, L., & Ahumada, A. Feedback and frequency variables in signal detection. Tech. Rpt. #30, Human Communication Laboratory, Dept. Psychol., UCLA, 1968. (b).

Gourevitch, G., Hack, M. H., & Hawkins, J. E., Jr. Auditory thresholds in the rat measured by an operant technique. *Science,* 1960, **131,** 1046–1047.

Gourevitch, V. & Galanter, E. A significance test for one parameter isosensitivity functions. *Psychometrika,* 1967, **32,** 25–33.

Green, D. M. Detection of multiple component signals in noise. *Journal of the Acoustical Society of America,* 1958, **30,** 904–911. [Reprinted in J. A. Swets (Ed.), *Signal detection and recognition by human observers,* New York: Wiley, 1964. Pp. 491–507.]

Green, D. M. General prediction relating yes–no and forced choice results. *Journal of the Acoustical Society of America,* 1964, **36,** 1042 (abstract).

Green, D. M., & Birdsall, T. G. The effect of vocabulary size on articulation score. In J. A. Swets (Ed.), *Signal detection and recognition by human observers: contemporary readings.* New York: Wiley, 1964. Pp. 609–619.

Green, D. M., & Luce, R. D. Detection of auditory signals presented at random times. *Perception & Psychophysics,* 1967, **2,** 441–450.

Green, D. M., & Luce, R. D. Detection of auditory signals presented at random times III. *Perception & Psychophysics,* 1971, **9,** 257–268.

Green, D. M., & McGill, W. J. On the equivalence of detection probabilities and well-known statistical quantities. *Psychological Review,* 1970, **77,** 294–301.

Green, D. M., & Moses, F. L. On the equivalence of two recognition measures of short-term memory. *Psychological Bulletin,* 1966, **66,** 228–234.

Green, D. M., & Swets, J. *Signal detection theory and psychophysics.* New York: Wiley, 1966.

Greenberg, G. Z. Frequency selectivity during amplitude discrimination of signals in noise. *Journal of the Acoustical Society of America,* 1969, **45,** 1438–1442. (a)

Greenberg, G. Z. Frequency-selective detection at three signal amplitudes. *Perception & Psychophysics,* 1969, **6,** 297–301. (b)

Greenberg, G. Z., & Larkin, W. D. Frequency response characteristics of auditory observers detecting signals of a single frequency in noise: The probe-signal method. *Journal of the Acoustical Society of America,* 1968, **44,** 1513–1523.

Gundy, R. F. Auditory detection of an unspecified signal. *Journal of the Acoustical Society of America,* 1961, **33,** 1008–1012. [Reprinted in J. A. Swets (Ed.), *Signal detection and recognition by human observers.* New York: Wiley, 1964. Pp. 187–198.]

Hall, J. L. Maximum-likelihood sequential procedure for estimation of psychometric functions. *Journal of the Acoustical Society of America,* 1968, **44,** 370 (abs.).

Hatfield, J. L., & Soderquist, D. R. Coupling effects and performance in vigilance tasks. *Human Factors,* 1970, **12,** 351–361.

Hecht, S., Schlaer, S., & Pirenne, M. H. Energy, quanta, and vision. *Journal of General Physiology,* 1942, **25,** 819–840.

Heinemann, E. G. The relation of apparent brightness to the threshold for differences in luminance. *Journal of Experimental Psychology,* 1961, **61,** 389–399.

Helson, H. *Adaptation-level theory.* New York: Harper, 1964.

Herrick, R. M. Psychophysical methodology: Comparison of thresholds of the method of limits and of the method of constant stimuli. *Perceptual and Motor Skills,* 1967, **24,** 915–922.

Herrick, R. M. Psychophysical methodology: comparisons within the method of limits. *Perceptual and Motor Skills,* 1969, **28,** 503–514.

Herrick, R. M. Psychophysical methodology: Deductions from the phi-gamma hypothesis and related hypotheses. *Perception & Psychophysics,* 1970, **7,** 73–78.

Hodge, M. H. The constant-ratio rule and identification tasks. Univ. of Georgia, Dept. of Psychology, Final report, 1962.

Hodge, M. H. Some further tests of the constant-ratio rule. *Perception & Psychophysics,* 1967, **2,** 429–437.

Hodge, M. H., Crawford, M. J., & Piercy, M. L. The constant-ratio rule and visual displays. Univ. of Georgia, Dept. of Psychology, Report 2, 1961.

Hodge, M. H., Piercy, M. L., & Crawford, M. J. The constant-ratio rule and lifted weights. Univ. of Georgia, Dept. of Psychology, Report 1, 1961.

Hodge, M. H., & Pollack, I. Confusion matrix analysis of single and multidimensional auditory displays. *Journal of Experimental Psychology,* 1962, **63,** 129–142.

Howarth, C. I., & Bulmer, M. G. Non-random sequences in visual threshold experiments. *Quarterly Journal of Experimental Psychology,* 1956, **8,** 163–171.

Jeffress, L. A. Stimulus oriented approach to detection. *Journal of the Acoustical Society of America,* 1964, **36,** 766–774.

Jerison, H. J. Signal detection theory in the analysis of human vigilance. *Human Factors,* 1967, **9,** 285–288.

Jerison, H. J., & Pickett, R. M. Vigilance: a review and re-evaluation. *Human Factors,* 1963, **5,** 211–237.

Jerison, H. J., Pickett, R. M., & Stenson, H. H. The elicited observing rate and decision process in vigilance. *Human Factors,* 1965, **7,** 107–128.

Kac, M. A note on learning signal detection. *I.R.E. Transactions on Information Theory,* 1962, **IT-8,** 126–128.

Katz, L. A comparison of type II operating characteristics derived from confidence ratings and from latencies. *Perception & Psychophysics,* 1970, **8,** 65–68.

Kiang, N. Y-S. *Discharge patterns of single fibers in the cat's auditory nerve.* Cambridge, Massachusetts: MIT Press, 1965.

Kinchla, R. A. A learning factor in visual discrimination. In R. C. Atkinson (Ed.), *Studies in mathematical psychology*. Stanford: Stanford Univ. Press, 1964. Pp. 233–249.

Kinchla, R. A. A comparison of sequential effects in detection and recognition. Experimental Psychology Series, Psychology Dept. of New York University, Tech. Rept. 1, 1966.

Krantz, D. H. Threshold theories of signal detection. *Psychological Review,* 1969, **76,** 308–324.

Kristofferson, A. B. Attention in time discrimination and reaction time. Washington, D.C.: NASA CR-194, 1965.

Kristofferson, A. B. A time constant involved in attention and neural information processing. Washington, D.C.: NASA CR-427, 1966.

Kristofferson, A. B. Attention and psychophysical time. *Acta Psychologica,* 1967, **27,** 93–100. (a)

Kristofferson, A. B. Successiveness discrimination as a two-state quantal process. *Science,* 1967, **158,** 1337–1339. (b)

Kristofferson, A. B. Sensory attention. Hamilton, Ontario: McMaster Univ. Tech. Rept. 36, 1969.

Kruskal, J. B. Multidimensional scaling by optimizing goodness of fit to a nonmetric hypothesis. *Psychometrika,* 1964, **29,** 1–27. (a)

Kruskal, J. B. Nonmetric multidimensional scaling: a numerical method. *Psychometrika,* 1964, **29,** 115–129. (b)

LaBerge, D. L. A recruitment theory of simple behavior. *Psychometrika,* 1962, **27,** 375–396.

Laming, D. R. J. *Information theory of choice-reaction times.* New York: Academic Press, 1968.

Larkin, W. D. Rating scales in detection experiments. *Journal of the Acoustical Society of America,* 1965, **37,** 748–749.

Larkin, W. D., & Norman, D. A. An extension and experimental analysis of the neural quantum theory. In R. C. Atkinson (Ed.), *Studies in mathematical psychology*. Stanford: Stanford Univ. Press, 1964. Pp. 188–200.

Larkin, W., & Greenberg, G. Z. Selective attention in uncertain frequency detection. *Perception & Psychophysics,* 1970, **8,** 179–185.

Lee, W. Detection theory, micromatching, and the constant-ratio rule. *Perception & Psychophysics,* 1968, **4,** 217–219.

Levine, J. M. The effects of values and costs on detection and identification of signals in auditory vigilance. *Human Factors,* 1966, **8,** 525–537.

Levitt, H. Testing for sequential dependencies. *Journal of the Acoustical Society of America,* 1968, **43,** 65–69.

Levitt, H. Transformed up–down methods in psychoacoustics. City Univ. of New York Graduate Center, mimeographed, undated.

Levitt, H., & Bock, D. Sequential programmer for psychophysical testing. *Journal of the Acoustical Society of America,* 1967, **42,** 911–913.

Levitt, H., & Rabiner, L. R. Use of a sequential strategy in intelligibility testing. *Journal of the Acoustical Society of America,* 1967, **42,** 609–612.

Levitt, H., & Treisman, M. Control charts for sequential testing. *Psychometrika,* 1969, **34,** 509–518.

Lindner, W. A. Recognition performance as a function of detection criterion in a simultaneous detection-recognition task. *Journal of the Acoustical Society of America,* 1968, **44,** 204–211.

Loeb, M., & Binford, J. R. Vigilance for auditory intensity changes as a function of preliminary feedback and confidence level. *Human Factors,* 1964, **6**, 445–458.

Luce, R. D. *Individual choice behavior.* New York: Wiley, 1959.

Luce, R. D. Detection and recognition. In R. D. Luce, R. R. Bush, & E. Galanter (Eds.), *Handbook of mathematical psychology,* Vol. I. New York: Wiley, 1963. Pp. 103–189. (a)

Luce, R. D. A threshold theory for simple detection experiments. *Psychological Review,* 1963, **70**, 61–79. (b)

Luce, R. D. Asymptotic learning in psychophysical theories. *British Journal of Statistical Psychology* 1964, **17**, 1–14.

Luce, R. D. A model for detection in temporally unstructured experiments with a Poisson distribution of signal presentations. *Journal of Mathematical Psychology,* 1966, **3**, 48–64.

Luce, R. D., & Green, D. M. Detection of auditory signals presented at random times, II. *Perception & Psychophysics,* 1970, **7**, 1–14.

Luce, R. D., & Green, D. M. A neural timing theory for response times and the psychophysics of intensity. *Psychological Review,* 1972, **79**, 14–57.

Mackworth, J. F. Decision interval and signal detectability in a vigilance task. *Canadian Journal of Psychology,* 1965, **19**, 111–117.

Mackworth, J. F. The effects of signal rate on performance in two kinds of vigilance tasks. *Human Factors,* 1968, **10**, 11–18.

Mackworth, J. F., & Taylor, M. M. The *d'* measure of signal detectability in vigilance-like situations. *Canadian Journal of Psychology,* 1963, **17**, 307–325.

Madansky, A. The fitting of straight lines when both variables are subject to error. *Journal of the American Statistical Association,* 1959, **54**, 173–205.

Markowitz, J. *Investigation of the dynamic properties of the neural quantal model.* Unpublished doctoral dissertation, Univ. of Pennsylvania, 1966.

Markowitz, J., & Swets, J. A. Factors affecting the slope of empirical ROC curves: comparison of binary and rating responses. *Perception & Psychophysics,* 1967, **2**, 91–100.

McGill, W. J. Neural counting mechanisms and energy detection in audition. *Journal of Mathematical Psychology,* 1967, **4**, 351–376.

McGill, W. J., & Goldberg, J. P. Pure-tone intensity discrimination and energy detection. *Journal of the Acoustical Society of America,* 1968, **44**, 576–581.

Miller, G. A., Heise, G. A., & Lichten, W. The intelligibility of speech as a function of the context of the test materials. *Journal of Experimental Psychology,* 1951, **41**, 329–335.

Nachmias, J. Effects of presentation probability and number of response alternatives on simple visual detection. *Perception & Psychophysics,* 1968, **3**, 151–155.

Nachmias, J., & Steinman, R. M. Study of absolute visual detection by the rating scale method. *Journal of the Optical Society of America,* 1963, **53**, 1206–1213.

Nakatani, L. H. *A confusion-choice stimulus recognition model applied to word recognition.* Univ. of California, Los Angeles, Dept. of Psychology, Ph.D. dissertation (TR 31), 1968.

Nakatani, L. H. Comments on Broadbent's response bias model for stimulus recognition. *Psychological Review,* 1970, **77**, 574–576.

Nakatani, L. H. Confusion-choice model for multi-dimensional psychophysics. *Journal of Mathematical Psychology,* 1972, **9**, 104–127.

Nickerson, R. J. Expectancy waiting time and the psychological refractory period. *Acta Psychologica,* 1967, **27**, 23–34.

Norman, D. A. Stochastic learning and a quantal model of signal detection. Proc. Joint Automatic Control Conference Symposium on discrete adaptive systems. *American Institute of Electrical Engineers,* 1962, 35–40. Reprinted in *Transactions of the I.E.E.E. on Applications and Industry,* 1964, **83,** 292–296.

Norman, D. A. Sensory thresholds and response bias. *Journal of the Acoustical Society of America,* 1963, **35,** 1432–1441.

Norman, D. A. Sensory thresholds, response bias, and the neural quantum theory. *Journal of Mathematical Psychology,* 1964, **1,** 88–120. (a)

Norman, D. A. A comparison of data obtained with different false alarm rates. *Psychological Review,* 1964, **71,** 243–246. (b)

Norman, D. A., & Wickelgren, W. A. Strength theory of decision rules and latency in retrieval from short-term memory. *Journal of Mathematical Psychology,* 1969, **6,** 192–208.

Ogilvie, J. C., & Creelman, C. D. Maximum-likelihood estimation of receiver operating characteristic curve parameters. *Journal of Mathematical Psychology,* 1968, **5,** 377–391.

Parducci, A., & Marshall, Louise M. Assimilation vs. contrast in the anchoring of perceptual judgments of weight. *Journal of Experimental Psychology,* 1962, **63,** 426–437.

Parducci, A., & Sandusky, A. Distribution and sequence effects in judgment. *Journal of Experimental Psychology,* 1965, **69,** 450–459.

Parducci, A., & Sandusky, A. J. Limits on the applicability of signal detection theories. *Perception & Psychophysics,* 1970, **1,** 63–64.

Parks, T. E. Signal-detectability theory of recognition: Memory performance. *Psychological Review,* 1966, **73,** 44–58.

Penner, M. J. Detection of sinusoids of uncertain frequency. Univ. of California, San Diego, Unpublished doctoral dissertation, 1970.

Pfafflin, S. M., & Mathews, M. Energy detection model for monaural auditory detection. *Journal of the Acoustical Society of America,* 1962, **34,** 1842–1852.

Pollack, I. Message uncertainty and message reception. *Journal of the Acoustical Society of America,* 1959, **31,** 1500–1508.

Pollack, I. Computer simulation of threshold observations by method of limits. *Perceptual and Motor Skills,* 1968, **26,** 583–586.

Pollack, I., & Decker, L. Consonant confusions and the constant ratio rule. *Language and Speech,* 1960, **3,** 1–6.

Pollack, I., & Hsieh, R. Sampling variability of the area under the ROC-curve and of *d'. Psychological Bulletin,* 1969, **71,** 161–173.

Pollack, I., & Norman, D. A. A nonparametric analysis of recognition experiments. *Psychonomic Science,* 1964, **1,** 125–126.

Pollack, I., Norman, D. A., & Galanter, E. An efficient non-parametric analysis of recognition memory. *Psychonomic Science,* 1964, **1,** 327–328.

Preston, M. G. Contrast effects and the psychometric judgments. *American Journal of Psychology,* 1936, **48,** 297–303. (a)

Preston, M. G. Contrast effects and the psychometric functions. *American Journal of Psychology,* 1936, **48,** 625–631. (b)

Robbins, H., & Munro, S. A stochastic approximation method. *Annals of Mathematical Statistics,* 1951, **22,** 400–407.

Rubenstein, H., & Pollack, I. Word predictability and intelligibility. *Journal of Verbal Learning and Verbal Behavior,* 1963, **2,** 147–158.

Schoeffler, M. S. Theory for psychophysical learning. *Journal of the Acoustical Society of America*, 1965, **37**, 1124–1133.

Schönemann, P. H., & Tucker, L. R. A maximum likelihood solution for the method of successive intervals allowing for unequal stimulus dispersions. *Psychometrika*, 1967, **32**, 403–417.

Schulman, A. I., & Greenberg, G. Z. Operating characteristics and a priori probability of the signal. *Perception & Psychophysics*, 1970, **8**, 317–320.

Senders, V., & Soward, A. Analysis of response sequences in the settings of a psychophysical experiment. *American Journal of Psychology*, 1952, **65**, 358–374.

Shepard, R. N. Stimulus and response generalization: A stochastic model relating generalization to distance in psychological space. *Psychometrika*, 1957, **22**, 325–345.

Shepard, R. N. Stimulus and response generalization: Deductions of the generalization gradient from a trace model. *Psychological Review*, 1958, **65**, 242–256. (a)

Shepard, R. N. Stimulus and response generalization: Tests of a model relating generalization to distance in psychological space. *Journal of Experimental Psychology*, 1958, **55**, 509–523. (b)

Shepard, R. N. Application of a trace model to the retention of information in a recognition task. *Psychometrika*, 1961, **26**, 185–203. (a)

Shepard, R. N. Role of generalization in stimulus-response compatibility. *Perceptual and Motor Skills*, 1961, **13**, 59–62. (b)

Shepard, R. N. The analysis of proximities: Multidimensional scaling with an unknown distance function. I. *Psychometrika*, 1962, **27**, 125–140. (a)

Shepard, R. N. The analysis of proximities: multidimensional scaling with an unknown distance function. II. *Psychometrika*, 1962, **27**, 219–246. (b)

Shepard, R. N. Analysis of proximities as a technique for the study of information processing in man. *Human Factors*, 1963, **5**, 33–48.

Shepard, R. N. Metric structure in ordinal data. *Journal of Mathematical Psychology*, 1966, **3**, 287–315.

Shipley, E. F. A model for detection and recognition with signal uncertainty. *Psychometrika*, 1960, **25**, 273–289.

Shipley, E. F. Dependence of successive judgments in detection tasks: correctness of the response. *Journal of the Acoustical Society of America*, 1961, **33**, 1142–1143.

Shipley, E. F. Detection and recognition: Experiments and choice models. *Journal of Mathematical Psychology*, 1965, **2**, 277–311.

Shipley, E. F. A signal detection analysis of a category judgment experiment. *Perception & Psychophysics*, 1970, **7**, 38–42.

Shipley, E. F., & Luce, R. D. Discrimination among two- and three-element sets of weights. In R. C. Atkinson (Ed.), *Studies in mathematical psychology*. Stanford: Stanford Univ. Press, 1964. Pp. 218–232.

Siebert, W. M. Some implications of the stochastic behavior of primary auditory neurons. *Kybernetik*, 1965, **2**, 206–215.

Smith, J. E. K. Stimulus programming in psychophysics. *Psychometrika*, 1961, **26**, 27–33.

Smith, J. E. K. Discussion on psychophysical testing. In *Conference on computer assisted testing*. Princeton, New Jersey: Educational Testing Service, 1966.

Smith, J. E. K. A note on the standard error of the estimates of TSD parameters from "Yes–No" experiments. University of Michigan, MMPP Tech. Rep. 69–8, 1969.

Speeth, S. D., & Mathews, M. V. Sequential effects in the signal-detection situation. *Journal of the Acoustical Society of America,* 1961, **33,** 1046–1054.

Stevens, S. S., Morgan, C. T., & Volkmann, J. Theory of the neural quantum in the discrimination of loudness and pitch. *American Journal of Psychology,* 1941, **54,** 315–335.

Stone, M. Models for choice-reaction time. *Psychometrika,* 1960, **25,** 251–260.

Stroud, J. M. The fine structure of psychological time. In H. Quastler (Ed.), *Information theory in psychology.* Glencoe, Illinois: Free Press, 1955.

Swets, J. A. Is there a sensory threshold? *Science,* 1961, **134,** 168–177. [Reprinted in J. A. Swets (Ed.), *Signal detection and recognition by human observers.* New York: Wiley, 1964. Pp. 122–144.

Swets, J. A. (Ed.). *Signal detection and recognition by human observers.* New York: Wiley, 1964.

Swets, J. A., & Birdsall, T. G. Deferred decision in human signal detection: a preliminary experiment. *Perception & Psychophysics,* 1967, **2,** 15–28.

Swets, J. A., & Green, D. M. Sequential observations by human observers of signals in noise. In C. Cherry (Ed.), *Information theory.* London: Butterworths, 1961. [Reprinted in J. A. Swets (Ed.), *Signal detection and recognition by human observers.* New York: Wiley, 1964. Pp. 221–242.]

Swets, J. A., Shipley, E. F., McKey, M. J., & Green, D. M. Multiple observations of signals in noise. *Journal of the Acoustical Society of America,* 1959, **31,** 514–521. [Reprinted in J. A. Swets (Ed.), *Signal detection and recognition by human observers.* New York: Wiley, 1964. Pp. 201–220.]

Swets, J. A., & Sewall, S. T. Stimulus versus response uncertainty in recognition. *Journal of the Acoustical Society of America,* 1961, **33,** 1589–1592. [Reprinted in J. A. Swets (Ed.), *Signal detection and recognition by human observers.* New York: Wiley, 1964. Pp. 431–446.]

Symmes, D. Self-determination of critical flicker frequencies in monkeys. *Science,* 1962, **136,** 714–715.

Tanner, T. A., Haller, R. W., & Atkinson, R. C. Signal recognition as influenced by presentation schedules. *Perception & Psychophysics,* 1967, **2,** 349–358.

Tanner, T. A., Jr., Rauk, J. A., & Atkinson, R. C. Signal recognition as influenced by information feedback. *Journal of Mathematical Psychology,* 1970, **7,** 259–274.

Tanner, W. P., Jr. Theory of recognition. *Journal of the Acoustical Society of America,* 1956, 28, 882–888. [Reprinted in J. A. Swets (Ed.), *Signal detection and recognition by human observers.* New York: Wiley, 1964. Pp. 413–430.]

Tanner, W. P. Jr., & Norman, R. Z. The human use of information, II. Signal detection for the case of an unknown signal parameter. *Transactions of the I.R.E. Professional Group on Information Theory,* 1954, 222–226.

Tanner, W. P., Jr., & Swets, J. A. A decision-making theory of visual detection. *Psychological Review,* 1954, **61,** 401–409.

Tanner, W. P., Jr., Swets, J. A., & Green, D. M. Some general properties of the hearing mechanism. Tech. Rep. No. 30, Electronic Defense Group, Univ. of Michigan, 1956.

Taylor, M. M., & Creelman, C. D. PEST: efficient estimates on probability functions. *Journal of the Acoustical Society of America,* 1967, **41,** 782–787.

Thomas, E. A. C., & Legge, D. Probability matching as a basis for detection and recognition decisions. *Psychological Review,* 1970, **77,** 65–72.

Thurstone, L. L. *The measurement of values.* Chicago: Univ. of Chicago Press, 1959.

Torgerson, W. S. *Theory and methods of scaling.* New York: Wiley, 1958.

Treisman, M. On the word frequency effect: Comments on papers by J. Catlin and L. H. Nakatani. *Psychological Review,* 1971, **78,** 420–425.

Verplanck, W. S., Collier, G. H., & Cotton, J. W. Nonindependence of successive responses in measurements of the visual threshold. *Journal of Experimental Psychology,* 1952, **44,** 273–282.

Verplanck, W. S., Cotton, J. W., & Collier, G. H. Previous training as a determinant of response dependency at the threshold. *Journal of Experimental Psychology,* 1953, **46,** 10–14.

Veniar, F. A. Signal detection as a function of frequency ensemble. I. *Journal of the Acoustical Society of America,* 1958, **30,** 1020–1024.

Wald, A. *Sequential analysis.* New York: Wiley, 1947.

Watson, C. S., & Nichols, T. L. Replication and revisions of Egan's method of free response. *Journal of the Acoustical Society of America,* 1966, **36,** 1247 (abstract).

Watson, C. S., Rilling, M. E. & Bourbon, W. T. Receiver-operating characteristics determined by a mechanical analog to the rating scale. *Journal of the Acoustical Society of America,* 1964, **36,** 283–288.

Wetherill, G. B. Sequential estimation of quantal response curves. *Journal of the Royal Statistical Society,* 1963, **25,** 1–48.

Wetherill, G. B. *Sequential methods in statistics.* London: Methuen, 1966.

Wetherill, G. B., Chen, H., & Vasudeva, R. B. Sequential estimation of quantal response curves: A new method of estimation. *Biometrika,* 1966, **53,** 439–454.

Wetherill, G. B., & Levitt, H. Sequential estimation of points on a psychometric function. *British Journal of Mathematical and Statistical Psychology,* 1965, **18,** 1–10.

White, C. T. Temporal numerosity and the psychological unit of duration. *Psychological Monographs,* 1963, **77** (Whole No. 575).

Wickelgren, W. A. Unidimensional strength theory and component analysis of noise in absolute and comparative judgments. *Journal of Mathematical Psychology,* 1968, **5,** 102–122. (a)

Wickelgren, W. A. Testing two-state theory. *Psychological Bulletin,* 1968, **69,** 126–130. (b)

Zwislocki, J., Maire, F., Feldman, A. S., & Rubin, H. On the effect of practice and motivation on the threshold of audibility. *Journal of the Acoustical Society of America,* 1958, **30,** 254–262.

Part IV

Scaling

Chapter 10

OVERVIEW OF PSYCHOPHYSICAL SCALING METHODS

F. NOWELL JONES

I. INTRODUCTION

The history of attempts to measure subjective events has been reviewed in another chapter. It was pointed out there that two main lines of approach have persisted from the day of Fechner and Plateau to the present. Essentially, Fechner's approach and its modern descendants use the discriminal capacity of the subject upon which to base a measurement formula, whereas those working in the spirit of Plateau utilize the presumed familiarity of the subject with the number system to obtain direct estimates of subjective magnitude. It is sometimes said (cf. Torgerson, 1958) that categorical methods are purely neither one nor the other of these approaches, and this point will be returned to later.

At the risk of some oversimplification, we may characterize the different approaches as follows. The "indirect," or Fechnerian methods, seem to be so called because considerable statistical manipulation is required for the construction of a measurement scale. Actually, data collection is "direct" for these methods, because what is required is direct judgments of differences among stimuli: Consider, for example, the method of constant stimulus differences. The so-called "direct" methods, on the other hand, require that judgments be made either according to some predetermined ratio given by the experimenter, or made in terms of, hopefully, real numbers. Thus the data collection involves a judgment in terms of a scale external to the stimuli themselves, but data reduction is straightforward. The categorical methods share with the direct methods the requirement that judgments be made on an external scale, but, on the other hand, data manipulation usually is based on the old Fechnerian approach. As we shall see, this last characterization may require some modification, since it is also possible to utilize categorical judgments at their face values, and ignore the methodology* based on discriminability.

II. THE INDIRECT METHODS

A. Introduction

The original Fechnerian idea was based on what he called Weber's Law (Fechner, 1860). That is, if discrimination requires a constant proportional increase in the stimulus, a function, $dr/R = K$, may be written for some probability of discrimination, and if we assume that this relationship holds for very small increments, we may regard this formula as giving the relationship between the stimulus and subjective increment. This leads to the famous Fechnerian statement that $S = k \log R$. A satisfying deriviation is given in Bock and Jones (1968).

Now, if what we need is the Weber fraction, and if we assume that it is constant over a long range of stimuli, any psychophysical method that yields a measure of discrimination will give us a subjective scale. In practice, however, this is not done, and so our attention is directed to those methods which are in common use. For more extensive general treatment of this topic, the reader is referred to Bock and Jones (1968), Guilford (1954), Torgerson (1958), or some of the specific references found in this chapter.

B. The Law of Comparative Judgment

Modern work on indirect scaling was begun by Thurstone, who published his famous Law of Comparative Judgment in 1927. According to him, the intellectual antecedents are Weber and Fechner. Essentially the idea was that a stimulus—whether physical or otherwise—gives rise to a hypothetical discriminal process within the subject which, for various

---

* More extended discussions of the methods and issues mentioned in this chapter may be found, for example, in Torgerson (1958), Ekman and Sjöberg (1965), and Zinnes (1969). An excellent textbook source is Engen (1971).

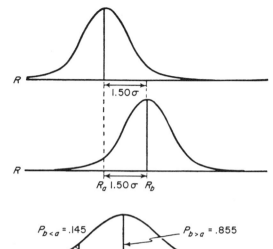

FIG. 1. Hypothetical dis-
criminal dispersions, showing
unequal variances and overlap.
[From Guilford (1954).]

random reasons, varies from presentation to presentation of the same stimulus. (This idea is also to be found in Fullerton and Cattell, 1892.) If the discriminal dispersions of two different stimuli have average values close enough together, and their variances are sufficiently large, these dispersions will overlap, as shown hypothetically in Fig. 1. If repeated measures are taken, and the shapes and variances of the dispersions are known, a measure of psychological distance can be calculated. To simplify matters, it is ordinarily assumed (Thurstone, Case V) that the dispersions are normal, that they are of equal variance, and that they are uncorrelated. An in-depth discussion of these assumptions is beyond the scope of this chapter. The reader is referred to the collection of papers in Thurstone (1959) and to the discussions in Bock and Jones (1968).

1. DATA COLLECTION METHODS FOR COMPARATIVE JUDGMENT

a. PAIR COMPARISONS. The most usual method of obtaining data for use in scaling according to the Law of Comparative Judgment is by means of pair comparisons. One may use either multiple trials for a single subject or obtain data from a sample of several subjects. Obviously, the meaning of the results will differ for these two cases, although the mathematics will not. From the judgments, which may be of preference, intensity, or any other desired attribute of the stimuli, one may obtain the proportion of trials on which each stimulus is judged more intense, preferred, etc., to each of the others. From these proportions, one may, usually using the assumptions of Case V, derive normal deivate estimates of psychological distance. A straightforward computational routine is to be found in Guilford (1954, Chap. 7). It should be noted that successive pairs along the continuum of interest must never be perfectly discriminated, for in that case, the distance between them is indeterminate.

The main advantage of the method of pair comparisons is that it yields an estimate of subjective distance over the range of whatever stimuli are used. Also, of course, it is possible to use stimuli that cannot be arranged on an objective dimension. Indeed, this is usually the case. One need not, therefore, know in advance which stimuli lie next to each other subjectively, a big advantage when dealing with, for example, food preferences.

There are two main disadvantages. First, there must be some degree of confusion between adjacent stimuli since, if not, we have seen that no estimate of distance is possible. This makes it difficult to design an investgation spanning a very large range without inordinately increasing the absolute number of stimuli, hence making the number of pairings [which will be $n(n-1)$, or half this amount if one disregards order] prohibitively large. It is possible to use a design with some pairings omitted (cf. Bock) & Jones, 1968, pp. 167f), but this also complicates matters. The second disadvantage is somewhat a corollary of the first. Even at best, the method requires a good many judgments for the amount of information extracted.

b. RANK ORDER. In the method of rank order, the subject is asked to arrange a set of stimuli in accordance with the amount of some property. For example, we might obtain ranks of composers, paintings, or foods according to the subjects's preferences. This is obviously a very much more rapid procedure than pair comparisons, at least so far as data collection is concerned. It should be noted that the method differs psychologically from the pair comparison method in a very real way: The stimuli are all present at the same time, hence the judgments are made in the context of the total range, whereas the total range enters into pair comparisons only by way of some memory process, if at all.

Deriving a scale from rank data is ordinarily accomplished in one of two ways. The first of these explicitly assumes that the stimuli were drawn from a population of stimuli that is normally distributed with respect to the property of interest. The obtained ranks, to be sure, represent a rectangular distribution. Each stimulus is assumed to represent an equal division of the total range of the property, and the assigned values are obtained by means of a table of normal deviates. In the simplest case, therefore, we, in effect, transcribe the data from percentiles to normal scores. Exact methods for doing this are outlined in Guilford (1954, Chap. 8).

The second method is derived from the law of comparative judgment. As in the case of pair comparisons we need repeated rankings, usually obtained by utilizing a sample of subjects. Logically we may regard the ranks as revealing comparisons among all of the pairs that may be assembled from the ranked stimuli. In other words, we proceed as though ranking involves comparison of each stimulus with every other. In view of the fact that the replications of the rankings show some variability, this permits us to derive proportions as in the case of pair comparisons. The usual way of going about this is also to be found in Guilford (1954).

The obvious advantage of the ranking method is that it is less time consuming than the method of pair comparisons. Also, increasing the number of stimuli does not increase the burden of the task nearly so much as it does in pair comparisons. It is still true, however, that the stimuli must not be so obviously different as to lead to no variability if we are to apply the method of scaling based on comparative judgment. This restriction is shared by the two methods.

C. Categorical Judgment

Although the logic underlying the treatment of categorical judgments for purposes of scaling is the Law of Comparative Judgment, it is convenient to treat this topic separately since, at least in Torgerson's opinion (Torgerson, 1958), categorical methods lie somewhat between the direct and indirect methods. If we should assume that numbers are but instances of categories, then the distinction between direct and categorical methods becomes tenuous indeed. Furthermore, data treatment can, and does, take the form of either the direct or indirect methods. That is, one may either take category placements at their face value, calculate mean category placements of stimuli, and use the resulting numerals as though they were on a scale of measurement, or one may rely on the Law of Comparative Judgment, calculate category boundaries, and use the resulting distances (from boundary to boundary) as measures. Bock and Jones (1968) give an extensive account of this latter approach, whereas the more "empirical" users of category judgments, especially Anderson (cf. Anderson, 1972b) and Parducci (cf. Parducci & Perrett, 1971) use the former.

1. FORMS OF DATA COLLECTION

Category judgments, although all deriving historically from the method of successive categories (cf. Guilford, 1954, for example), may be obtained in various ways which differ in detail. In the simplest case, the subject is presented with a succession of stimuli that he is to place in appropriate "piles" (whether real or symbolic), where the experimenter has decreed the number of piles to be used. The subject may, for example, be asked to place a series of weights in five piles, or indicate by numbers from one through five into which categories of liking a series of foods (or, rather, food names) should be placed. Sometimes verbal labels are used for the categories, e.g., a 5-point scale may be *like very much, like a little, neither like nor dislike, dislike a little, dislike very much.* The 9-point scale developed for the Quartermaster Corps (cf. Peryam, Polemis, Kamen, Eindhoven, & Pilgrim, 1960) is of this latter nature. For use with children, a scale of faces has been devised which ranges from smiling at one end to frowning at the other. Most extreme of all is the case where the subject marks off his judgments on a continuous line. The marks are later categorized with a ruler.

2. SPECIFIC JUDGMENTAL PROBLEMS

a. NUMBER OF CATEGORIES. It is generally accepted that reliable distinctions cannot be made beyond about seven categories. Nevertheless, even though apparent reliability may go down, it is sometimes desirable to have more categories for other reasons. If one intends to establish category boundaries, there must be some overlapping of stimulus placement, or the distances are indeterminate. This point was encountered previously in regard to pair comparisons. Second, the boundaries of the end categories cannot be established, so the more categories, the less overall indeterminancy one has. Finally, so-called "end effects," that is anomalous judgments in the end categories, are diminished by increasing the number of categories.

b. ANCHORING AND DISTRIBUTION EFFECTS. Elsewhere in this volume Parducci has considered in detail the question of context effects in judgment. The reader is referred to his chapter for a discussion of these topics. Suffice it to say here that, for practical purposes, one should avoid peculiar distributions of stimuli, and should consider assuring himself that the subject is familiar with the range of stimuli to be judged. One excellent way of doing this latter is to provide anchors just slightly above and below the range of stimuli given for judgment (cf. Anderson 1972a).

c. SCALING. It was already mentioned that two possible approaches to scaling from categorical data may be used. Guilford (1954), Torgerson (1958), and Bock and Jones (1968) all consider the case where category boundaries are to be established. Once these have been established, stimulus values may be calculated from them. The alternative method of simply calculating average category placement for each stimulus scarcely needs a *vade mecum.* The only serious trap lies in calculating the average stimulus value for each category, as might be the case where the stimuli are quantifiable on some external scale, e.g., weight, rather than calculating average category value for each stimulus. Thurstone (1959, p. 94) has made this point quite well.

An interesting and sophisticated approach to the scaling problem is to be found in discussions by Anderson (1972b and references therein). Termed "functional measurement," this approach both scales categorical judgments and provides an empirical check on the adequacy of the measurement model employed. This approach is discussed by Anderson in Chapter 9 of this volume, and will not be commented upon further here.

d. COMMENT. Categorical judgments in one form or another are the most common in use in practical situations. The scales are apparently easy for judges to use and give a great deal of information in a relatively brief time. Extensions of the analysis have been quite successful both on practical and theoretical grounds. For the practical successes we may give the predictions of food choices among soldiers (Peryam *et al.,* 1960). For the theoretical developments, the reader is referred to, especially, Bock and Jones (1968) and Anderson (1972b).

III. THE DIRECT METHODS

A. Methods Involving Judgments of Assigned Intervals

1. HISTORICAL

In 1872 Plateau published the results of some experiments he had conducted 20 years earlier in which eight artists were required to paint a gray midway between a given black and a given white. Because the perceived brightness relationships among the three resulting surfaces did not change with changes in illumination, Plateau concluded that the psychological *ratio* of one to two corresponded to a constant physical *ratio* of one to eight and thus the relationship between the two was to be represented as a power function. The history of subsequent events is treated in detail in several places (cf. Titchener, 1905; Fullerton & Cattell, 1892; Guilford, 1954). Unfortunately, the method did not seem to work out very well, since results from laboratory to laboratory were not reproducible.

It soon became apparent that after one had obtained results from a bisection experiment, it would be possible to require subjects to perform further bisections, thus both checking and extending the simpler case. If, instead of asking for successive bisections, an experimenter requires, in effect, a series of bisections to be made simultaneously, he arrives at the method of "equal-appearing intervals," which is the same as "successive categories" when the values of the stimuli are calculated by taking the intervals at their face values.

2. THORNDIKE'S APPLICATION

An early example of the application of equal-appearing intervals is the work of Thorndike (1910) who constructed a scale of penmanship. He asked 40 judges to sort some 1000 samples of penmanship into equally spaced piles. From these sortings it was possible to pick out a series of samples against which to rate other examples of penmanship.

3. EVALUATION

The method is described and discussed by Guilford (1954) in some detail. It is obvious that our faith in the results of such a scaling procedure will depend upon our assuring ourselves that the subject can actually make the judgments required. The results of methods described in this section do not normally gibe with the results obtained by a method of successive intervals. Deciding which, if either, approach, gives a "true" measure must depend upon the criteria one chooses for decision.

B. Fractionation Methods

1. DESCRIPTION

The procedural difference between a fractionation method and the methods discussed in the previous section is that, instead of there being two stimuli given to the subject between which he must place his response, one anchor is omitted and is assumed to be psychological zero. The subject is asked to give or to judge a stimulus that is, let us say, half as large as the one given or, possibly, one-third or any other fraction that the experimenter desires. The psychological assumption here is stronger than the one for simple bisection, in that bisection implies that the subject is able to make a judgment of equal sense distances, whereas the fractionation method assumes that he is able to make a ratio judgment.

2. DERIVATION OF SUBJECTIVE SCALE

The outcome of the method of fractionation as applied to a given sensory dimension is presumably a psychophysical scale. If one has a series of judgments yielding the physical magnitudes judged one-half of a corresponding series of stimuli, which extend over the range of possible values of a given dimension, one may construct a "half-judgment" plot where the x axis indicates the magnitude of the standards in physical units and the y axis indicates the physical magnitude of the stimuli judged as one-half. Since both axes are in physical units, it is necessary to find some, in this case arbitrary, unit for the subjective scale. One common way of accomplishing this goal is by assigning the value unity to the stimulus judged one-half the magnitude of the lowest standard stimulus. If we make this assignment, then the lowest standard stimulus must be given the value of 2. To get our

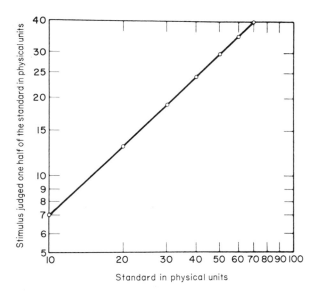

FIG. 2. Relation between given stimulus magnitudes and those judged one-half. [From Torgerson (1958).]

third point, which will represent the physical magnitude corresponding to four times our subjective unit, it is necessary to enter our plot in the y (the "judged" one-half axis) with the value just found. The discussion may be followed in Fig. 2. Reading from the line relating half judgments to the standards, we now find, on the x axis, the value that would have been the standard had the judgment actually been made. Since this is twice the value of the magnitude to which we had assigned the value 2, it must be 4 on our subjective scale. The rest of the scale is constructed in the same way. This procedure is explained in considerable detail in Torgerson (1958, pp. 97–101).

3. DATA COLLECTION

The judged fractional stimulus may be obtained, at least theoretically, by any standard psychophysical method. One of the most commonly used is the method of adjustment, wherein the subject is given control over a comparison stimulus, which he then proceeds to set at one-half the standard value. In a typical experiment of this type, Engen and Tulunay (1956) obtained fractional judgments of heaviness by providing subjects with a supply of shot which they were able to add to the comparison stimulus until it met the requirement of half-heaviness. Another common method for obtaining, in this case, half loudness judgments, is to provide the subject with an attenuator. This permits him to set a comparison loudness according to the experimenter's instructions. It is obvious that experimental control must take cognizance of all of the usual errors associated with the method of adjustment including the largely unknown influence of the movements involved in the adjustments themselves. One may, of course, use other methods that do not involve active adjustments on the part of the subject, such as the method of limits or a constant method. In these cases the subject is presented with a predetermined sequence and must judge whether or not a given stimulus is above or below the fractional value required.

4. VALIDITY

Although there seems to be relatively little dispute concerning the reliability of the method of fractionation, the problem of its validity is another matter. The most damaging criticism has come from Garner (1954), who has shown that the range of comparison stimuli presented to the subject for judgment almost completely controls his response. That is, judgments of half loudness tended to be made to the middle of a series of comparison stimuli even when their averages differed by as much as 20 dB. An argument that this simply demonstrates what can happen when one employs a bad experimental design is not compelling, since it implies that a well-designed experiment is one that gets the "proper" result. However, a number of sensory dimensions have been scaled at one time or another by the fractionation technique. The interested reader is referred to the table in Torgerson (1958, p. 95) for a list of references. It is probably fair to say that since the method of magnitude estimation, which we shall describe and discuss later, has come into general use, the method of fractionation has declined in popularity. No doubt one reason for this is that magnitude estimation is much more economical of subject time.

C. Methods of Multiple Production or Multiple Judgment

Closely related to judgments of fractions are judgments of multiples. In fact, some experiments concerned with fractionation have also included judgments of multiples; see, for example, Gieger and Firestone (1933), Ham and Parkinson (1932); and Hanes (1949). These experimenters achieved relatively good success, if success is defined as reliability, despite the fact that Fullerton and Cattell (1892) despaired utterly of being able to make such judgments reliably. In the articles referred to here and also in Torgerson's (1958) summary book, fractionation and judgments of multiples are considered together, although it is not necessarily clear that they represent the same psychological process. It is certainly true that many of the same methodological strictures hold—that is, they both run into the normal problems of psychophysical control and the same basic methodologies are available—but on the other hand, it is easy to think of a fractionation method, especially when it calls for a one-half judgment, as being a bisection judgment with zero as the lower anchor. One might also think of the judgment of multiples as involving an upper anchor that is the most intense stimulus of the particular kind that the subject has ever experienced. If this is the case, these judgments reduce to a method of equal sense distances or some variation thereof, and therefore do not, *prima facie,* yield ratio scales.

D. The Constant Sum or Ratio Partition Method

1. DESCRIPTION

From a suggestion by Metfessel (1947), Comrey (1950) has developed a method for obtaining a ratio scale of stimuli. Essentially, the method consists of dividing 100 points between pairs of stimuli in such a way that the assigned values indicate the relative amounts of some characteristic each contains.

The method devised by Comrey is based on a pair comparison format. Each stimulus is compared with each of the others, although not itself, according to the complete method of pair comparison, that is, each pair is judged twice, in random order, with the space or time error controlled. The original Comrey article explains and exemplifies his method of data reduction. Torgerson (1958) has provided an alternative method of analysis, which utilizes geometric instead of arithmetic means, and which provides for fallible data. Ekman (1958) has generalized the argument, and has provided a scaling procedure.

2. EVALUATION

One must speculate why this rather straightforward method has not been more widely applied. Probably its greatest handicap is the relative tediousness of data collection. Should one wish, for example, to scale 12 different magnitudes of sound, it would be necessary to obtain 123 judgments for each replication. Should we choose magnitude estimation, which will be discussed later, 120 judgments would suffice to give 10 replications of each judgment. Stevens (1956) criticized the method on the ground that it places more restrictions on the subject than is the case with magnitude estimation. This criticism is based on the premise that in magnitude estimation the subject really has an infinite series of numbers from which to pick. One may be permitted some doubt that such is genuinely the case.

E. Magnitude Estimation

1. DESCRIPTION AND ORIGIN

In the method of magnitude estimation, the subject is asked to assign appropriate numbers to a series of stimuli, presumably in accordance with the subjective impressions they elicit. The origins of this method are usually attributed to Richardson (1929) in his work on the intensity of fading afterimages, where judgments were always in terms of fractions. The credit for development of this method in its modern form must go to Stevens (1956, 1957).

2. EXAMPLE OF ACTUAL EXPERIMENT

The basic method may be illustrated by the following example (Jones, 1958): Three odors, benzene, heptane, and octane, were scaled by means of the magnitude estimation technique. Seven intensity levels of each of these were prepared by dilution in mineral oil. The instructions to the subject were ones commonly used in this type of experiment, namely:

> I am going to give you a bottle to sniff which contains an odor with an intensity which we shall arbitrarily call 10. I shall present you with some bottles containing the same odor but of different intensity, and you are to assign to each of these odors a number which represents its intensity relative to the standard. For example, if it is twice as intense as the standard, you will call it 20; if half as intense, you will call it 5. You may use any number you consider to be appropriate, including fractions. Do not let what you have previously called a given intensity influence your judgment, but assign the appropriate number to each stimulus.

In this particular experiment, the standard was presented before each comparison stimulus. The order of stimuli was the same for all three substances, and was determined for each individual subject from a table of random numbers. Two judgments were made for each intensity level. They were averaged by taking median judgments for each level for each substance, and the results with the three substances reduced to a common base are shown in Fig. 4.

It will be noted that in this particular experiment, averaging was accomplished by taking medians. Strictly speaking, this is somewhat inaccurate. It is logically correct to put the formula for the power function which is

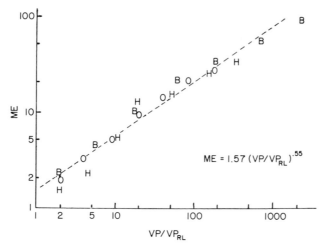

Fɪɢ. 3. Result of a typical magnitude estimation experiment. The letters refer to benzene, heptane, and octane. [From Jones (1958).]

typically obtained from magnitude estimates into its logarithmic form and average the logarithm of the judgments (cf. Jones & Marcus, 1961).

3. Other Designs

There are possible variants to some of the preceding procedures. First, it is possible to eliminate the standard completely and simply let each subject settle down to his own modulus. When this is done, the data from different individuals may be reduced to the same scale by application of appropriate constants. Second, if one does use a fixed standard, he may choose to present it only a few times at the beginning of each experimental session rather than inserting it before each judgment. Third, if a standard is used, it may be designated by some number other than 10. Within a reasonable range, it seems to make little difference. Fourth, the standard may be placed elsewhere than in the middle of the series, for example, at the top, or at the bottom. The resulting scales will not be enormously different (cf. Stevens, 1956; Jones & Woskow, 1966). Fifth, we may wish to pay some attention to the problem of order of judgment. This is probably best handled by using a systematic design which permits the assaying of ordinal effects (cf. Jones, Singer, & Twelker, 1962).

4. Discussion and Evaluation

The outcome of the preceding example is typical of the bulk of results obtained with this method. That is, most of the variance is accounted for by a power-function relationship between stimulus magnitude and assigned numerals. Since this outcome is in obvious contrast with the logarithmic law proposed by Fechner, herein lie the seeds of conflict. Stevens has been insistent that the true psychophysical law is the power function ordinarily obtained from magnitude estimation, and has made repeated attempts to demonstrate its validity. Some of the specific controversy will be reviewed in the succeeding paragraphs.

We might first ask how well the power function actually fits the data. We should particularly ask how well the function fits individual data, because, of course, the average function may not actually represent the results from any given individual. An extensive study of this question made by Pradhan and Hoffman (1963) found significant deviation from the power function, although, of course, the power function accounted for the bulk of the variance. When the deviations are at the lower end of the intensity scale, it is possible to apply the logical correction of subtracting the absolute threshold stimulus value from each stimulus intensity, as Stevens has suggested, thus making the complete formula as follows:

$$\psi = a(I - I_0)^b.$$

It is probably justifiable to conclude, especially in the absence of an alternate model, that, in the vast majority of carefully conducted experiments, most variance is accounted for by the power function, although, of course, this does not prove that some other function might not fit better.

Since it is obvious that this method depends upon the learned schema of numerals possessed by each subject, it is of interest to inquire into the problem of individual differences and also into the nature of these numerical schemata. That there are individual differences, there is no doubt whatsoever (cf. the long list of references in Zinnes, 1969). It does appear that an individual has, at any given time, a preferred range of numbers, which he tends to apply to whatever he is asked to judge. One result of this tendency is that he carries an individual exponent from situation to situation (Jones & Marcus, 1961) and that he tends to apply it to such things as pitch and loudness (see Jones & Woskow, 1962). Another consequence is the apparent increase in slope of the power function when the range of stimuli presented for judgment is reduced (cf. the discussion in Poulton, 1968). There is also some controversy over the form of the usual numerical schema. Does one's conception of the number series correspond to a linear scale? Or is it a logarithmic scale? If it is the latter, the power function results because there is a double logarithmic transformation—at the sensory input, and then in the numerical output. An exchange of notes between Ekman and Rosner illuminates this argument (Ekman, 1964; Ekman & Hosman, 1965; Ekman & Söberg, 1965; Rosner, 1965a,b). Rule (1971) has presented empirical evidence that the number series—from 1 to 10, at least—is represented subjectively as a power function of exponent .49.

Stevens has attempted to validate the results of magnitude estimation in two ways (cf. Stevens, 1971). The first of these is cross-modality matching, and the second is scaling by means of hand grip in comparison with the results of numerical judgment. In general, it may be said that if one asks an individual to match, let us say, a sound and a light, the slope of the relationship between a series of sounds and a series of light will be accurately predicted from the exponents for each. At the very worst this indicates a high degree of reliability for the method, although other functions, e.g., the logarithmic, also yield predictable relationships.

When a series of, say, sound intensities is scaled by means of a hand dynamometer, the results compare favorably with those obtained by numerical judgment. This is ordinarily interpreted as being a validation of the method of magnitude estimation. Unfortunately, the argument has a very serious flaw. When making a numerical judgment, the subject presumably has available to him an infinitude of responses. There is no ceiling. On the other hand, there is a very definite maximum for one's hand grip, and the dynamometer results are more analogous to, say, marking off a line according to the intensity of a stimulus (cf. McGill, 1960).

Some attempts have been made to relate subjective magnitudes to certain functions of the nervous system, a discussion by Mountcastle (1966) being one of the more interesting. He has reported obtaining a power-function relationship between input and thalamic activity in the somesthetic system, and even reports finding the same exponent as that reported in a magnitude estimation situation by Jones (1960). Another example is in an interesting report by Borg, Diament, Ström, and Zotterman (1968). However, it is not obvious that such neat relationships hold generally, and it is certainly true that if any degree of selection is permitted in the reading of, say, a cortical primary response, it should be possible to find some measure that would fit the power function. There is, however, evidence that there is a power-function transform at the receptor and that transmission thereafter is linear; this topic is beyond the scope of this chapter.

Quite a different approach has been made by Warren (cf. Warren & Warren, 1963), who argues that the judgments are learned. Interestingly, Fullerton and Cattell made very much the same argument in 1892 in discussing what they called the method of estimated amount of difference. They did not, however, explicitly state a square root law for sound and light, which is essential to the Warren position.

Further discussion and criticism can be found in Poulton (1968). His discussion is too detailed to repeat here, but essentially illustrates the lack of an obvious validating operation. It is true that Krantz, Luce, Suppes and Tversky (1971) assure us that they have gone a long way toward validating the power law, but since it is to appear in a second volume of their book, it was not available at the time this chapter was written. Possibly they will follow the "relational" theory of Krantz (1972) which postulates that the term "sensation" properly designates the result of a judgment of stimulus pairs. Although not, of course, identical, this approach is reminiscent of the Titchenerian idea of sensory distances (Titchener, 1905).

The most recent criticism of the power law and its typical method, magnitude estimation, has come from Anderson and his coworkers (cf. Weiss, 1972; Anderson, 1972a). Although the argument is too lengthy to be presented here in detail, it is of considerable general importance since it arises from an empirical rather than formal approach to measurement—an approach with which the author of this chapter sympathizes.

As we have mentioned in a previous section, Anderson has been conducting a series of investigations based on his concept of functional measurement (cf. Anderson, 1970). Interestingly, as applied to the validation of magnitude estimation, this approach leads to a test of the additive (or averaging) properties of various response methods. It is found that, when subjects are asked to average the magnitudes of two stimuli, category judgments are predictive of the results, magnitude estimates are not. The argument is, then, that the response scale in magnitude estimation is distorted. Beyond this negative assertion, the two variable analysis of variance design used by Anderson yields a subjective scale as well as a test for linearity within the same set of data.

References

Anderson, N. H. Functional measurement and psychophysical judgment. *Psychological Review,* 1970, **77,** 153–170.

Anderson, N. H. Cross-task validation of functional measurement. Center for Human Information Processing. Dept. of Psychology, Univ. of California, San Diego, Tech. Rept. No. 26, 1972. (a)

Anderson, N. H. Algebraic models in perception. CHIP Report No. 30, Univ. of California, San Diego, 1972. (b)

Bock, R. D., & Jones, L. V. *The measurement and prediction of judgment and choice.* San Francisco: Holden-Day, 1968.

Borg, C., Diament, H., Ström, L., & Zotterman, Y. Neural and psychophysical responses to gustatory stimuli. In D. R. Kenshalo (Ed.), *The skin senses.* Springfield, Illinois: Thomas, 1968.

Comrey, A. L. A proposed method for absolute ratio scaling. *Psychometrika,* 1950, **15,** 317–325.

Ekman, G. Two generalized ratio scaling methods. *Journal of Psychology,* 1958, **45,** 287–295.

Ekman, G. Is the power law a special case of Fechner's law? *Perceptual and Motor Skills,* 1964, **19,** 730.

Ekman, G. & Hosman, B. Note on subjective scales of number. *Perceptual and Motor Skills,* 1965, **21,** 101–102.

Ekman, G., & Sjöberg, L. Scaling, *Annual Review of Psychology,* 1965, **16,** 451–474.

Engen, T. Psychophysics II. Scaling methods. In J. W. Kling & L. A. Riggs (Eds.), *Woodworth and Schlosberg's experimental psychology,* 3rd ed. New York: Holt, 1971.

Engen, T., & Tulunay, Ü. Some sources of error in half-heaviness judgments. *Journal of Experimental Psychology,* 1956, **54,** 208–212.

Fechner, Gustav T. *Elemente der Psychophysik.* Leipzig: Breitkoph and Hartel, 1860.

Fullerton, G. S., & Cattell, J. McK. *On the perception of small differences.* Publications of the University of Pennsylvania, No. 2. Philadelphia: University of Pennsylvania Press, 1892.

Garner, W. R. Context effects and the validity of loudness scales. *Journal of the Acoustical Society of America,* 1954, **26,** 73–88.

Geiger, P. H., & Firestone, F. A. The estimation of fractional loudness. *Journal of the Acoustical Society of America,* 1933, **5,** 25–30.

Guilford, J. P. *Psychometric methods,* 2nd ed. New York: McGraw-Hill, 1954.

Ham, L. B., & Parkinson, J. S. Loudness and intensity relations. *Journal of the Acoustical Society of America,* 1932, **3,** 511–534.

Hanes, R. M. The construction of subjective brightness scales from fractionation data: a validation. *Journal of Experimental Psychology,* 1949, **39,** 719–728.

Jones, F. N. Subjective scales of intensity for three odors. *American Journal of Psychology,* 1958, **71,** 423–425.

Jones, F. N. Some subjective magnitude functions for touch. In G. R. Hawkes (Ed.), *Symposium on cutaneous sensibility.* Fort Knox, Kentucky: U.S. Army Med. Res. Lab., Report No. 424, 1960.

Jones, F. N., & Marcus, M. J. The subject effect in judgments of subjective magnitude. *Journal of Experimental Psychology,* 1961, **61,** 40–44.

Jones, F. N., Singer, D., & Twelker, P. A. Interactions among the somesthetic senses in judgments of subjective magnitude. *Journal of Experimental Psychology,* 1962, **64,** 105–109.

Jones, F. N., & Woskow, M. J. On the relationship between estimates of magnitude of loudness and pitch. *American Journal of Psychology,* 1962, **75,** 669–671.

Jones, F. N. & Woskow, M. J. Some effects of context on the slope in magnitude estimation. *Journal of Experimental Psychology,* 1966, **71,** 177–180.

Krantz, D. H. A theory of magnitude estimation and cross-modality matching. *Journal of Mathematical Psychology,* 1972, **9,** 168–199.

Krantz, D. H., Luce, R. D., Suppes, P., & Tversky, A. *Foundations of measurement,* Vol. I. New York: Academic Press, 1971.

McGill, W. The slope of the loudness function: A puzzle. In H. Gulliksen, & S. Messick (Eds.), *Psychological scaling.* New York: Wiley, 1960.

Metfessel, M. A proposal for quantitative reporting of comparative judgments. *Journal of Psychology,* 1947, **24,** 229–235.

Mountcastle, V. B. Neural replication of somatic sensory events. In J. C. Eccles (Ed.), *Brain and conscious experience.* New York: Springer-Verlag, 1966.

Parducci, A., & Perrett, L. F. Category rating scales: Effects of relative spacing and frequency of stimulus values. *Journal of Experimental Psychology Monograph,* 1971, **89,** 427–452.

Peryam, D. R., Polemis, B. W., Kamen, J. M., Eindhoven, J., and Pilgrim, F. J. *Food preferences of men in the U.S. armed forces,* Chicago: Quartermaster Corps, 1960.

Plateau, J. A. F. Sur la measure des sensations physique, et sur la loi qui lie l'intensité de ces sensations a l'intensité de la cause excitante. *Bulletin de l'Academie Royale, Belgique,* 1872, **33,** 376–385.

Poulton, E. C. The new psychophysics: Six models for magnitude estimation. *Psychological Bulletin,* 1968, **69,** 1–19.

Pradhan, P. L., & Hoffman, P. J. Effect of spacing and range of stimuli on magnitude estimation judgments. *Journal of Experimental Psychology,* 1963, **66,** 533–541.

Richardson, L. F. Imagery, conation, and cerebral conductance. *Journal of General Psychology,* 1929, **2,** 324–352.

Rosner, B. S. The power law and subjective scales of number. *Perceptual and Motor Skills,* 1965, **21,** 42. (a)

Rosner, B. S. Comment on note on numerical behavior. *Perceptual and Motor Skills,* 1965, **21,** 120. (b)

Rule, S. J. Discriminability scales of number for multiple and fractional estimates. *Acta Psychologica, Amsterdam,* 1971, **35,** 328–333.

Stevens, S. S. The direct estimation of sensory magnitudes—loudness. *American Journal of Psychology,* 1956, **69,** 1–25.

Stevens, S. S. On the psychophysical law. *Psychological Review,* 1957, **64,** 153–181.

Stevens, S. S. Issues in psychophysical measurement. *Psychological Review,* 1971, **78,** 426–450.

Thorndike, E. L. Handwriting. *Teachers College Record,* 1910, **11** (No. 2).

Thurstone, L. L. Psychophysical analysis. *American Journal of Psychology,* 1927, **38,** 368–389.

Thurstone, L. L. *The measurement of values.* Chicago: Univ. of Chicago Press, 1959.

Titchener, E. B. *Experimental psychology,* Vol. II. *Quantitative experiments,* Part II. *Instructor's manual.* New York: Macmillan, 1905. (Reprinted 1927.)

Torgerson, W. S. *Theory and methods of scaling.* New York: Wiley, 1958.

Warren, R. M., & Warren, R. P. A critique of S. S. Stevens' "New psychophysics." *Perceptual and Motor Skills,* 1963, **16,** 797–810.

Weiss, D. J. Averaging: An empirical validity criterion for magnitude estimation. Center for Human Information Processing, Dept. of Psychology, Univ. of California, San Diego, Tech. Rep. No. 26, 1972.

Zinnes, J. L. Scaling. *Annual Review of Psychology,* 1969, **20,** 447–470.

Chapter 11

PERCEPTUAL MAGNITUDE AND ITS MEASUREMENT

S. S. STEVENS

I. INTRODUCTION

Perceptual research has a concern with the art and the principles of scaling, because there is an obvious need to quantify the behavior of perceptual systems. It is one thing to know that the ear responds to sound and the eye to light, and that stimuli vary in intensity. But the posing of quantitative questions requires more than a listing of what is phenomenally obvious. Quantitative inquiry ought properly to begin with first-order issues, the chief one of which concerns the operating characteristics of the sensory systems—the input–output functions. The basic psychophysical problem thus becomes: How does sensation output depend on stimulus input?

Research in many laboratories has shown that the so-called psychophysical law is a power function. Sensory magnitude ψ increases in proportion to the stimulus ϕ raised to a power β. Thus we write $\psi = k\phi^{\beta}$, where k is a constant that depends upon units. Under some circumstances the value of ϕ may be altered by an additive constant representing the threshold, the value at which the stimulus first becomes effective. The sensation called "loudness" grows approximately as a power function of sound pressure. The exponent .6 is the conventional value that has been recommended by the International Organization for Standardization, but more recent evidence suggests that the value of the exponent may be close to $\frac{2}{3}$. Expressed in terms of sound energy rather than sound pressure, the loudness exponent becomes $\frac{1}{3}$. Brightness provides another example of the psychophysical power law, and for brightness the exponent is also close to $\frac{1}{3}$.

II. FECHNER'S LAW

We speak of the "psychophysical law" mainly because of its history. On a morning in the year 1850 the physicist G. T. Fechner was lying in bed, as he tells us, wondering how to connect the inner world of sensory magnitudes with the outer world of stimulus energy. It occurred to him that the correspondence lay in a simple principle: A relative increase in external energy corresponds to a fixed increment in subjective intensity. He later saw the relation between his new idea and the experiments of E. H. Weber, which showed that an increment to a stimulus becomes just noticeable when it reaches some fixed percentage of the original stimulus. Fechner made use of that relation to set up the equation

$$\Delta\psi = k(\Delta\phi/\phi).$$

Integration of that equation suggested that sensation ψ grows as the logarithm of the stimulus ϕ. The psychophysical law, according to Fechner, is a logarithmic function.

The logarithmic form of the psychophysical law still has adherents. It is still expounded in the numerous textbooks that deal with sensory systems, but change has been taking place. If the logarithmic law is no longer as highly regarded as it once was, the credit belongs, in large measure, to developments in acoustics.

As a testing ground for sensory principles, acoustics had two advantages. The first was that before 1920 acoustics was a backward science. Before the development of the vacuum tube, sound waves were so difficult to produce and control that a quantitative science was hardly possible. The second advantage was that those who made use of the new electronic tools in the 1930s did not have a long-established tradition to discourage the borrowing of useful ideas from other disciplines. In order to measure sound more conveniently, the acoustical workers borrowed from the transmission engineers the logarithmic decibel scale. Next they asked an obvious question: Is loudness proportional to decibels, as Fechner's law says it ought to be? The answer was plainly no. Simple listening tests made it clear that equal decibel differences did not mark off equal differences in loudness; and a sound of 50 dB did not seem half as loud as a sound of 100 dB. Actually, instead of sounding half as loud as 100 dB, a sound of 50 dB appears to be only about 2% as loud.

Beginning about 1930, direct experiments were started to determine how the perception of loudness grows with increasing sound pressure. Some of those early experiments were sponsored by commercial companies, because there was a practical engineering need to understand how the customer perceives loudness. In a novel method developed at the Bell Telephone Laboratories, the listener adjusted the loudness heard in one ear to match the loudness heard in both ears. On the assumption that loudness adds in the two ears, a loudness function was then derived. From those and other measurements, Fletcher (1938) proposed a loudness function that served many useful purposes, although the function was later modified.

The measurement of loudness did not go unchallenged, of course, for it represented a rather radical development. Fletcher's curve was the first empirically based scale of sensation that commanded wide agreement. Its adherents claimed that it measured the strength of an experience. But many people believed, and some still do, that such a measurement lies beyond the reach of science. It may indeed prove impossible to resolve the philosophic argument about the measurability of sensation, but we can at least measure what a person says about his sensory experience. For example, we can measure the point at which a person says that one sound seems equal to another, or the point at which one sound seems half as loud as another. The half-as-loud procedure, called fractionation, was popular in the 1930s and 1940s, but it has given way to more effective procedures.

III. THE POWER LAW

A turning point in psychophysics occurred when a battery of methods was applied to sensory measurement in both vision and hearing (Stevens, 1953). Since one of the methods, called bisection, showed a curious hysteresis effect when applied to loudness, the method of bisection was also tried with visual brightness. There too the same hysteresis effect was observed. An interesting outcome, to be sure, but what seemed more exciting was the close resemblance between sensory responses to light and sound when the data obtained with three different methods were compared. A new method, later to be known as magnitude estimation, in which the observer tries to assign numbers proportional to the apparent strength of his sensation, gave results that agreed fairly well with the two older methods—results indicating that in both vision and hearing, the sensation grows approximately as a cube-root power function of the stimulus intensity.

The next task was to explore the reach of the power function. Is it a general law, or does it hold only for vision and hearing? Experiments to answer that question have explored more than three dozen sensory and perceptual continua. The remarkable and quite unexpected result is that the psychophysical power law seems to hold in all sense modalities. The so-called distance senses, vision and hearing, are by no means special cases. In general, each sense modality has its own exponent, but the values of some of the exponents depend on such parameters as adaptation and contrast.

One of the advantages that we may hope to derive from a natural law lies in the constraints that it places on our expectations regarding the outcome of experiments. Prior to 1953, almost any outcome of a scaling experiment might have proved acceptable. Now, however, the accumulated inventory of some hundreds of power functions, covering nearly all the sense modalities, suggests that a suitable scaling operation must yield a highly restricted outcome. As the power law becomes more secure, the burden of proof tends to become inverted, so that it becomes the exception to the power law that alerts attention and demands demonstration. An unconfirmed exception no longer evokes much scientific interest. On the other hand, a confirmed exception, like some of those that have been repeatedly demonstrated for certain kinds of stimuli in hearing (Stevens, 1971a), may generate new attempts at understanding, for history has shown that the leverage inherent in a natural law makes it possible to pry new principles from seeming exceptions.

IV. CROSS-MODALITY MATCHING

Skepticism regarding people's ability to make numerical assessments of a sensory experience such as loudness has often been expressed, perhaps as well as ever by McGill (1960).

> Stevens' procedure capitalizes on our lifetime of commerce with quantification and estimation. Consequently, when the measurement is free of bias, the numbers are thought to represent loudness more or less accurately.
> But perhaps normal subjects seldom respond to the intensity of a sound in all the ways that numbers suggest. The responses may look or sound numerical, and they can often be plotted, but some sort of demonstration is demanded if we are to believe that they also have quantitative significance.

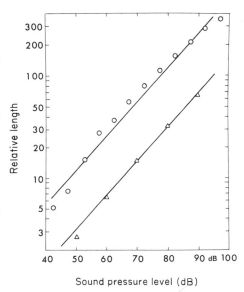

FIG. 1. Cross-modality matching of apparent length to apparent loudness. In one experiment (circles) the subject marked a distance from the left-hand end of a 6-inch line in order to indicate the apparent loudness of a tone of 1000 Hz (McGill, 1960). For the triangles the subject turned a knob to adjust a line of light projected on a wall in order to make its length appear to match the apparent loudness of a band of noise (Stevens & Guirao, 1963). Each experiment involved 10 observers.

In order to supply the needed demonstration, McGill proceeded to scale loudness by asking subjects to place a mark on a 6-inch line to indicate a distance from the left-hand end that would correspond to the apparent loudness of various intensities of a 1000-Hz tone. The median responses of 10 observers are plotted as circles in Fig. 1. The triangles are from another experiment involving length in which 10 observers adjusted a line of light projected on a wall in order to indicate the apparent loudness of a noise (Stevens & Guirao, 1963). The straight lines through the data represent power functions with the exponent $\frac{2}{3}$. In view of the constraints involved in the two procedures of length adjustment, especially with the 6-inch line segment, the two sets of data come remarkably close to the loudness functions for the two stimuli—a tone of 1000 Hz and a band of noise 500 to 5000 Hz. The loudness functions for both those stimuli are now known to depart somewhat from a simple power function and to exhibit a midlevel bulge. A power function can be approximated more closely if the stimulus approximates a critical band of noise centered at 3150 Hz. A $\frac{1}{3}$-octave band of noise at 3150 Hz has been proposed for the standard reference sound (Stevens, 1971a).

The method of direct cross-modality matching has been extended to a wide variety of continua, and has emerged as a powerful device for the measurement of subjective variables (Stevens, 1959). If, for example, loudness and brightness are both power functions of intensity, it becomes pertinent to ask what happens if an observer is instructed to adjust the level of a sound to make it seem as strong as the brightness of a given light? By matching loudness to brightness over a wide range of intensities, we should obtain a matching function that is also a power function. Not only that, but the exponent of the matching function should be given by the ratio of the exponents for loudness and brightness. Matching experiments between loudness and brightness, with each stimulus serving as the variable to be adjusted, have been carried out by J. C. Stevens and Marks (1965), who showed that the predicted results can be obtained.

If we neglect constants that depend only upon the choice of units, the argument can be expressed as follows. We assume that two sense modalities are governed by power laws

$$\psi_1 = \phi_1{}^a \quad \text{and} \quad \psi_2 = \phi_2{}^b,$$

and that the apparent sensations ψ_1 and ψ_2 are made equal by cross-modality matches at several different levels of stimulus intensity. The results of the cross-modality matches determine an equal sensation function. Since the procedure was designed to make

$$\psi_1 = \psi_2,$$

we can also write

$$\phi_1{}^a = \phi_2{}^b.$$

In terms of logarithms, we can further write

$$\log \phi_1 = b/a \log \phi_2.$$

In other words, in log–log (or decibel) coordinates, the equal sensation function becomes a straight line whose slope is given by the ratio of the two original exponents.

We therefore have at hand a method for validating a given sensory scale. Thus, for example, by means of cross-modality equations, loudness has been matched in one or another experiment to more than a score of different perceptual continua. Some of the results are shown in Fig. 2. There it can be seen that all the matching functions approximate power functions (straight lines in log–log coordinates). The slopes of the lines, which determine the matching exponents, accord quite well with the predictions based on the exponents of the various functions as determined in separate experiments. In addition to the 10 matching functions shown in Fig. 2, loudness matches have been used to scale at least that many other continua: the four basic tastes (Moskowitz, 1971), thermal discomfort for warm and for cold (J. C. Stevens, Marks, & Gagge, 1969), angular velocity (Brown, 1968), warmth on the back (J. C. Stevens & Marks, 1967), and whole-body vibration (Versace, 1963). Loudness has also been used to gauge

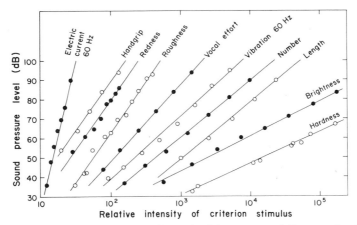

FIG. 2. Equal sensation functions determined by cross-modality matches between loudness and various criterion stimuli. Loudness was the variable that was adjusted in most of the experiments, but handgrip, vocal effort, and length were adjusted to match loudness. The relative positions of the functions have been adjusted for clarity. The slopes (exponents) are those determined by the data. [From Stevens, 1966.]

anxiety, both in a clinical setting (Peck, 1966) and in the classroom (Sullivan, 1969); and also to scale prestige of occupations, pronounceability of trigrams, and attitudinal statements about racism (Dawson & Brinker, 1971). Since loudness is so easy to produce and control, and since it can be varied over enormous ranges, it stands next to the number continuum with respect to the potential convenience afforded the experimenter who undertakes scaling.

Other families of matching functions have been based on matches involving handgrip (J. C. Stevens & Mack, 1959; Stevens, 1961a), brightness (Stevens, 1967), and various other continua (Stevens, 1968, 1969). The overall consistency of the total array of matching functions provides quantitative evidence that the question posed more than a century ago by Fechner is a tractable question that permits a scientific answer. The general psychophysical law follows the power-function form, not the logarithmic form that Fechner conjectured on October 22, 1850—a day celebrated by psychophysicists as Fechner Day. We celebrate the fact that Fechner posed the right question, even if it took a century to find the right answer.

V. THE ROLE OF EXPONENTS

What significance can we attach to the power-function form of the psychophysical law? Although the full significance is far from known, it is important to note that the power law can be summed up as a simple invariance: Equal stimulus ratios produce equal sensation ratios. The principle of ratio invariance seems to apply to all the sensory systems. An analogous principle holds for many of the functional relations in physics. Indeed, physical laws are most often power laws.

With physical laws, however, the exponents are usually integers or simple fractions, whereas the measured values of sensory and perceptual exponents rarely show such simplicity. Nevertheless, it is interesting to note that many of the sensory exponents approximate simple rational fractions. Table I shows typical measured values, and also a hypothetical set of values

TABLE I

MEASURED EXPONENTS AND THEIR POSSIBLE FRACTIONAL VALUES FOR
POWER FUNCTIONS RELATING SUBJECTIVE MAGNITUDE
TO STIMULUS MAGNITUDE

Continuum	Measured exponent	Possible fraction	Stimulus condition
Loudness	.67	$\frac{2}{3}$	3150-Hz signal
Brightness	.33	$\frac{1}{3}$	5° target in dark
Brightness	.5	$\frac{1}{2}$	very brief flash
Smell	.6	$\frac{2}{3}$	heptane
Taste	1.3	$\frac{3}{2}$	sucrose
Taste	1.4	$\frac{3}{2}$	salt
Temperature	1.0	1	cold on arm
Temperature	1.5	$\frac{3}{2}$	warmth on arm
Vibration	.95	1	60 Hz on finger
Duration	1.1	1	white noise stimuli
Finger span	1.3	$\frac{3}{2}$	thickness of blocks
Pressure on palm	1.1	1	static force on skin
Heaviness	1.45	$\frac{3}{2}$	lifted weights
Force of handgrip	1.7	$\frac{5}{3}$	hand dynamometer
Vocal effort	1.1	1	vocal sound pressure
Electric shock	3.5	3	current through fingers
Tactual roughness	1.5	$\frac{3}{2}$	rubbing emery cloths
Visual length	1.0	1	projected line
Visual area	.7	$\frac{2}{3}$	projected square
Angular acceleration	1.4	$\frac{3}{2}$	5-sec stimulus

that may characterize the exponents if, in fact, the sensory systems are to be thought of as governed by simple exponents under ideal conditions. Whatever the best values of the exponents may turn out to be, the point should be emphasized that, in all sensory systems studied thus far, equal stimulus ratios correspond to equal perceived ratios.

For the origin of the ratio invariance in the response of a sensory system, we may perhaps seek cues in the evolutionary history of the organism. In perceiving and reacting to the world, it is advantageous to an animal if the perceived relations among stimuli do not depend too strongly on the absolute magnitudes of the stimuli. Fortunately for our survival, perceived relations tend toward constancy. Thus, to take a simple example, the lengths of the sides of a triangle appear to maintain their relative proportions when the triangle is moved away from the viewer. Similarly, the ratio between the light and shaded parts of a photograph seem approximately the same under strong and under dim illumination. Relations among the sounds of speech remain much the same whether the speech is soft or highly amplified. The usefulness of those roughly constant relations under wide changes in stimulus levels is obvious—so obvious that we often take them for granted and fail to note their significance. The ratio invariance that underlies the psychophysical power law makes it possible for us to adjust adaptively to the rich patterning of the environment, despite the enormous ranges of stimulus energy to which we are subjected. Without a power-law operating characteristic in the eye, for example, our task of adjustment would presumably be made more difficult.

Those sense modalities that are subjected to wide ranges of energy tend to have low exponents, but that rule does not necessarily hold in reverse. For example, the sense of smell has a fairly low exponent, despite the fact that the effective range of odor concentrations is rather limited. But when the range of stimulus energy extends over more than a trillionfold, or more than 10^{12}, as it does in vision and hearing, there is an obvious need for the low exponents that nature has provided. The transducer nonlinearity, evidenced by a low exponent, seems to be nature's way of matching the input from the outside world to the needs of the central nervous system. By means of a nonlinear transducer, a billionfold change in sound energy becomes a thousandfold change in apparent loudness. To be sure, that is a large subjective change, but it seems not unreasonable that the nervous system should be able to process changes of a thousandfold. On the other hand, the neural processing of changes exceeding a billionfold would seem beyond reasonable possibility.

It may well be that the transmission and transfer processes in the central nervous system are limited to essentially linear transformations, as was suggested in a discussion by Sir John Eccles and V. B. Mountcastle at a Ciba

Symposium (Ciba, 1966). If central linearity, or some approximation thereto, turns out to be the general rule, then it becomes clear why the sense organs, which provide the window between world and brain, must also provide for nonlinear transductions, at least in some of the sense modalities. In those modalities for which the stimulus range is so large that it would overload the central system, the transducer must provide a compressor action, which it can do if its exponent is smaller than 1.0. In other sense modalities, however, where no compression appears to be needed, the exponent can be 1.0, which means that the function is linear. Or the exponent may be even larger. Thus several of the exponents in Table I are greater than 1.0, and the perceived magnitude grows as an accelerating function of the stimulus. Think how radically an accelerating function differs from Fechner's logarithmic function!

VI. NEURELECTRIC POWER FUNCTIONS

Although the physiological responses of the sense organs have often been said to be logarithmic, many of the actual recordings of neurelectric activity in sensory receptors, nerve fibers, and neural complexes have been shown to follow power functions. The major points of the electrophysiological evidence have been reviewed elsewhere (Stevens, 1970, 1971b). The electrical recording of nervous activity turns out to give highly variable results, but in many sense modalities the electrical potentials have been shown to grow as a power function of the stimulus intensity. There appears to be little question, therefore, that the sensory systems are capable of power transformations. Of course, every placement of an electrode does not yield a power function, but the effort to find such functions in neurelectric effects has proved rewarding.

Physiological power functions have been found by one or more investigators for each of the following sensory systems, and sometimes for various parts thereof:

Vision: receptor cell, ganglion cell, lateral geniculate, occipital cortex

Hearing: intracochlear nerve response, superior olivary complex, vertex (top of head)

Taste: chorda tympani (in human subjects), electrical pulse to tongue

Cutaneous: vibration, pressure, touch on hairy skin

Somesthetic: joint position, muscle stretch

Electric shock: pulses to skin

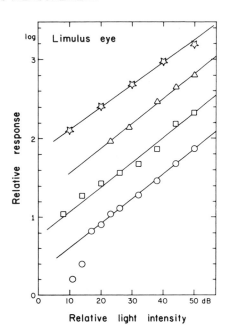

FIG. 3. Power-function responses in the eye of the horseshoe crab *Limulus*. The stars represent frequencies of nerve impulses recorded by Hartline and Graham (1932) from a single fiber of the optic nerve. Frequency was measured 3.5 sec after the onset of the light. The triangles, squares, and circles represent responses to .02-sec flashes of light, recorded with intracellular electrodes in single ommatidia. The plotted points represent the areas under oscillographs published by Fuortes and Hodgkin (1964). The straight lines in the log–log coordinates represent power functions. The slopes (exponents) are .29 (for the stars) and .32 (for the diamonds, squares, and circles). Both coordinates give relative values only. Eyes were dark-adapted.

In some of the physiological experiments, the recorded data can be described by power functions having approximately the same exponents as the corresponding psychophysical functions. More often, however, the experimental values of the neurelectric exponents have been characterized by lower values than the psychophysical exponents. The evidence seems to suggest that under optimal circumstances, with the electrode located in a place that samples the sense organ's behavior, the neurelectric response may exhibit an exponent as large as the psychophysical value. In other words, the psychophysical value appears to stand as an upper bound, and most neurelectric exponents fall below that upper bound, as though the function had been subjected to a power transformation.

Examples of power functions in the recorded responses of the *Limulus* eye are shown in Fig. 3.

VII. TWO KINDS OF PERCEPTUAL CONTINUA

The perceptual continua discussed in the foregoing pages have in common the feature that they concern intensity or amount. Scales of perceptual magnitude provide answers to the questions of how strong the sound, or the light, or the smell is. Intensity continua have been called prothetic, because many of them are based on a physiological process in which excitation is added to excitation already there. It is assumed, for example, that a light looks brighter than it is or a sound appears louder than it is because of added neural excitation.

Another kind of continuum is based on a different principle. Thus, when the pitch of a tone appears to rise, it is not because of added excitation, but because new excitation has been exchanged for excitation that has been removed. A substitution process of that kind underlies the typical continuum of the class known as metathetic (Stevens, 1957). Other metathetic continua are apparent position (azimuth) and apparent inclination.

The two physiological processes, the *additive* and the *substitutive,* mediate discriminations that follow dramatically different rules. Consider, for example, the just noticeable difference (jnd). On the scale of subjective pitch, which is measured in mels, the jnd is a constant size, namely, 1 jnd equals approximately 1 mel. Otherwise said, if we add up the jnd, as Fechner proposed to do, we obtain a scale that coincides with the scale of pitch obtained by the scaling methods of equisection and fractionation (Stevens & Volkmann, 1940a).

With loudness, on the other hand, the scale obtained by the adding up of jnd (which produces an approximately logarithmic function) fails to coincide with the sone scale of subjective loudness. In other words, the jnd for loudness are not constant in subjective size. Specifically, a jnd for white noise at 40 dB corresponds to a loudness difference of about .4 sone. At 100 dB, the difference reaches a value 50 times larger. Thus the subjective size of the jnd on a prothetic continuum grows rapidly as we go up the scale.

Another difference between prothetic and metathetic continua shows up on what are called *partition scales.* There are many kinds of partition scales, but they all have a crucial feature in common: They are created by requiring that the subject divide a segment of a continuum into parts. Now, whenever the subject performs the subdividing operation on a prothetic continuum, there results a systematic bias. Although he may try to equalize the subdivisions, the subject divides the lower end of the continuum into finer segments than the upper end. Experimental results have repeatedly shown that a linear, unbiased partition is rarely, if ever, achieved on a prothetic continuum.

On a metathetic continuum, however, the subject can perform a linear partition. In fact, the mel scale of pitch was constructed by asking subjects to adjust the frequencies on a special electronic piano in order to make the pitch distances appear equal from one key to the next. The data obtained by that method of equisection agreed with the ratio judgments obtained from the same listeners by the method of fractionation (Stevens & Volkmann, 1940a).

Except for their occasional uses on metathetic continua, it appears that partition scales have proved rather unsatisfactory as scaling devices. At best, the methods that require partitioning produce interval scales, not ratio scales. On interval scales the zero point is arbitrary, as on our ordinary temperature scales, Celsius and Fahrenheit.

VIII. CATEGORY SCALE

The most common and perhaps the least satisfactory form of partition scale is the category rating scale. In one of its simplest forms, the categories may be designated by a limited set of adjectives, such as large, medium, and small. Or the categories may be designated by a finite set of numbers, such as 1–6. Those were the numbers used for history's first recorded category scale, the scale of stellar magnitude, which dates from about 150 B.C., and which, in a much revised form, still serves the astronomer (Stevens, 1960). On prothetic continua the category scales are invariably nonlinear. When plotted against the scale obtained by magnitude estimation, for example, the data from category judgments produce a curve that is concave downward.

Examples of category scales for loudness are shown in Fig. 4, where they are plotted against the sone scale of subjective magnitude. There we see that it makes rather little difference whether the subjects use numbers

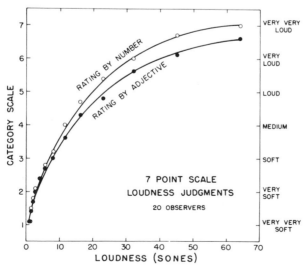

Fig. 4. The category scale produces a curvilinear function when plotted against the ratio scale of loudness. [From Stevens and Galanter, 1957.]

or adjectives. The forms of the two category scales are similar, because, whenever the subject is asked to categorize, he is forced to divide the continuum into parts or segments in order to make it conform to the limited, finite set of numbers or adjectives that he is required to use. In other words, he is obliged to attend to differences or distances. Under those circumstances, the subject is forced out of ratioing and into differencing, because the experimenter has precluded ratio judgments. The remedy, of course, is straightforward: Do not limit the subject to a finite set of numbers. If he is permitted to use any number that seems appropriate, he may produce a ratio scale, and, in fact, he usually does.

What we learn from category experiments is that the human being, despite his great versatility, has a limited capacity to effect linear partitions on prothetic continua. He does quite well, to be sure, if the continuum happens to be metathetic, but, since most scaling problems involve prothetic continua, it seems that category and other forms of partition scaling generally ought to be avoided for the purposes of scaling. If, for some reason, an unbiased interval scale is needed, it can be obtained from a ratio scale, for the ratio scale contains the interval scale (Stevens, 1946). The reverse is not possible, however. When only interval information is available, the ratio scale of the continuum cannot be recovered from the interval scale.

The conclusion, then, seems inescapable: For the purposes of serious perceptual measurement, category methods should be shunned. The deliberate and ill-conceived imposition of a limited set of response categories forces the subject into partitioning. At that point the hope for a ratio scale must fail.

IX. VIRTUAL EXPONENTS

Not only is the category scale concave downward, as in Fig. 4, but the bisection point in a bisection experiment tends to fall systematically lower than the magnitude scale would predict (Garner, 1954). For the bisection results it is possible to make use of a simple equation (Stevens, 1955) in order to determine the exponent of the power function that describes the results when a stimulus ϕ_2 is set to seem halfway between ϕ_1 and ϕ_3. The formula may be written

$$\phi_3{}^\alpha - \phi_2{}^\alpha = \phi_2{}^\alpha - \phi_1{}^\alpha.$$

The exponent α may be called the virtual or "as if" exponent in order to distinguish it from the actual exponent β, which governs the continuum (Stevens, 1971c). The virtual exponent is smaller than the actual exponent.

Category scales and other forms of partition scales can also be conveniently described by power functions. Thus the Munsell scale of lightness, which is a partition scale, has a virtual exponent of approximately $\frac{1}{3}$, whereas the actual exponent for lightness, as determined by magnitude estimation, is approximately 1.2 (Stevens & Galanter, 1957). Since the partition scale is, at best, an interval scale, the formula for the partition scale needs an additive constant P_0 to take care of the arbitrary zero. The equation may be written

$$P + P_0 = k\phi^\alpha,$$

where α is the virtual exponent.

The virtual exponents of some 29 category scales have been determined by Marks (1968). The virtual exponents ranged from high values that were roughly equal to half the values of the actual exponents down to a very low value (.06) for one of the nine category scales that Marks determined for brightness. The largest virtual exponent for brightness was .22.

The old astronomical scale of stellar magnitude—a visual category scale—gave an indeterminate exponent because the midpoint of the scale corresponded to a bisection below the geometric mean. That unusual bisection point probably results from the drastic skewness in the distribution of the stimuli in the heavens. There are thousands of times more dim stars than bright stars, and it seems that the astronomers adjusted their visual scale to make room, so to speak, for the many faint stars. Similar but less dramatic effects of skewed stimulus distributions have been exhibited many times in the laboratory (Stevens & Galanter, 1957). Except for that early astronomical scale, the virtual exponents of most partition scales appear to be positive. In fact, when conditions were made maximally easy for the observer to produce a simple bisection, the values of the virtual exponents for loudness (Stevens, 1955) and brightness (Stevens, 1961b) rose to within roughly 10% of the values of the actual exponents.

Much interest attaches to the fact that partitioning produces positive exponents, because there persists a wayward myth concerning the matter. The myth says that partition scales are logarithmic functions. If that were true, the virtual exponent would approach zero. But the virtual exponent is clearly greater than zero. As the virtual exponent becomes smaller, bisection falls closer and closer to the geometric mean. In practice, the bisection point seems always to fall well above the geometric mean.

If the virtual exponent fell near zero, a possible meaning would be that observers could not tell ratios from intervals (Torgerson, 1961). Experimental findings have demonstrated over and over, however, that observers can distinguish between ratios and intervals. That is, when observers match intervals, the results are not the logarithm of what they do when they match ratios. The logarithmic relation would obtain, if, when asked for equal differences, the observer produced equal ratios, or vice versa. As an experimental fact, such behavior does not usually occur.

The value of the virtual exponent lies between zero and the value of the actual exponent, but the exact location of the virtual exponent depends on the experimental circumstances. It seems to be a general rule that the value of the virtual exponent varies inversely with those factors that tend to increase the difficulty of the task. Difficulty tends to increase the noise load, which shows up in the consequent variability of the observer's behavior. Thus the partitioning called for in category scaling has usually produced a smaller virtual exponent than is produced on the same continuum by allowing the observer to set a bisection point. It appears that the noise load is less under bisection than under category scaling.

X. MAGNITUDE ESTIMATION OF INTERVALS

Another procedure that illustrates the operation of a virtual exponent calls for the experimenter to produce intervals and for the observer to make magnitude estimations of their apparent size. Instructive results were obtained by Beck and Shaw (1967) who asked 28 observers to judge loudness intervals of 5, 10, 15, and 20 sones. Each of the intervals was produced at four different levels on the stimulus scale. The median magnitude estimations for three of the intervals have been plotted in Fig. 5.

The circles show, for example, that a 20-sone interval is judged to be larger when it is produced at a low sound pressure level than at high sound pressure level. The other intervals exhibit the same general tendency; and the same overall trend is shown by the triangles, which were derived from experiments carried out by Dawson (1968).

The downward tilt of the lines in Fig. 5 exhibits in a dramatic fashion the operation of the bias that afflicts partitioning on prothetic continua. In a world in which equal intervals appeared equal to the perceiving subject, the four lines in Fig. 5 would be horizontal. Since the four lines are not horizontal, many facts can be explained. Thus it follows from the downward slopes in Fig. 5 that category scales must be curved when plotted against the magnitude scale, and that bisection points must fall below the value predicted by the magnitude scale.

The curves in Fig. 5 were constructed on the assumption that the virtual exponent is .3, or approximately half the size of the actual loudness exponent. The curves so constructed give a fair account of the data.

On the assumption that, when observers judge intervals, their results

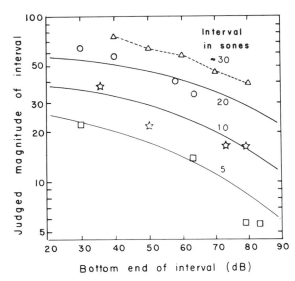

FIG. 5. The judgment of an interval of a constant size depends upon the location of the interval. Observers made magnitude estimations of sets of intervals 5, 10, 20, and approximately 30 sones wide. The stimulus level at the bottom end of the · interval is shown by the abscissa. The ordinate gives relative values only. As a constant interval moves upward in sound pressure level, the perceived size of the interval decreases. [Data from Beck and Shaw (1967); and (triangles) Dawson (1968).]

The three curves were generated by assuming that instead of the actual exponent of the sone scale .6, the observers used a virtual or "as if" exponent equal to .3.

can be described with the aid of a virtual exponent, we may ask what happens when the stimulus intervals presented are made to be equal, not in sones, but in units of a power function having an exponent equal to the virtual exponent. Beck and Shaw arranged such an experiment and obtained the expected results. The judged size of such an interval remained essentially constant, regardless of where it was placed on the stimulus continuum. In other words, when plotted as in Fig. 5 the judgments of constant intervals generated by the virtual power function described horizontal lines.

What happens, then, if the function used to generate the stimulus intervals has an exponent that is lower than the virtual exponent? The answer to that question is clear in some of Dawson's data, for he, in effect, allowed the exponent of the generating function to approach zero. In other words, he presented equal logarithmic (decibel) intervals. If plotted in Fig. 5, the results he obtained would describe a function that curves upward rather than downward. Specifically, for successive 10-dB intervals beginning at

40 dB, the magnitude estimations, averaged over four separate experiments, were 1.51, 1.89, 2.65, 4.14, and 9.1. Thus the interval 80–90 dB was judged to be about six times larger than the interval 40–50 dB.

From the three cases studied, then, a simple rule emerges. In the coordinates of Fig. 5, the curves will slope upward or downward, depending on whether the stimulus intervals are generated by a function whose exponent is smaller or larger than the observer's virtual exponent.

XI. PRODUCTION OF SUMS

If the virtual exponent is smaller than the actual exponent, an interesting question arises concerning the outcome of another kind of experiment, one that inverts the bisection procedure. We can turn the problem around, so to speak, and instead of asking the observer to produce segments, the experimenter can present the segments and ask the observer to produce what appears to him to be the whole, or the sum. In other words, the experimenter presents the partitions and asks what they are partitions of. Does the virtual function then remain convex, as it does when bisection is employed? If the observer's "as if" psychophysical function remains convex, it follows that the perceived whole should seem less than the sum of the perceived parts.

A series of experiments by Krueger (1970) gave evidence that the concept of the virtual exponent is useful not only in partitioning but also in summing. Observers were shown two or more line segments and were asked to produce a line that appeared equal to the sum. The line produced was longer than the sum of the separate lengths. For example, when shown two lines, each 1.5 inches long, the observers produced an average matching length of 3.55 inches. Krueger explored many of the factors that influence such a judgment and concluded that "apparent combined length did not equal, but exceeded, the sum of individual apparent lengths." In other words, there exists a convexity that suggests the operation of a virtual exponent having a value smaller than that of the actual exponent. For length of lines the actual exponent has been found to be close to 1.0. The exact value of the virtual exponent depends on numerous experimental variables.

XII. THE PARTITION PUZZLE

Many people have expressed one or another degree of dismay over the inability of observers to judge or produce linear partitionings on a prothetic continuum. "One of the long-standing puzzles," wrote Krantz (1970), "is why the scales obtained from category rating differ from those of magnitude estimation."

I find little to puzzle about in this matter—partly because the problem concerns only one class of scales. The various types of partition scales turn out to be linear on metathetic continua. It appears, therefore, that the problem of nonlinearity has to do, not with partitioning as such, but with the kind of continuum that is partitioned. Now, the two kinds of continua differ in several respects, this one in particular: On metathetic continua the absolute variability is constant; on prothetic continua the relative variability is constant. For example, the jnd for pitch corresponds to a fixed number of mels, all up and down the pitch continuum; but the jnd for loudness increases in number of sones with increasing location on the loudness continuum.

Given those basic facts, it appears that the puzzle loses much of its mystery. It would be more of a puzzle if two such different kinds of continua led to the same behavior on the part of a subject who attempts a partitioning. If there were no difference in the results of interval matching on the two kinds of continua, we would be faced with a most remarkable circumstance, for we could then measure infinitely small ratios. Imagine, for example, that a 1-sone interval appeared to have the same size regardless of its position on the loudness continuum. A 1-sone interval corresponds to 10 dB at a level of 40 dB and to .1 dB at 110 dB. Hence the observer would presumably be able to tell us that he perceives the decibel interval 40–50 dB as being equal to the interval between 110.0 and 110.1 dB. But two acoustic stimuli that stand to each other in the ratio that corresponds to .1 dB cannot be discriminated on more than a small percentage of trials. The jnd, defined as the ratio that is distinguishable on half the trials, is about .5 dB. In other words, if we are willing to assume that a prothetic continuum is like a metathetic continuum, and that an interval remains an interval of the same apparent size regardless of its location, then we can defeat Weber's law by having the observer judge or produce a 1-sone interval at those stimulus levels where 1 sone is far less than a jnd.

We see, therefore, that a contradiction is inherent in the assumption that a fixed size of subjective interval will appear constant all up and down the prothetic continuum. The contradiction suggests that we are concerned here with one of the basic and powerful principles of impotence: Measurement cannot be pushed to infinitely small ratios. If we are willing to postulate such a principle, then we must be careful what we say about absolute differences or partitions when the continuum involved is governed by Weber's law—the law that says that human variability is relative, not absolute. Weber's law applies to the distinguishing of stimulus differences on prothetic continua, where the error (variability, noise) is proportional to magnitude, i.e., the relative error is constant.

The principle of impotence also manifests itself in physical measurements, because on most physical continua we find the prothetic feature of a constant relative error, and seldom a constant absolute error. The precision of measurement is commonly stated as a percentage error, or alternatively, as 1 part in so many. For example, with a given class of mechanical procedures, involving gauges, blocks, and chains, we may be able to measure length to about 1 part in 10^4. Thus we might measure with an error of about 1 inch in a mile, but with an error of only a thousandth of an inch in a foot. If a mechanical device were wanted that would "judge" differences or intervals by responding when a given difference occurs, it would be futile to ask the device to respond to an increment of a thousandth of an inch if the input lengths were a mile long. Such a small increment would be lost in the noise, i.e., it would be small relative to the inherent variability.

The human observer shares many similarities with inanimate measuring devices, but he seems to differ in one important respect. When asked to judge intervals he can do so directly, so to speak. He does not need to measure the larger stimulus, then the smaller stimulus, and to subtract the one measurement from the other. Instead he seems able somehow to process directly his impression of the difference between the two stimuli and to respond with a number, or with some other form of matching operation. Nevertheless, his behavior is constrained by the same natural rules embodied in the principle of impotence that precludes infinite precision, and he behaves as though to effect a compromise. His virtual exponent decreases, so that absolute differences come to be judged more like relative differences. In that way his judgments do not violate the proscription against preserving as a clear perceptual difference the interval produced by a stimulus ratio that becomes vanishingly small as it moves on up the continuum. Instead, as shown by the curves in Fig. 5, the observer's judgment of a given difference trends downward when the location of the difference moves upward

That, it seems to me, is how it has to be on a prothetic continuum. I am puzzled that other people should be puzzled by the curves in Fig. 5 and by all the other partition results, such as category scales, equisections, bisections, etc., all of which speak the same message. They all tell us that in partitioning operations, the observer's results can be described by a virtual exponent, and that the value of the virtual exponent lies below that of the actual exponent. The smaller virtual exponent becomes a necessity if contradictions are to be avoided.

XIII. THRESHOLDS AND THE NQ

Although essentially worthless for ratio scaling, category procedures have an important and legitimate use in threshold measurements—the determination of boundaries between classes. In effect, all threshold measurements involve category methods, because the problem is to sort stimuli into categories or classes, e.g., those that can be heard and those that cannot, or those that are disturbing and those that are not, and so forth. Psychophysical thresholds are boundaries between classes. Although the boundary representing a sensory threshold may be sharp at any given instant in time, in a living organism the boundary behaves as though it were always moving about. Therefore we are forced to take repeated samples and to determine the location of the threshold boundary by way of a statistical decision. In practice, then, category boundaries become statistical concepts.

The experimental operations for determining any kind of threshold involve a procedure of matching either stimulus to category or category to stimulus. Procedures that utilize a so-called forced choice merely provide restricted alternatives, e.g., either louder or softer (no equal category). Or the procedure may force the subject to say where the stimulus occurred; he matches his perception to a category in space or time. The procedural variations on such category methods are potentially endless, but they all require the observer to perform some form of matching between stimuli and a category of response.

The denial that thresholds exist is a recurrent theme, dating back at least to 1884 when Peirce and Jastrow exhibited data on the judgment of small differences that seemed to agree with the predictions of the normal probability distribution. The judgments made by Peirce and Jastrow were of small changes in pressure on the skin of a finger. They judged the direction of the change, and they also rated on a 4-point category scale the confidence they felt in each judgment. The authors could find no evidence for a break that would indicate a steplike threshold. The poikilitic function relating size of pressure change to number of correct judgments showed no discontinuity, and hence no threshold in the sense of an abrupt change in a function. Concerning the discontinuous threshold, the authors said, "The introduction and retention of this false notion can only confuse thought."

Under most circumstances, to be sure, a clear-cut step does not manifest itself in threshold data. Rather the typical poikilitic function resembles the example shown in Fig. 6. But many studies have shown that there exist experimental arrangements under which observers having adequate powers of concentration can be made to yield evidence of a "neural quantum"

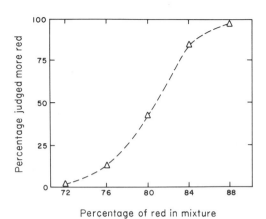

FIG. 6. A poikilitic function for judgments of redness obtained by the method of constant stimuli. The standard was a mixture of 80% red, 20% neutral gray. Each of four observers made 20 judgments of each of the five comparison stimuli, saying whether the comparison was more red or less red than the standard. Standard and comparison were presented alternately. [Data from Panek & Stevens, 1966.]

(NQ). Under three quite different procedures, various experimenters have obtained rectilinear poikilitic functions, cumulative response functions whose slopes are predicted by a simple step-function model of the NQ threshold (see Stevens, 1961c).

How the NQ model operates to predict a rectilinear poikilitic function, resulting from a rectangular distribution of responses to stimulus increments, is as follows:

A stimulus of a given magnitude excites, at a particular instant, a certain number of the NQ units, and it does so with a little to spare; that is to say, there is a small *surplus* excitation p, insufficient to cross the threshold of the unit next in line, but available to be combined with the stimulus increment $\Delta\phi$. When the increment $\Delta\phi$ is presented, it and the surplus p add together, and if their sum is large enough, they excite one or more additional NQ. Now, owing to an overall fluctuation in the sensitivity of the organism—a fluctuation that is large relative to the size of the NQ and slow relative to the time taken for a stimulus increment to be added and removed—one value of the surplus p is very nearly as likely to occur as any other value. Consequently, if we measure the size of the NQ in terms of the stimulus increment Q that will just succeed in always exciting it, the value of $\Delta\phi$ that is just sufficient to complement p and thereby excite one additional NQ is given by

$$\Delta\phi = Q - p. \tag{1}$$

A given $\Delta\phi$ will excite an additional NQ whenever $\Delta\phi \geqq Q - p$. Since p is distributed approximately uniformly over the interval $0 \leqq p \leqq Q$, the additional NQ is excited a proportion of the time r_1 given by

$$r_1 = \Delta\phi/Q. \tag{2}$$

Under the conditions of the experiments that produced the poikilitic functions in Figs. 7 and 8, the observer was not able to report when a single additional NQ was brought into play. The reason is presumably that the overall fluctuation in sensitivity is itself a process that produces randomly occurring increments and decrements, each equal in size to a single NQ. Against that fluctuating, steplike background, the observer adopts for his report the criterion of a double quantal jump. Since the single quantal jump is indistinguishable from the background, the observer presumably ignores it.

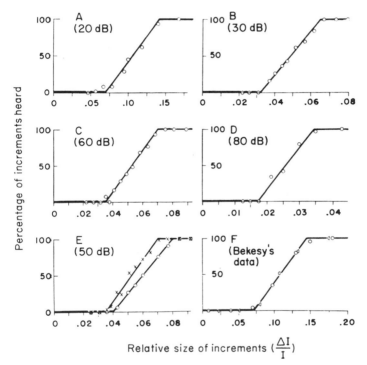

FIG. 7. Poikilitic functions measuring the neural quantum. The solid lines are the theoretical functions and the points show the obtained frequencies with which various increments in the intensity (sound pressure) of a 1000-Hz tone are heard as increases in loudness. The size of the NQ is measured by the point on the abscissa where the function first departs from zero. Except for plot B, the increments were passed through a sharply tuned filter. Each point is based on 50 to 100 responses. In plot E the circles were obtained at the first sitting; the crosses were obtained after a rest period during which the observer drank a cup of coffee.

Plot F: Békésy obtained the circles for an increase and the half circles for a decrease in intensity (ΔI positive and negative). Békésy's experimental method (constant stimuli) introduced an asymmetry (time error?) which has been eliminated in the plotting of Plot F. [From Stevens & Volkmann, 1940b; Békésy, 1930.]

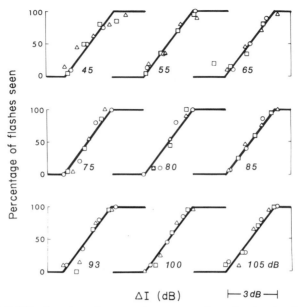

FIG. 8. Poikilitic functions for one observer at nine adapting levels of luminance expressed in decibels re 10^{-10} lambert. Each type of symbol represents a separate experiment. The lines of constant slope represent the form of the poikilitic function predicted by the NQ theory. [Data from Mueller, 1951.]

If two added NQ are thus needed to produce a response, Eq. (2) becomes

$$r_2 = (\Delta\phi - Q)/Q = (\Delta\phi/Q) - 1. \tag{3}$$

Or in terms of the percentage R of increments that an observer is able to detect, we have

$$R = 100(\Delta\phi/Q) - 1. \tag{4}$$

That is the equation that generates the lines in Figs. 7 and 8. The equation predicts two features of the poikilitic function, the slope and the rectilinearity.

A serious misconception has grown up concerning method, perhaps because several experimenters have used the procedure devised by Stevens and Volkmann (1940b) of adding an increment to a steady stimulus and of programming the increments in blocks of 25. It is sometimes alleged that the procedure of block presentation is a necessary condition. That is obviously not the case, because the data in plot F of Fig. 7 were obtained under a very different procedure. In fact, Békésy (1930) used the conventional method of constant stimuli, but with no time interval between the standard and the comparison stimulus.

Still a third method was used by Mueller (1951), who added brief 20-msec flashes, subtending a visual angle of 40 min, to a larger field subtending 12 degrees. An increment was presented every 10 sec but the different increments were presented in irregular order, not in constant-size blocks.

The results for the observer from whom most data were obtained are shown in Fig. 8. Three experiments are combined on each plot with each experiment indicated by a different symbol. Since the level of the steady field was varied over the wide range of almost a millionfold, or 59 dB, it is convenient to express the increment in logarithmic or decibel measure. A logarithmic measure entails that the slope predicted by the NQ theory will remain constant at all levels. Thus in Fig. 8, each poikilitic function rises from 0 to 100% when the increment increases by 3 dB, which represents a doubling of the size of the increment.

Each point in Fig. 8 is based on only 20 judgments, whereas the points in Fig. 7 represent 50–100 judgments. The slightly greater scatter in Fig. 8 may be due in part to that circumstance. Nevertheless, the consensus of the points seems clearly consistent with a rectilinear function exhibiting the prescribed slope.

In another visual experiment, Sachs, Nachmias, and Robson (1971) obtained very good NQ functions with a different type of visual target: vertical stripes having spatial frequency of 14 cycles per degree. The square target subtended $2\frac{1}{4}$ degrees on a side. The stripes were produced on the face of a cathode ray tube and the amplitude or contrast of the pattern could be varied from zero upward. The contrast increments lasted .76 sec. The observer responded if he saw the pattern. Catch trials were used on which no stripes were presented.

Sample results for two observers are shown in Fig. 9. Each function was determined on a different day. There is a slight day-to-day variation in the size of the NQ, but there is a systematic difference between the observers. Figure 9 gives only a small sample of the poikilitic functions obtained by the authors. Like Mueller, the authors describe their data by S-shaped curves. But the NQ function, which brings to bear the added power of specifying the slope of the function, appears to give an excellent account of the data.

As shown in Fig. 7, plot F, Békésy studied decrements as well as increments. It is interesting to note that results similar to those obtained by Békésy with randomized decrements were also obtained by Larkin and Norman (1964) when they used blocks of decrements. In one experiment the observer judged both increments and decrements, thereby producing two rectilinear poikilitic functions. Larkin and Norman found an asymmetry similar to that found by Békésy: the NQ for decrements was slightly larger than that for increments.

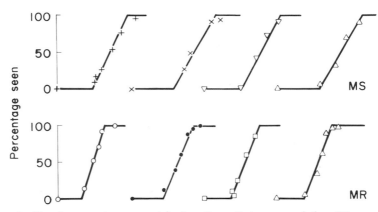

FIG. 9. The increment was a striped pattern that appeared for .76 sec on the face of a cathode-ray tube whose normal luminance was 83 dB (20 mL). The pattern of vertical stripes contained 14 stripes per degree. Data from two observers are shown. Each NQ function was determined on a different day. Increment size (contrast) was varied randomly from trial to trial and catch trials were included. [Data from Sachs, Nachmias, & Robson, 1971.]

Various parameters affect the NQ. For example, in the experiments of both Mueller (1951) and Stevens, Morgan, and Volkmann (1941), the Weber fraction $\Delta I/I$ decreased with intensity. A few of the other parameters that affect the measured size of the NQ have also been explored. Garner and Miller (1944) made an extensive study of the dependence of the NQ on the duration of the stimulus increment. They used two tonal frequencies, 500 and 1000 Hz, and two sound levels, 40 and 70 dB above threshold. Below about 250 msec the Weber fraction rises as duration decreases.

Miller (1947) used a white noise instead of a tone and showed that with a jittery noise stimulus, the scatter in the observers' judgments tends to obscure the rectilinearity of the poikilitic function. Nevertheless, the predicted slope was approximated by the 32 poikilitic functions obtained. An important feature of Miller's experiment was to show that the generalized Weber fraction $\Delta I(I + C)$ remains constant and thereby provides a good description of the size of the NQ for white noise over a wide range of stimulus intensity.

The foregoing sample of investigations shows that positive evidence for the NQ has been produced in experiments carried out under several different procedures and circumstances. To be sure, negative evidence has also been claimed by some investigators. The negative evidence has seemed less convincing, however. As I see it, the nature of the NQ problem creates an essential asymmetry, so that positive and negative findings do not command equal weight. The NQ hypothesis proposes that it may prove possible to produce evidence for a step function—an all-or-none process—provided sources of noise and variability are adequately suppressed. An investigator's failure to suppress the disturbing factors, whether in the procedure or in the observer, does not, therefore, constitute evidence against the hypothesis. If there were no positive evidence at all, the hypothesis would, of course, remain moot, but the absence of positive evidence can never foreclose the possibility of finding evidence for the NQ in a stepwise behavior of the poikilitic function. Actually, from the results of a dozen different investigators more than a hundred poikilitic functions have been plotted in a way that exhibits the form and slope predicted by the NQ hypothesis.

Note the contrast between the NQ hypothesis and the hypothesis for the logarithmic psychophysical law proposed by Fechner. Whereas the disproving of the NQ hypothesis would entail the proof of a universal negative, which is impossible, Fechner's hypothesis can be displaced by a demonstration that the psychophysical function actually takes a different form. Accordingly, the numerous psychophysical power functions thus far obtained have seemed adequate to force a revision in Fechner's conjecture. Thus far, however, the negative evidence for the NQ indicates only that some experiments have not succeeded.

References

Beck, J., & Shaw, W. A. Ratio-estimation of loudness-intervals. *American Journal of Psychology,* 1967, **80,** 59–65.

Békésy, G. v. Über das Fechnersche Gesetz und seine Bedeutung für die Theorie der akustische Beobachtungsfehler und die Theorie des Hörens. *Annalen der Physik,* 1930, **7,** 329–359. [English translation in Békésy, *Experiments in hearing.* New York: McGraw-Hill, 1960. Pp. 238ff.]

Brown, J. H. Cross-modal estimation of angular velocity. *Perception & Psychophysics,* 1968, **3,** 115–117.

Ciba Foundation Symposium. *Touch, heat and pain.* (A. V. S. de Reuck and J. Knight, Eds.) London: Churchill, 1966.

Dawson, W. E. An experimental analysis of judgments of sensory difference. Unpublished doctoral dissertation, Harvard University, 1968.

Dawson, W. E., & Brinker, R. P. Validation of ratio scales of opinion by multimodality matching. *Perception & Psychophysics,* 1971, **9,** 413–417.

Fechner, G. T. *Elemente der Psychophysik,* 1860. [Vol. I available in English translation as *Elements of psychophysics.* New York: Holt, 1966.]

Fletcher, H. Loudness, masking and their relation to hearing and noise measurement. *Journal of the Acoustical Society of America,* 1938, **9,** 275–293.

Fourtes, M. G. F., & Hodgkin, A. L. Changes in time scale and sensitivity in the ommatidia of *Limulus. Journal of Physiology,* 1964, **172,** 239–263.

Garner, W. R. A technique and a scale for loudness measurement. *Journal of the Acoustical Society of America,* 1954, **26,** 73–88.

Garner, W. R., & Miller, G. A. Differential sensitivity to intensity as a function of the duration of the comparison tone. *Journal of Experimental Psychology,* 1944, **34,** 450–463.

Hartline, H. K., & Graham, C. H. Nerve impulses from single receptors in the eye. *Journal of Cellular and Comparative Physiology,* 1932, **1,** 277–295.

Krantz, D. H. A theory of magnitude estimation and cross-modality matching. Michigan Mathematical Psychology Program, MMPP 70–6, July 1970.

Krueger, L. E. Apparent combined length of two-line and four-line sets. *Perception & Psychophysics,* 1970, **8,** 210–214.

Larkin, W. D., & Norman, D. A. An extension and experimental study of the neural quantum theory. In R. C. Atkinson (Ed.), *Studies in mathematical psychology.* Stanford, California: Stanford University Press, 1964. Pp. 188–200.

Marks, L. E. Stimulus-range, number of categories, and form of the category-scale. *American Journal of Psychology,* 1968, **81,** 467–479.

McGill, W. J. The slope of the loudness function: a puzzle. In H. Gulliksen & S. Messick (Eds.), *Psychological scaling: Theory and applications.* New York: Wiley, 1960. Pp. 67–81.

Miller, G. A. Sensitivity to changes in the intensity of white noise and its relation to masking and loudness. *Journal of the Acoustical Society of America,* 1947, **19,** 609–619.

Moskowitz, H. R. Intensity scales for pure tastes and for taste mixtures. *Perception & Psychophysics,* 1971, **9,** 51–56.

Mueller, C. G. Frequency of seeing functions for intensity discrimination at various levels of adapting intensity. *Journal of General Physiology,* 1951, **34,** 463–474.

Panek, D. W., & Stevens, S. S. Saturation of red: A prothetic continuum. *Perception & Psychophysics,* 1966, **1,** 59–66.

Peck, R. E. The application of thymometry to the measurement of anxiety. *International Journal of Neuropsychiatry,* 1966, **2,** 337–341.

Peirce, C. S., & Jastrow, J. On small differences of sensation. *Memoirs of the National Academy of Sciences,* 1884, **3,** (October 17), 3–11.

Sachs, M. B., Nachmias, J., & Robson, J. G. Spatial-frequency channels in human vision. *Journal of the Optical Society of America,* 1971, **61,** 1176–1186.

Stevens, J. C., & Mack, J. D. Scales of apparent force. *Journal of Experimental Psychology,* 1959, **58,** 405–413.

Stevens, J. C., & Marks, L. E. Cross-modality matching of brightness and loudness. *Proceedings of the National Academy of Sciences,* 1965, **54,** 407–411.

Stevens, J. C., & Marks, L. E. Apparent warmth as a function of thermal irradiation. *Perception & Psychophysics,* 1967, **2,** 613–619.

Stevens, J. C., Marks, L. E., & Gagge, A. P. The quantitative assessment of thermal discomfort. *Environmental Research,* 1969, **2,** 149–165.

Stevens, S. S. On the theory of scales of measurement. *Science,* 1946, **103,** 677–680.

Stevens, S. S. On the brightness of lights and the loudness of sounds. *Science,* 1953, **118,** 576.

Stevens, S. S. The measurement of loudness. *Journal of the Acoustical Society of America,* 1955, **27,** 815–820.

Stevens, S. S. On the psychophysical law. *Psychological Review,* 1957, **64,** 153–181.

Stevens, S. S. Cross-modality validation of subjective scales for loudness, vibration, and electric shock. *Journal of Experimental Psychology,* 1959, **57,** 201–209.

Stevens, S. S. On the new psychophysics. *Scandinavian Journal of Psychology,* 1960, **1,** 27–35.

Stevens, S. S. The psychophysics of sensory function. In W. A. Rosenblith (Ed.), *Sensory communication.* Cambridge, Massachusetts: M.I.T. Press, 1961. Pp. 1–33. (a)

Stevens, S. S. To honor Fechner and repeal his law. *Science,* 1961, **133,** 80–86. (b)

Stevens, S. S. Is there a quantal threshold? In W. A. Rosenblith (Ed.), *Sensory communication.* Cambridge, Massachusetts: M.I.T. Press, 1961. Pp. 806–813. (c)

Stevens, S. S. Matching functions between loudness and ten other continua. *Perception & Psychophysics,* 1966, **1,** 5–8.

Stevens, S. S. Intensity functions in sensory systems. *International Journal of Neurology,* 1967, **6,** 202–209.

Stevens, S. S. Tactile vibration: Change of exponent with frequency. *Perception & Psychophysics,* 1968, **3,** 223–338.

Stevens, S. S. On predicting exponents for cross-modality matches. *Perception & Psychophysics,* 1969, **6,** 251–256.

Stevens, S. S. Neural events and the psychophysical law. *Science,* 1970, **170,** 1043–1050.

Stevens, S. S. Perceived level of noise by Mark VII and dB(E). *Journal of the Acoustical Society of America,* 1971, **51,** 575–601. (a)

Stevens, S. S. Sensory power functions and neural events. In W. R. Loewenstein (Ed.), *Handbook of sensory physiology,* Vol. 1. New York: Springer-Verlag, 1971. Pp. 226–242. (b)

Stevens, S. S. Issues in psychophysical measurement. *Psychological Review,* 1971, **78,** 426–450. (c)

Stevens, S. S., & Galanter, E. H. Ratio scales and category scales for a dozen perceptual continua. *Journal of Experimental Psychology,* 1957, **54,** 377–411.

Stevens, S. S., & Guirao, M. Subjective scaling of length and area and the matching of length to loudness and brightness. *Journal of Experimental Psychology,* 1963, **66,** 177–186.

Stevens, S. S., Morgan, C. T., & Volkmann, J. Theory of the neural quantum in the discrimination of loudness and pitch. *American Journal of Psychology,* 1941, **54,** 315–335.

Stevens, S. S., & Volkmann, J. The relation of pitch to frequency: a revised scale. *American Journal of Psychology,* 1940, **53,** 329–353. (a)

Stevens, S. S., & Volkmann, J. The quantum of sensory discrimination. *Science,* 1940, **92,** 583–585. (b)

Sullivan, R. J. Subjective matching of anxiety to intensities of white noise. *Journal of Abnormal Psychology,* 1969, **74,** 646–650.

Torgerson, W. S. Distances and ratios in psychophysical scaling. *Acta Psychologica,* 1961, **19,** 201–205.

Versace, J. Measurement of ride comfort. New York: Society of Automotive Engineers, 1963, Report 638A.

Part V

**Multidimensional Scaling for
Measurement of Human Perception**

Chapter 12

MULTIDIMENSIONAL PERCEPTUAL MODELS AND MEASUREMENT METHODS

J. DOUGLAS CARROLL AND MYRON WISH

I. INTRODUCTION

Similarity, it can be argued, is the most fundamental of psychological relations. Every theory of behavior must deal with similarity in some way, most simply assuming it as an elementary undefined relation. William James (1890) for example, speaks of "association by similarity" as fundamental to human reasoning. James further discusses the absurdity of any behavioral theory based on *identity* of present and past stimulus situations. He points out that the probability of a particular brain state recurring identically is negligibly small, comparing it to the likelihood that an identical combination of waveforms should recur in the sea, all with their crests and hollows reoccupying identical places. This analogy can, of course, be extended to any *partial* brain-state, corresponding, say, to the pattern of neural activity evoked in the visual cortex by a particular distal visual stimulus at one particular point in time. Absolute perceptual identity of two stimuli almost certainly never occurs. What does occur is that two stimuli (which may be the "same" physical stimulus at two points in time) are perceptually very "similar" and are thus treated "as if" identical. That is, perception acts to group stimuli into more-or-less homogeneous classes based on degree of similarity. Without this ability to perceive nonidentical stimuli as similar, the perceptual world would forever be the "blooming, buzzing, confusion" of completely unique and unrelated events of which James speaks elsewhere.

In every scientifically recognized theory of learning (including Skinner's "nontheory") similarity is also an essential primitive. Recognizing this lack of recurrence of identical stimuli (or, for that matter, of identical responses) learning theorists from Pavlov on have adopted the twin principles of *stimulus* and *response generalization* (the eliciting of similar responses by similar stimuli) as principal building blocks of learning theory. Stimulus generalization is usually assumed to be a continuous (monotone nondecreasing) function of *degree* of similarity, which itself is treated as a continuous variable, but not otherwise defined very explicitly. One point is clear, however, about the implied definition of similarity used by students of learning: If stimuli are varied along a *single* physical dimension, the amount of generalization (and thus, presumably, the degree of similarity) of a second stimulus to a fixed stimulus usually decreases as the second stimulus moves farther away on this dimension. Thus similarity is defined, albeit vaguely, in terms of distance on one or more physical scales.

In multidimensional scaling, similarity is assumed to relate to some form of "distance" defined on *psychological* scales or dimensions. Similarity is taken as a primitive relation on pairs of stimuli. This relation is assumed to admit of degrees, that is to be orderable. Thus it is defined on at least an *ordinal* scale (the usual assumption in the so-called nonmetric multidimensional scaling methods). In some cases, it may be assumed to be measurable on an *interval scale* (the standard assumption for metric multidimensional scaling methods) or even on a *ratio scale*.

Multidimensional scaling methods are designed to find the dimensions, given the similarities. The typical input data consists of an $n \times n$ matrix (or, in the case of INDSCAL and other "three-way" methods, a *number* of such matrices) whose cell values indicate the similarity or dissimilarity of pairs of the n stimuli. Similarities or dissimilarities are generally assumed to measure (inversely or directly) the psychological *distance* between the stimuli or other objects. Coombs (1958) and Shepard (1962a) have proposed the more general term *proximities* to refer to numbers that (inversely) measure distance ordinally. We shall also use the term *antiproximities* to refer to numbers *directly measuring* distance on an ordinal scale. The term *proximity* is more general than similarity, which usually refers to direct judgments of stimulus similarity. In addition to absolute or comparative judgments of similarity, relatedness, association and the like, some common sources of proximities data in psychology and other behavioral sciences are "confusions" in a stimulus identification or "same–different" task, measures derived from stimulus generalization data, co-occurrence of stimuli, measures of interaction, or flow of information, and various measures of "profile similarity" derived from rating scales or other multivariate data. See Shepard (1972) and Wish (1972) for more detailed discussions of kinds of data appropriate for multidimensional scaling.

The central assumption underlying multidimensional scaling models for perception is that stimuli are "coded" internally in terms of continuously varying parameters or dimensions. The aim of multidimensional scaling is to "discover" the number of dimensions relevant to perception of the stimuli under consideration and to determine the stimulus coordinates on each dimension (that is, to determine the *dimensionality* and *configuration* of stimuli in *multidimensional space*). The problem of interpretation, then, is to identify physical or other correlates of these psychological dimensions, or to specify their psychological meaning in some way. It should be pointed out, however, that interpretation is sometimes configurational rather than dimensional; i.e., it entails description of meaningful clusters, regions, shapes or structures, symmetries, or other patterns in the multidimensional configuration. Furthermore "dimensions" need not actually vary continuously in the sense that all possible values will be evidenced, but may be more discretely valued, as would be the case if strong clustering occurred. See Torgerson (1965) for a discussion of this.

We are defining multidimensional scaling here in a fairly restricted way. A broader definition of the term could include a wide variety of other models and accompanying procedures for deriving "multidimensional scales" from (nonproximities type) data. For example, a number of multidimensional models exist for preferences (mostly for accounting for individual differences in preferences), and accompanying methods are available for deriving multidimensional stimulus configurations from preference data (see, e.g., Carroll, 1972; Coombs, 1964; Tucker, 1960). Various methods also exist (Carroll, 1969; Guttman, 1941; Lingoes, 1968) for handling purely categorical data (data, in Stevens's terms, on a *nominal* scale), based on models of varying types and degrees of generality. A method has even been devised (Carroll & Chang, 1972) enabling derivation of multidimensional structure from analogy completions data (assuming a model proposed by Rumelhart & Abrahamson, 1971) or from a kind of "multidimensional bisection" task, in which subjects choose a stimulus most nearly midway between two given stimuli.

The semantic-differential technique (Osgood, Suci, & Tannenbaum, 1957) and unidimensional psychophysical procedures (see Stevens, 1951) are probably about the most widely used alternatives to multidimensional scaling for measuring psychological dimensions. The major difficulty with these approaches is that they are so dependent on the researcher's a priori conceptions of the dimensions relevant to the domain. (This difficulty is also present in multidimensional scaling when applied to measures of profile similarity derived from semantic differential or other rating scales.) A dimension cannot be discovered by the semantic-differential technique unless it was first "guessed" by inclusion of an appropriate scale. Moreover the apparent importance of a dimension will probably depend more on the researcher's judgment, as reflected in his choice of scales and other aspects of experimental design, than on the subjects' responses. In the case of psychophysical scaling, there must be a physical correlate, or concomitant, to each psychological dimension, and the physical variables must be assumed not to interact in the psychophysical mapping. Whereas some modern methods allow relaxation of the assumption of a one-to-one relationship between physical and psychological dimensions, some fairly well-behaved psychophysical correspondence is required for any workable psychophysical scaling method. Another potential difficulty with both the semantic differential and psychophysical approaches is that some dimensions may not be amenable to effective articulation by any a priori unidimensional scale, whether defined verbally, behaviorally, or physically. Multidimensional scaling does not require such a priori definition of scales, but only some measure (behavioral or otherwise) of proximity of stimulus pairs. It should be kept in mind, on the other hand, that the dimensions do depend in some measure on the stimuli selected, the mode of presentation, and the particular kinds of judgments. (See Wish and Carroll, Chapter 13 in this volume.) No single data collection procedure is likely to provide a completely adequate description of the perceptual dimensions relevant to a stimulus domain.

While recognizing the validity and potential utility of such other approaches, as alternatives or as supplements, let us now focus on the topic of multidimensional scaling methods based on similarity judgments or other proximities data.

II. THEORETICAL AND MATHEMATICAL CONSIDERATIONS

A. Properties of a Proximity Function

Given a measure of proximity, defined on pairs of stimuli, we might ask what properties this measure should have. Assuming that the stimuli can be described in terms of a finite set of underlying dimensions, let x_{jt} represent the value of stimulus j on dimension t, and $\mathbf{x}_j$ stand for the vector (or point in the multidimensional space) representing the jth stimulus. Let $p(\mathbf{x}_j, \mathbf{x}_k) = p_{jk}$ be the proximity between j and k. Consider now the properties this function should have.

First, it would seem that as two stimuli "approach" one another, their proximities to any third stimulus should approach one another. That is,

$$\mathbf{x} \to \mathbf{y} \quad \text{implies} \quad p(\mathbf{x}, \mathbf{z}) \to p(\mathbf{y}, \mathbf{z}) \qquad \text{for all } \mathbf{z} \tag{1}$$

(where $a \to b$ means a approaches b). This *continuity* assumption, of course, says nothing about how $p(\mathbf{x}, \mathbf{y})$ should behave as $\mathbf{x}$ and $\mathbf{y}$ approach one another. It would seem, however, that any reasonable proximity function should have the property that no stimulus can be more proximal to some other stimulus than to itself. This implies

$$p(\mathbf{x}, \mathbf{y}) \leq \min [p(\mathbf{x}, \mathbf{x}), \ p(\mathbf{y}, \mathbf{y})] \tag{2}$$

Properties (1) and (2) would seem to be the least we would expect of any reasonable proximity measure. An additional property that might be assumed (but not always) is

$$p(\mathbf{x}, \mathbf{x}) = p(\mathbf{y}, \mathbf{y}) = p \qquad \text{for all } \mathbf{x} \text{ and } \mathbf{y}, \tag{3}$$

which says that all the "self-proximities" are the same. Equations (2) and (3) together imply that

$$p_{jk} \leq p_{ll} = p \qquad \text{for any } j, k, l. \tag{4}$$

[where $p_{jk} = p(\mathbf{x}_j, \mathbf{x}_k)$]

We may also add the following symmetry assumption:

$$p_{jk} = p_{kj} \qquad \text{for all } j, k \tag{5}$$

which says that order is irrelevant to proximities. Although for certain kinds of stimuli (e.g., sequentially presented auditory stimuli) this may not be realistic, such a symmetry assumption seems quite reasonable for most stimulus domains.

If we define the dissimilarity (or antiproximity) between j and k as

$$\delta_{jk} = p - p_{jk}, \tag{6}$$

then the following hold for δ:

$$\delta_{jk} \geq \delta_{jj} = 0 \qquad \text{(positivity)} \tag{7}$$
$$\delta_{jk} = \delta_{kj} \qquad \text{(symmetry)}, \tag{8}$$

making δ a *semimetric*. A semimetric defined on a space satisfies continuity plus all the metric axioms except the triangle inequality.

B. The Triangle Inequality

All we need add to such a semimetric to make it a *metric* (and thus, to make the stimulus space a *metric space*) is the triangle inequality. The triangle inequality states

$$d_{jl} \leq d_{jk} + d_{kl} \qquad \text{for all } j, k, l \qquad \text{(triangle inequality)} \tag{9}$$

where the d's are interpreted as *distances* between the entities referred to by the subscripts. If d satisfies properties (7), (8), and (9) (the metric axioms), it is a metric.

Since the proximities and thus the dissimilarities, δ, are assumed to be measured only ordinally, it is quite reasonable to assume that, among the class of permissible monotonic functions, there is at least one that will transform them into distances. In fact, it is trivial to do this for any finite set of points, simply by defining the monotone function by adding a suitably large constant to the mixed δ's (leaving the unmixed equal to 0). The smallest constant that will work is

$$c_{\min} = \max_{j,k,l} (\delta_{jl} - \delta_{jk} - \delta_{kl}) \tag{10}$$

so that we may define d by

$$d_{jk} = \delta_{jk} + c_{\min} \qquad \text{for } j \neq k; \tag{11}$$
$$d_{jj} = 0 \qquad \text{for all } j. \tag{12}$$

Of course, any larger constant $c > c_{\min}$ would also convert the δ's into d's satisfying the triangle inequality, but $c_{\min}$ is the smallest one that will do the job. In fact $c_{\min}$ is one of the estimates of the additive constant used to convert *comparative* (interval scale) distances into (ratio scale) distances in the now classical metric scaling procedures described in Torgerson (1958). This particular method of estimating the constant was justified by assuming that some set of three points lie exactly on a straight line in the multidimensional space. It seems simpler to us to justify it as the smallest additive constant guaranteeing satisfaction of the triangle inequality.

Thus we see that even this fairly trivial monotone function can convert essentially any set of dissimilarities into "distances" (i.e., numbers that at least satisfy the metric axioms). It is not unreasonable, therefore, to suppose that a more interesting function might be available to do this. As Shepard (1962a,b) has pointed out, the existence of a monotone function that assures satisfaction of the triangle inequality is not, in general, a very interesting condition—not, that is, without some other constraint. Shepard speaks of "low dimensionality" as being the right additional condition. This is not terribly interesting, either, unless the underlying metric (which is assumed monotonically related to proximities or antiproximities) is assumed to be Euclidean or a member of some fairly limited family of metrics. There is a kind of trading relation between dimensionality and complexity of the metric assumed. By assuming a sufficiently complex metric (which could still be continuously related to parameters of the stimulus space) one could obtain low-dimensional solutions in which distances relate monotonically to any proximities whatever. Thus, if we are considering the possibility of very general metric spaces, it would seem that Shepard's condition of low dimensionality must necessarily be supplemented by a condition of "simplicity of metric." After describing and illustrating some multidimensional scaling methods, we shall discuss some non-Euclidean metrics that have been considered in psychology.

C. Violations of the Metric Axioms

Let us assume we have a matrix of antiproximities (e.g., dissimilarities) for n stimuli or other entities. In the typical situation there is only a half-matrix, without diagonal, of data values. By imposing the constraint $\delta_{jk} = \delta_{kj}$, and treating the diagonals of the matrix (the δ_{jj}'s) as all tied at a value less than any of the nondiagonal δ's, the rest of the matrix could be filled in.

When the physical identity of a stimulus is not obvious (e.g., degraded acoustical or visual stimuli), it is common to collect proximities data associated with the diagonal cells (which indicate the dissimilarity between each stimulus and itself). In some cases it makes sense to collect data on both the (jk) and (kj) pairs—for example, when order effects are likely to occur. Systematic nonsymmetries (or any nonsymmetry not accountable for by chance) may cast doubt on the existence of an underlying metric space, since they imply violations of the symmetry axiom. Likewise, the failure of the self-dissimilarities to be equal to each other and less than any nondiagonal dissimilarities violates the positivity axiom of Eq. (7).

In some situations it is appropriate to take out row and column effects before analyzing the matrix of interactions by multidimensional scaling. An example of this is Coombs's (1964, 1971) analysis of journal citation data. The rationale for removing the main effects, is that differences in the overall number of citations made or received by a journal may distort the multidimensional representation of relatedness among the journals. In many instances the matrix of interactions will be more symmetric than the original data matrix.

If the violations of the metric axioms are severe, it is likely (but not certain) to be unreasonable and unproductive to seek a multidimensional representation of the data. Some indications of severe violations might be that the diagonal values were of about the same magnitude as the non-diagonal values, or that the rank ordering of proximity values in a row was unrelated to the ordering in the corresponding column. In most instances, however, the violations of the metric axioms are mild enough to justify a multidimensional scaling analysis. The simplest way to deal with nonsymmetries is to fit a multidimensional model to the nonsymmetric matrix, thereby providing a space for the symmetric part of the data. In effect the distance model could be regarded as a first approximation, and the nonsymmetries could be studied separately. For example, Wish (1967a,b) explored the nonsymmetries in matrices of confusions among Morse code signals and related rhythmic patterns, discovering that the probability of a "same" response to a pair of sequentially presented signals was greater when the shorter of the pair was presented first. The systematic nature of the nonsymmetries provides some information about the way such signals are stored and about the judgmental process.

Another approach to the problem of nonsymmetric matrices is to symmetrize the matrix by averaging the (jk) and (kj) entries. This might be expected to cancel out any significant order effects, leaving only the data that can be accounted for by an asymmetric distance model. A good example of this approach is provided by Shepard's (1957) analysis of stimulus generalization data. He proposed a rational model involving response bias to account both for asymmetries and for discrepancies in the diagonals, or self proximities. While this is an oversimplification, in essence, Shepard assumed that the observed probability p_{jk} of the response appropriate to stimulus k being given when stimulus j was presented is given by

$$p_{jk} = w_j^{(s)} w_k^{(r)} \pi_{jk}, \tag{13}$$

where $w_j^{(s)}$ and $w_k^{(r)}$ are weights associated with the jth stimulus and the kth response, respectively; and π_{jk} is a symmetric proximity measure satisfying (4) and (5), and assumed to be related by a decreasing monotonic function to distances in a metric space. (The monotonic function was assumed to be a negative exponential in Shepard's work, while the space was assumed to be Euclidean.)

Since, without loss of generality it is possible to assume the common value of π_{jj} and π_{kk} to be 1, Eq. (13) implies that

$$\pi_{jk} = p_{jk}p_{kj}/p_{jj}p_{kk} . \tag{14}$$

This method of symmetrizing was used by Shepard in his analysis of the Miller–Nicely data on confusions between consonant phonemes (to be discussed later in this chapter).

Another way to take into account the lack of symmetry and of maximality of the diagonal values (in a proximity matrix) is to treat the matrix as a conditional rather than as an unconditional proximity matrix. A row (column) conditional proximity matrix is one in which the order within a given row (column) is meaningful, but proximities in different rows (columns) are not comparable. Such a matrix generally arises when the row and column elements have different meanings or play different roles—for example, in a stimulus identification experiment in which the rows are associated with stimuli and the columns with responses, or when the entries in a row (column) indicate the rank order of similarity to the standard stimulus associated with that row (column). In terms of formal assumptions, the proximity matrix is row-conditional if and only if proximities are related to distances by

$$M_j(p_{jk}) \cong d_{jk} , \tag{15}$$

with M_j monotone nonincreasing.

The difference here is that we are assuming a different monotonic function for each j (corresponding to a row of the proximity matrix). A column-conditional matrix would be obtained by replacing M_j with $M_k{}^*$ in Eq. (15). In the unconditional case, there would just be a single unsubscripted M. The stimulus generalization paradigm that Shepard utilized could also be regarded as producing a row-conditional proximity matrix, although under Shepard's model, a suitable transformation of the matrix leads to an unconditional matrix.

Versions 4 and 5 of Kruskal's MDSCAL (Kruskal & Carmone, 1969) and certain programs in the Guttman and Lingoes series (Lingoes, 1966) have the facility to analyze row or column conditional proximity matrices, in effect fitting a different monotone function to each row (column). In principle, these programs can even handle data matrices in which the rows and columns represent distinct sets of elements—for example, stimuli and responses, or individuals and stimuli (as in the multidimensional unfolding model—see Coombs, 1964). A multidimensional scaling analysis of such a matrix would provide a "joint space" in which there was a point in the space for each row and for each column. The multidimensional space could conceivably reveal what kinds of stimulus–response or order effects were occurring. At one extreme, the jth row point and the jth column point may be very close together, suggesting no biases. At the other extreme, the column points may be related in a very systematic way to the row points, as, for example, by a tendency to shift in a specified direction. It should be pointed out, however, that there are difficulties in practice in determining a "nondegenerate" multidimensional space from such an "off-diagonal" or "corner matrix" (or from any matrix in which there are large blocks of missing data—see Carroll, 1972; Kruskal; 1972; Kruskal & Carroll, 1969).

Perhaps a more elegant way to account for nonsymmetries is to build them into the metric space model (see, e.g., Nakatani, 1972). This amounts, in one sense, to redefining distances in the space so as to drop the symmetry axiom of Eq. (5). In another sense, it might be viewed simply as superimposing an additional process onto the basic metric space model. This is the way Shepard apparently conceived of his response bias model—as a way of *preserving* the notion of symmetric distances rather than as defining asymmetric distances. The kind of bias parameters Shepard assumes could be introduced explicitly into the model, however, rather than simply being canceled out by averaging, thus creating a composite "asymmetric distance" model.

Kruskal (personal communication) has experimented with a model that provides for a nonsymmetric distance function. In this model the jth row point is related to the jth column point by a "drift vector," corresponding to a fixed shift in one direction. In a variant of the model, the appended vector might be the one pointing from one of the points toward (or away from) a specific fixed point in the space. This could be thought of as implying a kind of regression toward a stereotype or schema corresponding to the fixed point.

Keeping in mind the possibility of violations of the metric axioms, and other potential problems such as missing data, we shall restrict our attention for the moment to the standard case of a half-matrix (without diagonal) in which there are no missing entries. However, we do not necessarily restrict our attention to cases in which the metric axioms are satisfied. We shall, in fact, consider a sequence of increasingly general classes of proximity models, ranging from a very specific metric (the Euclidean) through various non-Euclidean metrics, to semimetrics (in which the triangle inequality is dropped) and finally the case in which all that is assumed is that similarity or proximity is *continuously* related to perceptual parameters. Cutting across this hierarchy is another distinction—that between so-called metric and nonmetric models and analyses, in which the proximities are treated as being on an interval (or stronger) scale, versus being merely ordinally measured.

III. METRIC, NONMETRIC, AND "CONTINUITY" SCALING

The distinction between metric and nonmetric multidimensional scaling was first made by Coombs (1958) and later elaborated by Kruskal (1964a), who used the term *nonmetric multidimensional scaling* to mean much the same as Shepard's (1962a,b) term *analysis of proximities*. The term has to do with the strength of the assumed scale properties of the data (proximities or antiproximities). In Stevens's terms, if the data are assumed to be measured on a ratio or interval scale, the analysis is (or ought to be) a metric one. If the data are assumed merely ordinal, then the analysis is (or ought to be) nonmetric.

For an analysis to be metric it is not necessary that the original data be linearly related to distances; only that they be convertible to at least interval scale distances by some known transformation. For example, Shepard's (1957) assumption of a negative exponential connecting proximities to distances meant that a logarithmic transformation would carry the (suitably symmetrized) proximities into ratio scale distances.

What might be called the "classical" metric method of multidimensional scaling is the one described in Torgerson's (1958) book. The theoretical basis for this was supplied by Young and Householder (1938), who proved a theorem that enabled determination of the minimum dimensionality of the space required to accommodate a given set of Euclidean distances among n points. A by-product of this theorem was a method of constructing the space, and indeed, of determining whether the distances could be accommodated in any Euclidean space. This constructive method was used by Richardson (1938) to implement the first known application of multidimensional scaling (see also Klingberg, 1941). The method essentially lay fallow until the early 1950s, when methodological improvements by Torgerson (1958), Messick and Abelson (1956) and others, together with the advent of high-speed digital computers, made it feasible to deal with fairly large data sets in cases of reasonably high dimensionality. This classical metric method can be outlined as follows:

Similarities data were first collected by one of several means, the most popular being the *complete method of triads* (in which the subject judges whether stimulus A is more like B or C for every triad A, B, C of stimuli) or the methods of equal appearing or of successive intervals (in both of which every pair of stimuli is placed in one of a series of ordered categories). These data were then typically put through one of the Thurstone-type undimensional scaling procedures to produce interval scale measures of distances (which were called comparative distances).

Since ratio scale distances were needed, the problem of estimating the "additive constant" arose. A number of methods were worked out for estimating this constant, the simplest (and possibly the best in a number of ways) being the estimate c_{min} defined in Eq. (10), which, as discussed earlier, is the smallest constant guaranteeing satisfaction of the triangle inequality. Some methods of data collection (e.g., Helm, 1964; Indow, 1960a,b) could plausibly be assumed to lead directly to ratio scale distances, so that many of these steps would be avoided. Once ratio scale distances were obtained, one proceeded to convert them to *scalar products*. Torgerson and others derived equations for calculating (estimated) scalar products around an origin placed at the centroid (or center of gravity) of all n points. (The Young–Householder results required placing the origin at one of the points, and getting scalar products of vectors from that point to the $n - 1$ remaining ones. This solution was unsatisfactory both esthetically and statistically.)

The simplest way to describe the conversion from Euclidean distances to scalar products is that one *double centers* the matrix whose general entry is $-1/2d_{ij}^2$. Double centering is equivalent to taking out both row and column effects in analysis of variance, leaving interaction numbers. In this case, the interaction numbers are the scalar products. The scalar product between stimuli j and k, usually called b_{jk} is defined as

$$b_{jk} = \sum_{t=1}^{m} x_{jt}x_{kt}. \tag{16}$$

In matrix notation, this can be written as

$$B = XX', \tag{17}$$

where B is the $n \times n$ matrix of scalar products and X is the (initially unknown) $n \times m$ matrix of coordinates of the n points in m dimensions. This equation looks a great deal like the fundamental equation of factor analysis, the main difference being that B replaces R (the correlation matrix). The matrix B can, in fact, be viewed as analogous to a covariance matrix, and methods closely related to factor analysis (or its statistical cousin, principal components analysis) can be used to determine the X matrix of appropriate dimensionality that best accounts for the scalar products. See Torgerson (1958) for further details.

A. Other Metric Scaling Techniques

In addition to this classical metric multidimensional scaling, there are other metric methods that are closely related to the newer nonmetric methods, in that they utilize computer-implemented iterative numerical procedures to fit a specified metric model to the data. This really amounts simply to replacing the monotone function central to the nonmetric methods with some specified function (linear, polynomial of some degree, or other) which may or may not be monotone.

Kruskal's MDSCAL, for example, allows use of polynomial functions up to degree 4 (including linear functions either with or without the constant term). The program used by Shepard to analyze the Miller–Nicely data (to be discussed subsequently) incorporated the explicit requirement that the function converting distances into proximities be a negative exponential. These approaches are metric in the general sense that interval-scale properties of the data are used. Of course, as functions with increasing numbers of parameters are used, this distinction becomes less and less meaningful; with enough parameters almost anything can be fit. (A monotone function, in a sense, has as many parameters as data points, but with strong inequality constraints on the values these parameters may legitimately assume.)

B. Nonmetric Multidimensional Scaling

The term *nonmetric multidimensional scaling* was first introduced by Coombs (1958), who had something in mind which is a little different from what is now called nonmetric scaling. The method Coombs and his co-workers proposed was based on nonmetric (i.e., merely ordinal) proximities data. It was nonmetric, too, in the sense that the space determined was not, in any well-defined sense, a metric space, since the values of stimuli on dimensions were defined only ordinally. There was, thus, no way to calculate interpoint distances, even if a specific metric such as the Euclidean was assumed. To do this, one would need to know the monotone function (different for each dimenison) transforming the rank order coordinates into at least interval scale coordinates. In this sense, i.e., that both data and solution are nonmetric, Coombs's procedure could be termed "doubly nonmetric."

It was Shepard (1962a,b) who first showed (by producing a computer algorithm) that it was possible to produce essentially metric solutions from such purely nonmetric (or ordinal) proximities data. These latter were metric in the dual sense that coordinates were defined up to interval scale and that the space *was* indeed a (Euclidean) metric space.

Shepard's method, which he called "analysis of proximities," started out with the n stimuli arranged in what might be called the "maximum entropy" configuration (a regular simplex in $n - 1$ dimensions—the multidimensional generalization of the equilateral triangle in two dimensions or the regular tetrahedron in three). He then introduced two processes, one tending to decrease dimensionality and the other to increase agreement with the data (in an ordinal sense). The dimensionality-reducing process is now primarily of historical interest. The approach to dimensionality estimation now almost universally used entails finding solutions in a number of different dimensionalities, and using the dimensionality versus goodness-of-fit curves in some way to judge how many dimensions are appropriate for the data. Shepard's notion, on the other hand, was to start in the highest possible dimensionality, but to impose forces tending to reduce that dimensionality to the smallest possible. Once that dimensionality was estimated, the best configuration in that smallest dimensionality was determined. The process he used to decrease the dimensionality (what he called the β process) was based on the idea of increasing large distances and decreasing small ones (one can see intuitively that this would tend to straighten out, say, a two-dimensional set of points on an arc of a circle into a one-dimensional set whose locus is a straight line). When this had seemingly reduced dimensionality as much as possible, the points were then projected exactly into a space of the "right" dimensionality, and the other, or α process, was continued in this "right" dimensionality (without the β process). The α process (which was used together with the β process in the first phase, and then alone) quite simply tended to increase distances between points that were too close together (relative to the ordinal proximities data) and to decrease distances between points too far apart. It did this by setting up what can be conceived as force vectors from each point, oriented either toward or away from each of the $n - 1$ other points. If the rank order of the distance were greater than (less than) that of the corresponding dissimilarity, the vector would be pointed away from (toward) the other point. The magnitude of the vector was proportional to the magnitude of the discrepancy. If the two rank orders agreed exactly, the force vector had zero magnitude, which is the same as saying there was no force vector in this case. These $n - 1$ force vectors (some possibly with zero magnitude) were then summed for each point, producing a resolution vector that could be thought of as the resolution of all the attractive and repulsive forces operating on that point. Each point was allowed to move in the direction of its resolution force vector a distance proportional to the magnitude of the force (the constant of proportionality being the α of the α-process, which corresponds to what numerical analysts would call the stepsize), and these new force vectors were computed. This process was continued until, ideally, the system was in perfect equilibrium (i.e., all force vectors had zero magnitude). Since this state of perfect equilibrium is seldom actually reached, however, in any such iterative procedure, some criterion of being close enough to equilibrium must be used.

In order to distinguish it from Shepard's rather different algorithm,

Kruskal borrowed Coombs's term nonmetric multidimensional scaling to describe his procedure. It is important to realize that it is the proximities data that are nonmetric in this case, not the solution. Some authors, notably Beals, Krantz, and Tversky (1968) call this ordinal rather than nonmetric scaling. This nomenclature, although possibly more appropriate, is not favored by usage. Green and Carmone (1970) have called methods such as those of Shepard and Kruskal nonmetric, whereas they call Coombs's procedure fully nonmetric (to emphasize that both data and solution are nonmetric).*

Kruskal's (1964) MDSCAL method improved Shepard's method in two important ways: (1) The notion of optimizing an explicitly defined measure of goodness (or badness) of fit was introduced; (2) an explicit numerical method, the method of gradients, or steepest descent was used.† Kruskal called his goodness-of-fit measure STRESS, defined in his original paper as

$$\text{STRESS} = \left[\frac{\Sigma_j \Sigma_k (d_{jk} - \hat{d}_{jk})^2}{\Sigma_j \Sigma_k d_{jk}^2} \right]^{1/2}, \tag{18}$$

where the d's are distances in the underlying metric space, and the $\hat{d}$'s are related to proximities data by a nonincreasing monotonic function. This formula for STRESS is now called STRESSFORM1. Another STRESS formula, called STRESSFORM2 has now been incorporated as the standard form. STRESSFORM2 differs only in the normalization factor in the denominator (under the radical). It is normalized by dividing by $\Sigma_j \Sigma_k (d_{jk} - \bar{d})^2$ rather than $\Sigma_j \Sigma_k d_{jk}^2$, where $\bar{d}$ is the mean of the d_{jk}'s.

Given a particular metric in the underlying space (Euclidean, say) *and* a particular dimensionality (say m), the objective was rigorously defined as that of minimizing STRESS over the class of all m-dimensional spaces (with the appropriate metric) *and* over the class of all nonincreasing monotonic functions. Formally, we can think of STRESS as a function of X, the coordinate matrix, and of M, the monotonic function converting proxim-

* The first author of this paper (Carroll) has used the term "fully nonmetric" elsewhere (e.g., Carroll & Chang, 1970; Carroll, 1972) to distinguish a technique whose solutions are completely invariant under monotone transformation of the data and which guarantees (at least "in principle") a perfect solution (one where rank order of distances agrees perfectly with that of the data) when one is possible. This was contrasted with what was called a "quasi-nonmetric" procedure, where one or the other (or both) of these conditions is only approximately true. This usage of the term should not be confused with that of Green and Carmone (1970). Perhaps this terminological difficulty could be resolved by calling the Coombs procedure "doubly nonmetric," as was suggested earlier.

† It has very recently been discovered by Kruskal and Carroll that Shepard's algorithm could in fact be characterized as a gradient method optimization of an explicitly defined measure of fit. This was not known at the time (1964), however. Furthermore, the measure of fit Shepard used as criterion in his method was different from the criterion being optimized.

ities into distances. If we represent that function as $S(X, M)$, we can set our task as the minimization over all X and M of STRESS $= S(X, M)$. Phrased in this way, this seems like a formidable task. However, Kruskal was able to take advantage of one very important simplification, which is expressed in the following seductively simple-looking formula

$$\min_{X,M} S(X, M) = \min_{X} [\min_{M} S(X, M)],$$

whose import is that if we can find a way to find the M minimizing S for a fixed X, then we are a long way toward our goal of minimizing S over X *and* M. It turns out that there is a well-defined and *finite* algorithm for finding the best M, given a specified X. Since the X matrix implies a set of distances, we could just as well assume that a set of fixed distances is given. The problem is to define the $\hat{d}$'s as a monotone function M of the δ's (the proximity, or antiproximity values) that minimize STRESS as defined in (18). Since the $\hat{d}$'s do not enter into the denominator, this is, in fact, equivalent to finding the g that minimizes the numerator; i.e., that produces the best least squares approximation to the $\hat{d}$'s. This problem of *least squares monotone* regression was first solved by van Eeden (1957a,b) and others (Bartholomew, 1959; Barton & Mallows, 1961; Miles, 1959) and was adopted by Kruskal (1964) to solve this problem of finding the best M. Since M could now easily be solved for any X, we can in effect redefine STRESS as a function of X alone; i.e.,

$$\text{STRESS} = S(X) = [\min_{M} S(X, M)],$$

so that the seemingly simpler problem now arises of finding X minimizing $S(X)$. The numerical method that Kruskal used to solve the problem actually turns out to be nearly equivalent to the α process described for Shepard's analysis of proximities. The major (and critically important) difference is that the algebraic magnitude of the discrepancy for points i and j is effectively defined to be proportional to $d_{ij} - \hat{d}_{ij}$. (This is not immediately obvious from Kruskal's gradient formula, but it can be established by some algebraic manipulation. The effective step-size, however, is changed somewhat.)

C. An Illustrative Application of Multidimensional Scaling

Before discussing further issues and details we would like to illustrate multidimensional scaling by an application to some data from Miller and Nicely's (1955) study of confusions among English consonants. The subjects in Miller and Nicely's experiment listened to female speakers read one-syllable stimuli, such as *pa, ta,* and *ka,* from randomized lists, and wrote down the consonant they heard after each syllable was spoken. There were 17 experimental sessions in each of which the speech transmission

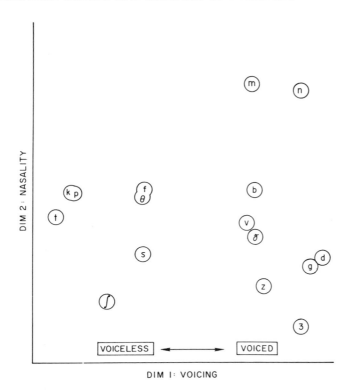

Fɪɢ. 1. Two-dimensional space from Shepard's (1973) analysis of data (see Table I) from Miller and Nicely's (1955) study of confusions among consonants.

circuit was degraded in a different way. In addition to the standard condition, which had a frequency response from 200 to 6500 Hz and a signal-to-noise ratio of 18 dB, there were five noise conditions (signal-to-noise ratio decreased from 12 dB to −12 dB in 6-dB steps), six low-pass filtering conditions (in which frequencies above a specified cutoff were filtered out) and five high-pass filtering conditions (in which the frequencies below a specified cutoff were filtered out).

Shepard (1973)* analyzed the pooled symmetrized matrix from the noise conditions, shown in Table I, by a variant of multidimensional scaling described earlier, in which an exponential rather than a monotonic fit was required. (Almost identical results were obtained by using a monotonic function; moreover, the best fitting monotonic function turned out to be very close to an exponential decay curve.) The two-dimensional (rotated) space obtained for these data is shown in Fig. 1. Shepard assigned the interpretation "voicing" to the horizontal dimension, since it distinguishes

* Despite the 1973 reference, the paper was actually written in 1965.

TABLE I

	p	t	k	f	θ	s	ʃ	b	d	g	v	ð	z	ʒ	m	n
p	—															
t	.229	—														
k	.432	.241	—													
f	.101	.057	.077	—												
θ	.124	.079	.084	.423	—											
s	.052	.050	.063	.066	.157	—										
ʃ	.038	.050	.047	.030	.048	.115	—									
b	.022	.013	.018	.046	.045	.024	.012	—								
d	.025	.022	.020	.025	.041	.031	.033	.058	—							
g	.013	.016	.030	.015	.039	.033	.021	.069	.342	—						
v	.016	.022	.020	.035	.040	.023	.020	.210	.059	.054	—					
ð	.028	.016	.018	.032	.031	.026	.018	.145	.094	.120	.338	—				
z	.025	.023	.025	.018	.033	.035	.017	.055	.106	.139	.080	.161	—			
ʒ	.019	.017	.019	.007	.017	.022	.012	.027	.089	.125	.029	.033	.136	—		
m	.025	.022	.021	.016	.019	.017	.012	.038	.024	.032	.030	.034	.121	.016	—	
n	.017	.018	.020	.012	.018	.013	.011	.024	.032	.030	.022	.028	.016	.030	.151	—

the voiced consonants (those, which, when spoken, produce vocal cord vibration) from their voiceless cognates. The interpretation "nasality" given to the vertical dimension reflects the fact that the two nasals, *m* and *n,* are separated from the other consonants.

Even though only two distinctive features (voicing and nasality) are explicitly mentioned in the labels for dimensions, Shepard does point out that some information regarding affrication and place of articulation is preserved in the two-dimensional space. For example, the stops are generally at opposite extremes of dimension 1, with the fricatives in between.

Shepard further clarified this configuration in particular, and the Miller and Nicely data in general, by applying Johnson's (1967) hierarchical clustering procedure to the same confusion matrix (Table I).

Johnson's hierarchical clustering procedure starts with the finest possible clustering (each point a separate "cluster") and proceeds to "merge" the two stimuli with the highest proximity value. (In case there is a tie for the most proximal pair, all pairs of points with the common value are merged simultaneously.) The newly merged cluster is treated as a separate point, so there are now (in general) $n - 1$, rather than n points. Distances must then be calculated between this point and the others. In the "maximum" method (used by Shepard) the distance of a cluster to another point (which may be another cluster) is taken to be the largest of the distances (smallest proximity) between the merged points; in the minimum method, it is the smallest distance (largest proximity). This process now continues, but with $n - 1$ points instead of $n,$ and does not end until all points are merged into a single large cluster. This process of continual merging produces a hierarchical clustering, which can be represented as a tree. The tree generated in this way for the Miller–Nicely data is shown in Fig. 2. The height of different nodes of the tree is then defined as the distance between the two points merged at that node. In the maximum method, this can also be shown to be the diameter of the largest cluster in the clustering, where diameter is defined as the largest distance between a pair of points in that cluster. If this process is applied to proximities rather than distances or antiproximities, the heights would be replaced by proximity levels that get smaller as one goes up the hierarchy. In Fig. 2, the heights have, in fact, been replaced by these proximity levels, and the tree is inverted so larger proximities are at the top. Perhaps in this case we should refer to the "depth" rather than "height" of the clusterings.

Figure 3 shows an embedding of results for five clustering levels (minimum intracluster proximity of .40, .20, .10, 05, and .025) in the multidimensional space for these data. These contours were drawn manually by Shepard. It is quite important to note, however, that they *could* be so drawn, without overlapping or crossing of cluster boundaries, and with

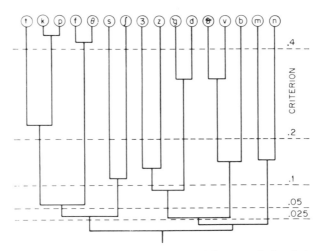

FIG. 2. Hierarchical clustering from Shepard's (1973) analysis of data (see Table I) from Miller and Nicely's (1955) study of confusions among consonants. Clusters at five levels (.40, .20, .10, .05, and .025) are indicated by dashed horizontal lines.

all the clusters appearing to be reasonably compact and connected. Since the two analyses (multidimensional scaling and hierarchical clustering) were done quite independently, there was no guarantee that this would happen. That it did tends to increase the credibility of both analyses, while also being quite helpful in interpretation of the multidimensional scaling solution.

As indicated by the three outermost curves, the clustering at the .025 level partitions the consonants into three broad clusters—the nasals, the voiced nonnasals, and the voiceless consonants. At the .05 level the voiceless and voiced consonants both subdivide, making five clusters in all. As the minimum intracluster value increases from .10 to .20 to .40, the number of clusters increases from 7 to 11 to 14. Twelve of the clusters at the .40 level contain a single consonant; the only two-element clusters at the .40 level are p, k (proximity = .432) and f, θ (proximity = .423).

Shepard also did separate hierarchical clusterings of the confusion matrices for each of the 17 experimental conditions. At the levels of each hierarchical clustering at which there were six clusters and five clusters, exactly the same clusters appeared for the four intermediate noise conditions (6, 0, −6, and −12 dB). In the two extreme conditions, the confusion rate was too low (at 12 dB) or too high (−18 dB) for stable clusters to be defined. The consistency in these and other clustering results led Shepard to conclude that "although signal-to-noise ratio is a powerful determiner

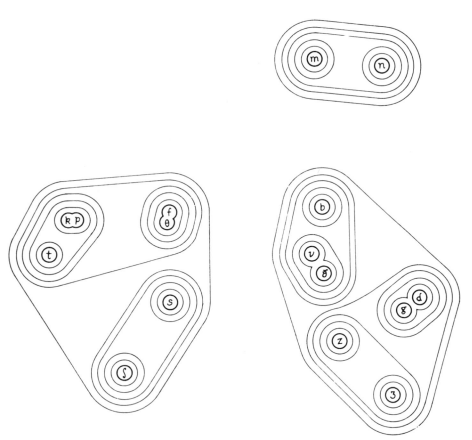

Fig. 3. Embedding of clusters from a hierarchical clustering analysis (Fig. 2) in the two-dimensional space (Fig. 1) for the same data (Table I). At a clustering level (lowest intracluster proximity) of .025, there are three clusters; while at a clustering level of .40, there are 14 clusters.

of overall level of confusion, it has little or no effect on the internal *pattern* of those confusions [Shepard, 1973]."

Whereas the clustering results for the low-pass filtering conditions were quite similar to those for the noise conditions, the clusterings for the high-pass filtering conditions were so different that they could not be embedded very well in the multidimensional space based on the "noise" conditions (see Shepard, 1973). The correspondence between results for the noise and low-pass filtering conditions is consistent with the fact (Miller & Nicely, 1955, p. 350) that the higher frequencies are more susceptible to masking by broadband, or white, noise, since the sound energy is generally weaker in the higher frequencies. In Chapter 13 in this volume (Wish & Carroll, 1974), we describe a later analysis of the Miller–Nicely data (Wish, 1970a), which gives more information about the confusion structure for high-pass filtering conditions and which allows for more direct and sensitive comparisons of the data for different kinds and degrees of acoustical degradations.

IV. NON-EUCLIDEAN METRICS AND SEMIMETRICS

Although most attention in multidimensional scaling has been given to the Euclidean metric, there are others that have been considered. The two principle classes are the so-called Minkowski r (or Lp, or power) metrics and the Riemannian metrics (principally, Riemannian metrics of constant, nonpositive curvature) which have a common intersection in the Euclidean metric. There is some evidence (Luneberg, 1947) that a Riemannian metric of constant negative curvature may be more appropriate than the Euclidean (which corresponds to the limiting case of constant *zero* curvature) for describing the geometry of visual space. This has been contested, however, by Indow (1967, 1968), whose results suggest that the internal geometry of visual space may well be Euclidean, while much of the evidence cited by Luneberg and others could be accounted for by nonlinearities in the *mapping* from physical to psychological space.

The Minkowski r-metrics are defined as:

$$d_{jk}^{(r)} = \left(\sum_{t=1}^{m} |x_{jt} - x_{kt}|^r \right)^{1/r}, \tag{19}$$

with r usually restricted to be greater than or equal to one. In the mathematical literature this is referred to as the Lp metric (the parameter p replacing r), while Beals, Krantz, and Tversky (1968) prefer to call it simply the power metric (r being the power).

As the parameter r varies in the Minkowski r-metric, we encounter three interesting special cases. To take the middle one first, $r = 2$ corresponds to the usual Euclidean metric. At the two extremes, $r = 1$ is the so-called "city block" or "Manhattan" metric, so called because of the analogy of effective distance between points in a city (e.g., Manhattan) laid out in a rectangular lattice of streets and blocks. This city block metric takes the very simple form

$$d_{jk}^{(1)} = \sum_{t} |x_{jt} - x_{kt}|, \tag{20}$$

that is, it is just a sum of absolute differences on the various dimensions.

This metric is psychologically appealing, since it might seem more plausible to assume processes corresponding to absolute differencing of values on dimensions than squared differencing (as in the Euclidean metric). It would seem, however, that one process is inherently no more nor less plausible than the other. When one thinks about it carefully, the neural circuitry for computing absolute differences would probably be at least as complicated as that for squared differences. The square-root operation at the end of the computation of the Euclidean function is not essential, since we are assuming proximities or dissimilarities to be only ordinally defined anyway. Also, there are other processes, such as the stochastic one suggested by Micko and Fisher (1970), that lead naturally to subjective distances that are Euclidean or to other varieties of power or Minkowski metrics.

At the other extreme, (for $r = \infty$), we have the so-called *maximum* or *dominance* metric, in which

$$d_{jk}^{(\infty)} = \max_t |x_{jt} - x_{kt}|, \tag{21}$$

that is, distance is given by the largest coordinate difference. This metric can be rationalized by invoking attentional factors. If the subject can attend only to one dimension at any one time, and if, furthermore, he attends to that dimension on which the two stimuli are most different, the resulting metric is this Minkowski ∞, or "dominance" metric (so called because the dimension with the largest difference "dominates" all the others). (This bears some resemblance to the lexicographic type of model discussed by Coombs, 1964.)

One point of interest about any particular metric is the set of *equidistance contours* it induces. Equidistance contours are simply the loci of equal distance from a particular point. Each point in the space has its own set of contours. The Minkowski r-family of metrics have the property that contours around every point have the same shape. This property is known as "translation invariance," since it implies that if two points are *translated* (moved by adding the same vector to both) in the same way, their distance remains unchanged. The Minkowski r-metrics also have the property that members of the family of equidistance contours for a particular point are mutually similar—in the strict geometric sense of this term. This means that the contours for two different values of d have the same shape, although they will have different sizes. In fact, if the origin is translated to the point whose contours we are considering, the curves for two different values of d are related by a multiplicative constant. If the two values of d are d_1 and d_2, the contour for the first will be just (d_1/d_2) times the contour for the second. This constant ratio rule for the contours implies that if three points, *a, b,* and *c,* fall in a straight line (with *b* between *a* and *c*), then $d_{ac} = d_{ab} + d_{bc}$.

This straight-line property does not necessarily hold for all metrics—for example, it does not hold, in general, for the Riemannian metrics. In fact, there are some metrics in which there may be *no* point "between" two arbitrary points, *a* and *c* (where we define *b* as being between *a* and *c* if and only if $d_{ac} = d_{ab} + d_{bc}$). This is a startling notion to contemplate, since it means that there is no geodetic (or shortest path) connecting such an *a* and *c*. The length of any connected path through other points in the space will necessarily be greater than the direct distance from *a* to *c*. It is as if one must get from *a* to *c* by going outside the space, somewhat analogous to traveling through time via the time warps so popular in science fiction. A simple example of such a space would be provided by a one-dimensional "space" consisting of a curved line in two or more dimensions, in which distance is defined as ordinary Euclidean distance in the larger space in which the curved line is embedded. Such a metric must satisfy the metric axioms, since it does in the larger space. Clearly, in this case, the geodetic distance determined by moving along the curve will, in general, be greater than the straight-line distance defined by going outside the curved one-dimensional space. In this case, of course, one might be tempted to argue that the real distance is the geodetic distance, since it is the only feasible one. (It does no good to know the distance "as the crow flies" if one is constrained to some less direct path.) This is, in fact, exactly the way in which the Riemannian metrics are defined—as geodetic distances defined in curved "spaces" embedded in higher-dimensional Euclidean space (e.g., the two-dimensional surface of a sphere embedded in three dimensions, which presumably is the functional geometry of the earth's surface).

Beals, Krantz and Tversky (1968) (see also Tversky & Krantz, 1970) following Busemann (1955) and Blumenthal (1953) use the term "metric with additive segments" to refer to a metric such that the geodetic distance always equals the actual distance (or, alternatively, such that there is always a point between every pair of points in the sense previously defined). Beals *et al.* argue that only metric spaces with this segmental additivity property should be considered as candidates for perceptual spaces. We prefer to leave this as an open question.

One example of a metric space that does not have the segmental additivity property is provided by what might be called the extended Minkowski *r*-metric defined by:

$$d_{jk}^{*(r)} = \sum_t |x_{jt} - x_{kt}|^r \qquad \text{for } 0 < r < 1. \tag{22}$$

While the Minkowski *r*-metric, as defined in (19), is usually restricted to $r \geq 1$, the modification in (22), in which the final $1/r$ power is omitted can, in fact, be shown to be a metric for r between 0 and 1. It satisfies all the metric axioms, including the triangle inequality, but it does *not* satisfy segmental additivity. This, incidentally, also provides a counterexample to something suggested by Shepard (1964), who seemed to indicate that no metrics were possible with concave (rather than convex) equidistance contours. The contours for this extended r-metric with $0 < r < 1$ are concave. The property they do fail to have, of course, is that of segmental additivity. Indeed, it is even possible to define metrics with concave contours that *do* satisfy segmental additivity, so long as it is not required that the segments (or geodetics) correspond to ordinary straight lines. The assertions Shepard made do hold, however, for the class of generalized *Minkowski* metrics he was considering. The generalized Minkowski metrics share the translation invariance and constant ratio rules discussed earlier for the more specialized Minkowski r-metrics, but with the family of similar contours allowed to have an arbitrary shape. They must be centrally symmetric, however, this being implied by the translation invariance property. It can also be shown that the contours must be convex (i.e., no straight line can intersect a contour in more than two points) if the triangle inequality is to hold.

Tversky and Krantz (1970) have provided an example of another metric that does not satisfy segmental additivity. This is the exponential metric, which can be defined as

$$d_{jk} = \log \left[1 + \sum_t \left(p^{|x_{jt} - x_{kt}|} - 1 \right) \right], \tag{23}$$

with $p > 1$. This metric satisfies segmental additivity only for points on lines parallel to coordinate axes.

Having broken the ice with our discussion of extended Minkowski r-metrics with r between 0 and 1, let us consider briefly another class, namely Minkowski r with *negative* r (here we need to reintroduce the final $1/r$ power once again). When r is negative, this "metric" is not a metric at all. The triangle inequality is not satisfied, nor can any reasonable transformation of the distances be found to assure satisfaction of that inequality. However, this class does provide an example of a *semimetric* with interesting properties. In particular, if *any* coordinate difference is 0, the distance is 0. As r approaches $-\infty$, we approach an especially interesting case that is a sort of mirror image of the $r = +\infty$ metric. As stated previously, the latter is sometimes called the maximum metric, because the distance between two points is the largest coordinate difference. The $r = -\infty$ semimetric might be called the *minimum* metric (or semimetric), since for it, the distance is the *smallest* coordinate difference. It is as though, in this case, the individual attends only to the single dimension on which the two stimuli are most similar. While this may seem unreasonable at first, a semimetric of this sort could account for a kind of paradox first suggested by William James (1890). James used an illustration involving three objects—the moon, a ball and a candle. He pointed out that the moon might be judged as similar to a ball because both are round, and similar to a candle because both provide light. A ball and candle are not, however, similar at all to one another. Shepard (1964) provides another example of this sort, involving the words "table," "fable," and "chair," and suggests that this implies a violation of the triangle inequality. Both of these cases, and others like them, could conceivably be accounted for by something like this "minimum semimetric," or by some other less extreme Minkowski negative semimetric. Hannes Eisler (personal communication) has described an actual set of data in which something very close to the minimum semimetric seemed to describe subjects' dissimilarity judgments.

We have thus described a generalization of the Minkowski r-metric in which r takes on all possible values except zero, but even this can be filled in, at least as a limiting case. This would correspond to a kind of "binary" metric, in which all points that are not identical are equally distant. All distances, then, are either 0 for identical points or a constant (which might as well be 1) for nonidentical points. (This is sometimes called the trivial metric by topologists). This sort of binary metric might provide a reasonable model for some situations; e.g., same–different judgments involving highly distinguishable stimuli. Thus, we see that this class of metrics and semimetrics is very general indeed. Some properties of these metrics are illustrated in Fig. 4.

A. Interdimensional Additivity and Intradimensional Subtractivity

The various Minkowski r-metrics, extended metrics, and semimetrics just discussed, as well as Tversky's exponential metric defined in Eq. (23) have the two properties of *inter*dimensional additivity and *intra*dimensional subtractivity. These properties were discussed by Shepard and Carroll (1966) (though these terms were not used) and have been extensively studied from an axiomatic standpoint by Beals, Krantz, and Tversky (1968) and more recently by Tversky and Krantz (1970). These properties are (in our notation)

$$d_{jk} = F\left\{\sum_t \varphi_t(x_{it}, x_{jt})\right\} \qquad \text{[interdimensional additivity]} \qquad (24)$$

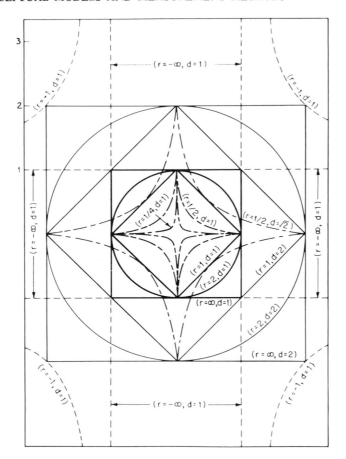

FIG. 4. Equidistance contours for Minkowski r-metrics [(———), $r \geq 1$] "extended" Minkowski r-metrics [(— — —), $0 \leq r < 1$] and Minkowski r-semimetrics [(– – –), $r < 0$]. The r parameter of the particular metric or semimetric is indicated in parentheses, together with the value of distance (d) generating the particular equidistance locus.

with F monotone increasing.

$$d_{jk} = G\{|y_{j1} - y_{k1}|, \quad |y_{j2} - y_{k2}|, \quad \ldots, \quad |y_{jm} - y_{km}|\}$$

$$\text{[intradimensional subtractivity], \quad (25)}$$

where $y_{jt} = f_t(x_{jt})$ and G is an increasing function in each of its arguments.

The functions f_t are, in a sense, redundant, since one may eliminate them by merely treating the y's rather than the x's as "the" dimensions.

They would be of interest, however, in the case where the x's correspond to known physical dimensions or are otherwise measured or known a priori.

Beals, Krantz, and Tversky prove that interdimensional additivity is implied by a kind of "context independence" property of the distances (or proximities) together with some very mild regularity conditions. This property (their A3) can be stated verbally as follows: If two stimuli, x and x' have equal values on dimension t, and two other stimuli, y and y', also have equal values (not necessarily the same as x and x') on that dimension, then the order of $p(x, y)$ and $p(x', y')$ (or of the corresponding d's, if one is dealing with distances) is dependent only on the values of the stimuli on the other $m - 1$ dimensions. (In particular, this order is not dependent on the pair of values on dimension t.) This says, in a rather general way, that the dimensions do not interact in their effects. While this kind of non-interaction, or independence certainly does not seem to be a *necessary* condition for a reasonable psychological metric, it does seem to be desirable. It might, in fact, provide the basis for an operational definition of *independent* perceptual dimensions.

The argument for intradimensional subtractivity, it would seem, is more direct. In the one-dimensional case the subtractive metric is the "natural" one (and in fact, the *only* one if segmental additivity is assumed). Some writers would, in fact, reserve the notion of unidimensionality for the case where the simple absolute difference metric holds. Even if the stimuli are multidimensional, if all but one dimension are held constant we are back to the one-dimensional case (implying the need for subtractivity). Furthermore, this one-dimensional subtractive metric should be independent of the constant values of the other dimensions and, in fact, must be if the independence condition already discussed is satisfied. If this is so, then intradimensional subtractivity must hold at least for cases in which only one dimension is varied. Whereas this does not *imply* that subtractivity must hold overall, it strongly suggests that this should be so; in fact, it *does* imply overall subtractivity if interdimensional additivity is also assumed. Although one could invent a metric for which subtractivity holds in the case where only one dimension is varied but not otherwise, it probably would be very strange. A kind of theoretical principle of parsimony would, then, strongly suggest the subtractivity property.

Beals, Krantz, and Tversky go on to establish that a metric that has both the interdimensional additivity and intradimensional subtractivity properties must be of the form

$$d_{jk} = \varphi^{-1} \left(\sum_t \varphi |x_{jt} - x_{kt}| \right), \tag{26}$$

with φ a superadditive (or convex) function.* (In this formula the redundant functions f_t are left out, or assumed to have been absorbed in the x's.) The Minkowski r, or power metric, is of this form, with $\varphi(u) = u^r$. Tversky's exponential metric as defined in Eq. (23) is of this form, with $\varphi(u) = p^u (p > 1)$.

In the later paper by Tversky and Krantz (1970) it is further established that, of the metric functions of the form in Eq. (26), the only ones satisfying segmental additivity are the Minkowski r, or power metrics (with $r \geq 1$). The 1968 paper by Beals, Krantz, and Tversky had established this only for the case in which the additive segments corresponded to algebraic straight lines; the 1970 Tversky and Krantz paper allows that this condition be dropped. This is a powerful result, in that it implies that, if one accepts the premise that all three of these properties (interdimensional additivity, intradimensional subtractivity, and segmental additivity) are necessary for the psychological metric, then the only permissible metrics are of the Minkowski-r type, with $r \geq 1$.

B. Methods Based on Non-Euclidean Metric

Kruskal's MDSCAL. (Kruskal & Carmone, 1970) and Young and Torgerson's (1967) TORSCA both have the capacity to fit specific non-Euclidean metrics—in particular, those of the Minkowski r class discussed earlier (the parameter r being read in by the user). It is possible to zero in on an optimal value of r by varying that parameter, looking at a curve of STRESS versus r, and seeking the value of r that minimizes STRESS. This was done by Kruskal (1964a), and has also been tried by Arnold (1971) and others.

Carroll and Chang (1967) developed a procedure a few years ago which they called "unknown metric scaling" that fit a metric with only the very general constraint (in addition to the metric axioms) that

$$\max_t |x_{jt} - x_{kt}| \leq d_{jk} \leq \sum_{t=1}^{m} |x_{jt} - x_{kt}|, \qquad (27)$$

which puts each distance between that predicted by the dominance (Minkowski ∞) and city block (Minkowski 1) metrics. The approach has not

* It would appear that these conditions could be weakened to interdimensional additivity combined with intradimensional subtractivity for one-dimensional stimulus pairs only. These two conditions together imply intradimensional subtractivity over the entire stimulus domain.

appeared very useful, however, mainly because of the difficulty in interpreting this very general metric whenever it departs from any of the "standard" forms. In two dimensions it is possible to look at equidistance contours, but these are not too helpful if the metric is not Minkowskian. In three or more dimensions it is almost impossible to interpret such a very general metric. Another reason for not pursuing this approach is that an analysis with Euclidean metric appears to be exceedingly robust even against very extreme departures of the metric from the Euclidean form.

A few workers [van de Geer, Batchelder (personal communications)] have pursued algorithms for fitting Riemannian metrics, but usually to stimulus spaces given a priori. To date, no one has, to the knowledge of the authors, developed a complete scaling algorithm utilizing a Riemannian metric. The same is true of the general Minkowski metric, in which the equidistance contours can take on any closed, convex, centrally symmetric shape, or the Finsler metrics, which bear the same relation to Minkowski metrics as the Riemannian does to the Euclidean (i.e., Finsler metrics are locally Minkowskian just as Riemannian are locally Euclidean).

C. Multidimensional Analysis Based on Continuity Principles

As suggested earlier, the most general assumption one can make regarding proximities is that they are *continuously* related to the underlying perceptual dimensions. There are also many other kinds of data (e.g., preferences, rating scale data, probabilities of choice or of other kinds of behavior) that might be supposed to be related continuously to underlying dimensions, but where the particular function is not known. If we have a matrix of data (which may be proximities) we say that the matrix is continuously related to underlying dimensions $x_j, \ldots, x_m$ if

$$y_{js} = f_s(x_{j1}, x_{j2}, \ldots, x_{jt}, \ldots, x_{jm}) \tag{28}$$

$||y_{js}||$ is a stimuli by variables matrix, y_{js} being the value of the jth stimulus on variable s, whereas x_{jt} is the value of stimulus j on *dimension* t. The function f_s is assumed only to be continuous in all its arguments (x_1 through x_t), and may or may not be the same for different values of s. In the case of a proximity matrix the "variables" would correspond to the stimuli, and so $f_s(\mathbf{x}_j)$ would be of the form of $p(\mathbf{x}_j, \mathbf{x}_s)$, where p is the proximity function. Since this proximity function is assumed only to be continuous, this would allow it to correspond to any metric or semimetric whatever, or even to violate the symmetry and diagonal maximality properties usually assumed for proximities.

Is it possible, given data having only this exceedingly general relation to underlying dimensions, to recover these dimensions? It turns out that it is, so long as the continuous functions (the f's) are relatively smooth. This admittedly vague concept of smoothness may be taken to mean essentially that the second derivatives are small relative to the spacing of the observation points, so that the functions are *locally* well approximated by linear functions.

Shepard and Carroll (1966) pursued the idea of continuity as a basis for finding the structure underlying multivariate data of the kind assumed here, and devised two different approaches to this problem. One, called *parametric mapping* (developed primarily by Carroll), utilized the principle of finding the m-dimensional space that optimized an index of "continuity" or "smoothness" (both terms are in quotes to indicate that it is not the precise mathematical meaning of these terms, but a vaguer, more empirical, meaning that is intended). The index used, called κ, was defined as

$$\kappa = \frac{\Sigma_j \Sigma_k d_{jk}^2 / D_{jk}^4}{\text{Normalizing Factor}} \tag{29}$$

where

$$d_{jk}^2 = \sum_s (y_{js} - y_{ks})^2 \tag{30}$$

and

$$D_{jk}^2 = \sum_t (x_{jt} - x_{kt})^2 \tag{31}$$

so that d_{jk} and D_{jk} are, respectively, Euclidean distances between stimuli j and k in the empirical data space and in the underlying (to-be-recovered) space defined by the x's.

The normalizing factor is defined so that the unconstrained minimum of κ is obtained when the recovered x-space is related to the y-space by a *similarity transformation* (which allows a rigid rotation, a central dilation, or uniform change of scale, and a possible shift of origin); that is to say, when the D's are proportional to the d's. If the dimensionality of the underlying space (m) is small, of course, this will not be possible, in general. Parametric mapping utilizes a numerical procedure based on the method of gradients or steepest descent to find the m-dimensional configuration that minimizes κ. For a further discussion of the rationale for this particular "index of continuity" and some applications of parametric mapping, see Shepard and Carroll (1966).

The other approach discussed in that paper, due primarily to Shepard, was called "locally monotone analysis of proximities." This method relies, in a sense, on the local linearity property already mentioned. The idea is that, if the function relating data to underlying dimensions is locally linear, a derived distance measure [such as the d^2 measure of Eq. (30)] should be locally related in a simple way (e.g., by a monotone function) to distances in the underlying space, although such a simple relation might not obtain globally (i.e., for larger distances). In principle, the property of "localness" should be defined in the underlying x-space, not in the y-space of the data (since the "mapping" whose continuity we are assuming is from x to y, not vice versa). However, except for extreme cases, involving, for example, points on closed curves or surfaces, what is local for one will also be local for the other. Using this fact, Shepard defined localness in terms of the data, so that two points for which the distance (as defined by some derived distance measure) was less than some criterial value were defined as local vis à vis each other (i.e., as close or neighboring points). The specific principle that was used in the locally monotone analysis of proximities was to attempt to enforce monotonicity between data and solution distances for such local points only. In practice this means that all distances greater than this cutoff value were simply ignored, or treated as missing data. Shepard, in fact, utilized Kruskal's MDSCAL program, with distances computed from the data playing the role of dissimilarities, and utilized the missing data options of MDSCAL to have the program ignore the large distances. (There is now an explicit option in the MDSCAL program that allows definition of "missing" data in terms of such a cutoff value.)

This approach worked remarkably well, as evidenced by an analysis by Shepard and Carroll (1966) of some color-naming data collected by Boynton and Gordon (1965). The stimuli were 23 spectral colors differing only in wavelength. The basic data consisted of the relative frequencies with which a group of observers applied four color names (blue, green, yellow, and red) to these stimuli. These data could be arranged in a 23×4 matrix of stimuli by color names, with relative frequencies as the cell entries. Shepard used a measure of profile dissimilarity that was actually equivalent to the "city block" metric (sum of absolute differences between the relative frequencies, summed across the four color names) but the results were quite similar when the "squared Euclidean distance" measure of Eq. (30) was used.

If overall global monotonicity was enforced, the two-dimensional configuration shown in Fig. 5 resulted. This figure looks remarkably like the classical color circle, but with corners corresponding roughly with the four color names that were used in The Boynton–Gordon study. However, when locally monotone proximity analysis was applied (using, in this case, only the 100 smallest of the total 253 profile dissimilarities) the one-dimensional solution shown in Fig. 6 resulted. Not surprisingly, the one dimension corresponded to the physical dimension of wavelength.

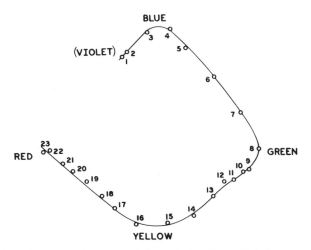

Fig. 5. Two-dimensional representation of the 23 profiles based on a nonmetric multidimensional scaling analysis of the *d* measures.

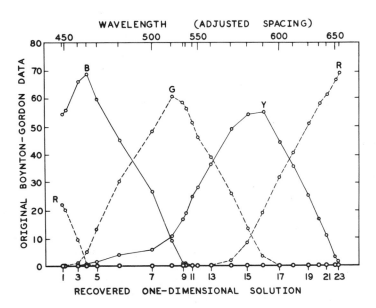

Fig. 6. One-dimensional solution based on a nonmetric MDS analysis of the 100 smallest *d* measures (line at bottom), with blue, green, yellow, and red components of original observation vectors plotted above. This is the analysis called by Shepard a "local analysis of proximities."

The plots appearing above the one-dimensional solution show how the original data are related to that dimension. It is clear that these four curves are relatively continuous, although they are not at all linear, or even monotonic. Shepard (1968) and Carroll (1968), in some unpublished joint work explored the application of such methods based on continuity principles to proximity data, where the proximities were defined by semimetrics that departed quite severely from the Euclidean (or any other) metric. A surprising practical conclusion of this work was that the Euclidean metric is exceedingly "robust" under even extreme departures from Euclidean metric. The practical import is that, in exploring the possibility of non-Euclidean metrics or semimetrics, it should suffice first to obtain the configuration by scaling the data assuming the Euclidean metric. Using the configuration so obtained, a detailed analysis can be done to uncover any systematic departures from the Euclidean metric.

D. Attentional Phenomena

It was Attneave (1950) who first suggested that attentional phenomena could strongly interact with the metric of the stimulus space. With the particular geometrical stimuli he used, a metric closer to the "city block" or Minkowski 1-metric seemed to account for his data better than the Euclidean (or Minkowski 2) metric. The important feature of his stimuli seemed to be that the dimensions could be easily isolated perceptually and attended to independently of one another. The suggestion Attneave made was that, in the case of such dimensions the summation of absolute differences formula incorporated in the city block metric was more appropriate than the square-root-of-sum-of-squared-differences Euclidean formula. The city block is, of course, the metric one would expect if subjects were judging some sort of interstimulus distance for each dimension independently, and then combining the distances additively to get an overall subjective distance. For stimuli such as colors, in which the dimensions could not be easily isolated, Attneave proposed that the more "wholistic" (and rotationally invariant) Euclidean metric was still appropriate.

Shepard (1964) has proposed the terms "analyzable" and "unitary" stimuli to cover these two cases. He argued that a metric somewhere between the Euclidean and city block was needed to account for similarity judgments involving analyzable stimuli. Shepard established this with highly analyzable geometric stimuli (circles of different sizes, with inscribed spokes varying in angle of inclination) by constructing series of stimuli that varied along lines in the physically defined space. The series was so constructed that one of the stimuli exactly matched the standard on one of the two dimensions and another in the series matched exactly on the second. The remaining stimuli effected compromises on the two dimensions. The subjects' task was to select the stimulus in the series that was closest to the standard.

If the psychological space had the same structure as the physical space *and* if its metric were Euclidean, neither of these two special stimuli (those that matched the standard on one dimension) should have been picked as closest to the standard, but rather a "compromise stimulus" which was "moderately close" to the standard on both dimensions. Shepard found, however, that very few subjects chose this compromise stimulus, or any of the intermediate stimuli. The distribution of choices (across subjects) was bimodal, with the two modes corresponding to the two stimuli which differed from the standard on only one of the two relevant physical dimensions. He interpreted this strong tendency of many subjects to match the standard stimulus on one of the two physical dimensions as implying that the perceptual metric was non-Euclidean, and, in particular, that it deviated from Euclidean toward the city block metric. He drew similar conclusions from an identification learning experiment involving eight stimuli, constructed in the same general manner as the earlier ones (again, the two dimensions were at least roughly equated for overall salience). In this case, Shepard concluded that the pattern of errors was inconsistent with the Euclidean metric.

In these studies, as well as the earlier ones reported by Attneave, there may be one serious logical flaw—the failure to distinguish carefully between possible nonlinearities in the psychophysical mapping from physical to psychological space and non-Euclideanness of the metric within the subjective perceptual space. This is exactly the same ambiguity in interpretation mentioned earlier in connection with Indow's (1968) argument for a representation of visual space as internally Euclidean, but with nonlinearities in the psychophysical mapping. Most of the results presented by both Attneave and Shepard could be accounted for by assuming a transformation of the physical space of the sort depicted in Fig. 7. This psychophysical mapping transforms a circle in the physical space, depicted on the left, into the kind of rounded square depicted on the right. This particular transformation could actually be accomplished by individual psychophysical functions for dimensions ϕ_1 and ϕ_2 of the ogival type pictured at the bottom of Fig. 7, which is, of course, a quite familiar kind of psychometric (if not psychophysical) function.

Shepard (personal communication) has argued that this possible interpretation is implausible because it is impossible to define a simple psychophysical mapping that will simultaneously transform *all* circles in the physical space into such rounded squares. Although this is true, all that is needed is that this be true for the particular set of stimuli Shepard used. Another

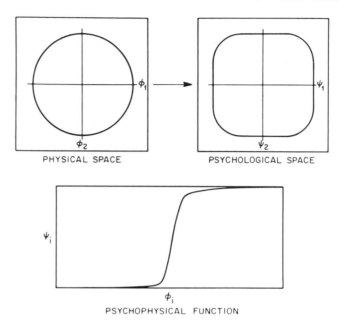

FIG. 7. Some of the results reported by Attneave (1950) and by Shepard (1964) could possibly be accounted for by a "psychophysical" mapping that would take the circular physical configuration on the upper left into the "rounded-square" psychological configuration shown on the right. Such a mapping could in fact result from psychophysical mappings $\psi_i = f_i(\phi_i)$ of the original form shown at the bottom.

problem is that only first choices were given. If more complete data were given, we could understand the metric better. Although we are at least moderately inclined toward Attneave's and Shepard's interpretations, we point out (as devil's advocates) the existence of this alternate interpretation so as to emphasize some of the possible pitfalls in this area, especially when generalizing from a particular relatively small and systematically selected set of stimuli to a larger population of stimuli.

In the case of the kinds of effects that Shepard reports, it seems to us that it is necessary to collect complete similarities data on a large set of stimuli that fill the space, and to show that it is not possible to account for these data adequately in terms of *any* configuration (of the appropriate dimensionality) involving a Euclidean metric. One way to approach this is to use multidimensional scaling to get the best fit in a Euclidean space, and then to look for systematic patterns in the residuals (actual distances minus predicted distances). If, for example, the metric tended toward the city block, one might expect pairs of stimuli varying on only a single dimension (unidimensional pairs) to have negative residuals and those differing on two dimensions (bidimensional pairs) to have positive residuals.

Experiments along exactly these lines were done by Hyman and Wells (1967, 1968) with results generally supportive of Shepard's interpretation (although there are some mild possible artifacts in their method that could partially account for their results). Generally speaking, we are willing to accept the proposition that, with analyzable stimuli, the metric tends to deviate from Euclidean toward the city block. It may, in some cases, even go *beyond* the city block to something like the extended Minkowski r-metrics, discussed earlier. We do, however, take this notion with some degree of reservation. With much real data such effects might be so small as to be masked effectively by noise or by other kinds of systematic distortions in the data.

E. Intra- and Interindividual Differences

Shepard presented evidence in the same paper we have just discussed of intra- and interindividual differences that have the character of shifts in salience or importance of dimensions within an individual over trials, or, more systematically, between individuals. Roughly speaking, he was able to divide his subjects into three major subgroups—one that tended (in the experiment described earlier) to choose the comparison stimulus that was exactly equal to the standard with respect to angle of inclination of the spoke, a second that tended to choose the stimulus that matched the standard in size, and a third group that apparently attended to differences on both dimensions. The third group seemed to weight the two dimensions equally, so that their distributions were generally unimodal, with modes somewhere in the center of the comparison sequence.

These data clearly imply intersubject differences in relative salience of the two dimensions. Shepard also suggests that some of his data may imply shifts of attention from trial to trial *within* the same individual. We are inclined to be a bit wary of this interpretation, however, since a more parsimonious interpretation may be possible in terms of either (or both) distortions in the psychophysical mapping or peculiarities in the internal perceptual metric. Any "shift of attention" that is systematically dependent on the pair of stimuli being judged *must,* we argue, be interpreted as one of these. Such a stimulus-dependent shift simply means that the metric (or, somewhat more generally, the similarity function) must be such as to take this shift into account. After all, in its most general definition the similarity function is just some continuous function of the pair of stimuli; thus, this is general enough to cover any effect that is a function only of the pair of stimuli. Since, as argued earlier, very little extra is added by assuming the similarity function to be monotonically transformable into a *metric,* it seems quite likely that this latter function could be so defined as to incorporate such systematic attentional shifts. (It may of course, be more elegant theoretically to postulate a relatively simple metric, e.g., Euclidean or city block, with a systematic attention shift imposed on it. But it would be just as consistent mathematically simply to redefine the metric or similarity function to include the attention shift). One metric, the so-called dominance metric, is, in fact, often interpreted in terms of such systematic shifts in attention; in this case, one attends solely to the dimension in which the greater difference is evidenced for the particular stimulus pair.

Thus it appears that the only convincing evidence for *intra*individual attentional shifts that cannot be viewed simply as a distortion in configuration or a change in metric (or similarity function) would entail within individual bimodality in the distribution of responses for a particular pair of stimuli (or in Shepard's paradigm, for a particular comparison series, with fixed standard). As it happens, Shepard did not replicate these series within individuals, nor do we know of any data that imply such intraindividual bimodality. While it is clear that changes in instructions or context can sometimes induce such shifts in attention (or at least lead to behavioral consequences that are consistent with such shifts), we are inclined to be a bit skeptical about such shifts occurring spontaneously within the same context or instructional set.

Let us return, then, to the question of systematic interindividual differences. We are, as will be seen, quite positively disposed toward this idea.

V. INDIVIDUAL DIFFERENCES IN PERCEPTION

The kind of differential attention to, or differential salience of, dimensions observed by Shepard illustrates a very important and pervasive source of individual differences in perception. While people seem to perceive the world in terms of very nearly the same dimensions or perceptual variables, they evidently differ enormously with respect to the relative importance (perceptually, cognitively, or behaviorally) of these dimensions.

Such differences in sensitivity or attention are presumably due in part to genetic differences (for example, differences between color-blind and color-normal individuals) and in part by the particular developmental history of the individual (witness the well-known, but possibly exaggerated, example of the Eskimos' presumably supersensitive perception of varieties, textures and colors of snow and ice). As suggested earlier, some attentional shifts might be due simply to instructional or contextual factors; but studies by Cliff, Pennell and Young (1966) have indicated that it is not really all that easy to manipulate saliences of dimensions in this way. (Recent studies by Gregson, 1974, suggest otherwise, however, at least with analyzable stimuli.) If a more behavioral measure of proximity were used, e.g., one based on confusions in identification learning, the differential weighting could be due at least in part to purely behavioral (as opposed to sensory or central) processes, such as differential gradients of response generalization. We shall generally, however, ignore the question of "where" the differential weighting occurs, and of how its etiology is to be divided between heredity and environment.

A. Differential Attention or Salience of Dimensions: The INDSCAL Model

The INDSCAL (for *IN*dividual *D*ifferences *SCAL*ing) model (Carroll & Chang 1970; Carroll, 1972, Carroll and Wish, Chapter 13) incorporates this notion of individual differences in the weights, or perceptual importances, of dimensions in a very explicit manner. The central assumption of the model has to do with the definition of distances for different individuals. As with ordinary, or *two-way*, scaling, these distances are assumed to relate in some simple way—e.g., linearly or monotonically—to similarities or other proximities. In INDSCAL, however, there is assumed to be a different set of distances for each subject. The distance between stimuli j and k for subject i, $d_{jk}^{(i)}$, is related to the dimensions of a "group" (or common) *stimulus space* by Eq. (32).

$$d_{jk}^{(i)} = \Big[\sum_{t=1}^{m} w_{it}(x_{jt} - x_{kt})^2 \Big]^{1/2},\tag{32}$$

where m is the dimensionality of the stimulus space; x_{jt} is the coordinate of stimulus j on the tth dimension of the "group" stimulus space, and w_{it} is the weight (indicating salience or perceptual importance) of the tth dimension for the ith subject. This equation is simply a weighted generalization of the Euclidean distance formula.

Another way of expressing the same model is provided by the following equations. We first define coordinates of what might be called a "private perceptual space" for subject i, by the equation

$$y_{jt}^{(i)} = (w_{it}^{1/2})x_{jt}\tag{33}$$

and then calculate ordinary Euclidean distances in terms of these idiosyncratic or private spaces, as shown in Eq. (34).

$$d_{jk}^{(i)} = \Big[\sum_{t=1}^{m} (y_{jt}^{(i)} - y_{kt}^{(i)})^2 \Big]^{1/2} = \Big[\sum_{t=1}^{m} w_{it}(x_{jt} - x_{kt})^2 \Big]^{1/2}\tag{34}$$

[The last expression was derived by substituting Eq. (33) into Eq. (32).] Thus the weighted distance formulation is equivalent to one in which each dimension is simply *rescaled* by the square root of the corresponding weight. This rescaling can be regarded as equivalent to turning the "gain" up or down, thus relatively increasing or decreasing the sensitivity of the total system to changes along the various dimensions.*

The input data for INDSCAL (as for other methods of what are now being called "three-way" scaling) comprise a three-way matrix of proximities (or anti-proximities) data, the general entry of which is $\delta_{jk}^{(i)}$, the dissimilarity (anti-proximity) of stimuli j and k for subject i. If there are n stimuli and N subjects, this three-way array, or matrix, will be $n \times n \times N$. The ith two-way "slice" through the third way of the matrix will result in an ordinary two-way $n \times n$ matrix of dissimilarities for the ith subject. The output in the case of INDSCAL (although not necessarily for other three-way scaling methods) consists of two matrices. The first is an $n \times m$ matrix, $X \equiv ||x_{jt}||$ of stimulus coordinates, the second an $N \times m$ matrix $W \equiv ||w_{it}||$ of subject weights. The input and output arrays for INDSCAL are illustrated in Fig. 8.

The coordinates described in the two matrices X and W can be plotted to produce two spaces, that we have called the group stimulus space (defined by X) and the subject space (defined by W). These two spaces, for a purely hypothetical data set, are illustrated in Fig. 9. Also shown in that figure are the idiosyncratic or "private" perceptual spaces for two of these subjects. Geometrically they are derived by stretching or shrinking each dimension by applying a rescaling factor, proportional to $w_{it}^{1/2}$, to the tth dimension. The tth weight, w_{it}, for subject i can be read off from the subject space by simply projecting subject i's point onto the tth coordinate axis.

It is easy to see that this would predict quite different patterns of similarity or dissimilarity judgments for subjects 2, 3, and 4. Subject 3 (who weights the dimensions equally, and so would have a private space that looks just like the group stimulus space) presumably judges A to be equally similar to B and D, since these two distances are equal in his private space. In contrast, subject 2 would judge A to be more similar to D than to B, (since A is closer to D), and subject 4 would judge A to be more similar to B than to D. There would, of course, be many other differences in the

---

* Tucker and Messick's (1963) "points of view" model which assumes that there are several clusters of subjects, each of which has its own private space, or point of view, (but with no necessary relation between spaces for different clusters) can be incorporated within the scope of INDSCAL. At the extreme the group stimulus space would include all dimensions represented in any one of the points of view, and an individual would have unit weights for all dimensions from the point of view he is identified with and zero weights on all dimensions from each of the others.

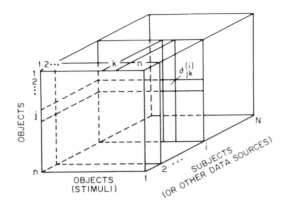

INPUT FOR INDSCAL
(OR OTHER THREE—WAY SCALING METHODS)

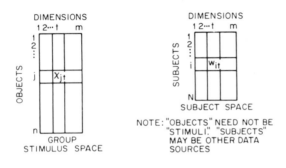

NOTE: "OBJECTS" NEED NOT BE
"STIMULI." "SUBJECTS"
MAY BE OTHER DATA
SOURCES

OUTPUT FROM INDSCAL

FIG. 8. A schematic representation of input for and output from INDSCAL. Input consists of N (≥ 2) $n \times n$ square symmetric data matrices (or half matrices) one for each of N subjects (or other data sources). $d_{jk}^{(i)}$ is the dissimilarity of stimuli (or other objects) j and k for subject (or other data source) i. This set of N square matrices can be thought of as defining the rectangular solid, or three-way array, of data depicted at top in the figure. (This is the form of the input for other three-way scaling methods also.) The output from INDSCAL consists of two matrices, an $n \times m$ matrix of coordinates of the n stimuli (objects) on m coordinate axes (or dimensions) and an $N \times m$ matrix of weights of N subjects for the m dimensions. These matrices define coordinates of the group stimulus space and the *subject space* respectively. Both of them can be plotted graphically, as in Fig. 9, and a private space for each subject can be constructed, as shown there, by applying the square roots of the subject weights to the stimulus dimensions, as in Eq. (33).

431

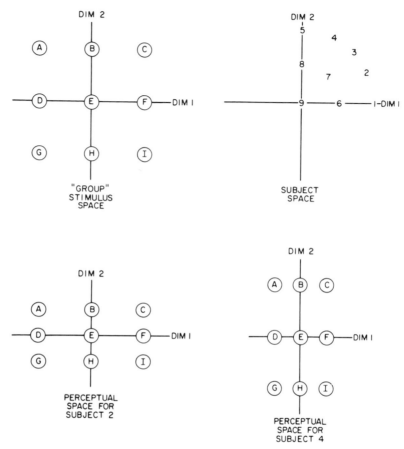

FIG. 9. Illustration of Carroll–Chang model for individual differences in multi-dimensional scaling. Weights (plotted in subject space) are applied to "group" stimulus space to produce individual perceptual spaces for subjects 2 and 4, shown in bottom of figure. (For purposes of illustration the dimensions are multiplied by the weights themselves, rather than by their square roots as is more technically correct.)

judgments of these three subjects, although all three are basing these judgments on exactly the same dimensions.

Two extreme cases are represented by subjects 1 and 5. These subjects are both "one dimensional," in the sense that each gives nonzero weight to only one of the two dimensions. Geometrically it is as though (if these were the only dimensions and the model were perfectly correct) subject 1 has simply projected the stimulus points down onto the dimension 1 axis, so that stimuli A, D, and G, for example, project into the same point, and so would be seen by this subject as being *identical*. Subject 5 exhibits the opposite pattern; he presumably attends only to dimension 2, and so would see stimuli A, B, and C as identical, for example.

Distance from the origin is also meaningful in this subject space. Subjects who are on the same line issuing from the origin, but at different distances from the origin, would have the same pattern of distances and therefore of *predicted* similarities or dissimilarities. They would have the same private space, in fact, except for an overall scale factor (which is not important for most purposes). The main difference between such subjects is that this same private space and pattern of predicted judgments account for less of the *variance* in the data for subjects who are closer to the origin. Thus, although subjects 3 and 7 in the illustrative example shown in Fig. 8 would have the same private space (the one corresponding to the group stimulus space) these two dimensions would account for more variance in the (hypothetical) matrix of subject 7 than of subject 3. Since subject 9 is precisely at the origin (indicating zero weight on both dimensions) he would be completely out of this space, that is, none of his data could be accounted for by these two dimensions. The unaccounted-for variance may be due to other dimensions not extracted in the present analysis, or simply to unreliability, or error variance, in the particular subject's responses. In this respect the square of the distance from the origin is closely analogous to the concept of communality in factor analysis. In fact, it is the square of the distance which is approximately proportional to variance accounted for. While this is only an approximation, it is generally a good one, and in fact is perfect if the coordinate values on dimensions are uncorrelated. The cosine of the angle between subject points (treated as vectors issuing from the origin) is approximately equal to the correlation between distances (more properly, scalar products) in their private perceptual spaces. Distances between these points are also meaningful—they relate approximately to "profile distances" between reconstructed distances (or, again more properly, scalar products) from the respective private perceptual spaces (where overall scale is included).

One of the most important aspects of INDSCAL is the fact that the dimensions are unique. In the psychological model the dimensions are supposed to correspond to fundamental perceptual or other processes whose strengths, sensitivities or importances, vary from individual to individual. Mathematically, the family of transformations induced by allowing differential weighting (which correspond geometrically to stretching or compressing the space in directions parallel to coordinate axes) will be different for different orientations of coordinate axes—that is, the family of admissible transformations is *not* rotationally invariant. This can be seen graphically by considering what kinds of private spaces would be generated in the illustrative case in Fig. 8 if the coordinate system of the group stimulus space were rotated, say, 45°. Instead of transforming the square lattice into various rectangular lattices, it would be transformed instead into various rhombus-shaped lattices. Rotating the coordinate system by something other than 45° would generate other families of rhombuses, generally a unique family for each different angle of rotation. These families are genuinely different, since they allow different admissible sets of *distances* among the objects or stimuli. Statistically speaking, a rotation of axes will generally degrade the solution in the sense that less variance will be accounted for in the data after such a rotation (even if optimal weights are recomputed for the rotated coordinate system). This dimensional uniqueness property is important because it obviates the need, in most cases, to rotate the coordinate system in order to find an "interpretable" solution. If one accepts the psychological model underlying INDSCAL, then these statistically unique dimensions should be psychologically unique as well. Indeed, practical experience has shown that the dimensions obtained directly from INDSCAL are usually interpretable without rotation (even in cases where there is little reason to believe the underlying model assumptions). Formal proofs of this uniqueness property of INDSCAL have been provided by Kruskal (personal communication) and by Harshman (1972a).

The INDSCAL model can be clarified by an application to some data on perceptions (or conceptions) of similarities among nations (Wish, Deutsch, & Biener, 1970). (See also the INDSCAL applications in Chapter 13 of this volume.) The subjects in the pilot study from which these data arose made pairwise ratings of similarities between 12 nations on a 9-point scale. After making these and other kinds of judgments, the subjects indicated their position on the Vietnam war. They were classified as "doves," "moderates," or "hawks" on the basis of their Vietnam opinions.

Figure 10 shows the group stimulus space obtained from a two-dimensional INDSCAL analysis of the proximities data (18 matrices of similarities between nations). The dimensions were interpreted *without rotation* as "political alignment" (or pro-Communist versus pro-Western) and "economic development." (A three-dimensional analysis of these data yielded an additional dimension that was roughly interpreted as "geography and culture"). Figure 10 shows the weights for subjects on the two dimensions of the subject space. The D, M, or H in a circle indicates whether the particular subject was classified as a dove, moderate, or hawk, respectively. One can observe that the political alignment dimension is more important for hawks than doves, whereas the reverse is true for the economic development dimension. In other words, the weights, or saliences, of these two dimensions depend on one's political orientation. (This result was replicated in a larger study—see Wish, 1970a and Wish, Deutsch, & Biener, 1970). Figures 10c and 10d show the private perceptual spaces for subjects 17 and 4, respectively. The horizontal stretching in subject 17's space reflects the higher weight on the horizontal than on the vertical dimension for that subject. Likewise, since subject 4 has a higher weight on dimension 2 than on dimension 1 his private space is vertically stretched.

Because of certain normalizing conventions (see Carroll & Chang, 1970, for details of the method) the distance of a subject's point from the origin of the subject space is approximately equal to the correlation between the original and reconstructed data [distances computed by Eq. (32)] for that subject. (As stated previously, the squared distance from the origin can be viewed as approximately equal to the variance of that subject's data accounted for by the INDSCAL solution.)

Ironically, distances in the group stimulus space are not immediately interpretable, except as they relate to the interstimulus distances of a hypothetical (or real) subject who weights all dimensions equally. This is because of the particular normalizing convention chosen for defining the group stimulus space and the subject space. Other conventions could have been chosen; in particular, the group stimulus space could be normalized so as to reflect the dimension weights for the "average" subject. The interpoint distances in the group stimulus space (under this different normalizing convention) could be interpreted as interstimulus distance for this "average" subject. In this case, of course, the subject space would also have to be normalized differently, and the distances and other aspects of this space would no longer have the direct interpretation mentioned above.

One point that ought to be made clear is that we are not particularly wedded to the Euclidean aspect of this model. As is so often the case, the (weighted) Euclidean metric was chosen for reasons of mathematical tractability, conceptual simplicity, and historical precedence. In the majority of stimulus domains (at least with nonanalyzable or unitary stimuli, or even apparently with analyzable stimuli when dimensionality gets large) the Euclidean seems to fit as well as any other metric. Furthermore, there is a great deal of evidence that methods based on it are quite robust, so that even if the basic metric is non-Euclidean, multidimensional scaling in a Euclidean space will usually recover the configuration quite adequately. We regard this particular choice of basic metric, then, as primarily heuristic and pragmatic, although it does seem on many grounds to be the best single one we could have chosen. It is, however, within the spirit of the INDSCAL model to assume a much wider class of weighted metrics. For example, an obvious generalization entailing Minkowski or power metric would be of the form:

$$d_{jk}^{(i)} = \left[\sum_{t=1}^{m} w_{it} |x_{jt} - x_{kt}|^r \right]^{1/r}, \tag{35}$$

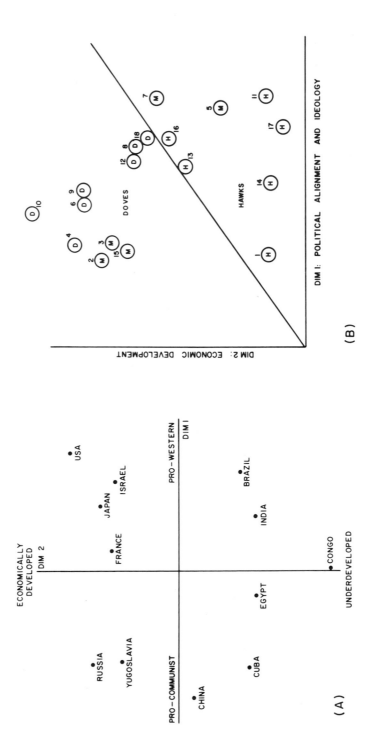

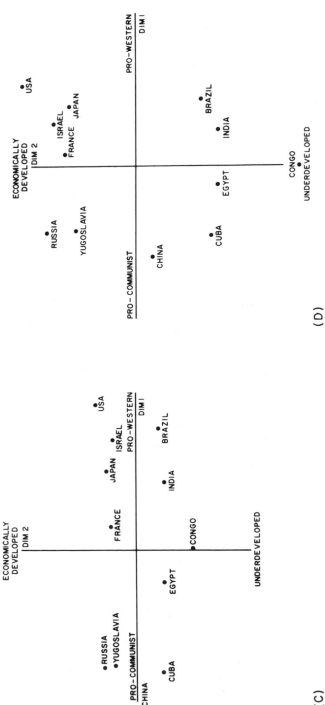

(C)

(D)

Fig. 10. Results from a two-dimensional INDSCAL analysis of data on judged similarities between 12 nations. The group stimulus space and subject space are shown in (A) and (B), respectively; private perceptual spaces for subjects 17 and 4 are shown in (C) and (D).

or, in terms of rescaling of dimensions, the private space would be defined
as:

$$y_{jt}^{(i)} = w_{it}^{1/r} x_{jt} \tag{36}$$

[and it will easily be seen that computing ordinary Minkowski r-metric
in this rescaled space, now involving the rth root of the weights, is equivalent to the weighted Minkowski r-metric in Eq. (35)].

In the more general cases of metrics with interdimensional additivity
or intradimensional subtractivity, the weighted generalization would be,
respectively:

(for interdimensional additivity)

$$d_{jk}^{(i)} = F\left\{ \sum_t w_{it}\varphi_t(x_{jt}, x_{kt}) \right\} \tag{37}$$

(for intradimensional subtractivity)

$$d_{jk}^{(i)} = G\{|y_{jt}^{(i)} - y_{kt}^{(i)}|, |y_{j2}^{(i)} - y_{k2}^{(i)}|, \ldots, |y_{jm}^{(i)} - {}_{km}^{(i)}y|\}, \tag{38}$$

where $y_{jt}^{(i)} = v_{it}x_{jt}$ [v_{it} is used advisedly, to distinguish it from w_{it}. As in
Eq. (26) the f_t's are omitted. The values F and G are both assumed to be
monotone increasing].

In case of both interdimensional additivity *and* intradimensional subtractivity, the correct weighted generalization would appear to be:

$$d_{jk}^{(i)} = F\left\{ \sum_t w_{it}\varphi_t(v_{it}x_{jt} - v_{it}x_{kt}) \right\}. \tag{39}$$

Following Tversky and Krantz, if we want this to be a proper metric
(i.e., to satisfy the metric axioms and segmental additivity along lines
parallel to the coordinate axes) $\varphi_1 = \cdots = \varphi_m = \varphi$ and $F = \varphi^{-1}$, with
φ convex.

Notice here that the w_{it}'s and v_{it}'s have independent effects, and cannot be combined into a single effect, as was the case with the weighted
power metrics. Of the two formulations, we would favor the rescaling one
as more basic and immediately psychologically meaningful, since it relates
directly to the kind of change in sensitivity to a dimension that is the
psychological basis of this model. Also, it generalizes easily to cases involving nonadditive metrics, whereas the weighted sum formulation clearly does
not.

The weighted power metric is the only case of an interdimensionally
additive metric in which the weighted-sum formulation and the rescaling
formulation are equivalent. This could conceivably be garnered as another
argument in favor of the weighted-power, or Minkowski r-metric, in the
case of perceptual phenomena. Clearly, again based on the results of

Tversky and Krantz (1970), if we assume this to be a metric with additive segments (for each individual), the distances must take the form of the weighted Minkowski r-metric of Eq. (39).

We may make the following somewhat more general assertion, relating the results of Beals, Krantz, and Tversky (1968) and of Tversky and Krantz (1970) to models for individual differences in perception. Assume the dimensions are the same for all individuals, but that the metric is (possibly) different for each individual. If interdimensional additivity, intradimensional subtractivity, and segmental additivity are assumed for each individual, the class of metrics must be of the form

$$d_{jk}^{(i)} = \left[\sum_{t=1}^{m} |y_{jt}^{(i)} - y_{kt}^{(i)}|^{r_i} \right]^{1/r_i}, \tag{40}$$

with

$$y_{jt}^{(i)} = f_{it}(x_{jt}). \tag{41}$$

If the functions f_{it} are assumed to be functions of t only (i.e., assumed to be the same across individuals, although not necessarily for different dimensions), they can be absorbed into the definition of the x's, in which case, the class of metrics are restricted to those of the form:

$$d_{jk}^{(i)} = [\Sigma w_{it}|x_{jt} - x_{kt}|^{r_i}]^{1/r_i} \tag{42}$$

a slight generalization of the weighted power metric, in which the power (as well as the pattern of weights) is allowed to be different for different individuals. The w_{it}'s were omitted from the more general formulation in Eqs. (40) and (41) because they could be absorbed into the function f_{it}.

There is some empirical evidence supporting the need for a generalization of INDSCAL such as that entailed in Eqs. (40) and (41) but with the f_{it}'s restricted to be monotonic (so that the x_{jt}'s are defined at least ordinally, rather than just nominally, as assumed by Tversky and Krantz). Typical of this evidence is the phenomenon noted by Wish when he attempted a four dimensional analysis of the nation data discussed here earlier. The political ideology dimension split into two separate dimensions which were highly correlated, but in a nonlinear fashion. They, in fact, appeared to amount to monotone rescalings of the same dimension. On one dimension the neutral nations were close to the Communist nations, with a large gap between the neutral and non-Communist nations. On the other dimension the neutral nations were close to the non-Communist nations with a large gap separating them from the Communist nations.

Data of this sort make it appear likely that a model like the one in Eqs. (40) and (41), but with the f's monotone, would fit a wide variety of situations. Development of a method to analyze data in terms of such a model has not yet been accomplished, however. Some other models for which analytic methods *are* available are discussed in what follows.

B. The IDIOSCAL Model and Some of Its Special Cases

The most general in what might be called the "Euclidean class" of models for multidimensional scaling is what has been called (Carroll & Chang, 1970, 1972; Carroll & Wish, 1973) the IDIOSCAL model, standing for *Individual Differences In Orientation SCALing*. (The name could also suggest *IDIOgraphic* or *IDIOsyncratic SCALing*. We shall not, however, speculate further as to other possible meanings of this acronym).

IDIOSCAL assumes distances are given by the *generalized* Euclidean metric, defined as:

$$d_{jk}^{(i)} = \left[\sum_s \sum_t (x_{js} - x_{ks}) c_{st}^{(i)} (x_{jt} - x_{kt}) \right]^{1/2} \qquad (43)$$

In vector and matrix form this can be written as:

$$d_{jk}^{(i)} = [(\mathbf{x}_j - \mathbf{x}_k) C_i (\mathbf{x}_j - \mathbf{x}_k)']^{1/2}, \qquad (44)$$

where $C_i \equiv \| c_{st}^{(i)} \|$ is an $m \times m$ matrix. The matrix C_i is generally assumed to be *symmetric and positive definite or semidefinite*. This is exactly the metric that would obtain if we defined a private perceptual space for individual i by a general linear transformation defined as:

$$y_{jt}^{(i)} = \sum_{s=1}^{m} x_{js} q_{st}^{(i)} \qquad (45)$$

which, in vector-matrix notation is

$$\mathbf{y}_j^{(i)} = \mathbf{x}_j Q_i \qquad (46)$$

and then computed ordinary Euclidean distances in these private spaces. It is easy to see that the matrix C_i in Eq. (43) is defined simply as

$$C_i = Q_i Q_i' \qquad (47)$$

for

$$\begin{aligned} [d_{jk}^{(i)}]^2 &= (\mathbf{y}_j^{(i)} - \mathbf{y}_k^{(i)})(\mathbf{y}_j^{(i)} - \mathbf{y}_k^{(i)})' \\ &= (\mathbf{x}_j - \mathbf{x}_k) Q_i Q_i' (\mathbf{x}_j - \mathbf{x}_k)'. \end{aligned} \qquad (48)$$

Another interpretation, closely related to this, is provided by decomposing the (symmetric, positive definite) matrix C_i into a product of the form:

$$C_i = T_i \beta_i T_i', \tag{49}$$

with T_i orthogonal and β_i diagonal. (This decomposition, which is closely related to principal components analysis, can always be done. If the C_i's are positive definite or semidefinite, the diagonal entries of β_i will be nonnegative.)

Then we can define

$$S_i = T_i \beta_i^{1/2}, \tag{50}$$

and clearly

$$C_i = S_i S_i' \tag{51}$$

Actually, S_i is just one way of defining the matrix Q_i in Eq. (46). Given any *orthogonal* matrix U, we may define

$$Q_i = S_i U, \tag{52}$$

and it will turn out that

$$Q_i Q_i' = S_i U U' S_i' = S_i S_i' = C_i. \tag{53}$$

Any Q_i satisfying (47) can be shown to be of the form in Eq. (52). The decomposition of C_i defined in Eqs. (50) and (51) (where U is the identity matrix) leads to a particularly convenient geometric interpretation, however. T_i can be interpreted as defining an orthogonal rotation of the reference frame, and thus the Individual Differences In Orientation (of the reference system) referred to earlier. The diagonal entries of β_i can be interpreted as weights analogous to the w_{it}'s in the INDSCAL model that are applied to this IDIOsyncratic reference frame.

C. The Tucker–Harshman Interpretation of C_i

Another possible way to decompose C_i is into a product

$$C_i = D_i R_i D_i, \tag{54}$$

where D_i is diagonal and R_i is symmetric (presumably positive definite, if C_i is) and with ones on the diagonal. If we think of C_i as analogous to a covariance matrix, R_i is analogous to the corresponding correlation matrix, and the diagonal entries of D_i to standard deviations. This conversion is very simple to implement—the diagonal entries of D_i are just the square roots of the diagonal entries of C_i, whereas R_i is defined by dividing rows and columns of C_i by that same term. We call this the Tucker–Harshman decomposition, because both Tucker (1972) and Harshman (1972b) have proposed models (to be discussed) in which this interpretation is utilized. They, in fact, do interpret R_i as a kind of matrix of subjective intercorrelations between dimensions.

D. Tucker's Three-Mode Scaling

Tucker's three-mode scaling (1972) uses his three-mode factor analysis (Tucker, 1963) (applied to a three-way matrix of derived scalar products) to implement an individual differences multidimensional scaling analysis. We need not, however, concern ourselves with details of the analysis here, but rather with the underlying model. Viewed as a special case of the IDIOSCAL model, it can be regarded as placing certain constraints on these C_i matrices; namely, that they be linear combinations of some smaller set of matrices. That is, it is assumed that

$$C_i = \sum_{s=1}^{S} a_{is} G_s \tag{55}$$

(where S presumably is less than the number of subjects). Each G_s is a symmetric matrix. Tucker does not specify this, but in some sense it seems desirable to assume that each G_s be positive definite or semidefinite, and that the a's be nonnegative (this guarantees positive definiteness or semi-definiteness of the C_i's). In this interpretation, each G_s could be viewed as defining a matrix for one of several idealized individuals, whereas each real individual can be viewed as having a matrix that is a linear composite of these idealized matrices.

E. Harshman's PARAFAC-2 Model

Richard Harshman's PARAFAC-2 (*PARA*llel *FAC*tors—*V*ersion 2) model can be viewed as another special case of IDIOSCAL in which the constraint placed on the C_i matrices (looked at in terms of the decomposition $C_i = D_i A_i D_i$) is essentially that

$$R_i = R \tag{56}$$

that is that R_i, the matrix of subjective intercorrelations among dimensions, is the same for all individuals, although the rescaling matrices D_i are allowed to differ.

In the Tucker three-mode formulation this decomposition of C_i into the product $D_i R_i D_i$ is not used in any essential way, although Tucker himself uses it very extensively in interpreting results of this analysis. The Tucker three-mode approach does not have the unique orientation of dimensions property that seems so important in INDSCAL (nor does the more general IDIOSCAL model have this property). Harshman's PARAFAC-2 model generalizes INDSCAL in that the dimensions are assumed to have different subjective intercorrelations. If the (common) R matrix assumed in

PARAFAC-2 is further restricted to be an *identity,* the model becomes equivalent to INDSCAL. Harshman has conjectured that PARAFAC-2 has the same dimensional uniqueness property as INDSCAL. No proof has been provided of this, however, and there is some reason to question this, at least as a general property. (It can, in fact, be proved that uniqueness does not hold unless there are more than two individuals or other data *sources,* in contrast to INDSCAL, where two sources are, in general, sufficient for a *unique* orientation of coordinate axes). Our current feeling is that uniqueness may obtain for PARAFAC-2 in some specific data situations, but not in all. Further interesting three-way generalizations of multidimensional scaling are no doubt waiting in the wings. Even "higher-way" generalizations have been proposed (Carroll & Chang, 1970, Carroll, 1972, Carroll & Wish, 1973). Other developments appear on the horizon, involving such things as hybrid models incorporating both discrete and continuous structure, methods of scaling based on very minimal assumptions, and entirely new kinds of postulated similarity structures. There is no doubt that the models and methods discussed in this paper have, quite literally, only begun to scratch the surface. We anticipate great forward strides within the next several years, both theoretically and methodologically.

References

Arnold, J. B. A multidimensional scaling study of semantic distance. *Journal of Experimental Psychology,* 1971, **90,** 349–372.

Attneave, F. Dimensions of similarity. *American Journal of Psychology,* 1950, **63,** 516–556.

Bartholomew, D. J. A test of homogeneity for ordered alternatives. *Biometrika,* 1959, **46,** 36–48.

Barton, D. E., & Mallows, C. L. The randomization bases of the amalgamation of weighted means. *Journal of the Royal Statistical Society,* Series B, 1961, **23,** 423–433.

Beals, R., Krantz, D. H., & Tversky, A. Foundations of multidimensional scaling. *Psychological Review,* 1968, **75,** 127–142.

Blumenthal, L. M. *Theory and applications of distance geometry.* Oxford: Clarendon Press, 1953.

Boynton, R. M., & Gordon, J. Bezold-Brüke hue shift measured by color-naming technique. *Journal of the Optical Society of America,* 1965, **55,** 78–86.

Busemann, H. *Geometry of geodesics.* New York: Academic Press, 1955.

Carroll, J. D. Parametric mapping of similarity data. In R. N. Shepard (Chm.), Comparison and tests of some alternative models for the geometric representation of psychological data. Symposium presented at the Mathematical Psychology meetings, Stanford, California, August 1968.

Carroll, J. D. Categorical conjoint measurement. Paper presented at the Mathematical Psychology meetings, Ann Arbor, August 1969.

Carroll, J. D. Individual differences and multidimensional scaling. In R. N. Shepard, A. K. Romney, & S. Nerlove (Eds.), *Multidimensional scaling: Theory and applications in the behavioral sciences*. Vol. 1. *Theory*. New York: Seminar Press, 1972. Pp. 105–155.

Carroll, J. D., & Chang, J. J. Multidimensional scaling with an unknown metric. Paper presented at special meeting of the Psychometric Society, Washington, D.C., September 1967.

Carroll, J. D., & Chang, J. J. Analysis of individual differences in multidimensional scaling via an N-way generalization of Eckart-Young decomposition. *Psychometrika*, 1970, **35**, 283–319.

Carroll, J. D., & Chang, J. J. SIMULES: *SIMU*ltaneous *L*inear *E*quation *S*caling. *Proceedings, 80th Annual Convention, American Psychological Association*, 1972, **7**, 11–12.

Carroll, J. D., & Wish, M. Models and methods for three-way multidimensional scaling. In R. C. Atkinson, D. H. Krantz, R. D. Luce, & P. Suppes (Eds.), *Contemporary developments in mathematical psychology*. San Francisco: Freeman, 1973.

Coombs, C. H. An application of a nonmetric model for multidimensional analysis of similarities. *Psychological Reports*, 1958, **4**, 511–518.

Coombs, C. H. *Theory of data*. New York: Wiley, 1964.

Coombs, C. H., Dawes, R., & Tversky, A. *Introduction to mathematical psychology*. New York: Wiley, 1971.

Cliff, N., Pennell, R. & Young, F. W. Multidimensional scaling in the study of set. *American Psychologist*, 1966, **21**, 707.

Green, P. E., & Carmone, F. J. *Multidimensional scaling and related techniques in marketing analysis*. Boston: Allyn & Bacon, 1970.

Gregson, R. A. M. Similarity judgments modified by feedback. *Acta Psychologica*, 1974, in press.

Guttman, L. The quantification of a class of attributes. In P. Horst (Ed.), with collaboration of P. Wallin and L. Guttman, *The prediction of personal adjustment*. New York: Social Science Research Council, 1941. Pp. 319–348.

Guttman, L. General nonmetric technique for finding smallest coordinate space for a configuration of points. *Psychometrika*, 1968, **33**, 469–506.

Harshman, R. A. Determination and proof of minimum uniqueness conditions for PARAFAC 1. U.C.L.A. Working Papers in Phonetics 22, March 1972, pp. 111–117. (a)

Harshman, R. A. PARAFAC2: Extensions of a procedure for "explanatory" factor analysis and multidimensional scaling. U.C.L.A. Working papers in phonetics #22, March 1972. (b)

Helm, C. E. Multidimensional ratio scaling analysis of perceived color relations. *Journal of the Optical Society of America*, 1964, **54**, 256–262.

Hyman, R., & Well, A. Judgments of similarity and spatial models. *Perception & Psychophysics*, 1967, **2**, 233–248.

Hyman, R., & Well, A. Perceptual separability and spatial models. *Perception & Psychophysics*, 1968, **3**, 161–165.

Indow, T. Applications of multidimensional scaling in perception. (this volume)

Indow, T. Two interpretations of binocular visual space: Hyperbolic and Euclidean. *Annals of the Japan Association for Philosophy of Science*, 1967, **3**, 51–64.

Indow, T. Multidimensional mapping of visual space with real and simulated stars. *Perception & Psychophysics*, 1968, **3**, 45–53.

Indow, T., & Kanazawa, K. Multidimensional mapping of Munsell colors varying in hue, chroma and value. *Journal of Experimental Psychology*, 1960, **59**, 330–336.

Indow, T., & Uchizono, T. Multidimensional mapping of Munsell colors varying in hue and chroma. *Journal of Experimental Psychology,* 1960, **59,** 321–329.

James, W. *The principles of psychology.* New York: Henry Holt & Co., 1890. 2 vols.

Johnson, S. C. Hierarchical clustering schemes. *Psychometrika,* 1967, **32,** 241–254.

Klingberg, F. L. Studies in measurement of the relations among sovereign states, *Psychometrika,* 1941, **6,** 335–352.

Kruskal, J. B. Multidimensional scaling by optimizing goodness of fit to a nonmetric hypothesis. *Psychometrika,* 1964, **29,** 1–27. (a)

Kruskal, J. B. Nonmetric multidimensional scaling: A numerical method. *Psychometrika,* 1964, **29,** 115–129. (b)

Krushal, J. B. Special problems and possibilities. Unpublished manuscript. Murray Hill, New Jersey: Bell Laboratories, 1972.

Kruskal, J. B., & Carmone, F. How to use M-D-SCAL (version 5M) and other useful information. Unpublished manuscript, Bell Laboratories, Murray Hill, New Jersey, 1970.

Kruskal, J. B., & Carroll, J. D. Geometric models and badness-of-fit functions. In P. R. Krishnaiah (Ed.), *Multivariate analysis II.* New York: Academic Press, 1969. Pp. 639–670.

Lingoes, J. C. An IBM 7090 program for Guttman-Lingoes smallest space analysis— RI. *Behavioral Science,* 1966, **11,** 322.

Lingoes, J. C. Recent computational advances in nonmetric methodology for the behavioral sciences. *Proceedings of the International Symposium: Mathematical and Computational Methods in Social Sciences.* Rome: International Computation Centre, 1966. Pp. 1–38.

Lingoes, J. C. The multivariate analysis of qualitative data. *Multivariate Behavioral Research,* 1968, **3,** 61–94.

Luneburg, R. K. *Mathematical analysis of binocular vision.* Princeton: Princeton University Press, 1947.

McGee, V. E. Elastic multidimensional scaling procedure. *Perceptual and Motor Skills,* 1965, **21,** 81–82.

Messick, S. J., & Abelson, R. P. The additive constant problem in multidimensional scaling. *Psychometrika,* 1956, **21,** 1–15.

Micko, H. C., & Fischer, W. Metric of multidimensional psychological spaces as a function of the differential attention to subjective attributes. *Journal of Mathematical Psychology,* 1970, **7,** 118–143.

Miles, R. E. The complete amalgamation into blocks, by weighted means, of a finite set of real numbers. *Biometrika,* 1959, **46,** 317–327.

Miller, G. A., & Nicely, P. E. An analysis of perceptual confusions among some English consonants. *Journal of the Acoustical Society of America,* 1955, **27,** 338–352.

Nakatani, L. H. Confusion-choice model for multidimensional psychophysics. *Journal of Mathematical Psychology,* 1972, **9,** 104–127.

Osgood, C. E., Suci, G. J., & Tannenbaum, P. H. The measurement of meaning. Urbana: University of Illinois Press, 1957.

Richardson, M. W. Multidimensional psychophysics. *Psychological Bulletin,* 1938, **35,** 659–660.

Roskam, E. E. *Metric analysis of ordinal data in psychology.* Voorschoten, Holland: University of Leiden Press, 1968.

Rumelhart, D. E., & Abrahamson, A. A. Toward a theory of analogical reasoning. (Tech. Rep. No. 18) San Diego: Center for Human Information Processing, University of California, 1971.

Shepard, R. N. Stimulus and response generalization: A stochastic model relating generalization to distance in psychological space. *Psychometrika*, 1957, **22**, 325–345.

Shepard, R. N. Stimulus and response generalization: Tests of a model relating generalization to distance in psychological space. *Journal of Experimental Psychology*, 1958, **55**, 509–523.

Shepard, R. N. Analysis of proximities: Multidimensional scaling with an unknown distance function. I. *Psychometrika*, 1962, **27**, 125–140. (a)

Shepard, R. N. Analysis of proximities: Multidimensional scaling with an unknown distance function. II. *Psychometrika*, 1962, **27**, 219–246. (b)

Shepard, R. N. Attention and the metric structure of the stimulus space. *Journal of Mathematical Psychology*, 1964, **1**, 54–87.

Shepard, R. N. Continuity versus the triangle inequality as a central principle for the spatial analysis of similarity data. In R. N. Shepard (Chm.), Comparison and tests of some alternative models for the geometric representation of psychological data. Symposium presented at the Mathematical Psychology meetings, Stanford, California, August 1968.

Shepard, R. N. A taxonomy of principal types of data and of multidimensional methods for their analysis. In R. N. Shepard, A. K. Romney, and S. Nerlove (Eds.), *Multidimensional scaling: Thory and applications in the behavioral sciences*. Vol I. New York: Seminar Press, 1972. (a)

Shepard, R. N. Psychological representation of speech sounds. In E. E. David & P. B. Denes (Eds.), *Human communication: A unified view*. New York: McGraw-Hill, 1972. (b)

Shepard, R. N., & Carroll, J. D. Parametric representation of nonlinear data structures. In P. R. Krishnaiah (Ed.), *Multivariate analysis II*. New York: Academic Press, 1966. Pp. 561–592.

Stevens, S. S. Mathematics, measurement and psychophysics. In S. S. Stevens (Ed.), *Handbook of experimental psychology*. New York: Wiley, 1951.

Torgerson, W. S. Multidimensional scaling: Part 1: Theory and method. *Psychometrika*, 1952, **17**, 401–419.

Torgerson, W. S. *Theory and methods of scaling*. New York: Wiley, 1958.

Torgerson, W. S. Multidimensional scaling of similarity. *Psychometrika*, 1965, **30**, 379–393.

Tucker, L. R. Intra-individual and inter-individual multidimensionality. In H. Gulliksen & S. Messick (Eds.), *Psychological scaling: Theory and applications*. New York: Wiley, 1960.

Tucker, L. R. Relations between multidimensional scaling and three-mode factor analysis. *Psychometrika*, 1972, **37**, 3–27.

Tucker, L. R., & Messick, S. J. Individual difference model for multidimensional scaling. *Psychometrika*, 1963, **28**, 333–367.

Tversky, A., & Krantz, D. H. Dimensional representation and the metric structure of similarity data. *Journal of Mathematical Psychology*, 1970, **7**, 572–596.

van Eeden, C. Maximum likelihood estimation of partially or completely ordered parameters. I. *Proceedings, Akademie van Wetenschappen*, Series A, 1957, **60**, 128–136. (a)

van Eeden, C. Note on two methods for estimating ordered parameters of probability distributions. *Proceedings, Akademie van Wetenschappen*, Series A, 1957, **60**, 506–512. (b)

Wish, M. A structural theory for the perception of Morse code signals and related rhythmic patterns. Center for Research on Language and Language Behavior, University of Michigan, 1967. (a)

Wish, M. A model for the perception of Morse code-like signals. *Human Factors,* 1967, **9,** 529–540. (b)

Wish, M. Comparisons among multidimensional structures of nations based on different measures of subjective similarity. In L. von Bertalanffy & A. Rapoport (Eds.), *General systems.* Vol. **15,** Society for General Systems Research, Ann Arbor, 1970. Pp. 55–65. (a)

Wish, M. An INDSCAL analysis of the Miller–Nicely consonant confusion data. Paper presented at meetings of the Acoustical Society of America, Houston, November 1970. (b)

Wish, M. Notes on the variety appropriateness and choice of proximity measures. Unpublished manuscript. Murray Hill, New Jersey: Bell Laboratories, 1972.

Wish, M., & Carroll, J. D. Applications of individual differences scaling to studies of human perception and judgment. In E. C. Carterette and M. P. Friedman (Eds.), *Handbook of Perception,* Vol II. New York: Academic Press, 1974. Pp. 449–491.

Wish, M., Deutsch, M., & Biener, L. Differences in conceptual structures of nations: An exploratory study. *Journal of Personality & Social Psychology,* 1970, **16,** 361–373.

Wish, M., Deutsch, M., & Biener, L. Differences in perceived similarity of nations. In A. K. Romney, R. N. Shepard, & S. Nerlove (Eds.), *Multidimensional scaling: Theory and applications in the behavioral sciences.* Vol. 2. *Applications.* New York: Seminar Press, 1972. Pp. 289–313.

Young, F. W., & Torgerson, W. S. TORSCA: A Fortran-4 program for Shepard–Kruskal multidimensional scaling analysis. *Behavioral Science,* 1967, **12,** 498.

Young, G., & Householder, A. S. Discussion of a set of points in terms of their mutual distances. *Psychometrika,* 1938, **3,** 19–22.

Chapter 13

APPLICATIONS OF INDIVIDUAL DIFFERENCES SCALING TO STUDIES OF HUMAN PERCEPTION AND JUDGMENT

MYRON WISH AND J. DOUGLAS CARROLL

I. INTRODUCTION

Since Shepard's (1962) and Kruskal's (1964a,b) pioneering break throughs in this area computerized procedures for both metric and non-metric multidimensional scaling (such as Kruskal's MDSCAL discussed in Chapter 12 in this volume) have been applied to data from a wide variety of fields. The typical multidimensional scaling input is an $n \times n$ matrix, whose cell values are based on some empirical "proximity measure" (see Coombs, 1964; Shepard, 1962, 1972a; Wish, 1972b)—for example, direct ratings of similarities or dissimilarities among stimuli, confusions in a stimulus identification experiment, word associations, co-occurrences of stimuli in a clustering task, communication or volume flow, and profile distances. The value δ_{jk} in cell (j, k) of the matrix shows, directly or inversely, the proximity between stimulus j and stimulus k. The output from multidimensional scaling is a single configuration of points. one point for each stimulus, in one or more dimensions. Distances between points reflect (as well as statistically possible for the data) the proximities of the associated stimuli; that is, the smaller the psychological distance between two stimuli (as shown in the proximities matrix), the closer the corresponding points in the multidimensional space.

In many applications of multidimensional scaling in the behavioral sciences, proximities data are obtained from several different subjects, or from the same subjects on different occasions or under different experimental conditions. In these instances, the data have been generally analyzed by means of (a) a single scaling (usually of a matrix of averaged proximities), treating the data from different individuals, occasions, conditions, etc., simply as experimental replications, or (b) a separate scaling of each subject's proximities data (arranged in a matrix), in effect treating the data from different subjects as unrelated.

Carroll and Chang (1969, 1970a) have developed a new multidimensional scaling method called INDSCAL, for INdividual Differences SCALing. INDSCAL is based on a model that relates "perceptual (or cognitive) structures" for different subjects or other data sources in a strong way, yet also permits large differences among them [see also Tucker and Messick's, 1963, "points of view" model, Tucker's, 1972, application of three-mode factor analysis (Tucker, 1964) to multidimensional scaling, McGee's; 1968, CEMD/DEMD, and Harshman's PARAFAC (1970) and PARAFAC-2 (1972)].

II. THE INDSCAL MODEL

The input to INDSCAL consists of two or more matrices of proximities, all pertaining to the same stimulus objects. Each matrix typically displays one subject's (or subgroup's) proximities data, but it could be based instead on data from another kind of *data source,* such as one of several experimental conditions, occasions, proximity measures, etc. It is assumed in the INDSCAL model that the proximities in each matrix are linearly* related to a kind of modified Euclidean distance between points, representing

---

* There are nonmetric versions, of INDSCAL (e.g., Carroll & Chang, 1970b), which require only a monotonic relationship between the proximities data and the spatial distances. However, this paper will discuss and use the metric version only.

stimuli, in a *group* (or composite) *stimulus space*. In Eq. (1), the mathematical equivalent of this assumption.

$$\delta_{jk}^{(i)} = L(d_{jk}^{(i)}),\tag{1}$$

where $\delta_{jk}^{(i)}$ is the proximity (or antiproximity) value associated with stimulus pair jk in matrix i, whereas $d_{jk}^{(i)}$ is the modified distance between these stimuli for subject (or source) i computed from the dimensions of the "group" stimulus space.

$$d_{jk}^{(i)} = \left(\sum_{t=1}^{r} w_{it}(x_{jt} - x_{kt})^2\right)^{1/2}.\tag{2}$$

In Eq. (2) x_{jt} and x_{kt} are the coordinates of stimulus j and stimulus k, respectively, on dimension t; while w_{it} indicates the weight, or perceptual (or statistical) importance, of dimension t in matrix i. This equation incorporates the assumption that $d_{jk}^{(i)}$ depends on the dimension weights for the particular source as well as on the coordinates in the r-dimensional "group" stimulus space. The $d_{jk}^{(i)}$'s can also be thought of as ordinary Euclidean distances in a "private" space for source i in which the stimulus coordinates, the $y_{jt}^{(i)}$'s, are given by

$$y_{jt}^{(i)} = (w_{it})^{1/2}x_{jt}.\tag{3}$$

Thus the private space for a particular individual or other data source can be thought of as being derived from the "group" stimulus space by differentially stretching (or shrinking) the dimensions in proportion to the square roots of the respective dimension weights.

The INDSCAL procedure determines, by means of an iterative least squares procedure, the stimulus coordinates (on the dimensions of the "group" stimulus space) and the dimension weights for subjects (which can be plotted in a "subject" space) that account for the maximum possible variance in the proximities data* in all matrices (the goodness of fit measure). The INDSCAL output also shows, for each subject or other data source, the correlation between the values in the particular proximity matrix and distances in the associated private space†. Chapter 12 provides a more detailed description of the INDSCAL model and method.

When the dimensions of the group stimulus space are normalized (so that the sum of squared coordinates on each dimension equals one), a

---

*INDSCAL actually accounts for the maximum variance in matrices of scalar products that are derived from the proximities data by a procedure described in Torgerson (1958).

† The correlational value for a subject is actually between a matrix of scalar products derived from his proximities data and a matrix of scalar products derived from his "private" space.

subject's weight on a dimension is approximately equal to the product–moment correlation between differences in stimulus coordinates on that dimension and proximity values in that subject's matrix. The squared weight indicates the proportion of variance in the matrix which can be accounted for by that dimension.* A dimension weight of zero can be thought of as meaning that the attribute associated with the dimension is irrelevant to the subject when he makes his judgments, i.e., he just does not perceive the stimulus differences specified by the dimension, or in any case, acts (in the particular task) as if he does not.

In solving for the stimulus coordinates and dimension weights the program finds the particular orientation of axes that maximizes the goodness-of-fit measure; that is, INDSCAL uses information latent in the variation among matrices to orient the dimensions *uniquely*. These axes, or dimensions, have a special status in INDSCAL, and might be assumed to correspond to fundamental psychological processes that have different saliences for different individuals or under different experimental conditions. The remarkable fact is that in most cases to date, the dimensions from INDSCAL could be interpreted *without rotation*. (As discussed in Chapter 12 of this volume, it is usually necessary to rotate the axes obtained from the earlier "two-way" multidimensional scaling procedures to interpret, the dimensions. This rotational, or interpretational, problem becomes increasingly formidable as the number of dimensions increases.) The uniqueness of orientation property of INDSCAL does not apply if all of the subjects have the same pattern (proportional profiles) of dimension weights. Otherwise the subjects are not really different! In fact, if the weights are proportional for any pair of dimensions, the orientation of axes within the corresponding plane of the group stimulus space is not unique.

Experimentation is generally needed to determine how many dimensions are appropriate for the data (Wish, 1972c); this involves analyses of the data in spaces of different dimensionality.† Although the overall proportion of variance accounted for always increases as dimensions are added, some of the higher dimensions may provide only a negligible improvement in

---

* The square of a weight underestimates the proportion of variance accounted for if, as is frequently the case, the dimensions of the group stimulus space are correlated.

† Except for a difference in the orientation of axes and weighting of dimensions, the stimulus configuration obtained from a multidimensional scaling of averaged proximities is very similar to the "group" stimulus space from an INDSCAL analysis. One can, therefore, save considerable computer time by using a multidimensional solution for averaged proximities as a starting configuration (instead of a random starting configuration) for an INDSCAL analysis. Another useful starting configuration for INDSCAL can be obtained from a preliminary IDIOSCAL (Carroll & Chang, 1972) analysis of the proximities data.

the goodness of fit measure. If, for example, a three-dimensional solution accounts for 10% more variance than a two-dimensional one, and a four-dimensional solution accounts for only 3% additional variance, one would probably conclude that not more than three dimensions are needed. Nevertheless, it may be worthwhile to keep a dimension that accounts for relatively little variance if it can be interpreted clearly and contributes to the general comprehension of the data. It might also be desirable to retain a dimension that is highly weighted by some subjects, but irrelevant to the rest (in other words, a dimension on which the variance of weights is high), despite the fact that its contribution to the total variance is small. (This is particularly true if the subjects with high weights on that dimension have some other characteristics in common.) Such a dimension would be lost if only the overall variance accounted for by each dimension were known.

III. INTRODUCTION TO APPLICATIONS

We shall now describe some applications of INDSCAL in several areas of human perception. The examples illustrate the wide range of stimuli as well as experimental methods that can be used in studies involving multidimensional scaling, and also demonstrate some special advantages of INDSCAL. In the applications to color perception (an area where a great deal was known about the stimulus structure beforehand), INDSCAL primarily serves to show the correspondence between the physical and psychological dimensions. In contrast the applications to perceptions (or conceptions) of rhythm and accent and of nations demonstrate that INDSCAL can reveal a great deal about psychological dimensions and individual differences not known a priori. Of course, if nothing were known about the stimuli, it would be impossible to interpret the dimensions! In the application to Miller and Nicely's data on consonant confusability (where each matrix is associated with a different kind of speech degradation), it is shown that INDSCAL can provide important information about the perceptual effects of different experimental conditions as well as about the stimuli.

IV. A REANALYSIS OF HELM'S COLOR PERCEPTION DATA

The subjects in Helm's (1964) study judged psychological distances among ten colors of constant saturation and brightness. The experimental task was to arrange triples of color chips into triangles such that the lengths of the three sides were proportional to the psychological distances between the colors of the chips at the vertices. Helm derived a matrix of psychological distances among colors for each subject from the subject's complete set of triadic judgments. There were actually two matrices apiece for two subjects who repeated the task on a second occasion (a month later).

Using a standard color discrimination test, Helm had determined that ten subjects had normal color vision, whereas four were deficient (in varying degrees) in red–green color vision. Matrices of perceived color dissimilarities for two of the subjects, one color deficient (CD1) and one with normal color vision (N7), are shown in Table I. Although one can readily see that these subjects differ markedly in their assessments of color differences—for example, in the matrix for CD1 red is closer to green (distance = 6.8) than to any other color, whereas in N7's matrix, red and

TABLE I

MATRICES OF PERCEIVED DISTANCES AMONG 10 COLORS FOR
TWO SUBJECTS IN HELM'S STUDY[a]

	1 RP	2 R	3 Y	4 GY1	5 GY2	6 G	7 B	8 PB	9 P1	10 P2
A. Dissimilarity matrix for Subject CD1										
1. Red–Purple		9.9	13.2	12.3	11.1	8.7	5.6	7.4	6.4	5.8
2. Red	9.9		7.3	7.9	6.9	6.8	9.9	13.1	12.7	12.1
3. Yellow	13.2	7.3		4.5	5.3	9.7	11.5	13.7	14.1	13.4
4. Green–Yellow (1)	12.3	7.9	4.5		5.3	8.6	12.5	13.4	14.1	13.1
5. Green–Yellow (2)	11.1	6.9	5.3	5.3		6.9	9.0	12.2	12.5	13.4
6. Green	8.7	6.8	9.7	8.6	6.9		6.7	9.7	11.3	9.9
7. Blue	5.6	9.9	11.5	12.5	9.0	6.7		5.5	7.4	5.4
8. Purple–Blue	7.4	13.1	13.7	13.4	12.2	9.7	5.5		4.2	4.0
9. Purple (1)	6.4	12.7	14.1	14.1	12.5	11.3	7.4	4.2		4.3
10. Purple (2)	5.8	12.1	13.4	13.1	13.4	9.9	5.4	4.0	4.3	
B. Dissimilarity matrix for Subject N7										
1. Red–Purple		7.1	10.2	11.1	12.5	11.8	9.9	8.6	4.3	2.9
2. Red	7.1		5.7	11.5	10.7	11.8	11.2	12.5	9.2	8.2
3. Yellow	10.2	5.7		6.7	8.9	9.4	11.3	12.5	11.9	10.5
4. Green–Yellow (1)	11.1	11.5	6.7		3.7	5.9	10.3	11.6	10.9	11.5
5. Green–Yellow (2)	12.5	10.7	8.9	3.7		3.6	8.2	9.8	11.3	11.1
6. Green	11.8	11.8	9.4	5.9	3.6		5.1	8.1	10.2	10.6
7. Blue	9.9	11.2	11.3	10.3	8.2	5.1		4.9	8.7	9.7
8. Purple–Blue	8.6	12.5	12.5	11.6	9.8	8.1	4.9		6.3	7.5
9. Purple (1)	4.3	9.2	11.9	10.9	11.3	10.2	8.7	6.3		3.0
10. Purple (2)	2.9	8.2	10.5	11.5	11.1	10.6	9.7	7.5	3.0	

[a] Standard color discrimination tests showed that subject CD1 was very deficient in red–green color vision, whereas Subject N7 had normal color vision.

green are judged to be very different (distance = 11.8)—inspection of the matrices for all subjects does not reveal the latent dimensions of color perception and their relative importance for different subjects. Accordingly, the complete set of matrices was used as input to INDSCAL (Carroll & Chang, 1970c; Wish & Carroll, 1971).

A. Results and Discussion

Over 90% of the variance in the matrices for all subjects was accounted for by a two-dimensional INDSCAL solution. Table IIA shows the coordinates for stimuli, and Table IIB shows the weights for subjects on these two dimensions. Table IIB also shows the proportion of variance in each matrix which can be accounted for by these two dimensions. The group stimulus space in Fig. 1a provides a graphic representation of the coordinates in Table IIA. The colors lie along the familiar color circle (see Shepard, 1962) rather than along a straight line, as is the case with the electromagnetic spectrum (whose visible portion ranges from a wavelength of about 400–700 mμ, that is, from violet to red). Basically, the fact that colors of constant brightness and saturation are represented on a circle rather than on a straight line reflects the fact that violet and red (which are at opposite ends of the physical continuum) are more similar psychologically than red and green (two colors much closer to each other on the physical spectrum). The circular representation also permits incorporation of the so-called "nonspectral" purples, which, psychologically, lie between violet and red. Of course, not all hues were actually represented in Helm's set of color chips; but it is fairly clear where the missing hues would fit into the picture.

The precise locations of the two coordinate axes describing this two-dimensional space are of particular interest, since, as we have said, the orientation of axes is *not* arbitrary in INDSCAL. The extreme points of dimension 1 are a purplish blue at one end and yellow at the other, while the extremes of dimension 2 are red and green. Thus, dimensions 1 and 2 could be labeled "blue–yellow" (or perhaps "purple–yellow") and "red–green," respectively. This fits in neatly with the opponent colors theory of Hering (1905), as elaborated in modern form by Hurvich and Jameson (1957). In fact, Michael Levine (personal communication) has conjectured that subject weights from an INDSCAL analysis of color perception data might be useful for measuring parameters associated with the two opponent processes in the Hurvich–Jameson theory.

Figure 1b, which plots the dimension weights shown in Table IIB, shows that the color-deficient subjects all have smaller weights on the "red–green" dimension than do the normal subjects. Furthermore, the order of weights

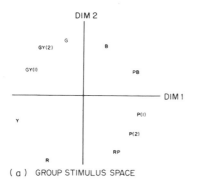

(a) GROUP STIMULUS SPACE

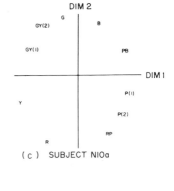

(c) SUBJECT NIOa

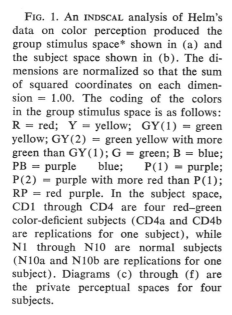

(b)   SUBJECT SPACE

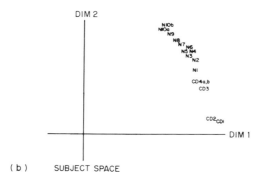

(d)   SUBJECT N7

FIG. 1. An INDSCAL analysis of Helm's data on color perception produced the group stimulus space* shown in (a) and the subject space shown in (b). The dimensions are normalized so that the sum of squared coordinates on each dimension = 1.00. The coding of the colors in the group stimulus space is as follows: R = red; Y = yellow; GY(1) = green yellow; GY(2) = green yellow with more green than GY(1); G = green; B = blue; PB = purple blue; P(1) = purple; P(2) = purple with more red than P(1); RP = red purple. In the subject space, CD1 through CD4 are four red–green color-deficient subjects (CD4a and CD4b are replications for one subject), while N1 through N10 are normal subjects (N10a and N10b are replications for one subject). Diagrams (c) through (f) are the private perceptual spaces for four subjects.

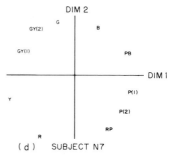

(e)   SUBJECT CD4a

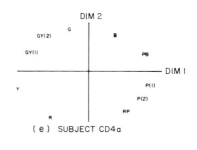

(f)   SUBJECT CDI

TABLE II

NUMERICAL RESULTS FROM AN INDSCAL ANALYSIS OF
HELM'S COLOR PERCEPTION DATA[a]

A. Stimulus Coordinates

Stimuli	Dimension 1	Dimension 2
Red–purple	.239	−.411
Red	−.248	−.468
Yellow	−.459	−.188
Green–yellow (1)	−.399	.184
Green–yellow (2)	−.294	.352
Green	−.119	.404
Blue	.165	.364
Purple–blue	.367	.171
Purple (1)	.392	−.131
Purple (2)	.334	−.277

B. Dimension Weights for Subjects

Subjects	Dimension 1	Dimension 2	R^b
CD1	.959	.107	.966
CD2	.913	.118	.923
CD3	.858	.337	.928
CD4a	.820	.397	.915
CD4b	.827	.390	.921
N1	.790	.475	.930
N2	.792	.549	.972
N3	.730	.608	.959
N4	.734	.615	.966
N5	.716	.621	.956
N6	.728	.636	.976
N7	.686	.672	.969
N8	.654	.693	.962
N9	.610	.738	.967
N10a	.547	.771	.954
N10b	.574	.784	.980

[a] The results are displayed graphically in diagrams (a) and (b) of Fig. 1.

[b] R is defined as the product–moment correlation between scalar products derived from subject's proximities data, and scalar products derived from the appropriately weighted dimensions of the "group" stimulus space.

is consistent with the relative degrees of deficiency (as reported by Helm) except for one small reversal (subject CD3 was least deficient by Helm's measures, and CD4 second least deficient, while the weight for CD4 on dimension 2 is slightly higher than that of CD3). This suggests that the patterns of dimension weights from INDSCAL might be useful for diagnosing the degree of red–green color weakness and perhaps also for diagnosing other deficiencies or anomalies of color perception. The high reliability of the subjects' weights (as shown by the closeness in Fig. 1b of the points for the two replications of subject CD4 and of subject N10) suggest that such an approach might compare quite favorably with standard procedures for measuring the degree and kind of color weakness.

Private spaces for four subjects, two of whose matrices appear in Table I, are shown in Figs. 1c–1f. While the private spaces for the normal subjects are reasonably circular, the spaces for the color deficient subjects look more like ellipses in which the major axis is the "blue–yellow" dimension and the minor axis is the "red–green" dimension. The more deficient the subject, the more elliptical the configuration—that is, the smaller the ratio of minor to major axis. Of course, there is considerable variation among the "normal" subjects themselves, with the more extreme (such as N10) bordering on blue–yellow color deficiency (which is much rarer than red–green deficiency). For such an extreme individual, the color circle is "deformed" into an ellipse whose major axis corresponds to the "red–green" dimension.

The strength of the INDSCAL model and method as revealed in this analysis is that it accommodates all these perceptual variations among subjects in a very parsimonious way. At the same time it tells us a great deal about color vision, which, if not precisely new and unexpected, confirms in an elegant way what has been worked out over the years by vision theorists.

V. PERCEPTION OF COLORS DIFFERING IN HUE, VALUE, AND CHROMA

Another set of data on color perception that were reanalyzed by the INDSCAL method were the Indow and Kanazawa (1960) data on judged similarities of 24 colors varying in all three physical parameters—hue, chroma and value. (*Chroma* corresponds roughly to the psychological attribute of saturation, and *value* to brightness.) Four subjects made complete judgments via Indow's method of multiple ratio judgments (see Chapter 14 in this volume by Indow for further explication of this method). The color circle was sampled in an essentially random way; there were four levels of chroma (2, 4, 6, and 8—higher numbers indicate greater saturation) and two general levels of Munsell value, called here high (for which the actual values ranged from 6.4 to 7.3) and low (ranging from 4.3 to 4.9).

A. Results and Discussion

Figures 2a and 2b show the 1–2 and 1–3 plane of the INDSCAL solution. As before, there was no rotation, so that the figures show the solution just as it emerged from the computer. Dimensions 1 and 2 seem to correspond rather well with a "red–green" and a "blue–yellow" dimension, respectively. Dimension 1, for example, ranges from a red at the left end to blue–green at the right; that is, it behaves almost exactly as one would expect. Dimension 2 ranges from a yellow (or green–yellow) at the bottom to a purple–blue at the top. A slight rotation (or linear transformation) might improve the orientation of dimension 2 mildly, but it nonetheless seems quite plausibly interpretable as a "blue–yellow" dimension. The concentric circles are "equichroma curves," ranging from Chroma 2 (inside) to Chroma 8 (outside). It should be pointed out that the equichroma curves and hue radii in Fig. 2a were drawn in by hand (with the arbitrary constraint that hue radii be straight lines, although they might more properly be represented as somewhat curved lines in this figure). No claim of optimality is made *vis à vis* these contours; they are provided purely to help interpret the figure. Figure 2b shows clearly that dimension 3 corresponds closely to Munsell value; i.e., all of the stimuli with Munsell value from 4.3 to 4.9 have low projections on dimension 3, while all with Munsell value from 6.4 to 7.3 have high projections.

Although Indow and Kanazawa (1960) obtained a similar configuration for the data (using an older two-way multidimensional scaling procedure for averaged data), they had to rotate the axes in order to find the structure shown in Fig. 2a. The uniqueness of orientation property of INDSCAL allowed us to find this structure *without* such rotation. The remarkable point is that this is true despite the fact that the individual differences in this case were very minimal. (INDSCAL relies on individual differences to orient the axes, so there is little guarantee of uniqueness with such small differences in weights.) The lack of individual variation can be seen in Figs. 2c and 2d which show the weights of the four subjects on the dimensions of the "group" stimulus space. It is not surprising that individual differences are so slight, since Indow and Kanazawa carefully avoided any subjects with deficient or anomalous color vision (as is typical in studies of color perception).

Now that this procedure is available for analyzing individual differences in perception, and for using such differences to specify perceptual dimensions more precisely, it would make sense for other investigators to collect proximities data from color deficient (or anomalous) as well as from color normal subjects. A study combining what we see as the principal virtues of the Helm and the Indow and Kanazawa studies would be very desirable. Following Indow and Kanazawa, all three parameters of color should be

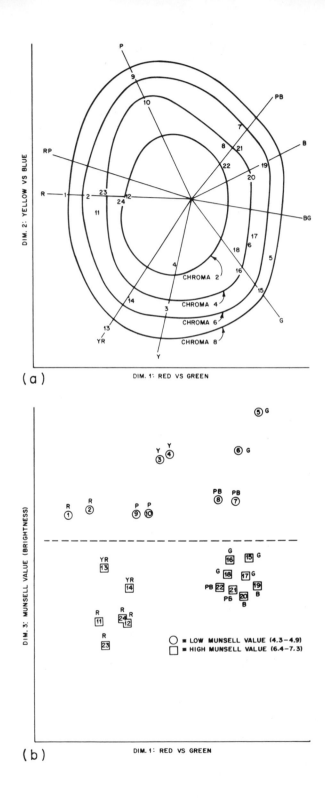

(a)

DIM. 2: YELLOW VS BLUE

DIM. 1: RED VS GREEN

(b)

DIM. 3: MUNSELL VALUE (BRIGHTNESS)

DIM. 1: RED VS GREEN

○ = LOW MUNSELL VALUE (4.3–4.9)
□ = HIGH MUNSELL VALUE (6.4–7.3)

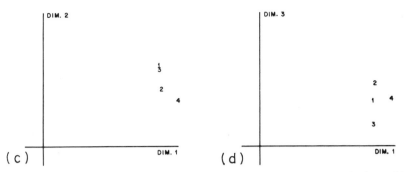

FIG. 2. Planes of the group stimulus space,* (a) and (b), and the subject space (c) and (d) from a three-dimensional INDSCAL analysis of the Indow and Kanazawa data on similarities among colors differing in hue, value (brightness) and chroma (saturation). The dimensions are normalized so that the sum of squared coordinates on each dimension = 1.00. The equichroma curves and hue radii in (a) were drawn in by hand to clarify the interpretation of results. The coding of the colors in the group stimulus space is as follows: R = red; RP = red–purple; P = purple; PB = purple–blue; B = blue; BG = blue–green; G = green; Y = yellow; YR = yellow–red. Despite the minimal variation in subject weights, the dimensions from INDSCAL were interpretable without rotation.

systematically varied, leading to a sample of stimuli that "fill" the three-dimensional color space as completely as possible. Following Helm, color deficient and anomalous subjects should be included—with as wide a range of deficiencies and anomalies as possible (ranging perhaps all the way from monochromats to normal trichromats, and including all possible variations between). It is hard to predict in advance just what this would lead to, but such a study has the potential to greatly increase our understanding of the phenomena of color vision. INDSCAL can, in principle, find dimensions that are not necessarily even linearly independent (so that one dimension *could* be a linear combination of two or more others). It is conceivable, then, that *more* than three dimensions would be required (to account for some of the anomalous cases, for example), but with linear or nonlinear dependencies among them. An INDSCAL analysis of the kind of data suggested here might shed light on such possibilities.

It should be kept in mind that the a priori knowledge about the dimensions of color perception was not communicated to the computer program that performed these INDSCAL analyses. The program saw only the subjects' data on proximities among the colors, and constructed the stimulus and subject spaces on the basis of this information alone. The fact that the axes from these and other applications (see the Bricker, Pruzansky, & McDermott, 1969, study of tones varying in waveform, modulation percentage, and modulation rate) correspond so well with the associated physical dimensions provide some justification for suspecting that the dimensions obtained in the applications that follow (where much less a priori information about the perceptual dimensions was available) might also correspond to fundamental psychological mechanisms or processes. Let us turn, then, from color perception to the perception of rhythm and accent in words and phrases.

VI. PERCEPTION OF RHYTHM AND ACCENT IN WORDS AND PHRASES

Two of the most common approaches to studying speech stress (which is sometimes defined as the articulatory effort involved in uttering a syllable or the perceptual prominence of that syllable to a listener) have been (1) to determine the relative importance of various physical correlates of stress (for example, intensity, duration, and pitch or pitch change) and (2) to develop rules for stress which give results in agreement with some linguists' conceptions of the correct stress patterns. The focus of this study was quite different. Its aim was to explore naive subjects' perceptions, or conceptions, of two attributes relevant to stress—rhythm and accent. Another motivation for doing this study was to relate the perceptual structure for rhythm and accent in speech to that obtained earlier for some three-component Morse-code-like rhythmic patterns (Wish, 1967a,b).

Eighteen students in a psychological measurement course (taught by the first author) participated in the experiment (Wish, 1969). Each subject judged the degree of *difference in rhythm and accent* between various three-syllable words and phrases. A page from the response booklet in which subjects recorded their ratings is shown in Fig. 3. Subjects were instructed to circle the number in each row which indicated how much the rhythm and accent of the word or phrase in that row differed from that of the standard stimulus at the top of the page (in this case, "pink grapefruit"). Subjects read the words silently rather than aloud, since they participated as a group during one class session. (In a study by Pruzansky and Wish, 1972, subjects spoke the stimulus pairs aloud in one session and listened to a speaker read the stimulus pairs in another session.) Each stimulus served as standard on one page of the booklet and as one of the comparison stimuli on each of the other 20 pages. The 21 words and phrases used as stimuli were selected to represent most of the rhythm and accent patterns for three-syllable words and phrases that occur in English.

After responding to every stimulus pair, subjects indicated their degree of prior musical and phonetics training and their native language. This

PINK GRAPEFRUIT

	No Difference									Very Different
1. personal	0	1	2	3	4	5	6	7	8	9
2. ice machine	0	1	2	3	4	5	6	7	8	9
3. garage door	0	1	2	3	4	5	6	7	8	9
4. aquaplane	0	1	2	3	4	5	6	7	8	9
5. enfranchise	0	1	2	3	4	5	6	7	8	9
6. teaspoonful	0	1	2	3	4	5	6	7	8	9
7. pineapple	0	1	2	3	4	5	6	7	8	9
8. big parade	0	1	2	3	4	5	6	7	8	9
9. string quartet	0	1	2	3	4	5	6	7	8	9
10. twilight zone	0	1	2	3	4	5	6	7	8	9
11. hot cross buns	0	1	2	3	4	5	6	7	8	9
12. field hockey	0	1	2	3	4	5	6	7	8	9
13. timbuctoo	0	1	2	3	4	5	6	7	8	9
14. creative	0	1	2	3	4	5	6	7	8	9
15. long meeting	0	1	2	3	4	5	6	7	8	9
16. the papoose	0	1	2	3	4	5	6	7	8	9
17. reduced fee	0	1	2	3	4	5	6	7	8	9
18. first-aid kit	0	1	2	3	4	5	6	7	8	9
19. aroma	0	1	2	3	4	5	6	7	8	9
20. interrupt	0	1	2	3	4	5	6	7	8	9

FIG. 3. A page from the response booklet in which subjects rated differences in rhythm and accent among 21 English words and phrases.

background data was used to divide the subjects into three subgroups (1) five native speakers of English who had prior musical or phonetics training, (2) eight native English speakers without musical or phonetics training, and (3) five subjects whose native language was not English.

Each page of a subject's response booklet determined a row of his proximities matrix (with diagonal values absent). Each matrix was symmetrized by arithmetically averaging the corresponding cells in the lower- and upper-half matrices [cell (j, k) and cell (k, j)]. The input to INDSCAL was a set of 18 matrices, one for each subject.

Before discussing the multidimensional results, brief mention will be made of the reliability of these data. If the correlation between values in the upper and lower halves of a subject's unsymmetrized matrix were used to measure the reliability of his data, one would conclude from the average correlation of .41 that the data for a single subject are very unreliable. An alternative way to assess reliability would be to compare both the subjects' weights and the stimulus configurations from (a) an INDSCAL analysis of the upper-half matrices for all subjects and (b) an INDSCAL analysis of the lower-half matrices for all subjects. In this regard, the correlations between stimulus coordinates on the corresponding *unrotated* dimensions of the two INDSCAL analyses were all over, .990, whereas the correlations between subjects' dimension weights from the two analyses were in the .80s and .90s. We can, therefore, place considerable confidence in the uniqueness of the multidimensional solution and in the reliability of the subjects' dimension weights.

A. Results and Discussion

Although five dimensions were needed to account adequately for the rhythm and accent comparisons of all subjects, no single individual had appreciable weights on more than three of these. As shown in Table III, dimensions 1 and 2 were most salient to subjects in the first subgroup, while dimensions 3 and 4 were most important to subjects in the second subgroup.* Mean weights on the fifth dimension did not differ much among subgroups. Although the percentage of variance accounted for by the five

* In this example the dimensions are not numerically ordered in terms of decreasing proportion of variance accounted for.

TABLE III

MEAN WEIGHTS ON FIVE DIMENSIONS FROM AN INDSCAL ANALYSIS OF
DATA ON JUDGED DIFFERENCES IN RHYTHM AND ACCENT
BETWEEN 21 ENGLISH WORDS AND PHRASES

Subgroups	Dimension 1	Dimension 2	Dimension 3	Dimension 4	Dimension 5	Proportion of variance accounted for
1. Five American Students with musical or phonetics training	.51	.42	.10	.18	.22	.65
2. Eight American students with no musical or phonetics training	.23	.12	.42	.33	.31	.54
3. Five foreign students (native language not English)	.21	.18	.18	.19	.28	.26
Randomly generated matrices of dissimilarities data for 24 hypothetical subjects	.16	.14	.15	.14	.14	.11

INDSCAL dimensions was much less for the foreign subjects (26%) than for those in Subgroup 1 (65%) or Subgroup 2 (54%), it is unlikely that the foreign subjects responded completely randomly. An estimate of random performance was obtained by generating random dissimilarities matrices for 24 hypothetical subjects. The percentage of variance in the hypothetical subjects' data accounted for by these five dimensions ranged from 5% to 17% with a mean of 11%.

Figure 4 shows that both of the dimensions that were highly weighted by subjects with musical or phonetics training are based on the precise stress patterns of the words and phrases. Dimension 1 distinguishes stimuli that are strongly accented on the middle syllable from those that are strongly accented at either or both extremes, whereas dimension 2 contrasts stimuli having primary stress at the beginning from those having primary stress at the end. It was interesting to discover that all of the native English speakers had higher weights on dimension 1 than on dimension 2. This means that stimuli with primary stress at one extreme are perceptually more similar in rhythm and accent to those with primary stress at the opposite extreme than either are to stimuli whose primary stress is on the middle syllable. In other words, stress relations between the adjacent syllables are perceptually more salient than stress relations between the nonadjacent syllables of these three-syllable stimuli. This may relate to the fact that stressed and unstressed syllables tend to alternate in English (see, for example, the "alternating stress rule" in Chomsky & Halle, 1968).

Figure 5 shows a plot of the dimensions that were most salient to subjects without musical or phonetics training. Dimension 3 separates the single-word stimuli from the phrases, while dimension 4 distinguishes phrases that have a word division between the first two syllables (first word has one syllable) from phrases that have a word division between the last two syllables (first word has two syllables). These results probably reflect the "untrained" subjects' lack of awareness of what the stress patterns for these stimuli are, since they made far more errors than the "trained" subjects when they rated in another task (after they completed the pairwise ratings of rhythm and accent differences) the strength of accent on each syllable of the words and phrases.

Dimension 5, which was moderately weighted by subjects in all three subgroups, was interpreted as "number of stressed syllables." As shown in Fig. 6, stimuli with one stressed syllable have low values, stimuli with two stressed syllables have intermediate values, and stimuli with three stressed syllables have high values on dimension 5. (The number of stressed syllables was estimated by means of the Chomsky and Halle stress rules.) Thus the total number of stressed syllables had some relevance to subjects' ratings of rhythm and accent differences, whether or not they were aware of or attended to the precise stress pattern.

Figure 7 dramatizes the extent of subgroup variation in patterns of dimension weights. The projection of a subject's point on the horizontal axis is equal to his combined weight (the square root of the sum of his squared

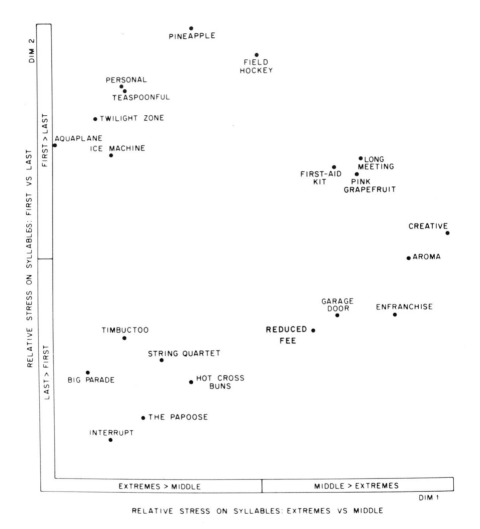

FIG. 4. Dimensions 1 and 2 from a five-dimensional INDSCAL analysis of subjective judgments of rhythm and accent differences among 21 English words and phrases. The dimensions are normalized so that the sum of squared coordinates on each dimension = 1.00. These two dimensions were most salient for native English speakers with musical or phonetics training.

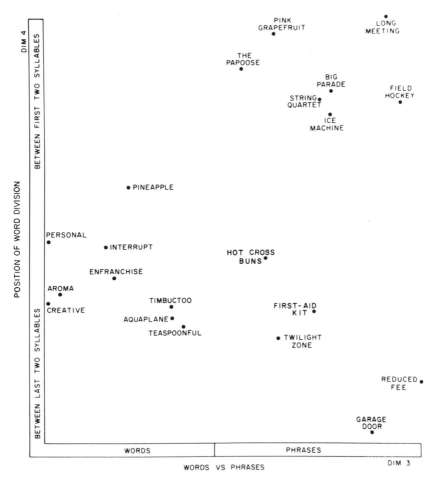

FIG. 5. Dimensions 3 and 4 from a five-dimensional INDSCAL analysis of subjective judgments of rhythm and accent differences among 21 English words and phrases. The dimensions are normalized so that the sum of squared coordinates on each dimension = 1.00. These two dimensions were most salient for native English speakers who had not had musical or phonetic training.

weights) on the first two dimensions, whereas the projection of his point on the vertical axis shows his combined weight on the third and fourth dimensions. While all of the native English speakers with musical or phonetics training have high weights on the former pair of dimensions and low weights on the latter pair, the opposite is true for native English speakers without such training. Since dimensions 1 and 2 are the only ones that deal with the relative stress on different syllables, we can conclude that the impression that appropriately trained subjects have of rhythm and accent has much in common with linguists' conceptions of stress. In contrast the "untrained" subjects responded to stimulus characteristics that are not indicated by conventional stress markings. Since the foreign subjects had low weights on both pairs of dimensions, their dissimilarity judgments must have been based on criteria different from those relevant to the native speakers of English. This result and other analyses not reported

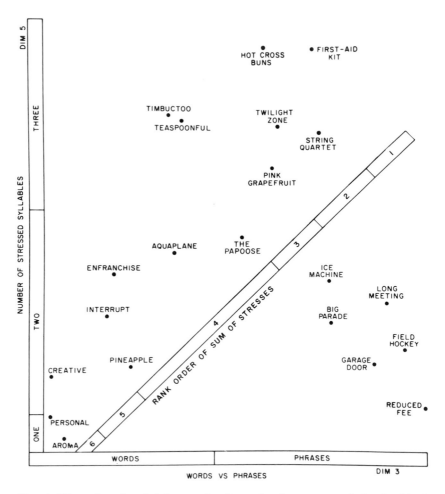

FIG. 6. Dimensions 3 and 5 from a five-dimensional INDSCAL analysis of subjective judgments of rhythm and accent differences among 21 English words and phrases. The dimensions are normalized so that the sum of squared coordinates on each dimension = 1.00.

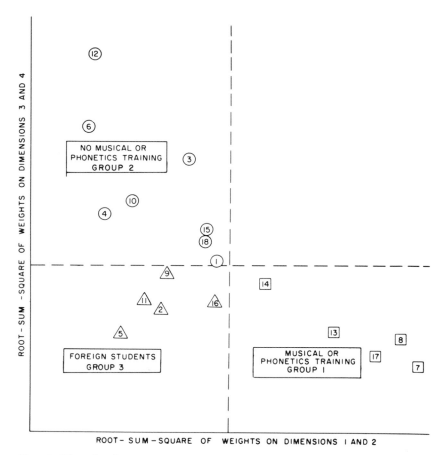

FIG. 7. Plot showing the relative importance of dimensions 1 and 2 (Fig. 4) versus dimensions 3 and 4 (Fig. 5) for 18 subjects who rated rhythm and accent differences among 21 English words and phrases. The projections of subject points on the horizontal axis indicate the combined (root-sum-square) weights on dimensions 1 and 2, while the projections on the vertical axis show the combined weights on dimensions 3 and 4.

here suggest that a person's perception of rhythm and accent in speech may depend in part on the stress rules appropriate to his own language. Since each of the foreign students had a different native language, no "common dimension" appeared for them.*

* The role one's language plays in the perception of rhythm and accent could be studied more effectively by selecting subsamples of subjects in which all subjects have the same language backgrounds, and perhaps by having subjects make judgments with respect to words in their own language as well as in English.

Although there are some ambiguities in the interpretation of these results, at least one point is clear—analyses of averaged data can sometimes yield misleading results. In this case, an analysis of averaged proximities data for all subjects would have failed to reveal that the "group" stimulus space as a whole is a composite of very different perceptual, or conceptual, structures, and that it does not reflect the judgments of any single individual.

Another point to be made is that the dimensions just described for the rhythm and accent data correspond relatively well with the dimensions arising from an earlier study (Wish, 1969) of perceptual confusions among three-component Morse-code-like rhythmic patterns. (The components were dots and dashes, as in the international Morse code; however, the intervals between components could be of either dot or dash duration.) For example, analogous to dimension 1 of Fig. 4 was a dimension in which stimuli at one extreme have a dash first and a dot last (first component longer than last), and stimuli at the other extreme have a dot first and a dash last. Likewise, a dimension interpreted as "number of dashes" corresponded to dimension 5, which was interpreted as "number of stressed syllables." Thus, despite great differences in the experimental procedures, the dimensions most salient to the perception of rhythm and accent in verbal stimuli also have some relevance for the perception of nonverbal auditory stimuli.

In all of the INDSCAL applications discussed so far, each matrix was based on the prox.mities data of a single subject; i.e., subjects provided the "third way" in the analyses. The last two examples, which illustrate the use of other kinds of data sources, demonstrate how INDSCAL can provide a valuable framework for comparing psychological effects of different experimental conditions, tasks, treatments, etc. In fact, the patterns of dimension weight for different acoustical conditions in the INDSCAL analysis of Miller and Nicely's consonant confusability data facilitated and reinforced the dimensional interpretations.

VII. PERCEPTION OF ACOUSTICALLY DEGRADED CONSONANTS

Miller and Nicely (1955) collected data on confusions among 16 English consonants under each of several conditions of noise (varying the signal-to-noise ratio), low-pass filtering (filtering out acoustical energy in the higher frequencies), and high-pass filtering (filtering out acoustical energy in the lower frequencies). The subjects listened to female speakers read C–V syllables (each syllable consisted of one of the 16 consonants followed by the vowel *a* as in f*a*ther), and tried to identify the consonant they heard after each syllable was spoken. In each of the 17 experimental sessions the speech was acoustically degraded in a different way. (Table IV shows the signal-to-noise ratio and the frequency range in hertz for each degradation condition.) A matrix of frequencies of stimulus–response confusions was derived for the data in each experimental condition. (All 17 nonsymmetric matrices are shown in the Miller and Nicely article.)

As described in Chapter 12 of this volume, Shepard (1972b, although the analysis was actually done in 1965) did a multidimensional scaling analysis of pooled data from the six noise conditions. (Wilson, 1963, did

TABLE IV

WEIGHTS FOR DEGRADATION CONDITIONS FROM AN INDSCAL ANALYSIS OF THE
MILLER AND NICELY DATA ON CONFUSIONS AMONG CONSONANTS

Degradation conditions		Weights on dimensions						
Signal-to-noise ratio	Frequency response in hertz	1	2	3	4	5	6	R^{2b}
Noise conditions								
1. 12 dB	200–6500	.40	.26	.27	.22	.35	.41	.66
2. 6 dB	200–6500	.47	.27	.26	.22	.39	.40	.72
3. 0 dB	200–6500	.52	.29	.25	.18	.43	.41	.81
4. −6 dB	200–6500	.63	.38	.25	.07	.39	.35	.89
5. −12 dB	200–6500	.73	.42	.26	.07	.25	.22	.91
6. −18 dB	200–6500	.55	.34	.23	.12	.08	.16	.53
Low-pass filtering conditions								
7. 12 dB	200–5000	.41	.29	.27	.23	.37	.38	.68
8. 12 dB	200–2500	.48	.30	.25	.19	.47	.38	.80
9. 12 dB	200–1200	.52	.28	.26	.07	.50	.37	.82
10. 12 dB	200–600	.50	.39	.28	.07	.48	.33	.84
11. 12 dB	200–400	.59	.41	.27	.03	.44	.32	.90
12. 12 dB	200–300	.70	.42	.20	.05	.32	.17	.85
High-pass filtering conditions								
13. 12 dB	1000–5000	.40	.23	.34	.32	.33	.45	.76
14. 12 dB	2000–5000	.33	.24	.49	.44	.24	.37	.81
15. 12 dB	2500–5000	.29	.26	.54	.43	.26	.34	.82
16. 12 dB	3000–5000	.18	.20	.62	.45	.24	.27	.80
17. 12 dB	4500–5000	.13	.20	.62	.40	.18	.21	.69
Proportion of variance accounted for by dimension		.24	.10	.13	.07	.13	.11	.78

a multidimensional scaling analysis for data from the second most extreme noise condition.) He interpreted the dimensions from a two-dimensional solution for these data as "voicing" and "nasality." In addition he embedded the results from hierarchical clustering analyses (Johnson, 1967) of data from each condition in the two-dimensional space for the noise conditions.

In the current application, the entire set of matrices from the Miller and Nicely study [each matrix was symmetrized by averaging the (i, j) and (j, i) cells] was used as input to a single INDSCAL analysis. This treatment of the data had two important advantages over the prior analyses: (1) The stimulus configuration included the dimensions relevant to all 17 experimental conditions and (2) quantitative information about the salience of different dimensions under different kinds and degrees of speech degradation was provided by the dimension weights (for experimental conditions).

A. Results and Discussion

The INDSCAL analysis revealed six interpretable dimensions,* shown in Figures 8, 9, and 10, which accounted quite well for the data in all 17 matrices. The first two dimensions (shown in Figure 8), interpreted as "voicing" and "nasality," correspond closely to those reported by Shepard. Dimensions 3 and 4 (Figure 9) labeled "sibilance" and "sibilant frequency," respectively, separate the lower frequency sibilants—ʃ (the *sh* sound in *sh*ow) and ʒ (the *zh* sound in *Zh*ivago)—and the higher fre-

* See footnote on page 464.

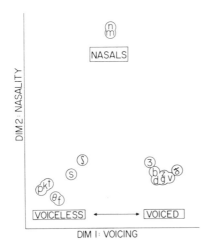

FIG. 8. Dimensions 1 and 2 of the group stimulus space from a six-dimensional INDSCAL analysis of the Miller and Nicely consonant confusability data. The dimensions are normalized so that the sum of squared coordinates on each dimension = 1.00. The input of INDSCAL was a set of 17 confusion (in a stimulus identification task) matrices, one for each experimental condition. (θ is the *th* sound in *th*in; ð is the *th* sound in *th*at; ʃ is the *sh* sound in *sh*ow; and ʒ is the *zh* sound in *Zh*ivago.)

FIG. 9. Dimensions 3 and 4 of the group stimulus space from a six-dimensional INDSCAL analysis of the Miller and Nicely consonant confusability data. The dimensions are normalized so that the sum of squared coordinates on each dimension = 1.00. The input to INDSCAL was a set of 17 confusion (in a stimulus identification task) matrices, one for each experimental condition. (θ is the *th* sound in *th*in; ð is the *th* sound in *th*at; ʃ is the *sh* sound in *sh*ow; and ʒ is the *zh* sound in *Zh*ivago.)

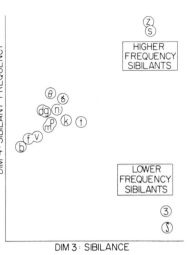

quency sibilants—*s* and *z*—from the nonsibilants and from each other. The fifth and sixth dimensions (Figure 10) differ considerably from the features which Miller and Nicely (1955) and others have proposed for these consonants. Dimension 5 separates the voiceless stops from the voiceless fricatives, whereas dimension 6 seems to distinguish voiced consonants according to whether there is a rising or falling second formant transition (from consonant to vowel).

As shown in Table IV, there is large but systematic variation in the patterns of dimension weights for different kinds and degrees of acoustical degradations. The relative importance of the "voicing" dimension increases with greater low-pass filtering or noise, and decreases with more extreme

FIG. 10. Dimensions 5 and 6 of the group stimulus space from a six-dimensional INDSCAL analysis of the Miller and Nicely consonant confusability data. The dimensions are normalized so that the sum of squared coordinates on each dimension = 1.00. The input to INDSCAL was a set of 17 confusion (in a stimulus identification task) matrices, one for each experimental condition. (θ is the *th* sound in *th*in; ð is the *th* sound in *th*at; ʃ is the *sh* sound in *sh*ow; and ʒ is the *zh* sound in *Zh*ivago.)

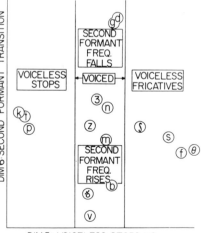

high-pass filtering. Likewise, the low-pass filtering and noise conditions have much higher weights on the "nasality" dimension than the high-pass filtering conditions. These results make sense, since most of the acoustical information distinguishing voiced from voiceless consonants, and nasals from nonnasals, is in the low-frequency range (sound energy in this range is removed by high-pass filtering). Since the sibilants differ from nonsibilants and from each other primarily in the frequency range above 2000 Hz, it is not surprising that the third and fourth dimensions are weighted much more highly by the high-pass filtering than by the low-pass filtering conditions.

Weights for the extreme noise conditions on the first four dimensions have been shown to be very similar to those of the severe low-pass filtering conditions and quite different from those of any high-pass filtering conditions.* In contrast, the weights for the extreme noise conditions on dimension 5 are closer to those for the high-pass than for the low-pass filtering conditions. The high weights on dimension 5 for the low-pass filtering conditions indicate that the low frequencies contain crucial information for distinguishing voiceless stops from voiceless fricatives; the low weights on dimension 5 for the extreme noise conditions (as well as for all high-pass filtering conditions) demonstrate that the sound energy in the low frequencies is not sufficiently audible in these conditions for voiceless stops to be distinguished from voiceless fricatives.

Unlike all the others, the sixth dimesnion is very important for the mild degradation conditions, and diminishes in perceptual salience as the degree of noise, low-pass filtering, or high-pass filtering increases. This means that the information in the intermediate frequencies, where the second formant transition occurs, is crucial for distinguishing consonants with a falling versus rising second formant transition.

The INDSCAL analysis of the Miller and Nicely data provides a clear picture of variations in consonant perception as a function of the degree and kind of acoustical degradation. The fact that weights on the dimensions are similar for acoustically similar conditions, and change gradually with acoustical changes, shows that the weights provide reliable and valid information concerning the perceptual saliences of dimensions. Moreover, the patterns of weights for conditions tell a great deal about the relative importance of sound energy in different frequency ranges for the identification of consonants.

It should be pointed out that the INDSCAL analysis of the Miller and Nicely data does not reveal *the* dimensions or *the* distinctive features of

---

* Since the noise had a flat spectrum, it interfered more with the higher frequencies in speech, which have less sound energy. Thus, its effect could be expected to be quite similar to that of low-pass filtering.

consonants. Instead, the results show how dependent the dimensions are on the particular acoustical conditions. In fact, Pruzansky's (1970) INDSCAL analysis of data on judged dissimilarities among the same consonants yielded quite different dimensions, which she interpreted as "continuants versus noncontinuants," "stops versus continuants and nasals," and "place and sibilance." Still other experimental tasks might bring out dimensions corresponding more closely to other distinctive features, such as place and manner of articulation. We can see, then, that the dimensions are not a function of the "stimuli" alone; they may depend on the experimental conditions, tasks, subjects, and other factors. By varying these parameters, we might gain additional insight into the processing of these and other speech sounds.

VIII. PERCEPTIONS OF NATIONS: SUBGROUP AND TASK VARIATION

In the final application, subgroup and task variation in multidimensional structures are both investigated. This example is a generalization of the pilot study on nation perception described in Chapter 12 in this volume.

Seventy-five Columbia University students from eight countries (Columbia, England, France, India, Korea, Thailand, United States, and Yugoslavia) participated in the study during the summer of 1968. All subjects (1) made pairwise ratings of similarities among 21 nations,* (2) sorted the nations (into mutually exclusive and exhaustive categories) with respect to overall similarity, (3) sorted the nations with respect to specific characteristics which they selected, and (4) rated the nations on 18 bipolar, or semantic-differential, scales. As will be described, 50 matrices of proximities among nations were derived from subjects' responses on these tasks.

A. Pairwise Similarity Ratings

A matrix of proximities was calculated for each nationality group and for the total group by averaging the pairwise similarity ratings of subjects in the particular group (see Wish, Deutsch, & Biener, 1972). In this way nine matrices were derived from the original 75 matrices for individual subjects.

* The coding of nations was as follows: BR = Brazil; CH = Mainland China; CO = Congo (Kinshasa); CU = Cuba; EG = Egypt; EN = England; ET = Ethiopia; FR = France; GR = Greece; IN = India; IO = Indonesia; IS = Israel; JP = Japan; MX = Mexico; PO = Poland; RU = Russia; S.A. = South Africa; SP = Spain; U.S. = United States; W.G. = West Germany; YU = Yugoslavia.

B. Sortings with Respect to Overall Similarity

A separate matrix was derived from the overall similarity sortings for each nationality group and for the group as a whole. The proximity value for a pair of nations in such a matrix was defined as the proportion of subjects in the particular group who put the two nations in the same category.

C. Sortings with Respect to Subject-Specified Characteristics

Each subject listed the most important ways in which nations differ from each other (all nations, not just those used as stimuli), and then sorted the nations (separately) with respect to the two most important characteristics specified. Proximity matrices were derived for the five characteristics which subjects most often listed and used as criteria for sortings—political aspects (44 sortings), economic aspects (40 sortings), culture or customs (21 sortings), race, religion, language, or social structure (18 sortings), and power or size (10 sortings). For example, the proximity values for a pair of nations in the matrix associated with the political aspects sortings was defined to be the porportion of the 44 sortings based on political aspects in which the two nations appeared in the same category.

D. Ratings on Bipolar Scales

1. A separate matrix of profile distances, or dissimilarities, was derived (from ratings on all 18 bipolar scales) for each nationality group and for the total group by using the following equation:

$$\delta_{jk}^{I} = \left(\frac{1}{18 n_I} \sum_{i \in I} \sum_{s=1}^{18} (Z_{js}^{(i)} - Z_{ks}^{(i)})^2 \right)^{1/2}, \tag{4}$$

where $\delta_{jk}^{(I)}$ is the profile dissimilarity between nation j and nation k for subgroup I; n_I is the number of subjects in subgroup I; and $z_{js}^{(i)}$ and $z_{ks}^{(i)}$ are the standardized ratings by subject i (one of the subjects in subgroup I) of nations j and k, respectively, on bipolar scale s.

2. A separate matrix of profile dissimilarities was also derived for each bipolar scale from ratings by all 75 subjects on the particular scale by use of the following formula:

$$\delta_{jk}^{(s)} = \left(\frac{1}{75} \sum_{i=1}^{75} (Z_{js}^{(i)} - Z_{ks}^{(i)})^2 \right)^{1/2}, \tag{5}$$

where $\delta_{jk}^{(s)}$ is the dissimilarity between nations j and k on scale s.

In order to make the matrices derived from the bipolar scales comparable with those for the pairwise similarities and the sortings, the dissimilarities computed by Eqs. (4) and (5) were converted to similarities by effectively taking the negatives of the δ-values. The matrices for these scales might be thought of as corresponding to matrices for 18 "ideal" subjects whose proximities data are based solely on the characteristic specified by a particular scale.

There were then three matrices for the group as a whole and three each for the eight nationality groups (one matrix per group was based on pairwise similarity ratings, one per group was based on sortings with respect to overall similarity, and one per group was derived from ratings on the bipolar scales). In addition, there was a proximity matrix associated with each of the 18 bipolar rating scales and with sortings with respect to each of five characteristics which subjects frequently listed as important ways in which nations differ. The entire set of matrices, 50 in all, served as input to a single INDSCAL analysis (Wish, 1972a). Separate analyses for the pairwise similarity ratings, sortings, and bipolar scale dissimilarities are reported in a previous paper (Wish, 1970a).

E. Results and Discussion

An interpretable nine-dimensional solution was obtained for these multimethod data, which provided a clearer and more complete picture of the dimensions of nation perception than separate multidimensional analyses of the pairwise similarity ratings, sortings, and bipolar scale dissimilarities. These dimensions were partitioned into three domains, or categories, of three dimensions each—a *political–evaluative* domain, a *potency* dimension, and an *ethnic–cultural* domain. In addition to three sets of dimension weights for each nationality group (since there were three matrices for each group), a set of dimension weights was obtained for each of 18 bipolar scales and for each of five subject-specified sortings. In the interpretation of stimulus dimensions that follows, reference will be made to the weights for scales and sortings on each dimension. These weights, which are shown in Table V, facilitated the interpretation of dimensions.

The dimensions comprising the political–evaluative domain are shown in Figure 11. The interpretation, "ideology and alignment," assigned to dimension 2 is perhaps more apparent than the others, since that dimension separates countries which are at opposite extremes of the political–ideological spectrum. The high weights on dimension 2 (see Table V) of the "individualistic," "many rights," and "aligned with U.S.A." scales and of the political aspects sortings provided additional support for its interpretation. The fact that the three most evaluative, or preference-related scales—"good,"

TABLE V

DIMENSION WEIGHTS FOR BIPOLAR SCALES AND SUBJECT-SPECIFIED SORTINGS, OBTAINED DIRECTLY FROM A NINE-DIMENSIONAL INDSCAL ANALYSIS OF MULTIMETHOD DATA ON PROXIMITIES AMONG NATIONS[a]

Bipolar scales	Political–evaluative domain			Potency domain			Ethnic–cultural domain			R
	Dim. 2	Dim. 3	Dim. 6	Dim. 1	Dim. 4	Dim. 9	Dim. 5	Dim. 7	Dim. 8	
1. Individualistic	.72[b]	−.04	.29	.01	.00	.00	.14	.06	.06	.806
2. Can change status	.49[b]	.22	.23	.16	.27	−.03	.02	.03	.02	.832
3. Many rights	.64[b]	.34	.10	.12	.10	.01	−.03	.03	.00	.866
4. Aligned with U.S.A.	.55[b]	.58[b]	−.09	−.05	.12	.03	−.02	.02	.05	.876
5. Good	.52[b]	.50[b]	.25	.05	.00	.01	.07	.01	.05	.882
6. I like	.47[b]	.51[b]	.08	.00	.04	.01	.12	.03	.07	.807
7. Similar to ideal	.42[b]	.36	.12	.24	.28	−.02	.01	.06	.01	.881
8. Peaceful	.36	.21	.10	−.06	.10	.03	.03	.08	.00	.494
9. Internally united	.14	.25	.67[b]	.00	−.12	.19	−.02	.09	.09	.786
10. Population satisfied	.22	.34	.45[b]	.22	.05	.12	.02	.13	.05	.838
11. Progressing	.20	.12	.43[b]	.18	.23	.03	.15	.07	.06	.781
12. Stable	.12	.24	.37[b]	.27	.18	.00	.04	.06	.07	.778
13. Industrialized	.09	.06	.11	.62[b]	.32	−.01	.02	.02	.01	.919
14. Rich	.19	.06	.00	.59[b]	.32	−.01	−.03	.04	.00	.867
15. Educated population	.11	.24	.15	.50[b]	.25	−.02	−.01	.04	.08	.869
16. Powerful	.09	−.05	.09	.15	.77[b]	.07	−.02	.02	.01	.903
17. Cultural influence	.16	.22	−.05	−.08	.70[b]	.00	.03	.06	.15	.782
18. Large	.03	.00	.01	.03	.17	.83[b]	.09	.04	.04	.887
			Specific sortings							
A. Political aspects	.63[b]	.17	.24	.15	.15	.00	.05	.14	.06	.876
B. Economic aspects	.02	.03	.07	.65[b]	.28	.00	.06	.10	.19	.912
C. Power or size	.09	.00	.18	.26	.42[b]	.20	.25	.11	.05	.831
D. Culture or customs	.14	.17	−.04	.34	.11	−.02	.43[b]	.42[b]	.28	.858
E. Race, language, social Aspects, or religion	.17	.03	.04	.35	.12	.02	.28	.53[b]	.33	.873

[a] Dim. 2 = Ideology and Alignment; Dim. 3 = Alignment and Average Preference; Dim. 6 = Internal Solidarity; Dim. 1 = Economic Development; Dim. 4 = Power and Influence; Dim. 9 = Size (Area); Dim. 5 = Contrast between African and Far-Eastern Nations; Dim. 7 = Contrast between African + Asian and "Spanish" Nations; Dim. 8 = Contrast between Latin-American and Eastern-European Nations.
[b] Weight greater than .40.

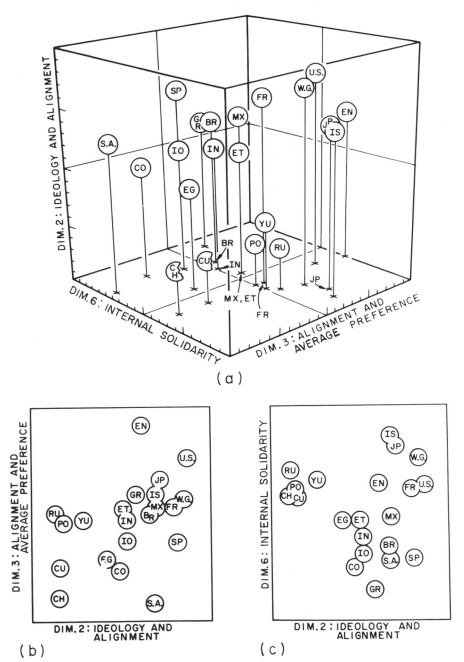

FIG. 11. The political–evaluative domain—three dimensions from a nine-dimensional INDSCAL analysis of multimethod data on proximities among 21 nations. The dimensions are normalized so that the sum of squared coordinates on each dimension = 1.00. Diagram (a) shows a three-dimensional perspective of Dim. 2 × Dim. 3 × Dim. 6, while Diagrams (b) and (c) show respectively, the Dim. 2 × Dim. 3 plane and the Dim. 2 × Dim. 6 plane. Coding of nations is indicated in Footnote 9.

"I like," and "similarity to ideal"—also have rather high weights on this dimension shows that political considerations are very important for subjects' preferences among nations. The high weights on dimension 3 for the most evaluative scales, along with moderate weights for some political scales, provided the rationale for its interpretation as "alignment and average preference." In fact, the correlation between projections on dimension 3 and the mean ratings of nations on the "I like" scale is .95. The justification for labeling dimension 6 as "internal solidarity" was the occurrence of high weights on that dimension for the "internally united," "population satisfied," "progressing," and "stable" scales.

Dimensions 1, 4, and 9, shown in Figure 12, measure three aspects of the potency of nations—"economic development," "power and influence" (or perhaps military and technological development), and "geographical size." Although these interpretations could have been made by observing which nations are at opposite extremes of these dimensions, the patterns of dimension weights for the bipolar scales bolster confidence in the dimensional interpretations. In this regard, note the high weights (Table V) on dimension 1 for the "industrialized," "rich," and "educated population" scales, and the economic aspects sortings, the high weights on dimension 4 for the powerful and cultural influence scales, and the high weight on dimension 9 for the "large" scale.

Dimensions 5, 7, and 8 (shown in Fig. 13), which comprise the ethnic–cultural domain, provide clusterings of nations based on culture, geographical location, race, religion, and other associated characteristics. As a matter of fact, the ethnic–cultural domain has a tetrahedron-like structure. The African, far eastern, "Spanish," and eastern European nations are at the vertices, while a western European cluster (composed of England, France, West Germany, and the United States) lies roughly in the center. The dimensional labels in Figure 13 indicate which cultural group are at opposite ends of the axes, and do not imply the existence of a continuum going from one extreme of a dimension to the other. Since every bipolar scale had low weights on all three of these dimensions, the rating scale data did not contribute to the interpretation of these dimensions. However, the moderate weights of the two cultural sortings (culture or customs, and race, religion, language, or social structure) on the ethnic–cultural dimensions does provide evidence that cultural considerations are relevant to all three dimensions.

In most multidimensional scaling applications in which semantic-differential as well as proximities data are collected, weights are not directly available for rating scales. Frequently, however (see, for example, Carroll, 1972; Green & Rao, 1972; Rosenberg, Nelson, & Vivekanathan, 1968; Wish, Deutsch, & Biener, 1972), the experimenter will use a linear regres-

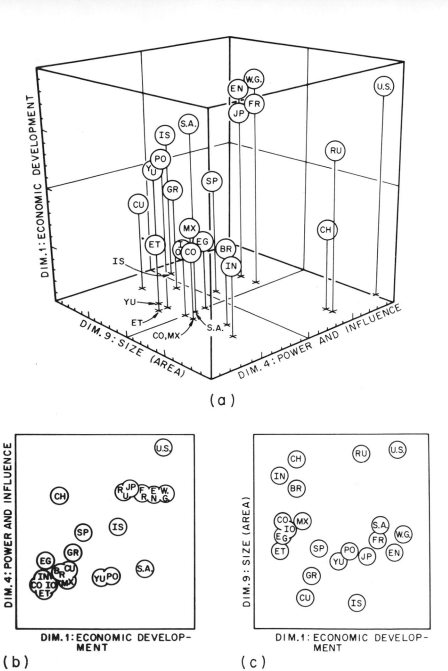

FIG. 12. The Potency domain—three dimensions from a nine-dimensional INDSCAL analysis of multimethod data on proximities among 21 nations. The dimensions are normalized so that the sum of squared coordinates on each dimension = 1.00. Diagram (a) shows a three-dimensional perspective of Dim. 1 × Dim. 4 × Dim. 9, while Diagrams (b) and (c) show, respectively, the Dim. 1 × Dim. 4 plane and the Dim. 1 × Dim. 9 plane. Coding of nations is indicated in the footnote on page 475.

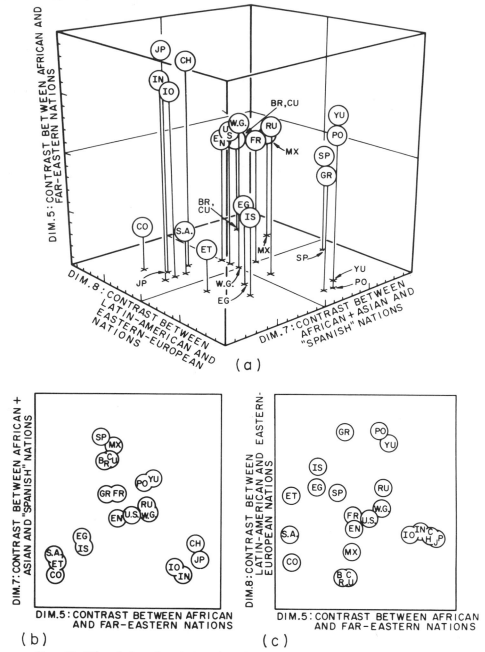

Fig. 13. The ethnic–cultural domain—three dimensions from a nine-dimensional INDSCAL analysis of multimethod data on proximities among 21 nations. Diagram (a) shows a three-dimensional perspective of Dim. 5 × Dim. 7 × Dim. 8, while Diagrams (b) and (c) show, respectively, the Dim. 5 × Dim. 7 plane and the Dim. 5 × Dim. 8 plane. The dimensions are normalized so that the sum of squared coordinates on each dimension = 1.00. Coding of nations is indicated in the footnote on page 475.

sion procedure to locate a vector in the multidimensional space for each rating scale (or for each physical property as in the Bricker, Pruzansky, and McDermott, 1969, study) such that projections of stimuli on that vector correlate maximally with mean ratings of stimuli on the particular scale (or with other measurements). The direction cosines of these vectors (with respect to the dimensions of the space) correspond to the optimal (normalized) regression weights for the respective dimensions for predicting mean ratings on the particular scales.

Table VI shows the results from such a linear regression (using Chang & Carroll's, 1968, PROFIT procedure) of mean ratings on the 18 bipolar scales onto the dimensions of the "group" stimulus space. The multiple correlations in the last column show how well mean ratings on each bipolar scale can be predicted from the nine INDSCAL dimensions. The normalized (sum of squares in each row = 1.00) regression weights, or direction cosines, show the relative importance of each dimension for predicting mean ratings on the particular scale.

Although the patterns of linear regression weights shown in Table VI correspond rather well with the dimension weights obtained directly from the INDSCAL analysis (Table V), there are some large discrepancies with respect to the dimensions of the political–evaluative domain. For example, the INDSCAL weights (Table V) on dimensions 2 are approximately equal to those on dimension 3 for the scales most relevant to preferences among nations—"good," "I like," and "similarity to ideal." In contrast, the weights for these scales determined from a linear regression of mean ratings (Table VI) are very high for dimension 3 and negligible for dimension 2. The fact that dimension 2 is unimportant for predicting *mean ratings* of nations on these preference-type scales may be misleading; that is, it might lead one to conclude (wrongly) that ideology and alignment are not important considerations for subjects' preferences among nations. As stated previously, however, Table V demonstrates that *differences in ratings* of nations on these scales can be predicted rather well from differences in coordinates of nations on the "ideology and alignment" dimension. Thus, although on the average, nations at opposite extremes of dimension 2 are about equally liked by the subjects in this study, individual subjects do have clear differences in preferences for pro-Communist and pro-Western nations.

Having described the stimulus dimensions and the patterns of dimension weights for the bipolar scales and sortings, we shall now discuss task and subgroup differences in the patterns of dimension weights. Figure 14a shows the weight of each dimension for the three major experimental

* The dimensions are normalized so that the sum of squared coordinates on each dimension = 1.00.

TABLE VI

Regression[a] Weights (from a Linear Regression Analysis) for Predicting Mean Ratings of 21 Nations on Each of 18 Bipolar Scales from indscal Dimensions[b]

Bipolar scales	Political-evaluation domain			Potency domain			Ethnic–cultural domain			Multiple R
	Dim. 2	Dim. 3	Dim. 6	Dim. 1	Dim. 4	Dim. 9	Dim. 5	Dim. 7	Dim. 8	
1. Individualistic	.63c	.20	−.65c	.28	.01	.00	−.06	−.12	−.19	.972
2. Can change status	.45	.49	.62c	.07	.38	−.11	.05	−.05	−.06	.968
3. Many rights	.54c	.68c	.40	.08	−.01	−.08	−.03	−.17	.21	.967
4. Aligned with U.S.A.	.81c	.49	−.16	.21	−.13	−.01	−.03	−.10	−.04	.995
5. Good	.22	.86c	.38	.03	−.16	.02	.14	−.03	−.16	.979
6. I like	.21	.94c	.10	−.19	−.09	.05	.09	.12	−.01	.976
7. Similar to ideal	.08	.73c	.18	.32	.46	−.22	.20	.11	−.07	.977
8. Peaceful	.28	.47	−.22	.28	−.70c	.07	.25	.14	−.04	.863
9. Internally united	−.15	.37	.82c	−.23	.06	−.24	−.14	.16	.07	.961
10. Population satisfied	.16	.42	.82c	.13	.20	−.19	−.10	−.06	.12	.982
11. Progressing	.15	−.03	.95c	−.04	−.07	.22	.16	.00	.02	.908
12. Stable	.01	.38	.72c	.52c	−.10	.19	.04	.07	.16	.929
13. Industrialized	−.12	.17	.19	.92c	.24	.09	.09	.00	−.05	.991
14. Rich	.01	.17	.14	.93c	.17	.10	−.16	−.08	−.14	.974
15. Educated population	−.16	.41	.16	.73c	.44	−.12	−.03	.10	.16	.994
16. Powerful	−.16	.01	.35	.43	.71c	.36	−.03	−.14	−.07	.988
17. Cultural influence	−.05	.35	−.18	−.19	.89c	.01	.04	.05	.10	.904
18. Large	.09	−.09	.05	.08	−.03	.98c	.11	−.02	.02	.995

[a] Regression weights are normalized so that the sum of squared weights for each bipolar scale equals 1.00.

[b] Dim. 2 = Ideology and Alignment; Dim. 3 = Alignment and Average Preference; Dim. 6 = Internal Solidarity; Dim. 1 = Economic Development; Dim. 4 = Power and Influence; Dim. 9 = Size (Area); Dim. 5 = Contrast between African and Far-Eastern Nations; Dim. 7 = Contrast between African + Asian and "Spanish" Nations; Dim. 8 = Contrast between Latin-American and Eastern-European Nations.

[c] Weights greater than .60.

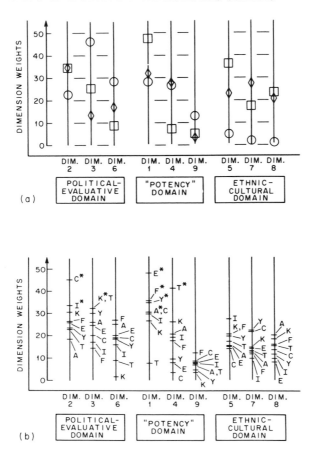

FIG. 14. Dimension weights for (a) three tasks and (b) eight nationality subgroups from a nine-dimensional INDSCAL analysis of multimethod data on proximities among nations. Weights associated with the pairwise ratings of similarities, the sortings (with respect to overall similarity), and the ratings on bipolar (or semantic-differential) scales are represented in Diagram (a) by squares, diamonds, and circles, respectively. Diagram (b) shows for each dimension, the average of the three weights on the dimension obtained for a nationality subgroup (one weight for the subgroup's pairwise ratings of similarities, one weight for the subgroup's sortings with respect to overall similarity, and one weight for the subgroup's bipolar scale ratings). An asterisk by the letter representing a subgroup (A for American (U.S.A.), C for Colombian, E for English, F for French, I for Indian, K for Korean, T for Thai, and Y for Yugoslav) indicates that the subgroup's highest weight is on that dimension.

tasks—pairwise similarity ratings (squares), sortings with respect to overall similarity (diamonds), and bipolar scale ratings (circles). Each set of weights is based on the matrix of averaged data for all subjects in a particular task.) This figure clearly shows that no single task (not even pairwise similarity ratings) elicits all of the dimensions, and that only two dimensions, "economic development" and "ideology and alignment," are weighted at least .20 by all three tasks. The bipolar scales have a high weight (greater than .30) on dimension 3 and moderate weights (between .2 and .3) on dimensions 1, 2, 4, and 6; the sortings have high weights on dimensions 1 and 2 and moderate weights on dimensions 4, 5, 7, and 8; and the pairwise similarity ratings have high weights on dimensions 1, 2, and 5 and moderate weights on dimensions 3 and 8. Overall, the patterns of dimension weights for the pairwise similarity ratings and the sortings with respect to overall similarity (the two direct measures of similarity) are rather similar to each other and quite different from the pattern for the bipolar scale ratings.

Figure 14b, which shows the average of the three subgroup weights (one for each task) on each dimension, demonstrates the extent of subgroup variation in dimension weights. For example, the subgroups from the more "developed" countries (U.S.A., England, France, and Yugoslavia) all have higher weights on the "economic development" dimension than on the "ideology and alignment" dimension, whereas the opposite is true of subgroups from the underdeveloped, or developing, countries (Colombia, India, Korea, and Thailand). The Korean and Thai subgroups have quite different conceptual structures (for nations) from the others—they have particularly high weights on the "alignment and preference" and "power" dimensions, and very low weights on the "internal solidarity" and "economic development" dimensions. It is shown elsewhere (Wish, Deutsch, & Biener, 1970, 1972; see also Carroll & Wish, Chapter 12 in this volume) that there are also systematic differences in patterns of dimension weights between political doves and hawks and between males and females. These results show that the salience of particular dimensions depends on the subject population as well as on the choice of experimental methods.

In summary, the INDSCAL analysis of these multimethod data provides a clearer and more complete picture of the dimensions of nation perception than separate analyses of matrices derived from each method (see Wish, 1970a):

1. The dimensions were easier to interpret, since dimension weights were directly determined for numerous bipolar scales and subject-specified sortings.
2. The multidimensional structure for each method was clarified by the inclusion of data based on other methods.
3. The data from different methods were easier to compare since a common frame of reference (the nine dimensions) was available.

SUMMARY

These applications illustrate the wide range of stimuli as well as experimental methods that can be studied by INDSCAL and other multidimensional scaling techniques. The stimuli ranged all the way from colors, which are concrete and well-defined physically, to rhythm and accent patterns of speech and to nations, which are so general and abstract that it is debatable whether we are dealing with *per*ception or *con*ception (in which higher intellectual processes interact strongly with or even replace purely sensory processes).

In the applications to the Helm and to the Indow and Kanazawa color similarity data, the dimensions obtained from INDSCAL *without rotation* correspond to basic physical dimensions previously described by vision theorists. Thus, although nothing really new was discovered, the results confirm in an elegant way what has been worked out over the years by vision theorists. The fact that the pattern of dimension weights was different for color-deficient and color-normal subjects in Helm's study suggests that dimension weights from INDSCAL may be useful for diagnosing deficiencies and anomalies in color perception.

In the other examples, where less a priori information was available about the perceptual dimensions, the unrotated axes could also be directly interpreted. If rotation of axes had been required, it would have been prohibitively difficult to make sense out of five-, six-, and nine-dimensional stimulus spaces.

In all but one application (the Indow and Kanazawa study), there were large differences in perceptual structures (as shown by the variability of dimension weights) among individuals and/or experimental conditions. Thus, the group stimulus spaces, which correspond (except for a rotation and weighting of dimensions) to the output from ordinary multidimensional scaling analyses of averaged data, provided only composite structures which did not directly reflect any single subject's perceptions. The strength of the INDSCAL model was illustrated by the fact that it could accommodate a wide variety of perceptual types within the framework of a single multidimensional space.

Even more significant than the actual presence of individual differences was the discovery of systematic relationships between dimension weights and other characteristics of the subjects or experimental conditions. In the study of nation perception, dimension weights for bipolar scales clarified and facilitated the dimensional interpretations. Likewise, the information about dimensions weights for different experimental conditions in Miller and Nicely's study of consonant confusability provided information about the relative importance of sound energy in different frequency ranges for the identification of consonants. As was suggested in the application to Helm's color perception data, dimension weights for subjects from studies of confusions among consonants or other speech stimuli may have diagnostic value—in this case for detecting the degree and kind of hearing loss.

Although much that we have learned about these stimuli *could* have been learned by use of the older multidimensional scaling methods, some of the conclusions relied heavily on special properties of the newer INDSCAL procedure: (1) *unique* determination of dimensions, eliminating (in most cases) the need for rotation of coordinate axes to attain interpretability; (2) a composite multidimensional space, derived from unaveraged proximities data, with respect to which different perceptual types can be more directly and reliably compared; and (3) quantitative information about the perceptual saliences of different dimensions for each subject (or other data source), and about the degree to which the multidimensional space as a whole reflects the perceptions or judgments of each subject (or other data source). In conclusion, INDSCAL provides a very general method of quickly and efficiently learning a great deal about the stimuli, the subjects, and the experimental conditions—information which can be quite useful for confirming or modifying prior hypotheses about perceptual dimensions and about variations in multidimensional structures.

References

Bricker, P. D., Pruzansky, S., & McDermott, B. J. Recovering spatial information from subjects' clusterings of auditory stimuli. Paper presented at the meeting of the Psychonomic Society, St. Louis, November 1969.

Carroll, J. D. Individual differences and multidimensional scaling. In R. N. Shepard, A. K. Romney, & S. Nerlove (Eds.), *Multidimensional scaling: Theory and applications in the behavioral sciences*, Vol. 1. New York: Seminar Press, 1972. Pp. 105–155.

Carroll, J. D., & Chang, J. J. How to use INDSCAL, a computer program for canonical decomposition of N-way tables and individual differences in multidimensional scaling. Bell Laboratories, unpublished report, 1969.

Carroll, J. D., & Chang, J. J. Analysis of individual differences in multidimensional scaling via an N-way generalization of "Eckart–Young" decomposition. *Psychometrika*, 1970, **35**, 283–319. (a)

Carroll, J. D., & Chang, J. J. A "quasi-nonmetric" version of INDSCAL, a procedure for individual differences multidimensional scaling. Paper presented at meetings of the Psychometric Society, Stanford, March 1970. (b)

Carroll, J. D., & Chang, J. J. Reanalysis of some color data of Helm's by INDSCAL procedure for individual differences multidimensional scaling. *Proceedings, 78th Annual Convention, APA*, 1970. Pp. 137–138. (c)

Carroll, J. D., & Chang, J. J. IDIOSCAL (*Individual Differences In Orientation SCALing*): A generalization of INDSCAL allowing *IDIO*syncratic reference systems as well as an analytic approximation to INDSCAL. Talk given at meetings of the Psychometric Society, Princeton, New Jersey, March 1972.

Chang, J. J., & Carroll, J. D. How to use PROFIT a computer program for property fitting by optimizing nonlinear or linear correlation. Bell Laboratories, unpublished manuscript, 1968.

Chomsky, N., & Halle, M. *The sound pattern of English*. New York: Harper & Row, 1968.

Coombs, C. H. *A theory of data*. New York: Wiley, 1964.

Green, P. E., & Rao, V. R. *Applied multidimensional scaling*. New York: Holt, 1972.

Guttman, L. A general nonmetric technique for finding the smallest coordinate space for a configuration of points. *Psychometrika*, 1968, **33**, 469–506.

Harshman, R. A. Foundations of the PARAFAC procedure: Models and conditions for an "explanatory" multi-modal factor analysis. Univ. of California, Los Angeles, unpublished manuscript, December 1970.

Harshman, R. A. PARAFAC2: Mathematical and technical notes. Univ. of California, Los Angeles, working papers in phonetics 22, March 1972. Pp. 30–44.

Helm, C. E. A multidimensional ratio scaling analysis of perceived color relations. *Journal of the Optical Society of America*, 1964, **54**, 256–262.

Horan, C. B. Multidimensional scaling: Combining observations when individuals have different perceptual structures. *Psychometrika*, 1960, **34**, 139–165.

Hurvich, L. M., & Jameson, D. An opponent-process theory of color vision. *Psychological Review*, 1957, 384–404.

Indow, T., & Kanazawa, K. Multidimensional mapping of Munsell colors varying in hue, chroma, and value. *Journal of Experimental Psychology*, 1960, **59**, 330–336.

Johnson, S. C. Hierarchical clustering schemes. *Psychometrika*, 1967, **32**, 241–254.

Kruskal, J. B. Multidimensional scaling by optimizing goodness of fit to a nonmetric hypothesis. *Psychometrika*, 1964, **29**, 1–27. (a)

Kruskal, J. B. Nonmetric multidimensional scaling: A numerical method. *Psychometrika*, 1964, **29**, 115–129. (b)

Kruskal, J. B., & Carmone, F. J. How to use MDSCAL (version 5M) and other useful information. Bell Laboratories, unpublished manuscript, 1969.

Lingoes, J. C. An IBM 7090 program for Guttman–Lingoes smallest space analysis— I. *Behavioral Science*, 1965, **10**, 183–184. (a)

Lingoes, J. C. An IBM 7090 program for Guttman—Lingoes smallest space analysis—II. *Behavioral Science*, 1965, **10**, 487. (b)

McGee, V. E. Multidimensional scaling of N sets of similarity measures: A nonmetric individual differences approach. *Multivariate Behavioral Research*, 1968, **3**, 233–248.

Miller, G. A., & Nicely, P. E. An analysis of perceptual confusions among some English consonants. *Journal of the Acoustical Society of America*, 1955, **27**, 338–352.

Pruzansky, S. Judgments of similarities among initial consonants using an auditory sorting apparatus. Paper presented at meetings of the Acoustical Society of America, Houston, November 1970.

Pruzansky, S., & Wish, M. Perception of rhythm and accent in English words and phrases. Paper presented at meetings of the Acoustical Society of America, Miami, November 1972.

Rosenberg, S., Nelson, C., & Vivekananthan, P. S. A multidimensional approach to the structure of personality impressions. *Journal of Personality and Social Psychology,* 1968, **9,** 283–294.

Rothkopf, E. Z. A measure of stimulus similarity and errors in some paired associate-learning tasks. *Journal of Experimental Psychology,* 1957, **53,** 94–101.

Shepard, R. N. The analysis of proximities: Multidimensional scaling with an unknown distance function. I, II. *Psychometrika,* 1962, **27,** 125–140; 219–246.

Shepard, R. N. Analysis of proximities as a technique for the study of information processing in man. *Human Factors,* 1963, **5,** 19–34.

Shepard, R. N. A taxonomy of some principal types of data and of multidimensional methods for their analysis. In R. N. Shepard, A. K. Romney, & S. Nerlove (Eds.), *Multidimensional scaling: Theory and applications in the behavioral sciences,* Vol. 1. New York: Seminar Press, 1972. Pp. 21–47. (a)

Shepard, R. N. Psychological representation of speech sounds. In E. E. David & P. B. Denes (Eds.), *Human communication: A unified view.* New York: McGraw-Hill, 1972. (b)

Torgerson, W. S. *Theory and methods of scaling.* New York: Wiley, 1958.

Tucker, L. R. The extension of factor analysis to three-dimensional matrices. In N. Fredriksen, & H. Gulliksen (Eds.), *Contributions to mathematical psychology.* New York: Holt, 1964. Pp. 109–127.

Tucker, L. R. Relations between multidimensional scaling and three-mode factor analysis. *Psychometrika,* 1972, **37,** 3–27.

Tucker, L. R., & Messick, S. An individual differences model for multidimensional scaling. *Psychometrika,* 1963, **28,** 333–367.

Wilson, K. V. Multidimensional analyses of confusions of English consonants. *American Journal of Psychology,* 1963, **76,** 89–95.

Wish, M. A structural theory for the perception of Morse Code signals and related rhythmic patterns. Center for Research on Language and Language Behavior, University of Michigan, 1967. (a)

Wish, M. A model for the perception of Morse code like signals. *Human Factors,* 1967, **9,** 529–540. (b)

Wish, M. Individual differences in perceived dissimilarity among stress patterns of English words. Paper presented at Psychonomic Society Meetings, St. Louis, October 1969.

Wish, M. Comparisons among multidimensional structures of nations based on different measures of subjective similarity. In L. von Bertalanffy & A. Rapoport (Eds.), *General Systems,* Vol. 15. Ann Arbor, Michigan: Society for General Systems Research, 1970. Pp. 55–65. (a)

Wish, M. An INDSCAL analysis of the Miller–Nicely consonant confusion data. Paper presented at meetings of the Acoustical Society of America, Houston, November 1970. (b)

Wish, M. Nine dimensions of nation perception: Cross-cultural and inter-task variation. *Proceedings 80th Annual Convention, APA,* 1972, 301–302. (a)

Wish, M. Notes on the variety, appropriateness, and choice of proximity measures. Bell Laboratories, unpublished manuscript 1972. (b)

Wish, M. Brief comments about dimensionality. Bell Laboratories, unpublished manuscript, 1972. (c)

Wish, M., & Carroll, J. D. Multidimensional scaling with differential weighting of dimensions. In F. R. Hodson, D. G. Kendall, & P. Tautu (Eds.), *Mathematics in the archaeological and historical sciences.* Edinburgh University Press, 1971. Pp. 150–167.

Wish, M., Deutsch, M., & Biener, L. Differences in conceptual structures of nations: An exploratory study. *Journal of Personality and Social Psychology,* 1970, **16,** 361–373.

Wish, M., Deutsch, M., & Biener, L. Differences in perceived similarity of nations. In A. K. Romney, R. N. Shepard, & S. Nerlove (Eds.), *Multidimensional scaling: Theory and applications in the behavioral sciences,* Vol. 2. New York: Seminar Press, 1972. Pp. 289–313.

Chapter 14

APPLICATIONS OF MULTIDIMENSIONAL SCALING IN PERCEPTION

TAROW INDOW

I. MULTIDIMENSIONAL SCALING (MDS)

A. Spatial Representation

For the sake of simplicity, the abbreviation MDS will be used to denote multidimensional scaling throughout this chapter. Kruskal and Carroll (1969), who have made significant contributions to the development of MDS, define it as follows: "MDS is a data analysis technique which constructs a configuration of points in space from some kind of information about the distances between the points [p. 650]." What are to be represented by points are objects, such as colors and persons, and the information from which the analysis is to start is, for example, color difference or dissimilarity in personality, etc. Hence, the fundamental data for MDS are an array of variables d_{jk} representing dissimilarity between two objects

j and k, where $j, k = 1, 2, \ldots, n$. The array will be called a dissimilarity matrix D. Usually D is a chaos of numbers, and by simple inspection, it is almost impossible to discern any tangible structure in D even if the structure really exists. At the final stage of MDS, if the analysis is successful, one will have a concrete picture of the underlying structure in the form of spatial representation. For example, an advertisement in *Science* (1966, **151**, 627), "Report from Bell Laboratories," shows an interesting three-dimensional illustration in which 10 words, differing only in the vowel sound such as *heed, had,* and *hid,* are represented as points; similar words that are frequently confused are located close to each other and dissimilar words that are rarely confused are located far apart. The configuration is a compact description of the perceptual relationship among the 10 words. Furthermore, if an appropriate set of coordinate axes is definable in the configuration, it will reveal what fundamental factors are responsible for causing the confusions.

Evidently, to have spatial representations as just described is useful in many different fields of psychology. For example, complexities of social attitudes or of opinions of various kinds have been analyzed by MDS (e.g., Messick, 1956; Morton, 1959, von Wright & Niemelä, 1966). Abelson and Sermat (1962) applied MDS to analyze 13 portraits, with the result that two fundamental factors, pleasant–unpleasant and tension–sleep, were found to be essential in determining similarity of emotional expression. Kuno and Suga (1966) gave a two-dimensional representation to the similarity of style of 11 piano pieces of music, from Scarlatti to Debussy. In this chapter, however, only applications of MDS in perceptual processes of more limited sense will be referred to and, because of limited space, the survey will not be exhaustive. Even in studies of perception of limited sense, the spatial representation is sought for with different purposes: either as a mere data reduction or as a quantitative model for making explicit the underlying psychological mechanism. This distinction will be discussed in Section I,C. Methods for obtaining the spatial representation are described in the next section.

B. Metric and Nonmetric Methods of Multidimensional Scaling

There are many different methods by which we can obtain some kind of spatial representation of psychological data: factor analysis, hierarchical clustering schemes (Johnson, 1967), multidimensional unfolding (Coombs & Kao, 1960), parametric mapping (Shepard & Carroll, 1966), etc. Conventionally, MDS comprises methods to obtain a configuration in a metric space from data that are directly related to similarity or dissimilarity between objects. It is also conventional to distinguish two different types of MDS: *metric* and *nonmetric*. Metric MDS is a mathematical method which is stated in terms of matrices (Young & Householder, 1938; Torgerson, 1952, 1958), whereas nonmetric MDS includes a variety of algorithms, none of which is describable in a neat mathematical formula (e.g., Guttman, 1968; Hayashi, 1969; Kruskal, 1964a,b; Lingoes & Roskam, 1971). As shown by Gleason (1967), all these procedures are similar in the fundamental structure. Because application of MDS is of primary concern in this chapter, the fundamental scheme of both types of MDS will be described only very briefly, and recent refinements of the mathematical aspect of MDS will not be touched upon (e.g., Micko, 1970; Micko & Fischer, 1970; Ramsay, 1969).

The notation to be used in the present chapter will be as follows: As already defined, d represents the distance-like relation between a pair of stimuli. If similarity rather than dissimilarity is at issue, as in the case of confusion between words, then s will be used instead of d. For simplicity, discussion will concern only distance if not otherwise stated. Notice that d is a *manifest variable* which is supposed to represent the perceptual relation under discussion, e.g., color difference as a perceptual entity. When necessary, this *latent variable* will be denoted by δ. Since δ can never be a manifest variable by itself, we must have an observable variable d to start with. Problems inherent in the process of converting δ into d will be discussed in Sections I,D, and III,B. Suppose that a configuration of n points has been constructed by MDS in an m-dimensional metric space, then the configuration and the space will be represented by $\{P_j\}$ and X^m, respectively. Note that X^m is not necessarily Euclidean. When only a Euclidean space is at issue, E^m will be used. Let $A = (a_{j\mu})$ denote a matrix of coordinates of P_j on a set of coordinate axes where $\mu = 1, 2, \ldots, m$. Ordinarily, such a set of axes are used that are orthogonal with the origin at the centroid of $\{P_j\}$. The matrix of interpoint distances of $\{P_j\}$ will be denoted by $\hat{D} = (\hat{d}_{jk})$. In nonmetric MDS, it will be necessary to define a monotonic regression curve of d upon $\hat{d}$, and the curve will be represented by $M(\hat{d})$. The plot of d against $\hat{d}$ will be called a *scatter diagram*.

Starting from the basic data D for n objects, MDS seeks for a configuration $\{P_j\}$ in X^m of the smallest possible dimension m that accounts for D in the following sense: In metric MDS, the interpoint distances $\hat{d}_{jk}$ of $\{P_j\}$ should numerically reproduce the given data d_{jk}, whereas in nonmetric MDS, the rank order among $\hat{d}_{jk}$ should coincide with the rank order among d_{jk} and hence such a set $\{P_j\}$ is sought for in which $\hat{d}$'s, when plotted against d's, yield the smallest possible scatter of points along a monotonic curve

$M(\hat{d})$. Hence, in order to evaluate the goodness of fit, Kruskal (1964) in his method of nonmetric MDS defined a measure called

$$Stress = \left\{ \sum_{j<k} [\hat{d}_{jk} - M(\hat{d}_{jk})]^2 \Big/ \sum_{j<k} \hat{d}_{jk}^2 \right\}^{1/2}. \tag{1}$$

Because the given data d's are fixed and $\hat{d}$'s are changeable through adjustment of $\{P_j\}$, $\hat{d}$'s are compared with $M(\hat{d})$. How the stress changes according to noise level in the data was studied by Wagenaar and Podmas (1971). It will be evident that, in order to be parsimonious, m has to be much smaller than n. In connection with a discussion to be stated later, the following remarks will be in order about the steps of procedure of both types of MDS and their implications:

A. *Metric Multidimensional Scaling* (Torgerson, 1952, 1958)

(M1)   From the basic data D, a matrix $B = (b_{jk})$ is determined where b_{jk} represents a scalar product of vectors from the origin to two points P_j and P_k and as is the case in factor analysis, a matrix A is obtained that minimizes

$$Q = \sum_j \sum_k \left(b_{jk} - \sum_\mu a_{j\mu} a_{k\mu} \right)^2.$$

Hence, by definition, $\{P_j\}$ is always in E^m and, therefore,

$$\hat{d}_{jk} = \left\{ \sum_\mu (a_{j\mu} - a_{k\mu})^2 \right\}^{1/2}. \tag{2}$$

(M2)   Unless the value of m is known in advance, B has to be complete and, therefore, D also. Being complete means that values of all the entries of the matrix are explicitly given.

(M3)   As in factor analysis, the dimensionality m is given by the number of such positive eigenvalues of B, λ_μ, $\mu = 1, 2, \ldots, m$, that are regarded significantly different from zero. The matrix A is determined from the eigenvectors corresponding to λ_μ. If there is any negative λ which is significantly different from zero, the set of objects cannot be embedded in a real Euclidean space.

(M4)   Metric MDS is not applicable to the data given in the form of similarity measure s unless s is converted into d according to a prescribed formula.

B. *Nonmetric Multidimensional Scaling* (Kruskal, 1964a,b)

(N1)   The space X^m is not necessarily Euclidean and the most widely used measure for $\hat{d}$ in X^m is what is called the Minkowski power metric (e.g., Beckenback & Bellman, 1961; Cross, 1965):

$$\hat{d}_{jk} = \left\{ \sum_{\mu} |a_{j\mu} - a_{k\mu}|^r \right\}^{1/r}, \qquad r \geq 1. \tag{3}$$

The Euclidean distance, Eq. (2), is a special case of Eq. (3) where the power $r = 2$. In principle, any other type of non-Euclidean distance can also be used.

(N2) Contrary to (M2), the basic data D are not required to be complete.

(N3) As the first step, an initial configuration of n points is defined in a space X of an arbitrary dimensionality, and through iterative procedures the final results will be obtained: The dimensionality m of X^m, the value of r in Eq. (3), $A = (a_{j\mu})$ for $\{P_j\}$, and the form of the monotonic curve $M(\hat{d})$ which reproduces the data d within the range of errors. The differences among the existing varieties of nonmetric MDS lie in their methods of how to carry out the iterations. The goodness of fit of $M(\hat{d})$ to d is given by the stress of Eq. (1) in the method of Kruskal.

(N4) For the similarity data, a decreasing monotonic function $M(\hat{d})$ is used to reproduce s.

Once A is determined by either method of MDS, we can plot $\{P_j\}$ in X^m and the relationship among n objects becomes visible. However, the coordinate axes obtained through the above-mentioned procedures, metric or nonmetric (if $r = 2$), may be quite arbitrary in nature and if it is desirable to have such coordinate axes, orthogonal or oblique, that represent some psychological attributes, it will be necessary to rotate the axes as in factor analysis. Recently, a new approach of metric MDS has been developed in which individual differences are taken into account (Carroll & Chang, 1970a,b; Carroll and Wish, 1971; Wish & Carroll, 1971). This method automatically gives psychologically meaningful axes, if they exist, and there is no room for rotation. The same is true with nonmetric MDS if $r \neq 2$.

It will be clear that nonmetric MDS is more flexible than metric MDS in many respects, especially since the ordinal property of d is used in nonmetric MDS. On the other hand, metric MDS has to start from the data d in terms of a metric appropriate for distance. Otherwise, there will be no hope of obtaining $\{P_j\}$ with interpoint distances $\hat{d}$ approximately equal to d. In nonmetric MDS, experimenters are relieved from the burden of obtaining such basic data d that faithfully behave as distances from the beginning. However, this flexibility may become a disadvantage for some applications. These problems will be discussed more fully in Sections III,B–D. Note, however, that the final results of nonmetric MDS are not nonmetric at all: $\{P_j\}$ and d are all metrics, and it was the insight of Shepard (1962a,b, 1966) that discerned the possibility that the metric structure is recoverable from the ordinal data of distance.

C. Data Reduction and Quantitative Model

Spatial representation of data is useful in extracting underlying metric structures in complexities of perceptual phenomena. A typical example may be what is called *color space,* which is not a perceptual space filled with colors, but a spatial representation of perceptual relationships among colors. Similarly most configurations referred to in this chapter are conceptual schemata, each used to visualize a certain perceptual relationship among objects in a spatial form. There will, however, be an exception: an attempt to give spatial representation to a visually perceived configuration of points. In this case, the obtained configuration is supposed to be a perceptual reality.

Except for visual space, what is obtained by MDS is always a conceptual schema. When constructing a conceptual schema, one has to bear in mind the purpose for which the schema is to be used. There seems to be two different roles that a schema may play: simple data reduction and quantitative psychological model (e.g., Tversky & Krantz, 1970). Of an obtained representation $\{P_j\}$, one will presuppose some psychological counterparts to $\hat{d}$, and this is what has been called a latent variable δ. And δ is tacitly assumed to be quantitative, at least in a vague sense. Then, by data reduction it is meant to have a compact and rather topological picture of the structure underlying the data, where either $\hat{d}$ or $M(\hat{d})$ is not necessarily supposed to be a faithful quantitative representation of δ. In order to have a quantitative psychological model, the relation between δ and $\hat{d}$ or $M(\hat{d})$ must be taken more seriously, because the ultimate aim lies in understanding psychological mechanisms which generate δ. This is called the problem of combination rules (Cross, 1965). For example, the question will be raised as to how the overall impression of color difference δ is related to differences in their respective attributes μ: hue, brightness, and saturation. In these cases, the correspondence between δ and $\hat{d}$, as well as the form of $\hat{d}$, such as given by Eq. (3), are of vital importance.

If, $r = 1$ in Eq. (3),

$$\hat{d}_{jk} = \sum_{\mu} |a_{j\mu} - a_{k\mu}|, \tag{4}$$

which is generally known as *city block* distance because the overall distance is given by the sum of distances on the respective dimensions (avenue and street). If $r = \infty$, it is easy to show (Beckenback & Bellman, 1961, 6.3) that

$$d_{jk} = \max_{\mu} |a_{j\mu} - a_{k\mu}|, \tag{5}$$

and the overall dissimilarity is completely dominated by the largest among differences on the respective dimènsions. Suppose that color difference is given by Eq. (5) and the largest difference is one on brightness for a given pair of colors, then the overall color difference is equal to that on brightness and differences on the other dimensions do not play any role. Only when differences on the respective dimensions are combined to generate overall dissimilarities between n objects in the manner given in Eq. (2), will it be possible to embed $\{P_j\}$ in a Euclidean space E^m. Furthermore, it cannot be taken for granted that any dissimilarity δ is always representable as distance $\hat{d}$ in X^m. There may be the case in which such a representation is just impossible no matter how complicated a structure is assumed with regard to X^m (Shepard, 1964). Because what MDS really does is to construct $\{P_j\}$ in X^m for a given data D, interest in this line of approach will be considerably lowered unless one is more or less convinced that d is proportional to or related to δ in an understandable form M^{-1}. We do not have any adequate operation to define δ as a quantitative variable. Nevertheless, δ as a conceptual construct is explicitly or implicitly behind most psychological studies, especially so in studies of perception.

D. Experimental Procedures to Scale Dissimilarity

In order to apply MDS, we have to have the basic data in the form of d or s. As in the example of confusion between words, which was mentioned in Section I,A, or in some examples to be stated later, sometimes the data are available that stand by themselves or how to define d or s will sometimes be self-evident. However, in most applications, some kind of judgment of dissimilarity is required to obtain d, and what kind of judgment should be used in defining d is not obvious.

Generally speaking, MDS can be applied to the dissimilarity matrix D defined for a group of subjects, N in number, or to D of each subject separately, or to D's of respective idealized individuals each representing a subgroup of subjects that has been shown to be homogeneous in its way of making judgments (Tucker & Messick, 1963). As mentioned in Section I,B, more efficient methods of dealing with individual differences is in progress.

Most traditional scaling procedures for quantifying an aspect of sensation, e.g., loudness, brightness, etc. (Krantz, 1972), can also be used to scale the dissimilarity between a pair of stimuli. Methods of ranking, rating, matching, successive intervals, paired comparisons, can be used for that purpose if a stimulus j is replaced by a pair of stimuli (j, k) or, if a pair of stimuli (i, j) are replaced by pairs of stimuli (i, j) and (k, l). When three stimuli i, j, and k are presented and comparison is made between (i, j) and (i, k), the procedure will be called the method of *triads*. When a number of stimuli $j = 1, 2, \ldots , n$ are presented with a fixed stimulus i and comparison is made among pairs $(i, 1)$, $(i, 2)$, $\ldots$ (i, n), the procedure will be called *multiple* comparison. When two stimuli pairs, (i, j) and (k, l), are compared or matched, the method will be called *pair* comparison or matching. When pairs of stimuli (i, j) are presented for comparison one by one, the method will be called *single* presentation. When judgments are obtained with all possible pairs or triads, the case will be called *complete*. In the cases of triads and multiple comparison, the results must ultimately be arranged in the form of D through appropriate procedures (Indow, 1968; Torgerson, 1952, 1958).

No matter what method of presenting stimuli is used, what the subject is required to judge is ultimately reduced to either difference or some ratio between two dissimilarities. It is analogous too that the subject makes judgment in terms of either difference or ratio between two sensations in scaling loudness, brightness, etc. According to the type of judgment, the term either *difference scaling* or *ratio scaling* will be used. It has been abundantly shown by Stevens (e.g., Stevens, 1961, 1971) that two different types of scaling of the same sensation yield two different scales which are not linear to each other. When both are power functions of stimulus intensity, the value of the exponent by ratio scaling tends to be larger than that by difference scaling. The magnitude of the difference in value of exponents changes according to modality, and the details of procedures. There seems to be no reason to expect the situation to differ with scaling of dissimilarity. Hence, which type of scaling was used to obtain d will be explicitly stated in each experiment.

In ratio scaling, the origin of d is absolutely fixed, which is not necessarily the case in difference scaling. Nonmetric MDS uses only the ordinal information of d and where the origin is defined, it is immaterial. Because the interpoint distance $\hat{d}$ has to be approximately equal to d in metric MDS, d must be defined in such a way that $d_{jj} = 0$, otherwise, even the dimensionality m would be affected (Messick & Abelson, 1956). Hence, when the original scale of dissimilarity is defined with an arbitrary origin, it must be converted by adding an appropriate constant to satisfy the required condition. A simple method of estimating the constant was described by Torgerson (1952, 1958) and an analytical method was given by Messick and Abelson (1956; see also Torgerson, 1958, and Indow & Shiose, 1958).

Sometimes, dissimilarity between a pair of stimuli is directly converted by the subject into a number or some other quantitative form, such as a length of line. This procedure is called *rating*. Sometimes, a pair of stimuli (k, l) are matched with regard to dissimilarity with another pair of stimuli (i, j) in the same modality. If the scaled value of d_{ij} is known in advance, the same value will be assigned to d_{kl}. This procedure or its variation is called *matching*, though there is no essential difference in the logical structure between rating and matching. When the frequency of a particular category of absolute judgment to a pair (i, j) or that of comparative judgment of (i, j) and (k, l) is used in a rather direct way to define d, the procedure will, if necessary, be called *counting*. When d is defined indirectly from the frequency in an analogous manner to Thurstone's methods of paired comparisons or of successive intervals (e.g., Torgerson, 1958), these procedures will be denoted by *Thurstonian PC* or *SI*, respectively.

II. EXAMPLES OF APPLICATION IN PERCEPTION

A. Munsell Color Space

The Munsell color solid is an arrangement of colors within a cylinder. The spacing of colors was determined originally by A. H. Munsell (1858–1918) and refined by a subcommittee of the Optical Society of America (O.S.A.). Each color is specified in terms of its principal attributes, H (hue), V (value), and C (chroma), where V represents lightness and C saturation. In contrast to the CIE (Commission International de l'Eclairage) colorimetric system, the Munsell color system is based on principles of color perception (e.g., Wyszecki & Stiles, 1967). It will be of importance to realize to what extent it is based on principles of color perception (Nickerson, 1969). The first report of the O.S.A. subcommittee (Newhall, Nickerson, & Judd, 1943) was based on some 3,000,000 color judgments made by 40 observers; the methodology is described more in detail in the preliminary report of the Subcommittee (Newhall, 1940). Further efforts to improve the spacing of the Munsell color system are continuing under the supervision of D. B. Judd.

In the introductory part of the preliminary report, it is stated that

> The ideal of this investigation is a psychological color solid in which cylindrical coordinates of Euclidean space represent the principal attributes of colors perceived as belonging to surfaces and equal linear extents represent equal sense-distance. Along the color scales there is a variation in but one attribute at a time, and the scalar graduations are perceptually uniform [Newhall, 1940].

From the operations employed, it is clear that the uniformity is limited to that along the respective attribute scales. Hence, the uniformity under discussion is more limited than the concept in the CIE uniform chromaticity scale (UCS) diagram (Graham, 1965; Wyszecki & Stiles, 1967), where an equal linear distance between a pair of colors varying both in hue and saturation should also represent an equal sense-distance. However, even the uniformities within the respective attributes will not be tenable unless a special rule of combination between H and C is presupposed, because the distance between two points (H_1, V, C_1) and (H_2, V, C_1) changes to the distance between two points (H_1, V, C_2) and (H_2, V, C_2), when C_1 changes to C_2, in a specified way in the coordinates under discussion. Both reports of O.S.A., preliminary and final, were not explicit on this problem. As mentioned in Section I,C, MDS is a method that is directly concerned with this kind of problem. According to Judd and Wyszecki (1963), "a uniform tridimensional color scale would be an important commercial as well as scientific achievement [p. 264]," and hence it will be of some help for the achievement to explore the uniformity of the Munsell color solid as a whole by means of MDS from a macroscopic point of view.

Of n colors which are held constant in an attribute, MDS always gave two-dimensional configurations in which two orthogonal axes corresponding to V and C were identified when H is held constant, polar coordinates corresponding to H and C were identified when V is held constant. Of n colors varying in all the three attributes, three-dimensional configurations were always obtained in which cylindrical coordinates corresponding to H, V, and C were identified. These results are summarized in Table I. Some studies were made for the purpose of examining the Munsell color space itself, and some studies were rather methodological and took the Munsell color space as an example to show the applicability of MDS. Both are included in Table I. All were under the condition that $r = 2$ in Eq. (3) and the space is Euclidean E^m, $m = 2$ or 3. Since the O.S.A. subcommittee did not define a standard scale for all the three attributes, the relative size of the present units has been a matter of dispute. Nickerson and Stultz (1944) consider that 1, 2, and 3 steps in V, C, and H, respectively are visually equivalent in the region of 5C and 1, 1, 2 steps in the region of 3C, whereas Bellamy and Newhall (1942) see the proportions as 1, 8, and 22 in the region of 6C. These proportions are given as a direct result of MDS. As will be stated later, the spacing of colors is problematic with regard to H, and only the proportion between steps in V and C in each study is given in Table I, except when V is held constant. Insofar as a Euclidean space is assumed, the proportion cannot be dependent upon the value of C. Attempts to give spatial representations to color names, instead of actual color chips, were made (Rapoport & Fillenbaum, 1968; Fillenbaum & Rapoport, 1971). Nonmetric MDS was applied to 17 monochro-

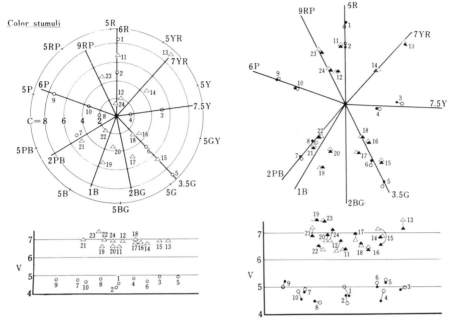

FIG. 1. Color stimuli in terms of Munsell hue, value, and chroma (renotation) and the three-dimensional configuration obtained from the complete matrix based on ratio judgments (four subjects) (Indow & Kanazawa, 1960). Unfilled circles and triangles by metric MDS and filled ones by nonmetric MDS. [From Indow (1963).]

matic-light stimuli to reproduce the hue circle by Boynton and Wagner (1972).

As examples, two configurations $\{P_j\}$ of n Munsell colors varying in all the attributes are shown in Figs. 1 and 3: one for $n = 24$ (Indow & Kanazawa, 1960; Indow, 1963) and the other for $n = 60$ (Indow & Ohsumi, 1972). The stimuli in terms of the Munsell renotation under the illumination used are also shown in the figures. The scatter diagrams of the respective cases are given in Figs. 2 and 4. Without going into details from viewpoint of color science (Indow, 1963), a few brief comments will be made.

1. In Figs. 1 and 2, the results of the two methods of MDS are plotted: unfilled circles and triangles for the metric and filled ones for the non-metric. Note that the two results are almost identical and the scatter diagram in Fig. 2 shows marked deviations from the identity relation $d = \hat{d}$ that has to be the case in metric MDS. Methodologically this finding is of interest because it suggests that metric MDS seems to be robust and

TABLE I
SUMMARY OF APPLICATIONS OF MDS TO MUNSELL COLOR SPACE

Investigator	Attributes		n	N	D	Method to present stimuli and judgment			MDS	V:C
	Constant	Varied								
1. Torgerson (1952, 1958)	5R	V.C.	9	38	group	triads complete	Thurstonian PC	difference	metric	1:2.3
2. Indow, Shiose (1956, 1958)	5R	V.C.	9	3	indiv.	triads complete	rating	difference	metric	1:2.3 1:3.0 1:3.1
3. Messick (1954)	5R	V.C.	8	42	group	triads complete	Thurstonian PC	difference	metric	1:2.5
	5R	V.C.	14	42	group	single complete	Thurstonian SI	difference	metric	1:1.9
4. Indow (Uchizono) (1960, 1963)	5V	H.C.	21	1	indiv.	multiple complete	rating	ratio	metric	
	5V	H.C.	21	3	group				nonmetric	
5. Helm Tucker (1962)	6V	H.C.	10	10	idealized	triads complete	rating	ratio	metric	
			4[a]		indiv.					
6. Hyman Well (1967)	5R	V.C.	9	6	indiv.	multiple complete	rating	ratio	metric	$\{P_{ij}\}$ not reported
	5R	V.C.	8	6	indiv.					
7. Ekman (1954) Shepard (1962)	not stated	wave-length[b]	14	31	group	single complete	rating	difference	nonmetric	
8. Ramsay (1968)	6V	H.C.	21	20	group	pair complete	rating	ratio	metric nonmetric	

504

9. Indow (Kanazawa) (1960, 1963)		H.V.C.	24	4	group	multiple complete	rating	ratio	metric nonmetric	1:1.8
10. Indow Matsushima (1969)	around 5R	H.V.C.[a]	15	6	group	pair matching (color difference to color difference) complete		difference	metric	1:11.2[c]
	around 5GY	H.V.C.[d]	15	6						1:2.9[c]
	around 4.8G	H.V.C.[d]	15	6						1:5.7[c]
	around 8.6B	H.V.C.[d]	15	6						1:5.5[c]
11. Indow Ohsumi (1972)		H.V.C.	60	5	group	pair matching with gray scale incomplete[e]		difference	nonmetric	1:2.8

[a] Subject with defective color vision.
[b] Monochromatic light.
[c] Two color patches were juxtaposed directly side by side.
[d] Varying within a local region.
[e] Limited within the range where degree of color difference is intuitively differentiated.

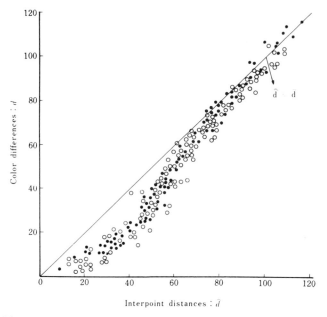

FIG. 2. The scatter diagram for the result in Fig. 1. The ordinate represents the scaled color differences and the abscissa the interpoint distances. Unfilled circles for metric MDS and filled ones for nonmetric MDS. [From Indow (1963).]

applicable to cases of which structures are not exactly as assumed in the model.

2. The colors of the same H appeared along a line segment in the order corresponding to C, and all the line segments converged into a single point at the center. The axis corresponding to V appeared orthogonal to the plane for H and C.

3. Although the order of H is as defined in the Munsell system, the spacing of H seems to deviate systematically from the Munsell notation. For example, the radius vectors representing BG, B, and PB are always too close to each other in both Figs. 1 and 3. The same tendency is observed in the results of Indow and Kanazawa (1960), Indow and Uchizono (1960), Ramsey (1968), and even in Ekman's (1954) data, analyzed by Shepard (1962), in which monochromatic lights were used instead of object colors. The tendency is not clear, however, in the results of Helm and Tucker (1962) nor in the reanalysis of their data (Carroll & Chang, 1970a; Wish & Carroll, 1971).

4. The value of stress defined in Eq. (1) was fairly small, which will be regarded as an evidence that the color space, as a whole, is Euclidean,

at least in the first approximation. The problem will be discussed more fully in Section III,A.

5. There is a marked curvilinearity in one scatter diagram (Fig. 2) and almost none in the other (Fig. 4). What is suggested by this finding will also be discussed in Section III,B.

6. Even if the color space is Euclidean as a whole, it does not necessarily imply that the region within which the subject can have tangible quantity-like impressions of color difference is unlimited. In the experiment with 60 colors, the comparisons were limited to a certain range of color differences, and, hence, D was incomplete. To establish the scope of perceptually

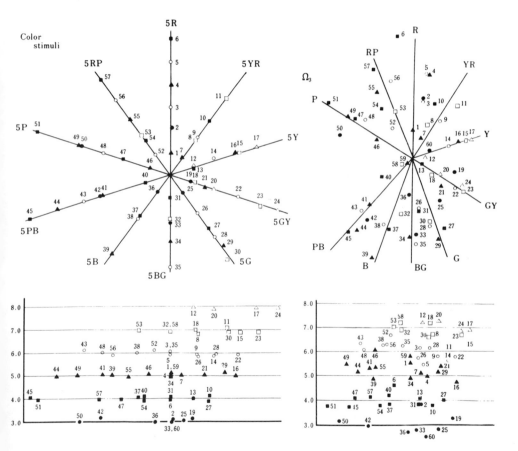

FIG. 3. Color stimuli in terms of Munsell hue, value, and chroma (renotation) and the three-dimensional configuration obtained by nonmetric MDS from the incomplete matrix of color differences based on difference judgments (five subjects). [From Indow & Ohsumi (1972).]

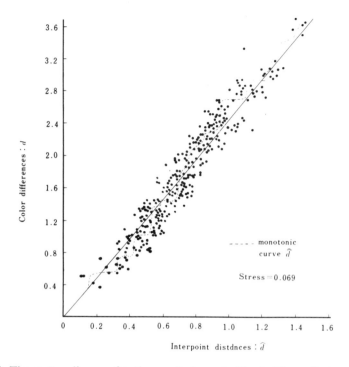

FIG. 4. The scatter diagram for the result shown in Fig. 3. The ordinate represents the scaled color differences and the abscissa the interpoint distances. [From Indow & Ohsumi (1972).]

natural information-processing is an interesting problem, but it is beyond the scope of this chapter.

B. Other Applications to Give Conceptual Schemata

For the purpose of showing that nonmetric MDS is a powerful tool for data reduction, an application of the method made by Shepard (1963) will be described in detail. The study is concerned with identifying international Morse code signals, 36 signals in total. A kind of confusion matrix, 36×36, was obtained by Rothkopf (1957). He had each of 598 subjects who were unfamiliar with the Morse code, judge whether two successively presented signals, j and k, were the same or different (single presentation). Each entry of the matrix is the percentage of "same" judgment, s_{jk}, which is certainly a measure of similarity between the two signals j and k (counting). If there is no error, $s_{jj} = 1$, and $s_{jk} = 0$ for $k \neq j$. In fact, the matrix is an array of 1260 numbers and it is almost impossible by inspection alone to discern any intelligible structure underlying this chaos of numbers. Shepard applied nonmetric MDS to extract information about how subjects perceive Morse code signals. Figure 5 shows the configuration $\{P_j\}$ obtained in E^2, which clearly indicates that the human information-processing system tends to analyze each signal primarily on the basis of two factors: the total number of components in a signal and the relative predominance of dots versus dashes among those components. In addition to these factors, the symmetry along time dimension seems to be another factor in confusability. Each pair of signals, differing only by a time reversal, is connected by line segments in Fig. 5 and these particular pairs all appear in close proximity. The scatter diagram is shown in Fig. 6, where points are more or less concentrated along a monotonic decreasing curve

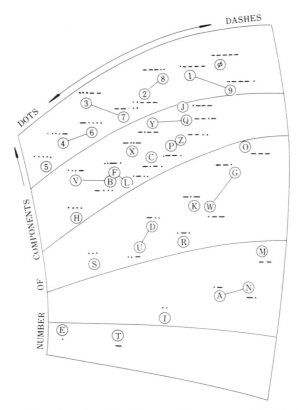

FIG. 5. The configuration for the Morse code constructed in Euclidean plane by nonmetric MDS from the complete matrix consisting of percentage of "same" judgments obtained by Rothkopf (1957). [After Shepard (1963).]

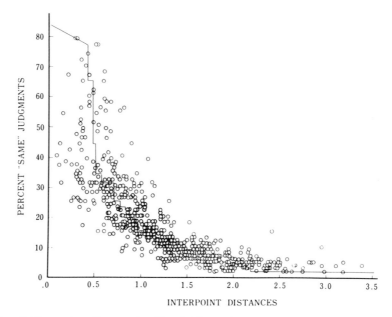

FIG. 6. The scatter diagram for Fig. 5. The ordinate represents the mean percentage of "same" judgments and the abscissa the interpoint distances. [After Shepard (1963).]

$M(\hat{d})$. Unfortunately, the value of stress was not given in the original article.

If what has been obtained in this study is interpreted as a compact description of the given data s_{jk}, there will be no problem. What factors are operating in determining $\hat{d}$ was made clear and the meaningful variable in practice, s, was found to be related to $\hat{d}$ in the form as given in Fig. 6. However, if interpreted as a quantitative perceptual model of how the confusability is determined by the perceptual similarity δ between two symbols, then we must worry about the relation between δ and $\hat{d}$ in Fig. 5. Nowhere in the analysis, is this relation directly touched upon. Hence, until some additional information becomes available, it is a matter of interpretation whether or not to regard $\hat{d}$ as being identical with δ and $M(\delta)$ in Fig. 6 as the functional relation between confusability and perceptual similarity.

Wilson (1963) applied MDS to the confusion matrices of English consonants taken from the study by Miller and Nicely (1955); one for 6 stopped consonants and the other for 16 consonants. The consonants were presented to five subjects and the matrices analyzed were for signal-to-noise ratio of -12 dB for a 200–6500-Hz channel. Because he used the metric procedure, he had to convert s_{jk}, the frequency that a consonant j

is identified as k, into a distance-like variable d_{jk} in advance (M4 in Section I,B) and the following two formulas were used:

$$d_{jk}^{(1)} = 0.5 \log \left(\frac{s_{jj} \times s_{kk}}{s_{jk} \times s_{kj}} \right);$$

$$d_{jk}^{(2)} = \left(1 - \frac{s_{jk} + s_{kj}}{s_{jj} + s_{kk}} \right)^{1/2}.$$

The former $(d^{(1)})$ was the formula derived by Shepard (1957) from his model of stimulus and response generalization whereas the latter $(d^{(2)})$ was the formula by Wilson on the assumption that independent differences in cue should have additive effects in reducing the value of s. When the metric procedure was applied to the matrices consisting of $d^{(1)}$ and $d^{(2)}$, respectively, somewhat different configurations were obtained in the data for both 6 and 16 consonants. Note that the difference is not a simple distortion of configuration but concerned with interpretation of the factors underlying the information processing under discussion. Here is a typical example of the trouble we encounter whenever we do not have an unambiguous way of defining the basic data. Similar analyses were made with 11 Dutch vowel sounds, one from the similarity judgments and one from the confusion matrix, both by nonmetric MDS (Pols, van der Kamp, & Plomp, 1969; van der Kamp & Pols, personal communication). The two configurations obtained in E^3 were in close agreement. In the similarity judgment, the stimuli were presented by the method of triads and s was defined by counting from 18 subjects. The stress of the case was 1.6%. In some sense, they seem to regard $\hat{d}$ for the similarity judgment as the operational definition of δ and used it as the criterion with which the result for the confusion matrix and the result of the physical analysis of the stimuli were compared.

Of 15 musical intervals (S) consisting of two simultaneous sinusoids and 15 musical intervals (C) consisting of two simultaneous complex tones, both always kept at a mean value of 500 Hz and a 55–60-dB level, nonmetric MDS was applied to the respective matrices of similarity. Each of these matrices was obtained by exactly the same method as in the preceding example with a group of 16 subjects. The values of stress were about 11% for $m = 3$ in the two analyses, S and C, respectively. In the subspace E^2, it was found that musical intervals are ordered along a U-shaped curve in accordance with their width: frequency difference between two component tones. In other words, extremely narrow intervals are located very far apart along the curve but sound rather similar to human ears and fairly close to each other in E^2. Some additional findings were also described in the original article (Levelt, van de Geer, & Plomp, 1966).

Metric MDS was applied to taste sensation by Yoshida (1969) and non-metric MDS to taste mixtures by Gregson (1965, 1966, 1968) and Gregson and Russell (1965a,b). Yoshida (1968a,b) also tried to give some spatial representations to the complexities of touch with the aid of metric MDS. There are a number of studies in which MDS has been applied to analyze perception of visual forms, from random patterns to letters through geometrical figures, and also forms in memory (Carroll & Chang, 1970b; Hyman & Well, 1967, 1968; Julesz, 1967; Kuennapas, 1966, 1967, Kuennapas & Janson, 1969; Kuennapas, Maelhammar, & Svenson, 1964; and Shepard & Chipman, 1970). Of these studies, the results concerning the combination rules will be described in Section III,A.

C. Binocular Visual Space

In vision, touch, and sometimes in audition, perception itself is of spatial character. For example, stars in the night sky are perceived as being embedded in a hemisphere-like surface. Note that there is no astronomical reason that they must appear in that way. It might be of interest to raise questions as follows: What is the real shape of night sky in perception, how does it differ from person to person; What geometry is most adequate to describe the visual space; and so on. With the hope of providing some answers to these questions, a series of attempts were made to apply metric MDS to configurations of small light points in a dark room and also to real stars in the night sky (Indow, 1968). The stimuli were always observed binocularly and hence these situations correspond to what has been called *binocular visual space* by Luneburg (1947, 1948, 1950). Conditions of all the experiments are summarized in the left half of Table II. In each experiment, the subject made ratio judgments (ratings) about perceptual distances δ_{jk} between all possible pairs (j, k) of n points. The subject himself was always counted as a point and the remaining $(n - 1)$ points were arranged sometimes randomly in a three-dimensional space, sometimes on a hemisphere, and sometimes in the plane of the eye level. It is of importance that distances from the subject to points j have been included in the same way as distances between pairs of points (j, k). Except in the case of Expt. 2.1, all the light points were visible and, hence, the multiple comparison was made (see Section I,D). In Expt. 2.1, only three light points, or two when the subject acted as a point, were visible at a time and the remaining light points were turned off in a manner similar to the method of triads (Matsushima & Noguchi, 1967). The subject was allowed to move his head and eyes freely in observing the stimuli widely scattered in space, except in Expt. 5, where the head was fixed and all the light points were within the range of sight under this condition. Each

TABLE II

BRIEF DESCRIPTION OF EXPERIMENTAL CONDITIONS AND RESULTS: APPLICATIONS OF METRIC MDS TO BINOCULAR VISUAL SPACE[a]

Experiment Year Experimenter	Description	Number of stimuli n (Dimension) [Repetition of judgments]	Condition of head	Subjects	Eigenvalues λ_μ					$d:\hat{d}$	
					1	2	3	4	5	M/R[c]	RMS/R[d]
Expt. 1 1963 Miyauchi	Light points randomly arranged	18 (3) [4]	free	TI	659	283	159	−1.8	—	−.016	.054
				EI	693	280	167	*		−.011	.030
				TK	670	262	161	69	*	−.003	.043
				KM	554	175	153	36	*	.012	.037
Expt. 2.1 1965 Miyauchi	Light points randomly arranged	16 (3) [4]	free	EI	412	139	128	*		−.001	.036
				TK	390	107	91	*		−.003	.059
				YN	414	152	116	26	17	−.007	.049
				HM	322	111	98	19	11	−.002	.045
Expt. 2.2 1965 Miyauchi	The same as in Expt. 2.1 method of triads	17 (3) [4]	free	EI	286	118	99	21	17	.011	.064
				TK	299	103	91	27	20	.027	.059
				YN	252	118	100	28	23	.012	.066
				HM	321	97	92	29	18	.010	.053
Expt. 3 1962 Matsushima	Light points on a sphere of $r^* = .04$[b]	17 (3) [4]	free	TI	11.6	3.1	1.6	*		−.023	.046
				EI	7.6	3.0	1.7	—		−.042	.042
				TK	9.3	3.0	1.5	—		−.013	.039
Expt. 4 1962 Matsushima	Stars of about the same brightness	12 (3) [2]	free	TI	5.9	2.2	1.8	*		−.019	.038
				TK	8.3	2.5	1.3	—		−.040	.076
Expt. 5 1963 Nishikawa	Light points in the eye level	15 (2) [4]	fixed	TI	215	48	*	*		−.001	.038
				EI	195	47	*	*		−.008	.027
				TK	597	260	*	*		.001	.032
				KM	641	313	*	*		−.007	.033
				YN	566	246	*	*		.000	.023
				YI	169	36	*	*		.009	.056

[a] From Indow (1968).
[b] Angle of convergence in radians.
[c] The mean of $(d - \hat{d})$ over the range of $\hat{d}$.
[d] The root-mean-square of $(d - \hat{d})$ over the range of $\hat{d}$.

pair of points was judged by each subject four times, except in Expt. 4 as shown in the third column of Table II.

Metric MDS was used throughout, and, hence, the configurations of light points $\{P_j\}$ were constructed in Euclidean spaces E^m, $m = 2, 3$. Some of the results are given in the right half of Table II: eigenvalues λ_m and λ_{m+1}, where m indicates the dimensionality of E^m adopted. An asterisk and a dash, respectively, in Table II represent that the iterative procedure did not converge and that the computation was terminated before obtaining λ due to some rules in the program of calculating λ_μ. Both take place when eigenvalues of almost the same value are to follow. It will be clear, therefore, that there are abrupt drops from λ_m to λ_{m+1} and further decreases from λ_{m+1} on are very small. In other words, the dimensionality of E^m was unambiguously determined in each case. In the last two columns of Table II, two indices for the goodness of fit were given where M and RMS represent the mean and the root-mean-square of $(d_{jk} - \hat{d}_{jk})$ respectively and R represents the range of d_{jk}. The index RMS/R has about the same meaning as the stress of Eq. (1). As examples, four scatter diagrams are given in Fig. 7, where plots A, B, and C are examples of the relatively close, medium, and poor coincidence between d and $\hat{d}$. Plot D is the only case where a considerable degree of the same curvilinearity as in Fig. 2 was observed. From these results, it may be concluded that binocular visual

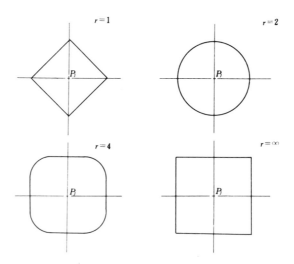

FIG. 7. Four representative examples of scatter diagram for Table II (application of metric MDS to binocular visual space). Plots A, B, and C shows examples of the relatively good, medium, and poor fit and D the only example where a curvilinear trend was observed. Of the two values in each plot, the upper represents M/R and the lower RMS/R. [From Indow (1968).]

space is, at least as the first approximation, describable in terms of Euclidean geometry. According to Expt. 4, the perceived night sky was not completely spherical, and its schematic picture is shown by the dotted curves in Fig. 8, where the continuous curves represent a hemisphere of a constant radius. We shall discuss the negative values that are predominant in M/R later.

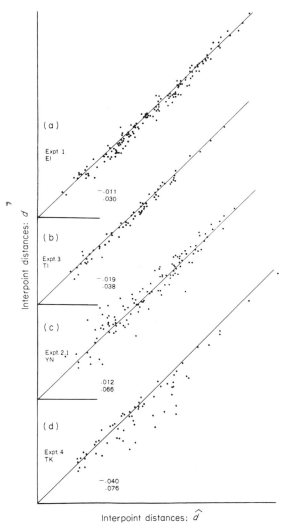

FIG. 8. Schematic representation of the perceptual sky (dotted curves) obtained in Expt. 4 in Table II. Solid curve represent a spherical surface. [From Indow (1968).]

Suppose that nonmetric MDS is applied to reproduce the shape of night sky, in which the subject is not included as a point and no 'judgment is made on perceptual distances from the subject to the stars. From the logic of nonmetric MDS, we will have the configuration of points developed to a flat surface E^2. As a data reduction, coupled with the obtained $M(\hat{d})$, this is a perfect representation for the given data. However, the result is meaningless as a picture of the sky in perception. Here is a clear distinction between a data reduction and a quantitative psychological model. In contrast to the other examples in Sections II,A,B, the model herein is concerned with the geometry of binocular visual space. As will be described in Section III,C, there is no a priori reason that binocular visual space must be Euclidean. In the other cases, quantitative psychological models are always concerned with the combination rules. Hence, discussion will be made with the combination rules first in Section III,A.

III. SIGNIFICANCE OF MULTIDIMENSIONAL SCALING IN STUDIES OF PERCEPTION

A. Analyzable or Unitary Percept

Any tangible entity in perception such as a color, sky, etc., will be called a *percept*. In some percepts, several attributes or parts are perceptually distinctive and in some others, they are not. A face as a percept comprises perceptually distinctive features: its shape and color, eyes, nose, mouth, and also the shapes, colors and positions of these parts. A color as a percept may be described in terms such as hue, brightness, saturation, and surface texture, if systematically compared with other colors. However, at first glance, or to the layman, these attributes are not very distinctive. Everyone can tell how the eyes or nose looks in a given face. This is not the case with the attributes of a given color. Let us call the former an analyzable percept and the latter a unitary percept.

More or less in connection with the development of MDS, the following conjecture has been gradually consolidated (Attneave, 1960, 1962; Shepard, 1964, Torgerson, 1958). The combination rule for overall dissimilarity δ may change its form according to the extent to which the different dimensions inherent in the percept are distinctive and separable. Between analyzable percepts, the overall dissimilarity is apt to take the form of a city block distance where $r = 1$ in Eq. (3). Between unitary percepts, δ will be given by the Euclidean distance where $r = 2$. If there is such a dimension that perceptually dominates the others, the distance with $r = \infty$ will provide the better description of the δ. Hyman and Well (1967,

1968) demonstrated the two following points. The overall dissimilarity d between geometrical figures, such as parallelograms varying in size and tilt or circles-with-radius varying in size and tilt, is accounted for in terms of the city block distance where the two respective attributes correspond to a street or an avenue, whereas, color difference d between red colors varying in V and C is Euclidean. Furthermore, when the two attributes were made perceptually distinct by presenting colors appropriately, then the city-block model held with d (multiple comparisons, complete ratio scaling by rating, metric MDS). With three- or four-component taste mixtures (e.g., sucrose, sodium chloride, citric acid, and quinine sulphate), it was shown (single presentation, complete difference scaling by rating, nonmetric MDS) that the dissimilarity was described by the power metric $r = 6 \sim 10$ in X^3 or X^4, where each dimension μ corresponds to each of the taste qualities (Gregson, 1966; Russell & Gregson, 1966).

As a matter of course, much has to be done to test the conjecture just stated. There is no logical reason for the overall dissimilarity δ of unitary percepts not being in any other form than the Euclidean model. Hence, if it has really been established of color space that the Euclidean model holds at least within a given range, it will be a great contribution to the study of perception. The foregoing experiment by Hyman and Well was made of colors which were held constant in H. In a plane of given H, V and C constitute the orthogonal axes μ. However the relation between H and C is not that simple in a plane of given V. Nevertheless, the studies summarized in Section II,A, show results favorable toward the possibility that the color space is Euclidean even when variation of H is involved. Of colors varying in H and C, Kruskal (1964a) showed that the results due to r between 2.0 to 2.5 gave the best fit to the data when r was varied from 1.0 to 5.0.*

Insofar as the neighborhood of a given stimulus is concerned, it will be possible to design experiments, with no use of MDS, to make clear the combination rules operating therein, no matter what the combination rules are. It will be tedious, however, to repeat the experiment with a number of stimuli, and application of MDS will open the way for macroscopic approaches to the problem although possible forms of the combination rules to be dealt with are rather limited. Presumably, a number of cases will be discovered in studies of perception that follow the combination rules which are not in the scope of Eq. (3). Such discoveries will also be great

* If a plane of constant V is Euclidean, then the dimensions in Eq. (3) cannot be H. and C. As Euclidean model is the only case where no a priori coordinate axes are presupposed, the coordinates μ can be any parameters. Hence, there is the possibility that color is really unitary in the sense that the subject does not analyze the percepts into any components in judging color differences.

contributions. Perhaps for the study of perception, MDS would ultimately be as useful in providing opportunities to discover how reality differs from the model assumed in MDS as in providing perfect descriptions to some sets of perceptual phenomena.

B. Problems in Scaling Dissimilarity

From the viewpoint of the modern development of axiomatic approaches to the problem of measurement and scaling (e.g., Krantz, Luce, Suppes, & Tversky, 1971; Luce, Bush, & Galanter, 1963), the problem is twofold in MDS: scaling of d and spatial representation of d in order to provide information on δ. The former involves about the same problems as in the ordinary scaling of unidimensional cases and, as to the latter, a set of axioms were given which have to be satisfied to lead to a spatial representation (Beals, Krantz, & Tversky, 1968; Krantz, 1967; Tversky & Krantz, 1969, 1970). Indeed, MDS is a complex of axioms, and to apply MDS to the data arranged in the form of D is a kind of gamble. If it works, one will accept the whole result, though the possibility still remains that the success is due to a fortuitous combination of axioms, not all of which are true taken individually. If it does not work, one will not be able to tell what axiom(s) may be responsible for the failure. However, the situation will be the same for all models utilizing more than one axiom (Martin, 1965, p. 240).

If stated very briefly, the structure of metric MDS is as follows. Discussion will be limited to d obtained by the ratio scaling through rating in pair comparisons (see Section I,D). Then the theorems developed by Krantz (1972) for scaling sensation can be extended in the obvious manner to the scaling of dissimilarity (Indow, in preparation). Suppose that the subject assigned ratios in a consistent manner to pairs of stimuli, and the ratio given to (i, j) and (k, l) be p, then there exists such scales as f and g:

$$f(i, j)/f(k, l) = g(p). \tag{6}$$

By taking a set f' and g', we can define d^R as follows:

$$f'(i, j) = d_{ij}^R, \qquad g'(p) = p \tag{7}$$

However, as shown by Krantz, there exists other sets of scales,

$$d_{ij} = \alpha(d_{ij}^R)^{1/\beta}, \qquad g(p) = p^{1/\beta}, \tag{8}$$

where α, $\beta > 0$. Furthermore, d as the input to metric MDS has to fulfill the properties of distance and, for example,

$$d_{ik} = d_{ij} + d_{jk}, \tag{9}$$

for any P_j on the segment connecting P_i and P_k in E^m. Suppose that there is such a d of Eq. (8) that is linearly related with $\hat{d}$. Unless $\beta = 1$, Eq. (9) is not satisfied with d^R and if $\beta > 1$, d^R is concave upward when plotted against $\hat{d}$. This is exactly what is observed in Figs. 2 and 4. Whenever color difference is scaled by ratio judgment, the same cuvilinearity appears in the scatter diagram and the curvilinearity seems to disappear with d^D that is obtained by difference scaling (Fig. 4). The requirement given in Eq. (9) is a matter of difference between d's and if d exists which satisfies Eq. (9), then it seems to be obtainable by difference scaling. Furthermore, as stated in Section I,D, if d^D and d^R are related in the form of Eq. (8), we can expect $\beta \geq 1$. Notice that we cannot predict from either d^D or $\hat{d}$ ratio judgments in the form e.g., $\hat{d}_{ij}/\hat{d}_{kl}$, except in the case where $\beta = 1$.

In binocular visual space, d represents visual length, and it is well known that the two types of scaling lead to an almost identical result in this case and therefore β is close to 1. Presumably, this may be the reason that the curvilinearity is not conspicuous in the scatter diagrams with d^R as shown by examples A, B, and C in Fig. 7. However, if scrutinized, the curvilinearity concave upward, though very slight, will be detectable in A and B. The same is true in most of the remaining scatter diagrams of the experiments referred to in Table II. This is one of the reasons that M is apt to be negative as shown in Table II. Even if there is no constant deviation in the negative direction in the scatter diagram, the curvilinearity tends to make M negative because of the higher concentration of points in the central region.

C. Euclidean Representation of Non-Euclidean Space

Suppose that two rows of small light points are presented in the dark, all in the eye level, and that the farthest pair is fixed. Let us call the rows of stimuli a *parallel alley* when the remaining light points are so arranged that the two rows appear "parallel." And let us call them a *distance alley* when they are so arranged that all the interpoint distances between the corresponding points appear to be equal. Obviously, both alleys should be identical in a Euclidean space. In fact, the two alleys do not coincide and the distance alley lies outside the parallel alley. This empirical fact led Luneburg (1947, 1948, 1950) to an interesting idea that binocular visual space be a hyperbolic space. From some theoretical analyses, he conjectured that binocular visual space be a Riemannian space of a constant curvature K. Also from some theoretical analyses, he assumed relatively simple mapping functions from the physical space of stimuli to the Euclidean map of binocular visual space, and he showed that the discrepancy of the two alleys can be accounted for as a natural consequence of the hyperbolic property of binocular visual space: $K < 0$. The model has only two parameters: the Gaussian total curvature K in the line-element on the Euclidean map, and σ in the mapping functions which is concerned with the effectiveness of convergence. If the values of these parameters of a subject are estimated, the whole properties of his binocular visual space are quantitatively deductible. The model has been further elaborated by Blank (1953, 1957, 1958a,b, 1959), and a series of experimental studies have been made (Foley, 1964, 1966; Hardy, Rand, & Rittler, 1951, 1953; Indow, Inoue, & Matsushima, 1962a,b, 1963; Shipley, 1957a,b; Zajaczkowska, 1956a,b).

Under exactly the same condition with Expt. 5 in Table II, and also with the subjects, from TI to KM, the discrepancy of the two alleys was repeatedly confirmed and K was around $-.30$ for the respective subjects (Indow, Inoue, Matsushima, 1962b). The scale of space is so defined that $-1 < K$, if binocular visual space is hyperbolic. If it is elliptic, $K > 0$. If Euclidean, $K = 0$, of course. According to the Luneburg's model, it is imperative to conclude that binocular visual system is hyperbolic. However, as stated in Section II,C, we would give to the binocular visual space the Euclidean picture by metric MDS with the high degree of reproducibility as shown in Fig. 7 (Nishikawa, 1967). These contradictory results threw doubt on the sensitivity of metric MDS to non-Euclidean property, especially when the space was Riemannian where $K \gtrless 0$. Notice that the power-metric of Eq. (3) is non-Euclidean in an entirely different way when $r \neq 2$. In essence, it is similar to a Euclidean space except for the size of the unit distance around a point varying according to direction (Fig. 9).

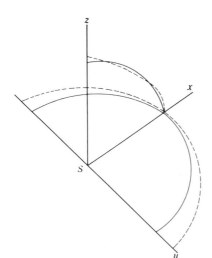

FIG. 9. Euclidean graphs of unit circles around a point P_j for Minkowski r-metric in two-dimensional case. Distance between P_j and any point on the locus makes $\hat{d} = 1$ in Eq. (3).

An attempt to incorporate the elliptic geometry into metric MDS was made by van de Geer.

Given the value of K and σ, it is possible, under the scheme of Luneburg, to calculate d_{jk} in the given perceptual space X^m of Riemannian character with a given configuration of n points $\{Q_j\}$ in the physical space. Under each of 20 pairs of values for K and σ, D was constructed with the same $\{Q_j\}$ consisting of 16 points plus a point corresponding to the subject which are scattered in the plane as in Expt. 5. The set $\{P_j\}$ was always obtained in a Euclidean plane E^2 by metric MDS. The report will be made in detail elsewhere (Indow & Matsushima, in preparation). Three examples of scatter diagram are given in Fig. 9, where A represents the case ($K = -.50$, $\sigma = 11$), which is the most representative of the results in

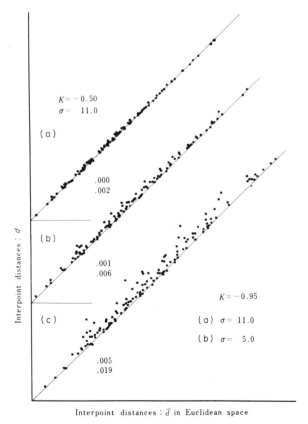

FIG. 10. Three examples of scatter diagram in the applications of metric MDS to various hyperbolic spaces. The ordinate represents geodesics given by K and σ, and the abscissa the interpoint distances of the configuration in Euclidean space.

the alley and other related experiments, B and C, the cases of $(K = -.95,$ $\sigma = 11)$ and $(K = -.95, \sigma = 5)$, respectively. Because of the condition $-1 < K$, B and C represent almost the farthest deviations from the Euclidean property. Surprisingly enough, however, not only A, but also B exhibit almost perfect fit of the Euclidean model. The case C showed the worst fit among the 20 pairs of K and σ. Nonetheless, the scatter is fairly small and no curvilinear trend is observed. Pairs of values in Fig. 10 represent M/R and RMS/R respectively as in Fig. 7. For the purpose of making intuitive the deviations of X^2 from E^2 in A, B, and C, the discrepancies of the two alleys are shown in Fig. 11. Only the curves on the right side of the alleys are given where the continuous curves inside represent the parallel alleys. The discrepancies in B and C are much larger than usually observed in actual experiments. Nevertheless, the Euclidean model reproduced d with the degree shown in Fig. 10.

Any Riemannian manifold X^m may be embedded in an Euclidean space $E^{m'}$ if $m' \geq m(m+1)/2$. However, the embedding under discussion was achieved without adding any extra dimension and evidently it is possible only at the sacrifice of distortion of the configuration. In other words, as the case mentioned at the end of Section II,C, the $\{P_j\}$ obtained does not represent anything in reality.

The author came across the same flexibility of metric MDS when he

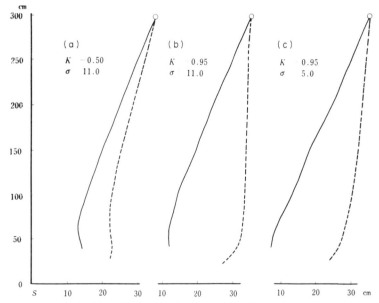

FIG. 11. Theoretical parallel (continuous) and distance (dotted) alleys for the three cases in Fig. 10. The respective alley curves on the right side only.

applied it to matrices of color differences which are claculated through formulas of non-Euclidean property: the 1964 CIE (U*V*B*) formula; the NBS formula (Judd & Wyszecki, 1963; and Wyszecki & Stiles, 1967); the Nickerson's (1936) formula, and the MacAdam, modified 1965 Friele, formula (Chickering, 1967) (Indow & Matsushima, 1969). Each of these formulas except U*V*W* are non-Euclidean in a different way. Color differences were calculated by these formulas with the set of 15 colors in the four local regions each, which were used in the Indow and Matsushima's (1969) experiment. The goodness of fit of the Euclidean model in terms of M/R and RMS/R are given in Table III as in Table II. With the (U*V*W*) formula and the NBS formula, the fit was perfect and with the other two formulas the fit was, in general, a little worse than those in the empirical applications to binocular visual space (Table II). The detailed description of this study will be made elsewhere (Indow & Matsushima, in preparation). Once again, it was shown that the non-Euclidean basic data did not result in large and/or systematic deviations in the scatter diagram but resulted in a satisfactory apparent fit of an Euclidean model. What has been obtained here by metric MDS is a reduction of the given data in the form of a compact and more tractable Euclidean configuration. It will be misleading, however, if interpreted as the quantitatively faithful description of the structure underlying the basic data.

D. Concluding Remarks

The two sets of examples described in Section III,C should be taken as a warning. If metric MDS is so flexible, evidently, nonmetric MDS would be more so. As a tool for data reduction, the flexibility is obviously an advantage. However, as a method of obtaining a quantitative psychological model, it poses a problem. Suppose that we have no auxiliary information or hypothesis about the underlying structure of the given data, and by applying MDS, we have obtained $\{P_j\}$ in X^m with sufficiently high reproducibility in the scatter diagram. If MDS be such a method of giving the satisfactory fit only to the data of the structure as assumed in the model, we would regard the obtained result as a faithful picture of the quantitative structure underlying the data. The examples showed that this was not the case.

Of the two sets of examples stated in Section III,C, we had the information as to how d_{jk} were generated in advance, and, hence, we could tell that the result obtained by MDS was misleading in these cases. In a practical situation, however, nothing is known in advance; how to define d_{jk}, what the possible combination rules are, and what attributes μ are involved. Hence, the only practical way of making effective use of MDS would be to supplement with some auxiliary information. When Isaac (1970) ap-

TABLE III

Goodness of Fit of Euclidean Model to Color Difference by Formulas
(All Possible Pairs of 15 Colors Varying in H, V, C)[a]

Formula	Around 5R		Around 5GY		Around 4.8G		Around 8.6B	
	M/R	RMS/R	M/R	RMS/R	M/R	RMS/R	M/R	RMS/R
Nickerson	−0.02	0.04	−0.02	0.05	−0.06	0.10	−0.01	0.06
MacAdam–Friele–Chickering	−0.04	0.07	−0.02	0.02	−0.03	0.06	−0.05	0.10
NBS	0.00	0.00	0.00	0.00	0.00	0.00	0.00	0.00
U*V*W*	0.00	0.00	0.00	0.00	0.00	0.00	0.00	0.00

[a] From Indow & Matsushima (1969).

plied nonmetric MDS to the dissimilarity matrix concerning facial expression, he tried to supply the auxiliary information by carrying out an additional experiment. Certainly, MDS is not such a method that discloses the truth at a single blow. However, there are a number of problems that need such a macroscopic approach as MDS, at least as the first step.

Once we obtain $\{P_j\}$ in X^m with colors of sufficiently large number, we can design new experiments and focus upon testing some further problems of the configuration or of the combination rules. Remember that, of object colors, what perceptual attribute is covariant with what colorimetric property of stimulus is not self-evident a priori. Hence, we cannot even define a series of chromatic colors varying along a perceptually single dimension* unless we have such a framework as $\{P_j\}$. As discussed before, we do not have any direct method to define the latent variable δ such as perceptual color difference or perceptual interpoint distance in binocular visual space, which means that we have a wide degree of freedom to define δ in indirect ways. Hence, assume that the following fact has been gradually consolidated through repeated applications of MDS. A particular scale d always leads to $\{P_j\}$ of which pattern is understandable from, or consistent with, the auxiliary information and of the combination rules or geometry which are relatively simple in form. Then, we will be able to give the operational definition to δ, color difference or perceptual distance, that the scale d represents δ which follows the combination rules or the geometry under discussion. This is the parsimony in science.

Acknowledgments

The first draft of this chapter was prepared in February 1971. However, it was almost completely rewritten while the author was a visiting member of The Institute for Advanced Study from 1971 to 1972, due to a grant from the Alfred P. Sloan Foundation. The author would like to express his warmest thanks to R. Duncan Luce for making the opportunity to come to The Institute possible.

References

Abelson, R. P., & Sermat, V. Multidimensional scaling of facial expressions. *Journal of Experimental Psychology,* 1962, **63,** 546–554.

* For example, it is well known that loci of perceptually constant hue in the chromaticity diagram are, except in a few cases, not so simple as given by straight lines connecting the achromatic point with the respective dominant wavelengths. The distinction between "analyzable" and "unitary" is often made in terms of stimulus, e.g., "the form of the metric may depend upon the extent to which the different dimensions of stimuli are perceptually distinct [Shepard, 1964, p. 59]." In Section III,A, the distinction was made in terms of perceptual dimensions because the correspondence between two dimensions is not clear in many cases.

Attneave, F. Dimensions of similarity. *American Journal of Psychology,* 1950, **63,** 516–556.

Attneave, F. Perception and related areas. In S. Koch (Ed.), *Psychology: A study of a science,* Vol. 4. New York: McGraw-Hill, 1962, 619–659.

Beals, R., Krantz, D. H., & Tversky, A. The foundations of multidimensional scaling. *Psychological Review,* 1968, **75,** 127–142.

Beckenback, E., & Bellman, R. *An introduction to inequalities.* New York: Random House, 1961.

Bellamy, B. R., & Newhall, S. M. Attributive limens in selected regions of the Munsell color solid. *Journal of the Optical Society of America,* 1942, **32,** 465–473.

Blank, A. A. The Luneburg theory of binocular visual space. *Journal of the Optical Society of America,* 1953, **43,** 717–727.

Blank, A. A. The geometry of vision. *British Journal Physiological Optics,* 1957, 1–30.

Blank, A. A. Axiomatics of binocular vision. The foundation of metric geometry in relation to space perception. *Journal of the Optical Society of America,* 1958, **48,** 328–334. (a)

Blank, A. A. Analysis of experiments in binocular space perception. *Journal of the Optical Society of America,* 1958, **48,** 911–925. (b)

Blank, A. A. The Luneburg theory of binocular space perception. In S. Koch (Ed.), *Psychology, A study of a science.* Study I, Vol. 1, New York: McGraw-Hill, 1959, 395–426.

Boynton, R. M., & Wagner, H. G. Color differences assessed by the minimally distinct border methods. In J. J. Vos, L. F. C. Friele, & P. L. Walraven, (Eds.) *Color metrics.* AIC/Holland, c/o Institute for Perception TNO, Soesterverg, 1972.

Carroll, J. D., & Chang, J. J. Reanalysis of some color data of Helm's by INDSCAL procedure for individual differences multidimensional scaling. Proceedings of 78th Annual Convention, American Psychological Association, 1970, 137–140. (a)

Carroll, J. D., & Chang, J. J. Analysis of individual differences in multidimensional scaling via an N-way generalization of "Eckart-Young" decomposition. *Psychometrika,* 1970, **35,** 283–319. (b)

Carroll, J. D., & Wish, M. Measuring preference and perception with multidimensional models. *Bell Laboratories Record,* 1971, May, 147–154.

Chickering, K. D. Optimization of the MacAdam-modified 1965 Friele color-difference form. *Journal of the Optical Society of America,* 1967, **57,** 537–541.

Coombs, C. H., & Kao, R. C. On a connection between factor analysis and multidimensional unfolding. *Psychometrika,* 1960, **25,** 219–231.

Cross, D. V. Metric properties of multidimensional stimulus generalization. In D. I. Mostofsky (Ed.) *Stimulus generalization.* Stanford: Stanford University Press, 1965, 72–93.

Ekman, G. Dimensions of color vision. *Journal of Psychology,* 1954, **38,** 467–474.

Fillenbaum, S., & Rapoport, A. *Structure in the subjective lexicon.* New York: Academic Press, 1971.

Foley, J. M. Desarguesian property in visual space. *Journal of the Optical Society of America,* 1964, **54,** 684–692.

Foley, J. M. Locus of perceived equidistance as a function of viewing distance. *Journal of the Optical Society of America,* 1966, **56,** 822–827.

Gleason, T. C. A general model for nonmetric multidimensional scaling. Technical Report MMPP67-3, University of Michigan, Michigan Mathematical Psychology Program, 1967.

Graham, C. H. (Ed.) *Vision and Visual perception.* New York: Wiley, 1965.

Gregson, R. A. M. Representation of taste mixture cross-modal matching in a Minkowski r-metric. *Australian Journal of Psychology,* 1965, **17,** 195–204.

Gregson, R. A. M. Theoretical and empirical multidimensional scalings of taste mixture matchings. *British Journal of Mathematical and Statistical Psychology,* 1966, **18,** 59–75.

Gregson, R. A. M. Simulating perceived similarities between taste mixtures having mutually interacting components. *British Journal of Mathematical and Statistical Psychology,* 1968, **21,** Part I, 117–130.

Gregson, R. A. M., & Russell, P. N. Psychophysical power law exponent value for sucrose intensity. *Perceptual and Motor Skills,* 1965, **20,** 294. (a)

Gregson, R. A. M., & Russell, P. N. Problems and results in the scaling of intermodal and intramodal complex taste similarities by D metrics. University Canterbury, Department Psychology and Sociology Research, Project 8, 1965. (b)

Guttman, L. A general nonmetric technique for finding the smallest coordinate space for a configuration of points. *Psychometrika,* 1968, **33,** 469–506.

Hardy, L. H., Rand, G., & Rittler, M. C. Investigation of visual space. *Archives of Ophthalmology,* 1951, **45,** 53–63.

Hardy, L. H., Rand, G., Rittler, M. C., & Boeder, P. *The geometry of binocular space perception.* Knapp Memorial Laboratories, Institute of Ophthalmology, Columbia University College of Physicians and Surgeons, 1953.

Hayashi, C. Distance and dimension from a statistical viewpoint. (published in Japanese from Yoron Kagaku Kyokai), 1969.

Helm, C. E. & Tucker, L. R. Individual differences in the structure of color-perception. *American Journal of Psychology,* 1962, **75,** 437–444.

Hyman, R., & Well, A. Judgments of similarity and spatial models. *Perception & Psychophysics,* 1967, **2,** 233–248.

Hyman, R., & Well, A. Perceptual separability and spatial models. *Perception & Psychophysics,* 1968, **3,** 161–165.

Indow, T. Two kinds of multidimensional scaling methods as tools for investigating color space from the macroscopic point of view. *Acta Chromatica,* 1963, **1,** 60–71.

Indow, T. Multidimensional mapping of visual space with real and simulated stars. *Perception & Psychophysics,* 1968, **3,** 45–53.

Indow, T., Inoue, E., & Matsushima, K. An experimental study of the Luneburg theory of binocular space perception (1). The 3- and 4-point experiments. *Japanese Psychological Research,* 1962, **4,** 6–16. (a)

Indow, T., Inoue, E., & Matsushima, K. An experimenal study of the Luneburg theory of binocular space (2). The alley experiments. *Japanese Psychological Research,* 1962, **4,** 17–24.

Indow, T., Inoue, E., & Matsushima, K. An experimental study of the Luneburg theory of binocular space (3). The experiments in a spacious field. *Japanese Psychological Research,* 1963, **5,** 10–27.

Indow, T., & Kanazawa, K. Multidimensional mapping of Munsell colors varying in hue, chroma and value. *Journal of Experimental Psychology,* 1960, **59,** 330–336.

Indow, T., & Matsushima, K. Local multidimensional mapping of Munsell color space. *Acta Chromatica,* 1969, **2,** 16–24.

Indow, T., & Matsushima, K. Euclidean representation of four color difference formulae. (to appear in *Farbe*)

Indow, T., & Ohsumi, K. Multidimensional mapping of sixty Munsell colors through nonmetric procedure. In J. J. Vos, L. F. C. Friele, & P. L. Walraven, (Eds.) *Color metrics*. AIC/Holland, c/o Institute for Perception TNO, Soesterverg, 1972.

Indow, T., & Shiose, T. An application of the method of multidimensional scaling to perception of similarity or difference in color. *Japanese Psychological Research*, 1956, **3**, 45–64.

Indow, T., & Shiose, T. A note on an application of the method of multidimensional scaling to perception of similarity or difference in color. *Japanese Psychological Research*, 1958, **5**, 21.

Indow, T., & Uchizono, T. Multidimensional mapping of Munsell colors varying in hue and chroma. *Journal of Experimental Psychology*, 1960, **59**, 321–329.

Issac, P. D. Dissimilarity judgements and multidimensional scaling configuration as indices of perceptual structure: A study of intra-individual consistencies. *Perception and Psychophysics*, 1970, **7**, 229–233.

Johnson, S. C. Hierarchical clustering schemes. *Psychometrika*, 1967, **32**, 241–254.

Julesz, B. Some recent studies in vision relevant to form perception. In Wathen-Dunn, W. (Ed.), *Models for the perception of speech and visual form*. Cambridge, Mass.: Massachusetts Institute of Technology Press, 1967, 136–154.

Judd, D. B., & Wyszecki, G. *Color in business, science, and industry*, (2nd ed.). New York: Wiley, 1963.

Krantz, D. H. Rational Distance functions for multidimensional scaling. *Journal of Mathematical Psychology*, 1967, **4**, 226–245.

Krantz, D. H. A theory of magnitude estimation and cross-modality matching. *Journal of Mathematical Psychology*, 1972, **9**, 168–199.

Krantz, D. H. Visual scaling. In D. Jameson, & L. M. Hurvich (Eds.), *Visual psychophysics*, Chapter 26. Berlin: Springer, 1972, 660–689.

Krantz, D. H., Luce, R. D., Suppes, P., & Tversky, A. *Foundations of Measurement*. Volume 1. *Additive and polynomial representations*. New York: Academic Press, 1971.

Kruskal, J. B. Multidimensional scaling by optimizing goodness of fit to a nonmetric hypothesis. *Psychometrika*, 1964, **29**, 1–27. (a)

Kruskal, J. B. Nonmetric multidimensional scaling: A numerical method. *Psychometrika*, 1964, **29**, 115–129. (b)

Kruskal, J. B., & Carroll, J. D. Geometrical models and badness-of-fit functions. *Multivariate Analysis*, 1969, **2**, 639–671.

Kuennapas, T. Visual perception of capital letters; multidimensional ratio scaling and multidimensional similarity. *Scandinavian Journal of Psychology*, 1966, **7**, 189–196.

Kuennapas, T. Visual memory of capital letters; multidimensional ratio scaling and multidimensional similarity. *Perceptual and Motor Skills*, 1967, **25**, 345–350.

Kuennapas, T., & Janson, A. J. Multidimensional similarity of letters. *Perceptual and Motor Skills*, 1969, **28**, 3–12.

Kuennapas, T., Maelhammar, G., & Stevenson, O. Multidimensional ratio scaling and multidimensional similarity of simple geometric figures. *Scandinavian Journal of Psychology*, 1964, **5**, 249–256.

Kuno, U., & Suga, Y. Multidimensional mapping of piano music. *Japanese Psychological Research*, 1966, **8**, 119–124.

Levelt, W. J. M., van de Geer, J. P., & Plomp, R. Triadic comparisons of musical intervals. *British Journal of Mathematical and Statistical Psychology*, 1966, **19**, Part II, 163–179.

Lingoes, J. C., & Roskam, E. A mathematical and empirical study of two multidimensional scaling algorithms. Technical Report MMPP 71–1, University of Michigan, Michigan Mathematical Psychology Program, 1971.

Luce, R. D., Bush, R. R., & Galanter, E. *Handbook of mathematical psychology,* Volume 1, New York: Wiley, 1963.

Luneburg, R. K. *Mathematical analysis of binocular vision.* Princeton, Princeton University Press, 1947.

Luneburg, R. K. Metric methods in binocular visual perception, Studies and Essays. *Courant Anniversary Volume.* 1948, 215–240.

Luneburg, R. K. The metric of binocular visual space. *Journal of the Optical Society of America,* 1950, **40,** 637–642.

Martin, E. Concept identification. In R. R. Luce, R. R. Bush & E. Galanter, (Eds.), *Handbook of mathematical psychology,* Volume 3, New York: Wiley, 1965, pp. 205–267.

Matsushima, K., & Noguchi, H. Multidimensional representation of binocular visual space. *Japanese Psychological Research,* 1967, **9,** 85–94.

Messick, S. J. The perception of attitude relationships: A multidimensional scaling approach to the structuring of social attitudes. Ph.D. Thesis, Princeton University, 1954.

Messick, S. J. The perception of social attitudes. *Journal of Abnormal and Social Psychology,* 1956, **52,** 57–69.

Messick, S. J., & Abelson, R. P. The additive constant problem in multidimensional scaling. *Psychometrika,* 1956, **21,** 1–5.

Micko, H. C. A 'halo' model for multidimensional ratio scaling. *Psychometrika,* 1970, **35,** 199–227.

Micko, H. C., & Fischer, W. The metric of multidimensional psychological spaces as a function of the differential attention to subjective attributes. *Journal of Mathematical Psychology,* 1970, **7,** 118–143.

Miller, G. A., & Nicely, P. E. An analysis of perceptual confusions among some English consonants. *Journal of Acoustic Society of America,* 155, **27,** 338–352.

Morton, A. S. Similarity as a determinant of friendship: A multi-dimensional study. A Technical Report from Princeton University and Educational Testing Service, 1959.

Newhall, S. M. Preliminary report of the O.S.A. Subcommittee on the spacing of the Munsell colors. *Journal of the Optical Society of America,* 1940, **30,** 617–654.

Newhall, S. M., Nickerson, D., & Judd, D. B. Final report of the O.S.A. Subcommittee on the spacing of the Munsell colors. *Journal of the Optical Society of America,* 1943, **33,** 385–418.

Nickerson, D. The specification of color tolerances. *Textile Research,* 1936, **16,** 509.

Nickerson, D. History of the Munsell color system. *Color Engineering,* 1969, **7** (5), New York: Chromatic Communication, Inc.

Nickerson, D., & Stultz, K. F. Color tolerance specification. *Journal of the Optical Society of America,* 1944, **34,** 550–570.

Nishikawa, Y. Euclidean interpretation of binocular visual space. *Japanese Psychological Research,* 1967, **9,** 191–198.

Pols, L. C. W., van der Kamp, L. J. Th., & Plomp, R. Perceptual and physical space of vowel sounds. *Journal of Acoustic Society of America,* 1969, **46,** 458–467.

Ramsay, J. O. Economical method of analyzing perceived color differences. *Journal of the Optical Society of America,* 1968, **58,** 19–22.

Ramsay, J. O. Some statistical considerations in multidimensional scaling. *Psychometrika,* 1969, **34,** 167–182.

Rapoport, A., & Fillenbaum, S. A structural analysis of the semantic space of color names. Multilithed Report No. 60, The L. L. Thurstone Psychometric Laboratory, University of North Carolina, 1968.

Rothkopf, E. Z. A measure of stimulus similarity and errors in some paired-associate learning tasks. *Journal of Experimental Psychology*, 1957, **53**, 94–101.

Russell, P. N., & Gregson, R. A. M. A comparison of intermodal and intramodal methods in the multi-dimensional scaling of 3-component taste mixtures. *Australian Journal of Psychology*, 1966, **18**, 244–254.

Shepard, R. N. The analysis of proximities: Multidimensional scaling with an unknown distance function I. *Psychometrika*, 1962, **27**, 125–139. (a)

Shepard, R. N. The analysis of proximities: Multidimensional scaling with an unknown distance function II. *Psychometrika*, 1962, **27**, 219–246. (b)

Shepard, R. N. Analysis of proxities as a technique for the study of information processing in man. *Human Factors*, 1963, **5**, 33–48.

Shepard, R. N. Attention and the metric structure of the stimulus space. *Journal of Mathematical Psychology*, 1964, **1**, 54–87.

Shepard, R. N. Metric structures in ordinal data. *Journal of Mathematical Psychology*, 1966, **3**, 287–315.

Shepard, R. N., & Carroll, J. D. Parametric representation of nonlinear data structures. In P. R. Krishnaiah, (Ed.) *Multivariate analysis: Proceedings of the first international symposium of multivariate analysis*. New York: Academic Press, 1966.

Shepard, R. N., & Chipman, S. Second-order isomorphism of internal representations: shapes of states. *Cognitive Psychology*, 1970, **1**, 1–17.

Shipley, T. Convergence function in binocular space: I. A note on theory. *Journal of the Optical Society of America*, 1957, **47**, 795–803. (a)

Shipley, T. Convergence function in binocular visual space: II. Experimental report. *Journal of the Optical Society of America*, 1957, **47**, 804–821. (b)

Stevens, S. S. The psychophysics of sensory function. In W. A. Rosenblith (Ed.), *Sensory communication*, Cambridge, Mass., Massachusetts Institute of Technology Press, 1961. Pp. 1–33.

Stevens, S. S. Issues in psychophysical measurement. *Psychological Review* 1971, **78**, 426–480.

Torgerson, W. S. Multidimensional scaling: Theory and method. *Psychometrika*, 1952, **17**, 401–419.

Torgerson, W. S. *Theory and methods of scaling*. New York: John Wiley, 1958.

Tucker, L. R., & Messick, S. An individual differences models for multidimensional scaling. *Psychometrika*, 1963, **28**, 333–367.

Tversky, A., & Krantz, D. H. Similarity of schematic faces: A test of interdimensional additivity. *Perception and Psychophysics*, 1969, **5**, 124–128.

Tversky, A., & Krantz, D. H. The dimensional representation and the metric structure of similarity data. *Journal of Mathematical Psychology*, 1970, **7**, 572–596.

van der Geer, J. P. The application of non-euclidean geometry in psychological scaling (unpublished, mimeographed manuscript from The Center for Advanced Study in the Behavioral Sciences, Stanford, 1969).

van der Kamp, L. J. Th., & Pols, L. C. W. Perceptual analysis from confusion between vowels (personal communication).

von Wright, J. M., & Niemela, P. On the ontogenetic development of moral criteria. *Scandinavian Journal of Psychology*, 1966, **7**, 65–75.

Wagenaar, W. A., & Padmos, P. Quantitative interpretation of stress in Kruskal's multidimensional scaling technique. *Journal of mathematical and statistical Psychology*, 1971, **24**, 101–110.

Wilson, K. V. Multidimensional analyses of confusions of English consonants. *American Journal of Psychology*, 1963, **76**, 89–95.

Wish, M., & Carroll, J. D. Multidimensional scaling with differential weighting of dimensions. In S. R. Hodson, D. G. Kendall, and P. Tautu (Eds.), *Mathematics in the archeological and historical sciences*. Edinburgh University 1971, pp. 150–167.

Wyszecki, G., & Stiles, W. S. *Color Science: Concepts and methods, quantitative data and formulas*. New York: John Wiley, 1967.

Yoshida, M. Dimensions of tactual impressions. *Japanese Psychological Research*, 1968, **10**, 123–137. (a)

Yoshida, M. Dimensions of tactual impressions. *Japanese Psychological Research*, 1968, **10**, 157–173. (b)

Yoshida, M., & Saito, S. Multidimensional scaling of the taste of amino acids. *Japanese Psychological Research*, 1969, **11**, 149–166.

Young, G., & Housholder, A. S. Discussion of a set of points in terms of their mutual distances. *Psychometrika*, 1938, **3**, 19–22.

Zajaczkowska, A. Experimental determination of Luneburg's constants σ and K. *Quarterly and Journal of Experimental Psychology*, 1956, **8**, 66–78. (a)

Zajackzowska, A. Experimental test of Luneburg's theory. Horopter and alley experiments, *Quarterly and Journal of Experimental Psychology*, 1956, **46**, 514–527. (b)

AUTHOR INDEX

Numbers in italics refer to the pages on which the complete references are listed.

SUBJECT INDEX

A

Accent, INDSCAL applied to perception of, 462–470

Acoustics, psychophysical law and, 362–363

Adaptation-level theory, 19, 128, 220
  memory bias and, 66–67
  multiplying models and, 274–276
  range effects and, 131
  range–frequency theory compared with, 245–246

Adding models, 226

Additive structures, in algebraic models, 177–180

Additivity, interdimensional, 416–419, 438

Algebraic models, 175–187, 216–218, 285
  linear and averaging,
    applications, 233–259
    assumptions and analyses, 220–233
  multiplying, 259
    applications, 266–280
    assumptions and analyses, 259–266

Ambiguity, modulation of perception and, 102, 103

Analogy completions, multidimensional model for, 394

Analysis, 216

Analysis of proximities, *see* Scaling, nonmetric

Analysis of variance,
  linear models and, 223
  for multiplying model, 262–264

Analyzable percept, multidimensional scaling and, 516

Anchoring, 78–79, 131–132, 232
  in categorical judgment, 348
  in comparative judgment, 276–277

Animals, as experimental subjects, 89–91

Anticipations, false, 326

Antiproximities, 393

Anxiety, use of loudness to gauge, 366–367

Apparent inclination, 372

Apparent position, 372

Arousal, labeling, 147

Assimilation effects, 244

Attention
  auditory, 46–47

dimensional, 47–48
  speech and, 48–51
  concepts in, 29–33
  divided, 27–28
  intermodality, 33–36
  meaning and, 51–52
  non-Euclidean metric and, 424–429
  vigilance and, 329
  visual, 46
    color selection, 45–46
    dimensional, 37–41
    interocular, 36–37
    spatial factors in, 42–45

Attentive combination, 27–28
  absolute judgments and, 41
  auditory, 47
  serial and parallel processing in, 32
  speech and, 48–49

Attentive integration, 28–29
  absolute judgments and, 40–41
  speeded, 38–39

Attentive selection, 27
  absolute judgments and, 41
  auditory, 47–48
  serial and parallel processing in, 32–33
  speech and, 49–50
  speeded, 37–38

Attitudes
  balance principle and, 160
  estimation of, 155–156
  ethnic identification and, 146–147
  impression formation and, 150
  multidimensional scaling in, 494
  use of loudness to gauge, 367

Attraction, interpersonal, 160–161

Attribution
  causal, 153–155
  of traits and dispositional states, 149–155

Auditory detection, sequential effects and, 322, 323

Averaging models, *see under* Algebraic models

Azimuth, 372

B

Balance principle, attraction and, 160

Belief, probability and, 96

Bias, 62, *see also* Response bias
  adaptation level and, 66–67

HANDBOOK OF PERCEPTION

EDITORS: *Edward C. Carterette and Morton P. Friedman*

Department of Psychology
University of California, Los Angeles
Los Angeles, California

Volume I: Historical and Philosophical Roots of Perception. 1974

Volume II: Psychophysical Judgment and Measurement. 1974

Volume III: Biology of Perceptual Systems. 1973

Volume V: Seeing. 1975

IN PREPARATION

Volume IV: Hearing

Volume VII: Language and Speech

```
    5
B   6
C   7
D   8
E   9
F   0
G   1
H   2
I   3
J   4
```